Financial Forensics Body of Knowledge

Founded in 1807, John Wiley & Sons is the oldest independent publishing company in the United States. With offices in North America, Europe, Australia, and Asia, Wiley is globally committed to developing and marketing print and electronic products and services for our customers' professional and personal knowledge and understanding.

The Wiley Finance series contains books written specifically for finance and investment professionals as well as sophisticated individual investors and their financial advisors. Book topics range from portfolio management to e-commerce, risk management, financial engineering, valuation, and financial instrument analysis, as well as much more.

For a list of available titles, visit our Web site at www.WileyFinance.com.

Financial Forensics Body of Knowledge

DARRELL D. DORRELL
GREGORY A. GADAWSKI

John Wiley & Sons, Inc.

Published by John Wiley & Sons, Inc., Hoboken, New Jersey.
Published simultaneously in Canada.

Library of Congress Cataloging-in-Publication Data:

Dorrell, Darrell D.
Financial forensics body of knowledge / Darrell D. Dorrell, Gregory A. Gadawski. — 1
p. cm. (Wiley finance ; 616)
Includes bibliographical references and index.
ISBN 978-0-470-88085-2 (hardback); ISBN 978-1-118-21896-9 (ebk);
ISBN 978-1-118-21897-6 (ebk); ISBN 978-1-118-21898-3 (ebk)
1. Financial crimes. 2. Forensic accounting. 3. Fraud investigation. I. Gadawski, Gregory A. II. Title.
HV6769.D675 2012
363.25′6—dc23 2011034183

10 9 8 7 6 5 4 3 2 1

This book is dedicated to the citizens of the United States of America, and those who gave their lives to defend its foundational values and precepts, established by the Declaration of Independence, *the* Constitution, *and the* Bill of Rights. *The book's contents compel rational thought and decision making based upon facts, evidence and integrity. Thus, America's citizens can restore, sustain, and strengthen our core beliefs that* "... all men are created equal, that they are endowed by their Creator with certain unalienable Rights, that among these are Life, Liberty and the pursuit of Happiness ..." *Re-orienting America with our beginnings will counter recent stridencies making demands* "For the benefit of the few, to the detriment of the many." *American citizens will once again learn that we are* "... one Nation under God ..." *and the world's citizens will benefit from America's strengths, leadership and commerce. God bless America!*

Contents

Preface xi

Acknowledgments xv

Introduction 1

What Is a Methodology? 1
Why Was This Book Written? 4
How to Use This Book 10
About the Book's Website 10
How This Book Is Organized 11

PART ONE
Financial Forensics Tools, Techniques, Methods, and Methodologies

CHAPTER 1
Foundational Phase 21
Assignment Development Stage 21
Scoping Stage 36
Conclusion 54

CHAPTER 2
Interpersonal Phase 55
Interviews and Interrogation Stage 56
Behavior Detection 62
Background Research Stage 73
Conclusion 77

CHAPTER 3
Data Collection and Analysis Phase: Part I 79
Data Collection Stage 79
Surveillance Stage 111
Confidential Informants Stage 114
Undercover Stage 117
Laboratory Analysis Stage 119
Confirmation Bias: Clinical Thinking 122
Aberrant Pattern Detection: What's the Difference? 131
Forensic Lexicology: How to Analyze Words Like Numbers 150
Conclusion 172

CHAPTER 4
Data Collection and Analysis Phase: Part II 173
Analysis of Transactions Stage 173
The Myth of Internal Control 175
Financial Statements—Written Confessions 181
60-Second Method 185
Forensic Indices 204
Forensic Financial Analysis 212
Conclusion 252

CHAPTER 5
Data Collection and Analysis Phase: Part III 255
FSAT—Financial Status Audit Techniques 255
Applying Digital Analysis Techniques in Financial Forensics Investigations 270
Valuation & Forensics—Why & How 287
Valuation's Orphan 294
Conclusion 314

CHAPTER 6
Trial and Reports Phase 315
Trial Preparation Stage 315
Testimony and Exhibits 318
Weapon (WPN) 320
Reports and Exhibits: Tips and Techniques 325
Post-Assignment 333
Conclusion 334

PART TWO
Financial Forensics Special Topics

CHAPTER 7
Counterterrorism: Conventional Tools for Unconventional Warfare 337
Stop the Money—Stop the Terrorists 337
Civil Tools Used by Federal Law Enforcement 338
The Civil Statutes as Counterterrorism Weapons 339
Why Use Civil Laws in Addition to Criminal Laws? 341
Discussion of Alter Ego 343
Alter Ego Literature 348
Alter Ego Jurisdictional Examples 358
The Challenges of Alter Ego Investigation 361
Fraudulent Transfer 372
Solvency 374
Forensic Accounting Techniques 378
Alter Ego, Fraudulent Conveyance, and Solvency Matters in Action 384
What Target-Rich Scenarios Can Be Exploited? 386

Forensic Accounting: Counterterrorism Weaponry 391
Financial Statements—The Sources of Data 395
When Financial Statements Contain Laundered Money 403
When No Records Have Been Prepared by the Terrorist 408
Summary of Forensic Accounting Observations 413
A Forensic Accounting Methodology to Support Counterterrorism 415
Summary 421
Conclusion 423

CHAPTER 8
Civil versus Criminal Law Comparison 445
Comparison 457
What If You Suspect Embezzlement?—The Three Big *Don'ts* and Several *Do's* 457
Conclusion 469

Appendix
Forensic Inventory: Forensic Tools, Techniques, Methods, and Methodologies 471

Bibliography 517

About the Authors and Contributors 521

Index 529

Preface

The genesis of this book dates to 9:50 A.M. EST, Friday, June 29, 2001. I will explain that in a moment.

Since that date, thousands of forensic operators throughout North America have received training in all or some of this book's content. They include a cross-section of both the public and private sector and comprise (alphabetically) analysts, attorneys, attorneys general, auditors, bankers, certified public accountants (CPAs), chief financial officers (CFOs), consumers, controllers, district attorneys, fiduciaries, internal auditors, investigators, investment bankers, journalists, judges, law enforcement (federal, state, and local), non-CPAs, professors, prosecutors, retirees, students, treasurers, and others. They represent publicly held companies, privately held companies, non-profits (NPOs) non-governmental organizations (NGOs), and many branches of government, including FBI, SEC, USDOJ, state and local agencies, and others.

Throughout the training, attendees consistently requested the content in book format. There were two primary reasons for their requests. First, the training and (now) this book constitute the most all-inclusive codified financial forensics body of knowledge known to exist. Most other financial references focus myopically on fraud to the detriment of all other financial arenas. Their narrow focus contradicts the vital need for guidance in *all* financial dimensions, that is, performance measurement, investment, regulation, and reporting, in addition to fraud. Therefore, the all-inclusive nature of the tools, techniques, methods, and methodologies of this body of knowledge integrate fraud as a subset. As the saying goes, "*If you understand financial forensics, you understand fraud, but not vice versa.*"

Also, even though this book's content is substantially available through the Financial Forensics Academy™ training and Internet site, this book contains more explanation. Books are often preferred for their physical characteristics, ready availability, and go-anywhere features. Furthermore, experienced forensic operators know that books can be more persuasive in court than electronic contents.

Returning to 9:50 A.M. EST, Friday, June 29, 2001 ...

That was the last day of my weeklong attendance at the FBI National Academy in Quantico, Virginia. I delivered a financial forensics training session to about 250 FBI Special Agents earlier in the week. My security clearance permitted me to attend many other briefings and training during the week, including FBI, CIA, US Marshals, Federal Reserve, and others.

While I searched for an auditorium seat for the 10 A.M. session, the FBI Training Director sought me out and asked me to deliver the 10 A.M. presentation ad hoc. A matter of national emergency had diverted the assigned speaker. The training director did not describe the national emergency but was visibly distressed. I misinterpreted his distress as anxiety due to the last-minute speaker absence.

Terrorists attacked the United States 74 days later, on September 11, 2001. Post-9/11 analysis indicates the June 29 national emergency was one of the precursors to the attack.

Like most Americans, I remember precisely what I was doing when I learned of the September 11 attacks. Furthermore, like most Americans, words cannot express the anguish that I suffered. I can summarize, however, by saying that, for 24 hours, my mind reeled, seeking ways to join America's war against terrorism. I knew that even if I could talk my way into the military, there was no way my wife would permit me to enlist. Consequently, I agonized through dozens of scenarios playing out how I might contribute to America's fight.

I had an epiphany almost exactly 24 hours later—I could crystallize three critical facts that I had learned at Quantico. First, I learned that FBI Special Agents and law enforcement specialists in general deploy financial crimes methodologies in their assignments. The methodologies may vary by agency, but they share certain commonalities with the financial investigations conducted by forensic operators and some CPAs.

Second, I learned that terrorists covet the annihilation of anyone whose beliefs differ from theirs. Terrorists execute their subhuman life goals of obliteration by subsisting on tiny amounts of money. This may seem counterintuitive, but they can, and do when necessary, operate on a shoestring. For example, $20,000 was the estimated cost necessary for all the terrorists' expenses for the October 2000 boat-bomb that killed 17 Navy sailors, wounded 35, and nearly sunk the USS Cole. The US Navy's Arleigh Burke–class destroyer cost $984 million to launch. Before 9/11, small sums of money were off the radar screen of investigators, since large sums, for example, drugs and money laundering, had received nearly all the attention. Consequently, new forensic tools, techniques, methods, and methodologies were crucial to address both large and small sums of money in both civil and criminal investigations.

Finally, I realized that the financial forensics methodology that my firm developed in the late 1990s could capture both civil and criminal investigation parameters for *all* financial matters, whether large or small. We published the codified methodology through the United States Department of Justice, Executive Office for United States Attorneys, National Advocacy Center in two issues: "Counterterrorism: Using Conventional Tools for Unconventional Warfare," *United States Attorneys' Bulletin* 53, no. 2 (March 2005) and "Forensic Accounting: Counterterrorism Weaponry," *United States Attorneys' Bulletin* 53, no. 3 (May 2005).

Nearly everyone who received training in this book's content applauds it by citing two factors as unique. First, they cite the methodology, a method suited for virtually any financial forensic matter. The methodology is an interactive process map that mirrors military mission–specific doctrine. Military strategists know that "*No battle plan survives first encounter with the enemy.*" Therefore, military operators must be so well trained in their mission that they can course-correct the instant combat surprises appear. Likewise, forensic operators know that "*No investigation plan survives first encounter with the people and money.*" Training in a foundational methodology, therefore, ensures continual progress during any assignment.

Second, the methodology presently contains 250–plus or minus unique tools, techniques, methods, and methodologies that apply to virtually *any* large or small financial matter—civil, criminal, and dispute. This permits forensic operators to draw from a vast contemporary toolkit optimized for every assignment. The advantages are obvious: the right tools ensure more efficient and effective assignments; using the proper tools nullifies the dictum "*Owning only a hammer, everything begins to look like a nail.*" New forensic tools, techniques, methods, and methodologies continually update the toolkit. Therefore, forensic operators can rely on the methodology since it is quite literally never out of date. Furthermore, the methodology mirrors the process of an assignment, so that tool selection matches the assignment progress.

Greg and I, as the authors of this work earnestly desire that the contents of this book will help redefine the financial forensics profession and serve financial originators, users, and regulators.

DARRELL D. DORRELL and GREGORY A. GADAWSKI
July 2011, Lake Oswego, OR

Acknowledgments

I have struggled during the past several months contemplating how I could possibly distill my life's innumerable blessings and thank those who have led me to this book. The obvious dilemma is that if I covered everyone who made significant contributions to my personal and professional life, it would exceed the length of this book. Alternatively, a succinct acknowledgement would inevitably exclude many, many people.

My wife, Cindy, is the single most important person to me on the face of the Earth and is the greatest blessing that I have ever received, closely followed by our daughters. She gave her gifts of beauty, intelligence, sophistication, independence, athleticism, and personality to our three beautiful, smart, sophisticated, independent, athletic, and personable daughters of our marriage, Heather, Heidi, and Holly. Heidi and Heather have brought three brilliant, handsome, and athletic grandsons, Gavin and Wyatt, and Bond into our family. They each uncannily resemble me. Naturally, our daughters' husbands, Craig and Chris, are an essential part of the equation! We are proud to have them as sons-in-law.

Our extended families are a key part of our lives, including Bob and Dolores Smith, Kevin Smith, Dr. Wendy Smith, Perry Smith, PE, and Barry Smith and their families.

Our friends, associates, and colleagues, especially those at **financialforensics**®, Heidi, Janet, and Kevin, mark another blessing. Their integrity, commitment to excellence, and devotion to the profession are exemplary. Other people have profoundly influenced this book (often in ways unknown to them) including (chronologically), Rev. Vergil DeFreece, Terry Callaway, Eric Harris, JD, William Smart, Sid Robertson, Kenneth Docter, Mark Lutchen, Dr. J. Vernon McGee, Ron Decker, Dr. James Dobson, Dr. F. Owen Black, Dr. Charles Swindoll, Richard and Kathy Snyder, David and Charles Fein, and Greg and Hiromi Hadley.

Our clients inspire us! We have worked with some of the most outstanding people in America, and their professional passion and entrepreneurial perseverance motivates us to be the best possible forensic operators.

Likewise, our colleagues throughout the United States have demonstrated a continual striving for excellence and have both contributed ideas and reinforced the effectiveness of the tools, techniques, methods, and methodologies constituting our portfolio.

Finally, my father, John, who gave his life to defend America and ensure the freedoms and privileges that we enjoy today, was key to the foundational values and principles of my early years. His early life struggles with abandonment, his daily (and hourly) combat to survive during World War II, as a Japanese POW, his extraordinary encounters with history, and his short life after the War personify him as part of the Greatest Generation. I owe him more than I can ever articulate.

A singular note about Greg Gadawski: We have been friends and business partners for more than 10 years, and he exemplifies the saying "Select your business partner more carefully than your spouse." He has supported me throughout the odyssey of building and growing our unique practice and perhaps more important, invariably redirects me to the proper course. He has uncommon talent in the financial forensics discipline and will inexorably achieve his place of international eminence in the profession.

DARRELL D. DORRELL

I would like to acknowledge all of those who have collectively contributed to the development of the Forensic Accounting/Investigation Methodology (FA/IM ©), the Forensic Accounting Academy™, and ultimately this book. It has been a long and tedious process that would not have been possible without the contributions of some of the best and brightest forensic operators in the world.

Furthermore, I would like to thank all of those who continue to contribute to advancement of the field of financial forensics. These are the people who are constantly developing or refining the countless tools and techniques for our profession. Their contributions have been invaluable, as we must always strive to be better, more efficient, and one step ahead of the bad guys.

I would like to thank all of our co-workers at **financialforensics**® for the extraordinary patience they exercised with Darrell Dorrell and me during the compilation of this book, and consistently on a day-to-day basis. Their support and contributions have been critical to our success and personal development.

Naturally, I would like to thank my wife for her continued love and support. She is my best friend and partner in life. She has blessed me with a handful of beautiful children and I look forward to spending the rest of my life with her by my side.

Finally I would like to acknowledge the person that has made all of this possible, Darrell Dorrell. Darrell encouraged me to enter the profession of financial forensics and ever since then he has been a great friend and business partner. Darrell is truly a visionary and it is a blessing to work alongside him every day. It is an immense understatement to say that without Darrell Dorrell none of this would have been possible.

GREGORY A. GADAWSKI

Introduction

This book describes and illustrates the copyrighted, trademarked, and patent-in-process (through the USPTO[1]) financial forensics/forensic accounting methodology. It can be deployed as-is in this book or through its comprehensive software-driven, Internet-based financial forensics methodology, Forensic Accounting/Investigation Methodology©, or FA/IM©. Other financial forensics methodologies are also described, both inside and outside of FA/IM. They include 60-Second Method, BIC, FSAT, and ICE/SCORE©, among others.

FA/IM has been delivered for nearly ten years throughout the United States in training sessions ranging from 1 or 2 hours, 1 or 2 days, or through our signature 5-day Forensic Accounting Academy©. Naturally, shorter sessions cover less content.

The numerous participants' responses have been nearly universal, stating that:

"It is the most comprehensive tool that I have ever seen" or

"I have never seen the forensic process demonstrated so logically" or

"I love the fact that it is continually updated" or

"I can leave the session with tools for immediate use" or

"This is what the accounting profession should have produced."

The methodology and its tools can be deployed whether or not the software is accessed through subscription. A thorough read through of this book enables a forensic operator to deploy the methodology and its embedded tools, techniques, methods, and methodologies in civil, criminal, and dispute matters. However, the book's content, augmented by the software-driven, Internet-based methodology gives forensic operators more accessibility and ensures continually updated leading-edge content.

WHAT IS A METHODOLOGY?

Skilled forensic operators routinely deploy methodologies, but their clients and other parties occasionally need explanation regarding the term *methodology*. Simply put, a methodology is a formal or informal way of doing things. Merriam-Webster defines a methodology as "A body of methods, rules, and postulates employed by a discipline; a particular procedure or set of procedures."[2] Virtually everyone uses methodologies on a day-to-day basis.

[1] United States Patent and Trademark Office.

[2] www.merriam-webster.com/dictionary/methodology.

The following examples summarize simple methodologies encountered on a day-to-day basis.

- Baristas follow a methodology to make a latte, depending upon the size, ingredients, toppings, and other customer preferences.
- Grade-school children follow a methodology to add, subtract, multiply, and divide numbers by hand, "... carry the nine..."
- Users follow a methodology to launch a software program. That is, the user enters a user ID, followed by a password.
- Law enforcement officers follow a methodology to clear jammed semiautomatic pistols, consisting of "tap, rack, bang."
- Cashiers use a methodology to close out the till at the end of their shift.
- Health enthusiasts follow a methodology when working out, such as warm-up and stretch, workout, and cool-down.
- Men follow a methodology when getting ready in the morning, comprising the tasks of teeth-brushing, flossing, shaving, and other ablutions.

The preceding examples outline simple methodologies used for a wide variety of purposes. Methodologies also exist for more complex activities, as indicated next.

- Corrections officers follow a methodology when returning prisoners to their cells and securing the facility.
- Pilots follow a preflight methodology to ensure safety.
- Hairstylists follow a methodology when trimming, cutting, shaping, styling, or other actions, depending on the customer's preference.
- Chefs follow a methodology when preparing various dishes.
- Accounting firms follow a methodology to plan and execute audits.
- Medical assistants follow a methodology after a patient checks in for a physician's visit.
- Housekeepers follow a methodology to clean hotel rooms.
- Reporters follow a methodology[3] when writing articles and columns.

The list of example methodologies is literally endless, but the point is clear—methodologies are integral to human beings. Also, methodologies have existed since man's earliest days. For example, nearly 2,000 years ago Moses was instructed, "See to it that you make everything according to the pattern shown you on the mountain."[4] However, none of the above examples provided one-to-one comparison for forensic operators. Forensic operators need a wide array of technical capabilities, any of which may be necessary depending upon the facts and circumstances of each assignment. Certain disciplines, though especially the military, law enforcement,

[3] Reporters seldom know how much of their article will be used since it is partly dependent upon available space. Consequently, reporters write articles containing the most important facts at the beginning of the article, followed by successively less-important facts so that if anything is cut, it will be less important to the article.

[4] Hebrews 8:5, NIV.

and firefighters, serve as useful models for forensic operators. A few of them are listed here.

- *United States Marine Corps*—The official mission of the Marine Corps is established in the National Security Act of 1947, amended in 1952. Marines are trained, organized, and equipped for *offensive* amphibious employment and as a "force in readiness." According to the Act, Marines stand prepared to meet mission requirements.[5]
- *82nd Airborne Division*—The mission of the 82nd Airborne Division is to, within 18 hours of notification, strategically deploy, conduct forcible entry parachute assault, and secure key objectives for follow-on military operations in support of US national interests.[6]
- *Delta Force*—The unit commonly referred to as Delta Force is the US Army's special operations unit organized for the conduct of missions requiring a rapid response with surgical application of a variety of unique skills while maintaining the lowest possible profile of US involvement.[7] They plan and conduct a broad range of special operations across the operational continuum.
- *LAPD SWAT*—Los Angeles Police Department's SWAT (Special Weapons and Tactics Team) responds upon the request of the Incident Commander (IC) to barricade and hostage episodes or suicide intervention, or both, as well as initiate service of high-risk warrants for all department entities.[8]
- *FDNY*—Fire Department of New York—As first responders to fires, public safety, and medical emergencies, disasters, and terrorist acts, FDNY protects the lives and property of New York City residents and visitors. The department advances public safety through its fire prevention, investigation, and education programs. The timely delivery of these services enables the FDNY to make significant contributions to the safety of New York City and homeland security efforts.[9]

When one reviews the shortlist of preceding examples (there are several hundred good examples not listed), a sense of awe, respect, skill, courage, and other positive attributes prevail. Each of the preceding examples has a common trait: They embody *superbly trained* experts—*superbly trained.*

In most cases, they constantly train in their mission, their objectives, their tools, their methodologies, and every other factor to continually refine their skills. In fact, many train their entire career with scant opportunity to deploy their capabilities. The constant training focused on their respective missions enables them to achieve their respective mission objectives.

More important, though, they are so superbly trained that *they can deviate from their mission* and still be successful. The capability to deviate is necessary because

[5] www.lejeune.usmc.mil/2dfssg/med/files/103.htm.

[6] www.globalsecurity.org/military/agency/army/82abn.htm.

[7] Ibid.

[8] www.lapdonline.org/inside_the_lapd/content_basic_view/848.

[9] www.nyc.gov/html/fdny/html/general/mission.shtml.

combat and emergencies invariably present them with unexpected circumstances. Military strategists and combat veterans know that "*No battle plan survives first encounter with the enemy.*" Therefore, military operators must be so well trained in their mission that they can course-correct the instant combat surprises appear.

Forensic operators are no different—the public anticipates, the courts expect, and the profession requires forensic operators who are superbly trained in their craft—*superbly trained*.... Consequently, forensic operators know, "*No investigation plan survives first encounter with the people and money.*" Forensic operators serve at the pointy end of the spear and cannot function without appropriate tools, techniques, methods, and methodologies.

That is the purpose of FA/IM and the other financial forensic methodologies detailed in this book. It permits forensic operators to continually train for and refine their craft so that they approach every assignment superbly trained, with the ability to deviate. A methodology also defines training needs, since forensic operators can compare their skill sets with the comprehensive requirements codified by a methodology.

The Forensic Accounting/Investigation Methodology, or FA/IM, gives every forensic operator a specific tool that permits continual refinement of skills for everyone's benefit. Furthermore, it provides forensic operators the means by which to deviate from the assignment when the need arises.

WHY WAS THIS BOOK WRITTEN?

This book should have been written (or at least begun) about 100 years ago. That time horizon, that is, circa 1910 to 1930, is significant because of the preconditions and convergence of seminal economic, political, scientific, and social events reliant upon financial information. Complete discussion of such events is outside the scope of this book, but the discussion in this section makes the case.

Perhaps the single most startling example is contained in the September 26–28, 1904, proceedings of the Congress of Accountants held during the St. Louis World's Fair. The following extraction from the proceedings summarizes the need for this book.

> *The rise of large corporations in the decades before the [C]ongress...and some spectacular panics and stock market crashes—underscored the importance of proper accounting procedures and financial reporting. This gathering of accountants at the dawn of the new century was intended as an event at which the attendees could consider what kinds of services and procedures businesses required and* what the profession must do to meet those needs. *(Emphasis added.)*

Not knowing the date of original publication, one could easily place this quote within a few years of today's date. Indeed, the authors often display this quotation without a date and ask forensic operator training attendees to date the extract based on the text content. Invariably, the proffered dates fall very near the year *2000*. That is about 100 *years* after its publication. Simply stated, the same problems that faced accountants 100 years ago still exist today. Therefore, this book addresses such problems through its financial forensics tools, techniques, methods, and methodologies.

This Is a How-To Book

This book is a how-to book. It contains, describes, and illustrates more than 250-plus-or-minus forensic operator tools, techniques, methods, and methodologies. The term *forensic operator* is used throughout this book to identify financial forensics-capable personnel. It was derived from the *special operator* term that describes USSOCOM[10] Special Forces military personnel. Furthermore, *forensic operator* reflects the *necessity* for personnel to possess *unique and specific* skills, knowledge, experience, education, training, and integrity to function in the financial forensics discipline. The Forensic Inventory in the Appendix details the striking similarities between the job descriptions of the two titles, that is, *special operator* and *forensic operator.*

This book achieves its how-to status through seven unique features.

First, the vast majority of training and literature offered as financial forensics and forensic accounting training largely discusses the *what* of the discipline, not the *how* of the discipline. For example, the guidance offered by training and literature tells forensic operators to *carefully analyze the financial documents* but give few, if any, of the tools necessary to achieve such guidance. The few tools given are typically recitations of other publications. This book remedies that dilemma.

Second, this book purposely contains substantial content never before published within the financial forensics discipline, particularly as part of a comprehensive methodology. This feature is critically necessary for CPA forensic operators in particular. The accounting profession advises they label themselves forensic accountants despite providing a dearth of tools, techniques, methods, or methodologies for such a designation. Other professions, such as law enforcement, regulators, and so forth, do not make the same mistake; they gain legitimate training and expertise before attempting to do the work. Labeling oneself as forensic operator without commensurate skills is akin to trying to do a different job with the same tools. This book remedies that dilemma.

Third, a great deal of content in existing training and literature is highly duplicative. For example, many publications readily cite others' works within its own contents, sometimes without attribution. Some contain substantial portions of print merely reproducing what is already available from the public record, for example, statutes, ordinances, and so forth. Although some duplication and republishing may be in order, forensic operators need and seek new tools, techniques, methods, and methodologies. This book remedies that dilemma.

Fourth, this book presents five unique training and learning options for forensic operators. Forensic operators can:

1. Use this book on a standalone basis.
2. Use this book augmented by its optional Internet subscription content from the Financial Forensics Academy™ at www.financialforensicsacademy.com.

[10] United States Special Operations Command, *Department of Defense Dictionary of Military and Associated Terms,* Joint Publication 1-02, April 12, 2001 (as amended through September 30, 2010), Joint Chiefs of Staff (not classified).

3. Use the Internet site as a standalone tool.
4. Attend the 1- or 2-hour, 1- or 2-day, or 5-day Academy CPE sessions.
5. Combinations of the above.

The Internet site has the decided advantage of the continual, real-time update of new tools, techniques, methods, and methodologies, although subsequent book editions will, of course, also contain the new material. Previously, forensic operators had to look to numerous disparate sources for limited guidance. This book remedies that dilemma.

Fifth, this book gives forensic operators legitimate authority, as evidenced by its pedigree. For example, the Forensic Accounting/Investigation Methodology (FA/IM) that our firm created and formalized was originally published through the United States Department of Justice. In addition to that, the American Bar Association published descriptions of the methodology in a family law book.[11] The rigorous and scrupulous reviews and editing of both publication sources give forensic operators significant confidence in the contents. Continuing references in courtroom settings and forensic reports further substantiate the tools, techniques, methods, and methodologies. Forensic operators continually seek to increase their confidence level in the tools they deploy. This book remedies that dilemma.

Sixth, this book serves as an ideal quality control and training tool within the forensic operator's environment. It can serve in academic environments, public sector organizations, accounting firms, law enforcement, regulators, military, and other venues to support forensic operator training and assignment execution. Many forensic operators function in an environment in which parties have vast differences in skill, knowledge, education, experience, and training. This book remedies that dilemma.

Finally, this book spans the gamut of financial information. It provides guidance to financial information originators, users, and regulators, thus establishing a single source for all parties. Most other publications offer a narrow focus, compelling users to seek multiple sources. This book remedies that dilemma.

The Definition of Financial Forensics

This book defines financial forensics and forensic accounting by the following phrase: *The art & science of investigating people & money.*© The definition dates from circa 1993[12] and the following exhibit symbolizes the definition's transcendence.

Exhibit I.1 conceptualizes the universe of financial forensics tools, techniques, methods, and methodologies within the octagon shape. That is, the octagon represents every forensic technique on the face of the Earth. The ovals, such as "Economic Damages" and "Performance Auditing," and so forth, represent different (noninclusive) services typically provided by forensic operators. The ovals also reflect two other factors. First, each displays significant overlap with the universe of financial

[11] Miles Mason, Sr., JD, CPA, *The Forensic Accounting Deskbook—A Practical Guide to Financial Investigation and Analysis for Family Lawyers*, American Bar Association, 2011.
[12] **financialforensics**®.

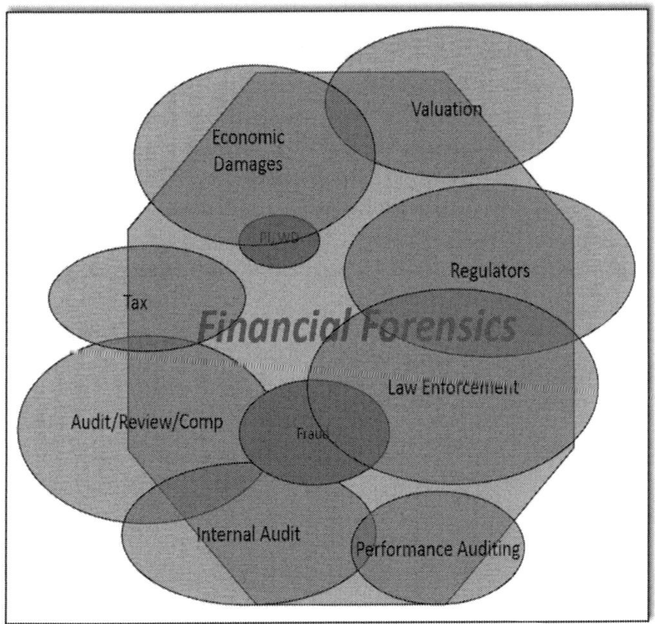

EXHIBIT I.1 Financial Forensics

forensics tools, techniques, methods, and methodologies or overlap with other services. This symbolizes how the collection of forensic tools, techniques, methods, and methodologies in this book almost universally to forensic services. That is, forensic operators should use common tools in virtually all assignments, thus increasing their proficiency.

Second, each oval displays a portion *outside* the financial forensics universe. That reflects the reality that certain service area requirements do not necessarily require financial forensics capabilities. For example, certain Financial Accounting Standards Board (FASB) requirements may fall outside the financial forensics universe. Also, statutes, precedents, jurisdictional requirements, and other guidance fall outside the financial forensics universe.

Furthermore, the figure places fraud within its appropriate context, as discussed in the Preface, that is, a subset of the financial forensics supra discipline. Forensic operators conducting fraud assignments indeed fall within the scope of financial forensics, but most financial forensics assignments fall outside the fraud realm. This book describes this broader scope and detail while still addressing fraud.

Finally, the public would be astonished to know that *no* definition of financial forensics exists that even approaches the essence of our work. Forensic accounting and financial forensics had various definitions in the past, all inadequate. In fact, some consider it akin to *debate* because of the root of the word *forensic.*[13] Those misguided souls fail to consider the context of the root. That is, the Roman forum

[13] 1650s, from L. *forensis* "of a forum, place of assembly," www.etymonline.com/index.php.

was the center of the world in its time. All legal, financial, societal, economic, cultural, moral (and immoral) laws, and mores derived from the Roman forum, where all roads led to Rome. Caesar was assassinated at the forum, and all manner of scheming and plotting took place there. It was anything but civil debate. Likewise, forensic operators function in career-ending and even life-ending environments. Such a realization germinated the CombatCPA© genre, as explained in the Appendix. Therefore, forensic operators must be realistic about the risks associated with such a dangerous undertaking, further substantiating the essential need for sophisticated tools, techniques, methods, and methodologies.

Events Converging about 100 Years Ago

The following events summarize those economic, political, scientific, and social events converging during the 1910 to 1930 time frame. They do not comprise an exhaustive treatment of the events but serve to illustrate the convergence of key points.

Economic Events

- 1896—The legal recognition of the CPA designation became effective April 17, 1896.[14,15]
- 1904—The Congress of Accountants convened at the St. Louis World's Fair. (See preceding extract.)
- 1907—The Panic of 1907 was a U.S. financial crisis triggered when large corporate failures caused business and Wall Street brokerage failures. Stock market prices collapsed and short-term legislation lead to the formation of the Federal Reserve System.
- 1909—Publication of the *Cyclopedia of Commerce, Accountancy, Business Administration*, American Technical Society, Chicago. This 10-volume set contains extensive guidance regarding financial techniques, including instructions for finding fraud in financial statements.
- 1917—The naming of the American Institute of Accountants (AIA) occurred. The AIA was the successor to the American Association of Public Accountants (AAPA), which dated to 1887. The AIA restricted membership to CPAs in 1936. The AIA became the American Institute of Certified Public Accountants in 1957.[16]
- 1919—America emerged from World War I as a creditor rather than a debtor nation, and Wall Street supplanted London as the world's investment capital.[17]

[14] Dale L. Flesher, Gary J. Previts, and Tonya K. Flesher, "Profiling the New Industrial Professionals: The First CPAs of 1896–97" (*Business and Economic History* 25, no. 1, 1996).

[15] American Institute of Certified Public Accountants, 2011.

[16] American Institute of Certified Public Accountants, 2011.

[17] www.nyse.com.

- 1929—The stock market crash occurred October 29, 1929, precipitating the Great Depression, which arguably continued until the 1941 onset of World War II.

Political Events

- 1913—The Owen-Glass Federal Reserve Act created the Federal Reserve System.
- 1913—16th Amendment (Amendment XVI) to the United States Constitution ratified Congress's right to impose a federal income tax.
- 1933—The U.S. Congress passed the Securities Act of 1933.
- 1934—The U.S. Congress passed the Securities Exchange Act of 1934, which created the Securities and Exchange Commission, or SEC. The 1933 and 1934 Acts catapulted the growth of the accounting and auditing profession in support of financial reporting.

Scientific Events

- 1911—Frederick Winslow Taylor, "The Father of Scientific Management" copyrighted his work *The Principles of Scientific Management.*
- 1917—The Industrial Revolution peaked roughly coincident with the United States's April 16, 1917, entry into World War I.
- 1920s—The source of the popular DuPont model (ROI, or return on investment) was F. Donaldson Brown, of E. I. du Pont de Nemours and Company's treasury department.
- 1924—The International Business Machines Corporation (IBM) became the successor to the Computer Tabulating Recording Company. Herman Hollerith had formed the predecessor company after inventing a punch-card tabulating machine for the 1890 U.S. census.[18]
- 1925—The disciplines of statistics and probability were widely applied by 1925 and thus were available to accountants charged with evaluating financial statements. Commonly applied techniques included regression and correlation (1888), the normal distribution curve (1889), standard deviation (1894), chi-square test (1900), probability (1907), and ANOVA (1920), among others.
- 1931—Alphonse Gabriel "Al" Capone is indicted for tax evasion and eventually sentenced to prison. The federal government used a forensic accounting technique known as the indirect method to help prosecute the case.
- 1934—Benjamin Graham and David Dodd published *Security Analysis.* Graham and Dodd were Columbia University professors who codified the foundational tenets of financial analysis for investors. Their 736-page book contains techniques to evaluate the quality of earnings contained within financial statements. Significant portions of the text describe analytical techniques still useful today. Some of the reference phrases include *padded income account, manipulated accounting, misleading artifices,* and other techniques, all still pertinent today. Warren Buffet wrote that he considers this book as one of the four most treasured books that he owns.

[18] U.S. Census Bureau history.

Social Events

- 1910 to 1930—The Industrial Revolution stimulated the flow of residents from the countryside to cities to gain industrial employment.
- 1920—19th Amendment (Amendment XIX) to the United States Constitution ratified prohibiting the denial of voting rights for any U.S. citizen based on sex. This Amendment culminated the women's suffrage movement.
- 1921—The Emergency Quota Act restricted legal immigration into the United States due to the burgeoning inflows. It established numerical limits on European immigrants and used the quota system to control the limits.
- Circa 1923—Oliver Gingold of Dow Jones coined the phrase *blue chip* while standing by the stock ticker of the brokerage firm that later became Merrill Lynch.[19] It is believed this is a reference to the blue chip being the highest denomination in old poker chip sets.

We are convinced that this book will fill the vacuum in financial forensics training and education for the near term. We are also confident that this book will serve as the foundation for continuing research, development, discovery, and application of continually more sophisticated tools, techniques, methods, and methodologies. The financial world grows more complex each day and it is essential that forensic operators have access to weapons that, at a minimum, keep pace with the change, and eventually overtake it.

HOW TO USE THIS BOOK

This book applies to nearly *everyone* originating or relying upon financial information, ranging from novice to expert. It contains tools that transcend the needs of anyone falling within the three basic classes of people who rely upon financial information: originators, users, and regulators. They are defined in Exhibit I.2.

A Reader Lookup Table in Exhibit I.3 permits nearly everyone to find exactly what is needed within. Merely identify the Reader category say, "Investor" and note the • under the respective chapters. Thus, an investor would read the chapters so indicated. If seeking a type of matter say, "Due Diligence," complete the same process.

ABOUT THE BOOK'S WEBSITE

Additional content is available for download at www.wiley.com/go/financial forensics. The website includes 12 actual BLINDED financial forensics reports related to the discussions in Chapter 6. The reports cover a wide range of matters—civil, criminal, and dispute, thus providing forensic operators with reference material applicable to the matter(s) at hand.

[19] www.djindexes.com.

EXHIBIT I.2 Three Classes of People Reliant Upon Financial Information

Explanation	Originators	Users	Regulators
Description	This category includes those who *originate* (directly or indirectly) financial information for any purpose. It comprises individuals, households, publicly held entities, privately held entities, government organizations, NPOs, and others.	This category includes those who *use* (that is, rely upon) the financial information produced by originators for any purpose.	This category includes those who *regulate* the financial information submitted by originators or users or both. It includes civil regulators, criminal regulators, military, and others.
Types	Typical examples of *originators* include CEOs, CFOs, controllers, accounting clerks, application specialists, expense report filers, income tax return filers, and others.	Typical examples of *users* include auditors, CPAs, CAs,[20] boards of directors, investors, lenders, professors, insurers, brokers, executives, consumers (e.g., personal financial planning, 401(k) management), valuators, attorneys, insurance providers, and others.	Typical examples of *regulators* include civil regulators (SEC, IRS, FTC, and others), criminal regulators (FBI, DEA, IRS, state police international, federal, state, local law enforcement), military (counterterrorism), and others.

HOW THIS BOOK IS ORGANIZED

This book is based upon the most comprehensive financial forensics/forensic accounting body of knowledge and methodology known to exist, FA/IM© (Forensic Accounting/Investigation Methodology©). The methodology is a copyrighted, trademarked and patent-in-process (through the USPTO[21]) technique built upon a software-based, user-interactive process map with context-sensitive hyperlinks. It has been delivered a few hundred times to thousands of attendees throughout the United States, receiving very positive reviews.

[20] Chartered Accountants.

[21] United States Patent and Trademark Office.

EXHIBIT I.3 Reader Lookup Table

Reader Lookup Table	Introduction and Methodology				Financial Forensics Tools, Techniques, Methods and Methodologies													Special Topics		Appendices		
					Chapters																	
					1		2		3				4, 5		6							
Reader / Topic	Preface	Acknowledgments	Authors	Introduction	Assignment	Scoping	Behavior Detection	Background	Data Collection	Surveillance	Informants	Undercover	Laboratory	Analysis	Preparation	Reporting	Post-Assignment	Terrorism	Fraud	Inventory	Bibliography	Index
Accountant	•			•	•	•	•	•	•				•	•	•	•	•	•	•	•	•	•
Alter Ego							•	•					•	•		•		•				•
Attorney	•			•	•	•	•	•	•	•	•	•			•	•		•	•	•	•	•
Auditor	•			•	•	•	•	•	•	•	•	•	•	•	•	•		•	•	•	•	•
Background Research					•	•	•	•	•							•						•
Banker/Lender	•			•	•	•	•	•	•				•	•	•	•			•	•	•	•
Behavior Detection							•	•		•	•	•										•
Board Director	•			•	•	•	•	•	•				•	•	•			•	•	•	•	•
Broker, Securities	•			•	•	•	•	•	•				•	•	•	•		•	•	•	•	•
Business Owner							•	•										•	•	•	•	•
CEO							•	•										•	•	•	•	•
CFO/Controller	•			•	•	•	•	•	•				•	•	•	•	•	•	•	•	•	•
Counterterrorism	•			•	•	•	•	•	•	•	•	•	•	•	•	•	•	•	•	•	•	•
Damages	•			•	•	•	•	•	•	•	•	•	•	•	•	•		•				•
Document Request							•	•														•
Due Diligence							•	•		•	•	•	•	•	•	•		•	•	•	•	•
Engagement Letter							•	•														•
Financial Analyst	•			•	•	•	•	•	•						•		•	•	•	•	•	•

Forensic Operator	•	•		•	•	•	•	•	•	•	•	•	•	•	•	•	•	•	•	•	•	•
Fraud	•			•	•	•	•	•	•	•	•	•	•	•	•	•	•	•	•	•	•	•
Fraudulent Transfer/Conveyance	•			•	•	•	•	•	•	•	•	•	•	•	•	•	•	•	•	•	•	•
Internal Auditor	•			•	•	•	•	•	•	•	•	•	•	•	•	•	•	•	•	•	•	•
Interview/Interrog							•	•		•	•	•										•
Investigator	•			•	•	•	•	•	•	•	•	•	•	•	•	•	•	•	•	•	•	•
Investor	•			•	•	•	•	•	•	•	•	•	•	•	•	•	•	•	•	•	•	•
Journalist	•			•	•	•	•	•	•	•	•	•	•	•	•	•	•	•	•	•	•	•
Jurist	•			•	•	•	•	•	•							•		•	•	•	•	•
Lost Profits							•	•		•	•	•	•	•		•						•
Law Enforcement	•			•	•	•	•	•	•	•	•	•	•	•	•	•	•	•	•	•	•	•
Management	•			•	•	•	•	•	•									•	•	•	•	•
Marital Dissolution	•			•	•	•	•	•	•	•	•	•	•	•	•	•	•		•	•	•	•
Money Laundering	•			•	•	•	•	•	•	•	•	•	•	•	•	•	•	•	•	•	•	•
Professor	•			•	•	•	•	•	•				•	•		•		•	•	•	•	•
Public Sector	•			•	•	•	•	•	•				•	•		•	•	•	•	•	•	•
Regulator	•			•	•	•	•	•	•	•	•	•	•	•	•	•	•	•	•	•	•	•
Reporting, Forensic							•	•								•	•	•	•	•	•	•
Retiree							•	•										•				•
Single Parent							•	•										•				•
Shareholder	•			•	•	•	•	•	•				•	•	•	•	•	•	•	•	•	•
Solvency/Insolvency	•			•	•	•	•	•	•	•	•	•	•	•	•	•	•	•	•	•	•	•
Student							•	•								•		•				•
Valuation	•			•	•	•	•	•	•	•	•	•	•	•	•	•	•	•	•	•	•	•

The book comprises the contents of FA/IM© and can be used as a stand-alone tool. Alternatively, it can be supplemented by the subscription based methodology and related training sessions.

FA/IM© mirrors any forensic assignment and functions left-to-right, top-to-bottom. It comprises 4 Phases, 13 Stages, and 5 Actions per Stage. Each chapter describes the respective Phase, Stage, and Actions, and contains the pertinent reference material. The 250-+/− specific forensic accounting/financial forensics tools, techniques, methods, and methodologies are contextually described throughout the book.

The following outline describes the respective chapter content, organized into two parts. Part 1 contains the financial forensics tools, techniques, methods, and methodologies. Part 2 contains special topics, including significant content on counterterrorism. Also, fraud-related content compares the civil and criminal law processes in financial forensics matters, and provides specific advice for anyone encountering a potential embezzlement in an organization.

Part One: Financial Forensics Tools, Techniques, Methods, and Methodologies

Chapter 1: Foundational Phase This chapter lays the foundation for the overall methodology as described by the detailed content. The two stages in this phase of the methodology, Assignment Development and Scoping, permit the forensic operator to accurately scope an assignment before launching an assignment.

The *Assignment Development* stage contains conflict resolution recommendations and is supported by chain of custody, conflict resolution, sample engagement letter, and entity-party chart descriptions and example formats.

The *Scoping* stage contains forensic timeline, genogram, document request, data catalog, and document map descriptions and example formats. They enhance the foundation and will be continually updated throughout the respective assignment.

Chapter 2: Interpersonal Phase This chapter highlights the *Interview and Interrogation* and *Background Research* stages and includes an example deposition matrix. The discussion permits forensic operators to continually loop back to refine and enhance the data gathered during subsequent phases and stages.

The *Interview and Interrogation* stage addresses the process of eliciting information through interviews, interrogation, and introduces behavior detection techniques such as facial mapping.

The *Background Research* stage is purposely summarized, since most forensic operators enlist specialists to conduct such research. Thus, the focus is on select resources the forensic operator should access.

Chapters 3, 4, 5: Data Collection and Analysis Phase—Parts I, II, and III This phase comprises three chapters, that is, 3, 4, and 5, segmented as Parts I, II, and III, respectively. The phase contains the majority of content since this is where most of the pick-and-shovel work occurs in forensic assignments. The respective chapters introduce techniques, discuss their application, and provide examples of output. The content is very descriptive and it is likely that most forensic operators will spend most of their time in this phase. The contents follow.

Chapter 3: Data Collection and Analysis Phase—Part I This chapter contains a detailed description of a versatile submethodology ICE/SCORE©. It can be used as a stand-alone methodology or in parallel with the overall methodology. Forensic operators will use it as a training tool for a wide variety of client and subject targets. Also, the proof of cash technique is explained as a logical extension of the ICE/SCORE technique.

The *Surveillance—Electronic and Physical, Confidential Informants,* and *Undercover Stages* are lightly treated in this book because the actual training contains sensitive techniques typically pertinent in law enforcement, counterterrorism, and military applications. Nonetheless, they still apply to all other forensic operators. For example, in civil litigation, surveillance sometimes consists of merely driving by opposition facilities. Specifically, the authors worked on a matter where it was suspected that the third shift of a frozen-foods company was selling inventory for cash. One of the authors parked nearby during several third shifts to observe and document traffic. Likewise, in another matter, a forensic operator stationed a staff accountant in a parking lot to observe, document, and count the number of cars serviced by a car wash during a defined period. That information was used to compare to the opposition's claims. In such circumstances, surveillance applies to forensic operators, but lacks law enforcement authority.

The *Confidential Informants* stage has similar implications for non–law enforcement matters. For example, forensic operators routinely chat with company employees to informally learn about the business.

The *Undercover* stage is often conducted by forensic operators in civil matters. For example, assuming counsel concurs, it is routine practice to phone opposition's subject company to query parties regarding products, services, pricing, and the like. Done properly, it is merely gathering information generally available to anyone who would phone the company.

WAR STORY

The authors are familiar with a CPA who tried to do forensic work without training. He was assisting an attorney who represented the wife in a marital dissolution. The day before trial he called the husband (an investment advisor) pretending to be a high-net-worth individual and obtained a great deal of information. Naturally, such a process, known as pretext actions, is at least unethical and perhaps illegal. During trial the next day, while the CPA spouted forth his newfound knowledge, he was asked on cross-examination how he obtained the information. He happily explained how clever he was, whereupon the judge dismissed him and suggested he seek counsel. Both the CPA and attorney were sanctioned by their respective professional associations.

The *Laboratory Analysis* stage contains new and powerful forensic tools. They include instructions and training regarding avoiding confirmation bias, which affects nearly every forensic operator. Aberrant pattern detection provides a unique perspective regarding data uncommonly considered by forensic operators. Also, forensic lexicology instructs forensic operators how to quantify words like they do numbers.

Companion Section—Valuation and Litigation: This unique section identifies foundational content for forensic operators seeking rapid insight into valuation and similar assignments. The content references sections essential to such assignments including confirmation bias, aberrant pattern detection, forensic indices, forensic financial analysis, valuation & forensics—why & how and valuation's orphan.

Chapter 4: Data Collection and Analysis Phase—Part II The *Analysis of Transactions* stage begins with this chapter and contains tools more familiar to forensic operators but with dimensions beyond common knowledge.

The Myth of Internal Control provides surprising insight that clarifies the state of auditing today. The *60-Second Method* is a very simple methodology that serves as a training tool for clients and a framework for trial testimony. *Financial Statements—Written Confessions* outlines a unique perspective of financial statements that forensic operators will welcome. *Forensic Indices* introduces insight into the dozens of techniques to assess financial statement veracity, surprisingly unknown to most CPAs, although non-CPA financial specialists know them well. *Forensic Financial Analysis* outlines a comprehensive analytical framework and a method of quantifying results in support of an ultimate conclusion.

Chapter 5: Data Collection and Analysis Phase—Part III The *Analysis of Transactions* stage continues with this chapter and contains knowledge particularly suited to investigating financial statements and related data. In addition, the content is essential for forensic operators who practice valuation for any purpose.

FSAT—Financial Status Audit Techniques summarizes the IRS' long-established investigation methodology. *Data Mining and Digital Analysis* synthesizes techniques almost unavoidable by forensic operators since so much of financial data is digitally stored. *Valuation & Forensics—Why & How* is a persuasive discussion of *why* valuation cannot be competently conducted without using forensic techniques. Finally, *Valuation's Orphan* addresses the most under-represented issue in valuation: assessment and derivation of economic benefit streams.

Chapter 6: Trial and Reports Phase This chapter contains actual content taken from many forensic assignments. A chapter summary highlights the key report components specific to forensic operator output. Although the content is from actual assignments, certain portions are BLINDED to prevent identification of any parties, entities, and so forth. This precaution is taken even though virtually all of it is already public record through the courts. The reports cover Alter Ego, Damages, Damages/Lost Profits—2 Reports, Forensic Accounting—Shareholder Oppression, Fraud—Individual, Fraud—Institutional, Fraudulent Transfer, Marital Dissolution—Forensics and Valuation, Observations Matrix, Solvency, Valuation—Matrix, and Valuation—Report Card. Due to size restrictions, the reports reside online, and are available for download at www.wiley.com/go/financialforensics.

Part Two: Financial Forensics Special Topics

This part contains two components. The first discusses counterterrorism using financial forensics as explained in two monographs originally written by the authors and published by the United States Department of Justice. The contents elaborate on using civil laws and financial forensics in the fight against terrorism. They were published in USDOJ's *Bulletin,* which is the technical reference source for US attorneys prosecuting matters on behalf of the United States. They are titled: "Financial Forensics I—Counterterrorism: Conventional Tools for Unconventional Warfare," vol. 53, no. 2, March 2005 issue, and "Financial Forensics II—Forensic Accounting: Counterterrorism Tactical Weaponry," vol. 53, no. 3, May 2005 issue. Forensic operators are encouraged to maintain a counterterrorism vigil when executing forensic assignments.

The second component has two specific fraud-related segments to augment the fraud techniques throughout the book. First, *Civil versus Criminal Comparison* compares and contrasts how the two types of forensic matters course their way from beginning to end. Also, *What If You Suspect Embezzlement?*—The Three Big Dont's and Several Do's is a first-aid-like reference for anyone experiencing potential embezzlement.

* * *

We are confident that forensic operators will find virtually all of the content covered in this book useful and helpful. Nearly all the contents of this book are original and cannot be found in other, allegedly similar publications. Readers can use it in a variety of ways depending on the facts and circumstances of the assignment at hand. Regardless of approach, we are confident that it will be an indispensable tool and commonly cited reference when supporting analysis and opinions.

PART One

Financial Forensics Tools, Techniques, Methods, and Methodologies

CHAPTER 1

Foundational Phase

Forensic operators must initiate assignments by clearly identifying and documenting the entities, parties, and ownership interests in the matter at hand. This phase is essential and cannot be disregarded since it charts the vector for the remainder of the assignment, notwithstanding subsequent refinements.

ASSIGNMENT DEVELOPMENT STAGE

Purpose of Stage

This action anchors the forensic assignment and shapes the context and defines the framework for assignment execution. See Exhibit 1.1.

The objective of this action is to complete necessary policy and procedural due diligence before taking any steps toward launching the assignment. This is the starting point for all forensic assignments.

Specific actions include:

- Identify *all* parties in the matter, internal and external. This includes, but is not limited to: plaintiff and defendant, petitioner and respondent, prosecutor and defendant, claimant and disputant, etc., including legal and regulatory parties.
- Correlate the matters of law, as applicable.
- Establish technical requirements.
- Uniquely identify the assignment with a client or case number or both.

References

This action confirms access to pertinent technical references, whether currently available or requiring acquisition. Technical resources comprise written materials and training, including self-study, webinar, and live classroom training.

The objective of this action is to ensure that necessary technical resources are at hand.

Specific actions include:

- Search, for example, the Internet for pertinent technical reference sources.
- Develop a list of required sources.
- Compare required sources against currently available sources.
- Acquire sources not otherwise available.

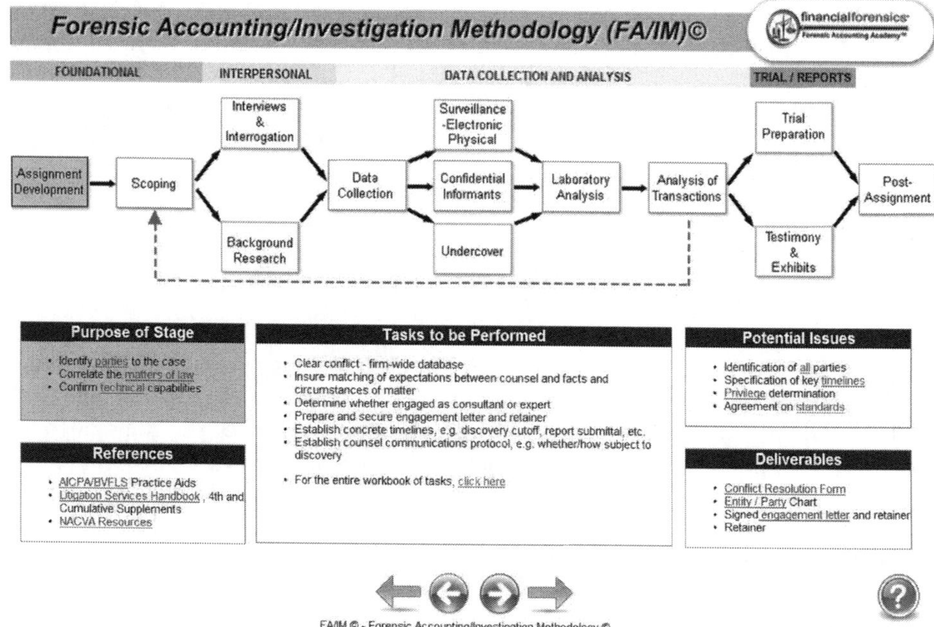

EXHIBIT 1.1 Assignment Development

Example of Reference Sources The following reference sources serve to jump start the forensic operator. The Key Internet Sites and Key Reference Materials are not all-inclusive but provide starting points from which to build resources. Also, refer to the bibliography.

Key Internet sites

- All forensic operators
  www.financialforensicsacademy.com
  www.fjc.gov
  - "Reference Manual on Scientific Evidence," *Reference Guide on Economic Losses in Damages Awards*, by Mark A. Allen, Robert E. Hall and Victoria A. Lazear.
- CPA forensic operators
  www.financialforensicsacademy.com

Key Reference materials

- All forensic operators
  - *Financial Forensics Body of Knowledge*, published by John Wiley & Sons.
- CPA forensic operators
  - *Litigation Services Handbook: The Role of the Financial Expert, 4th ed.*, published by John Wiley & Sons. Also, earlier editions and supplements contain significant additional material.

Tasks to Be Performed

This action outlines likely tasks but is not a checklist since each forensic assignment is unique. Use the tasks as a guideline and modify according to the unique facts and circumstances of the assignment.

The objective of this action is to ensure that the forensic operator *thinks through* the assignment from inception to completion before launching activities.

Specific actions include:

- Initiate full-and-false inclusion[1]

  The full-and false inclusion technique is *foundational* to financial forensics yet is foreign to many forensic operators and thus routinely overlooked. It is the *single most important element* of financial forensics yet is unknown or disregarded by untrained forensic operators. The technique is indispensable because it identifies the evidence essential to the forensic assignment at hand.

  Full-and-false-inclusion testing serves as the real-time map continuously constructed by the GPS-like capabilities of financial forensics. (See the following chain of custody.)
- Initiate chain of custody[2]

  The chain of custody is the fraternal twin of full-and-false inclusion. The term is familiar to forensic operators with criminal investigation backgrounds. Chain of custody likewise applies in civil and mere dispute matters just as it applies in criminal matters. (See full-and-false inclusion, above.)
- Formally clear conflict.
- Confirm the expectations of the responsible party(s). This could include a testimony role, consulting role, advisory role, or other capacity.
- Confirm the applicable laws, jurisdiction, regulations, precedent, and other requirements to ensure compliance.
- Confirm internal technical capabilities or alternatively, identify technical assistance, or initiate specific training.
- Search for pertinent technical reference sources via, for example, the Internet.

Example Chain of Custody Form *Note:* The following example chain of custody form (see Exhibit 1.2) permits all forensic operators to establish and maintain a contemporaneously documented trail of data and evidence. There are no generalized requirements for chain of custody forms except those unique to the forensic operator's organization. Nonetheless, it is often essential in both criminal and civil matters.

Descriptors: Each portion is self-explanatory regarding completion, with N/A indicated as necessary.

Custody: The prenumbered chain of custody forms trace to the chain of custody issue log. Both the chain of custody issue log and the chain of custody forms are permanently maintained in the evidence (work paper, library, etc.) room or locker.

---

[1] Full-and-false inclusion testing commences with inception and continues throughout the duration of the assignment. It continually determines the appropriate universe of data under investigation. Full-and-false inclusion testing ensures that all appropriate data is included and extraneous data is excluded. It symbolizes the yellow crime-scene tape of a forensic assignment.

[2] The documented trail that authenticates evidence.

NOTE: The following Example Chain of Custody form permits all forensic operators to establish and maintain a contemporaneously documented trail of data and evidence. There are no generalized requirements for Chain of Custody forms except those unique to the forensic operator's organization. Nonetheless, it is often essential in both criminal and civil matters.

Descriptors: Complete each self-explanatory section unless "N/A" is indicated.

Custody: The pre-numbered Chain of Custody forms traced to the Chain of Custody Issue Log. Both the Chain of Custody Issue Log and the Chain of Custody forms are permanently maintained in the evidence (workpaper, library, etc.) locker.

CHAIN OF CUSTODY FORM			**No. FO987654**
FORENSIC OPERATOR AGENCY			
Assignment Title:	**Assignment #:**	**Date Established:**	
Primary Party Responsible:	**Signature/Date:**		
Secondary Party Responsible:	**Signature/Date:**		
Assigned Item Number:	**Location:**		**Page ___ of ___**
Item Description:			
Item Identifiers: (S/N, model number, mfr.)			

ITEM	DATE/TIME	FROM	TO	REASON
	Date: Time:	Name: Signature:	Name: Signature:	
	Date: Time:	Name: Signature:	Name: Signature:	
	Date: Time:	Name: Signature:	Name: Signature:	
	Date: Time:	Name: Signature:	Name: Signature:	
	Date: Time:	Name: Signature:	Name: Signature:	
	Date: Time:	Name: Signature:	Name: Signature:	
	Date: Time:	Name: Signature:	Name: Signature:	
	Date: Time:	Name: Signature:	Name: Signature:	
	Date: Time:	Name: Signature:	Name: Signature:	
	Date: Time:	Name: Signature:	Name: Signature:	

EXHIBIT 1.2 Chain of Custody Form

Potential Issues

This action prompts the forensic operator to consider the boundaries of the people, parties, entities, timelines, data, output, cost, technical standards, and related criteria pertinent to the respective assignment. The suggested list is not an all-inclusive checklist since each forensic assignment is unique. Use the tasks as a guideline and modify according to the unique facts and circumstances of the assignment.

The objective of this action is to ensure that the forensic operator contemplates exigencies that may surface during the assignment. The forensic operator can minimize exigencies (to the extent possible) by diligent attention to this action.

WAR STORY

Plaintiff's counsel contacted a partner of an international accounting firm seeking his expert witness assistance. The forensic partner cleared the matter through his national office and began work. About three months later, defendant's counsel contacted a partner in the same accounting firm, seeking his expert witness assistance. The second partner did not follow procedure but began work immediately. Three months later an expert report exchange disclosed that the accounting firm was assisting both plaintiff and defendant. The accounting firm paid substantial damages and the second accounting partner is no longer with the firm.

Specific actions include:

- Confirm expectations of responsible parties.
- Confirm respective responsibilities of responsible parties.
- Agree upon criteria for success among responsible parties.
- Determine the extent of privilege,[3] if any.
- Confirm cost expectations of involved parties.
- Confirm pertinent technical standards.
- Confirm expectations of output composition.
- Confirm timelines (hearings, disclosures, discovery cutoff, report exchange, depositions) throughout the duration of the assignment.

Deliverables

The objective of this action is to identify and eventually finalize deliverables pertinent to the assignment. The forensic operator always develops deliverables designed with

[3] Privilege. A particular and peculiar benefit or advantage enjoyed by a person, company, or class, beyond the common advantages of other citizens. An exceptional or extraordinary power or exemption. A peculiar right, advantage, exemption, power, franchise, or immunity held by a person or class, not generally possessed by others. Black, *Henry C. Black's Law Dictionary* 6th ed. St. Paul, MN: West Publishing, 1990.

From: [ ]
Sent: Sunday, May 08, 2011 1:00 PM
To: Darrell Dorrell
Subject: Example Conflict Resolution

Partners: Please indicate affirmatively whether you have a conflict with the following.

MATTER: Criminal

Financial Statement Manipulation. Prosecution claims Chief Executive Officer and Chief Financial Officer fraudulently overstated their publicly held company's financial statements for at least the three most recent fiscal years.

Our responsibility is to lead the financial forensics analysis into the financial statements and underlying data, e.g., journal entries, board minutes, statement notes, and related evidence. The Special Agent team will support us directly. We will also testify at trial.

PROSECUTION (Our Client)

Federal government agency (NAME), spearheaded by Prosecutor #1 (NAME) and Prosecutor #2 (NAME). Supported by financial crimes specialists, Special Agent #1 (NAME) who requested our assistance. He will lead a team of Special Agents and Analysts who will be available to us for specific tasks.

DEFENDANTS

CEO (NAME) and CFO (NAME) of publicly held company (NAME). They were responsible for the three years of allegedly manipulated financial statements which resulted in a run-up and collapse of its publicly traded stock. They are named parties in a shareholder suit which will be deferred while the criminal suit progresses.

They are being individually defended by Large Law Firm #1 and Large Law Firm #2. Both law firms specialize in defense of white collar crime.

OTHER

Timing: Depositions will begin within 60 days, so we need to launch the assignment immediately. Also, we will prepare a Deposition Matrix for each deposed party. Trial is tentatively set, but likely to be set over per defendants' counsel.

Data: Imaged hard drives were already secured and are being investigated by the federal agency's computer forensic specialists.

EXHIBIT 1.3 Example Conflict Resolution Email

the end in mind so as to maximize efficiency. Document compliance with policies and procedures.

- Commonly communicate understanding.
- Provide tangible evidence of assignment progress.
- Serve as reference points continually updated as necessary.
- Complete necessary policy and procedural paperwork required by the forensic operator's environment.
- Prepare necessary deliverables.

Example Deliverables The following deliverables are frameworks for the forensic operator, who will modify them to comply with their respective internal and other requirements.

Example Conflict Resolution Email Format *Note:* The preceding sample conflict resolution email format (see Exhibit 1.3) includes typical considerations pursuant to assignment acceptance. The format can take almost any form, but the contents of the document must include the following and other firm- or agency-specific policy matters.

- *Addressed:* The email addresses *all* internal parties familiar with potential conflicts.
- *Affirmative Response:* The affirmative response permits the forensic operator's organization to maintain a continuously updated database of parties to avoid future conflicts.
- *Role:* The explanation clearly identifies the forensic operator's testifying role.
- *Timing:* Timing expectations ensure accommodation with the forensic operator's availability.

Example Engagement Letter *Note:* The following sample engagement letter obviously applies to forensic operators who practice as CPAs. Nonetheless, even non-CPA practitioners can refer to the contents for generalized guidance to construct similar letters of understanding.

SAMPLE ENGAGEMENT LETTER

PRIVILEGED AND CONFIDENTIAL
PREPARED AT REQUEST OF COUNSEL DURING LITIGATION

DATE

Mr. Litigator/Prosecutor
Law Firm/Agency
ADDRESS
CITY STATE, ZIP

Re: Litigator/Prosecutor

Dear Mr. Litigator/Prosecutor:
This letter documents our conversations and confirms that we have cleared conflict and begun work. This letter then confirms the engagement of our firm to provide analysis and consulting services in assisting you in your representation of SUBJECT/PARTY.

The Nature of Our Professional Responsibilities and Ethics

We practice as certified public accountants, CPAs. Therefore, we are compelled to meet a wide variety of ethical, legal, professional, and technical standards. These requirements reflect our fiduciary capacity and comprise a set of standards exceeding virtually any other profession.

We hold our ethical, legal, professional, and technical practice responsibilities in the highest regard, particularly the hallmark of our profession, *independence*. It is through independence that we serve the public's interest in providing unbiased, objective, and technically correct opinions on financial matters, whether in court or in private transactions.

The authorities governing our ethical, legal, professional, and technical practice actions include:

AICPA—American Institute of Certified Public Accountants. This national body, in connection with the Financial Accounting Standards Board (FASB) and related entities establishes financial reporting requirements commonly known as Generally Accepted Accounting Principles (GAAP). The AICPA rules of professional conduct contain twelve (12) rules organized into the following categories:

100–Independence, integrity, and objectivity

200–General and technical

300–Responsibilities to clients

400–Responsibilities to colleagues (superseded, that is, no longer in force)

500–Other responsibilities and practices

State—State State Board of Accountancy.[4] This body, authorized by statutes has as its primary purpose to protect the public interest. It is the principal government state agency that issues CPA licenses and certificates. The state laws governing certified public accountants generally follow the Uniform Accountancy Act (UAA), but where conflicts arise, state law prevails. The board rules specifically refer to breach of fiduciary duty as a part of general prohibitions against dishonesty and fraud under statutes. Virtually all states have similar provisions.

[4] A partner of our firm presently serves on the State's Complaints Committee.

Statutes—State Society of Certified Public Accountants. This body furthers the interests of CPA members, and coordinates professional requirements with the AICPA through the joint ethical enforcement program (JEEP).

SEC—Securities and Exchange Commission. This U.S. law enforcement government body governs financial reporting requirements for all publicly held and certain privately held businesses and transactions.

IRS—Internal Revenue Service. This U.S. Treasury body is responsible for administering the laws and collections processes concerning revenue for the federal government.

Jurisdictional Requirements—The federal, state or local jurisdiction may govern the specific approach to the opening period.

Other Professional Bodies—The unique nature of our forensic accounting practice compels us to apply additional professional and ethical standards from the following:

ACFE—American College of Forensic Examiners

ACFE—Association of Certified Fraud Examiners

ASA—American Society of Appraisers

IBA—Institute of Business Appraisers

IMA—Institute of Management Accountants

IMC—Institute of Management Consultants

NACVA—National Association of Certified Valuation Analysts

We strive to meet and exceed the preceding standards through our firm's guidance as summarized here:

Our Mission Statement: (list mission statement here)

The Definition of Forensic Accounting Is: The art & science of investigating people & money.[5]

Background and Scope

You have requested that we assist you with analysis and consultation in connection with the just-referenced matter. We are also prepared to provide testimony at deposition and trial should you decide that to be appropriate. At this point, however, we are serving as consultants; thus, we understand the work performed by us will be *confidential,* constituting a portion of your work product, and is to be regarded by us as being covered by the *attorney-client* and attorney work-product privileges. This will apply even after you are no longer a client.

We understand that all communications between us and you and your firm, whether oral or written, as well as any materials or information developed

[5]Circa 1993.

or received by us during this engagement, are protected by applicable legal privileges and, therefore, will be treated by us as confidential. Accordingly, we agree, subject to applicable law or court order, not to disclose any of our communications, or any of the information we receive or develop in the course of our work for you, to any person or entity apart from your office, or such other persons or entities as your office may designate. We are committed to safekeeping your confidential information. We maintain physical, electronic, and procedural safeguards to protect your information.

Our analysis and results will be completed in accordance with the pertinent consulting standards set by the American Institute of Certified Public Accountants (AICPA).

We will document the results of our work in the form of various calculation schedules and narrative reports that will be provided to and discussed with you. Such documents will provide sufficient support for conclusions, yet maintain cost-effectiveness in preparation. The results will be explained and refinements, if any, will be incorporated during work sessions that may be required.

Any written reports or other documents that we prepare are to be used only for the purpose of this engagement and may not be published or used for any other purpose without our express written consent.

Team Assigned

The team assigned to your work will consist only of professionals individually qualified to conduct the requisite analysis.

Lead Team Member and Bio: He has extensive experience in financial forensics, business litigation, and business valuation and has testified many times in various courts.

Project Team Member and Bio: He has extensive experience in financial forensics, business litigation, and business valuation and has testified many times in various courts.

The previous will be supported by other professionals and technical specialists as necessary.

To learn more about our firm, examine our Internet site at the following Internet address: www.InternetAddress.com

The Fees Necessary to Complete the Work

It is not presently possible to estimate the fees that we may incur during this project. However, we will invoice you biweekly so that you are kept apprised of our progress and your fee investment. That will permit you and your client to assess whether additional investigation is warranted.

The fee investment involved depends upon the nature and extent of available information, as well as the developments that may occur as work progresses. It is our intention to work closely with you and structure our work so that our fees are kept to a minimum. Our fees are not contingent upon any results obtained by you or your client in this matter. We neither warrant nor predict the results or outcome of this matter.

Regardless of the outcome of this matter, we understand that you and your client will compensate us for the time and expenses (if any) incurred. _______ (Initial here)

Our billing rates for are as follows:

Principals, range per hour ________

Other professionals, range per hour ________

Technical staff, range per hour ________

Possible average, range per hour ________

These fees for our services are based on the actual time expended on the engagement at the standard hourly rates for the individuals assigned. We capture our time daily in detail and round to the nearest tenth (.10) of an hour. Our billings are generally self-explanatory, but please let us know if you have questions about them.

In addition, we are reimbursed, at cost, for any travel and out-of-pocket expenses, such as long-distance telephone charges, reproduction costs, supplies, etc. It is our understanding that you and your client will be responsible for paying our fees and reimbursement of our out-of-pocket expenses.

Before commencing work on this engagement, we require a retainer approximating the expected peak time that we might invest during our work. Based upon our initial understanding of our involvement in this case, we are requesting a retainer in the amount of $xx,xxx. The retainer amount *is not* representative of a total fee estimate for this matter.

Note that this retainer will be applied to the final invoice on this engagement. _______ (Initial here) Any unused retainer will, of course, be refunded.

Bills will be submitted periodically as the work progresses and *are due and payable upon receipt.* Interest on unpaid bills is accrued at a rate of 1.5% per month. We reserve the right to halt further services until payment is received on past due invoices.

Our billings are due upon receipt.[6] _______ (Initial here)

If we should be required to testify, we require that we be paid in full for all work performed to date prior to our testimony. _______ (Initial here)

Our hourly rates are subject to change from time to time due to increased experience of our staff and changing market conditions. We will advise you

[6]Note that our insistence on timely payment is, of course, related to prudent business practices. More important, however, late or overdue billing payments discovered by opposing counsel have often been used to *convince a jury that such condition impairs the objectivity and independence of the expert.*

immediately if our rates are being adjusted. You will be responsible for fees at the increased rates.

If you or your client disagree with or question any amount due under an invoice, you shall communicate such disagreement to us in writing within thirty (30) days of the invoice date. Any claim not made within that period shall be deemed waived.

In the event that formal collection procedures are required, you and your client agree to pay all expenses of collection and all attorney's fees and costs actually incurred by our firm in connection with such collection, whether or not suit is filed thereon. If litigation is required regarding collection of the account, we will be paid our hourly rates for all the time actually expended by our firm in connection with such action.

Indemnifications

The following items are recommended by the AICPA[7] when CPAs serve as expert witnesses.

You, your firm, and we agree that any controversy or claim arising out of or relating to this contract, or the breach thereof, or the services performed by us shall be settled by binding arbitration before a single arbitrator in accordance with the commercial arbitration rules of the arbitration service of CITY, and judgment on the award rendered by the arbitrator may be entered in any court having jurisdiction thereof. Any arbitration shall be initiated at the ASP offices in CITY, STATE, and all hearings shall be conducted at said offices. In the event an arbitration or litigation (including but not limited to any proceeding to compel arbitration) is initiated to resolve or settle any dispute or claim between the parties, the prevailing party shall be entitled to recover from the nonprevailing party or parties its reasonable costs, including but not limited to reasonable attorney's fees and fees of our firm incurred in connection with the arbitration or litigation. In agreeing to arbitration, we acknowledge that in the event of a dispute over fees, each of us is giving up the right to have the dispute decided in a court of law before a judge and jury and, instead, is accepting the use of arbitration resolution.

You, the law firm, or the court itself will advise us, with sufficient notice, of the work to be performed by us and the requirement (if any) for our appearance in court. Should information become known that would make our continued involvement in the engagement inappropriate, or should the attorneys or parties involved in this litigation change, we reserve the right to withdraw from this engagement.

Our work, to be performed under your direction, is to perform such tasks as may be identified during the course of this engagement. However, we may refuse to perform any act that we deem a violation of law, public policy, or our professional ethical standards, and in such event, we may withdraw from the engagement without penalty.

[7]American Institute of Certified Public Accountants.

If we believe that you or your client has provided materially untruthful information, which may affect our conclusions, we may withdraw from the engagement without penalty.

You and your client agree that NAME OF ENTITY will not be liable for incidental or consequential damages even if we have been advised of the possibility of such damages, with respect to any event associated with this engagement.

By acknowledging acceptance of the terms of this engagement, your firm represents and warrants that it has the authority from your client to employ us on the terms and conditions set forth herein, including but not limited to the provisions mentioned with respect to arbitration of disputes and claims.

If we are required to present, represent, defend, or otherwise testify in court regarding this engagement, your firm, your client, or the court will advise us, with sufficient notice, of the work to be performed by us and the requirement, if any, for appearance in court.

You and your client agree to hold NAME OF ENTITY, its partners, shareholders, employees, and their heirs harmless from any and all liabilities, costs, and expenses relating to this engagement (and those of our legal counsel) incurred by reason of any action taken or committed at your direction and taken by us in good faith, and you agree to indemnify us for any such action taken at your direction.

If the arrangements described in this letter are acceptable to you and your client and the services outlined are in accordance with your requirements, please sign, date and forward a copy to us in the envelope provided along with the $7,500 retainer.

The terms of this letter are subject to change if not executed and returned to us within fifteen (15) days of the date of this letter.

We look forward to assisting you in this matter. If we can provide you with any additional information, please call us at (999) 888-7888, or email us at NAME@NAME OF ENTITY.com or NAME2@NAME OF ENTITY.com.

Very truly yours,
NAME
Principal
NAME OF ENTITY

Accepted by: ________________
Dated: ________________
Mr. Litigator/Prosecutor *or* as specified, that is, Subject/Party
Title:________________
Please Print Name: ________________

Accepted by: ________________
Dated: ________________
Client of Litigator/Prosecutor *or* as specified, that is, Subject/Party
Title:________________
Please Print Name: ________________

Entity-Party Charts: Assignment Playbook Forensic operators must identify the entities and parties central to a forensic assignment. This is especially true when a subject party(s) holds (or held) an ownership interest in one or more entities. A simple diagram, that is, entity-party chart is very useful and helps establish benchmarks for investigation.

The definition of an entity-party chart is a visual representation of entity structure, party ownership, and relationships. The entity-party chart is more comprehensive than a simple organization chart. The entity-party chart conveys entity(s) structure, entity interests, entity(s) relationships, party(s) ownership, key financial characteristics, and other indicators.

How to Construct an Entity-Party Chart Entity-party charts be constructed using a wide array of simple tools. The tools can range from hand-drawn pencil and paper or flip charts. Excel, Word, and PowerPoint will all construct entity-party charts. Each has their own embedded tools to construct limited scope entity charts, typically referred to as organization charts. Exhibit 1.4 is an Excel example that illustrates a simple entity chart. Both Word and PowerPoint features are virtually identical.

Actual Examples Hand-drawn or Excel (or other Microsoft products) are adequate for simple entity-party charts, but the authors have used Excel drawing tools to construct more robust visuals. The entity-party chart Exhibit 1.5 is from an actual matter involving contested ownership transfers. The chart displays all the structures, ownership interests, timing, transfers, and key financial measures in a single visual. The court used the document to understand the matter at hand.

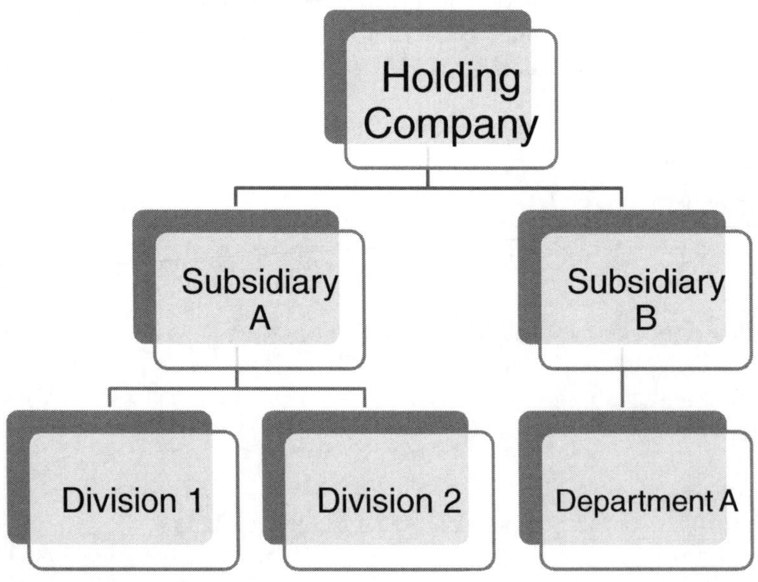

EXHIBIT 1.4 Entity-Party Chart (simple)

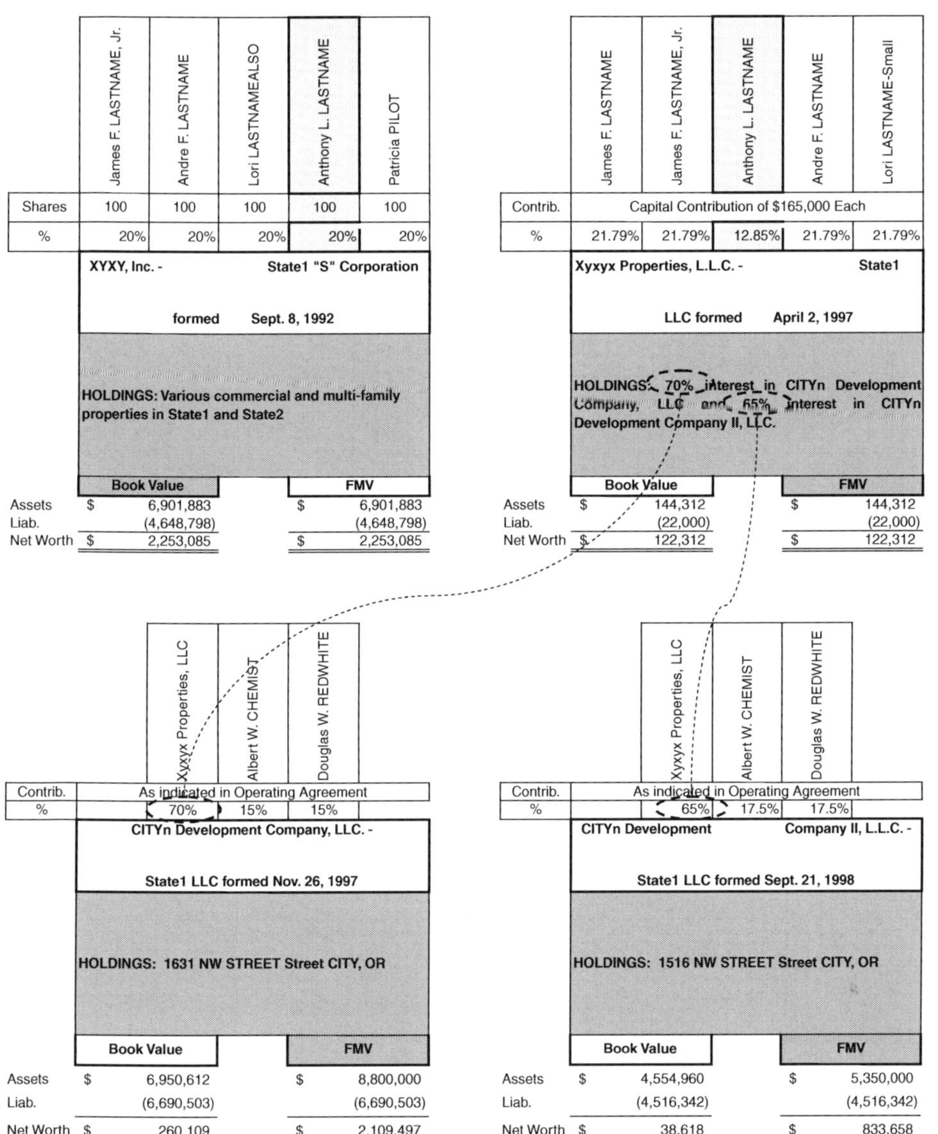

EXHIBIT 1.5 Entity-Party Chart (detailed)

Another entity-party chart is from an actual matter involving a fraudulent conveyance matter. The chart emphasizes the transition of the various entity structures that fraudulently conveyed assets over time. The keyed legend explains key transactional points. The chart also displays all the structures and ownership interests in a single visual. The court used the document to rule upon allegations and facts. See Exhibit 1.6.

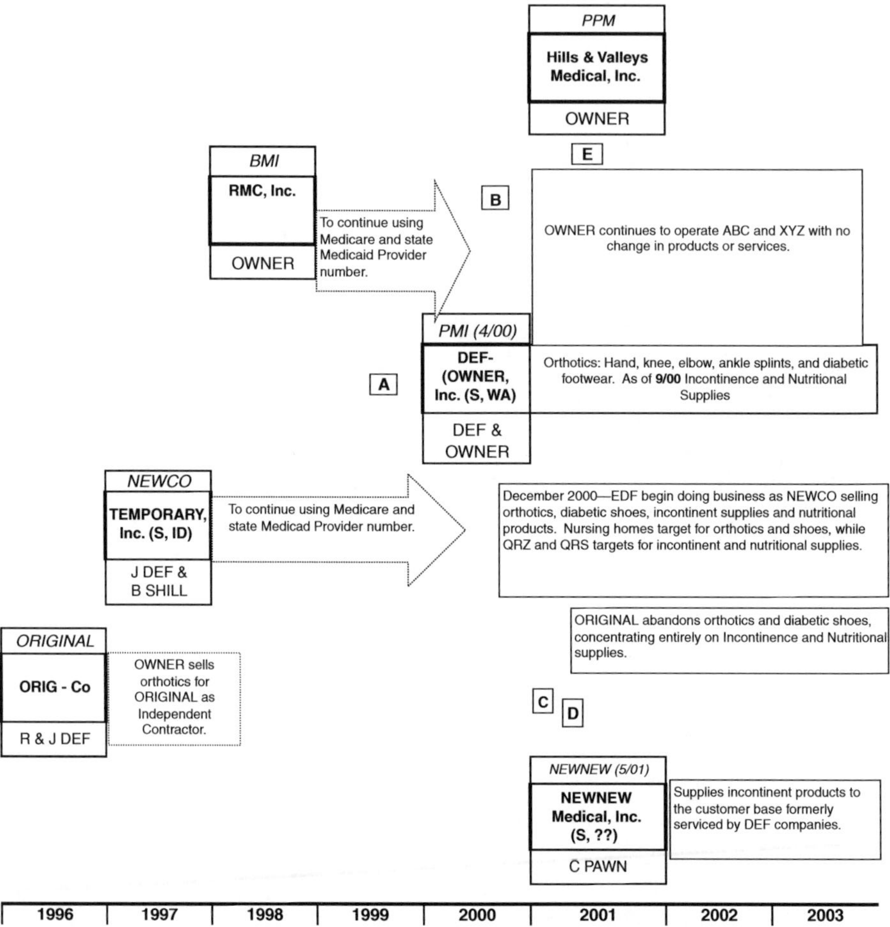

Note: Entity legend is "Type" and "State," e.g. (S, WA) refers to "S" corporation in Washington.
PLAINTIFF, Inc. is "dba" Hills & Valleys Rehab.
AFH - Adjult Family Homes.
ALH - Assisted Living Homes.
A - October 1999—DEFENDANTS approach PLAINTIFF about joining; see Business Plan.
B - November 2000—PLAINTIFF advises DEFENDANTS that he intends to separate. Suggests they take customer base they developed and continue doing business as NEWCO.
C - February 2001—DEFENDANTS raided by the FBI and shortly lose their Medicare Provider Number under NEWNEW, Inc.
D - April 2001—DEFENDANTS begin doing business (again) under the OLDCO name. Did not notify State of Washington. Operated until September 2001 when they closed it.
E - PLAINTIFF incorporates NEWOLD and OLDNEW, Inc., purchases inventory of SSS and absorbs outstanding obligations.

EXHIBIT 1.6 Entity-Party Chart

SCOPING STAGE

Purpose of Stage

This action establishes the scope of the forensic assignment and accommodates its refinement as necessary. See Exhibit 1.7.

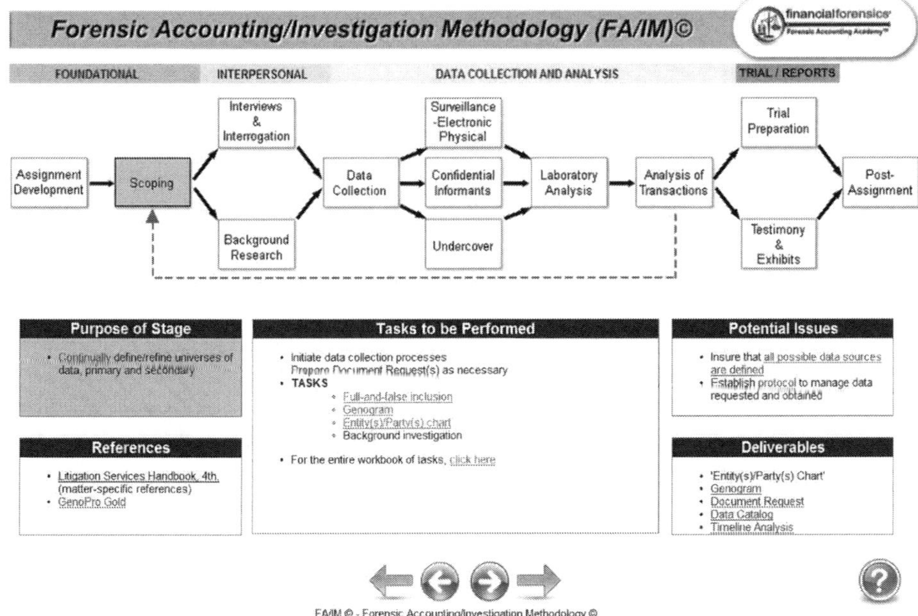

EXHIBIT 1.7 Scoping

The objective of this action is to define a forensic operator's roles and responsibilities as defined by the responsible parties.

Specific actions include:

- Define and document the forensic operator roles and responsibilities.
- Refine, modify, and document roles and responsibilities throughout the assignment as necessary.
- Other actions as required.

References

This action confirms that the intended scope complies with the forensic operator's internal and professional requirements.

The objective of this action is to validate the forensic operator's authority to proceed as intended.

Specific actions include:

- Validate the actions executed in the preceding assignment development stage.
- Other actions as required.

Example Reference Sources The following reference sources serve to jump-start the forensic operator. The Key Internet Sites and Key Reference Materials are not all-inclusive, but provide starting points from which to build resources. Also, refer to the bibliography.

Key Internet sites

- All forensic operators
  www.financialforensicsacademy.com
  www.fjc.gov
  - "Reference Manual on Scientific Evidence," *Reference Guide on Economic Losses in Damages Awards*, by Mark A. Allen, Robert E. Hall and Victoria A. Lazear.
- CPA forensic operators
  www.financialforensicsacademy.com

Key Reference materials

- All forensic operators
  - *Financial Forensics Body of Knowledge,* published by John Wiley & Sons
- CPA forensic operators
  - *Litigation Services Handbook: The Role of the Financial Expert, 4th ed.,* published by John Wiley & Sons. Also, earlier editions and supplements contain significant additional material.

Tasks to Be Performed

This action outlines likely tasks but is not an all-inclusive checklist since each forensic assignment is unique. Use the tasks as a guideline and modify according to the unique facts and circumstances of the assignment.

The objective of this action is to ensure that the forensic operator begins the assignment with proper foundational compliance.

Specific update actions include:

- Reconsider full-and-false inclusion and update if necessary.
- Reconsider chain of custody and update if necessary.
- Develop or update entity(ies)/party(ies) chart.
- Other actions as required.

Specific actions include:

- Develop forensic timeline.
- Develop genogram.
- Prepare document request(s), discovery request(s), et al. as necessary.
- Develop data catalog.
- Develop document map.
- Initiate data collection through appropriate channels, for example, court, counsel, subpoena, et al.
- Other actions as required.

Potential Issues

This action prompts the forensic operator to consider the boundaries of the potential data sources throughout the assignment that may eventually convert to evidence.

The objective of this action is to ensure that the forensic operator establishes and maintains sufficient data management protocols.

Specific actions include:

- Insure that all possible data sources are defined.
- Establish protocol to manage data requested and obtained.
- Other actions as required.

Deliverables

The objective of this action is to identify and eventually finalize deliverables pertinent to the assignment. The forensic operator always develops deliverables designed with the end in mind so as to maximize efficiency. This does not suggest that forensic operators are prescient regarding report content, trial exhibits, or any other output. Rather, it reflects the relationship between conceptualized output and ease in formulating data.

Specific actions include:

- Prepare necessary deliverables.
- Other actions as required.

Example Deliverables The following deliverables are frameworks for the forensic operator who will modify them to comply with their respective internal and other requirements.

Example Forensic Timeline: Storyboard[8] The forensic operator must be an exceptional communicator; merely identifying the facts or even finding the smoking gun is not adequate. The parties to the matter must discern the facts, circumstances, and evidence to permit them to arrive at the forensic operator's same conclusion. Prosecutors, law enforcement, litigators, defense counsel, and others often discuss the story of the case. There is no more effective tool than a forensic timeline to convey that story to the Triers of fact.

A forensic timeline is a visual representation of the key events in a forensic assignment. It chronologically depicts events to provide a clear and organized portrayal of the entire assignment, or selected time segments within an assignment. The forensic timeline is useful in all facets of an assignment because it portrays events in a storyboard format—just as the key events unfolded. Human beings[9] tend to think in terms of timelines, such as life events from birth to death, with key events such as marriage, children, graduation, military service, employment, etc. chronologically presented within.

---

[8] A visual portrayal of events (often chronological) accompanied by explanatory text. The technique is often used in visual and other media production, including movies, commercials, television shows, theater plays, and so on.

[9] Western cultures, in particular, think left to right, similar to reading this book.

Forensic operators sometimes mistakenly consider timelines pertinent only for trial-related exhibit support. However, a forensic timeline continually assists in setting and refining the scope of an assignment. Furthermore, timelines are most effective throughout the duration of an assignment, and continually updated and refined throughout. Savvy prosecutors, litigators, and forensic operators understand that the evidence presented in a timeline chronology helps all parties formulate the events in their mind. The logical structure often forms the foundation for opening arguments, witness sequencing, and closing arguments in addition to serving several other purposes. Furthermore, timelines provide a facile platform upon which to overlay all or selected portions of trial events.

A review of deposition transcripts is an excellent opportunity to develop a forensic timeline. Attorneys often organize their deposition plan to follow a timeline sequence. However, the dynamic nature of the deposition often results in disrupting the chronology in order to establish key facts. Forensic timeline software permits the forensic operator to identify key events matching the transcript flow but automatically reorders the events in the proper chronology.

How Are Forensic Timelines Used? Forensic timelines are quite versatile and serve multiple purposes in forensic assignments, including the following:

- *Learning tool*—A forensic timeline is an essential learning tool for all parties. That is, it establishes and refines assignment boundaries for the parties pursuing the matter. Furthermore, it clarifies and amplifies the key facts for the judge, jury, or other parties involved in resolving the assignment. This characteristic underscores the critical need to begin the forensic timeline coincident with assignment initiation.
- *Assignment boundaries*—A forensic timeline establishes and updates (as necessary) all aspects of an assignment. This includes defining the start and completion (as can best be determined at the time), involved parties, potential documents, current events, and virtually all other elements of a forensic assignment.
- *Evidence scoping*—A forensic timeline assists all parties with determining whether evidence may still exist. For example, existing document retention laws complicate the prospects of obtaining banking information exceeding seven years in the past.
- *Interactive storyboard*—A forensic timeline serves as a forensic operator's storyboard to capture and display the key events in a forensic assignment.

How to Construct a Forensic Timeline Forensic operators construct forensic timelines using a wide array of simple tools. The tools range from hand-drawn pencil and paper to specialized software available from the Internet. Also, Excel, Word, and PowerPoint all contain SmartArt and related tools and graphics that help construct forensic timelines. The usefulness of the Microsoft tools, though, declines in direct proportion to the complexity of the forensic assignment. Consequently, forensic operators typically prefer timeline software.

The authors have used various software tools to develop forensic timelines. inData Corporation (www.indatacorp.com) offers one of the more user-friendly and inexpensive timeline tools, titled TimelineXpress. Although designed within a suite of software products, TimelineXpress runs effectively as a standalone tool. It

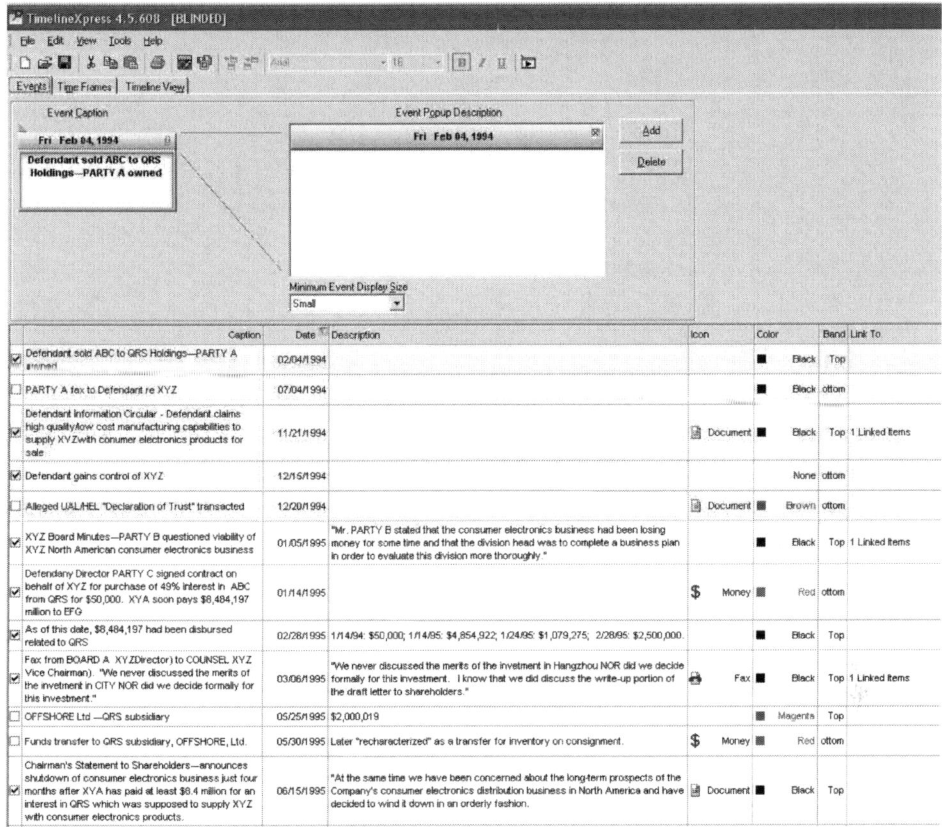

	Caption	Date	Description	Icon	Color	Band	Link To
☑	Defendant sold ABC to QRS Holdings—PARTY A owned	02/04/1994			Black	Top	
☐	PARTY A fax to Defendant re XYZ	07/04/1994			Black	ottom	
☑	Defendant Information Circular - Defendant claims high quality/low cost manufacturing capabilities to supply XYZwith conumer electronics products for sale	11/21/1994		Document	Black	Top	1 Linked Items
☑	Defendant gains control of XYZ	12/15/1994			None	ottom	
☐	Alleged UAL/HEL "Declaration of Trust" transacted	12/20/1994		Document	Brown	ottom	
☑	XYZ Board Minutes—PARTY B questioned viability of XYZ North American consumer electronics business	01/05/1995	"Mr. PARTY B stated that the consumer electronics business had been losing money for some time and that the division head was to complete a business plan in order to evaluate this division more thoroughly."		Black	Top	1 Linked Items
☑	Defendany Director PARTY C signed contract on behalf of XYZ for purchase of 49% interest in ABC from QRS for $50,000. XYA soon pays $8,484,197 million to EFG	01/14/1995		$ Money	Red	ottom	
☑	As of this date, $8,484,197 had been disbursed related to QRS	02/28/1995	1/14/94: $50,000; 1/14/95: $4,854,922; 1/24/95: $1,079,275; 2/28/95: $2,500,000.		Black	Top	
☑	Fax from BOARD A XYZDirector) to COUNSEL XYZ Vice Chairman). "We never discussed the merits of the invetment in CITY NOR did we decide formally for this investment."	03/06/1995	"We never discussed the merits of the invetment in Hangzhou NOR did we decide formally for this investment. I know that we did discuss the write-up portion of the draft letter to shareholders."	Fax	Black	Top	1 Linked Items
☐	OFFSHORE Ltd —QRS subsidiary	05/25/1995	$2,000,019		Magenta	Top	
☐	Funds transfer to QRS subsidiary, OFFSHORE, Ltd.	05/30/1995	Later "recharacterized" as a transfer for inventory on consignment.	$ Money	Red	ottom	
☑	Chairman's Statement to Shareholders—announces shutdown of consumer electronics business just four months after XYA has paid at least $8.4 million for an interest in QRS which was supposed to supply XYZ with consumer electronics products.	06/15/1995	"At the same time we have been concerned about the long-term prospects of the Company's consumer electronics distribution business in North America and have decided to wind it down in an orderly fashion.	Document	Black	Top	

EXHIBIT 1.8 Timeline Sample—Event View

is downloadable for $129 or available on a "try before you buy" basis. Also, the learning curve is short.

The following steps illustrate how TimelineXpress input and output processes are common to most other similar products.

- First, spreadsheet-like entry accommodates key event entry. The data fields consist of a brief description, date, explanation (if required), color, icon (if desired), location above or below the midline, and hyperlink (file, document, video, audio, Internet, and so on) (if desired). Manual presequencing of date order entry is not important. The timeline software automatically reorders the entry with each additional event. Various color options are useful to designate common events, documents, and other contents meriting attention. (See Exhibit 1.8.)
- Next, time frames with selected explanations provide context with respect to the overall assignment. The time frame horizons can vary from the overall assignment, thus accommodating comparison against key events. (See Exhibit 1.9.)
- Perhaps the most compelling and persuasive reason to use timeline software is the ability to hyperlink clarifying content. The hyperlinks can consist of documents,

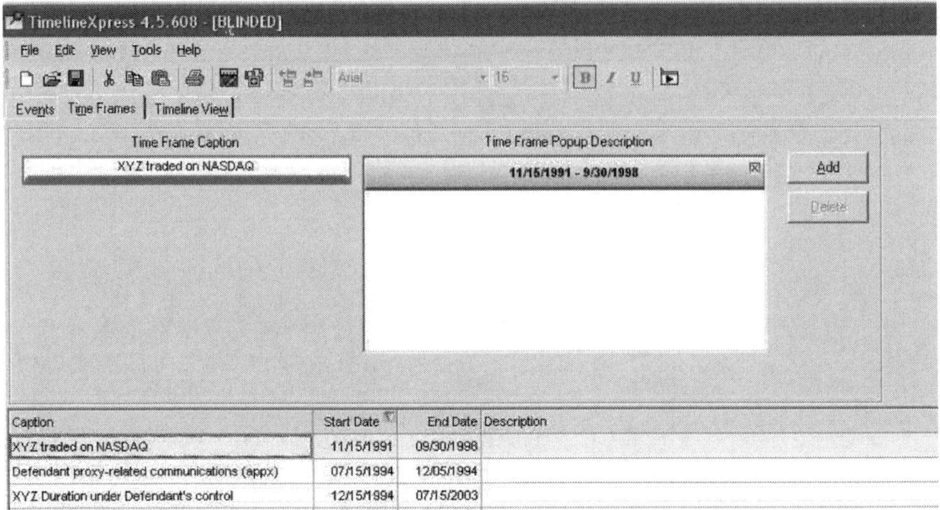

EXHIBIT 1.9 Timeline Timeframe Sample

files, photographs, videos, audios, Internet access, and virtually any other file type. The redacted hyperlink example illustrates how an invoked document looks after selecting its respective event. (See Exhibit 1.10.)

- Finally, the last screen displays the entire timeline. During a live presentation, however, most software accommodates a progressive build that can walk the participants step-by-step from the beginning to the end of the forensic assignment. (See Exhibit 1.11.)

Synergies Between and

As we have demonstrated, has achieved excellent growth over the last four and a half years and is proud of its track record. It see as a company much like others which has assisted in the past — a company in need of focus and direction and the kind of assistance which the is uniquely positioned to provide. is convinced that there are significant operational synergies which will result from association with These include:

- has a number of low-cost production facilities producing high quality products (many of which are ISO 9000 certified) providing a reliable and cost efficient source of electronic consumer products for distribution business. distribution business will benefit immediately from being able to offer its customers high quality products at competitive favourable prices.
- interests in the telecommunications industry in are complementary (rather than competitive) with interests. is prepared (subject to shareholder approval) to combine part of its existing telecommunication business with that of Together these interests would constitute a formidable force in the telecommunications industry in
- experience in conducting business in will be invaluable to owns and successfully operates three state-of-the-art, low cost manufacturing facilities in with an annual output exceeding US$200 million and a workforce of over 10.000.
- has very strong research and development resources. employing over 270 qualified engineers and scientists, which resources would be made available to
- comprises approximately 130 companies, including three companies listed on the and one company listed on the (with market capitalizations of approximately US$315 million, US$85 million, US$57 million and US$95 million, respectively). A link between and will result in a higher profile for in the .
- Establish an effective investor relations office at dedicated to providing all shareholders with timely and accurate reports of the Company's business and financial operations.

EXHIBIT 1.10 Annual Report—MD&A Page

EXHIBIT 1.11 Timeline View

WAR STORY

A forensic operator analyzed and distilled 12,000 pounds of discovery into cogent testimony. During the 10-day trial, counsel used the timeline software for both opening and closing arguments and during the forensic operator's extensive direct examination. The judge issued a bench ruling in favor of the forensic operator's client, and cited the software as crucial to gaining understanding in the extremely complex matter.

Example Genogram: Relationship Maps A genogram is an essential tool for the forensic operator. Furthermore, genograms accelerate a forensic operator's understanding of the people component of any assignment.

"*The art & science of investigating people & money*"[10] is the definition of financial forensics.[11] Competent forensic operators know that the people component of the financial forensics doctrine implies two principles. First, the people component is *more important* than the money component. That is because "*if you understand the people, the money is easy.*" The behavior (habits, patterns, relationships, hobbies, etc.) of the assignment subjects leads forensic operators to the answers about the money. Thus, skilled forensic operators launch the people component first, and continually investigate the people while executing the money component.

Second, a classic paradox hobbles the great majority of forensic operators; they are least skilled in the people (primary) component but most skilled in the money (secondary) component. The statement does not criticize forensic operators but reflects the state of financial forensics training today. This disparity in skill sets invariably yields suboptimum assignment results. Forensic operators who lack skill in people investigation, or who have a skill imbalance fall prey to human nature. They tend to do what they know since they are not trained to do what is needed.

WAR STORY

A former county deputy started his own forensics practice after retiring. He was very skilled in eliciting confessions from financial crimes suspects. However, when confessions were not forthcoming, he lacked the skills to investigate the money component.

The Genogram Is a People Tool A genogram is a visual display of the people and relationships in a forensic assignment. A genogram is best described as a relationship map since it depicts the people and relationships among assignment subjects. The genogram benefits forensic operators since "*if you understand the people, the money*

[10] Circa 1993, copyright by **financialforensics®**, all rights reserved.

[11] The terms *financial forensics* and *forensic accounting* are used interchangeably unless otherwise indicated.

is easy." It permits the forensic operator to isolate patterns of subject behavior and identify other parties meriting further investigation. Isolating key indicators of the subjects' behavior leads to additional points of investigation.

Who Uses Genograms? Many different professional disciplines have used genograms for decades. The disciplines include (alphabetically) attorneys, educators, family therapists, forensic operators, genealogists, intelligence analysts, law enforcement, military, nurse practitioners, physicians, psychiatrists, psychologists, researchers, social workers, and others.

Intelligence Analysts, Law Enforcement, and the Military

Forensic operators intuitively understand why intelligence analysts, law enforcement, and the military are skilled users of genograms. Whenever people knowledge is crucial, such as in criminal matters, the more that is known about the subject, the greater the likelihood of apprehension and prosecution or termination.

Actual Genogram Example The following sample genogram supported both civil and criminal matters related to embezzlement. A federal court convicted the controller of a business of embezzling more than $5 million from his employer in only two years. The genogram supported the investigation and eventual recovery of funds that flowed from the business through the controller to his various personal relationships. The initial draft form of the genogram displays the parties and relationships before their finalization.

Genograms consist of only three components: shapes, connectors, and colors. Rectangles represent male subjects while circles represent female subjects. Both the rectangles and circles can contain additional information such as age, descriptors, photographs, and other facts. Connectors establish and identify the type of (past and present) relationship between parties. Connector composition ranges from solid lines to dotted and dashed lines. Colors amplify the connectors. For example, a blue connecting line represents an existing relationship, while a red connecting line indicates a former relationship.

The primary subject in the center of the following genogram[12] represents the convicted embezzler. The red connector to the circle (former wife) adjacent to the suspect has two hash marks through it, indicating that a former marriage terminated due to divorce. The red connector flows downward between the former husband and wife indicating three children born during the former marriage. All three children show marriage relationships, and the red connectors to the two daughters indicated an estranged relationship with their father. The blue connector illustrates that the son has an existing relationship with his father.

The red connector continues beyond the primary subject's former wife to another rectangle (male) indicating a former same-sex relationship. The former same-sex relationship no longer exists as indicated by the single[13] hash mark. The connector

[12] GenoPro software constructed the example genogram.

[13] The federal government does not recognize same-sex "marriages" and only six states permit them. Therefore, only a single hash mark is necessary, since the relationship was informal.

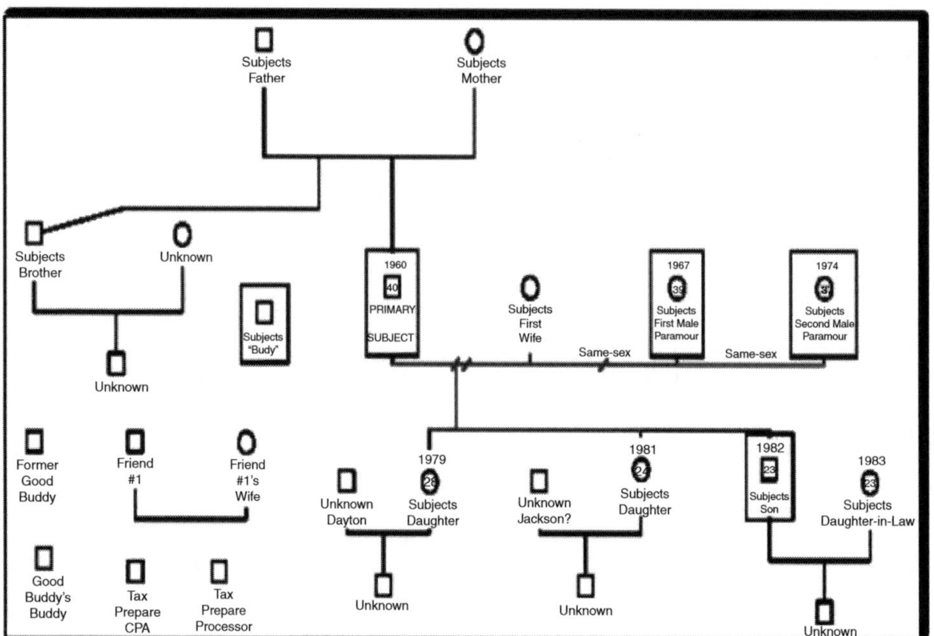

EXHIBIT 1.12 Genogram

continues to another rectangle (male) same-sex relationship, but is colored blue to denote an existing relationship.

Another connector flows upward from the primary subject to his parents. A connector flows from the parents indicating the primary subject had a married brother who had at least one child. Other male and female subjects have no direct connections to the primary subject. The unconnected symbols indicate relationships that lack definition (at the time of initial construction), and must be further explored. See Exhibit 1.12.

The example genogram supported both civil and criminal matters after finalization. The genogram supported the prosecution and conviction of the embezzler and supported the civil pursuit and recovery of assets for the benefit of the company.

How to Construct a Genogram Forensic operators can construct genograms using a wide array of simple tools. The tools can range from hand-drawn pencil and paper to specialized software available from the Internet. Also, Excel, Word, and PowerPoint will all construct genograms. Standardized genogram symbols, connectors, and colors ensure consistent interpretation by users.

Genogram software is the most effective tool since it is purpose-built and easily updated. GenoPro has a large installed base of genogram software at www.genopro.com. The software is very inexpensive ($49 for a 1-user license), is easy to use, and provides a free evaluation copy. GenoPro provides tutorials, significant support, and example templates.

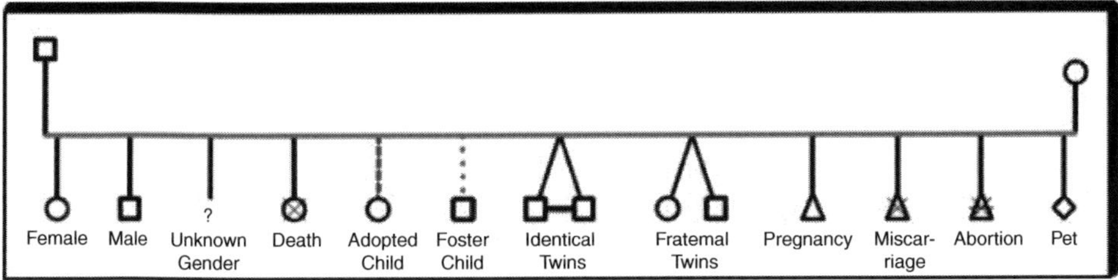

EXHIBIT 1.13 Genogram Legend—Types of People

GenoPro software applies standardized shapes, connectors, and colors. The associations of relationships among subjects include the following alternatives:

- Family
- Social
- Partnerships
- Business divisions

The standardized symbols for the various subjects include the following (see Exhibit 1.13):

- Female
- Male
- Unknown gender
- Death
- Adopted child
- Foster child
- Identical twins, and so on

Some of the standardized color-coded detailed lines include the following, as shown in Exhibit 1.14.

Social and even emotional relationships can be depicted among the subjects. For example, it may be necessary to understand how various parties emotionally relate to one another. Potentiality for collusion is obvious to most forensic operators who would benefit from such information. Alternatively, legal counsel may need to know about a history of hatred or violence between parties. There are numerous emotional relationship symbols, including those shown in Exhibit 1.15.

- Most genogram software will display subject-specific detailed information. Such features significantly enhance the usefulness of the genogram, making this

EXHIBIT 1.14 Genogram Legend—Relationships

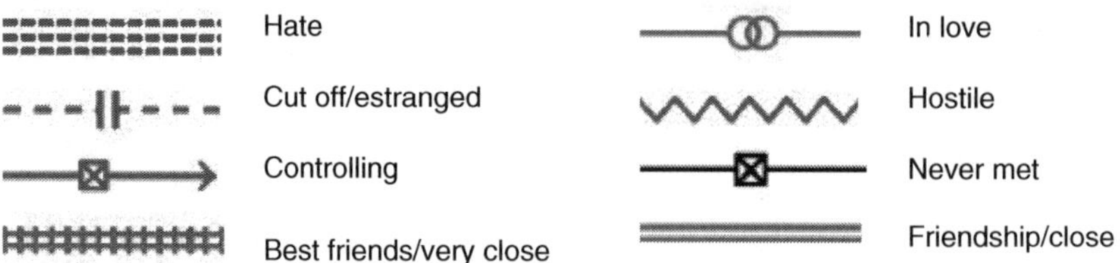

EXHIBIT 1.15 Genogram Legend—Relationships—Extended

interpretation easy to achieve, even for those unfamiliar with genogram techniques. Examples of detailed information include the following:

- Birth place
- Name history (maiden, name change, aka, etc.)
- Education history
- Occupation history
- Photographs (subject at different ages, homes, automobiles, etc.)

Behavior patterns typically emerge after mapping out relationships. Understanding past relationships in coincidence with key events, may be critical to the forensic operator. For example, a genogram could reveal prior patterns of decision making detrimental to a sibling in a shareholder oppression matter.

The Genesis of Genograms Genograms trace to at least the 1970s,[14] with techniques developed by Dr. Murray Bowen. Dr. Bowen trained as a psychiatrist at the Menninger Foundation in Topeka, Kansas, and devoted his life to developing a science of human behavior. He was a professor at Georgetown University Medical Center and founded the Georgetown Family Center in 1975. His work formalized the Bowen Theory, which is still in use today.[15]

The definitive work on genograms is *Genograms in Family Assessment*, 3rd ed. (W. W. Norton & Company, Inc., 2002), by Dr. Monica Goldrick and Dr. Randy Gerson. The first edition (1985) formalized and codified the symbols, connectors, and colors still used by professionals today.

Example Data Catalog: Information Sources Even simple data catalog procedures provide valuable benefits to the forensic operator. The following example illustrates basic data catalog procedure output. This example is entirely maintained within the firm's time and billing system, thus permitting access to anyone working on the respective assignment.

Forensic operators typically receive many types and kinds of data throughout an assignment. The data can range from electronic copies to hardcopy printouts to photographs to blueprints to video and audio recordings, ad infinitum. It is essential that the forensic operator maintain a contemporaneous record of data received and thus accommodate the recurring need to search through the data.

There is no magic per se regarding the format or procedures to be used. At a minimum, however, contemporaneously updated lists contain a brief description of

[14] www.ancestrylibrary.com.
[15] www.thebowencenter.org.

the data received, the date received, the method of receipt, and other descriptors necessary for the assignment. In some cases, it helps to list Bates numbers and sequences, numbers of pages received, or other identifiers. Also, in very large cases, a formal cataloging number process augmenting the Bates numbers may be helpful. The chain of custody process and the data cataloging process obviously exhibit many commonalities. Therefore, combining the two techniques will increase efficiency.

Furthermore, it is often necessary to list information sources used by the forensic operator. Such a requirement is typical in most jurisdictions, called for by professional standards and customary in other circumstances.

How to Implement a Data Catalog A few simple procedures implement a simple data catalog process as the following indicates (see Exhibit 1.16):

- Assign responsibility to a single person through which all data received must flow.
- Upon receipt, that person stamps the date received on the respective data, enters it on a list, and forwards it for analysis.
- The forwarding of the data could be to an individual on the assignment or filed within the assignment work papers, depending upon internal protocols.

Example Document Map: Visual Production Sometimes, simpler is indeed better, as illustrated by the document map.

Forensic operators know that evidence comes in a seemingly endless array of formats, including documents, data, testimony, photographs, audio recordings, videos, and formulas, among others. In civil and criminal matters, the subpoena and discovery process is a key method for obtaining the evidence. However, both processes are often needlessly complicated by the production dance between opposing parties.

For example, forensic operators are often tasked with preparing customized discovery requests. Such requests are ordinarily executed by counsel through a subpoena and other methods. Counsel forwards the production to the forensic operator upon receipt and instructs him to initiate his investigation. Unfortunately, the forensic operator often determines that significant data has not been produced—and thus begins the production dance.

Mapping the Documents The opposing parties inevitably launch escalating volleys of phone calls, emails, correspondence, filings, hearings, motions to compel, etc. in the pursuit of obtaining sufficient evidence to proceed. This sparring continues until one (or both) side stops dancing due to frustration, cost, diminishing benefits, imminent timelines, and other factors.

The disparities typically pivot upon disagreements regarding what was or was not produced by the respective parties. That is, Party A subpoenaed evidence it believes Party B did not produce and vice versa. Reaching agreement is often complicated by several factors. They include the sheer quantity of documents, document definitions (e.g., Party A believes an income statement is more properly titled a profit and loss statement, etc.), and other matters.

Fortunately, a simple but powerful tool can shortcut the discovery dance: the document map. The document map serves two critical purposes in resolving discovery disputes. First, it visually conveys to all parties (including the court) the facts of

3/29/07—Received via email from Client Contact a scanned copy of the complaint, printed a hard copy for file. JCM

4/13/07—Received via FedEx a binder of materials concerning certain matters alleged in the complaint. JCM

5/4/07—Mailed engagement letter packet including $10,000 retainer request. JCM

5/9/07—Received via FedEx the signed engagement letter and $10,000 retainer. Received a DVD that contains: (1) depositions of Defendant's representatives; (2) XYZ's and Defendant's public filings; and (3) the documents produced by Defendant in the underlying action, which we have indexed. Also received three CDs, each of which contains a "binder" of documents and deposition excerpts (taken from the materials contained in the DVD) relating to certain of the transactions referred to in the complaint: (1) the red CD is the binder for the Pre-/ Post-transactions; (2) the blue CD in the binder for the China JV joint venture; and (3) the yellow CD in the binder for the SUBSIDIARY transaction. JCM

5/15/07—Received via FedEx two binders containing the following documents:

1. Notice of Motion (for an order dismissing complain for lack of personal jurisdiction and failure to state a claim upon which relief can be granted);
2. Memorandum of Law in Support of Defendant's Motion for an Order Dismissing Action;
3. Former Auditor's Memorandum of Law Opposition to Defendant's Motion to Dismiss;
4. Declaration of Declarant in Opposition to Defendant's Motion to Dismiss;
5. Defendant's Reply to Memorandum of Law in Furthuer Support of its Motion to Dismiss.
   JCM

5/16/07—Received via FedEx 12 dividers with:

1. A copy of the complaint filed December 20, 2006. Defendant the Defendant Parent's request for judicial notice;
2. A copy of the original complaint;
3. A conformed copy IN Re Failed Importer Technologies Shareholder Litigation;
4. Complaint for Alter Ego Relief;
5. Subscription Agreement made December 15, 1994;
6. U.S. SEC Form 20-F Annual Report for January 31, 1995;
7. U.S. SEC Form 20-F Annual Report for January 31, 1996;
8. U.S. SEC Form 20-F Annual Report for January 31, 1997;
9. U.S. SEC Form 20-F Annual Report for January 31, 1998;
10. U.S. SEC Form 20-F Annual Report for January 31, 1999;
11. U.S. SEC Form 20-F Annual Report for January 31, 2000;
12. U.S. SEC Form 20-F Annual Report for January 31, 2002; & The Defendant Parent.
    JCM

EXHIBIT 1.16 Data Catalog

5/16/07—Received via hand delivery from Litigator Contact;

1. Defendant's notice of motion and motion to quash service of summons for lack of personal jurisdiction; Memorandum of points and authorities in support thereof; Declaration of Co-Declarant filed concurrently.
2. Notice of hearing on Demurrer and Demurrer of Defendant the Defendant Parent to Plaintiffs' complaint; Memorandum of points and authorities in support thereof.
3. Defendant the Defendant Parent's amended notice of hearing demurrer and motion to quash. JCM

5/17/07—Received via email from Litigator Contact Client Contact's Excel files containing detailed history of Defendant and XYZ financial statements, and 3 PowerPoint files containing animations of China JV, Pre- and SUBSIDIARY. Placed on "S." DDD

5/18/07—Received via FedEx: 1. Summaries of the depositions of Defendant Party 1, Defendant Party 2, Defendant Party 5, Defendant Party 6, Defendant Party 3, and Defendant Party 4. 2. Defendant's annual reports for 1995, 1997, 1998, 1999, and 2006. 3. Documents relating to the proxy contest. 4. Three California cases concerning alter ego (Sonora Diamond, Associated Vendors and Automotriz). 5. Defendant's responses to our written discovery requests, which contain the requests themselves. 6. XYZ's by-laws dated October 10, 1995. JCM

5/21/07—Received via FedEx, a set of XYZ (and subsidiary) board minutes for the period December 1, 1994, to May 29, 1996, which were prepared in connection with the underlying XYZ litigation. JCM

5/25/07—Received via email from Litigator Contact a Detailed Cash Analysis, and the Litigator Contact 2 Declaration, both in .pdf. DDD

6/04/07—Emailed a .pdf scanned copy of Chapter 29—Alter Ego of the Wagner Handbook to Litigator Contact per DDD. JCM

6/12/07—Received via hand delivery from Litigator Contact a spreadsheet of DefendantTel Technologies Inc. (XYZ) Cash Analysis (Excludes Consolidated Joint Venture Activities) from 1995–2002. JCM

6/12/07—Received via Litigator Contact:

1. Letter to Mr. Law Officer from Defendant 7 regarding Report of Fraud Against Early Bad Guy & Others.
2. Letter to Mr. Law Officer 2 from Defendant 7 Report Of Cheating Against China National Pte. Ltd.
3. From Defendant Party 2 DefendantTel Management Notes on Meeting May 3, 1996.

EXHIBIT 1.16 *(Continued)*

4. Defendant Parent List of banks, bank account numbers, and bank addresses of all the banks which Suntel has accounts.
5. Defendant Parent Schedule showing the December 13 cash and fixed deposits of XYZ Hong Kong.
6. Defendant Tel Technologies Inc. Meeting notes from August 2.

Copy made for DDD. cs

6/21/07—Received during meeting with Litigator Contact copies of matters discussed during DefendantTel Management Meeting—August 2. Also received DefendantTel Management Meeting notes. JCM

6/21/07—Received via email from Para-Legal (Litigator Contact's secretary) latest Litigator Contact 2 Declaration in DRAFT. Printed for Litigator Contact since he was on-site with us today. DDD

EXHIBIT 1.16 Data Catalog (*Continued*)

production. Second, effort is focused where it is most needed, that is, the disputed production.

The document map can be easily constructed using Excel, although Word, PowerPoint, and many other applications can also be used. It can consist of a one-page summary with successively detailed worksheets, or a single, comprehensive worksheet, depending upon need.

The sample document map is based on an actual example focusing on bank statement production. It comprises a few basic categories, all driven by the facts and circumstances of the case. It contains a few simple descriptors in columns and rows as described here.

Columns

- Report—Identifies the respective document.
- Bank—Identifies the bank.
- Description—Describes the document.
- A/C No.—Account number or other descriptor.

  Note: Listing only the last four digits of bank accounts may be necessary when the document map might make its way into the public record.
- Year—Self-explanatory, can be annual, quarterly, monthly, or any combination thereof.

Rows

- USA Operations—Other operating territories can be listed as necessary.
- MAS 200—The general ledger used by the entity.
- Internally Prepared—The source of the financial documents.
- Tax Returns—For the respective years.
- Legend—The legend is limited only by imagination.
- Color-coding (or shading/fill since colors may not be apparent when printed in black and white, such as when copies are made).

The sample document map in Exhibit 1.17 clearly indicates the status of all pertinent documents at a glance. Furthermore, the document map can be readily

Document Map
XYZ Company
Updated 5/12/10

Report	Bank	Description	A/C No.	Year				2009												2010				
				2007	2008	2009	2010	Jan	Feb	Mar	Apr	May	Jun	Jul	Aug	Sep	Oct	Nov	Dec	Jan	Feb	Mar	Apr	May
U.S. Operations																								
CPA Review—ABC CPA																								
CPA Review—MNO CPAs																								
MAS 200																								
General Ledger Detail																								
General Journal Detail Report of Entries																								
Accounts Receivable Cash Receipts Detail																								
Inventory Management Detail Report																								
Inventory Sales History Report																								
Accounts Payable Invoice Detail																								
Accounts Payable Check Register	BANK X	Operating Account	9999																					
Accounts Payable Check Register	BANK X	Payroll Account	8888																					
Accounts Payable Check Register	BANK X	Escrow Accounts	7777																					
Internally Prepared																								
XYZ Quarterly Reports																								
XYZ Monthly Disbursement Rpts																								
XYZ Operating Rpt																								
XYZ Monthly Import Report																								
Tax Returns				2007	2008	2009	2010																	
U.S. Operations																								
Brazilian Operations																								

Legend
- Not Applicable
- We have the document
- Document requested
- In process
- Not available timely

EXHIBIT 1.17 Document Map

updated as status changes. There is no magic to the format contained here—construct it according to the facts and circumstances of the respective assignment.

The court immediately benefits from this simple tool. The judge and opposing parties can readily refer to the visualization of the disputed documents. The clarity of the document map permits the court to readily discern what extent production has or has not occurred. Most important, attention is focused on the disputed documents so that efforts can be directed toward resolution.

Tax return production is a classic example of the benefit of the document map. Specifically, tax returns are invariably produced without the supporting schedule. The document map directs effort to where it is most needed—resolution of current production.

CONCLUSION

This phase is titled *Foundational* for good reason: It is the base from which all subsequent activities proceed. It is a form of authentication; for example, a bank statement must be authenticated by a bank representative to establish its authenticity for the court. Only then can it proceed to be used as evidence. Failure to establish the foundation through requisite assignment development and scoping procedures leads to errors, or worse.

This chapter covered several specific forensic operator tools, including, conflict resolution, entity-party charts, engagement letter, chain of custody form, forensic timeline, genogram, document request, data catalog, and document map. They were each explained, supported by examples, and included sources for additional support. The tools are easy to build, learn, and use, and often become part of the report or trial exhibits, or both, due to their intuitive contents. They convey a great deal of information in small packages.

The following chapter addresses the interpersonal phase, which is the logical progression from the results gained in this chapter. It summarizes nearly obsolete interviewing suggestions that were de rigueur 40 years ago. Then it progresses to more contemporary interrogation methods that are routinely taught, especially to law enforcement and certain elements of the military. Finally, behavior detection is introduced, including complementary techniques, such as facial mapping.

Also, background research is introduced with an emphasis on Internet tools, techniques, and resources. However, non-Internet, that is, pick-and-shovel, gumshoe, and similar guidance is outlined, since it often fills in gaps unavailable through other means.

CHAPTER 2

Interpersonal Phase

In this chapter, the "people and money"[1] principle is deployed through the dictum "*If you understand the people, the money part is easy.*" That is because money-related deception (through journal entries, financial statement manipulation, corruption, and so forth) cannot be effected without people involvement. Put another way, "Nothing happens until someone does something." The principle also frames the sequence of investigation and remedies unbalanced forensic operator people skill sets. Forensic assignments should begin with, continue with, and end with interviews, interrogation, research, and analysis into the *behavior* of the people (directly and indirectly) involved. The people starting point focuses and accelerates all subsequent activities and leads to successful, efficient, and effective forensic assignments.

Unfortunately, forensic operators often possess an unbalanced people and money skill set since their knowledge, education, experience, training, and familiarity tend to emphasize one skill set at the expense of the other. For example, law enforcement specialists are often heavily skilled in the people component of the principle, resulting from their training in interviews and interrogation. However, they invariably lack commensurate skill depth in the money component of the principle. Conversely, forensic operators with deep money skills typically lack commensurate abilities to interview, interrogate, or deploy behavior detection skills with people.

Therefore, this chapter introduces the people and money principle and emphasizes three essential elements comprising the people component. That is interviewing, interrogation, and behavior detection are all three essential and integrated elements and are interdependent with one another. For example, an auditor with 30 years' experience has probably been through interview training but knows little about interrogation or behavior detection. Likewise, regulators may have interrogation training, but know little about behavior detection.

Interviewing and interrogation techniques are discussed first, and then behavior detection is addressed. The limitations of a book prevent comprehensive discussion of behavior detection. Nonetheless, the contents serve as a primer to permit forensic operators to continually build upon the knowledge.

[1] For purposes of the principle, "money" is defined as the quantitative aspect of forensic assignment.

This chapter remedies the skill imbalance between people and money components for forensic operators. That is a forensic operator with light people skills but heavy money skills will benefit, and vice versa.

INTERVIEWS AND INTERROGATION STAGE

Purpose of Stage

This action initiates the people component of a forensic assignment and continually refines the context and framework for assignment execution. Therefore, it flows logically from the preceding foundational phase. See Exhibit 2.1.

The objective of this action is to plan and execute data collection from the people directly and indirectly involved in a forensic assignment. It ordinarily progresses logically from interviews to interrogation while comprising behavior detection. However, the descriptors do not suggest discrete tasks, rather a continuum of analysis depending upon the party(s), their potential for involvement, and other factors.

Specific actions include:

- Identify all parties in the matter, internal and external, present and past. (Note: Former employees are often a rich source of information that could not otherwise be obtained. Naturally, counsel, or whoever is directing the assignment must authorize such access and potential evidence.)
- Establish an interview or interrogation plan while deploying behavior detection techniques throughout.

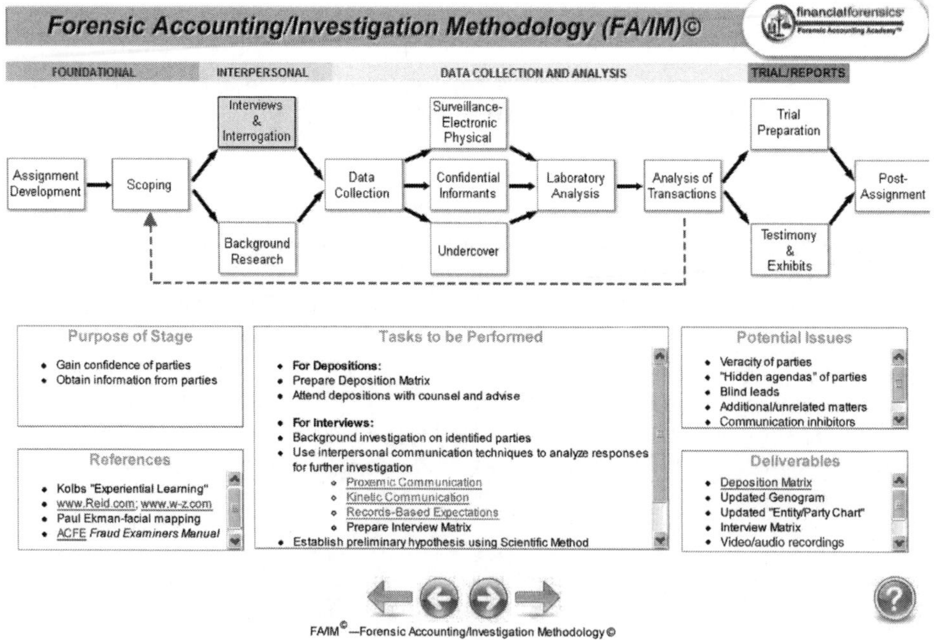

EXHIBIT 2.1 Interviews and Interrogation

References

This action initiates the live, face-to-face encounter with all parties potentially possessing information important for the forensic assignment. It also identifies technical references for forensic operators seeking refreshers or incremental interviewing, interrogation, or behavior detection techniques.

The objective of this action is to ensure that the people aspect yields information useful for the forensic assignment.

Uncommonly rich (but disparate) sources of people information are found on various Internet sites, and typically fall within the social media category. Most social media sources are free and sometimes yield facts simply unavailable elsewhere. Most significantly, people often post statements and life details on the sites that could not be found elsewhere.

WAR STORY

A forensic operator was assisting wife's counsel with forensic investigation into the divorcing couple's assets. The forensic operator found information independently posted by the husband and the husband's office manager. The husband's information was found on a dating site. The office manager information was found on LinkedIn and described the strength of the husband's business, how their customer base was increasing, new people were being hired to meet demand, and similar comments indicating a thriving business. The forensic operator joined a dating site where the husband was rumored to be listed. She found that the husband was making business claims similar to the office manager and even posted a photo of a new Harley Davidson he had purchased. During a subsequent deposition, wife's counsel asked business-related questions of the husband, to which he indicated a "doom and gloom" tale and denied questions about customer growth, hiring new employees, and so forth. Then, wife's counsel disclosed the social media data, thus impeaching the husband's veracity.

Example of Reference Sources The following reference sources serve to jumpstart the forensic operator. The Key Internet Sites and Key Reference Materials are not all-inclusive but provide starting points from which to build resources. Also, refer to the bibliography.

Key Internet sites

- All forensic operators

  Selected leading social media sites are alphabetically summarized below. The forensic operator should gain familiarity (directly or indirectly) with their respective features and limitations.

  Caution: It is essential that the forensic operator comply with pertinent legal and policy guidance regarding using pretext or subterfuge methods when collecting personal information about a party in a forensic assignment. Also, personal credit information is a high-risk arena requiring legal and policy compliance. Gathering and using personal information is an ever-evolving discipline and compels the forensic operator to deploy continual vigilance.

- Blogs: Web log is the root of the term's contraction. Blogs are usually created and maintained by a special interest user or group. The sites typically comprise regular entries of commentary from parties with specific interests. (Note: Receiverships and similar matters often attract bloggers and provide rich sources of easily obtained data.) Blogs are located via various sources, but a quick Google search directs effectively directs queries.
- Facebook: www.facebook.com. Facebook is a personal (compared to professional, e.g., LinkedIn) site accessible by others using a user-designated acceptance of their Facebook account. Discussion forums can be set up among common interest groups, thus providing certain professional attributes to the site. Also, user events are sometimes listed in timeline format. Facebook presently claims more than 700 million users.
- LinkedIn: www.linkedin.com. A professional (compared to personal, e.g., Facebook) site. Parties can often be reviewed at a high level without permission and some events comprise timeline elements.
- Plaxo: www.plaxo.com. A personal gateway links with Facebook, Twitter, and other sites for user updates.
- StumbleUpon: www.stumbleupon.com. This is a news site of sorts, reflecting user-generated input. It has certain common interest features and can link to other sources. They presently claim 11 million users.
- Twitter: www.twitter.com. A micro-blog within which real-time short messages are exchanged among users, that is, tweets. Some high-profile Twitter users such as celebrities have large numbers of followers. Businesses are beginning to use it more frequently to announce events, new products, promotions, and so on.

Dating sites can be rich sources of information, but forensic operators should gain counsel, direction, or other authority before accessing and attempting to use as evidence. Also, they are typically subscription-based and their terms and conditions should be viewed before accessing for forensic assignment purposes. They are listed alphabetically next.

- Chemistry: chemistry.com. Subscription site claiming 15 million members, and connects subscribers based upon personality and interpersonal criteria.
- ChristianMingle: www.christianmingle.com. Subscription site (with basic free option) claiming 5,000,000 members, and cost-effectiveness compared to other Christian sites.
- eHarmony: www.eharmony.com. Subscription site claiming more than 9 million members, and claims to focus on long-lasting relationships using 29 proprietary criteria.
- Match: www.match.com. Subscription site claiming more than 20 million members, and connects subscribers based upon personality and interpersonal criteria.
- Perfect Match: www.perfectmatch.com. Subscription site claiming 11-plus million members, with an up-front free "personality assessment" and matching.
- Spark: www.spark.com. Subscription site claiming more than a million members, requiring them to upload photos.

A few Internet sites offer interviewing and interrogation training (on-line and/or textual references) as reflected by the following summary.

- Humintell: www.humintell.com. This is a resource site for forensic operators seeking training on interpreting facial expressions during interviews to determine veracity and other conditions. It offers free on-line training for up to one year.
- John E. Reid: www.reid.com. This site offers highly regarded text and training resources. It is the source of The Reid Technique®, a well-known method of interviewing and interrogation taught to law enforcement.
- NASS-USA: www.nass-usa.com. This site, offered by New Age Security Solutions specializes in aviation and transportation security. They offer their proprietary Behavior Pattern Recognition (BPR) within their services. It is a behavior detection methodology built upon seven essential elements.
- Wicklander-Zulawski & Associates, Inc. www.w-z.com. This site offers highly regarded text and training resources on interviewing and interrogation techniques.

- CPA forensic operators
  www.financialforensicsacademy.com

Key Reference materials

- All forensic operators
  - *Anatomy of Interrogation Themes*, by Louis C. Senese
  - *Criminal Interrogations and Confessions*, by Fred E. Inbau, et al.
  - *Essentials of the Reid Technique: Criminal Interrogations and Confessions*, by Fred E. Inbau, et al.
  - *Experiential Learning: Experience as the Source of Learning and Development*, by David A. Kolb
  - *Financial Forensics Body of Knowledge*, by Darrell D. Dorrell and Gregory A. Gadawski
  - *Fraud-Related Interviewing*, by Don Rabon and Tanya Chapman
  - *Ragnar's Guide to Interviews, Investigations, and Interrogations: How to Conduct Them, How to Survive Them*, by Ragnar Benson
  - *Interviewing and Interrogation*, by Don Rabon and Tanya Chapman.
  - *Investigative Discourse Analysis*, by Don Rabon
  - *Persuasive Interviewing*, by Don Rabon
  - *Practical Aspects of Interview and Interrogation*, by David Zulawski and Douglas Wicklander
  - *The Investigator's Little Black Book: The Investigative Resource Used by Thousands of Private Investigators, Law Enforcement Agencies, Media Organizations*, by Robert P.I. Scott.
  - *Unmasking the Face: A Guide to Recognizing Emotions from Facial Expressions*, by Paul Ekman and Wallace V. Friesen
  - *War Fighting*, by A.M. Gray
- CPA forensic operators
  - *Litigation Services Handbook: The Role of the Financial Expert, 4th ed.*, published by John Wiley & Sons. Also, earlier editions and supplements contain significant additional material.

Tasks to Be Performed

This action outlines likely tasks, but is not an all-inclusive checklist since each forensic assignment is unique. Use the tasks as a guideline and modify according to the unique facts and circumstances of the assignment.

The objective of this action is to ensure that the forensic operator *thinks through* the people aspect of the assignment from inception to completion before launching activities. It also ensures that legal and policy requirements are met.

Specific actions include:

- Prepare an interview[2] matrix.
- Conduct an interviews, interrogations, and behavior detection analysis.
- Document and prioritize key findings.

Specific actions for interviews, interrogation, and behavior detection include:

- Background investigation on identified parties (see section in this chapter).
- Develop a strategy customized to each person.
- Use interpersonal communication techniques to analyze responses for further investigation, including the following noninclusive techniques:
  - Proxemic communication.
  - Kinetic communication.
  - Clothing worn by the subject.
  - Physiological considerations, for example, circadian rhythms, proximate environmental factors, and external environmental factors, for example, weather changes.
  - Records-based expectations.

Potential Issues

This action prompts the forensic operator to consider the potential constraints affecting the process, including legal, policy, cultural (e.g., race, ethnicity, biological, language, etc.), and other factors germane to the environment. The suggested list does not provide as an all-inclusive checklist since each forensic assignment is unique. Use the tasks as a guideline and modify according to the unique facts and circumstances of the assignment.

The objective of this action is to ensure that the forensic operator contemplates exigencies that may surface during the assignment. The forensic operator can minimize such constraints (to the extent possible) by diligent attention to this action.

Specific actions include:

- Validate intended actions with appropriate authorizing parties, for example, counsel, agency director, etc.

---

[2] The term *interview* is generic in this sense and could include interrogation and behavior detection.

- Contemporaneously document understanding before proceeding with interviews, interrogation, or behavior detection techniques.

WAR STORY

A forensic operator was tasked with determining who was conducting third-shift thefts in a large teaching hospital. The nursing staff was ruled out through video surveillance, which left housekeeping staff, visitors, patients, vendors, and walk-ins. The forensic operator spent several nights through the entire 11 P.M. to 7 A.M. shift and elected to interrogate certain housekeeping staff. During the interrogation of a Cambodian immigrant, the forensic operator observed the staff member's aversion to eye contact. He concluded that the staff member's actions indicated deception and anxiety. However, the forensic operator subsequently pulled the staff member's personnel file and discussed his background with management (a task that he should have done before interrogating). He learned that the Cambodian's history of torture and brutality during the Khmer Rouge reign had conditioned the housekeeper to avert eye contact. The housekeeper was removed from the target list and another housekeeping staff member was later identified as the thief.

Deliverables

The objective of this action is to identify and eventually finalize deliverables pertinent to the assignment. The forensic operator always develops deliverables designed with the end in mind so as to maximize efficiency.

This action prompts the forensic operator to identify pertinent deliverables throughout the assignment. Deliverables serve multiple purposes, including:

- Maintains a common and consistent focus on the objectives of the assignment.
- Promotes efficiency by the continual building of the output, as opposed to a last-minute rush to aggregate findings.
- Permits progressive review by other parties.

The objective of this action is to document the data, findings, observations, and ancillary information resulting from the interviews, interrogation, and behavior detection.

Specific actions include:

- Updated deposition or interview matrix.
- Updated genogram.
- Updated entity or party chart.
- Video or audio recordings or both.
- Preliminary hypothesis.

BEHAVIOR DETECTION

Behavior Detection is a technique developed by the Israeli Security Agency (ISA) that allows trained professionals to detect people with harmful intentions, such as carrying out a terrorist attack. The techniques are applicable to virtually any forensic assignment involving people. Consequently, forensic operators must gain familiarity with the pertinent tools and techniques.

Behavior detection is deployed through a technique known as CICO (Concentric In-Concentric Out). Simply stated, CICO recognizes that behavior detection comprises anything and everything that might represent a cause or effect of a subject's behavior. The Concentric-In component starts conceptually with a very wide circle encompassing the subject company's and parties' business footprint and progressively becomes focused on the site. That is, a business with operations in three states would require consideration of the physical (e.g., weather, traffic flow), economic (e.g., state of the economy, labor force), cultural (e.g., deep South versus New England) and all other factors that could possibly impact the business now and in the pertinent past.

For example, abrupt barometric pressure changes are known to affect some people's behaviors. Thus, if an interview occurs coincident with significant declines or increases, it is possible that interview subjects could be commensurately affected to a certain extent. Likewise, the day of the week and the time of day could have an impact on behavior. Specifically, circadian rhythms[3] are physical, mental, and behavioral changes that follow a roughly 24-hour cycle, responding primarily to light and darkness in an organism's environment. Virtually any living organism, including humans, is subject to the impact of such a cycle. Consequently, forensic operators benefit from knowing their timing with respect to themselves and to their subjects.

The Concentric-Out component starts conceptually with a very narrow circle encompassing the subject's eyes[4] and progressively expanding to include the forehead and temples, face,[5] throat, shoulders, upper diaphragm, and torso. Then, it starts conceptually again with a very narrow circle encompassing the subject's feet and progressively expanding to include the legs, knees,[6] thighs, and lower midsection.

All the while the forensic operator notes the subject's hands since they are very mobile and often expressive.

Finally, the forensic operator knows that the beginning of an interview offers the "calibration" opportunity. That is, by asking general, noninvasive questions a subject's behavior can be calibrated. Then, when sensitive questions trigger different behaviors they often flag avenues for additional inquiry.

---

[3] www.nigms.nih.gov/Education/Factsheet_CircadianRhythms.htm

[4] The progressive nature of the Concentric-Out technique mirrors individual behavior detection techniques.

[5] The human face is the only location on the body where the muscles are attached directly to the skin. Consequently, stress-induced physiologies typically manifest themselves through the face and related body parts.

[6] Knees can be very telling, suggestive of the subject's desire to leave by pointing toward the exit.

WAR STORY

A forensic operator arrived at the headquarters of a business that was the subject of a forensic assignment: the large business had suffered from seemingly unexplainable monthly gross profit swings. The CEO greeted him Monday morning and introduced him to the large accounting staff. Early Monday evening, the CEO asked his opinion of the CFO, controller, and other accounting staff. The forensic operator explained that he had not yet talked with them. The CEO seemed slightly puzzled but not concerned. Tuesday evening the CEO repeated the same question. The forensic operator again indicated that he had not yet talked with the accounting staff. The CEO was more puzzled and rather curious about the delay. Late Wednesday evening, the CEO pointedly inquired whether the forensic operator had talked with the accounting staff. At that point, the forensic operator indicated that he had indeed talked with them. When the CEO inquired why it took "so long" the forensic operator stated that he had first been meeting with other departments, for example, purchasing, marketing, warehousing, and others. That permitted him to *understand* the business before talking with the accounting staff, thus enabling him to evaluate their answers to his questions.

Verbal and Nonverbal Cues

Forensic operators who use both verbal and nonverbal cues are better at detecting lies. There are numerous resources available to the forensic operator regarding interview and interrogation techniques. Yet to be effective, the interviewer should obtain a working knowledge of ancillary tools such as proxemics, paralinguistic communications, and micro-expression recognition. These tools assist the forensic operator in detecting deception cues, thereby enhancing the interview process and overall investigation results.

Interviewing is one of the most essential steps of every forensic assignment. This book defines financial forensics and forensic accounting as *the art & science of investigating people & money*. The interpersonal phase of the Forensic Accounting/Investigative Methodology is therefore vital to understanding the people aspect of the investigation.

All forensic operators should strive to become adept at interviewing techniques. Management and employees possess much-needed knowledge regarding the organization and other employees. As such, effective interviews can reduce investigation time and provide stronger evidence to support the findings.

Also, interviewing is important in all forensic accounting matters. Many people associate interviewing solely with fraud investigations. However, meaningful interviews benefit all forensic matters, including audit, litigation consulting, business valuation, and others.

Forensic operators may also conduct interrogations or admission-seeking interviews. Interrogations are slightly more complex, as it often involves the questioning of an uncooperative witness while the objective is often to obtain a confession from a suspect.

Regardless of the task at hand, interview or interrogation, the interviewer must be able to assess the veracity or truthfulness of the information received. All forensic operators should follow the principles of independence, integrity, and objectivity. As such, they cannot blindly accept all statements as being the truth and are obligated to exercise some degree of skepticism. Obviously, fraud investigators need to be able to determine if witnesses or suspects are being truthful. Also, auditors should assess the veracity of statements made by management or employees. And even litigation consultants should exercise some skepticism when interviewing their client or client's attorney, as they are clearly advocates for *their* position.

The forensic operator must develop some basic behavior detection skills to assess the truthfulness of a witness or interviewee. The relationship between interviewing, interrogation, and behavior detection is illustrated in Exhibit 2.2.

Regardless of the type of engagement, behavior detection is a skill set that a forensic operator should apply throughout the entirety of the interview or interrogation process.

The Lie Lying has been described as embellishing, concealing, or omitting information, falsification of information, or ambiguity. Generally, a lie is a falsification or omission that misstates the truth. People may lie for a variety of reasons but the primary motivations are for personal gain or the avoidance of undesired consequences.

People will defend themselves by lying until the pain of their conscience becomes unbearable or until outside influences prompt them to reveal their guilt. A confession is often a combination of both factors, outside influences and the liar's conscience. Sometimes, a small amount of influence will produce a confession and in other instances perpetrators will carry the lie with them to their grave. There are rarely voluntary confessions, as almost all confessions are a response to a stimulus, regardless of how small that stimulus.

Lying is not easy work and usually causes a fair amount of stress for the liar. The fact that lying is a stressor contributes to a trained professional's ability to detect lies. Liars typically exhibit symptoms, subtle or not, of the stress from lying.

There are a multitude of reasons why people do not detect lies. Sometimes people just do not want to detect lies because they prefer to trust others or detecting the lie may not be in their best interest. However, the primary reason people do not detect lies is the lack of training in how to do so. Because of their lack of training, people

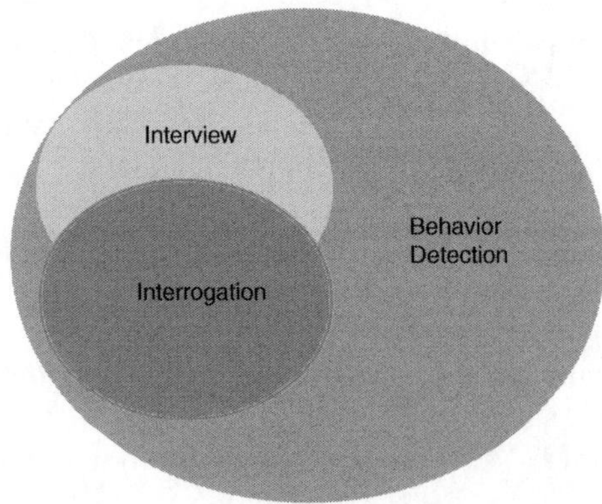

EXHIBIT 2.2 Behavior Detection (Circles)

often fail to recognize reliable clues to deception or will label the wrong behaviors as deception signals.

Identifying lies can be challenging, as they are usually interspersed with the truth or subtle variations of the truth. Even highly trained professionals only correctly identify a fraction of the lies they are exposed to.

Detecting the Lie Early landmark studies found that over 90 percent of communication was nonverbal. Subsequent studies have refined this number, but the consensus is that approximately two-thirds of our communication is nonverbal. Nonverbal communication consists of vocal and physical communication. Vocal communication consists of changes in pitch, tone, or pauses. Physical communication includes expressions, gestures, and general physical movements. To properly identify deceptive behavior, the interviewer must be able to look and listen at the same time.

Behavior is generally a response to some stimulus. In an interview, the stimulus is predominately a question. Conversely, other actions or inactions can serve as a stimulus, too. Deceptive behavior will usually begin within five seconds of a stimulus. If the behavior is delayed longer than five seconds, the interviewer cannot be certain of its cause.

Deceptive behaviors usually occur in clusters of two or more. The behaviors should follow within seconds of each other and isolated behaviors should be ignored. Generally, the greater the cluster of deceptive behaviors, the greater the likelihood of deception. Transient or isolated behaviors should be disregarded. Deceptive behaviors may be verbal or nonverbal.

To properly identify deceptive behaviors, the forensic operator should establish a baseline for the interviewee. How does the interviewee normally act? Do they have a twitch or any other physical trait that could be misread as a deceptive behavior? Interviewers should be careful to not misconstrue general nervousness as a deceptive behavior.

Verbal Cues Verbal cues focus on what is being said and require the interviewer to actively listen. The following are some verbal cues to deception that an astute interviewer should follow up on:

- Repeating of the question or failure to understand simple terms—often viewed as a tactic to buy time and generalize an answer.
- Overly specific answers—"I did not steal $1,000." The interviewee does not deny all stealing, but only that he did not steal "$1,000."
- Detour statements—"As I said before..." or "That reminds me of..."
- Invoking of religion—"I swear to God" or "As God is my witness..."
- Statements that fail to answer the question—"That's a good question."

Truthful answers are typically direct and spontaneous as the interviewee has nothing to hide and the facts are his allies.

Nonverbal Cues Nonverbal cues are typically harder to detect than verbal cues. They require the forensic operator to actively listen to and observe the actions of the interviewee. This is difficult, as most people can concurrently listen and observe for short burst of time. Not only does the forensic operator have to process what the interviewee is saying but also has to process how the interviewee is saying it and what physical behaviors are exhibited in the response.

Some common nonverbal cues are grooming, touching the face, clearing throat, covering of orifices (particularly the mouth), and sweating. Yet, once again, the forensic operator must be careful to not misconstrue behavioral false positives such as sweating, blushing, and general tension. It is normal for interviewees to exhibit some level of general nervousness and this is why the forensic operator must establish a behavioral baseline for each interviewee. This is usually accomplished in the first part of the interview process.

Nonverbal cues to deception are classified as follows:

Negation Cues—Negation cues are contact with the head or face that covers any orifice (mouth, eyes, nose, or ears). Can also include scratching or rubbing of the same orifices.

Aversion Cues—Aversion cues are major aggressive movements of the body away from the interviewer. Can include whole body leans but may also be limited to simple movement of the head or the legs.

Performance Cues—Performance cues are exaggerated physical gestures intended to oversell the response. May include extended shaking of the head or other overly animated gestures.

Contradiction Cues—Contradiction cues can be observed on three levels: verbal, nonverbal, and verbal/nonverbal. Verbal contradiction is when the voice pitch or volume is not consistent with what is being said. Nonverbal contradiction is when physical characteristics are not congruent (piercing stare while smiling). Verbal/nonverbal contradiction is when the physical movements are not congruent with what is being said (nodding agreement while saying no).

Control Cues—Control cues are an attempt to suppress normal gestures or reactions, such as sitting on the hands or jamming the hands into pockets.

The forensic operator should familiarize herself with proxemics, kinetic communication, and paralinguistic communication to further her detection and understanding of nonverbal cues. *Proxemics* was coined by Edward Hall during the 1950s and 1960s and has to do with the study of our use of personal space and how various differences in that use can make us feel more relaxed or anxious. Kinetic communication entails observation of the body and physical responses. Finally, paralinguistic communication is analysis of volume, pitch, and voice quality during communication.

Facial Mapping and Micro-Expressions

In 1954, Dr. Paul Ekman began researching facial expressions and body movement as the subject of his master's thesis.[7] Since then, Dr. Ekman has authored or... co-authored multiple books regarding the study of human emotions and their relations to facial expressions. One of the key principles observed is that facial expressions are

[7] www.paulekman.com/about-ekman.

not culturally determined but are rather universal. Some of the observable expressions include anger, disgust, fear, joy, sadness, surprise, and contempt. Dr. Ekman eventually developed the *F*acial *A*ction *C*oding *S*ystem (FACS) to categorize every conceivable human facial expression.

Dr. Ekman's research included the study and analysis of micro-expressions. Micro-expressions are very brief, less than a second, facial expressions that often occur when people attempt to deliberately conceal their true emotions as a response to a certain stimulus.[8] Detection of micro-expressions is nearly impossible without proper training and experience. However, the ability to spot and correctly identify micro-expressions could be an invaluable tool for the forensic operator. As such, those forensic operators who frequently conduct interviews or interrogations should be trained and proficient in micro-expression recognition.

Deposition Matrix: "What Should I Ask?"

Depositions are often taken in civil matters. If they are properly executed they provide a rich source of potential evidence regarding the respective matter. However, a gap often exists between a forensic operator's information needs and counsel's deposition objectives. Consequently, a tool known as a deposition matrix is pivotal in bridging the gap between forensic operators and counsel.

One of most effective applications of the deposition matrix is to e-mail it to counsel for his review. It gives counsel the opportunity to ask clarifying questions of the deponent. In addition, it provides counsel the technical education to determine whether the answer they receive during a deposition is reasonable. Then, while discussing it on the telephone, the matrix can be refined as required. Footnoted comments amplify matter considerations. However, caution is essential, since the deposition matrix may be subject to disclosure. Therefore, seek guidance from counsel before finalizing.

Attorneys often seek guidance from forensic operators regarding what questions to ask a deponent, suspect, and other parties. The process may be the only opportunity to establish evidence crucial to a matter. Occasionally, forensic operators sit with counsel and provide real-time suggestions. Rarer still, the court occasionally permits the forensic operator to proffer questions. Regardless of conditions, questions prepared in advance of depositions make the process most effective. Advance preparation is essential, since counsel may lack sufficient expertise and vocabulary to understand the testimony delivered.

What Is a Deposition Matrix? A deposition matrix is a document that provides counsel with a strategy or detailed questions, or both, when deposing a party. The deponent can be the opposing party, a witness who has information relevant to the matter, the opposing expert witness, or other party. Depositions take place during the discovery phase of the civil law process. During a deposition, the opposing attorney questions the party in order to gather information for trial purposes. The answers given in a deposition will typically not change at trial; if they do, counsel points out the discrepancy(s) to the court. The deposition provides counsel the opportunity to identify and explore the substance of a witness's testimony to avoid

[8] www.paulekman.com.

surprises. The deposition matrix helps guide its user to explore all vital subjects and follow-up responses.

How to Use a Deposition Matrix Typically, when preparing to depose a party, counsel solicits suggestions from the forensic operator for general subjects to cover, and specific questions to be asked. It is optimal for the expert to be present at the deposition if possible. However, there are many reasons, for example, jurisdiction, local rules, strategies, and so forth, that experts do not attend depositions. The deposition matrix is therefore the next-best alternative.[9]

The deposition matrix serves multiple purposes. For example, it:

- Guides counsel in obtaining data the forensic operator needs for analysis.
- Informs counsel with background regarding the nature and type of business and related factors.
- Enables counsel to become familiar with the nature of the data and ultimate objectives of the opposing forensic operator's analysis.
- Enables counsel to precisely focus his efforts in deposition, thus excel in the eyes of all the parties in the deposition, that is, his client and the opposition.

How to Construct a Deposition Matrix The deposition matrix provides a structured format containing specific questions tailored to the matter. It is likely that the matrix will contain some similar general content regarding the deponent or the subject of the litigation. For example, when deposing an opposing forensic operator, the deposition matrix will likely contain background questions applicable when questioning any opposing forensic operator. However, inquiries regarding his opinion or report are unique to the matter. See Exhibit 2.3.

This section illustrates an example deposition matrix containing the structured deposition matrix format that comprises industry and functional guidance, specific questions, and guidance regarding potential follow-up questions. The sample deposition matrix pertains to the deposition of an accountant for a restaurant. Much of the content applies to the deposition of any party who handles the finances of a restaurant. However, the matter-specific questions, say, a claim of lost profits versus employee theft require distinctly different questions.

The structure of the matrix is the most important element and contains the following five basic components:

1. *Deposition Objective*—This section is a goal-setting technique and serves to clarify and validate a mutual understanding between counsel and the forensic operator of the deposition. The example provides a schematic of the generic accounting function to assist counsel with questioning.
2. *Nature of the Restaurant Business*—This section outlines categories comprising all aspects of the business.
3. *Category of Inquiry*—These sections alert counsel to the major category of the inquiry. It also enables the forensic operator to parcel out the various areas in as much or as little detail as desired.

---

[9] The deposition matrix is typically prepared even when the forensic operator attends the deposition.

Possibilities that depend highly on the matter include:

a. Relationship (parties, entities) background
b. Employment or professional history or both
c. Education and training
d. Roles and responsibilities
e. Claim-specific matters, extent of loss, damages, etc.

4. *Specific Questions*—This section provides sample verbiage that guides counsel in deposing the party(s). Note also that this technique is particularly useful when deposing experts, since they will recognize the operative terms and perceive counsel as more technically savvy. This encourages honesty in deponent responses.
5. *Comments and Clarifications*—This section explains the information the forensic operator seeks, but perhaps more importantly it provides a road map for counsel to use in follow-up and related exploratory queries.

The example deposition matrix follows. It is abbreviated for illustrative purposes.

Category of Inquiry **Specific Questions**

Deposition Objective: Determine, through inquiry of Mr. PARTY, the nature and extent of ENTITY transactional capture, aggregation and controls in support of the Cash Receipts Journal and its eventual posting into the General Ledger. The hierarchy of information is composed of:

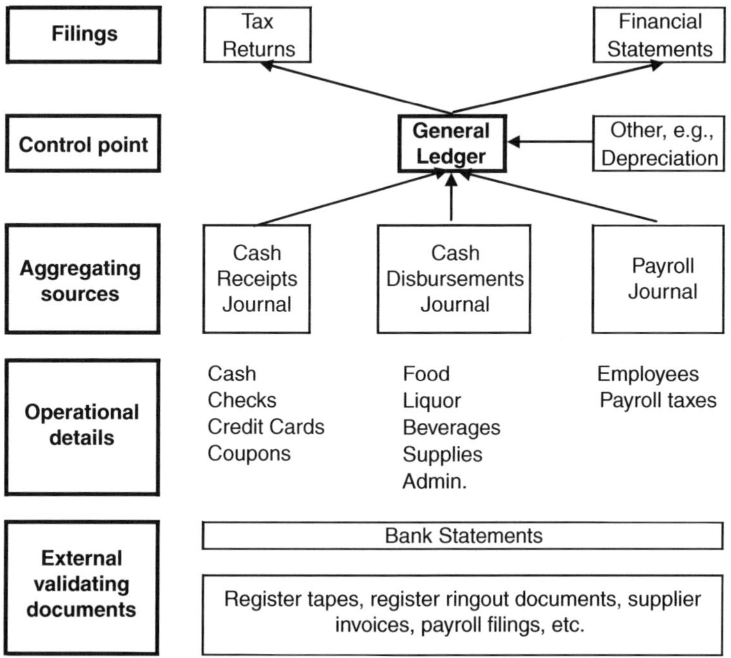

EXHIBIT 2.3 Deposition Matrix

Category of Inquiry	Specific Questions

Such knowledge serves multiple purposes:

1. **To validate/refute his reported financial results**—If controls were weak and reported financial results not supported by transaction data, then Plaintiff may have misrepresented (intentionally or unknowingly) ENTITY results.
2. **To establish a baseline for "before and after" results**—A "before and after" comparison (i.e. ownership transition period) must be based on supportable data to validate differences.
3. **To isolate whether key variables changed after the ownership change**—If the same controls, policies and procedures were maintained post-acquisition then opposition has less opportunity to claim that Defendant's impact was the result of a business decline.

Note: Also, refer to attached Document Request Checklist for additional details. The Questions are stated as general for guidance to accommodate flexibility.

Nature of the Restaurant Business: The restaurant business is cash- and consumable-intensive and financial misrepresentation can result from the following:[10]

1. **Supplier:** Shorting shipments, overpricing/unauthorized substitution, and employee (or other party) collusion on payments.
2. **Customer:** Similar to employee, above but less direct opportunity although employee "friend" connections possible.
3. **Owner:** Lowest level of controls is on owner, thus opportunity greatest for all of the preceding items.
4. **Regulators:** Graft is the most likely possibility for this category, such as payoffs to officials to skirt requirements.
5. **Employee:** Cash theft, cash skimming, cash "forgiveness," e.g., foregoing cover charge, inventory (liquor/food) theft, "friend" collusion, supplier collusion, payroll misreporting.

Controls Hierarchy: A hierarchy of controls should exist (in various forms) as summarized below:

1. **Company Policies:** A code of ethics and employee awareness that employee fraud is not tolerated and will subject the employee to prosecution. Also, job descriptions should be clear, supervisory levels enforced, etc.
2. **Foundational Controls:** Such controls range from physical (e.g., locks, alarms, etc.) to procedural (e.g., register ringout) to supervisory (e.g., review/approval of preparer reconciliations), etc.
3. **External Accountability:** Including insurance policy coverage for amounts similar to claims made by owner, etc.

Comments/Clarifications

Background	Describe the history and nature of your involvement with the ENTITY including its purchase and operations.	This will provide foundation, perhaps generate additional questions and shed light on the nature of Plaintiff's involvement in the operations of the business.

EXHIBIT 2.3 Deposition Matrix (*Continued*)

[10] See Chapter 3 for the section titled, ICE/SCORE©.

Category of Inquiry	Specific Questions	Comments/Clarifications
Employment (Restaurant and Other)—Current and History	Provide a detailed description of your employment history, pre- and post-ENTITY ownership. Who is your current employer and what is your position? What duties does your current position entail? What are your annual earnings from employment? (Base compensation, bonuses, benefits, etc.) Also, ask what compensation levels were in prior positions held.	This will assist us in establishing an earnings history for Plaintiff. It will also give a starting point to verify against other sources (i.e., Income Tax Returns, lifestyle analysis). Note that in ANY business enterprise, there are 3 primary responsibilities (below) that must be accounted for; identification of each party's "assignment" will support valuation assumptions. ❑ Finance (startup and continuing) ❑ Marketing ❑ Operations
Roles and Responsibilities	Please describe the day-to-day Roles and Responsibilities for yourself at the ENTITY.	This will help us pinpoint key control points in the decisions regarding receipts and expenditures.
Informational Chain of Custody	Determine EACH PERSON who was responsible for recording transactions, ranging from point of entry to the general ledger.	The chain of custody indicates who had access to records and thus the degree of difficulty of manipulation.

The following questions are operationally specific and responses will likely lead to additional clarification. This background will help construct a comprehensive "before and after" analysis, thus simultaneously establishing consistent continuity while countering claims by opposition.

Specific Operational Items for Management Inquiry	1. Days open? 2. Hours open? 3. Number of shifts? 4. Average number of employees on each shift? 5. Did employees work the same shift on a regular basis? 6. If not, how were shifts rotated? How were different shifts recorded? 7. Who set up the room? 8. What was the average set-up time? 9. How was set-up rotated? 10. If stations were not rotated, how were they assigned?	1. Any recurring/non-recurring cycles, e.g. open/close of college season, resulted in customer flow changes. Also, seasonality impacts, e.g., winter/spring. Also, traffic flow (e.g., major construction projects) and/or competition (restaurants opening/closing) impacts? Finally, what key events occurred during his ownership, e.g. 9/11, fires, floods, etc.?

EXHIBIT 2.3 Deposition Matrix (*Continued*)

Category of Inquiry	Specific Questions	Comments/Clarifications
Specific Operational Items for Management Inquiry	11. What was the seating capacity of the restaurant? 12. Were tips pooled and split among waitpersons? 13. How were tips split? 14. If tips were not split, was there a practice of tipping out? To whom and at what rate?	2. Were any employees ever caught stealing; were they prosecuted? 3. Note that 8% is the amount the IRS routinely "assumes" for tips.
Common Methods and Indications of Under Reporting Income (Source: Ed Hynes and Walt Matysik, Restaurant Accounting Controls 2000 (Edmonds, Wa: Restaurant Seminar Institute, Inc., 2000), pgs. 109 to 113.)	1. Record a smaller sales amount on the daily operating report than is shown on the cash register tape. This reduces the amount of cash that must be deposited for the day. 2. Regular cash overages. This is an indication that sales are not being recorded, and a breakdown in controls. 3. Collect the side income (e.g., vending machine proceeds, T-shirt revenue, gambling fees, and admission charges) and do not include the income on the daily operating report. 4. Collect directly from special customers, parties, and banquets and do not report the income on the daily operating reports. 5. Purchase food and supplies for personal consumption without reimbursing the restaurant. 6. Deposit supplier rebates into the owner's person account without recording the payments in the books and records. 7. Purchase food for friends, charge them, and do not record any amounts collected and pocket the funds.	1. Ask him EACH of these questions and gauge his response with regard to how deep to continue. 2. Such amount, i.e., "Cash Over-Short" should be reported in the financial records as a separate account. 3. Supplier rebates should be separately recorded in the financial statements as a separate account.

EXHIBIT 2.3 Deposition Matrix (*Continued*)

Category of Inquiry	Specific Questions	Comments/Clarifications
Methods Perpetrated by Employees (Source: Ed Hynes and Walt Matysik, Restaurant Accounting Controls 2000 (Edmonds, Wa: Restaurant Seminar Institute, Inc., 2000), pgs. 109 to 113.)	1. Employee doesn't ring up sale and keeps cash. 2. Short ring; Under-ring the correct price of item and pocket the difference. 3. Service and collecting while register is reading between shift changes. 4. Claiming a phony walk out and keeping money received from the customer. 5. Cooks requesting wine for the kitchen—and drinking the wine rather than using it for a menu item. 6. Picking up customer's cash and claiming it as a tip when the customer thought they were paying the bill. 7. Wrapping food, etc., and dropping into garbage can for later retrieval. 8. Fictitious coupon sales. Manager or employee accumulates coupons and exchanges them for cash. 9. Producing surplus food (such as sandwiches) so it can be taken home. 10. Mobile catering drivers purchasing and selling their own inventory for profit.	

EXHIBIT 2.3 Deposition Matrix (*Continued*)

BACKGROUND RESEARCH STAGE

Purpose of Stage

This action can yield data, evidence, and clues not otherwise attainable. It follows the interview and interrogation stage in this book but can be conducted in advance or concurrently. See Exhibit 2.4.

The objective of this action is to gather facts for verification and testing for subject veracity. For example, knowing the answer to certain questions before asking them assists the forensic operator in evaluating subject honesty.

Specific actions include:

- Obtain validating data (in advance or following).
- Obtain refuting data (in advance or following).

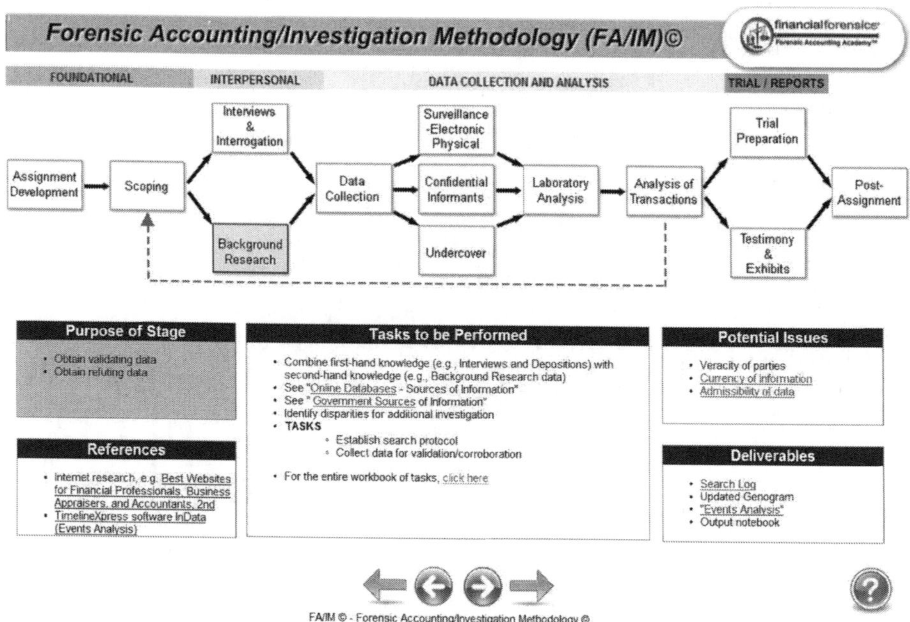

EXHIBIT 2.4 Background Research

WAR STORY

A forensic operator assisting the wife's counsel was advised that the "husband was lying" about his business ownership interests. Although this is a common claim in marital dissolution, the forensic operator performed a quick search using www.veromi.com, one of the free Internet sites previously indicated. The husband claimed ownership in only two business interests. However, when the forensic operator conducted a reverse telephone and address lookup, he found several other businesses registered at the same address. He searched the secretary of state records for each business and found two familiar names that had previously surfaced during a free search. The husband had registered two businesses in a son-in-law's name and one business in his son's name. The husband was impeached during deposition.

References

This action ensures that all pertinent data is obtained with or without cooperation from the subject(s). This not only bolsters the forensic operator's findings; it also accelerates the process of interviews, interrogation, behavior detection, and data collection. It can also lead to midcourse corrections in planned tasks.

The objective of this action is to ensure that all pertinent data is obtained and to uncover previously undisclosed facts, data, and evidence.

Example of Reference Sources The following reference sources serve to jump start the forensic operator. The Key Internet Sites and Key Reference Materials are not all-inclusive, but provide starting points from which to build resources. Also, refer to the bibliography.

Key Internet sites

- All forensic operators

  Many Internet sites offer reference sources, but the following sites reflect the authors' short list. Third-party information aggregators and providers offer vast amounts of information. It is expensive (with some exceptions); thus forensic operators should either access outside specialists or assign an internal party to become their go-to specialist.

  - BlackBook: www.blackbookonline.info. This is a gateway site to hundreds of additional sources, many of which are free. The authors consider this the "point of entry" for all Internet related investigations. Its contents facilitate subsequent information searches.
  - KnowX: www.knowx.com. This is an extraordinarily rich site for forensic operators to conduct progressive levels of people related business, people and asset evidence. It has a learning curve, but is well worth the time and money necessary to become proficient.
  - Skip Trace: www.skiptraceseminar.com. This site provides extraordinary training for forensic operators seeking people information not otherwise available through conventional sources.
  - Spokeo: www.spokeo.com. This site is a people search engine comprising vast amounts of information ranging from a large variety of public information sources. It reports the data in very informative formats, including earnings, occupation, marital status, age and other categories. It is very cost-effective.
  - Veromi: www.veromi.com. This is a gateway site that aggregates people-specific information. Its contents are free at the first level and provide progressively more expensive information depending upon the length of time the user desires to access the site.

Reference materials

- All forensic operators

  Third-party information aggregators and providers provide vast amounts of information. It is expensive (with some exceptions); thus forensic operators should either access outside specialists or assign an internal party to become their go-to specialist.

  - Accurint: www.Accurint.com
  - *Business Background Investigations: Tools and Techniques for Solution-Driven Due Diligence* by Cynthia Hetherington. Checkpoint: www.CheckPoint.riag.com
  - Tudor, Jan Davis. Super Searchers on Mergers & Acquisitions: *The Online Secrets of Top Corporate Researchers and M&A Pros*, Medford, NJ: CyberAge Books, 2001.
  - KnowX: www.KnowX.com
  - LexisNexis www.LexisNexis.com

- PACER: Public Access to Court Electronic Records (PACER) is an electronic access service that provides case and docket information from federal appellate, district and bankruptcy courts. In addition, the PACER case locator functions via the Internet. "PACER is provided by the federal Judiciary in keeping with its commitment to providing public access to court information via a centralized service." http://www.pacer.gov/
- WestLaw—http://west.thomson.com/westlaw/
- Local Court Access systems

Tasks to Be Performed

This Action outlines likely tasks, but does not provide an all-inclusive "checklist" since each forensic assignment is unique. Use the tasks as a guideline and modify according to the unique facts and circumstances of the assignment.

The objective of this Action is to insure that the forensic operator gathers all pertinent data.

Actions include:

- Combine firsthand knowledge (e.g., interviews and depositions) with secondhand knowledge (e.g., background research data).
- Identify disparities for additional investigation.
- Establish search protocol.
- Collect data for validation and corroboration.

Potential Issues

This action prompts the forensic operator to consider the boundaries of the people, parties, entities, timelines, data, output, cost, technical standards, and related criteria pertinent to the respective assignment. The suggested list is not an all-inclusive checklist since each forensic assignment is unique. Use the tasks as a guideline and modify according to the unique facts and circumstances of the assignment.

The objective of this action is to ensure that the forensic operator contemplates exigencies that may surface during the assignment. The forensic operator can minimize exigencies (to the extent possible) by diligent attention to this action.

Specific actions include:

- Determine the veracity of parties.
- Consider the currency of collected data (Internet data can be quite outdated).
- Determine whether data is admissible in the respective proceedings.

Deliverables

This action prompts the forensic operator to update and generate pertinent deliverables throughout the assignment.

Specific actions include:

- Updated search log.
- Updated genogram.
- Updated events analysis.
- Updated timeline analysis.
- Updated output notebook.

CONCLUSION

The people component of this interpersonal phase and its related stages, interviews and interrogations (including behavior detection), and background research is often the richest and most productive with respect to veracity assessment and assignment acceleration. The amount of time spent in this interpersonal phase varies considerably, depending upon the nature of the assignment. For example, if subject contact is limited, say, to depositions, the face-to-face time is obviously limited. However, the time that can be spent in background research has no practical limits, subject, of course, to the law, policy, and other factors.

The risk regarding background research compels forensic operators to use highly skilled research specialists to the extent necessary. Two of the references mentioned, above Jan Tudor and Cynthia Hetherington, are very cost-effective and fill any gaps in the forensic operator's knowledge. Nonetheless, the forensic operator should become familiar with the basic sources listed here to gather foundational data and thus provide more refined guidance to specialist resources.

CHAPTER 3

Data Collection and Analysis Phase: Part I

This chapter initiates the data collection and analysis tasks within a forensic assignment. This phase often represents the largest proportion of time, money, and related resources within a forensic assignment. This typically reflects the large amount of data and the commensurate analytical tasks. Accountants sometimes try to shortcut an assignment by immediately launching this phase since they are often more comfortable with the numbers. Such impulsivity is usually counterproductive, and merely an impetuous response to the dictum, "Not knowing what to do, one does what one knows." Consequently, the distinction between effort and results is blurred. Therefore, forensic operators starting with this phase are counseled to reconsider the prerequisite phases, that is, foundational and interpersonal.

Proceeding through the various stages arms forensic operators with a significant array of tools, techniques, methods, and methodologies previously unknown to many. The sheer number of such tools reinforces the essential need for a methodology within which to capture and apply them to forensic assignments' respective unique facts and circumstances.

DATA COLLECTION STAGE

Purpose of Stage

This action formally defines the data collection plan based upon previously completed stages, such as behavior detection and background research. It permits the forensic operator to subsequently launch data collection efforts and initiate analysis commensurate with appropriate techniques. See Exhibit 3.1.

The objective of this action is to determine the extent of data available as evidence, and the additional or repetitive tasks necessary to obtain all feasible data.

Specific actions include:

- Define the data collection plan based upon data already obtained, and additional data to be requested.
- Obtain data and other information.
- Surface evidence from all feasible sources.

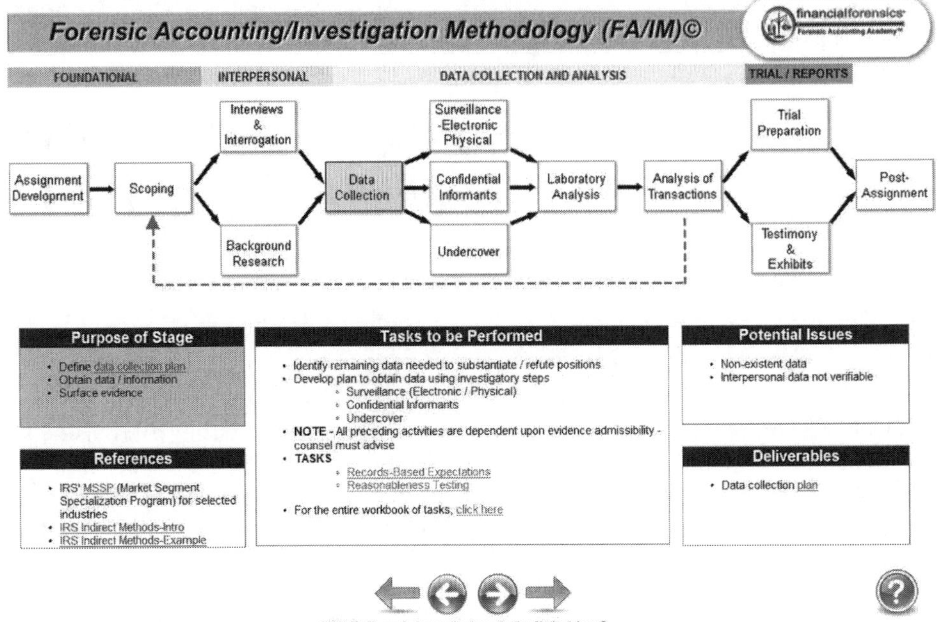

EXHIBIT 3.1 Data Collection

References

This action identifies and accesses all feasible guidance for data collection. Such guidance typically includes the type of industry, the nature of the entity, and the structure of the data capture techniques.

The objective of this action is to ensure that necessary technical resources are consulted to the extent necessary to identify additional data to be obtained.

Reference sources include:

- Internal Revenue Service Market Segment Specialization Program (MSSP) manuals for selected industries.

Example Reference Sources The following reference sources serve to jumpstart the forensic operator. The Key Internet Sites and Key Reference Materials are not all-inclusive, but provide starting points from which to build resources. Also, refer to the bibliography.

- Key Internet sites
  - All forensic operators
    - www.financialforensicsacademy.com
    - www.irs.gov/businesses/small/article/0,,id=108149,00.html
    - This site links to the IRS audit technique guides (ATGs) that provide examination techniques, common and unique industry issues, business practices, industry terminology and other information intended to support examiners for specific market segments, for example, construction, executive

compensation, farmers, hardwood timber, etc. The ATGs are quite detailed and specific, and some approach 200 pages of industry-specific instruction. The table of contents for the construction industry is contained within this chapter.[1]

- Key reference materials
  - All forensic operators
    - *Financial Forensics Body of Knowledge*, by Darrell D. Dorrell and Gregory A. Gadawski.

Tasks to Be Performed

This action outlines likely tasks, but is not an all-inclusive checklist, since each forensic assignment is unique. Use the tasks as a guideline and modify according to the unique facts and circumstances of the assignment.

The objective of this action is to ensure that all feasible and potentially pertinent data is obtained and considered for analysis. This stage is a likely point to enter the iterative loop back through preceding stages, if necessary.

Specific actions include:

- Identify remaining data needed to substantiate or refute positions.
- Develop a plan to obtain data using the following investigatory steps:
  - Surveillance (electronic or physical)
  - Confidential informants
  - Undercover
- *Note:* All preceding activities depend upon the admissibility of evidence. Counsel must advise on this.
- Establish records-based expectations regarding the nature, type, and veracity of data.
- Conduct reasonableness testing to the extent practicable and necessary. Note that the term *reasonableness testing* implies empirical observations and conclusions, not professional judgment.[2] For example, if a six-year CAGR (compound annual growth rate) of a subject's personal expenses approximate, say 7.8 percent, it can only be deemed reasonable by comparing to some standard. The potential standards include itself, for example, that represents the steady historical growth; benchmarks, for example; other expense reports; or a statistical measure using standard deviation; t-statistic; etc.

Potential Issues

This action prompts the forensic operator to consider the boundaries of the people, parties, entities, timelines, data, output, cost, technical standards, and related criteria

---

[1] Note that the IRS periodically updates their ATGs and Internet site. Consequently, certain previously available ATGs were removed and can be found at www.unclefed.com.

[2] See Appendix for a definition of *professional judgment.*

pertinent to the respective assignment. The suggested list is not an all-inclusive checklist since each forensic assignment is unique. Use the tasks as a guideline and modify according to the unique facts and circumstances of the assignment.

The objective of this action is to ensure that the forensic operator contemplates exigencies that may surface during the assignment. The forensic operator can minimize exigencies (to the extent possible) by diligent attention to this action.

Specific potential issues include:

- Data authentication
- Undisclosed data.
- Altered data.
- Varying versions of the same data.
- Varying definitions of the purportedly same data.
- Nonexistent data.
- Interpersonal data not verifiable.

Deliverables

This action prompts the forensic operator to identify or generate deliverables pertaining to the assignment.

The objective of this action is to document the source, timing, and nature of the various documents, information, and other potential evidence. Also, the assembly of such records may be a logical source for inclusion in exhibits and reports. Furthermore, it may be required in certain court proceedings.

Specific actions include:

- Data collection plan.
- Data request to opposing party(s).
- Data status, say by a document map.
- Chain of custody log update.

Sample Deliverables The following deliverables are frameworks for the forensic operator who will modify them to comply with their respective internal and other requirements:

- Updated data collection plan.
- Updated document map.
- Forensic Document Request.

Example Forensic Document Request *Note:* The following example forensic document request includes typical items sought in a forensic assignment. The format can take almost any form, but the contents of the document must specify the documents sought.

FORENSIC DOCUMENT REQUEST

DATA AND POTENTIAL EVIDENCE

SUMMARY

Forensic operators routinely prepare Forensic Document Requests to identify the data, documents, and other potential evidence necessary to complete their investigation. The following example Forensic Document Request illustrates the items in a shareholder dispute involving a call center in the Southeastern United States. The cause of action was a shareholder dispute, but the plaintiff (the forensic operator's client) strongly suspected that shareholders, and possibly some of the executive management had been skimming receipts and spending substantial sums on personal items. Therefore, the items requested go beyond the typical shareholder dispute matter, but subtle indications (e.g., bank statements) avoid alerting opposition to such strategy.

Forensic Document Requests vary from terse to voluminous and everywhere in between. Perhaps the Single Most Important Factor driving the content of a Forensic Document Request is the strategy employed by counsel. Some attorneys prefer to take a conciliatory approach early on in the hopes of receiving more, rather than less production. Alternatively, other attorneys prefer a very aggressive approach early on, thus setting the stage for continued battle. Regardless, forensic operators take their guidance from the intent of counsel in constructing a Forensic Document Request.

Displaying alternative formats to counsel is often helpful in order to agree upon the final form. Forensic Document Requests can take many forms, but the following example contains certain key features proven useful over many years. The features include the following.

- ❑ The instructions to the responding party specify both hard copy and electronic content;
- ❑ The Forensic Document Request exists in both hard copy and electronic versions, and accommodates the responding part(y)'s specific notations for each item.
- ❑ The specific nature of the requested items makes it difficult for opposition to object regarding "vague" descriptions.
- ❑ Comments throughout, including requests for questions and clarifications avoid contention and invite discourse. Additionally, the contents make clear that further requests may be forthcoming, thus subtly encouraging their compliance during the first round of production.
- ❑ Logical categories using the SCORE© methodology facilitate the respondent's review and completion of the document. The SCORE© acronym derives from well-known strategic planning stakeholder techniques which consider all the potential impacts to the entity's future operations by identifying all-encompassing categories. SCORE© provides a convenient mnemonic for the forensic operator to identify sources of control and correlating data categories. Those categories include Suppliers, Customers, Owners, (defined as investors and lenders), Regulators (a catchall term referring to IRS, SEC, etc. and anything else that might be necessary, e.g., weather, competition, politics, etc.), and Employees. (Refer to the ICE/SCORE© section in this book.)

The explanatory options following each request, "Enclosed," "N/A," and "Comments" encourage respondents to explain and clarify their production. In addition, the "checklist" format facilitates respondent's completion to include all the contents.

CONCLUSION

The Forensic Document Request is a critical task executed early in the assignment and merits considerable attention. To do otherwise could limit the forensic operator's ability to complete a thorough investigation.

ASSIGNMENT: Forensic Accounting

DATA REQUEST CHECKLIST PURSUANT TO MEDIATION

TODAY'S DATE:

Matter: Plaintiff
v.
Defendant A, Defendant B, and Defendant C
Likely As-of Date(s): **(tbd)**
Entities Include: Defendant A, Defendant B, and Defendant C

In each case where existing, we require ELECTRONIC documents in addition to hard-copy compliance. Specify the format for electronic compliance, which can remain in a native state or downloaded format, e.g., ASCII-delimited. In addition, PASSWORDS, if any must be provided with native state files.

This request covers documents and data 2003 to date.

General Instructions: The process that we deploy in forensic assignments compels us to develop a keen insight into and understanding of the entity(ies) requiring a conclusion. The data below is the "starting point" for achieving such understanding, and may in fact be sufficient to reach the objective(s). *However, further details may be requested, either in data form and/or interviews/depositions.*

It may **not** be necessary to individually provide data in each case below; some sources often provide multiple elements of the data, e.g., CPA-prepared financial statements, income tax returns, etc. Comments are included in ***bold, italics*** to clarify such items. Highlighted items specify essential data.

You can forward the information in any manner including copies, faxes, email, diskette, etc. although we prefer both electronic and hard-copy where possible.

If you have any questions please contact us at 999–999–9999 or PartyA@forensicoperator.com.

Financial Statements (Balance Sheet, Income Statement & Statement of Cash Flows)

1. All historical annual financial statements including those prepared by an outside party, CPA firm, and those prepared internally from inception to date.
   - ❑ *It is possible that income tax returns, below comprise the data.*
   - ❑ Enclosed
   - ❑ N/A
   - ❑ Comments:____________________________________

2. All annual federal and state (where applicable) income tax returns (including supporting schedules and statements) from inception to date.
   - ❑ Enclosed
   - ❑ N/A
   - ❑ Comments:____________________________________

3. All annual federal and state (where applicable) excise and/or sales tax returns from inception to date.
   - ❑ Enclosed
   - ❑ N/A
   - ❑ Comments:____________________________________

4. Copies of year-end, adjusting, or other Journal entries (including support) for the above-referenced financial statements.
   - ❑ Enclosed
   - ❑ N/A
   - ❑ Comments:____________________________________

5. All annual (where applicable) K-1s for the years from inception to date.
   - ❑ Enclosed
   - ❑ N/A
   - ❑ Comments:____________________________________

6. Interim financial statements (Quarterly or Monthly) for inception through current as available.
   - ❑ *This request might be met by providing an electronic file, e.g., QuickBooks if appropriate.*
   - ❑ Enclosed
   - ❑ N/A
   - ❑ Comments:____________________________________

7. Copies of any budgets, forecasts, or projections spanning inception to date and future years. Please also note when these were prepared, the purpose of preparation, and what assumptions that drove them.
   - ❑ Enclosed
   - ❑ N/A
   - ❑ Comments:____________________________________

8. **List of subsidiaries or other businesses in which the subject entity has an economic interest (if any) together with their financial statements matching the periods above.**
   - ❑ Enclosed
   - ❑ N/A
   - ❑ Comments:____

9. **The extent, if any to which the entities and/or assets were declared as collateral, proof of income, ability to repay or other representations, for other, supposedly unrelated entities and/or businesses.**
   - ❑ Enclosed
   - ❑ N/A
   - ❑ Comments:____

10. **The extent, if any to which Call Centers, Inc. has access to and/or is employing business assets or interests.**
   - ❑ Enclosed
   - ❑ N/A
   - ❑ Comments:____

11. **Explanation of significant non-recurring and/or non-operating items appearing on <u>any</u> of the financial statements and/or income tax returns, if not detailed in the footnotes.**
   - ❑ Enclosed
   - ❑ N/A
   - ❑ Comments:____

12. **Copies of all bank, credit union, money market, and other containing checking, savings, and other transactions, including reconciliations.**
   - ❑ Enclosed
   - ❑ N/A
   - ❑ Comments:____

13. **Copies of support identifying transfers into or out of any accounts under control of the parties and/or entities.**
   - ❑ Enclosed
   - ❑ N/A
   - ❑ Comments:____

14. **Copies of insurance policies, including business interruption, executive coverage, et al.**
   - ❑ Enclosed
   - ❑ N/A
   - ❑ Comments:____

15. **Copies of key business management tools used by owners and executives, typically identified as "flash" reports, "scorecard" reports, "vital signs" reports, et al.**
   - ❑ Enclosed

- ❑ N/A
- ❑ Comments:______________________________

Other Financial Data (to be prepared on ANNUAL BASIS)

16. An electronic copy of the accounting general ledger maintained by the Company, e.g., QuickBooks or equivalent spanning the years noted above.
    - ❑ *A PDF file of the general ledger detail is an option.*
    - ❑ *Please indicate version and password as applicable.*
    - ❑ Enclosed
    - ❑ N/A
    - ❑ Comments:______________________________

17. List of items comprising significant other asset balances, e.g., <u>equipment,</u> including original cost and accumulated depreciation from inception to date.
    - ❑ *It is possible that such information is contained in the income tax return. However, detailed schedules of assets and depreciation are often missing from the income tax returns. If so, you may need to ask your CPA for these.*
    - ❑ Enclosed
    - ❑ N/A
    - ❑ Comments:______________________________

18. Annual accounts receivable listing, preferably aged.
    - ❑ Enclosed
    - ❑ N/A
    - ❑ Comments:______________________________

19. Annual accounts payable listing, preferably aged.
    - ❑ Enclosed
    - ❑ N/A
    - ❑ Comments:______________________________

20. List of notes payable and other interest-bearing debt including supporting lending documentation (promissory notes specify loan date, term, interest rate, monthly payment, etc.). Loan amortization schedules are helpful.
    - ❑ *A copy of any outstanding loan documents is also requested.*
    - ❑ *Also, copies of any loan applications pertaining to prior existing or anticipated loans.*
    - ❑ Enclosed
    - ❑ N/A
    - ❑ Comments:______________________________

21. List of items comprising significant "other" liability balances, if any.
    - ❑ Enclosed
    - ❑ N/A
    - ❑ Comments:______________________________

22. **Schedule of revenue by lines of business, property or investment, and/or type of transaction for each period that an income statement (historical or future periods) is obtained. Also, the gross profit by lines of business, if applicable.**
    - ❑ ***If other sources do not capture such information, (e.g., general ledger) then we can clarify with discussions.***
    - ❑ Enclosed
    - ❑ N/A
    - ❑ Comments:____

23. **Schedule of officers' and directors' compensation, by person for each year in which financial information has been presented.**
    - ❑ Enclosed
    - ❑ N/A
    - ❑ Comments:____

24. **Copies of any business plans, past and present. Please note the date of preparation.**
    - ❑ Enclosed
    - ❑ N/A
    - ❑ Comments:____

SUPPLIERS

25. **Copies of ALL correspondence with any suppliers and/or manufacturers from inception. This includes: liquor, beer, wine, food (meats, fish, produce, bakery items, et al.), condiments, equipment, supplies, et al.**
    - ❑ Enclosed
    - ❑ N/A
    - ❑ Comments:____

26. **Copies of any major supplier contracts whether or not included with the preceding item.**
    - ❑ Enclosed
    - ❑ N/A
    - ❑ Comments:____

CUSTOMERS

27. **Major customers/clients, e.g., Oracle added/dropped during the period covered by the financial statements for all the years included above.**
    - ❑ Enclosed
    - ❑ N/A
    - ❑ Comments:____

28. **Schedule of all hours of operation, including holidays.**
    - ❑ Enclosed
    - ❑ N/A
    - ❑ Comments:____

29. Copies of any major customer contracts.
    - ❑ Enclosed
    - ❑ N/A
    - ❑ Comments:____

30. Detailed description of means and methods of sales and marketing employed by the Company from inception, including copies of any/all correspondence, contracts, etc. related to same.
    - ❑ Enclosed
    - ❑ N/A
    - ❑ Comments:____

31. Copies of menus, brochures, price lists, catalogs, or other service/product sales information.
    - ❑ Enclosed
    - ❑ N/A
    - ❑ Comments:____

32. Major products/services added/dropped during the period covered by the financial statements for all the years included above.
    - ❑ Enclosed
    - ❑ N/A
    - ❑ Comments:____

OWNERS/LENDERS/INVESTORS

33. History statement, including a description of how long in business, and details of any changes in ownership and/or any bona fide offers recently received during the time.
    - ❑ Enclosed
    - ❑ N/A
    - ❑ Comments:____

34. List of all prior/existing owners, stockholders or partners, showing the amount of stock or percentage of ownership held by each person and/or entity.
    - ❑ Enclosed
    - ❑ N/A
    - ❑ Comments:____

35. Copy of any Stockholder, Membership, Operating, and similar Agreements, including the Corporate Charter, Articles of Incorporation, Bylaws, and Buy-Sell or similar agreements.
    - ❑ Enclosed
    - ❑ N/A
    - ❑ Comments:____

36. Minutes, resolutions, memoranda and other actions, including all Board of Directors' meetings.
    - ❑ Enclosed

- ❑ N/A
- ❑ Comments:____

37. **Details of transactions with related parties, in any form, e.g., leases, rents, merchandise purchases, et al.**
    - ❑ Enclosed
    - ❑ N/A
    - ❑ Comments:____

38. **Schedule of officers' and directors' compensation by person for each year in which financial information has been presented.**
    - ❑ Enclosed
    - ❑ N/A
    - ❑ Comments:____

39. **Copies of significant leases and loans, including notes receivable and notes payable.**
    - ❑ Enclosed
    - ❑ N/A
    - ❑ Comments:____

40. **Details of any contingent liabilities (such as guarantees, warranties, or derivative financial instruments) or off balance sheet financing (such as letters of credit).**
    - ❑ Enclosed
    - ❑ N/A
    - ❑ Comments:____

41. **Copies and identification of liquor, beer, wine, and related federal, state, and local licenses.**
    - ❑ Enclosed
    - ❑ N/A
    - ❑ Comments:____

REGULATORY

42. **Description of business position relative to competition and any factors that make the business unique.**
    - ❑ Enclosed
    - ❑ N/A
    - ❑ Comments:____

43. **Listing of key competitors, including location and other competitive advantages.**
    - ❑ Enclosed
    - ❑ N/A
    - ❑ Comments:____

44. Published articles about the Company and/or its industry contained in professional journals, magazines, and other publications that contain information about the Company and/or its industry.
    - ❑ Enclosed
    - ❑ N/A
    - ❑ Comments:____________________________________

45. Copies of correspondence regarding sales tax audit in progress.
    - ❑ Enclosed
    - ❑ N/A
    - ❑ Comments:____________________________________

46. Copies of correspondence from any other taxing or regulatory authorities from inception to date.
    - ❑ Enclosed
    - ❑ N/A
    - ❑ Comments:____________________________________

47. Copies of any US Customs reporting (imports AND exports) since inception.
    - ❑ Enclosed
    - ❑ N/A
    - ❑ Comments:____________________________________

48. Names and addresses/phone numbers and Internet URLs of professional associations which pertain to the Company's industry.
    - ❑ Enclosed
    - ❑ N/A
    - ❑ Comments:____________________________________

49. Knowledge of recent sales of business similar to the Company.
    - ❑ Enclosed
    - ❑ N/A
    - ❑ Comments:____________________________________

50. Copies of compliance filings, e.g., periodic reporting to lenders.
    - ❑ Enclosed
    - ❑ N/A
    - ❑ Comments:____________________________________

51. List the major industry publication(s) of interest to management.
    - ❑ Enclosed
    - ❑ N/A
    - ❑ Comments:____________________________________

52. List of any of the following including details and indications of ownership:
    a. Patents.
    b. Copyrights.
    c. Trademarks, Trade Names, Trade Dress, Trade Secrets.
    d. Similar intangibles, identifiable or otherwise.
    e. Other.

- ❑ Enclosed
- ❑ N/A
- ❑ Comments:____

EMPLOYEES

53. Organization chart indicating key and total employees and brief biographical summary of key people summarizing experience, education, work history, etc.
- ❑ Enclosed
- ❑ N/A
- ❑ Comments:____

54. Copies of employment agreements currently in force.
- ❑ Enclosed
- ❑ N/A
- ❑ Comments:____

55. Reports of other consultants/banks, etc., including previous business valuations for the Company or related entities.
- ❑ Enclosed
- ❑ N/A
- ❑ Comments:____

56. Appraisals on specific assets such as land, machinery, equipment, etc., if any.
- ❑ Enclosed
- ❑ N/A
- ❑ Comments:____

57. Reports from insurance agents regarding business interruption and property/casualty as well as key person life insurance.
- ❑ Enclosed
- ❑ N/A
- ❑ Comments:____

58. Copies of all insurance policies maintained by the individuals and/or entities.
- ❑ Enclosed
- ❑ N/A
- ❑ Comments:____

59. Copies of employee bonding coverage.
- ❑ Enclosed
- ❑ N/A
- ❑ Comments:____

60. Reports of independent auditors other than the financial statements, e.g., Annual Management Letter, periodic analysis, etc.
- ❑ Enclosed
- ❑ N/A
- ❑ Comments:____

61. Copies of payroll filings, including 940s, 941, et al.
- ❑ Enclosed
- ❑ N/A
- ❑ Comments:__________________________________

62. Copies of any union or collective-bargaining contracts.
- ❑ Enclosed
- ❑ N/A
- ❑ Comments:__________________________________

63. Copies of any employee contracts, non-competes, non-disclosures, et al.
- ❑ Enclosed
- ❑ N/A
- ❑ Comments:__________________________________

64. Items not specifically listed but that would provide useful information are also encouraged to be provided.
- ❑ ***As a general rule, "If in doubt" about whether to provide a document, please provide it. We prefer more rather than less documentation***
- ❑ Enclosed
- ❑ N/A
- ❑ Comments:__________________________________

ICE/SCORE

ICE/SCORE is a simple methodology that enables the forensic operator to either rely upon or *modify* self-reported[3] data to arrive at a correct and defensible evidence-based conclusion. Furthermore, its straightforward and step-by-step structure permits others, that is, triers of fact, to grasp the reasoning and conclusions, since it is objectively supported by unbiased data and evidence.

Thinking Outside the . . . Triangle The ICE/SCORE methodology is a subset of FA/IM,[4] and its simple two-part, three-step structure can be considered a micro methodology. It parallels the evidence[5]-based analysis techniques used by judicial systems (civil and criminal), law enforcement, the military, the IRS, etc. It functions in virtually *any* forensic assignment that requires data[6] validation, refinement or rebuttal regarding evidence, and is thus *not* restricted to merely financial matters.

---

[3] Data compiled or reported or both by any person or entity without the benefit of independent oversight or attestation.

[4] Forensic Accounting/Investigation Methodology—FA/IM, described in this text.

[5] Any species of proof, or probative matter, legally presented at the trial of an issue, by the parties and through the medium of witnesses, records, documents, exhibits, concrete objects, and so on, for the purpose of inducing belief in the minds of the court or jury as to their contention. *Black's Law Dictionary* 6th ed. (St. Paul, MN: West Publishing, 1990), 555.

[6] Organized information generally used as the basis for an adjudication or decision. Commonly organized information, collected for a specific purpose. *Black's Law Dictionary* 6th ed. (St. Paul, MN: West Publishing 1990), 395.

ICE/SCORE's foundational premise is logical simplicity: it progressively evaluates and rates the reliability of a subject's (person, business, company, department, division, government, nonprofit, NGO,[7] or any other entity) self-reported data by comparison to itself and control data. Control data apply from both within (through ICE) and outside (through SCORE) the subject's self-reporting system.[8] A strong correlation between self-reported and control data suggests greater reliability of the subject data, while weak correlation suggests lesser reliability.

WAR STORY

During a financial crimes presentation of ICE/SCORE to a large police department, the expression "score some ice" was coined. *Ice* is a street name for crystal methamphetamine. It thus provided the officers with an easy way to remember the name of the methodology.

The subject's data can be virtually *anything* prepared by or pertaining to the subject. The subject's data can be quantitative or qualitative. The qualitative data can consist of words, pictures, numbers, testimony, dates, financial, operational, statistical, weights, temperatures, colors, or any other characteristics purported to represent the subject's self-reported data.

ICE/SCORE is an acronym designed for ease of intuitive memory and implementation. This section details its components later and include the following:

ICE Components			
Internal	*I*	(*I*CE)	Subject's Internal data
Control	C	(ICE)	Subject's Control data
External	*E*	(IC*E*)	Subject's External data
SCORE Components			
Suppliers	*S*	(*S*CORE)	Subject's Suppliers
Customers	C	(SCORE)	Subject's Customers
Owners	O	(SCORE)	Subject's Owners
Regulators	*R*	(SCO*R*E)	Subject's Regulators
Employees	*E*	(SCOR*E*)	Subject's Employees

The following visual (Exhibit 3.2) illustrates the overall ICE/SCORE methodology and its components.

How Does ICE/Score Work? ICE/SCORE is a two-part methodology executed by completing three successive steps in sequence. At the successful completion of each

[7] Nongovernmental organization, for example, the American Red Cross.

[8] Signifies the boundaries of data captured (whether or not self-reported) under any person's or entity's control, also known as *On-Book*; data under any person's or entity's control but *not* captured is referred to as *Off-Book*.

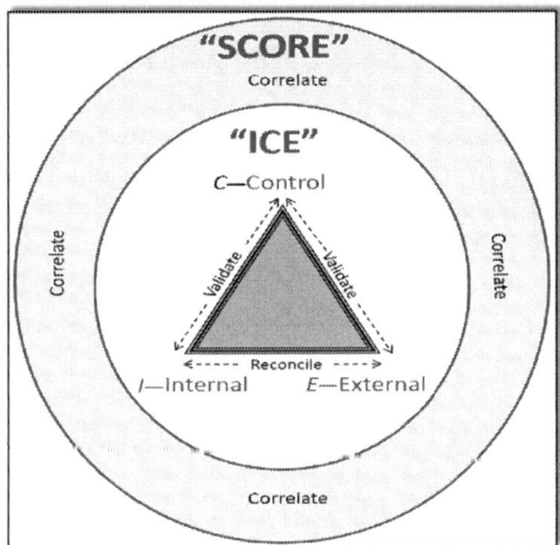

EXHIBIT 3.2 ICE/Score Diagram

step, the reliability of the subject's self-reported data can be progressively assessed. Therefore, successful completion of Step 1 results in reliability levels from none to low; successful completion of Step 2 results in reliability levels from low to medium; and successful completion of Step 3 results in reliability levels from medium to high. The ranges of assessment permit observations that reflect the reliability of the data within each step.

The following visual (Exhibit 3.3) illustrates the steps within the methodology and the concomitant progressive reliability rating of the subject's data. The narrative following explains the diagram in detail.

Step 1: ICE—Reconcile Step 1 initiates the first half of the methodology and consists of reconciling the subject's self-reported internal and external data. Common examples of internal and external data include management-prepared financial statements and income tax returns, respectively. Regardless of source, the internal and external data originates within the subject's self-reporting system.

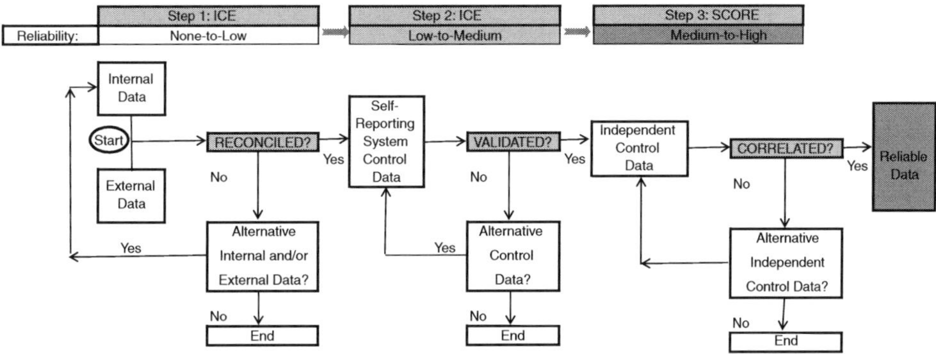

EXHIBIT 3.3 ICE/Score Steps Flow Chart (Reconciled, Validated, Correlated)

The objective of Step 1 is to determine the extent of corroboration between the two sources of self-reported data, that is, internal and external. For example, a subject's management-prepared financial statements and income tax returns will typically reconcile with little difficulty. Any reconciling differences will likely consist of timing and noncash items, for example, cash versus accrual, depreciation, etc. errors notwithstanding. Therefore, if Step 1 is successfully reconciled, Step 2, validation of control data can be undertaken.

If Step 1 cannot be successfully reconciled, a fundamental problem exists, and Step 2, validation cannot be pursued until (if) Step 1 is resolved. If Step 1 is not initially successful, the internal and external data should be reviewed to determine whether sufficient commonalities exist to permit reconciliation. Such commonalities include relevancy of data content, commonality of data content, time period consistency, sufficient drill-down[9] detail, etc.

If Step 1 cannot be completed, alternative internal and external data may need to be considered. If Step 1 still cannot be completed after considering alternative data, then the data reliability conclusion must be none to low. That is, the data cannot be validated beyond the face of the self-reported content. Thus, if Step 1 cannot be completed, there is no need to continue—efforts toward Steps 2 or 3 without Step 1's foundation are pointless.

Even when Step 1 results in successful reconciliation of internal and external data, a subject's self-reported data cannot be considered reliable beyond none to low. That is because the Step 1 reconciliation merely corroborates two sources of data produced by the *same party(s) from the same self-reporting system*. Consequently, no independent data from outside the self-reporting system can validate the self-reported data. Nonetheless, successful reconciliation is a favorable indicator and provides a solid foundation upon which to apply Step 2, validation of related control data.

Description of Step 1 Data to Be Used Internal and external data are defined next.

I (*I*CE)—*Internal:* Any internal records prepared or used, or both, by the subject. Such records purport to track some type of subject activity and typically consist of business, management, production, operational, financial, and other records.

For example, during a valuation, a business typically submits management-prepared, that is, internal financial statements to be used in the appraisal of its respective interests. Alternatively, the records in a damages or lost profits matter might reflect the labor hours, miles driven, gallons produced, or other similar output measures of a particular business unit. Finally, a governmental unit might provide output measures for department activity, such as the number of forms processed, number of citizens served, number of phone calls received, etc.

Regardless of the composition of the Internal data, the critical point to remember is that the data reflects the internal activities as self-reported by the subject.

E (IC*E*)—*External:* Any external records reported to or prepared, or both, by outside parties using the subject's internal records.

For example, during a valuation, a company typically provides CPA-prepared, that is, external tax returns to be used in the appraisal of its respective interests.

[9] An investigative process that moves from top to bottom. It starts with summary information and moves downward through successively more detailed supporting data to focus on the pertinent component parts.

Alternatively, in a damages or lost profits matter, the subject's import or export self-reporting to U.S. Customs might reflect volume activity that could be used to reconcile to internal records. Finally, a governmental unit's head-count budget request could be compared to internal payroll records.

A subject's management-prepared financial statements (internal data) often significantly differ from the respective income tax returns (external data), and they typically require some level of reconciliation. Thus, Step 1 is the logical point from which to conduct reconciliation.

A forensic operator routinely reconciles the internal and external data, noting any differences. A successful reconciliation (even with minor differences) could suggest a none-to-low rating regarding the reliability of the data. The reconciliation could also serve other purposes. For example, forensic operators typically conduct such reconciliations in valuation assignments to identify economic benefit stream components, and to identify normalization[10] adjustments. Even if the internal and external data readily reconcile, such results cannot be considered a strong measure of its reliability. That is because the data, both internal and external, reflect those items as self-reported by the subject.

Regardless of the composition of the external data, the important point to remember is that the data reflects the external activities as self-reported by the subject. The following visual (Exhibit 3.4) illustrates the relationship and successful reconciliation between the subject's self-reported internal and external data. The same visual (Exhibit 3.4) also illustrates the triangle aspect of the methodology. The triangle is widely known to represent the strongest of all geometric and structural shapes. That is because the three points of the triangle (in this case represented by internal, external, and control) are all mutually dependent upon one another. Also, any alteration to any one of the points affects one and probably both of the other points.

PUTTING IT INTO PRACTICE

Self-Reported Data

It is essential to maintain an attitude of healthy skepticism regarding data you receive from clients, the opposition, through formal discovery or through your own research. That is the rationale for referring to data as self-reported. Such a posture does not suggest a lack of respect for your client, but rather that your client expects you to provide straightforward answers.

A Caution Although successful completion of Step 1 is a positive indicator, the forensic operator must maintain an attitude of healthy skepticism regarding any self-reported data. There are abundant examples of high-profile public and private entities whose internal and external data were relied upon by a wide variety of parties, including auditors, tax authorities, investors, bankers, and other lenders, suppliers, employees, and others whose data proved grossly unreliable. The consequences of such false reliance are inevitably substantial.

[10] Normalizations are adjustments to financial statements to eliminate the distortion of nonoperating, nonmarket, and nonrecurring events.

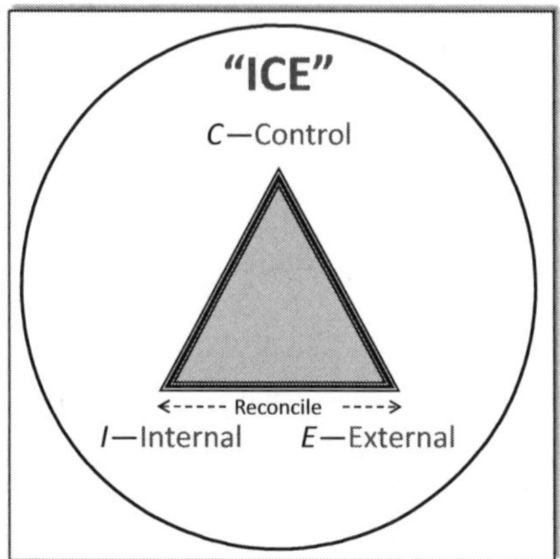

EXHIBIT 3.4 ICE Diagram
(Reconcile—Bottom of Triangle)

The nature of the internal and external data used by the methodology has, by definition, a *potentially* high level of reliability. That is, the self-reporting party is representing that the data reflects the entity's activities. Furthermore, such data are likely to be the most visible to parties outside the entity, so the universe of reconciled data is quite limited with respect to the remainder of the subject's captured data. Consider, for example, that a detailed set of the subject's financial statements reflects the top of the pyramid with respect to the underlying transaction details. There are literally thousands of individual transactions that make up the financial statements. Consequently, the forensic operator cannot impute reliability upon the underlying transactions or financials even when Step 1 is successfully reconciled.

Therefore, if a reliability conclusion falls at the low end of the low-to-medium scale, it may be warranted to conduct additional reconciliations to strengthen the degree of reliability.

Assuming that Step 1 has been successfully completed, the Step 2 portion of the methodology can be pursued.

Step 2: ICE—Validate Step 2 completes the second half of the methodology and consists of validating the subject's control data by comparison against the subject's self-reported internal and external data. Bank statements[11] are often considered a form of control data that can be used to validate the internal and external data. Regardless of source, control data is typically generated by a third party and driven by or identified by the subject's self-reporting system. That is, even though the subject's control data was derived incidentally to self-reported internal and external data, it must be independent of such data. Regardless, it is critical that the control data be *outside* the subject's ability to manipulate.

The objective of Step 2 is to find and correlate data that independently validates the internal and external data reconciled during Step 1. For example, a subject's bank statements are directly related to and dependent upon the subject's self-reported

[11] Naturally, this presumes that bank statements are obtained directly from the bank. The authors have seen many examples of both sophisticated and amateurish computer graphics manipulation of bank statement contents.

data. Typical examples of such Step 1 data include the management-prepared financial statements and income tax returns mentioned in the preceding discussion of internal and external data, respectively. Bank statements can be used to validate internal and external data using the proof-of-cash technique described later in this section appendix.

Before attempting completion of Step 2, Step 1 must have been successful. If Step 2 results in disparities, a fundamental problem exists, and Step 3 correlation cannot be pursued until (if) Step 2 is successfully completed. To complete Step 2, review the control data to determine whether the internal and external data are sufficiently common to permit validation. This process is similar to that in Step 1, but it is essential to use control data outside the subject's ability to manipulate.

If Step 2 cannot be completed, alternative control data may need to be considered. If Step 2 still cannot be completed, then the data reliability conclusion must be none to low. That is, the data cannot be validated beyond Step 1 reconciliation of internal and external data. Thus, if Step 2 cannot be completed, then there is no need to continue—efforts toward Step 3 without Step 2's foundation is pointless.

Assuming that Steps 1 and 2 are both successful, one can *preliminarily* conclude that the subject's self-reported data is reliable within the low-to-medium range. A preliminary conclusion is necessary for two reasons. First, the ICE technique (Steps 1 and 2) uses data self-reported by the subject, which may differ from fact to varying degrees because of error or manipulation or both. Second, the ICE technique (unaccompanied by SCORE) considers only activity within or related to the subject's self-reporting system. Activity outside the self-reporting system would be overlooked by relying upon ICE alone, thus creating the need for Step 3, correlation.

C (ICE)—*Control:* Any records driven by internal and external data, but not subject to manipulation. Such records are typically prepared by third parties and made available by the subject coincident to the business operations. Bank statements represent an excellent example of control records.

The following visual (Exhibit 3.5) illustrates the validation process using control data between the subject's self-reported internal and external data after reconciliation.

The preceding visual (Exhibit 3.4) also illustrates the triangle aspect of the methodology. The triangle is widely known to represent the strongest of all geometric

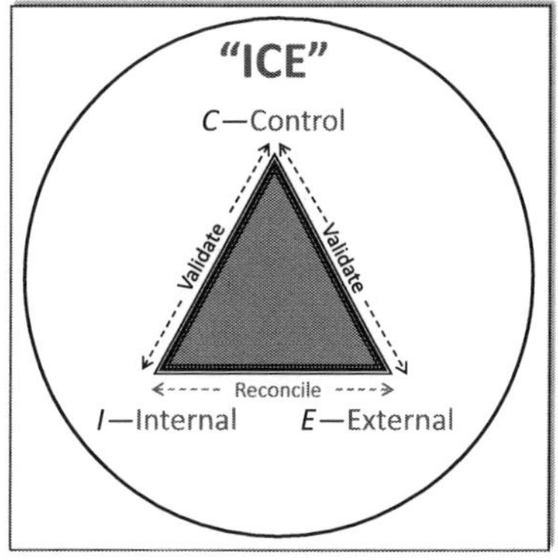

EXHIBIT 3.5 ICE Diagram (validate—right and left side of triangle)

and structural shapes. That is because the three points of the triangle (in this case represented by internal, external, and control) are all mutually dependent upon one another. Also, any alteration to any one of the points affects one and probably both of the other points.

The authors often observe forensic operators in training who mistakenly believe that by completing only Steps 1 and 2, and thus completing the triangle, that their forensic analysis is complete. Such a presumption is a gross and often fatal error. Such faulty thinking initiated the origin of the "Thinking outside the . . . triangle" phrase. Similar to "Thinking outside the box," a forensic operator must think outside the triangulation of the methodology.

The following visual (Exhibit 3.5A) demonstrates an actual example of the failure to use ICE. Note that the two internal sources agreed to the penny. The discrepancies were identified only when compared against an external control source, in this case bank statements.

Terminating forensic analysis before completing the third and final step, that is, SCORE, would preclude discovery of data outside the subject's self-reporting system. Significantly, experienced forensic operators know that the most interesting data reside *outside* the subject's self-reporting systems.

Assuming that Steps 1 and 2 have been successfully completed, the SCORE portion of the methodology can then be pursued.

Step 3: Correlate using SCORE Step 3 correlation is the second half of the methodology and completes the third and final step. Step 3 focuses on correlating independent data *outside* (but related to) the subject's self-reporting system to the Steps 1 and 2 results from ICE.

The objective is to correlate data *independent* of the subject's self-reporting system to the results from ICE (Steps 1 and 2) and obtain correlation to increase the

Internal | Internal | External

FOOD COMPANY
Missing Deposits Summary
May 31, 2006 to March 4, 2008

Cash on Computer Input Sheet	Total on Computer Input Sheet	Date on Bank Deposit Slip	Subtotal: Cash	Subtotal: Checks	Total per Bank Slip	Date Bank Statement	Total per Bank Statement	Diff betw slip & statement	Missing Cash
$ 408.00	$ 7,246.11	Thursday, July 06, 2006	$ 408.00	$ 6,838.11	$ 7,246.11	Missing		$ (7,246.11)	$ (408.00)
$ 656.00	$ 4,904.25	Wednesday, August 16, 2006	$ 656.00	$ 4,248.25	$ 4,904.25	Missing		$ (4,904.25)	$ (656.00)
$ 191.05	$ 4,686.26	Wednesday, May 31, 2006	$ 191.00	$ 4,495.21	$ 4,686.21	Missing		$ (4,686.21)	$ (191.00)
$ 206.00	$ 5,658.63	Thursday, October 19, 2006	$ 206.00	$ 5,452.63	$ 5,658.63	Missing		$ (5,658.63)	$ (206.00)
$ 508.00	$ 5,085.91	[illegible]	$ 508.00	$ 4,577.91	$ 5,085.91	Missing		$ (5,085.91)	$ (508.00)
$ 331.86	$ 5,851.02	[illegible]	$ 332.00	$ 5,519.16	$ 5,851.16	Missing		$ (5,851.16)	$ (332.00)
$ 695.00	$ 6,368.68	Friday, December 15, 2006	$ 695.00	$ 5,673.68	$ 6,368.68	Missing		$ (6,368.68)	$ (695.00)
$ 251.00	$ 8,292.30	[illegible] 2007	$ 251.00	$ 8,041.30	$ 8,292.30	Missing		$ (8,292.30)	$ (251.00)
$ 672.00	$ 7,195.10	[illegible] 2007	$ 672.00	$ 6,523.10	$ 7,195.10	Missing		$ (7,195.10)	$ (672.00)
$ -	$ 6,058.80	Wednesday, August 15, 2007	$ -	$ 6,058.80	$ 6,058.80	Missing		$ (6,058.80)	$ -
$ 605.00	$ 3,920.29	Monday, September 10, 2007	$ 605.00	$ 3,315.29	$ 3,920.29	Missing		$ (3,920.29)	$ (605.00)
$ 461.00	$ 6,423.85	Thursday, September 27, 2007	$ 461.00	$ 5,962.85	$ 6,423.85	Missing		$ (6,423.85)	$ (461.00)
$ 930.00	$ 10,897.74	Friday, October 26, 2007	$ 930.00	$ 9,967.74	$ 10,897.74	Missing		$ (10,897.74)	$ (930.00)
$ 509.00	$ 6,975.99	Tuesday, November 20, 2007	$ 509.00	$ 6,466.99	$ 6,975.99	Missing		$ (6,975.99)	$ (509.00)
$ 247.00	$ 11,532.53	Wednesday, December 12, 2007	$ 247.00	$ 11,285.53	$ 11,532.53	Missing		$ (11,532.53)	$ (247.00)
$ 866.00	$ 6,393.04	Friday, December 28, 2007	$ 866.00	$ 5,527.04	$ 6,393.04	Missing		$ (6,393.04)	$ (866.00)
$ 214.00	$ 10,809.43	Wednesday, January 23, 2008	$ 214.00	$ 10,595.43	$ 10,809.43	Missing		$ (10,809.43)	$ (214.00)
$ 170.00	$ 8,973.08	Wednesday, January 30, 2008	$ 170.00	$ 8,803.08	$ 8,973.08	Missing		$ (8,973.08)	$ (170.00)
$ 207.00	$ 11,833.03	Monday, February 11, 2008	$ 208.00	$ 11,625.03	$ 11,833.03	Missing		$ (11,833.03)	$ (208.00)
$ 823.00	$ 6,071.72	Wednesday, February 13, 2008	$ 823.00	$ 5,248.72	$ 6,071.72	Missing		$ (6,071.72)	$ [illegible]
				TOTAL	$ 145,177.85			$ (145,177.85)	$ (8,952.00)

Amounts Agree

Theft

EXHIBIT 3.5A Failure to Use ICE Diagram

assessment of reliability. This process is similar to Step 2, where control data helped validate reconciled data from Steps 1 and 2.

Identifying data used for Step 3 correlation can be challenging to those unfamiliar with investigation methodologies. The challenge stems from two basic factors. First, there appears to be a seemingly endless source of independent control data, thus presenting an obstacle that is more imagined than real. Second, and probably more pronounced, is the forensic operator's lack of familiarity with even basic measures of statistical correlation. Regardless of the SCORE data used, there are two overriding criteria: Control data must be outside (but related to) the subject's self-reporting system, and the control data must be outside the subject's ability to manipulate.

The nature of a subject's operations provides a rich source of guidelines regarding SCORE data. For example, a coin-operated laundry could boast well-maintained and easily reconciled books and records, and a proof of cash could yield no discrepancies. In that case, both Step 1 and Step 2 (ICE) would have been successfully completed. However, concluding that the coin-operated laundry's records are "just fine" would be premature and quite possibly wrong. Despite the success of ICE, the subject's self-reported data were not correlated to data *outside* the subject's self-reporting system. Furthermore, the only way to know for sure, say, whether all receipts were indeed reported would be to look *beyond* the self-reporting system to an independent source of correlating data, using SCORE. In such a case, water utility gallon usage would provide independent control data against which to compare the subject's self-reporting system.

The SCORE Model The SCORE model was developed to provide forensic operators with a convenient means of identifying correlating data. See Exhibit 3.6.

The SCORE acronym derives from well-known strategic planning stakeholder techniques that consider all the potential impacts to the entity's future operations by identifying all-encompassing categories. SCORE provides a convenient mnemonic for the forensic operator to identify sources of control and correlating data categories. Those categories include *S*uppliers, *C*ustomers, *O*wners, (defined as investors and lenders), *R*egulators (a catchall term referring to IRS, SEC, etc. and anything else that might be necessary, for example, weather, competition, politics, etc.), and *E*mployees.

The SCORE acronym goes one step further by specifying that either units (U) or money ($) flow into or out of a business (or government, nonprofit, marriage, department, etc.) depending upon the stakeholder category. For example, units (U) of iron ore flow into a steel mill while money ($) flows out in exchange for the ore. Therefore, the following schedule provides a quick reference for each of the stakeholder categories so that the forensic operator can determine what units or money or both might pertain to the subject business.

SCORE's stakeholder data categories consist of:

S (*S*CORE): ***Suppliers*** provide units (U) to the business in exchange for money ($) paid by the business. For example, an electric utility provides kilowatts of power (U) paid for ($) by the business. The same flow is true of virtually every type of business or nonbusiness operation. In a grocery chain, canned goods, produce, meats, dairy items, (U) etc. flow into the business, which pays money ($) that flows out of the business.

"SCORE"

	Flow of $ and/or Units	
Stakeholder	In	Out
S–Suppliers	U	$
C–Customers	$	U
O–"Owners" Investors/Lenders	$	$
R–Regulators	n/a	$
E–Employees	U	$

EXHIBIT 3.6 SCORE Stakeholder and Flow of Funds Chart

C (sCORE): *Customers* provide money ($) to the business in exchange for units (U) produced by the business. For example, patients (and insurance companies) provide money ($) to a hospital in exchange for health care services (U). The same flow is true of virtually every type of business or non-business operation. For example, taxpayers provide money ($) to governmental units for safety and related services (U); tenants provide money ($) to property owners for the rental (U) of office space, etc. Consequently, the nature of the business helps identify sources of customer information that provide additional control points.

O(scORE): *Owners* (investors and lenders) provide money ($) to the business in exchange for money ($) produced by the business. For example, investors provide startup capital in exchange for dividends and eventual gains, and lenders provide funds in exchange for interest payments to rent their money. Consequently, the nature of the business helps identify sources of owner information that provide additional control points.

R (scoRE): *Regulators* may not *directly* provide units (U) (licenses, permits, etc.) to the business even though the business provides money ($) (taxes, fees, filings, etc.). Regardless, an intangible economic exchange takes place for the right to stay in business. For example, the SEC regulates and enforces compliance with publicly held companies regarding the veracity of their financial statements, which accommodates investor transactions and capital markets. Consequently, the nature of the business helps identify sources of regulator information that provide additional control points.

E (scorE): *Employees* produce units (U) (hours, miles, pieces, etc.) in exchange for money ($) paid by the business. For example, in an accounting firm, employees complete tax returns (U) in exchange for compensation ($); cashiers provide customer interface services (U) in a bank in exchange for compensation ($); pilots fly planeloads (U) of passengers in exchange for compensation ($), etc. Consequently, the nature of the business helps identify sources of employee information that provide additional control points.

Disposition of Step Three If Step 3 cannot be completed, alternative independent control data may need to be considered. If Step 3 still cannot be completed, then the data reliability conclusion must be low to medium. That is, the data cannot be validated beyond Steps 1 and 2, that is, reconciliation and validation, respectively.

Assuming that Step 3 results in a favorable comparison against independent control data, one can conclude that the subject data is reliable within the medium-to-high range. This does not guarantee reliability, however. The conclusion merely indicates that the data extant correlates to the subject's self-reporting system, and the likelihood of manipulation is reduced to a nominal level.

The following visual (Exhibit 3.7) illustrates the successful completion of Step 3, correlation.

During a valuation, a forensic operator typically correlates self-reported sales with an independent variable, often GDP[12] or GSP[13] to determine whether the measure could be used for forward-looking financial estimates. In smaller businesses, more local measures may be appropriate. For example, labor sector measures reported by the subject's respective state may serve as a benchmark for businesses trends. Alternatively, in a damages or lost profits matter, the subject's industry outlooks could be compared to internal and external reporting. Finally, a governmental unit's measure of certified teachers compared to state funding could be compared to internal and external self-reporting.

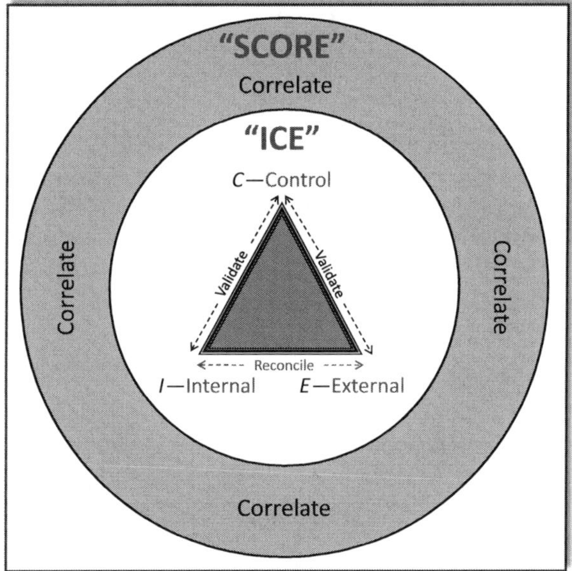

EXHIBIT 3.7 ICE/SCORE Diagram (ICE section faded)

[12] Gross Domestic Product—The total annual value of all goods and services produced by labor and capital within a country's borders.

[13] Gross State Product—The total annual value of all goods and services produced by labor and capital within a state's borders.

WAR STORY

A grocery store chain was convinced that a store manager was stealing register cash. However, scrupulous comparisons of register tapes, cash closeouts, deposits, and other tests of the store's seven registers all tied out. The reporting system appeared to be accurate. After a late shift, though, the internal auditor noted that the store had *eight* registers in operation—the manager had been operating his own private register.

The SCORE categories can also be used to find various control data categories within Step 2 of the ICE tasks. Bank statements served as control data in the earlier ICE example to validate internal and external financial statements. In that case, the bank was a supplier of services to the subject business. Typically, there will be several sources of control data for the respective subject entity, and thinking through the SCORE categories permits the forensic operator to identify them.

If one (or more) of the SCORE data categories correlates with the findings of the ICE activities, then the forensic operator has achieved the highest degree of reliance (or rebuttal) upon the self-reported data. That is, the self-reporting system was properly reconciled *and* independently validated. Note that such validation may include either confirmation or rebuttal that the system is valid, depending upon the respective assignment objectives. Consequently, favorable conclusions for Steps 1, 2, and 3 tend to support a medium-to-high rating of reliability.

If Step 3 cannot be completed, at least the forensic operator can fall back on the reliability rating established through Step 2, and can demonstrate the attempt to complete Step 3.

The following visual (Exhibit 3.8) illustrates the successful completion of all three steps within the ICE/SCORE methodology and its structure.

Is SCORE Really Necessary? Forensic operators are sometimes tempted to terminate analysis after successfully completing Steps 1 and 2. That is because they incorrectly believe that with reconciliation of internal and external data, and validation by control data they have tested data both inside and outside of the subject's self-reporting system. If they make such an observation, they have overlooked the very essence of the methodology.

Why? Because control data derives from and consists of data *related to* the subject's self-reporting system. Consequently, all such analysis depends upon the subject's self-reporting system. Therefore, the forensic operator overlooked any activity *unrelated* to the self-reporting system.

In other cases, forensic operators ignore Step 3, SCORE, because of their inability to identify data outside the self-reporting system that can be used to assess the system's veracity, or their lack of understanding of even basic statistical correlation.

Finally, some forensic operators attempt to jump directly to Step 3, SCORE. This is also an error, since SCORE may be so indirectly related to Steps 1 and 2 that one gains no assurance whatsoever regarding internal and external self-reporting system corroboration. Ignoring Step 3 is an unacceptable use of the methodology

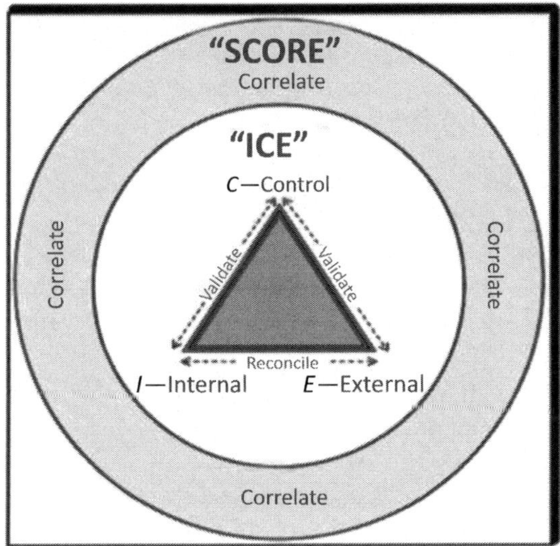

EXHIBIT 3.8 ICE/SCORE Diagram

and exposes the forensic operator to criticism or cross-examination impeachment or both.

A simple example demonstrates why the methodology cannot be used piecemeal. Assume that a divorce action requires the valuation of a business interest—in this case, a family-owned specialty grain commodities broker. Furthermore, assume that the forensic operator dutifully completed ICE (the first half of ICE/SCORE), successfully reconciling internal and external data, and successfully validated control data through the proof-of-cash method. Also, assume that all the data tied out very well.

However, the non-moneyed spouse continued the ubiquitous refrain: "*My husband (wife) is hiding money (assets).*" Flawless execution of the ICE portion of the methodology would have done nothing to resolve that issue. Recall that even though data reliability is potentially assessed as low to medium, the actions have merely *validated what was self-reported* by the subject.

Furthermore, assume the forensic operator sensed that something was . . . *just not quite right*. Therefore, SCORE (the second half of the ICE/SCORE methodology) identified data *outside* the subject's self-reporting system, but could not corroborate the reconciled data with the outside data.

By using SCORE guidelines (described earlier) the forensic operator determined that *S*uppliers (in this case, the rail freight shipping company) would be an excellent source to corroborate the self-reported data. Consequently, the forensic operator compared rail freight shipping manifests to the grain elevator's order entry system. By comparing the actual output reported as shipped by the rail freight shipping company to the representative quantities on the grain elevator's order entry records, it became clear that a discrepancy existed.

That is, the independent control (from SCORE) data demonstrated that actual (shipped) activity exceeded the amount contained in the grain elevator's self-reported data. The forensic operator applied that relationship to the excess to derive underreported income. Furthermore, after adding back the unreported estimate, the overall measures fell more closely within expected forensic and industry parameters.

The preceding example is a clear case—among many—in which failing to apply SCORE would have lead to a failed assignment.

Where Can It Be Used? ICE/SCORE is extremely versatile and can be used in virtually any financial forensics matter, whether or not financial data is involved. Its versatility applies to formal and informal matters, civil and criminal matters, plaintiff and defendant, petitioner and respondent. It can be used independently in very simple matters, independently in very complex matters, as a front-end to FA/IM or throughout FA/IM.

ICE/SCORE applies in virtually all types of assignments, including, but not limited to, the following alphabetized practice areas:

Auditing and Agreed-Upon Procedures: Used to determine risk assessment and virtually any audit testing and agreed-upon procedures tasks.

Damage or Lost Profits: Used to establish and validate (or refute) estimates of damages and lost profit.

Family Law: Used to determine the reliability of income and asset self-reporting by all parties, and valuing business interests.

Fraud: Used to prove or disprove civil or criminal fraud, or both, in personal and business matters.

Government: Used to conduct performance-auditing assignments.

Internal Auditors: Used to conduct operational analysis in support of financial self-reporting.

Investors: Used to assess the veracity of investment self-reporting.

Law Enforcement: Used to train law enforcement officers who lack specific financial training.

Lenders: Used to assess the veracity of credit applications.

Litigation: Used in virtually any matter requiring application of evidence and indicators, for example, alter ego, breach of contract, fraudulent transfer, malpractice, solvency or insolvency, et al.

QDE[14] *and FAB*[15]*:* Used to determine the validity of documents by comparison to evidence and indicators not subject to manipulation by the party(s).

Regulators: Used to validate or refute contents of various documents, for example, SEC filings, PPMs (private placement memorandums), income tax returns, customs filings, and virtually any other regulatory filing.

Valuation: Used to establish and validate rights and restrictions, economic benefit streams, rates of return, and secondary adjustments.

---

[14] Questioned Document Examination.

[15] Fake, Altered, or Borrowed documents.

Proof of Cash The proof of cash technique is a lost art to CPAs. The proof-of-cash technique was a routine audit procedure many years ago, before risk-based auditing became standard practice. Today, few auditors apply the procedure and fewer still are even aware of its existence. Regardless, it is an excellent technique to compare *actual* bank deposits, withdrawals, and transfers to *reported* bank deposits and withdrawals.

The proof-of-cash technique is similar to a bank reconciliation but is more detailed and extensive. It is sometimes labeled "four-way bank reconciliation." The technique validates whether a subject's records reflect its bank deposits, withdrawals, and transfers.

Necessary Information The information required to perform a proof of cash (example on the following page) is straightforward and consists of:

All bank statements (obtain *originals* directly from the bank) for the respective period.

The subject's check register (or equivalent), which captures reported deposits and withdrawals for the same period.

Listings with verified totals for:

Outstanding checks at each period's beginning and end.

Outstanding deposits at each period's beginning and end.

Total receipts and disbursements for the period.

Note: Such totals will enable you to conduct a proof of cash for virtually any period, that is, annual, monthly, multiyear, partial year, etc.

Procedure to Complete the Proof of Cash The following procedures describe how to perform a proof of cash for an annual period from January 1 through December 31, 2012.

1. Starting point *Begin 12/31/11 (December 31, 2011)*—Beginning of the period under analysis. These steps pertain to the "Balance per Bank."

   Line 1: Record the balance per bank as of the last day (that is, December 31, 2011) of the statement (previous year-end), shown as $1,250 in the example.

   Line 2a: Add deposits not yet received or recorded by the bank, shown as $335. These are also referred to as deposits in transit.

   Line 3a: Subtract outstanding checks from the books and the bank at the same date, shown as $25.

   Line 4: Comprises the total of lines 1, 2a and 3a, shown as $1,560.

   These steps pertain to the "Balance per (Subject's) Books."

   Line 5: Record the cash balance per the subject's books as of December 31, 2011, shown as $1,560.

   Lines 6, 7, 8, and *9:* Should not require entries unless any items were not posted to the subject's records *at the end* of the previous fiscal year.

Line 10: Comprises the total of lines 5 through 9 and should be the *same* as line 4.

2. Next Step *Received 2012*—Recording receipts for the year. These steps pertain to the "Balance per Bank."

    Line 1: Enter the total deposits for 2012 *according to the bank statements,* shown as $10,305 in the example.

    Line 2a: Subtract deposits recorded by the bank belonging to 2011 (same as Line 2a, Step 1, shown as ($335)).

    Line 2b: Add deposits in transit not yet received or recorded by the bank as of December 31, 2012, shown as $450 (same as Line 2b, December 31, 2012).

    Line 4: Comprises the totals of Lines 1 through 2b, $10,420 in this example. See the note in Step 2a.

    These steps pertain to the "Balance per (Subject's) Books."

    Line 5: Enter the total receipts for 2012 according to the subject's books, shown as $10,170.

    Line 8: Add (or subtract) all known differences between the subject books and the bank, shown as $200.

    Line 9: Add (or subtract) interest received (or charged) from the bank and not recorded in books, shown as $50.

    Line 10: Comprises the total of Lines 5 through 9, shown as $10,420. This should compare with line 4, column 2, shown as $10,420.

3. Next Step *Disbursed 2012*—Recording disbursements for the year. These steps pertain to the "Balance per Bank."

    Line 1: Enter the total disbursements and charges for 2012 *according to the bank statements,* shown as ($9,830).

    Line 3a: Subtract charges and outstanding checks recorded by the bank in 2012, but actually belonging to 2011, shown as $25, which should be the same amount as column 1.

    Line 3b: Add outstanding checks not yet cleared by the bank at December 31, 2012, shown as ($265).

    Line 4: Comprises the totals of Lines 1 through 3b, shown as ($10,070).

    These steps pertain to the "Balance per (Subject's) Books."

    Line 5: Enter total disbursements for 2012 according to the subject's books, shown as ($10,100).

    Line 6: Add bank service charges unrecorded on the subject's books, shown as ($25).

    Line 7: Add returned NSF checks not recorded on the subject's books, shown as ($70).

    Line 8: Add or subtract other known differences between the subject books and the bank, shown as $125.

    Line 10: Comprises the totals of Lines 5 through 8, etc. This should compare with line 4, column 3.

4. Ending Point *End 12/31/12 (December 31, 2012)*—Ending of the period under analysis. These steps pertain to the "Balance per Bank."

   Line 1: Record the *balance per the bank* as of December 31, 2012 (the last bank statement date), shown as $1,725.

   Line 2b: Add deposits at the current period's end (December 31, 2012, in the example), shown as $450, the same amount on Line 2b, "Received 2012."

   Line 3b: Subtract the total outstanding checks at December 31, 2012, shown as ($265), the same amount on Line 3b, "Disbursed 2012."

   Line 4: Comprises the totals of Lines 1 through 3b, shown as $1,910.

   These steps pertain to the "Balance per Subject's Books."

   Line 5: Record the cash balance per the subject's books at the end of 2012, shown as $1,630.

   Line 6: Subtract the bank service charge, if not posted to subject books, shown as ($25).

   Line 7: Subtract NSF checks returned but not posted, shown as ($70).

   Line 8: Add or subtract other known differences between the subject's books and the bank, shown as $325.

   Line 9: Add interest received from the bank not posted to the subject books, shown as $50.

   Line 10: Comprises the totals of Lines 5 through 9, shown as $1,910. This should compare with Line 4, "End December 31, 2012."

5. To reconcile outstanding differences and thus identify unreported deposits, withdrawals, or income, apply the following procedures.

   Line 10 of "End December 31, 2012," shown as $1,910, should compare with the subject's adjusted cash on hand.

   The following steps, after accounting for any differences should balance:

   Begin with the amount on Line 10 of "Begin December 31, 2011," shown as $1,560.

   Add the amount on Line 10 of "Received 2012," shown as $10,420.

   Subtract the amount on Line 10 of "Disbursed 2012," shown as ($10,070).

   After preparing the proof of cash using the known amounts, any reconciling differences can be isolated and categorized in the schedule. This will identify errors and misreporting. Typical unaccounted-for items include:

   Incorrect totals or subtotals in the subject's books.

   Transfers to or from other accounts were overlooked.

   Voided or canceled checks may have been purposely used.

   NSF checks were not properly reversed from the subject's books.

   Discrepancies between receipt, disbursement, or transfer amounts between the bank and the subject's books.

Inconsistent transaction dates; for example, holding open cutoff dates.
Bank charges not posted to the subject's books.
Bank interest not recorded on the subject's books.

The following visual (Exhibit 3.9) illustrates a versatile proof-of-cash form, both blank and completed. The reader is encouraged to reproduce the form, say, in Excel

Body of Knowledge
Proof of Cash
Exercise

Description	Line	Column 1 Beginning Bank Reconciliation 12/31/2011	Column 2 Receipts	Column 3 Disbursements	Column 4 Ending Bank Reconciliation 12/31/2012
Balance per Bank:	1	1,250			
Deposits in transit:	2				-
December 2011	a				
December 2012	b				
Outstanding Checks:	3				
per list 12-31-2011	a				
per list 12-31-2012	b				
ADJUSTED BALANCE	4				
Balance per Books:	5	1,560	10,170	(10,100)	
December Service charge:	6				
NSF Checks returned:	7				
Bank transfers, errors in recording, other adjustments	8				
Interest posted, by bank:	9				
ADJUSTED BALANCE (same as line 4)	10	1,560			

INSTRUCTIONS—Complete the 4-column proof of cash using the data contained below. All boxes require an entry. Shaded areas do not require entry.
HINT—Remember that all rows total across and columns total down. If done correctly, the ending Adjusted Balance per Bank and per Book for each column will match.

Proof of Cash Data Table	**12/31/11**	**12/31/12**
Outstanding checks at beginning and end of year	25	265
Outstanding deposits at beginning and end of year	335	450
Yearly total receipts per Bank		10,305
Yearly total disbursements per Bank		9,830
NSF customer checks not reversed out of the books		70
Interest recorded by the Bank not posted on the books		50
Service charges per bank statement		25
Cash transfers not recorded on Books		200
Checks you may have canceled or voided		125

EXHIBIT 3.9 Proof of Cash Exercise

and using the preceding information, complete the proof of cash. Then, compare the results to the completed form; they should be identical. Once the proof-of-cash technique is familiar, the forensic operator will routinely deploy it in pertinent forensic assignments.

SURVEILLANCE STAGE

Purpose of Stage

This action establishes the plan to execute through surveillance,[16] techniques to gather evidence. Forensic operators sometimes assume that surveillance can be conducted only by military or law enforcement agencies. In the strictest sense, that is correct. However, any form of *legal* observation (after receiving approval from counsel, the director, and so on) is a type of surveillance. For example, a civilian forensic operator observing third-shift produce deliveries to cash customers is a means of gathering surveilled evidence pertaining to damages. See Exhibit 3.10

The objective of this action is to acquire data, evidence, and other information pertinent to the forensic assignment. Such data is typically obtained by sources other

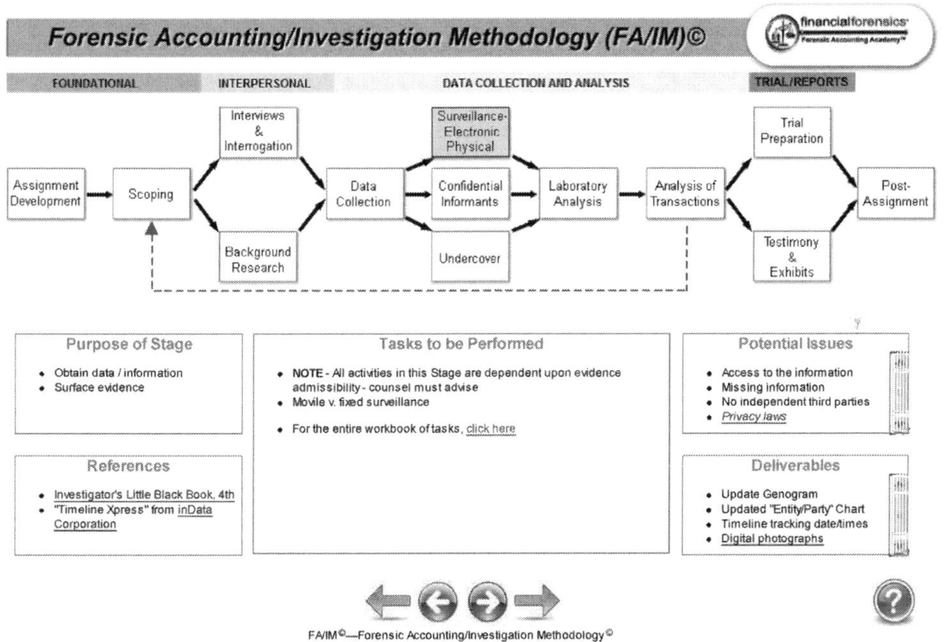

EXHIBIT 3.10 Surveillance—Electronic or Physical

[16] Continual or intermittent covert observation of a party(s) who is a suspect or potential suspect in order to obtain evidence pursuant to an assignment.

than those voluntarily or procedurally (e.g., response to subpoena) submitted by the subject.

Specific actions include:

- Obtain approval to proceed with planned surveillance, whether civilian or otherwise.
- Ensure data, evidence, and other information is legally admissible.
- Collect and document the surveillance including date(s), time(s), parties involved, and ancillary support, for example, photographs, if permissible.

WAR STORY

History's first record of a forensic accountant does not name him (or her), but documents the catastrophic results of the investigation. Under the circumstances, the forensic accountant probably conducted surveillance and reported the transgressors. In the New Testament, Acts 5 (NIV), documents a man and wife who failed to properly report their transaction. Selected portions of the chapter follow: 1 Now a man named Ananias, together with his wife Sapphira, also sold a piece of property. 2 *With his wife's full knowledge he kept back part of the money for himself*, but brought the rest and put it at the apostles' feet. 3 Then Peter said, "Ananias, how is it that Satan has so filled your heart that you have lied to the Holy Spirit and have *kept for yourself some of the money you received for the land*? 4 Didn't it belong to you before it was sold? And after it was sold, wasn't the money at your disposal? What made you think of doing such a thing? You have not lied to men but to God." 5 When Ananias heard this, *he fell down and died.* And great fear seized all who heard what had happened. 6 Then the young men came forward, wrapped up his body, and carried him out and buried him. 7 About three hours later his wife came in, not knowing what had happened. 8 Peter asked her, "*Tell me, is this the price you and Ananias got for the land?*" "*Yes,*" *she said,* "*that is the price.*" 9 Peter said to her, "How could you agree to test the Spirit of the Lord? Look! The feet of the men who buried your husband are at the door, and they will carry you out also." 10 *At that moment she fell down at his feet and died.* Then the young men came in and, finding her dead, carried her out and buried her beside her husband. 11 Great fear seized the whole church and all who heard about these events. (*Emphasis added.*)

References

This action confirms access to pertinent technical references, whether currently available or requiring acquisition. Technical resources referred to include written materials and training, including self-study, webinar, and live classroom training.

The objective of this action is to ensure that necessary technical resources are at hand and are deployed as required.

Specific actions include:

- Search, for example, the Internet for pertinent technical reference sources.
- Develop a list of required sources.
- Compare required sources against currently available sources.
- Acquire sources not otherwise available.

Example of Reference Sources The following reference sources serve to jumpstart the forensic operator. The Key Internet Sites and Key Reference Materials are not all-inclusive, but provide starting points from which to build resources. Also, refer to the bibliography.

Key Internet sites

- All forensic operators
  www.iacsp.org (International Society of Certified Surveillance Professionals)

Key Reference materials

- All forensic operators
- *Financial Forensics Body of Knowledge,* by Darrell D. Dorrell and Gregory A. Gadawski
- *Countering Hostile Surveillance: Detect, Evade, and Neutralize Physical Surveillance Threats*, by ACM IV Security Services
- *Rural Surveillance: A Cop's Guide to Gathering Evidence in Remote Areas*, by Van Ritch
- *Secrets of Surveillance: A Professional's Guide to Tailing Subjects by Vehicle, Foot, Airplane, and Public Transportation*, byACM IV Security Services
- *Surveillance Countermeasures: A Serious Guide to Detecting, Evading, and Eluding Threats to Personal Privacy*, by ACM IV Security Services
- *Understanding Today's Police* 3rd. ed., by M.L. Dantzker

Tasks to Be Performed

This action outlines likely tasks but is not an all-inclusive checklist since each forensic assignment is unique. Use the tasks as a guideline and modify according to the unique facts and circumstances of the assignment.

The objective of this action is to ensure that the forensic operator effectively executes civilian, military, or law enforcement surveillance admissible to the proper venue and without exposing the forensic operator to harm.

Specific actions include:

- *Note:* All activities in this stage depend upon the admissibility of evidence. Counsel must advise on this.
- Consider mobile versus fixed surveillance.

Potential Issues

This action prompts the forensic operator to consider the boundaries of the people, parties, entities, timelines, data, output, cost, technical standards, and related criteria pertinent to the respective assignment. The suggested list is not an all-inclusive checklist since each forensic assignment is unique. Use the tasks as a guideline and modify according to the unique facts and circumstances of the assignment.

The objective of this action is to ensure that the forensic operator contemplates exigencies that may surface during the assignment. It also ensures that the forensic operator obtain admissible evidence.

Specific potential issues include:

- *Privacy laws:* Privacy laws vary considerably, depending upon the venue, jurisdiction, and state and local variations. For example, in certain states, phone conversations can be recorded and used in civil matters, while other states insist that such recording be pre-announced.
- Inadmissible evidence.
- Access to the information.
- Missing information.
- No independent third parties.

Deliverables

The objective of this action is to identify and eventually finalize deliverables pertinent to the assignment. The forensic operator always develops deliverables designed with the end in mind so as to maximize efficiency.

The objective of this action is to confirm authorization to proceed with civilian, military, or law enforcement surveillance.

Specific actions include:

- Update genogram
- Updated entity or party chart
- Update timeline tracking dates and times
- Log digital photographs or videos

CONFIDENTIAL INFORMANTS STAGE

Purpose of Stage

This action establishes the plan to access confidential (or open) informants to gather evidence. Forensic operators sometimes assume that confidential (or open) informants can be conducted only by military or law enforcement agencies. However, any form of legal information gathering (after receiving approval from counsel, the director, and so on) is a type of informant access. For example, a civilian forensic operator casually discussing the CEO's incoming phone call volume with the receptionist is a means of accessing an informant to gather evidence. See Exhibit 3.11.

The objective of this action is to acquire data, evidence, and other information pertinent to the forensic assignment. Such data is typically obtained by sources other than those voluntarily or procedurally (e.g., response to subpoena) submitted by the subject.

Specific actions include:

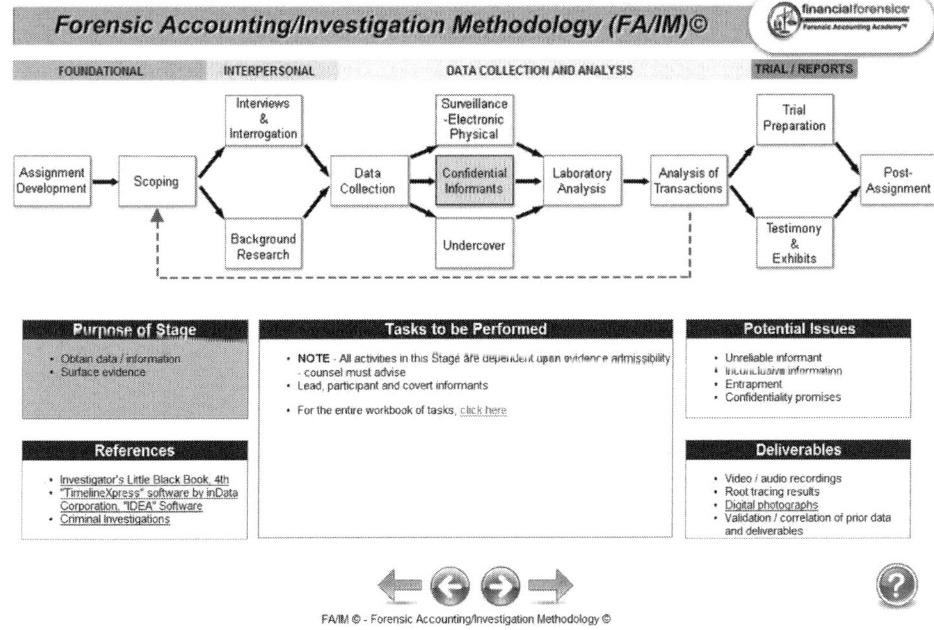

EXHIBIT 3.11 Confidential Informants

- Obtain authorization to proceed.
- Obtain data and other information.
- Document the evidence.

References

This action confirms access to pertinent technical references, whether currently available or requiring acquisition. Technical resources referred to include written materials and training, including self-study, webinar, and live classroom training.

The objective of this action is to ensure that necessary technical resources are at hand and deployed as required.

Example of Reference Sources The following reference sources serve to jumpstart the forensic operator. The Key Internet Sites and Key Reference Materials are not all-inclusive, but provide starting points from which to build resources. Also, refer to the bibliography.

Key Internet sites

- All forensic operators
  www.confidentialinformant.org
  www.crimetime.com/informants.htm

Key Reference materials

- All forensic operators
- *Aguilar–Spinelli Test,* Spinelli v. United States, 393 U.S. 410 (1969)
- *Financial Forensics Body of Knowledge*, by Darrell D. Dorrell and Gregory A. Gadawski
- *Ragnar's Guide to Interviews, Investigations, and Interrogations*, by Ragnar Benson
- *Ragnar's Guide to Interviews, Investigations, and Interrogations: How to Conduct Them, How to Survive Them*, by Ragnar Benson
- *Understanding Today's Police* 3rd ed., by M.L. Dantzker
- See also, references cited in Chapter 2, Interviews and Interrogations Stage
- See also, references cited in this chapter, Surveillance Stage

Tasks to Be Performed

This action outlines likely tasks, but is not an all-inclusive checklist since each forensic assignment is unique. Use the tasks as a guideline and modify according to the unique facts and circumstances of the assignment.

The objective of this action is to ensure that the forensic operator effectively executes communication with confidential (or open) informants that yield evidence admissible to the proper venue and without exposing the forensic operator to harm.

Specific actions include:

- *Note:* All activities in this stage depend upon the admissibility of evidence. Counsel must advise on this.
- Develop the assumed identity to gather data and other information.
- Document all data and other information gathered.
- Investigate observed lifestyle changes.

Potential Issues

This action prompts the forensic operator to consider the boundaries of the laws, ordinances, regulations, policies, and related constraints pertinent to the respective assignment. The suggested list does not provide an all-inclusive checklist, since each forensic assignment is unique. Use the tasks as a guideline and modify according to the unique facts and circumstances of the assignment.

The objective of this action is to ensure that the forensic operator contemplates exigencies that may surface during the assignment. It also ensures that the forensic operator obtains admissible evidence.

Specific potential issues include:

- No guarantee of confidentiality
- Veracity of parties.
- Unrelated actions.
- Predication.
- Entrapment.
- Engagement and personal risks.

Deliverables

This action prompts the forensic operator to identify pertinent deliverables throughout the assignment.

The objective of this action is to confirm authorization to proceed with civilian, military, or law enforcement surveillance.

Specific actions include:

- Video or audio recordings.
- Digital photographs.
- Lifestyle analysis.

UNDERCOVER STAGE

Purpose of Stage

This action establishes the plan to access confidential (or open) informants via undercover to gather evidence. Forensic operators sometimes assume that undercover evidence can be conducted only by military or law enforcement agencies. However, any form of legal information gathering (after receiving approval from counsel, the director, and so on) is a type of undercover access. For example, a civilian forensic operator phoning a company's customer service line to gain information generally available to the public is a means of accessing undercover evidence. See Exhibit 3.12.

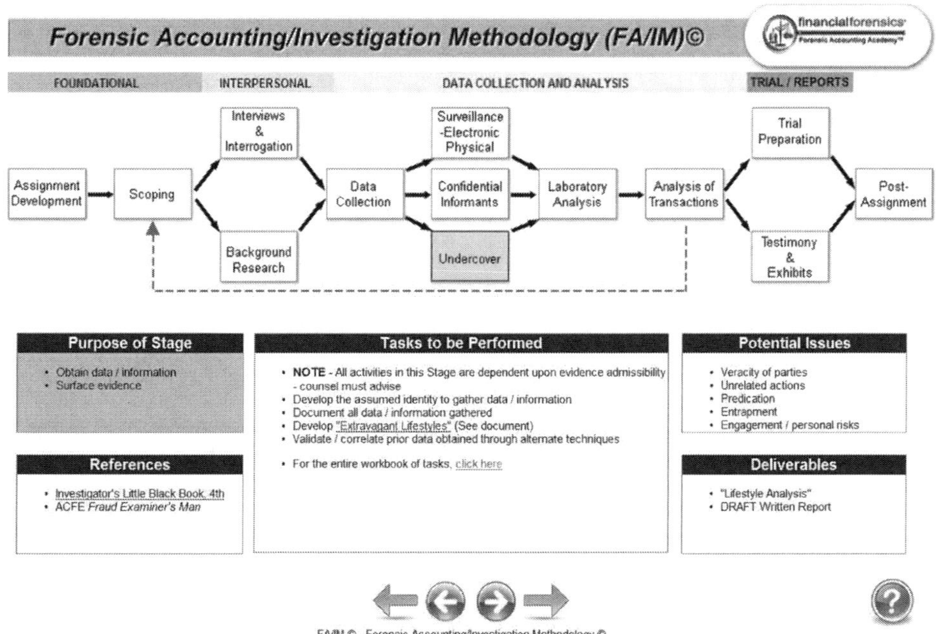

EXHIBIT 3.12 Undercover

The objective of this action is to acquire data, evidence, and other information pertinent to the forensic assignment. Such data is typically obtained by sources other than those voluntarily or procedurally (e.g., response to subpoena) submitted by the subject.

Specific actions include:

- Obtain authorization to proceed.
- Obtain data and other information.
- Document the evidence.

References

This action confirms access to pertinent technical references, whether currently available or requiring acquisition. Technical resources comprise written materials and training, including self-study, webinar, and live classroom training.

The objective of this action is to ensure that appropriate forensic techniques are applied and that the results are correctly interpreted.

Example Reference Sources The following reference sources serve to jumpstart the forensic operator. The Key Internet Sites and Key Reference Materials are not all-inclusive, but provide starting points from which to build resources. Also, refer to the bibliography.

- **Key Internet sites**
  - All forensic operators
    - www.financialforensicsacademy.com
    - www.undercover.org. (International Association of Undercover Officers)
- **Key Reference materials**
  - All forensic operators
    - *Financial Forensics Body of Knowledge*, John Wiley & Sons
    - *Disguise Techniques: Fool All of the People Some of the Time* by Edmond A. MacInaugh
    - *Methods of Disguise: Revised and Expanded*, by John Sample
    - See also, references cited in Chapter 2, Interviews and Interrogations Stage
    - See also, references cited in this chapter, Surveillance Stage

Tasks to Be Performed

This action outlines likely tasks, but does not provide an all-inclusive checklist, since each forensic assignment is unique. Use the tasks as a guideline and modify according to the unique facts and circumstances of the assignment.

The objective of this action is to ensure that the forensic operator effectively executes communication with the undercover informants that yield evidence admissible to the proper venue and without exposing the forensic operator to harm.

Specific actions include:

- Perform any additional indirect or direct analytical forensic techniques as needed, and have output reviewed by a second set of eyes.
- Validate and correlate prior data obtained through alternate techniques.

Potential Issues

This action prompts the forensic operator to objectively assess and evaluate whether results are conclusive or require reconsideration. Also, the results may not support the matter's original objectives, thus compelling the forensic operator to advise decision makers of the status.

The objective of this action is to ensure that the forensic operator conducts objective, independent analysis with respect to the foundational data.

Specific potential issues include:

- No guarantee of confidentiality
- Veracity of parties.
- Unrelated actions.
- Predication.
- Entrapment.
- Engagement and personal risks.

Deliverables

This action prompts the forensic operator to assemble pertinent deliverables throughout the various completed tasks. Naturally, the deliverables are a function of the various tools, techniques, methods, and methodologies deployed.

Example Deliverables The potential deliverables resulting from this stage are frameworks for the forensic operator who will modify them to comply with their respective internal and other requirements. Specific examples are found in the following sections.

- Genogram or entity or party chart
- Deposition matrix or interview matrix
- Search log or background investigation
- Event analysis or timeline tracking
- Lifestyles analysis

LABORATORY ANALYSIS STAGE

Purpose of Stage

This action launches detailed analysis comprising virtually any type of data, including analysis of words. The sections that follow comprise confirmation

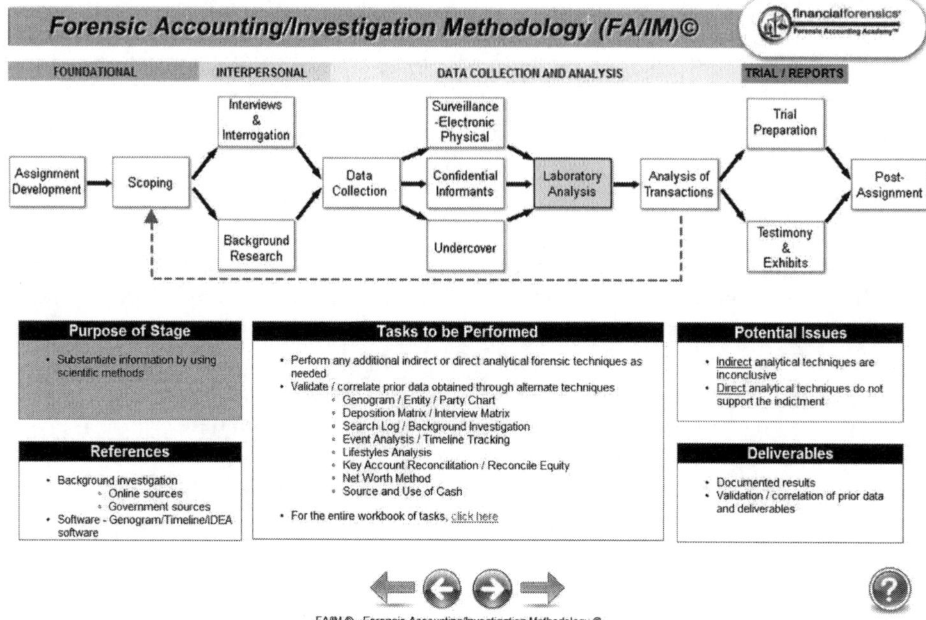

EXHIBIT 3.13 Laboratory Analysis

bias, aberrant pattern detection and forensic lexicology. Significantly, discussion regarding recognition and avoidance of confirmation bias advises forensic operators to the insidious impact of bias—conscious and unconscious. Forensic operators are expected to provide objective and independent conclusions based upon unbiased analysis since incorrect opinions result from bias distortions. See Exhibit 3.13.

The objective of this action is to analyze data and information pertinent to the forensic assignment. Likewise, analysis may identify subsequent or additional data that compels collection.

Specific actions include:

- Insure sufficient, relevant data is at hand.
- Conduct objective and independent analysis using empirical techniques.
- Document the findings.

References

This action confirms access to pertinent technical references, whether currently available or requiring acquisition. Technical resources comprise written materials and training, including self-study, webinar, and live classroom training.

The objective of this action is to ensure that appropriate forensic techniques are applied and that the results are correctly interpreted.

Example Reference Sources The following reference sources serve to jumpstart the forensic operator. The Key Internet Sites and Key Reference Materials are not all-inclusive, but provide starting points from which to build resources. Also, refer to the bibliography.

- **Key Internet sites**
  - All forensic operators
  - www.financialforensicsacademy.com
  - www.khanacademy.com
  - www.statsoft.com
  - Key reference materials
  - All forensic operators
  - *Financial Forensics Body of Knowledge,* by Darrell D. Dorrell and Gregory A. Gadawski
  - *Statistics Hacks.* Sebastopol, by Bruce Frey.
  - *How to Lie with Statistics*, by Darrell Huff.
  - *Statistical Techniques in Business and Economics* 4th ed., by Robert D. Mason.
  - *The Drunkard's Walk: How Randomness Rules Our Lives*, by Leonard Mlodinow.
  - *Questioned Documents,* 2nd ed., by Albert S. Osborn.
  - *Envisioning Information*, by Edward R. Tufte.
  - *The Visual Display of Quantitative Information*, by Edward R. Tufte.

Tasks to Be Performed

This action outlines likely tasks, but does not provide an all-inclusive checklist, since each forensic assignment is unique. Use the tasks as a guideline and modify according to the unique facts and circumstances of the assignment.

The objective of this action is to ensure that the forensic operator effectively executes empirically sound analysis not otherwise evident to those lacking commensurate skills. Specific actions include:

- Confirm results of analysis and findings.
- Request additional data as required.

Potential Issues

This action prompts the forensic operator to objectively assess and evaluate whether results are conclusive or require reconsideration. Also, the results may not support the matter's original objectives, thus compelling the forensic operator to advise decision makers of the status.

The objective of this action is to ensure that the forensic operator conducts objective, independent analysis with respect to the foundational data.

Specific potential issues include:

- Findings do not support original premise
- Findings lack persuasiveness due to inconclusive results
- Findings are insufficient to refute opposition.

Deliverables

This action prompts the forensic operator to assemble pertinent deliverables throughout the various completed tasks. Naturally, the deliverables are a function of the various tools, techniques, methods, and methodologies deployed.

Example Deliverables The potential deliverables resulting from this stage are frameworks for the forensic operator who will modify them to comply with their respective internal and other requirements. Specific examples are found in the following chapters.

- Aberrant pattern detection output
- Forensic lexicology output.

CONFIRMATION BIAS: CLINICAL THINKING

Confirmation bias is insidious and requires continual practice to avoid it since it is inherent in human nature. The preceding contents permit forensic operators to deliver more effective and more efficient services while simultaneously defending against opposition attack.

Note: This topic begins a Companion Section to the other five sections listed in Exhibit 3.14. Each section stands on its own. However, it is recommended that they be used together to gain a complete picture of their application to a forensic assignment. When read collectively, read them in ascending order, starting with confirmation bias, then, progressing to pattern detection, and so on.

The forensic operator faces the greatest danger[17] at the beginning of an assignment. That is because it is the most likely time for confirmation bias[18] to take root and yield disappointing or even disastrous results. The following definition of confirmation bias applies in this book.

> *The human tendency that, after forming a viewpoint, one seeks and assimilates reinforcing data, and rejects rebutting data.*[19]

---

[17] Notwithstanding violence encountered in hostile, law enforcement, and military assignments.

[18] Confirmation bias has been traced at least as far back as Thucydides (circa 460 BC to circa 395 BC) a Greek historian. Since then, numerous writers, academics, psychologists, and psychiatrists have extensively studied the phenomenon.

[19] Sometimes known as *confirmatory* or *myside* bias.

EXHIBIT 3.14 Companion Sections: Valuation and Litigation

Companion Sections	Contents	How to Use
Confirmation Bias (page 122)	This section describes the intellectual and professional perspective necessary to avoid bias when analyzing data.	Use as a training or reminder reference, or both, before beginning assignments. It can also be required reading when training staff.
Aberrant Pattern Detection (page 131)	This section describes how to identify whether data and any resultant pattern(s) are aberrant. It applies empirical approaches to determine whether a pattern is aberrant.	Use whenever analyzing the data and patterns supporting evidentiary observations and conclusions foundational to opinions.
Forensic Indices (page 204)	This section describes various methods for analyzing the quality of reported earnings and the resultant impact on the income statement, balance sheet and statement of cash flow.	Use whenever analyzing audited, reviewed, compiled, or other types of financial statements. Also, use whenever developing forward-looking financial statements, including valuation, damages, and (page 301) similar forensic assignments.
Forensic Financial Analysis (page 212)	This section provides a model for analyzing data—financial or otherwise. It contains several descriptive statistics within a progressively sophisticated schema to evaluate and score a data set.	Use whenever empirical analysis of one or more data sets is necessary. Also, use when comparing data sets against one another.
Valuation & Forensics—Why & How: (page 287)	This section describes why valuation and litigation assignments must include forensic tools, techniques, methods, and methodologies.	Use whenever executing valuation and litigation assignments requiring opinions regarding value and/or forward-looking economic benefit streams.
Valuation's Orphan (page 294)	This section describes how to analyze and derive economic benefit streams.	Use whenever developing forward-looking financial statements, including valuation, damages, and similar forensic assignments.

Two extreme examples illustrate the point. The objective in bowling is to knock down all 10 pins with the first of two balls released down the alley. Right-handed bowlers aim for the number 1 and number 3 pins pocket, to the right of the number 1 (head) pin. After release, the ball usually heads in a direction away from the pocket. Despite the inevitable absence of a strike, the bowler invariably moves his body so that it appears (to the bowler) as if the ball will strike the pocket. This is a classic case of confirmation bias: the bowler started with a viewpoint of where the ball should strike, created (the appearance of) data by altering the line of site and rejected the inevitable failure.

The "Great War"[20] was a classic example of confirmation bias. Gunpowder originated in China about the ninth century.[21] Weapons rapidly exploited gunpowder's capabilities and spread throughout the world. Military and gunpowder technology kept pace with weaponry until World War I. Military doctrine still called for massed troops charging open-field across a broad front. However, the industrialization (machine guns, high explosives, mechanization, and chemical warfare) of World War I resulted in unprecedented carnage. Nonetheless, both sides generally continued using outmoded military tactics until near the end of the war. Military tacticians' confirmation bias carried a viewpoint that massed troop charges would overcome the enemy. The tacticians assimilated irregular nominal tactical gains (for both sides) as reinforcement of their outmoded doctrine, and generally rejected the ghastly daily death tolls.

The preceding example does not criticize the military. Military tactics kept pace with technology for centuries preceding World War I; indeed, the U.S. military is among the most innovative, agile, and successful of all large-scale organizations. However, both examples illustrate the consequences of confirmation bias.

The consequences of forensic assignment confirmation bias ordinarily fall on a scale of magnitude between the two examples. Nonetheless, the outcome can be disastrous for the forensic operator's agency, practice, department, or career.

Why Do Forensic Operators Care about Confirmation Bias?

Forensic operators throughout the globe serve three different types of roles as they carry out various forensic assignments. The three roles include independent, enforcement, and consultative roles. Furthermore, they conduct the assignments with respect to the three major classes of financial information, comprising originators, users, and regulators. Forensic operators can be found serving in any role (*assuming* appropriate training and knowledge) depending upon the client or employer, and some cases, serving in combined roles. Exhibit 3.15 summarizes the classes and typical financial information encountered during assignments.

Descriptions of the three primary roles served by forensic operators follow.

Independent The independent forensic operator ordinarily practices within a professional services firm. The independent assignment typically requires expert witness services whereby the forensic operator assists a trier of fact (in legal matters) or a decision maker(s) (in nonlegal matters) in understanding the evidence extant. The

[20] World War I.

[21] Jack Kelly, *Gunpowder: Alchemy, Bombards, and Pyrotechnics: The History of the Explosive that Changed the World* (New York: Perseus Books, 2005), 2–5.

EXHIBIT 3.15 Three Classes of People Reliant Upon Financial Information

Explanation	Originators	Users	Regulators
Description	This category includes those who *originate* (directly or indirectly) financial information for any purpose. It comprises individuals, households, publicly held entities, privately held entities, government organizations, NPOs, and others.	This category includes those who *use* (that is, rely upon) the financial information produced by originators for any purpose.	This category includes those who *regulate* the financial information submitted by originators or users or both. It includes civil regulators, criminal regulators, military, and others.
Types	Typical examples of *originators* include CEOs, CFOs, controllers, accounting clerks, application specialists, expense report filers, income tax return filers, and others.	Typical examples of *users* include auditors, CPAs, CAs,[22] boards of directors, investors, lenders, professors, insurers, brokers, executives, consumers (e.g., personal financial planning, 401(k) management), valuators, attorneys, insurance providers, and others.	Typical examples of regulators include civil regulators (SEC, IRS, FTC, and others), criminal regulators (FBI, DEA, IRS, state police, international, federal, state, local law enforcement), military (counterterrorism), and others.

forensic operator receives such an assignment from a party seeking to prove or rebut a particular viewpoint, that is, plaintiff, defendant, petitioner, respondent, claimant, etc.

Independence is critical in this role and the forensic operator can only advocate for her opinion, not the opinion of the party.[23] Fortunately, many (if not most) assignments convey a certain degree of self-validation that benefits the forensic operator. For example, a plaintiff who brings a civil suit has sufficiently identified facts and circumstances that convince an attorney (and the court) of the need for adjudication. Therefore, the discovery, analysis, and investigation executed by the forensic operator may indeed support the plaintiff's position.

[22] Chartered Accountants.

[23] Notwithstanding a coincidental one-to-one match between a plaintiff's position and an expert's opinion.

WAR STORY

A forensic operator diligently determined a plaintiff's damage claim approximating $10 million. Both the plaintiff and his counsel concurred with the damages claim until a pretrial work session. The plaintiff unexpectedly demanded $30 million testimony from the forensic operator under threat of lawsuit and nonpayment of fees. The forensic operator refused and testified to $10 million, with which the jury agreed. Despite the $10 million judgment, the plaintiff wanted $30 million and refused to pay the remainder of the forensic operator's fees. The forensic operator lost several thousand dollars in fees but avoided a lawsuit. Unfortunately, the plaintiff sued his attorney, who spent a considerable sum successfully defending himself and his firm during the next three years.

The defendant rebuts the accusations and thus seeks an expert to assist in rebutting the plaintiff's position. The same self-validation that benefited the plaintiff's expert likewise benefits the defendant's expert. Therefore, the discovery, analysis, and investigation executed by the forensic operator may indeed support the defendant's position.

The independent role sometimes places forensic operators in untenable positions. For example, if the findings are contrary to the party's position, the forensic operator must apprise his client of the matter's weaknesses. Such findings sometimes surface only after the assignment is well under way and significant time and money have already been expended. Nonetheless, the independent assignment responsibilities compel full disclosure regardless of whether the news is good or bad.

Confirmation bias can have disastrous consequences on the independent forensic operator. Therefore, the forensic operator cannot permit confirmation bias to affect the investigation regardless of the apparent strengths and weaknesses of an assignment. There are two primary reasons that confirmation bias can be disastrous to a forensic operator serving an independent role. First, the failure to consider and apply contrary data places the expert in a biased position. He loses his independence in the eyes of the parties, and becomes an advocate. More importantly, the failure to consider and apply contrary data could cause the expert to be wrong in his position, thus embarrassing him, contributing to the matter's defeat, and jeopardizing his career.

Enforcement The enforcement role comprises forensic operators in civil (SEC, IRS, FTC, etc.), law enforcement (FBI, DEA, state, and local), and military (e.g., counterterrorism) assignments. The enforcement role significantly differs from the preceding independent role, but is still vulnerable to confirmation bias. The forensic operator receives enforcement assignments from regulators seeking to enforce the violation of laws, ordinances, or regulations, etc.

The enforcement forensic operator typically may serve an advocacy role in contrast to the independent role discussed earlier. Independence, per se, is not required in the strict sense. Nonetheless, enforcement authorities expect an unbiased assessment of the evidence, both pro and con to the matter. Similar to the independent matters mentioned before, many (if not most) enforcement assignments convey a certain degree of self-validation that benefits the forensic operator. For example, the enforcement or regulating agency that brings an action has sufficiently identified facts and circumstances to convince internal decision makers and the court of adjudication. Therefore, the discovery, analysis, and investigation executed by the forensic operator may indeed support the enforcement position.

The enforcement role sometimes places forensic operators in untenable positions. For example, if the findings are contrary to the regulator's position, the forensic operator must apprise leading parties of the matter's weaknesses. Such findings sometimes surface only after the assignment is well under way and significant time and money have already been expended. Nonetheless, the enforcement assignment responsibilities compel full disclosure regardless of whether the news is good or bad.

Confirmation bias can have disastrous consequences on the enforcement forensic operator. Therefore, the forensic operator cannot permit confirmation bias to affect the investigation regardless of the apparent strengths and weaknesses of an assignment. There are two primary reasons that confirmation bias can be disastrous to a forensic operator serving an enforcement role. The reasons relate to, but differ from those summarized earlier in the independent role. First, the failure to consider and apply contrary data could result in opposition challenges to the regulator for which they are unprepared to respond.

Second, the failure to consider and apply contrary data could cause the forensic operator to be wrong in his position, thus embarrassing him and jeopardizing his career and the regulator's reputation.

Most importantly, though, failure to consider contrary data could jeopardize the operation, its assets, and even the lives of the participants. Furthermore, the people and money cost of a failed operation could extend beyond the involved parties, and include innocent victims. For example, a failed SEC action could permit a swindler to continue his exploitation of other investors. Law enforcement and military matters can have even greater consequences, such as resulting in the loss of life.

Consultative The consultative role could apply in either or both independent actions and enforcement actions. In effect, the consultative forensic operator provides advice and counsel to those prosecuting the respective matter. A forensic operator could serve in a capacity, say, assisting the CIA or the NSA in investigating financial evidence leading to a terrorist. Naturally, it is in everyone's best interest (except for the terrorist) to identify, locate, and destroy the target. Therefore, the forensic operator's analysis and investigation tends to emphasize those factors contributing to destroying the target. Alternatively, expert witnesses sometimes serve in a consultative capacity pursuant to litigation matters.

The consultative forensic operator typically serves an advocacy role; independence, per se, is not required in the strict sense. Naturally, such assistance must comply with ethical, professional, and legal requirements pertinent to the matter. Nonetheless, parties relying upon his guidance expect him to provide an unbiased assessment of the evidence, both pro and con to the matter. Similar to the matters discussed earlier, many (if not most) consultative assignments convey a certain degree of self-validation that benefits the forensic operator.

The consultative role sometimes places forensic operators in untenable positions. For example, if the findings are contrary to the leading party's position, the forensic operator must apprise pertinent decision makers of the matter's weaknesses. Such findings sometimes surface only after the assignment is well under way and significant time and money have already been expended. Nonetheless, the consultative assignment responsibilities compel full disclosure regardless of whether the news is good or bad.

Inexperienced forensic operators view the consultative role as less restrictive than both the independent and the enforcement roles. Nonetheless, the risk of confirmation bias is still very high. Confirmation bias can have disastrous consequences on the consultative forensic operator. The degree of consequences is directly proportional to the parties at risk. Thus, the forensic operator cannot permit confirmation bias to affect the investigation regardless of the apparent strengths and weaknesses of an assignment.

There are three primary reasons that confirmation bias can be disastrous to a forensic operator serving a consultative role. The reasons relate to, but differ from those summarized earlier in the independent and enforcement roles. First, the failure to consider and apply contrary data could result in opposition challenges to the consultative party for which they are unprepared to respond.

Second, the failure to consider and apply contrary data could cause the forensic operator to be wrong in his position, thus embarrassing him and jeopardizing his career and the consultative party's reputation.

Most importantly, though failure to consider contrary data could jeopardize the operation, its assets, and even the lives of the participants. Furthermore, the people and money cost of a failed consultative operation could extend beyond the involved parties, and include innocent victims. For example, a failed operation could permit terrorists to continue killing innocent victims and disrupting peaceful society.

Combination Roles The roles summarized here typically function discretely from one another, but can on occasion, overlap in forensic assignments. For example, a forensic operator serving in a consultative role could transition to an independent (e.g., expert witness) role if warranted by circumstances.

How to Defeat Confirmation Bias: Two Methods

There is good news and bad news about defeating confirmation bias. The bad news is that the forensic operator must constantly manage personal confirmation bias, since it is an inherent human trait. The good news is that there are two primary methods to counter confirmation bias, the self-actualization[24] method and the aberrant pattern detection method. The aberrant pattern detection method is a separate section. Both methods yield two simultaneous benefits. First, the forensic operator begins to rely more on the science of investigation and less on the art of investigation. That permits him to minimize the use of the "professional judgment" phrase when testifying and writing reports. Parties to a matter intuitively (and correctly) conclude that the more

[24] Abraham Maslow, *Motivation and Personality,* 150: "The full use and exploitation of talents, capacities, potentialities, etc."

times a forensic operator uses the professional judgment phrase during testimony, the less science there is in the opinion.

Second, increased reliance on the science in a forensic assignment communicates more effectively to the parties in a matter, thus countering *their* confirmation bias. That benefit moves the parties closer to the forensic operator's own data-driven conclusions.

The Self-Actualization Method The self-actualization method permits the forensic operator to practice countering confirmation bias, at no cost and on a daily basis. There is only one condition to using the self-actualization method: that the forensic operator holds at least one deeply held belief (religion, politics, et al) regarding an emotionally charged topic. The authors have never encountered a forensic operator who failed to meet that criterion.

The self-actualization method does not attempt to change the forensic operator's viewpoint regarding any deeply held belief. Rather, it compels the forensic operator to *deliberately* seek out and *consider* data contrary to his deeply held emotionally charged matters. This exercise conditions the forensic operator to conduct similar practices in forensic assignments. For example, a plaintiff defines his viewpoint during an initial work session. That session permits the forensic operator to gain an understanding of the theory of the case with respect to the plaintiff. That initial work session plants the seeds of confirmation bias unless the forensic operator takes the steps outlined next.

The forensic operator must consider the opposing parties' (defendant's) viewpoint based upon the facts and the circumstances presented to him from the plaintiff's viewpoint. That does not suggest that the forensic operator should become sympathetic to the defendant's position. It does suggest, however, that the more that is known about both viewpoints, the more likely the success of the investigation. Knowing more about both viewpoints permits preparation of both supporting and rebutting potentialities.

Practicing the self-actualization method begins to refine the way a forensic operator thinks about and reasons with data and evidence. The refined thinking process transitions into the writing process, which transitions into the testimony process, ad infinitum. The transition benefits all parties to a matter since the forensic objective thought process flows throughout the assignment actions. Furthermore, the emotional aspects of an assignment decline.

Put Another Way . . . If the forensic operator has learned to rationally address personal emotionally charged subjects, how much more effective will he be in technical matters, such as financial analysis?

The self-actualization method is easy to practice. The following steps permit its use on a daily basis.

Mentally identify a personal list of deeply held beliefs. There is no end to the potential list of beliefs, but they must be personally important and significant to the forensic operator. The beliefs could include (alphabetically), abortion, balancing the federal budget, capital punishment, fluoridation of water supplies, government control, gun control, income taxes, motorcycle helmet laws, no-fault divorce, no-fault insurance, offshore drilling, privacy laws, separation of church and state, speed limits, etc.

The authors use simple examples to illustrate the concept while instructing the two-day and five-day Financial Forensics Academy. Specifically, the participants are asked to complete the following phrase: "*Separation of church and* _____ (fill in the blank)." Typically, participants quickly indicate that the word *state* completes the phrase. Then, the authors query the participants regarding the source of the phrase. Invariably, suggestions of "Constitution" and Bill of Rights/First Amendment" tend to be the most common replies. Since varying answers have been suggested, the authors ask for a vote that results in a consensus answer. The alternatives for voting are given by listing the documents foundational to the United States's formation. The dates and documents follow.

1620—Mayflower Compact

1776—Declaration of Independence (July 4th)

1781—Articles of Confederation declared "in force"

1787—Constitution is initially ratified

1791—Bill of Rights adopted

Typically, the majority of the participants vote on the Constitution or First Amendment as the source of the phrase. After voting on the preceding list, the authors point out that the phrase "separation of church and state" is in none of the previous documents. Its sourcing is a *1947* Supreme Court ruling in Everson versus Board of Education. Furthermore, Associate Justice Hugo Black adopted the phrase from an *amicus curiae* (friend of the court) brief prepared by the ACLU.

Occasionally, a participant will become animated with a deeply held belief contrary to the facts of the phrase. But that is the point—to practice comparing *facts* to one's belief. The facts will either confirm or deny the belief. Most importantly, it illustrates the challenge that forensic operators face when delivering opinions in trial, which is basically an argument regarding two dichotomous positions.

Mentally prioritize the beliefs into A, B, and C strata. The A items comprise the matters most personally sensitive, while the C items comprise the least personally sensitive matters.

Select a C item as the initial subject. A C item permits the forensic operator to transition into the process. A items may potentially be so emotionally charged that the forensic operator inherently avoids the personal conflict or cannot objectively consider contrary data.

It does not matter what position the forensic operator may hold for the C item. For the purpose of this practice, it is only important to identify a deeply held belief.

Topic X is the example selected for this section. There are only two possible viewpoints regarding Topic X, Red or Blue. Red is the viewpoint selected for this section.

This section is passionately committed to Topic X-Red. Therefore, the following suggestions identify sources of data upon which to launch the self-actualization process.

Written Material Deliberately seek out, read, and consider articles covering Topic X-Blue, the position contrary to the section's Topic X-Red. Start with smaller articles that will deliver less shock to emotionally charged topics. Gradually, increase the size of the articles reviewed and considered. Note each contrary data point and consider its respective strengths and weaknesses. Compare and contrast the data points against deeply held beliefs. The logical progression of written material may even progressively lead to white papers, treatises, or books arguing opposing points of view. There is a direct correlation between complexity and argument composition of contrary data, to the benefit received in countering confirmation bias.

Television and Radio News Programs Deliberately seek out, read (or listen to), and consider new programs covering Topic X-Blue, the position contrary to the section's Topic X-Red. Start with less polarizing program hosts that will deliver less shock to emotionally charged topics. Gradually, increase the length of time devoted to the programs. There is a direct correlation between complexity and argument composition of contrary data, to the benefit received in countering confirmation bias.

Personal Conversation Deliberately seek out and converse with parties you know to be in favor of Topic X-Blue, the position contrary to the section's Topic X-Red. The conversation is educational and not exploitive. In some cases, it is advisable to inform the party regarding the nature of the conversation; that party might even reconsider their confirmation bias, and thus benefit from the conversation as well.

The preceding discussion enables the forensic operator to refine analytical expertise deployed in forensic assignments. There is a direct correlation between complexity and argument composition of contrary data, to the benefit received in countering confirmation bias.

The preceding examples are not limiting, but rather suggestive to illustrate how easily forensic operators can practice countering confirmation bias.

ABERRANT PATTERN DETECTION: WHAT'S THE DIFFERENCE?

Patterns inherently exist within data and are essential to support forensic observations and opinions. Patterns are ubiquitous within forensic assignments and transcend financial data into operating, marketing, and virtually any kind of data.

Patterns can be discerned, measured, and interpreted using one or a combination of visual, time, and variation techniques. Significantly, such analysis preempts the mere professional judgment preface to opinions. Aberrant pattern detection is far more rigorous and empirical to the trier(s) of fact than merely stating "It looks to me like it significantly deviates."

Experienced forensic operators understand that "data[25] derives patterns[26] and patterns derive evidence."[27] Data can measure *anything* tangible or intangible, real or imagined, factual or hypothetical, qualitative or quantitative. Data's most attractive attribute, though, is patterns. Data contains an inherent display of patterns, the absence of patterns, or unexpected occurrences within patterns. The forensic operator's challenge is to *measure* pattern aberration (or stability) rather than merely state that a pattern aberration exists. This technique is aberrant pattern detection. Its functionality transcends all aspects of financial forensics. In addition, it applies to literally all types of data analysis.

A simple illustration demonstrates how even qualitative indicators can be measured and tested for patterns. For example, many physicians' offices display a pain scale in their examining rooms. The most familiar scale may be the Wong-Baker FACES Pain Rating Scale.[28] It comprises a pain scale from 0 to 10, with a cartoon drawing of a happy face progressing along the scale to a decidedly unhappy face.

Forensic operators can apply similar techniques when using data to make observations and form opinions. A simple illustration demonstrates how even qualitative indicators can be measured and tested for patterns. Suppose, for example, that an assignment involved quantifying the cloudiness of today's weather. Such a measurement is decidedly qualitative, assuming that NOAA's National Weather Service data is unavailable.

The first step requires establishing a standard of measurement. One approach consists of establishing a personal scaling range from the least cloudy day to the cloudiest day in one's personal experience. The personal scaling could range from 1 to 10, with 1 representing a cloudless day, and 10 representing the cloudiest day. Then, today's cloudiness measure calibrates against the newly derived personal scaling range, thus establishing a cloudiness score.

The objectivity and precision of today's cloudiness scale improve when including scores (and possibly scaling) from other observers. Finally, the cloudiness measurement could be a single point, say, 7 out of the scale of 1 to 10, or a range such as 6 to 7 out of a scale of 1 to 10. A cloudiness range, such as the 6 to 7 example reflects variation in the score, and gives representation to the variance likely from others' scores.

---

[25] Data—Facts or representations such as occurrences, measurements, times, colors, and so on.

[26] Pattern—A natural or chance configuration (frost *patterns*) (the *pattern* of events); a reliable sample of traits, acts, tendencies, or other observable characteristics of a person, group, or institution (a behavior *pattern*) (spending *patterns*). www.merriam-webster.com/dictionary/pattern.

[27] Evidence—Any species of proof, or probative matter, legally presented at the trial of an issue, by the parties and through the medium of witnesses, records, documents, exhibits, concrete objects, and so on, for the purpose of inducing belief in the minds of the court or jury as to their contention. *Black's Law Dictionary* 6th ed. (St. Paul, MN: West Publishing, 1990) 555.

[28] From Marilyn J. Hockenberry and David Wilson, *Wong's Essentials of Pediatric Nursing* 8th ed. (St. Louis: Mosby, 2009).

Today's cloudiness score is a moderately interesting measurement. However, the *patterns* of cloudiness yield more informative (and meaningful) data. In other words, did cloudiness increase or decrease over time, say, in the last 30, 60, or 90 days. Cloudiness patterns (among numerous other topics) are important because they can identify trends and unusual or unexpected occurrences within a trend.

Forensic operators routinely study patterns to identify key pattern behaviors (known as trends) and unexpected occurrences within patterns. They can sometimes make such observations and support conclusions by mere observation of the patterns; patterns can exhibit clearly increasing or decreasing trends. More often, though, patterns require empirical analysis to accurately describe their behaviors. The section titled Forensic Financial Analysis explains many of the techniques. The remainder of this section, though, displays actual examples of aberrant pattern detection used in civil and criminal matters.

How to Deploy Aberrant Pattern Detection

Chapter 2 explained the people & money© principle. *Patterns* form the linkage between people & money. That is, where money is concerned, peoples' actions emit numerous trails evidenced by patterns. Consequently, forensic operators innately seek patterns by observing raw data.

Data and Patterns Human beings depend upon information from data and patterns every hour of every day. For example, note the following list of example data encountered in everyday life.

- Emails
- Miles per gallon
- Blood pressure
- Checkbook balance
- Golf scores
- Credit card balance
- Billable hours
- Weather patterns
- Traffic delays
- Sports team records
- Calorie count
- Opinion polls

The preceding data's value increases when the inherent data-related patterns surface because the patterns significantly aid in decision making. Compare the preceding list of data to the corollary patterns that follow and note the increase in value.

Data	Pattern
Emails	How many "flagged for follow-up"?
Miles per gallon	Is a tune-up necessary?
Blood pressure	Increasing or decreasing?
Checkbook balance	Enough until end of month?
Golf scores	Staying ahead of my brother?
Credit card balance	Regular payments for credit score?
Billable hours	Did I meet my monthly target?
Weather patterns	Is a storm coming?
Traffic delays	Will I be late for my meeting?
Sports team records	Will they make the playoffs?
Calorie count	Below my target?
Opinion polls	Will my candidate win?

Data is important in forensic assignments, and patterns are arguably more important in many circumstances. Therefore, forensic operators must be skilled in identifying, displaying, and interpreting patterns. Pattern discernment is the forensic operator's primary goal, but empirical measurement of pattern aberration (or stability) is the secret to the goal. Aberrant pattern detection is an indispensable tool in forensic assignments, and essential to forensic operators.

Fortunately, virtually every forensic assignment is a target-rich environment comprising a wide variety of data. Virtually all of it lends itself to aberrant pattern detection.

Categories of Data and Patterns The aberrant pattern detection process requires the forensic operator to find, capture, and measure data and patterns to determine whether they yield evidence. Also, patterns invariably require display, such as those contained in a trial exhibit. Patterns generally fall into one (or a combination of) three categories as follows.

- *Visual*—Self-evident patterns typically require little or no formal measurement. For example, the life expectancy of U.S. residents has increased since 1900. Although this pattern may be understood by most adults, an exhibit validates the increasing trend.
- *Time*—Self-evident event patterns occur throughout the duration of the assignment. They ordinarily require little or no formal measurement. For example, there is a direct cause-and-effect correlation between reduced income taxes and increased U.S. economic output. A timeline demonstrating the tax reductions followed by economic increases falls within this category.
- *Variation*—Variations in patterns support a conclusion by using measurement. Measurement can establish whether a pattern falls into one or more of the following categories: increasing, decreasing, stable, no pattern, and variation within a pattern.

The following visuals that served in actual assignments supply guidelines to jumpstart the forensic operator. The actual assignment scenarios contain a summary of the scenario, the source of data, the method of pattern detection, the pattern observed, and a summary of the assignment results.

Aberrant Pattern Detection—Visual

Visual aberrant pattern detection is intuitively appealing. However, forensic operators need skill to identify, capture, display, and report the patterns so they are similarly appealing to the pertinent audience. Some patterns are so visually compelling that their display begs the question of measurement.

Did Revenue Increase? *Actual Scenario:* This assignment involved a compensation dispute between the company owner and the CEO. One part of the CEO's compensation package depended upon a revenue increase over the duration of his leadership. Therefore, one part of the forensic assignment required measurement to determine whether revenue increased or decreased over the CEO's tenure.

Source of Data: Audited financial statements.

Pattern Detection Method: Visual.

Pattern Observed: Increasing.

Outcome: Exhibit 3.16 clearly indicates revenue increased over time. Consequently, a credible challenge of that observation would be difficult.[29]

Forensic assignments seldom consist of the simple observation discernible here. Nonetheless, simpler is often better.

Did the Executives Act Properly in a Fiduciary Capacity? *Actual Scenario:* The assignment involved convincing the court that corporate officers effectively looted and squandered investor funds. More than 5,000 investors responded to a glossy

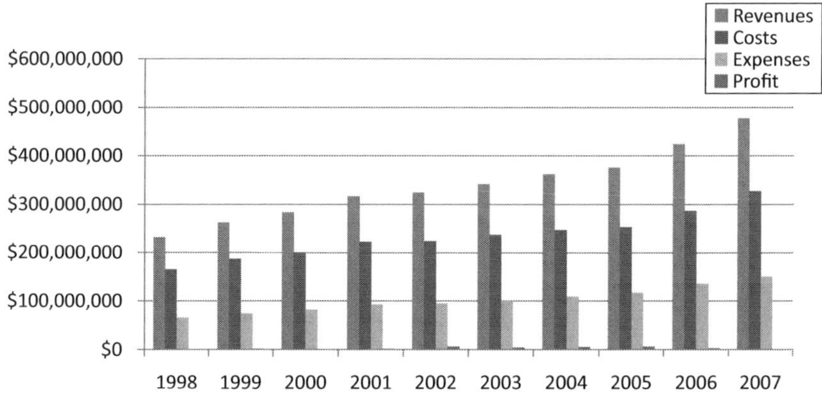

EXHIBIT 3.16 XYZ Income Statement Components Bar Chart

[29] This presumes that the data contains consistent parameters such as time horizons and account classifications, among others. The data driving the graph does indeed contain consistent data parameters.

EXHIBIT 3.17 Cascading Indicators

$102,034,100	The total cash dispersed by SUSPECT X for alleged operating expenses, automobiles, boats, artwork, jewelry, parties, and furniture and equipment during the alleged fraud's existence.
$91,154,854	The total funds that investors and lenders tendered to SUSPECT X during the alleged fraud's existence.
$165,475	The book balance of SUSPECT X's various bank accounts as of the date of the financial statements.
$15,300	The total amount paid in, categorized by SUSPECT X as Investor Relations during the alleged fraud's existence.
11,000	The number of inter- and intra-bank transfers among the various SUSPECT X bank accounts.
5,248	The estimated number of individual investors identified as placing funds with SUSPECT X during the alleged fraud's existence.
$3,910	The total interest income earned by SUSPECT X from the $102,034,100 that passed through executives' hands.
130	The estimated number of automobiles, boats, other watercraft, trucks, motorcycles, trailers, and a fire truck purchased by SUSPECT X during the alleged fraud's existence.
23	The number of entities formed during the existence of SUSPECT X's alleged fraud, including C corporations, LLCs, sole proprietorships, PLLCs, etc.
6	The number of years of SUSPECT X's existence through the report date.
5	The number of parties named in the original TRO.
2	The number of foreign countries where SUSPECT X holds an entity, and still holds one or more bank accounts, i.e. Nevis and the Bahamas.
0	The number of federal, state, and local income tax returns filed by SUSPECT X management for its 23 entities throughout its six years of existence.

PPM[30] brochure, and contributed more than $100 million within a three-year period. The complexity of the case called for an exhibit that summarized the myriad facts while detailing the executives' misuse of funds. The following exhibit draws one's eye to the left-hand side of the document and follows the natural downward flow of large to small numbers, from top to bottom. The simple listing of facts ranging from $102 million expended down to zero tax returns filed effectively communicated the findings. Federal prison was the sentence for certain executives, one of whom remains incarcerated at the time this section was written.

Source of Data: All case discovery, including financial documents, corporate communications, ISP[31] records, deposition transcripts, informal interviews, witness statements, board minutes, general ledger, etc.

Pattern Detection Method: Visual.

Pattern Observed: Various declining indicators.

Outcome: Exhibit 3.17 clearly indicates investment inflows were substantial, but executives and management squandered nearly all of the funds, and failed to act in a fiduciary capacity.

[30] Private Placement Memorandum.

[31] Internet Service Provider.

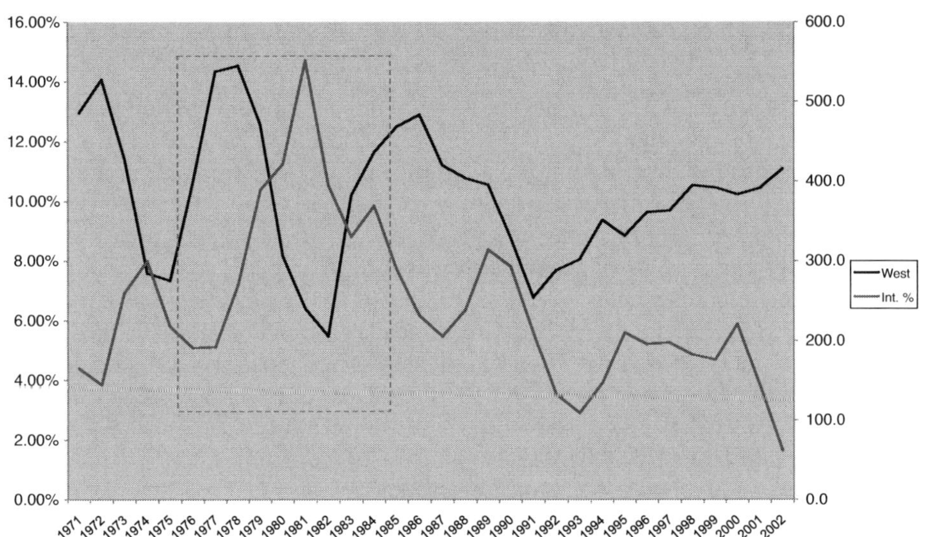

EXHIBIT 3.18 Devastating Economic Impacts from 1976 to 1985: Sales Plummeting and Interest Rates Soaring
Source: U.S. Census Bureau 000s for Housing.

Did the Executives Exercise Corporate Governance? *Actual Scenario:* The following case involved an alter ego matter tracking through federal courts for 18 years. The original contract pivoted upon an unusual condition during the relevant time: the divergence of soaring interest rates and plummeting home sales during the 1980 to 1982 time horizon. Adults intuitively understand that lower interest rates tend to result in higher home sales. However, the case at bar made it necessary to demonstrate the exact opposite of expectations for the relevant time horizon. Also, the visual demonstrated some counterintuitive findings, where declining interest rates did not result in increasing home sales. See Exhibit 3.18.

The visual demonstrated three findings for the court, two of which were contradictory. First, the visual reinforced intuitive understanding and demonstrated that changing interest rates tend to affect home sales (1971 to 1974 and 1995 to 2002). Second, it demonstrated counterintuitive findings that declining interest rates tracked with declining home sales (1976 to 1980 and 1986 to 1995). Finally, it demonstrated the unusual divergence for the relevant time horizon, 1980 to 1983, contained within the rectangle in the upper left quadrant of the visual. It demonstrated the extraordinary events when interest rates were approaching 16 to 20 percent and more.

The judge cited the strength of the evidence as delivered through the various visuals, and issued a bench ruling in favor of the client at the end of the 10-day trial. The judge stated that it was her first bench ruling delivered during eighteen and a half years on the bench.

Source of Data: US Department of Commerce, and the Federal Reserve, among others.

Pattern Detection Method: Visual.

Pattern Observed: Correlating, convergent, and divergent.

Outcome: The court found for the forensic operator's client, the defendant, and did not permit the federal government to pierce the corporate veil.

Aberrant Pattern Detection—Time

Time-based patterns demonstrate cause-and-effect and other conditions. Formal measurements, per se, are often not necessary, but can augment findings. Time-based patterns are appealing because humans experience life, and tend to think in terms of time-based events. In Western culture, time and patterns flow from left to right, mirroring how the written word is constructed.

Actual Scenario: The following case involved a Switzerland-based global company with operations in Portland, Maine and Hong Kong, among many other locations. Executive management believed a male senior vice president was having an affair with his subordinate, a female vice president based in Portland, Maine.

The likely affair violated strict company policies, but it also created considerable dissension within company ranks. Furthermore, the senior vice president was eligible for a substantial profit-sharing bonus approximating several hundred thousand dollars. Executive management informally confronted the parties about the concerns and immediately thereafter one party's laptop was "lost," and the other party wiped clean the company-issued hard drive. The party claimed the need to restore the hard drive as the reason to wipe it clean. Unfortunately, the company's well-meaning IT manager attempted to restore the wiped data. This effort violated the chain of custody protocol and thus precluded using any of the recovered data for analysis.

The forensic operator learned that the parties had spent inordinate amounts of time with one another beyond the needs of their respective position responsibilities. However, two factors confronted the forensic operator. First, the absence of data from the parties' respective hard drives precluded their use. Second, the company's fiscal year-end was imminent. Consequently, if the senior vice president merely delayed his termination, the large bonus would inure to him. There was simply inadequate time to conduct lengthy data collection and analysis.

Therefore, the forensic operator sought readily accessible data that betrayed the parties' locations over time. The company payroll data captured time in only limited categories, but the categories were useful for the circumstances. The categories included vacation, PTO (personal time off), and location-specific indication.

The visual in Exhibit 3.19 compared the two parties' respective locations during the 10 most recent months. The days highlighted in blue indicated the male's travel status, and the days highlighted and pink indicated the female's travel status. Four observations immediately surfaced. First, the female spent a great deal of time in Portland, Maine, where the male was based, and who happened to not be traveling at the time. Second, the male spent a great deal of time in Hong Kong, where the female was based, and who happened to be not traveling at the time. Third, both parties managed to spend several weekends at common locales even when a return home would have been more logical. Finally, when both parties were traveling, it was often to a common location, such as London and other locales.

Source of Data: Payroll and vacation records.

Pattern Detection Method: Time overlap, aka the "togetherness index."

Pattern Observed: Unusual occurrences of common time spent together.

Outcome: Both parties resigned and the bonus-eligible executive was thus compelled to forgo the substantial payment, and to avoid spousal disclosure.

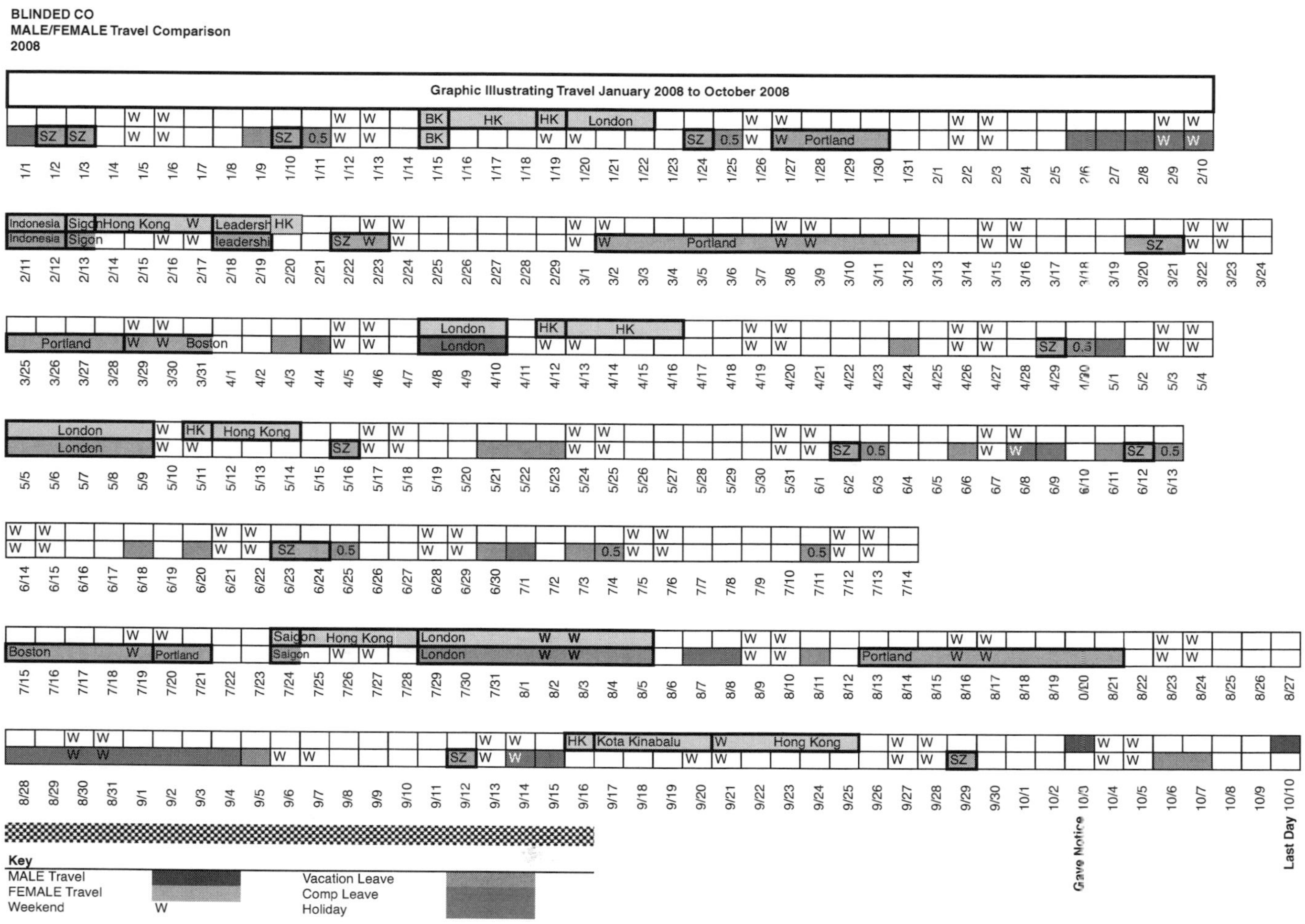

BLINDED CO
MALE/FEMALE Travel Comparison
2008

Graphic Illustrating Travel January 2008 to October 2008

1/1 – 2/10

Male: W W | W W | BK | HK | HK | London | W W | W W | W W
Female: SZ | SZ | W W | SZ | 0.5 | W W | BK | W W | SZ | 0.5 | W | W | Portland | W W | W W

1/1 1/2 1/3 1/4 1/5 1/6 1/7 1/8 1/9 1/10 1/11 1/12 1/13 1/14 1/15 1/16 1/17 1/18 1/19 1/20 1/21 1/22 1/23 1/24 1/25 1/26 1/27 1/28 1/29 1/30 1/31 2/1 2/2 2/3 2/4 2/5 2/6 2/7 2/8 2/9 2/10

2/11 – 3/24

Male: Indonesia | Sigon | Hong Kong | W | Leadersh | HK | W W | W W | W W | W W | W W
Female: Indonesia | Sigon | W W | leadershi | SZ | W | W | W | W | Portland | W W | W W | SZ | W W

2/11 2/12 2/13 2/14 2/15 2/16 2/17 2/18 2/19 2/20 2/21 2/22 2/23 2/24 2/25 2/26 2/27 2/28 2/29 3/1 3/2 3/3 3/4 3/5 3/6 3/7 3/8 3/9 3/10 3/11 3/12 3/13 3/14 3/15 3/16 3/17 3/18 3/19 3/20 3/21 3/22 3/23 3/24

3/25 – 5/4

Male: W W | W W | London | HK | HK | W W | W W | W W
Female: Portland | W W | Boston | W W | London | W W | W W | W W | SZ | 0.5 | W W

3/25 3/26 3/27 3/28 3/29 3/30 3/31 4/1 4/2 4/3 4/4 4/5 4/6 4/7 4/8 4/9 4/10 4/11 4/12 4/13 4/14 4/15 4/16 4/17 4/18 4/19 4/20 4/21 4/22 4/23 4/24 4/25 4/26 4/27 4/28 4/29 4/30 5/1 5/2 5/3 5/4

5/5 – 6/13

Male: London | W | HK | Hong Kong | W W | W W | W W | W W
Female: London | W W | SZ | W W | W W | W W | SZ | 0.5 | W W | SZ | 0.5

5/5 5/6 5/7 5/8 5/9 5/10 5/11 5/12 5/13 5/14 5/15 5/16 5/17 5/18 5/19 5/20 5/21 5/22 5/23 5/24 5/25 5/26 5/27 5/28 5/29 5/30 5/31 6/1 6/2 6/3 6/4 6/5 6/6 6/7 6/8 6/9 6/10 6/11 6/12 6/13

6/14 – 7/14

Male: W W | W W | W W | W W | W W
Female: W W | W W | SZ | 0.5 | W W | 0.5 | W W | 0.5 | W W

6/14 6/15 6/16 6/17 6/18 6/19 6/20 6/21 6/22 6/23 6/24 6/25 6/26 6/27 6/28 6/29 6/30 7/1 7/2 7/3 7/4 7/5 7/6 7/7 7/8 7/9 7/10 7/11 7/12 7/13 7/14

7/15 – 8/27

Male: W W | Saigon | Hong Kong | London | W W | W W | W W | W W
Female: Boston | W | Portland | Saigon | W W | London | W W | W W | Portland | W W | W W

7/15 7/16 7/17 7/18 7/19 7/20 7/21 7/22 7/23 7/24 7/25 7/26 7/27 7/28 7/29 7/30 7/31 8/1 8/2 8/3 8/4 8/5 8/6 8/7 8/8 8/9 8/10 8/11 8/12 8/13 8/14 8/15 8/16 8/17 8/18 8/19 8/20 8/21 8/22 8/23 8/24 8/25 8/26 8/27

8/28 – 10/10

Male: W W | W W | HK | Kota Kinabalu | W | Hong Kong | W W | W W
Female: W W | W W | SZ | W W | W W | W W | SZ | W W

8/28 8/29 8/30 8/31 9/1 9/2 9/3 9/4 9/5 9/6 9/7 9/8 9/9 9/10 9/11 9/12 9/13 9/14 9/15 9/16 9/17 9/18 9/19 9/20 9/21 9/22 9/23 9/24 9/25 9/26 9/27 9/28 9/29 9/30 10/1 10/2 10/3 10/4 10/5 10/6 10/7 10/8 10/9 10/10

Gave Notice (10/3)
Last Day (10/10)

Key
MALE Travel
FEMALE Travel
Weekend W
Vacation Leave
Comp Leave
Holiday

EXHIBIT 3.19 "Male-Female Travel Comparison" Chart 2008

Actual Scenario: A large mental health NPO[32] advised its primary public sector funding source of an imminent crisis. The NPO stated that it was unexpectedly several million dollars short of funding necessary to cover its payroll, due in four days. The primary funding source was shocked by the disclosure, since the NPO had earned clean audit opinions for the last several years. Furthermore, the NPO's quarterly and monthly funding reporting had signaled no financial problems.

The primary funding source immediately enlisted support from the various other funding sources and they managed to cover the current payroll. The various funding sources contacted a forensic operator to determine what happened in the NPO. The forensic operator immediately launched internal investigation efforts amid hostile NPO parties, and more importantly, rapidly implemented tools necessary for the funding sources to prevent surprises and continuing occurrences of funding shortages. Furthermore, he orchestrated a weekly all-hands telephone conference to ensure that all parties were communicating, in compliance with remote provisions.

The high-profile matter generated a media frenzy (television, newspapers, blogs, and so on) that referred to the "forensic auditor"[33] brought in to diagnose problems. Naturally, in a high-profile crisis matter, all parties want immediate answers and immediate resolutions, even though resolutions often take considerable time to implement. Therefore, the forensic operator used selected key findings to convey the problems while simultaneously identifying near-term resolutions. Two visuals (among others), shown here, identified the problems and led to the dismantling of the NPO into smaller, more manageable pieces.

Source of Data—Audited financial statements.

Pattern Detection Method: Elapsed time between the fiscal year-end (FYE) and the date of the audit opinion. The forensic operator perused the audit opinions[34] for the six most recent years available. The NPO had selected new auditors within the last five years and had one predecessor audit opinion available. A rapid review of the audit highlighted certain key indicators. First, a simple but telling measure regarding financial statements' quality results from comparing the length of time that the audit opinions following the respective fiscal year-end. As noted, auditor 1 required 6.6 months to issue the audit opinion. Then, auditor 2 required additional time, 7.9 months to issue the audit opinion. An increase in time required by a successor auditor is not necessarily unusual because of transitional considerations. Furthermore, the successor auditor steadily decreased the elapsed time, thus suggesting improved quality of the financial statements. However, the most recent audit opinion time gap dramatically increased. Such a change could be (as in this case, was) an indication of trouble within financial statement quality.

The second simple but telling measure regarding financial statement quality results by noting the restatements required by the successor auditors. Restating financial statements by successor auditors is, again, not necessarily unusual. However, the additional restatement for the June 30, 2005, fiscal period does indeed suggest problems. Unfortunately, the funding sources lacked even basic financial statement

---

[32] Nonprofit organization.

[33] A contradictory term, or oxymoron, akin to conducting a wellness check on a corpse.

[34] Naturally, the forensic operator conducted a great deal more analysis than merely perusing the audit opinions.

EXHIBIT 3.20 (Elapsed Time—FYE versus Audit Opinion Date)

Auditor	Auditor 1			Auditor 2		
Fiscal Year-End (FYE)	June 30, 2002	June 20, 2003	June 30, 2004	June 30, 2005	June 20, 2006	June 30, 2007
Opinion Date	Jan. 16, 2003	Feb. 24, 2004	Dec. 29, 2004	Dec. 15, 2004	Nov. 27, 2006	Mar. 5, 2008
Opinion: Months After FYE	6.6	7.9	6.0	5.4	4.9	8.2
Restated?	No	Yes	No	Yes	No	No

analysis capabilities. Consequently, they were completely caught off guard by the sudden shortage of funding.

The schedule in Exhibit 3.20 compares and contrasts the two auditors' elapsed time from fiscal year-end date to the date of the audit opinion. In addition, it indicates the two restatement periods suggesting additional audit problems.

A different way of viewing the data, Exhibit 3.21 illustrates the sudden departure from the steady decline of the elapsed time. If the NPO's primary funding sources had merely looked beyond and behind the audit opinion, they would likely have been forewarned about the deteriorating financial conditions.

Actual Scenario: (continued)

Source of Data—Board of director minutes.

Pattern Detection Method: Time insufficiency.

Pattern Observed: The NPO had a long-time employee who served as the board of directors' secretary during many years of board meetings. She dutifully transcribed and formalized the minutes in great detail and filed them in case it was necessary to

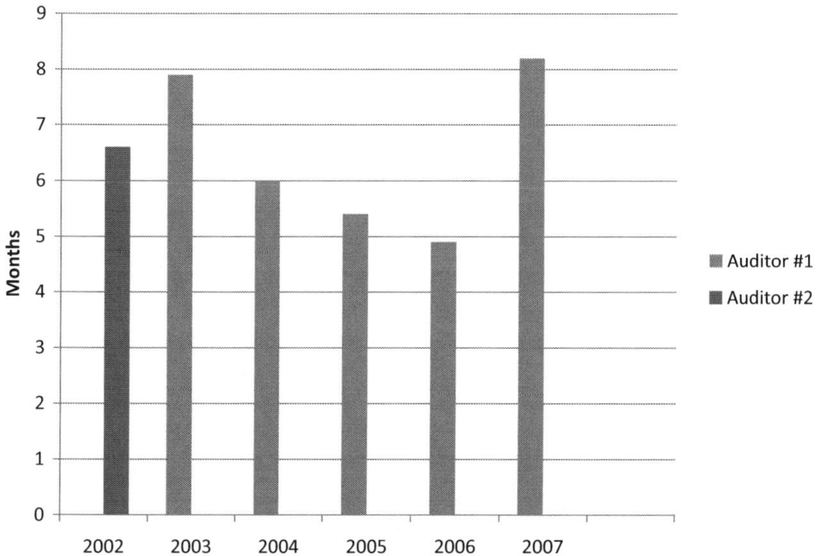

EXHIBIT 3.21 "Months from FYE to Audit Opinion Date" Bar Chart

review the contents. She told the forensic operator that she had never been asked by *anyone* for copies of prior board minutes, including the auditors.

When the forensic operator observed the extensive written record, he noted significant time aberrations. Generally, there was an inverse relationship between the duration of board meetings and the complexity of the respective matter. That is, very short board meetings were held for complex matters, and very long board meetings were held for mundane matters. The board of directors' minutes demonstrated inadequate time devoted to significant decisions affecting the provider's financial condition. The forensic operator highlighted key aspects of the minutes' contents for the forensic report.

Outcome: When the report was eventually made public, the media immediately identified and publicized the disparity between time and complexity. Also, the agency was forced to dramatically downsize so that several other agencies assumed the duties.

The media noted that during a four-month time frame, only three board meetings occurred, indicating only 18, 17, and 22 minutes, respectively. Put another way, the board devoted only 57 minutes over the four months indicated. Exhibit 3.22 illustrates an example of the redacted minutes.

But I Like an Optimistic Forecast *Actual Scenario:* A forensic operator executed a business valuation to determine the fair market value of a business's closely held shares pursuant to a family oppression lawsuit. The business operated in a market very sensitive to economic outlooks and five-to-seven-year business cycles. That is, if the U.S. economy was strong and appeared to be growing, the business value increased, and vice versa. The relationship was tested and validated using regression analysis, comparing subsets of the US gross domestic product (GDP), for example, private domestic investment (PDI), etc. with the company's revenue. Virtually all the regression showed a very strong correlation.

The opposing appraiser stressed the expected strong growth of the U.S. economy by selecting a single source upon which to base his observation. The forensic operator believed the preponderance of the evidence indicated a much slower growing economy. Consequently, the outlook for the U.S. economy was a pivotal difference between the two appraisers assisting the opposing parties.

The forensic operator simply compared multiple sources demonstrating their diversion. Coincidentally (or purposely), the opposing valuator selected the single source of U.S. economic output forecast higher than any other forecast. Consequently, he significantly overstated the value of the entity. The single source was the White House's estimation of the U.S. economy's future, indicated by "Obama 2010." That source was significantly greater (and showed smaller declines) than virtually all sources. When the parties viewed the visual shown in Exhibit 3.23 the disparity was self-evident. The opposing appraiser could provide neither subjective nor objective reasoning for his selection of the source.

Source of Data: Comprehensive business valuation from opposition.

Pattern Detection Method: Comparison of GDP future estimates.

Pattern Observed: Comparison to the preponderance of evidence.

Outcome: The opposing appraiser's report was discredited and the parties accepted the forensic operator's conclusion.

EXHIBIT 3.22 Mental Health Provider Summary of Meeting Minutes

NO-NAME COUNTY
Mental Health Provider, Inc.
Preliminary Forensic Accounting Diagnosis
May 2, DATE

Date, Time Length of Meeting	Key Items	Comments
18 minutes 5:52–6:10 P.M.	"... meeting to discuss CEO's employment contract. Upon review Board member approved the contract language; however the discussion around salary increase has been deferred to the 1st of the year. During that discussion the Board will decide if the salary increase will have a retro payout. (Name) also presented the bonus calculation figures for Board review. Members approved the figures and once the year-end financials have been finalized the bonus dollars will be paid." "The Board approved the bonus calculations for (CEO) which will be paid once the June 30, 2007 year-end financials have been finalized."	
October 23, 2007 Upland Commons 17 minutes 6:30–6:47 P.M.	(Resolution authorizing Non-Profit Housing, Inc. to act on behalf of Non-Profit Behavioral Healthcare, Inc.)	
No November Board Meeting		
December 9, 2007 Board Chair's Home 22 minutes 3:58–3:20 P.M.? (probably 4:20 P.M.)	Financial Update—"(Name) presented the October 2007 Income Statement and Balance Sheet with Board members. We had a surplus of $60,000 in October. We continue to improve cash month to month. Our YTD loss is $202,000, but we plan to break even by the end of January 2008. We exceeded the projected revenue by $13,000. This jump was due to an increase in productivity standards (sic), going from 50% to 55%. At the end of October we were fully drawn on our line of credit; however, we've paid down the line by $500,000 by the 21st of November and paid another $250,000 today. We did not have to draw to meet the November payroll. Our cash increased by $455,000, or 32% in October, again due to the increase in productivity standards. (sic)	

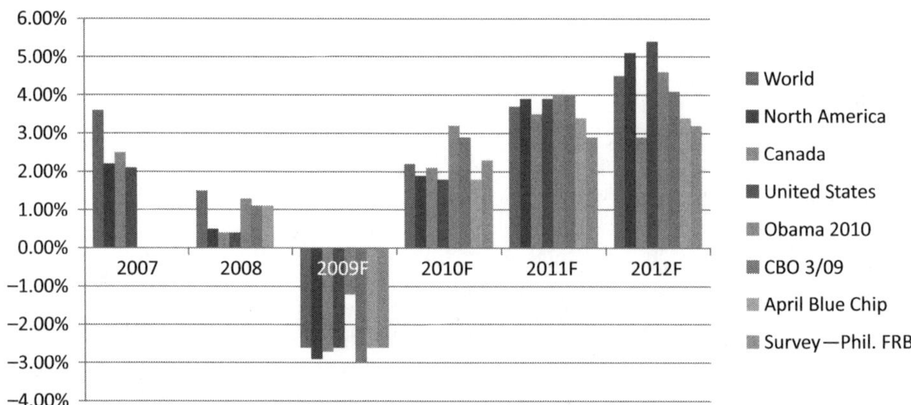

EXHIBIT 3.23 Year-to-Year Percentage GDP Change Bar Chart
Source: Moody's and as indicated.

Manipulation? What Manipulation *Actual Scenario:* A forensic operator was tasked with evaluating the leadership performance of the CEO installed in the late 1990s. The CEO directed sweeping financial and operational business changes that moved the private company toward financial distress despite growth in the respective industry. In particular, he effected a 2003 leveraged buyout of the private company through a quasi-reorganization that burdened the company with substantial debt.

The chairman became concerned and hired three different financial firms to individually opine on the value of the business and conclude whether the CEO's decisions had improved, rather than diminished its financial condition. One firm was a national valuation firm, one was an investment banking house, and one was a forensic operator. Two of the three firms performed typically valuation-related financial analysis, but the forensic operator used forensic methods such as CRO, TATA, and others to supplement his analysis. The forensic operator constructed two visuals, one simple and one complex, to counter the three firms' viewpoints.

Source of Data: Financial statement aberrations.

The forensic operator used the simple visual shown in Exhibit 3.24 to demonstrate unusual or unexpected occurrences within the financial statements for the

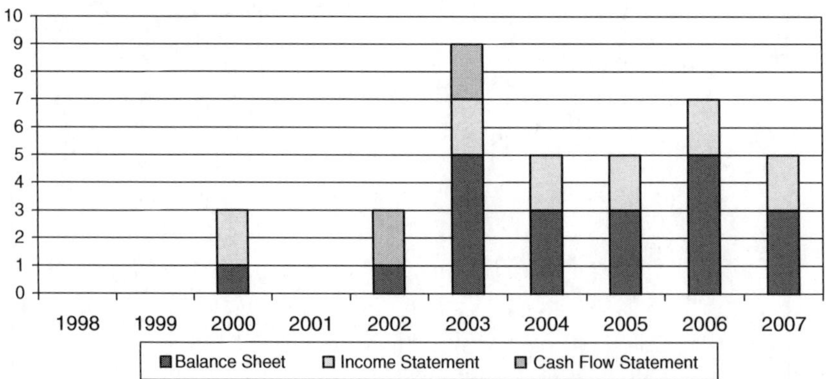

EXHIBIT 3.24 Annual Indicators—Balance Sheet, Income Statement, Cash Flow Chart

respective years. For example, in 2002, a substantial amount of goodwill appeared on the balance sheet after an acquisition.

There was little disagreement surrounding the facts supporting the visual contents. The other two firms had already pointed out the same factors, but had not noted their aberrant pattern. By merely pointing out the obvious pattern, the forensic operator demonstrated the aberrant occurrences in the financial statements that followed the CEO's decisions. He merely tabulated the occurrence of aberrant events for each of the three financial statements, resulting in an unmistakable before-and-after pattern.

Pattern Observed: Unusual financial statement events after CEO's hiring.

Actual Scenario: continued.

Source of Data: Audited financial statements.

Pattern Detection Method: Visual before-and-after comparison.

Pattern Observed: Unusual financial statement events after CEO's hiring.

After displaying and explaining the preceding visual, the forensic operator then displayed a more complex version containing similar conclusions. Specifically, he constructed a detailed financial analysis using only common financial ratios to illustrate the before-and-after financial condition of the company with respect to the CEO's hiring. Since the parties had already seen and thus understood the simpler version, the more complex version was a logical extension of the analysis.

The forensic operator prepared the analysis for that same time horizon, 1998 to 2007. He calculated and measured the typical ratios encountered by investors and lenders, consisting of liquidity, coverage, leverage, operating, and selected other ratios. Importantly, he color-coded the visual to represent the time before the CEO's hiring and the time after the CEO's hiring. Then he established a benchmark and icon for each of the ratios, indicating whether their preferred trend was to increase, decrease, or remain stable represented by the ↑, ↓, and ~, symbols, respectively.

Source of Data: Audited financial statements.

Pattern Observed: Scoring declined.

Having established the preferred trend for each measure, the forensic operator then scored the trend for the two periods, that is, before and after the CEO's hiring. The scores were indicated as better, worse, or no change represented by the symbols √, x, and ~, respectively. The preponderance of indicators clearly suggests that the company's financial condition worsened after the CEO's hiring. Also, the scores are individually tallied at the lower right-hand corner of the visual in Exhibit 3.25 to dispel any doubts regarding the measurement. The parties were convinced that the CEO's decisions had caused the financial condition of the company to deteriorate.

Source of Data: Audited financial statements.

Pattern Detection Method: Visual and quantitative.

Pattern Observed: Significant aberration during a key period.

Outcome: The forensic operator's forensic analysis discovered that the CEO was manipulating earnings by overstating inventory in order to fabricate the net income. The manipulation had not been noticed by the other two firms, but the forensic operator used the TATA (Total Accruals to Total Assets) index. When he reported the findings to the chairman and the other two firms, the other two firms were unaware of the implications and were dismissed by the chairman. The forensic operator continued the assignment and the CEO separated from the company. See Exhibit 3.26.

	Median Qrtl RMA Curr Yr	1998	1999	2000	2001	2002	2003	2004	2005	2006	2007	Pref. Direction Up	Pref. Direction Down	1998-2001 Better	1998-2001 Worse	2002-2006 Better	2002-2006 Worse
LIQUIDITY RATIOS:																	
Current Ratio	1.2	1.05	0.93	1.00	0.97	0.9	1.1	1.1	0.9	0.9	1.0	↑			✗		✗
Quick (Acid-Test) Ratio	0.4	0.3	0.3	0.3	0.3	0.3	0.4	0.4	0.3	0.3	0.3	↑			✗		✗
Revenue/Accounts Receivable	78.3	83.0	124.0	93.1	89.5	93.8	83.9	67.5	80.3	92.6	61.4	↑			✗	✓	
Average Collection Period	4.7	4.4	2.9	3.9	4.1	3.9	4.4	5.4	4.5	3.9	5.9		↓	~			✗
Inventory Turnover	14.6	9.2	9.6	9.7	10.5	10.0	10.0	9.6	9.0	9.3	9.3	↑		✓			✗
Days' Inventory	25.0	39.7	38.0	37.6	34.8	36.5	36.5	38.0	40.6	39.2	39.2		↓	✓			✗
COGS/Payables	19.1	18.2	18.2	16.9	21.6	18.7	17.8	20.8	16.9	16.2	15.1	~		~			✗
Days' Payables	19.1	20.1	20.1	21.6	16.9	19.5	20.5	17.5	21.6	22.5	24.2	~		~			✗
Revenue/Working Capital	81.0	161.5	-103.5	9046.8	-311.9	-124.0	65.8	160.2	-64.8	-59.3	309.3	↑			✗		✗
COVERAGE RATIOS:																	
Times Interest Earned	3.9	1.2	1.4	1.2	1.4	2.5	2.6	1.9	2.1	1.3	1.1	↑		✓			✗
NI+Non-Cash Expenditures / Current L.T. Debt	4.8	0.6	0.6	1.0	0.8	1.0	1.6	1.8	1.5	1.3	1.5	↑			✗		✗
LEVERAGE RATIOS:																	
Fixed Assets/Tangible Worth	1.7	4.0	4.2	5.5	5.1	3.6	4.4	5.1	6.2	N/A	N/A	↑		✓		✓	
Debt-to-Tangible Net Worth	2.1	5.2	5.6	7.4	6.9	4.7	7.2	8.8	10.4	N/A	N/A		↓		✗		✗
Debt-to-Equity	2.1	4.1	4.2	4.6	4.5	3.4	3.9	3.7	3.6	N/A	N/A		↓		✗		✗
OPERATING RATIOS:																	
Gross Profit Margin	26.00%	28.9%	28.8%	29.2%	29.6%	31.0%	30.6%	31.7%	32.8%	32.5%	31.5%	↑		✓		✓	
EBT/Tangible Worth	22.60%	9.2%	15.2%	12.6%	16.7%	42.3%	53.5%	55.3%	80.6%	N/A	N/A	↑		✓		✓	
EBT/Total Assets	6.30%	1.4%	2.2%	1.4%	2.0%	7.0%	5.9%	4.9%	N/A	2.1%	0.6%	↑		~			✗
Fixed Asset Turnover	9.1	3.5	3.7	3.6	3.8	4.1	4.9	5.1	4.7	5.1	5.7	↑		✓		✓	
Total Asset Turnover	4.5	2.2	2.2	2.2	2.3	2.4	2.4	2.3	2.2	2.3	2.5	↑		~		~	
EXPENSE TO REVENUE RATIOS:																	
% Deprtn., Depltn., Amort./Revenue	1.50%	1.9%	1.9%	1.8%	1.9%	1.7%	1.7%	1.5%	1.6%	1.7%	1.5%		↓		✗		✗
% Officer's &/or Owner's Compensation/Revenu	0.00%	0.3%	0.3%	0.3%	0.3%	0.3%	0.2%	0.2%	0.2%	0.1%	0.0%	↑		~			✗
Cash Flow Ratios:																	
Operating Cash Flows (OCF)		N/A	0.4	0.2	0.3	0.3	(0.1)	0.3	0.3	0.2	0.3	↑		~			✗
Cash Interest Coverage		N/A	3.2	1.8	2.4	3.6	1.3	2.6	3.3	2.1	2.2	↑		✓		✓	
Cash Flow to Total Debt		N/A	0.2	0.1	0.1	0.2	(0.0)	0.1	0.2	0.1	0.1	↑			✗		✗

	1998-2001		2002-2006	
Better	8	33.3%	6	25.0%
Worse	9	37.5%	17	70.8%
Same	7	29.2%	1	4.2%
	24	100.0%	24	100.0%

Risk Management Association, Philadelphia, PA 2003
RMA SIC Code is 4451, Supermarkets and Other Grocery (except Convenience) Stores

Legend	
↑	Should increase
↓	Should decrease
~	Should remain same

EXHIBIT 3.25 Ratio Analysis Spreadsheet

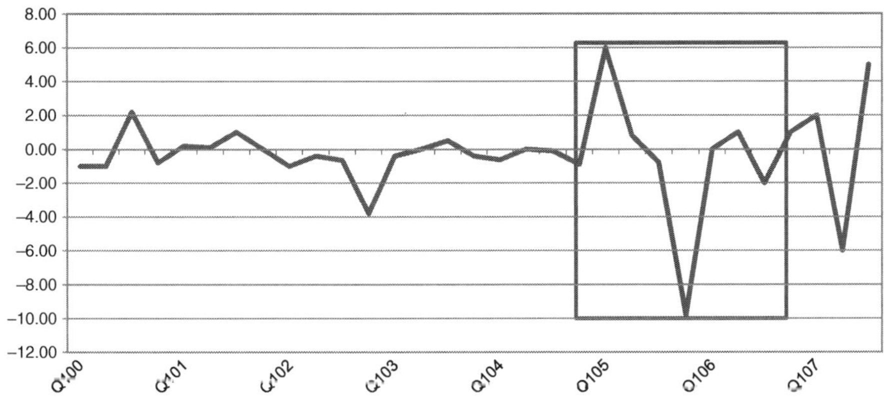

EXHIBIT 3.26 Accrual to Assets Ratio Line Chart

Aberrant Pattern Detection—Variation

Visual aberrant pattern detection is intuitively appealing. However, forensic operators need skill to identify, capture, display, and report the patterns so that they are similarly appealing to the pertinent audience. Some patterns are so visually compelling that their display begs the question of measurement.

Did the Line Items Increase Significantly? *Actual Scenario:* A government agency deployed investigators on various assignments and reimbursed them for expenses. The agency's policy required each expense item to be individually listed. Since each investigator was assigned to a unique territory, the expense line items varied from other territories, but remained stable within a territory. An informer claimed that one investigator was overstating expenses, but refused to identify the investigator. Based upon the circumstances, the forensic operator determined that a significant aberration within a territory identified the suspect. The agency's director concurred, but insisted on empirical measures to identify whether or not an aberration existed in the line items.

Source of Data: Expense report line items.

Pattern Detection Method: Variation—chi-square.

Pattern Observed: Aberrant.

Outcome: The forensic operator measured the number of line items within each territory for a five-year horizon. Using chi-square, the forensic operator determined that investigator C's line items displayed significant aberrations relative to the other investigators. The agency used the findings to approach the investigator.

A chi-square test measured differences in the number of line items to identify an out-of-the-ordinary difference. Using such a technique avoids the judgmental assessment of which, if any, of the line items were significantly different.

The Expense Report Line Item table in Exhibit 3.27 categorizes each investigator's line item total by year. The chi-square formula is summarized here:

$$\text{Chi-square} = \Sigma\,(\text{Observed frequency} - \text{Expected Frequency})^2/\text{Expected Frequency}$$

In essence, the formula that derives chi-square sums the squares of the difference between the observed frequency (each actual category line item count per year),

EXHIBIT 3.27 Expense Report Line Items

Category	Year 1	Year 2	Year 3	Year 4	Year 5	Year 6
A	1,110	1,225	1,210	1,200	1,225	1,194
B	650	660	680	640	620	650
C	770	860	740	848	775	799
D	843	915	877	896	873	881
E	512	530	552	498	572	533

minus the expected frequency (each category line item average for each year). After summing, the product is divided by the expected (average) frequency for each year. "Observed frequencies" refer to the actual data per year, and "expected frequencies" refers to a measure of central tendency, that is, the mean for each year.

The chi-square formula produced the table shown in Exhibit 3.28. Note the chi-square conclusions ranging from a low of three to a high of 14 in the schedule. Tables of critical chi-square values at the 5 percent level of significance indicate that with five categories of data (Years 1 through 5) a chi-square score beyond 9.49 is significant. Consequently, category C, which illustrates a chi-square score of 14, indicates that its occurrence is beyond mere chance. That is, the forensic operator is 95 percent confident that the aberrations did not occur by chance. Therefore, investigator C's line items were out of the ordinary and identified the cheating investigator.

Which Expenses Display the Most Variation? *Actual Scenario:* A forensic operator was investigating the concealment of fraudulent transactions. The subject allegedly journalized the theft into a few operating expense accounts in the hope that the amounts went unnoticed. The time was limited in the matter, thus it was essential to effectively deploy effort toward those accounts offering the greatest promise.

Source of Data: Operating expense line items.

Pattern Detection Method: Variation—mean average deviation (MAD).

Pattern Observed: Aberrant.

Outcome: The forensic operator measured whether accounts exhibited aberrant properties by the mean average deviation (MAD) technique. It is derived by the average of the absolute differences between each value for an account, and the average of the values in an account. The forensic operator used Excel to conditionally format the aberrant amounts as displayed in Exhibit 3.29.

The following section, titled "Forensic Financial Analysis," describes several other techniques that empirically measure aberration.

EXHIBIT 3.28 Σ (Observed Frequency – Expected Frequency)^2/Expected Frequency

Category	Year 1	Year 2	Year 3	Year 4	Year 5	Chi-Square
A	6	1	0	0	1	8
B	—	0	1	0	1	3
C	1	5	4	3	1	14
D	2	1	0	0	0	3
E	1	0	1	2	3	7

	2007	2008	2009	2010	2011	2012	Minimum	Maximum	Mean	MEAN ABSOLUTE DEVIATION
Sales wages	1,025,618	1,822,733	1,007,490	682,526	421,532	1,107,715	421,532	1,822,733	1,011,269	307,420
Sales health insurance	43,296	71,423	31,944	39,088	-	94,899	-	94,899	46,775	24,257
Sales payroll tax	99,933	162,421	173,230	94,518	14,162	107,740	14,162	173,230	108,667	39,439
Commissions	226,409	144,320	150,409	118,585	136,078	125,297	118,585	226,409	150,183	25,484
Advertising	449,044	298,086	529,502	139,568	87,343	(24,414)	(24,414)	529,502	246,522	179,023
Marketing/Consulting	-	-	-	-	-	210,210	-	210,210	35,035	58,392
Camera/art/die cut work	100,507	222,323	88,735	10,741	22,840	76,054	10,741	222,323	86,867	50,322
Demo & training supplies	7,703	11,936	34,593	9,067	2,156	23,591	2,156	34,593	14,841	9,501
Samples	21,644	23,842	47,408	5,469	4,078	41,641	4,078	47,408	24,014	13,674
Contest expense	29,046	27,656	24,174	4,841	8,755	3,605	3,605	29,046	16,346	10,613
Packaging	17,254	15,617	10,328	1,788	14,486	30,705	1,788	30,705	15,030	6,162
Promotions & gifts	104,403	75,742	196,164	188,377	123,225	8,633	8,633	196,164	116,091	53,165
Charitable donations	58,091	35,218	19,135	19,008	3,252	27,868	3,252	58,091	27,095	13,297
Freight	1,820,964	2,442,133	3,544,871	3,741,616	1,926,630	1,786,144	1,786,144	3,741,616	2,543,726	733,011
Training, education & recruiting	58,784	69,196	230,316	92,982	8,018	5,730	5,730	230,316	77,504	56,096
Service & maintenance	55,205	38,972	56,900	91,951	71,266	30,395	30,395	91,951	57,448	16,107
Uniforms	-	7,575	-	5,290	-	37,855	-	37,855	8,453	9,801
Working supplies	313,104	218,077	21,239	199,457	227,913	237,594	21,239	313,104	202,897	61,700
Kitchen supplies	-	-	38,233	22,730	41,543	34,216	-	41,543	22,787	15,210
Research & development	23,144	94,526	115,100	82,874	3,936,975	2,219,101	23,144	3,936,975	1,078,620	1,332,945
Cleaning	13,318	22,286	45,213	42,105	30,305	49,941	13,318	49,941	33,861	11,892
Safety & health	19,359	31,144	48,752	26,428	16,553	34,836	16,553	48,752	29,512	8,732
Miscellaneous	57,927	53,168	34,220	42,918	11,575	34,702	11,575	57,927	39,085	12,253
Admin wages	685,847	2,141,636	2,436,771	1,976,895	2,054,424	4,236,169	685,847	4,236,169	2,255,290	720,786
Misc labor wages	-	-	-	1,019,772	221,606	740,530	-	1,019,772	330,318	366,555
Admin health insurance	49,678	94,098	172,504	142,499	-	146,824	-	172,504	100,934	53,009
Misc labor health insurance	-	-	-	(1,066)	83,123	151,384	(1,066)	151,384	38,907	52,231
Mec. Labor health insurance	-	-	-	-	-	41,350	-	41,350	6,892	11,486
Admin payroll tax expense	67,896	184,889	115,510	177,342	149,907	315,534	67,896	315,534	168,513	57,409
Misc labor payroll tax expense	-	-	-	78,549	-	106,479	-	106,479	30,838	41,117
Worker's comp insurance	122,639	89,828	144,004	169,656	126,645	284,042	89,828	284,042	156,136	47,142
Member's health insurance	-	102,999	116,378	-	-	104,088	-	116,378	53,911	53,911
Employee benefits	-	-	-	-	-	902	-	902	150	251
Life insurance	27,998	31,293	24,713	25,354	22,201	52,559	22,201	52,559	30,686	7,493
Disability	-	20,652	27,536	27,536	27,536	20,652	-	27,536	20,652	6,884
Contract labor	3,577	21,832	8,856	4,564	6,526	9,138	3,577	21,832	9,082	4,269
Building lease	629,301	764,319	787,496	1,318,470	1,618,944	2,262,727	629,301	2,262,727	1,230,210	503,171
Building repairs	48,317	26,903	33,860	13,207	26,218	14,131	13,207	48,317	27,106	9,322

EXHIBIT 3.29 Expenses Analysis Spreadsheet Highlighted (Min, Max, Mean, MAD)

FORENSIC LEXICOLOGY:[35] HOW TO ANALYZE WORDS LIKE NUMBERS

Forensic operators continually seek new tools, techniques, methods, and methodologies for the increasingly complex forensic assignments encountered today. Therefore, it is essential that they use every available technology. Forensic lexicology is a powerful weapon that is easily deployed using nominal effort. The results invariably exceed requisite efforts. Furthermore, after simple methods, for example, Microsoft Word's "Readability Statistics," successively more complex and powerful tools can be deployed.

Forensic assignments contain data in many basic forms with perhaps the two most prevalent forms being numbers and words. The numbers come from a variety of sources, including financial statements, general ledgers, journal entries, purchase orders, journal vouchers, payroll checks, inventory records, and the like. Word sources include opposition briefs, testimony transcripts, interview notes, financial document contents, financial statement notes, expert witness reports, etc. Although forensic operators tend to spend the majority of their time analyzing numbers, words can also generate forensic understandings not otherwise available.

Forensic operators often lack specific tools to analyze the words in a forensic assignment. Even forensic operators gifted with sophisticated reading, review, and comprehension talents seek to accelerate and refine their observations. Also, detailed and objective word analysis can be more persuasive than generalized statements during testimony such as "I read the transcript and noted the occurrence of certain words multiple times." It is merely a matter of knowing how to analyze the words and coax the content out of them.

Fortunately, empirical word analysis has been in practice in various forms for centuries. The techniques range from labor-intensive translations of ancient manuscripts all the way to today's software algorithms designed specifically for word analysis. Word analysis techniques are not necessarily intuitive (until you understand them), but yield insights otherwise unavailable through the mere reading and notation of documents.

This section illustrates various forensic lexicology techniques and progresses from basic word analysis through progressively sophisticated methods. However, the contents of the section are by no means exhaustive. The field is vast, complex, and dynamic and many books would be necessary for adequate topic coverage. This section introduces the subject and describes several tools that are immediately applicable in financial forensic assignments.

How to Analyze Words

Forensic operators understand that people exhibit patterns reflecting virtually every aspect of their behavior. Their language, mannerism, accents, body movement, breathing, vocabulary, and other personal manifestations represent who they are, their very identity. Also, forensic operators understand the difficulty in trying to

[35] Lexicology is a branch of linguistics concerned with the signification and application of words. See www.merriam-webster.com.

change or disguise such behavior. Examples have been anecdotally demonstrated in movies in which a party working undercover is inadvertently exposed by a minor slip of the tongue or other mishap. Subjects in a forensic assignment are no different.

Therefore, forensic operators continually seek behavioral measurements to identify or reject a subject's identity or veracity regarding claims. Some forensic operators possess innate skills they intuitively deploy to exploit mannerism. However, objective criteria for discernment and measurement are essential, since such gifts are rare and difficult to prove in civil and criminal matters. Furthermore, behavioral patterns often change under stress, thus some means of stabilizing data and measurements is essential.

The written word offers such criteria. Words are the result of thought (conscious or otherwise) and yield clues into a subject's mind. Even audio or video transcriptions yield word patterns, especially when a subject provides few written records.

Words contain information conveyed overtly, subtly, or subconsciously. For example, reading about the same event as reported by two different news sources could lead one to believe there were actually two *different* events. It is widely acknowledged[36] that media bias is pervasive in the United States, journalistic integrity notwithstanding. Media's words contain reporting bias (subconscious or otherwise) within the words they use and distorts the facts.

Words in forensic matters are no different. If supposedly neutral media sources routinely contain bias, how much more so will the parties to a dispute? That is, the parties under investigation create the words, and thus overtly, subtly, or subconsciously include a bias spin—a bias in order to deceive. By ferreting out the bias, forensic operators can find the facts and present them in the proper venue.

There are several reasons forensic operators should analyze words beyond their apparent content. For example:

- The facts and evidence can be validated or refuted, since distortions often occur in written documents.
- Consistency of viewpoints can be assessed, such as determining when or whether an expert changed an opinion over the life of the matter.
- Consistency of testimony can be assessed, such as determining whether or not a subject changed his story regarding a crime while being interrogated at various times.
- The authenticity of authorship is measurable within expert reports in order to determine where or whether other parties engineered the expert's opinion.

Although the preceding examples are not exhaustive, they illustrate why the forensic operator should apply forensic lexicology techniques to the words in a forensic assignment.

The following contents lay out progressively more sophisticated methods of analyzing words. The techniques present little difficulty in their application and produce output that is easily discernible and defensible. Furthermore, the cost in each case is free or nominal.

---

[36] "Even Harvard Finds the Media Biased," *Investor's Business Daily*, November 2, 2007.

Intuition

Every forensic operator has developed some discernment techniques that identify word content and patterns. For example, some forensic operators reorganize copious notes taken in parallel to a document's linear structure. Other forensic operators use self-sticking notes to capture observations gleaned from reading through documents. Some use various software tools, whether or not designed for the purpose, to attempt to organize their thoughts.

While those techniques may be effective in some smaller matters, larger complex matters often require more powerful analytical tools. Furthermore, intuitive techniques lack the empirical support produced by more sophisticated methods.

Microsoft Word Microsoft Word contains some very basic but useful tools for word analysis. Microsoft Word software contains embedded tools available that analyze virtually any text captured in a Word document. Even if the forensic operator has only hard copy with which to work, those documents will convert to text format, which Word software can then analyze. Scanning and converting hard copy documents produces .pdf, .txt, .rtf, .doc, .docx, and other file formats useful for detailed analysis.

Once a document resides in Microsoft Word, the page count and word count (number of words contained in the document) are constantly displayed in the lower left-hand corner of the screen. Furthermore, by selecting portions of the document, that is, single paragraph, multiple paragraphs, page, or multiple pages, the words in the respective selection compare to the total words in the document. This could accommodate a simple test for boilerplate content in an expert report. That is, by determining 78 percent of the report content is boilerplate, the implication is that only 22 percent was specifically written for the matter at hand.

Microsoft Word also provides some simple style testing that is useful for forensic purposes. When Microsoft Word runs a spelling and grammar check on a Microsoft Word document, it produces comparative grammar and style results. The results include counts of words, characters, paragraphs, and sentences. The results also include averages for sentences per paragraph, words per sentence, and characters per word. Finally, the results include readability measures such as the percentage of passive sentences, the Flesch Reading Ease scale and the Flesch-Kincaid Grade Level scale.

The Flesch[37] Reading Ease scale is a method to measure content readability and dates to many decades ago. The scale ranges from about 100 for the highest readability (easiest, that is, each sentence contains only two one-syllable words) to 0 for the lowest readability. The Flesch-Kincaid[38] Grade Level scale measures readability levels, according to U.S. grade school levels. For example, a Flesch-Kincaid Grade Level scale of 8 suggests that a typical eighth-grader could read the document, a Flesch-Kincaid Grade Level scale of 11 suggests that a typical 11th-grader could read the document, and so forth.

---

[37] The *Harvard Law Review* scores in the low 30s.

[38] J. Peter Kincaid, R. P. Fishburne, R. L. Rogers, and B. S. Chissom, *Derivation of New Readability Formulas (Automated Readability Index, Fog Count, and Flesch Reading Ease Formula) for Navy Enlisted Personnel* (Naval Air Station, Memphis: Chief of Naval Technical Training, Research Branch Report 8-75, 1975).

Interestingly, the two measurements contain some divergence. For example, the Flesch[39] Reading Ease Scale indicates the higher the score the greater the readability. However, the Flesch-Kincaid Grade Level suggests lower grade school levels to reflect lower complexity. Taken literally, that suggests that an ideal document would have a high Flesch Reading Ease Scale, and a low Flesch-Kincaid Grade Level scale. Therefore, the forensic operator must be familiar with the scoring techniques to ensure that the written content matches the likely reader audience to maximize their grasp and absorption of the written content.

The following example illustrates the power of a very simple word analysis tool, that is, the techniques contained in Microsoft Word. Three documents from an actual forensic assignment served for analysis. The same firm produced the three documents, but they covered different topics. Even though the same party allegedly prepared all three documents, it was necessary to determine authorship authenticity. Forensic lexicology results indicate that one person authored two of the documents, but a different person authored the third document. The reader is asked to use the Microsoft Word analysis that follows to identify the errant document.

The authors converted each document from hard copy to Word format. Then, the authors ran the "Review" and "Spelling and Grammar" routines from within Word. At the completion of each routine the "Readability Statistics" dialogue boxes in Exhibit 3.30 were displayed.

The schedule in Exhibit 3.31 comparatively displays the "Readability Statistics" results to provide comparative clues in order to identify the document prepared by two authors.

Significantly, note the disparity in size among the three documents as indicated by the number of words, characters, paragraph, and sentences. Document 2 is the largest, while documents 1 and 3 are similar in size. The size disparity illustrates how the techniques apply without regard to document size.

The "Counts" measurements, next, summarize the results from the source documents.

- *Words per document*—disparate size, with no usable indication of authorship.
- *Characters per document*—disparate size, with no usable indication of authorship.

Readability Statistics	1	2	3
Counts			
Words	6238	11913	5351
Characters	34827	67449	28911
Paragraphs	219	427	142
Sentences	302	564	280
Averages			
Sentences per Paragraph	2.1	2.0	3.6
Words per Sentence	18.7	18.8	17.7
Characters per Word	5.3	5.4	5.2
Readability			
Passive Sentences	18%	25%	17%
Flesch Reading Ease	31.5	27.7	40.9
Flesch-Kincaid Grade Level	13.4	14.0	11.8

EXHIBIT 3.30 Readability Statistics (3 sets of results)

[39] The *Harvard Law Review* scores in the low 30s.

EXHIBIT 3.31 Readability Statistics

	Document 1	Document 2	Document 3
Counts			
Words	6,238	11,913	5,351
Characters	34,827	67,449	28,911
Paragraphs	219	427	142
Sentences	302	564	280
Averages			
Sentences per paragraph	2.1	2.0	3.6
Words per sentence	18.7	18.8	17.7
Characters per word	5.3	5.4	5.2
Readability			
Passive sentences	18%	25%	17%
Flesch Reading Ease	31.5	27.7	40.9
Flesch-Kincaid Grade Level	13.4	14.0	11.8

- *Paragraphs per document*—disparate size, with no usable indication of authorship.
- *Sentences per document*—disparate size, with no usable indication of authorship.

The "Averages" measurements, next, summarize the results from the source documents.

- *Average sentences per paragraph*—documents 1 or 2 compare favorably, and document 3 is nearly double the average of documents 1 and 2.
- *Average words per sentence*—average converges for all three documents, with no usable indication of authorship.
- *Average characters per word*—average converges for all three documents, no usable indication of authorship.

The "Readability" measurements, next, summarize the results from comparing them to the source documents.

- *Passive sentence content*—documents 1 and 3 contain similar percentages, suggesting document 2 is unique.
- *Flesch Reading Ease*—documents 1 and 2 contain similar steals, while document 3 is divergent.
- *Flesch-Kincaid Grade Level*—documents 1 and 2 contain similar scores, while document 3 is divergent.

Some of the measurements are common across all three documents, that is, the raw measurement of "Characters per Word" ranging from 5.2 to 5.4. Other measurements show significant differences, such as the raw measurement of "Sentences per Paragraph." These differences begin to identify the documents' authorship. Most telling, though, are the two Flesch measures, the Flesch Reading Ease Scale and the

Flesch-Kincaid Grade Level. The Flesch Reading Ease Scale scores of 31.5 and 27.7 for documents 1 and 2 are very similar; document 3 is an outlier. The Flesch-Kincaid Grade Level scores of 13.4 and 14.0 for documents 1 and 2 are also very similar; document 3 is an outlier. Consequently, it is logical to conclude that the same author created documents 1 and 2. Document 3 was created by a different author. The facts of the assignment are consistent with the Microsoft Word analysis.

The forensic utility of Microsoft Word's readability analysis is admittedly limited. However, the illustration clearly demonstrates how even simple forensic lexicology can lead to significant forensic observations.

Linguistic Style Analysis Technique (LSAT) The logical progression beyond the simple measurement techniques embedded in Microsoft Word consists of deploying linguistic style analysis technique (LSAT) methods. Law enforcement, the military, counterterrorism analysts, forensic operators, and others routinely deploy LSAT. The technique evaluates veracity in verbal and written statements. Skilled LSAT analysts parse content into structural components, for example, terms, phrases, and the like in order to compare (and develop) the facts. One of the United States's leading authorities is Sergeant Bob Shaffer,[40] of the Loveland, Colorado, Police Department. Sergeant Shaffer regularly conducts training on the technique.

Detailed treatment of the topic is beyond the scope of this section but a simple example illustrates the technique. In a recent forensic assignment, the plaintiff claimed that he was promised an ownership interest in his employer's business. When the business sold for a substantial sum, the plaintiff filed suit, demanding payment for his supposed ownership interest. The plaintiff's allegations centered upon claimed conversations with the owner during which the owner allegedly made the promise. The plaintiff used three different nouns during his description of the promise during his lengthy video depositions. He used a mixture of the terms *part, percentage,* and *portion* in his assertions. For example, he claimed, "I was promised a ______ (part, percentage or portion) of the business when it sold."

Plaintiff's attorney used the same three nouns in his various briefs, but a forensic operator noted an apparent discrepancy in the proportion of the terms' usage by the plaintiff's counsel. The plaintiff's attorney appeared to employ a different proportion of terms that gave a contextual edge to his client's claims. Specifically, within the context of the allegations, the words *portion* and *percentage* were more advantageous to his client.

The forensic operator used LSAT to compare and contrast the two sources, that is, the plaintiff's deposition transcripts and the plaintiff's counsel's briefs. The two analyses are reproduced next.

The plaintiff's deposition transcripts used the three nouns 21 times as indicated in the table shown in Exhibit 3.32 and illustrated in Exhibit 3.33.

The plaintiff's deposition transcripts also contained the three nouns, but in different proportions. Plaintiff used the noun *part* 90 percent of the time and the other two nouns, that is, *portion* and *percentage,* only 5 percent of the time. In comparison, plaintiff's counsel's briefs also used the same three nouns, but the proportions were significantly different. The term *part* was used only 43 percent of the time, as indicated by Exhibits 3.34 and 3.35.

[40] www.linguisticstatementanalysis.com/index.php.

EXHIBIT 3.32 Plaintiff's Deposition Transcripts

Plaintiff's Deposition	Occurrences	Percentage
"Portion"	1	5%
"Part"	19	90%
"Percentage"	1	5%
	21	**100%**

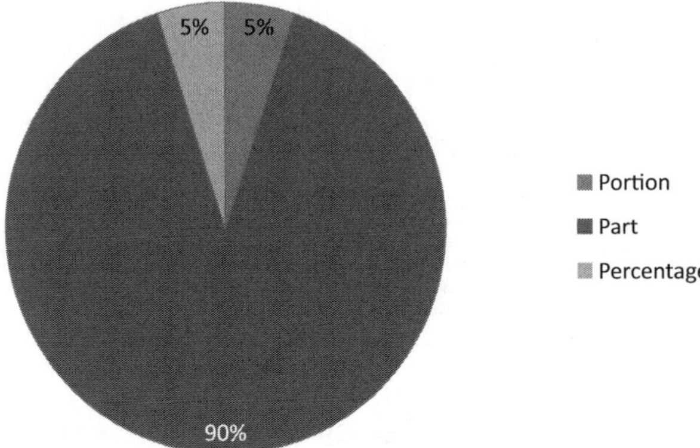

EXHIBIT 3.33 Defendant's Plaintiff's Deposition—Sale Pie Chart (*Portion, Part, Percentage*)

EXHIBIT 3.34 Plaintiff's Counsel Briefs

Plaintiff's Counsel	Occurrences	Percentage
"Portion"	35	35%
"Part"	42	43%
"Percentage"	22	22%
	99	**100%**

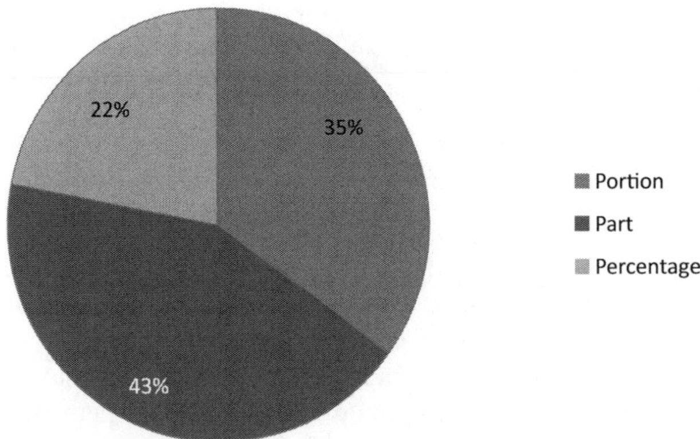

EXHIBIT 3.35 Counsel's Briefs—Sale Pie Chart (*Portion, Part, Percentage*)

Based upon the forensic operator's analysis, defendant's counsel used the preceding visuals as support for a motion for summary judgment, arguing that plaintiff's counsel had distorted (consciously or unconsciously) the facts of the case to favor his client. The judge agreed and struck that component of the claim from the matter.

myWordCount The first example in this section used Microsoft Word's limited readability techniques to compare documents. Even though Microsoft Word can analyze only one document at a time, repeated analysis provides data so that multiple documents can be compared. Fortunately, several software products provide forensic operators with additional significant features. Typically, such software measures, analyzes, and helps improve readability, grammar, and style content. Likewise, they support comparisons and analysis of authorship.

One writing software product is particularly well suited to forensic lexicology. That product is known as myWordCount by myWriterTools.[41] Its entry-level version can be downloaded for $14.95 and is very user-friendly. The learning curve is very short and a forensic operator can have the software up and running in only minutes.

The following summary compares the various measurements and illustrates data available to analyze one or more documents. Significantly, the individual measures empirically analyze word-driven composition.

myWordCount collects and compares readability and other document statistics, but will also drill deeply within a document and compare phrases, word counts, occurrences, and several other measurements. The following example illustrates the drill down within one document to explore the features. A deposition transcript of William Jefferson Clinton from the public domain[42] is used to illustrate the analysis. The transcript was converted to .txt format, although the software analyzes different file formats.

The first visual, Exhibit 3.36, involves a word count comparison. The first step involved selecting the file, the deposition transcript, in text mode (.txt). Next, the "Count Words" button was selected and resulted in the screen shown in Exhibit 3.36. The words are listed in descending order according to the number of occurrences, and can be sorted in various ways. Words are also measured for proximity to one another. The word *that* was used 741 times throughout the transcript, 607 times within 50 words, 97 times within 50 to 100 words, etc. The columns can be selected and sorted according to the analysis required. Next, the "Graph Highlighted Word" button was selected and resulted in Exhibit 3.37.

The visual produced by the tool is reproduced in Exhibit 3.37. The bar graph visual contains what would be color-coded references for each page of the transcript, indicating the frequency of occurrence and within the word ranges as indicated. For example, the word *that* is highlighted in red to indicate its occurrence within 50 words of separation. Likewise, the word *that* is highlighted in purple to indicate its occurrence within 50 to 100 words of separation. Simultaneously, the pertinent text is displayed to the left with the word *that* color-coded to indicate occurrence and placement.

The next visual, Exhibit 3.38, displays a phrase count comparison, and can be displayed for 2-word, 3-word, 4-word, and 5-word phrases. The "Count Phrases"

[41] www.mywritertools.com.

[42] www.washingtonpost.com/wp-srv/politics/special/pjones/docs/clintondep031398.htm.

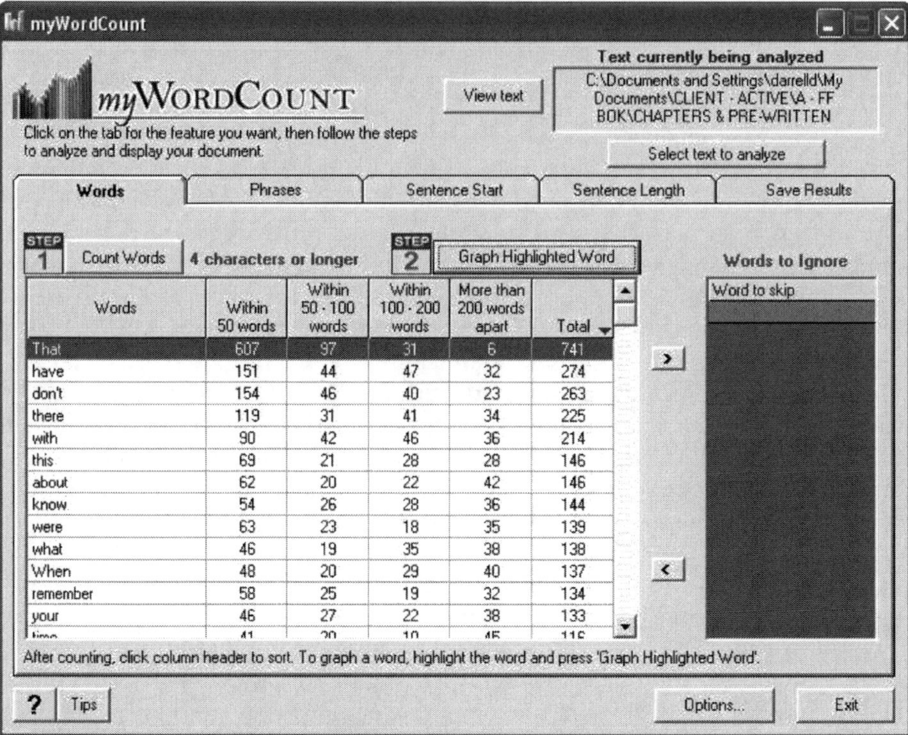

EXHIBIT 3.36 Count Words

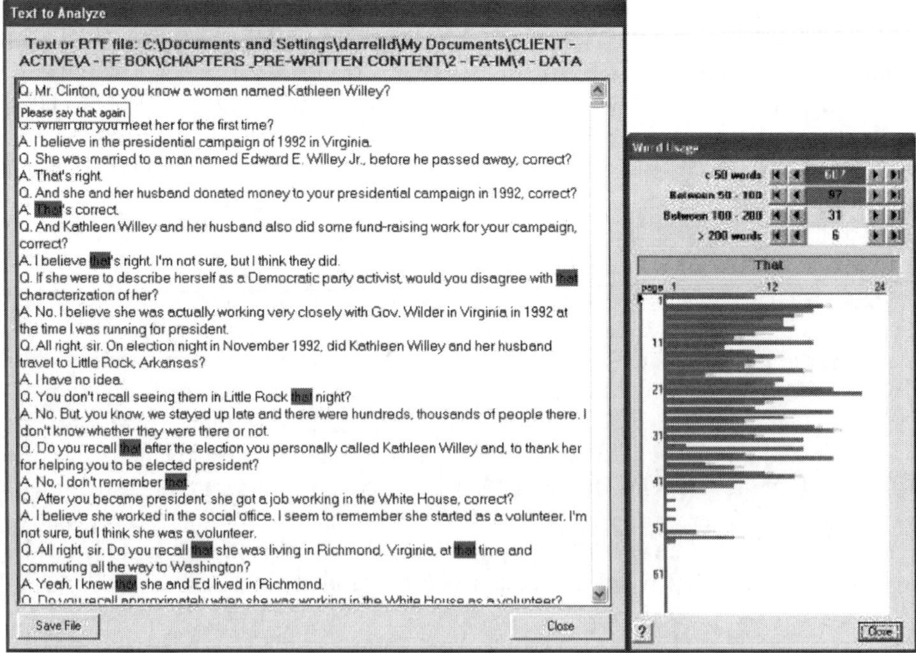

EXHIBIT 3.37 Text to Analyze Box; Word Usage Box

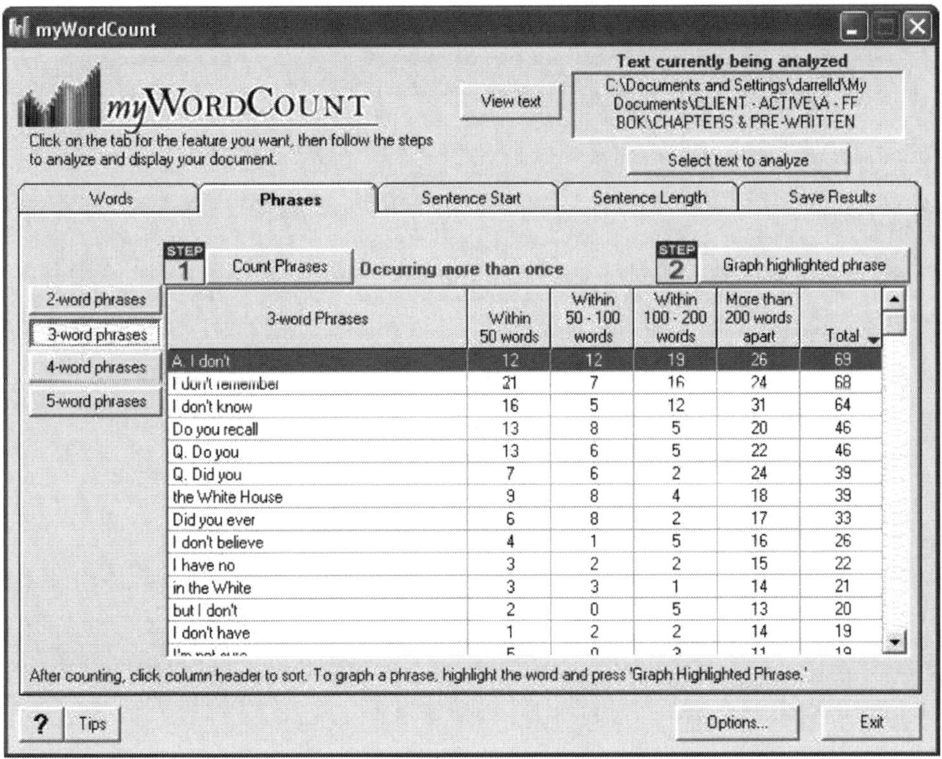

EXHIBIT 3.38 Three-Word Phrases

button was selected and resulted in the preceding screen. The phrases are listed in descending order in total, and also in comparison to other words. The 3-word phrase "I don't remember" was used 68 times throughout the transcript. Since the document is a deposition transcript, a certain uniqueness must be considered, such as the Q and A designations. This is apparent when observing variations of "A. I don't" which was used 69 times as a 2-word phrase, "I don't know" was used 64 times as a 3-word phrase, and "I don't know" was used 16 times as a 4-word phrase not shown. Likewise, "don't remember" was used 75 times as a 3-word phrase (not shown). The columns can be selected and sorted according to the analysis required. Next, the "Graph Highlighted Phrase" button was selected and resulted in Exhibit 3.39.

The visual produced by the tool is shown in Exhibit 3.39. The bar graph visual contains what would be color-coded references for each page of the transcript, indicating the frequency of occurrence and within the word ranges as indicated. In this case, "*I don't*" was selected. Simultaneously, the pertinent text (in this case, page 1) is displayed to the left with the words "*I don't*" color-coded to indicate placement.

The next visual, Exhibit 3.40, involves a sentence-start comparison, and can be displayed for 1-word, 2-word, and 3-word sentence starts. The "Count Start-of-Sentence Phrases" button was selected and resulted in Exhibit 3.40. The phrases are listed in descending order in total, and also in comparison to other words. The three-word phrase "I don't remember" was used 19 times as the start of a sentence

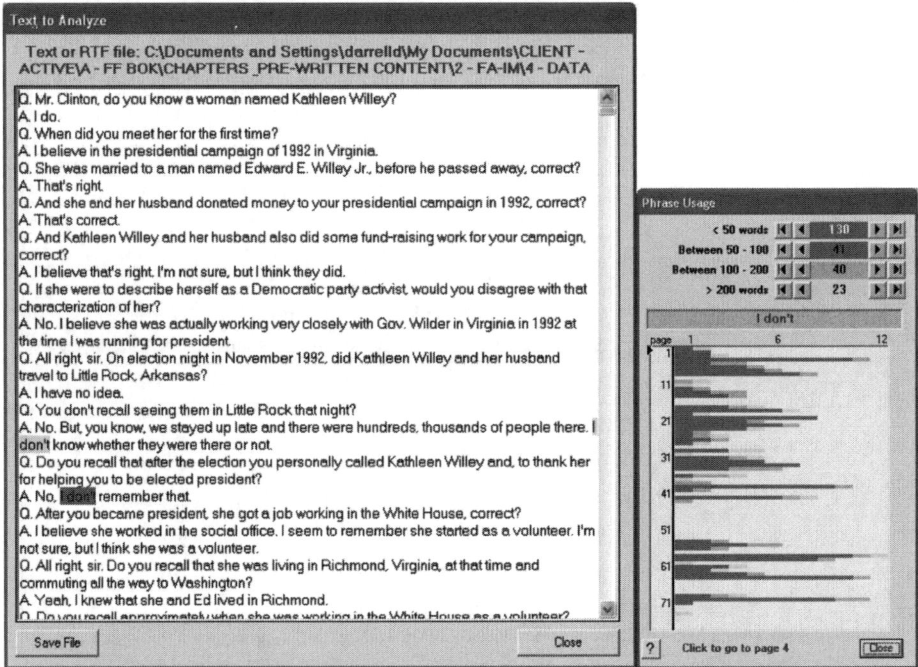

EXHIBIT 3.39 Text to Analyze Box; Phrase Usage Box

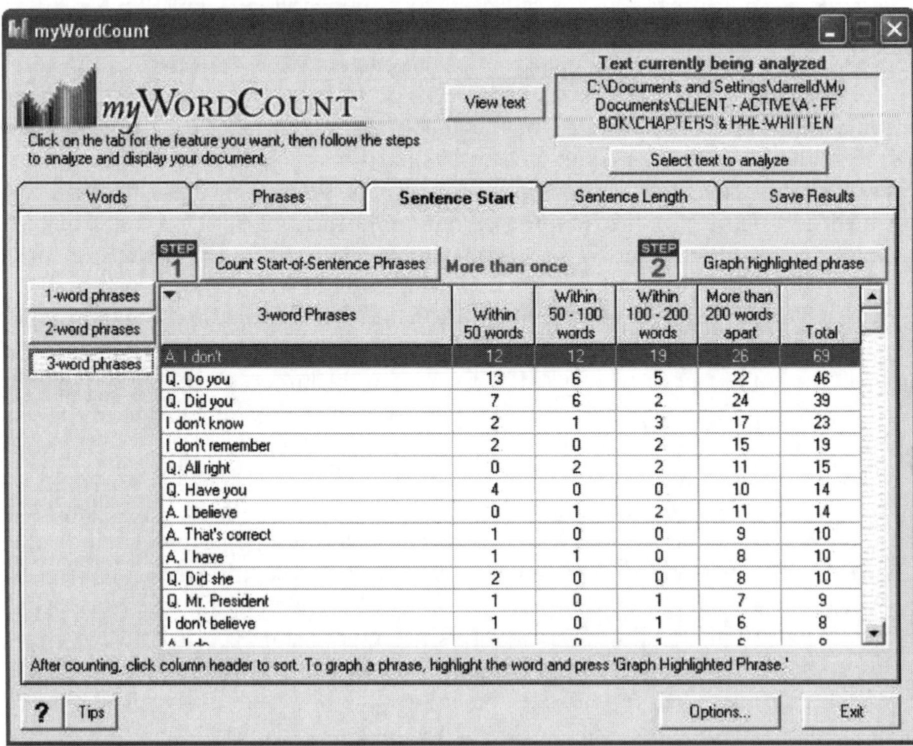

EXHIBIT 3.40 Sentence Start 3-Word Phrases

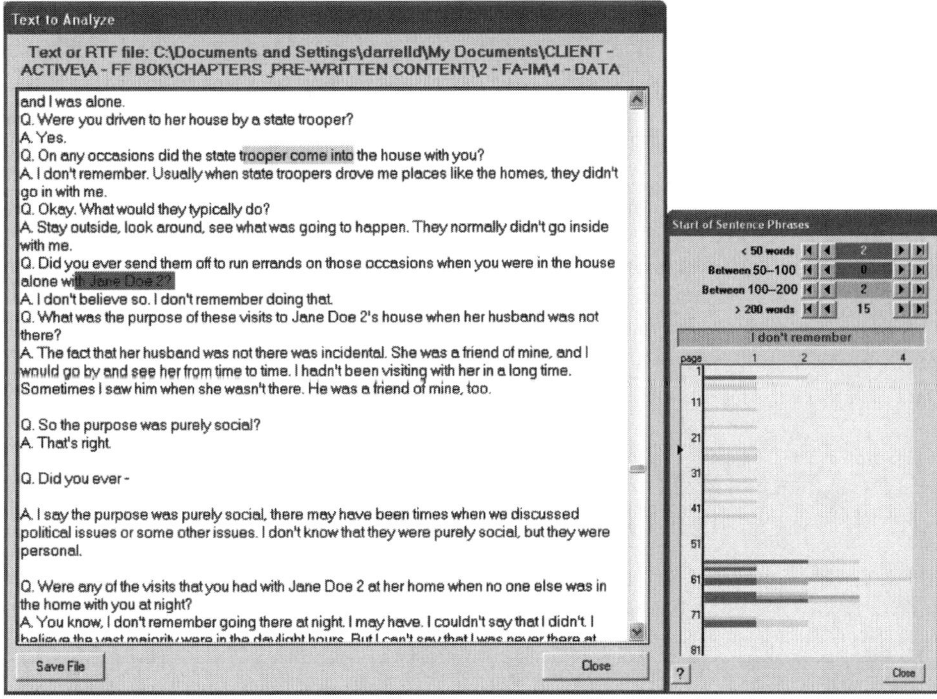

EXHIBIT 3.41 Text to Analyze Box; Start of Sentence Phrases Box

throughout the transcript. The columns can be selected and sorted according to the analysis required. Next, the "Graph Highlighted Phrase" button was selected and resulted in Exhibit 3.41.

The visual produced by the tool is shown in Exhibit 3.41. The bar graph visual contains what would be color-coded references for each page of the transcript, indicating the frequency of occurrence and within the word ranges as indicated. In this case, the "Jane Doe 2" phrase was selected. Simultaneously, the pertinent text (in this case, page 1) is displayed to the left with the word *that* color-coded to indicate placement.

The next visual, Exhibit 3.42, involves a sentence-length analysis. The bar graph illustrates sentence-length comparison throughout the document. In the deposition transcript analyzed, the average sentence was 13.5 words and the longest sentence was 146 words. Knowing that the average sentence length was 13.5 words permits the forensic operator to focus on those sentences that were longer or shorter since they could represent a deviation from the pattern, and a conscious or subconscious motivation by the deponent to distort testimony. In particular, those sentences exceeding 40 words merit further inquiry.

The last visual of myWordCount, Exhibit 3.43, illustrates a wide variety of means by which to capture the analytical results. The output is captured in a convenient format for easy reference and the detail file can be accessed later as necessary, for example, courtroom presentation.

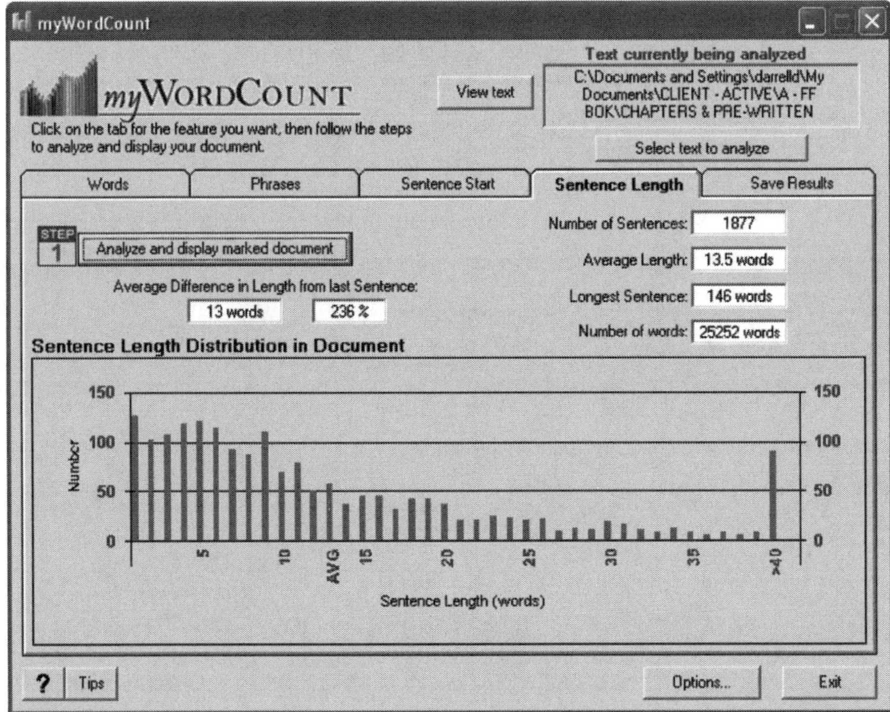

EXHIBIT 3.42 Sentence Length Analysis

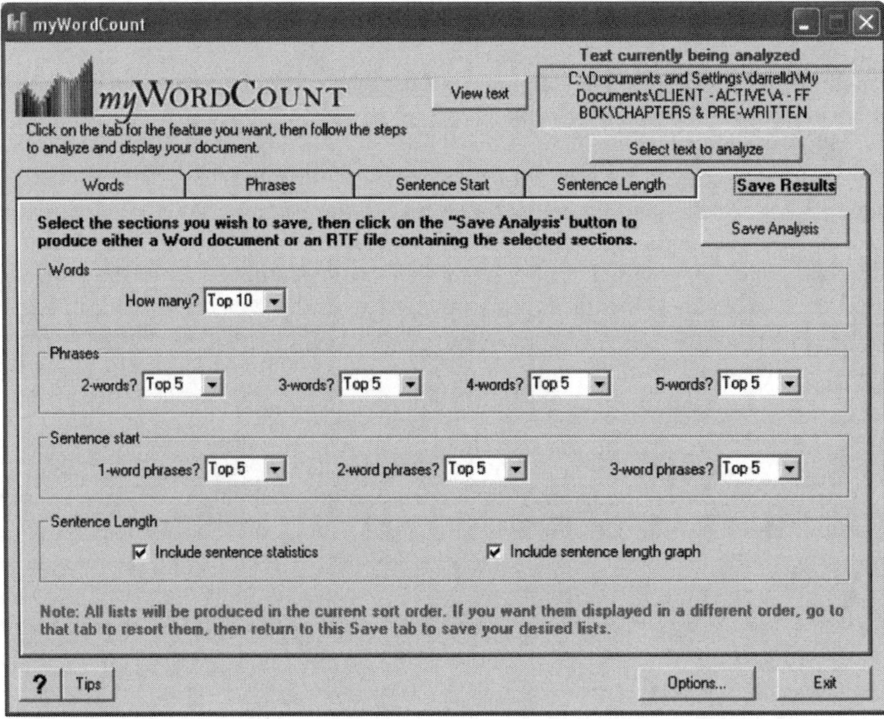

EXHIBIT 3.43 Save Results

The myWordCount software adds a potent weapon to the forensic operator's arsenal. It is very easy to use, very inexpensive, and provides considerable power to analyzing words.

Stylometry Stylometry tests for author authenticity, plagiarism, multiple authors, and other factors. It is commonly employed in universities to test for student plagiarism. It has also been used in high-profile matters, such as determining to what extent Shakespeare was the true author of the various works attributed to him. It has further been applied to other fields, including music and art and is emerging as a tool to analyze financial statement notes. Stylometry can become quite mathematically complex, but access to software has made this technique commonly available to virtually anyone needing to forensically examine the words within a document.

The following example uses a freeware resource known as Signature,[43] authored by Dr. Peter Millican of Oxford University and Dr. Patrick Juola of Duquesne University. Stylometry tests authorship (among other factors) to determine whether a forensic expert's client (attorney or defendant or both) had significant influence in the expert's report wording. In this example, two different reports of different size were purported to be authored by the same opposing expert witness. The two reports were received in hard copy, scanned, and converted to PDF and then text files (.txt), respectively. The text files (BLINDA.txt, and BLINDB.txt), were then loaded into the Signature program and the diagnostics produced as summarized in Exhibit 3.44.

The first test consisted of comparing word count for the two documents. The Signature program conveniently produces visuals supporting its analysis, thus making observations very straightforward. Exhibit 3.44 indicates that BLINDA contained 20,893 words while BLINDB contained 6,133 words. Furthermore, the distributions of the various word lengths are indicated. For example, one-character words (such as I) occurred 4.91 percent and 5.14 percent of the time for BLINDA and BLINDB, respectively. Likewise, six-character words occurred 9.18 percent and 9.16 percent, for BLINDA and BLINDB, respectively. Consequently, word lengths matched very closely within the two documents.

The second test, in Exhibit 3.45 compared the sentence lengths for the two documents. The visual indicates BLINDA contained 1,853 sentences while BLINDB contained 407 sentences. However, sentence lengths between the two documents varied somewhat. Specifically, one-word sentences occurred 24.3 percent and 10.3 percent for BLINDA and BLINDB, respectively. One-word sentences are very unusual, except for explanations such as answers to questions, and headers with a document. Therefore, that disparity could be disregarded based upon the nature of the document.

Other disparities, such as 14-, 15-, 16-, and 17-word sentences, merit attention. BLINDA contained sentences of that length for 4.42 percent, 5.41 percent, 4.18 percent, and 4.42 percent, of the time compared to BLINDB's similar length sentences occurring 1.62 percent, 1.67 percent, 1.89 percent, and 1.83 percent of the time. This disparity suggests authorship differences between the two documents.

The third test, in Exhibit 3.46 compared paragraph lengths for the two documents. The preceding visual indicates a large disparity in one-sentence paragraphs

[43] www.philocomp.net/?pageref=humanities&page=signature.

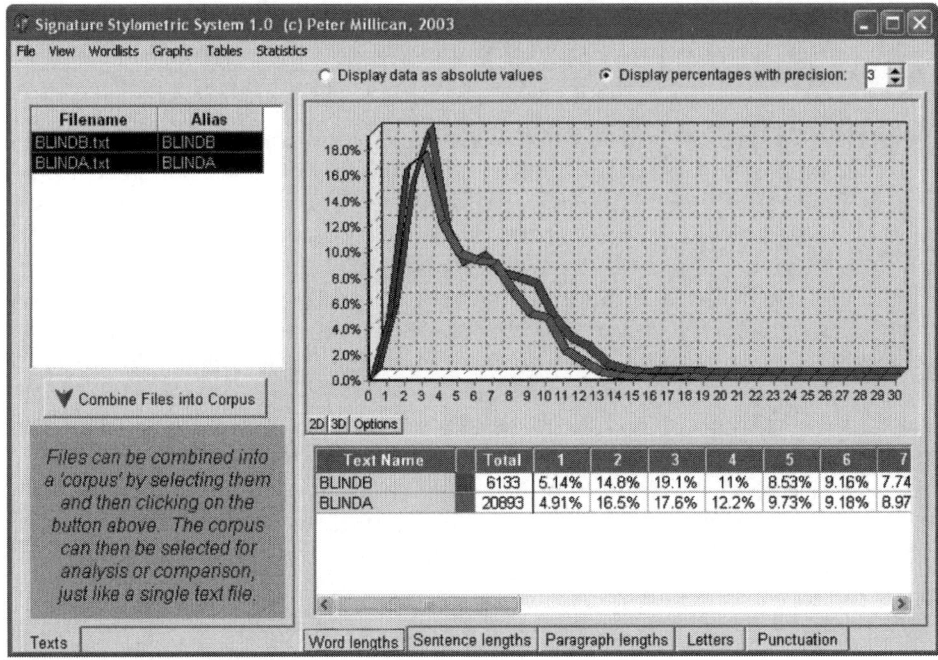

EXHIBIT 3.44 Words and Word Lengths

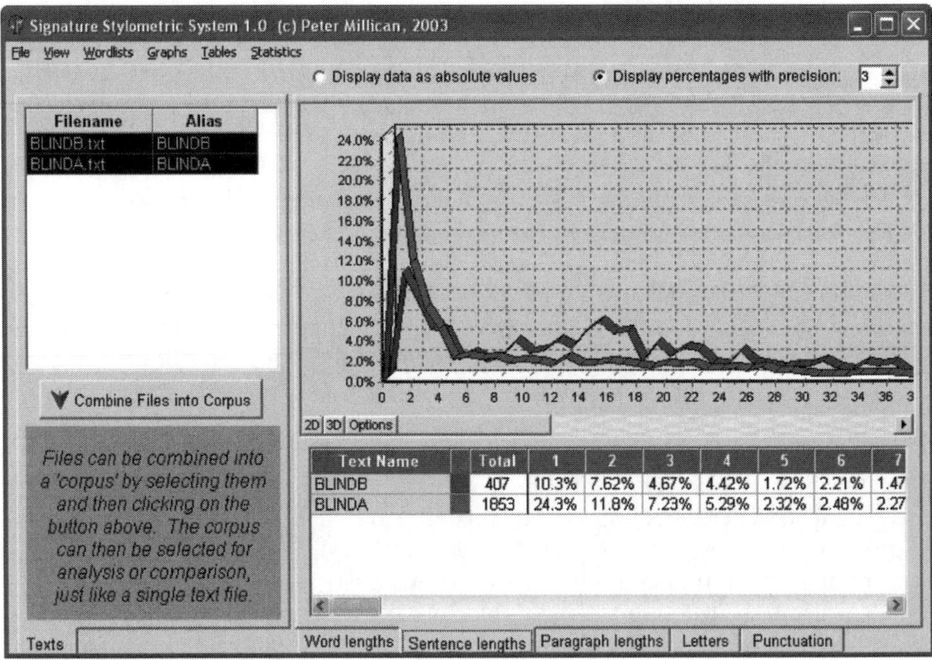

EXHIBIT 3.45 Sentence Lengths

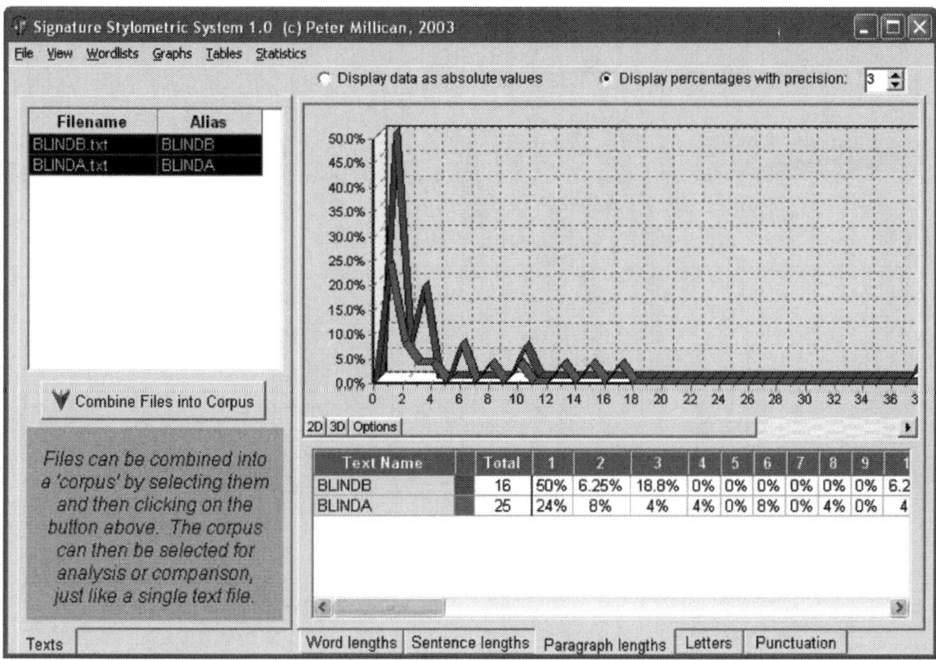

EXHIBIT 3.46 Paragraph Lengths

between the two reports. Based upon the nature the report, the finding can be disregarded since a one-sentence paragraph is relatively unusual, and may also reflect headers within the document. Other disparities such as four-word paragraphs, six-word, and eight-word paragraphs merit attention and suggest different authorship.

The fourth test, in Exhibit 3.47, compared letter usage for the two documents. The comparison indicates strong similarity regarding letter usage except for certain letters, including two vowels, E and O, and three consonants, F, N and S, which demonstrated strong variance. The respective chi-square test discussed later indicates statistically different usage.

The fifth test, in Exhibit 3.48 compared the punctuation usage for the two documents. The visual indicates a large disparity in the use of the period and the dash punctuation. That is, BLINDA used the period a great deal more than BLINDB, while BLINDB used the dash more than BLINDA. BLINDA's usage of the period is easily explained since BLINDA contains 1,853 sentences to BLINDB's 407 sentences. The dash usage disparity is unusual, however, since that type of punctuation is a personal style matter rather than a word count matter. Consequently, the dash disparity suggests different authors and suggests different authors, depending upon the nature of the documents.

The sixth test, Exhibit 3.49, displayed punctuation and keywords to compare the two documents. The forensic operator then prepared a word list and produced the following output after running the analysis.

The seventh test, Exhibit 3.50, compared the usage of seven keywords between the two documents. Obvious disparities include words such as *sales, expense, exhibit, respectively,* and others between the two documents. Since keywords are highly

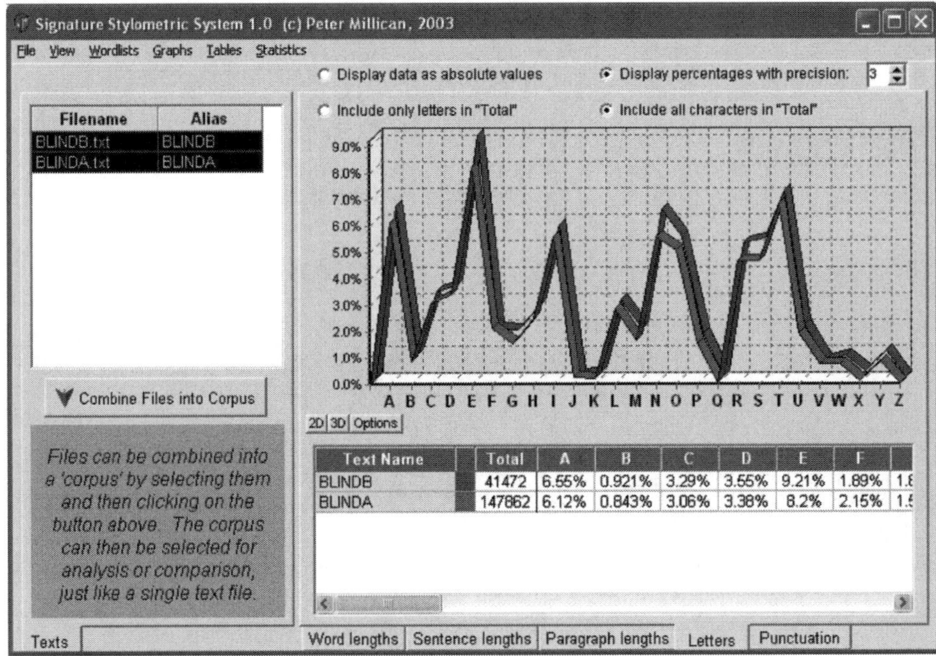

EXHIBIT 3.47 Letters

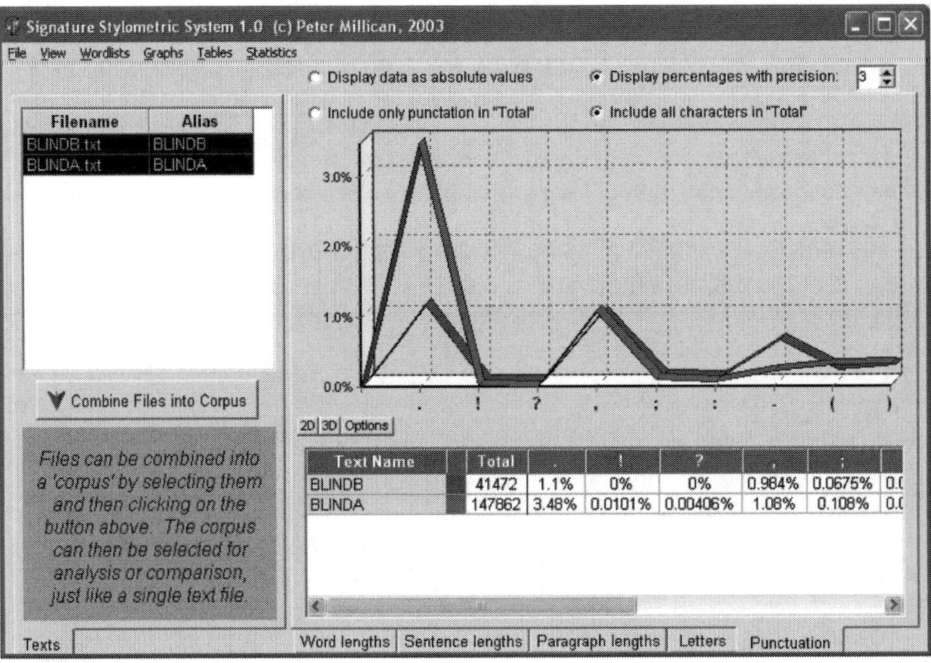

EXHIBIT 3.48 Punctuation

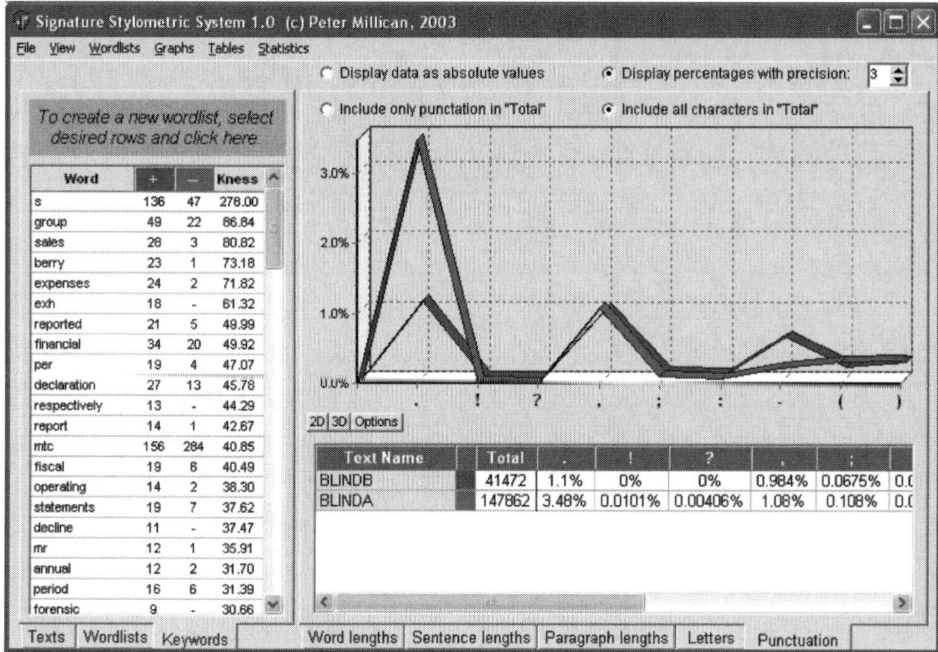

EXHIBIT 3.49 Punctuation and Key Words

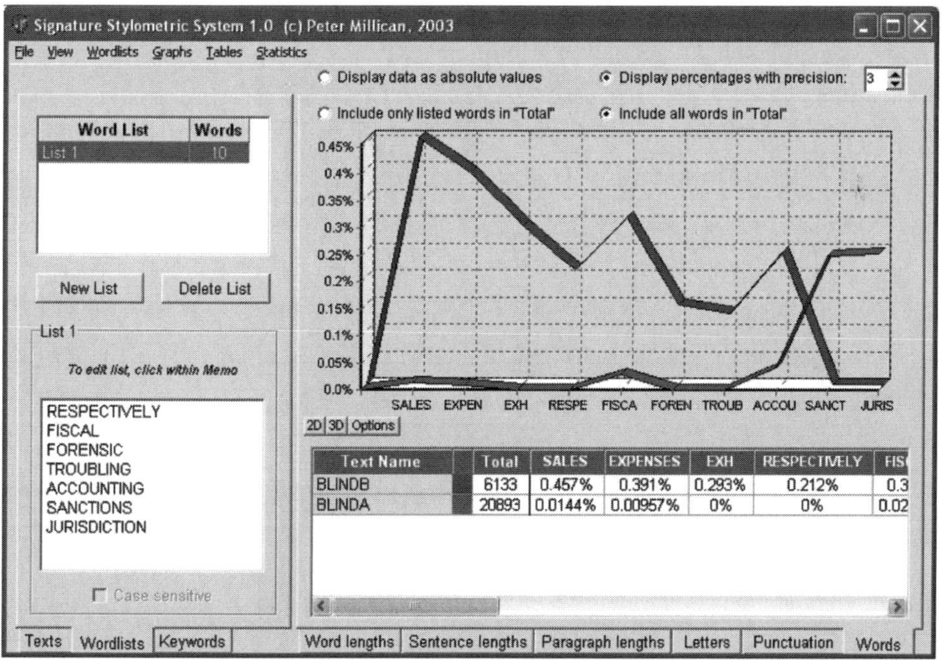

EXHIBIT 3.50 Word Selections

Chi-square significance test

Choice of Texts

Sample text: BLINDB

Reference text: BLINDA

Swap

Include sample in reference (if not already)

The chi-square test is available only if exactly two texts have been selected for analysis. When this is the case, the controls below will automatically test for significance based on the parameters entered.

Apply Yates' correction to chi-square

Choice of Data Columns

Apply chi-square test to all data columns

Select columns from 2 to 8

Treatment of unselected columns

Ignore unselected columns

Treat others as one data column

Separate others into lower/higher

Columns: 7 Degrees of freedom: 6 Chi-square: 33.328

The aim of this test is to assess the significance of the measured differences between the 'sample' and the 'reference' texts.

In this case the difference is very highly significant, at the 0.1% (0.001) level. Chi-Square 0.1% value = 22.46

Word lengths | Sentence lengths | Paragraph lengths | Letters | Punctuation | Words

EXHIBIT 3.51 Chi-Square Significance Test—Columns 2 to 8 (Word Lengths)

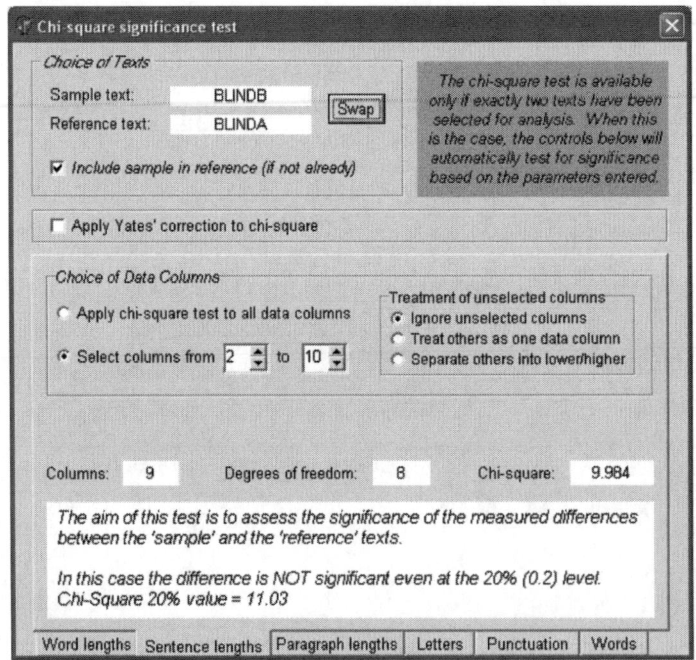

EXHIBIT 3.52 Chi-Square Significance Test—Columns 2 to 10 (Sentence Lengths)

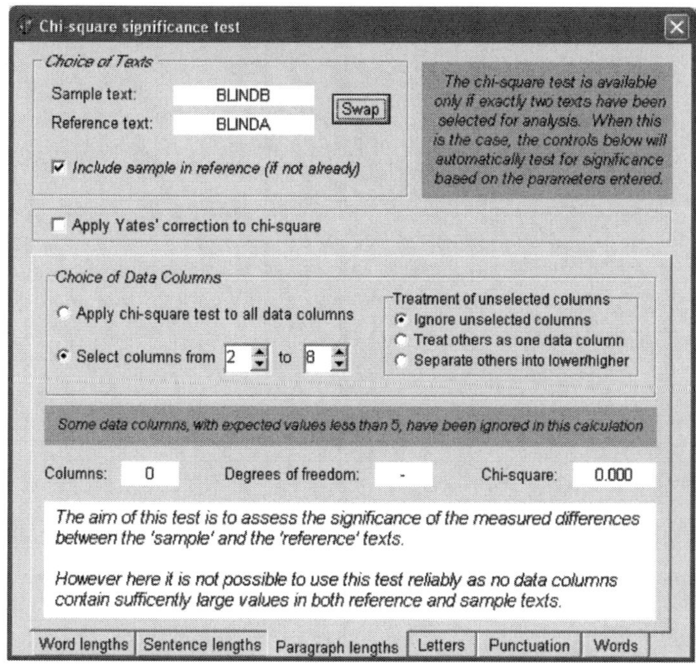

EXHIBIT 3.53 Chi-Square Significance Test—Columns 2 to 8 (Paragraph Lengths)

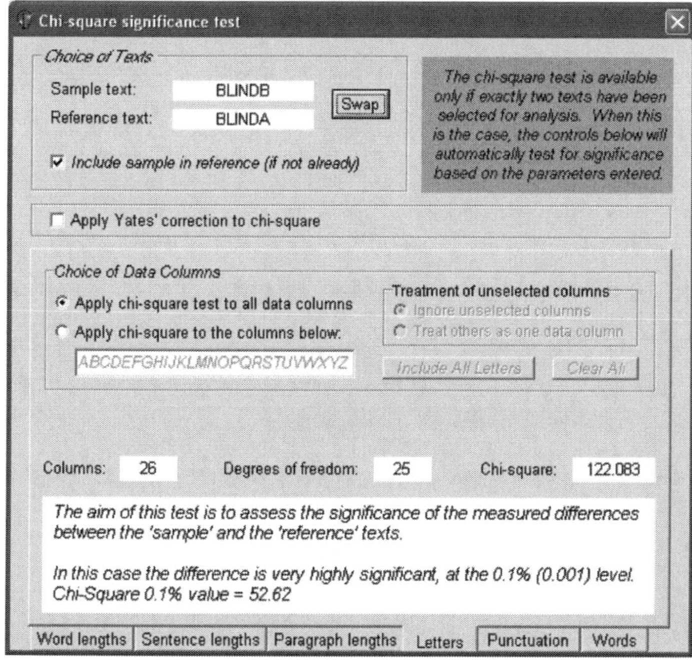

EXHIBIT 3.54 Chi-Square Significance Test (Letters)

Chi-square significance test

Choice of Texts

Sample text: BLINDB

Reference text: BLINDA

Swap

Include sample in reference (if not already)

The chi-square test is available only if exactly two texts have been selected for analysis. When this is the case, the controls below will automatically test for significance based on the parameters entered.

Apply Yates' correction to chi-square

Choice of Data Columns

Apply chi-square test to all data columns

Apply chi-square to the columns below:

. ! ? , ; : - ( )

Treatment of unselected columns

Ignore unselected columns

Treat others as one data column

Include All Punct'n

Clear All

Some data columns, with expected values less than 5, have been ignored in this calculation

Columns: 7 Degrees of freedom: 6 Chi-square: 628.510

The aim of this test is to assess the significance of the measured differences between the 'sample' and the 'reference' texts.

In this case the difference is very highly significant, at the 0.1% (0.001) level. Chi-Square 0.1% value = 22.46

Word lengths | Sentence lengths | Paragraph lengths | Letters | Punctuation | Words

EXHIBIT 3.55 Chi-Square Significance Test (Punctuation)

Chi-square significance test

Choice of Texts

Sample text: BLINDB

Reference text: BLINDA

Swap

Include sample in reference (if not already)

The chi-square test is available only if exactly two texts have been selected for analysis. When this is the case, the controls below will automatically test for significance based on the parameters entered.

Apply Yates' correction to chi-square

Choice of Data Columns

Apply chi-square test to all data columns

Apply chi-square to the columns below:

Treatment of unselected columns

Ignore unselected columns

Treat others as one data column

Include All Words

Clear All

Some data columns, with expected values less than 5, have been ignored in this calculation

Columns: 8 Degrees of freedom: 7 Chi-square: 182.972

The aim of this test is to assess the significance of the measured differences between the 'sample' and the 'reference' texts.

In this case the difference is very highly significant, at the 0.1% (0.001) level. Chi-Square 0.1% value = 24.32

Word lengths | Sentence lengths | Paragraph lengths | Letters | Punctuation | Words

EXHIBIT 3.56 Chi-Square Significance Test (Words)

Measurement	BLINDA	BLINDB	Comments	Difference? Yes	Difference? No	Explanation
Word Count	20,893	6,133		n/a		
Word Length	Relatively similar		One-character word % similar		X	
Sentence Count	1,853	407		n/a		
Sentence Length	4.6%	1.8%	14-17 word sentences averaged	X		
Paragraph Count	25	16	Disparaty due to text headers	n/a		
Paragraph Length			Disparity due to style differences	n/a		
Character Count	147,862	41,472	Nearly identical	n/a		
Character Usage						
Punctuation Usage			Disparity due to size difference	n/a		
Key Word Usage:						
Sales	0.01%	0.46%		X		
Expenses	0.01%	0.39%		X		
Exh	0.00%	0.23%		X		
Respectively	0.00%	0.21%		X		
			Total	**5**	**1**	
Chi-Square						
Word Length	33.328		Very highly significant at 0.1% level	X		See one-character comment, above
Sentence Length	9.984		Difference NOT significant even at 20% level		X	
Paragraph Length	0		Insufficient data	n/a		
Character Usage	122.083		Very highly significant at 0.1% level	X		
Punctuation Usage	628.51		Very highly significant at 0.1% level	X		
Word Usage	182.972		Very highly significant at 0.1% level	X		
			Total	**4**	**1**	

EXHIBIT 3.57 Word Count, Word Length, Sentence Count, and So On

representative of personal style, the preceding results strongly suggest involvement from two different authors. Such findings go beyond mere intuition such as when the forensic operator may be tempted to observe that a nonfinancial party would be less inclined to use financial terms. Although this is a logical observation, it takes on more legitimacy through the empirical testing and measurements discussed by the remainder of this section.

Statistical significance determines to what extent, if any, variance exists among the various tests already displayed. The following statistical conclusions use chi-square to determine whether or not statistical significance is evidenced in the data.

The first chi-square test, Exhibit 3.51, indicates that the word length difference is very highly significant and thus shows legitimate disparity.

The second chi-square test, Exhibit 3.52, indicates that the sentence length difference is not as significant, and this cannot be used to determine author composition.

The third chi-square test, Exhibit 3.53, indicates that analysis cannot be complete because of a lack of sufficiently large values.

The fourth chi-square test, Exhibit 3.54, indicates that the letter usage difference is very highly significant, which suggests that the two documents reflect different authors.

The fifth chi-square test, Exhibit 3.55, indicates that the punctuation usage difference is very highly significant, which suggests that the two documents reflect different authors.

The sixth chi-square test, in Exhibit 3.56, indicates that the word usage difference is very highly significant, which suggests that the two documents reflect different authors.

Exhibit 3.57 is a comparative summary that captures output from both myWordCount and Stylometry analysis. The column labeled "Difference?" demonstrates that both myWordCount and Stylometry found distinct differences between BLINDA and BLINDB, thus indicating different authors. The preceding example illustrates how even simple analysis can yield insights that would otherwise simply not be available. Stylometry can become much more complex, yet the cited example should provide sufficient motivation to begin applying the tool in forensic matters.

CONCLUSION

This phase, Part I of Data Collection and Analysis, introduced forensic operators to the rationale and logical approach to analytical methods. At this point, even jaded and seemingly experienced forensic operators realize that a vast repertoire of tools, techniques, methods, and methodologies exists beyond the tools they have routinely deployed for years. This does not necessarily suggest that they were performing inadequate work, rather that new horizons for exploration and learning are virtually unlimited.

The next section, Part II of Data Collection and Analysis, takes analytical tools even further. It introduces additional new tools, techniques, methods, and methodologies for deployment to not-yet-discussed realms of investigation.

CHAPTER 4

Data Collection and Analysis Phase: Part II

This chapter continues the data collection and analysis tasks within a forensic assignment. In addition, it contains submethodologies and other instructive techniques for analyzing financial reporting usable with ICE/SCORE. Experienced forensic operators should not presume to know the techniques discussed in this chapter. A small time investment yields substantial returns for anyone taking the time to peruse the guidance.

This chapter also contains instructive content for nonfinancial types, say detectives who have little or no financial or accounting background. For example, step-by-step techniques simplify how nearly all types of financial reporting are readily analyzed. The 60-Second Method and BIC technique quickly illustrate the approach. Other contents also provide useful reference for clients and others seeking assistance from forensic operators.

ANALYSIS OF TRANSACTIONS STAGE

Purpose of Stage

This action continues the forensic assignment using the tools, techniques, methods and methodologies described below. See Exhibit 4.1.

The objective of this action is to apply specifically pertinent technical methods pursuant to the assignment execution.

Specific actions include:

- Obtain sufficient relevant data to provide credible evidence.
- Apply the specific tools as required.

References

This action accommodates application of pertinent technical references, whether currently available or requiring acquisition.

The objective of this action is to ensure that necessary technical resources are identified and applied.

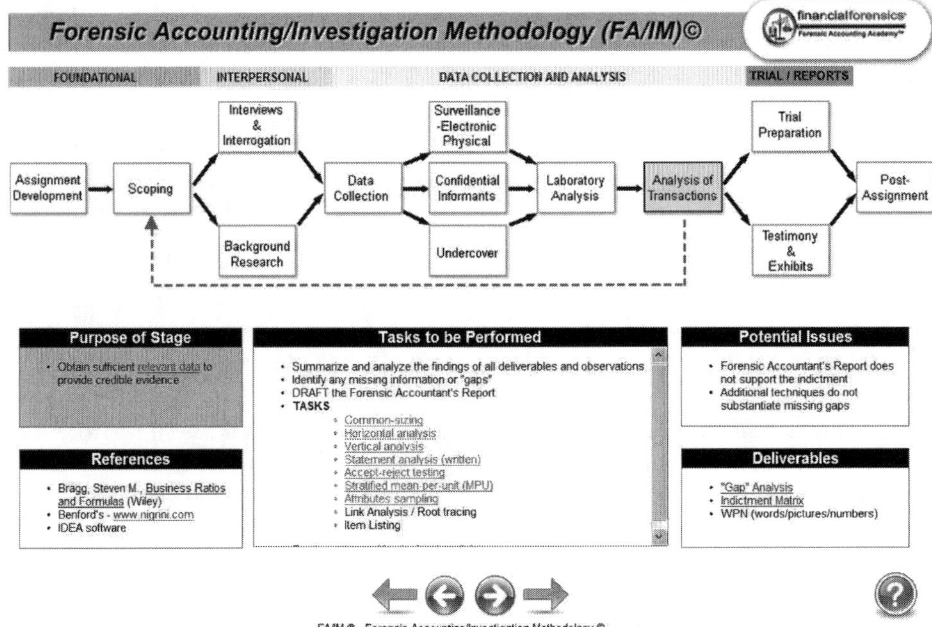

EXHIBIT 4.1 Analysis of Transactions

Example of Reference Sources The following reference sources serve to jumpstart the forensic operator. The Key Internet Sites and Key Reference Materials are not all-inclusive, but provide starting points from which to build resources. Also, refer to the bibliography.

Key Internet sites

- All forensic operators
  www.audimation.com
  www.financialforensicsacademy.com
  www.khanacademy.com
  www.nigrini.com
  www.statstoft.com

Key Reference materials

- All forensic operators
  - *Analyzing Financial Statements*, by American Bankers Association
  - *Business Ratios and Formulas 2nd ed.*, by Steven M. Bragg
  - *Financial Forensics Body of Knowledge,* by Darrell D. Dorrell and Gregory A. Gadawski
  - *Income Reconstruction: A Guide to Discovering Unreported Income.* by Kalman Barson
  - *Statistics Hacks*, by Bruce Frey
  - *The Cartoon Guide to Statistics*, by Larry Gonick and Woollcott Smith
  - *The Classic 1934 Edition - Security Analysis*, by Benjamin Graham and David Dodd

Tasks to Be Performed

This action outlines likely tasks but is not an all-inclusive checklist since each forensic assignment is unique. Use the tasks as a guideline and modify according to the unique facts and circumstances of the assignment.

The objective of this action is to ensure that the forensic operator considers the assignment requirements from inception to completion to ensure efficient and effective techniques application.

Specific actions include:

- Perform any additional indirect or direct analytical forensic techniques as needed.
- Validate and correlate prior data obtained through alternate techniques.
- Summarize and analyze the findings of all deliverables and observations
- Identify any missing information or "gaps"
- DRAFT findings or conclusions

Potential Issues

This action prompts the forensic operator to consider the implications of available data within the context of applicable and defensible techniques.

The objective of this action is to ensure that the forensic operator maximizes the complement of data and techniques.

Specific potential issues include:

- Indirect analytical techniques are inconclusive.
- Direct techniques do not support the indictment.

Deliverables

The objective of this action is to identify and eventually finalize deliverables pertinent to the assignment. The forensic operator always develops deliverables designed with the end in mind so as to maximize efficiency.

The objective of this action is to progressively develop analytical results within the context of likely output.

Specific actions include:

- Documented results.
- Validation and correlation of prior data and deliverables.

THE MYTH OF INTERNAL CONTROL

The general public holds auditors responsible for fraud detection, despite auditors' adamant insistence to the contrary. The concept of internal control, foundational to audit opinions is likewise misunderstood. The confusion exists even within the auditing profession regarding the definition of internal control, as evidenced by the contents of this section. Therefore, this section is a primer for those unfamiliar with a fundamental accounting and auditing concept, internal control. To know that it is also a necessary refresher for everyone else—including accountants and auditors—surprises many.

WAR STORY

One of the authors trained the audit department of an accounting firm in forensic techniques. While discussing their firm's internal control checklist, the author noted there were no tasks listed to learn the operations of the subject business or its industry. When he asked a lead auditor how he learned about each business under audit, the auditor replied, "Well, I am not expected to really *understand* the business—I just 'audit' it."

That observation results from various acknowledgments of confusion in the literature, including COSO, AICPA, and the SEC:

> *Over the last several years,* some auditors have expressed confusion *relating to the concept of internal control and, specifically, internal control over financial reporting as well as documenting their understanding of internal control.* Part of this confusion *may arise from the definition of internal control itself.*[1] *(Emphasis added.)*
>
> *Internal control* means different things to different people. *This causes* confusion *among businesspeople, legislators, regulators and others. The resulting miscommunication and different expectations cause problems within an enterprise. Problems are compounded when the term, if not clearly defined, is written into law, regulation or rule.*[2] *(Emphasis added.)*
>
> *Over the last several years, practitioners in public practice* have expressed confusion *relating to the concept of internal control and, specifically, internal control over financial reporting.*[3] *(Emphasis added.)*
>
> *As noted in the Proposing Release, there's been* some confusion over *the exact meaning and scope of the term* internal control, *because the definition of the term has evolved over time.... From the outset, it was recognized that internal control is a broad concept that extends beyond the accounting functions of a company.*[4] *(Emphasis added.)*

---

[1] "Identifying and Communicating Internal Control Deficiencies under SAS 115," American Institute of Certified Public Accountants, Lewisville, Texas, 2011, adapted from Thomas A. Ratcliffe and Charles E. Landes, "Understanding Internal Control and Internal Control Services" (AICPA, 2009) and COSO's "Internal Control over Financial Reporting—Guidance for Smaller Public Companies" vol. 1, Executive Summary (2006).

[2] "Internal Control—Integrated Framework," The Committee of Sponsoring Organizations of the Treadway Commission (COSO), 1992, 1994, page 3, www.coso.org.

[3] Thomas A. Ratcliffe, and Charles E. Landes, "Understanding Internal Control and Internal Control Services," *Journal of Accountancy*, White Paper, September 2009.

[4] "Final Rule: Management's Report on Internal Control over Financial Reporting and Certification of Disclosure and Exchange Act Periodic Reports," Securities and Exchange Commission (SEC), August 14, 2003.

If auditors are confused, what is everyone else's understanding? And, more important, what can clarify the matter? The phrase "Those who cannot remember the past are condemned to repeat it"[5] is particularly appropriate for internal control and gives us direction. Therefore, this section brings readers up to date on internal control, starting with its recent origin in 1949. Then, observations are crystallized and addressed with specific recommendations to remedy the circumstances.

Historical Development

Internal control is a newborn concept compared to the long existence of accounting and reporting techniques. Artifacts from antiquity indicate that accounting-related procedures paralleled the development of civilization and were integral to a civilized society's growth. For example, Tally sticks representing records of commerce in the Mesopotamian Valley date to about 3500 BC.[6]

Curiously, many accounting historians point to the "... first signs of internal control ..."[7] since that period, and many subsequent articles refer to the signs of internal control without evidence of its existence. This is not to criticize the many authors, but rather to note that the "signs" to which they refer did not relate to internal control as we know it. Instead, the procedures they noted were more "checks and balances" focused than internal control focused. It is as if the authors retroactively imputed internal control to the circumstances. The contents of ancient records reflect obvious checks and balances such as separation of duties, oversight, and outside accountability.[8] However, there is no mention of the concept of internal control similar to its use today, until the 1949 definition posited by the American Institute of Accountants. Consequently, the view that internal controls have long existed is not accurate, especially with respect to the term's contemporary usage.

Professor David Hay's[9] "Internal Control: How It Evolved in Four English-Speaking Countries" contains a particularly on-point history of internal control development. Dr. Hay is the head of the Department of Accounting and Finance, and is professor of auditing at the University of Auckland, New Zealand. Highlights of his work summarize a pre-1992 chronology, which follows, and the reader is encouraged to acquire a copy of his work for more detail.

- *1920s* and *1930s*—Internal control was first included in professional statements. Also, audit procedures began to focus more on financial reporting rather than financial fraud.

[5] George Santayana, *Reason in Common Sense*, vol. 1, *The Life of Reason*, 1905.

[6] Nicholas Apostolou and D. Larry Crumbley, "The Tally Stick: The First Internal Control?" *The Forensic Examiner* (Spring 2008): 60–62.

[7] Willard E. Stone, "Antecedents of the Accounting Profession," *Accounting Review* (April 1969): 284–285.

[8] T. A. Lee, *Journal of Accounting Research* 9, no. 1 (Spring, 1971): 150–157.

[9] David Hay, "Internal Control: How It Evolved in Four English-Speaking Countries," *Accounting Historians Journal* 20, no. 1 (June 1993).

- *1936*—The American Institute of Accountants (predecessor to the American Institute of Certified Public Accountants) defined "internal check and control" as:

  > *Those measures and methods adopted within the organization itself to* safeguard the cash and other assets *of the company as well as to check the clerical aspects of the book-keeping [AIA 1951]. (Emphasis added.)*

  Note the reference to "... safeguard the cash and other assets ... "
- *1949*—the American Institute of Accountants issued its definition of internal control:

  > *Internal control comprises the plan of organization and all of the coordinate methods and measures adopted within a business to* safeguard its assets, *check the* accuracy and reliability *of its accounting data, promote operational efficiency, and encourage adherence to prescribed management policies [AIA 1949, 6]. (Emphasis added.)*

  Note the references to "... safeguard its assets ...," and "... accuracy and reliability ..."
- *1958*—The AICPA (the 1957 successor to the American Institute of Accountants) narrowed the definition and divided internal control into two parts: accounting controls and administrative controls. The committee on auditing procedure stated that an auditor is primarily concerned with accounting controls "*... because they bear directly on the reliability of financial data*" [AICPA 1958, 67].
- *1973*—The AICPA modified the definition and revised the distinction between accounting control and administrative control. One objective of internal control, the "*safeguarding of assets,*" was *narrowed* to "*the procedures and records* that are concerned with *safeguarding assets.*" (Emphasis added.)
- *1977*—The Foreign Corrupt Practices Act was enacted. It required corporations to comply with the AICPA's 1973 definition of internal accounting control.
- *1985*—The National Commission on Fraudulent Financial Reporting (Treadway Commission) was set up by the AICPA and other accounting organizations. The commission commented that instances of fraudulent financial reporting involved transactions "*under management's direct control and not part of the system of internal accounting controls.*" [National Commission on Fraudulent Financial Reporting 1987, 29–30].
- *1988*—The AICPA replaced the definition of internal control with the new, broader description of "*internal control structure.*" SAS No. 55 contained language, including "... the policies and procedures established to provide reasonable assurance that specific entity objectives will be achieved." SAS number 55 also changed the standard concerning internal control for generally accepted auditing standards. Previously, "a proper study and evaluation" was the operative language, which was replaced by "a sufficient understanding of the internal control structure." The change was not intended to imply that a reduced scope was required. AICPA officeholders described the intent of the change "to broaden the auditor's responsibility to consider internal control and planning" [Guy and

Sullivan 1988, 38] and "expanding the auditor's responsibility for determining how internal control works." [Temkin and Winters 1998, 86.]

- *1992*—The Committee of Sponsoring Organizations of the Treadway Commission (COSO) produced the "Internal Control—Integrated Framework," redefining internal control. The following extract comes from Chapter 1, but the document requires reading in its entirety (163 pages) to attempt grasping the gist of their definition. The accompanying evaluation tools workbook comprises 209 pages. Therefore, 372 pages are necessary to define and describe internal control.

> *Internal control is defined as a* process, *effected by an entity's people, designed to accomplish specific objectives. The definition is broad, encompassing all aspects of controlling a business, yet facilitates a directed focus on specific objectives. Internal control consists of five interrelated components, which are inherent in the way management runs the enterprise. The components are linked and serve as criteria for determining whether the system is effective. (COSO 1992, 1994). (Emphasis added.)*

The five components described by the COSO document include:

1. Control environment.
2. Risk assessment.
3. Control activities.
4. Information and communication.
5. Monitoring.
   - *2002*—Congress enacted the Sarbanes-Oxley Act (SOX) in reaction to corporate financial scandals, including Adelphia, Enron, Tyco, and WorldCom. The Act intended to "protect investors by improving the accuracy and reliability of corporate disclosures made pursuant to the securities laws." Section 404 of the Act is unquestionably the most expensive and time-consuming aspect of SOX implementation. Section 404 requires management's assessment of the company's controls, referred to in Section 302. The details for both management and auditors were determined by accounting firms under close oversight of a specially created organization, the Public Company Accounting Oversight Board (PCAOB).
   - *2002*—The AICPA released SAS No. 99, "Consideration of Fraud in a Financial Statement Audit," superseding SAS No. 82, which took effect on December 15, 1997. It was released coincident to, and likely resulting from, the same financial scandals that propelled Congress to enact SOX. SAS No. 99 comprises 52 pages and more than 25,000 words. It uses the term *brainstorming* one time, and the term *forensic* one time. Neither of the words is defined, but it refers to brainstorming as "An exchange of ideas..." The creator of brainstorming, however, Alex Osborn, defined a formalized process to be deployed before brainstorming activity is effective.
   - *2009*—The AICPA released "Understanding Internal Control and Internal Control Services," a White Paper. This document attempts to explain the intent of the integrated framework.

- From 2003 to date, several corporate scandals take the measure of previous internal control efforts, including Royal Ahold; Parmalat; Health South; Nortel; Chiquita Brands; AIG; Bernie Madoff; Anglo-Irish Bank; Siemens; Satyam Computer Services; Lehman Brothers; Group Danone; Hewlett-Packard; and foreclosure-related scandals, including Fannie Mae, Freddie Mac, GMAC, Bank of America, JPMorgan, and Wells Fargo, among others. The list could be longer; the SEC filed 681 enforcement cases for FY2010.[10] Nonetheless, the point is served.

Observations

Based upon the preceding and many years of professional experience, the authors observe certain key implications of internal control. They are organized into three categories, societal, economic, and professional factors, as follows.

Societal Factors The key societal factors identified by the authors include:

- The public continues to believe that auditors are responsible for finding fraud during an audit. This is not an observation resulting from empirical analysis. Rather, it is gleaned from many years of professional experience and encounters with all spectrums of people.
- The public's expectations of auditors' capabilities are set by media and entertainment sources, thus increasing the chasm between expectations and auditors' existing skill sets.
- The auditing profession continues to distance itself from the public's fraud expectations and away from safeguarding company assets toward increased accuracy and reliability in financial reporting.
- Post-secondary curricula have not kept pace instructing students in the wide variety of forensic tools, techniques, methods, and methodologies that identify earnings manipulation.

Economic Factors The key economic factors identified by the authors include:

- Following World War II, the U.S. economy, market, and population have grown in size, complexity, reliance upon technology, and widely varying levels of sophistication. These conditions make it less and less feasible that auditing can be conducted merely by "pick-and-shovel manpower," and thus must rely more heavily on forensic tools, techniques, methods, and methodologies.
- The public increasingly relies on capital markets as a source of personal wealth, directly related to long-term and retirement finances. Consequently, significant declines tend to attract a great deal of attention.

---

[10] "FY 2010 Performance and Accountability Report," United States Securities and Exchange Commission, page 11.

Professional Factors

- The accounting and auditing professions continue to confuse fraud and forensics, focusing most effort on fraud activities. However, forensic tools, techniques, methods, and methodologies are much more comprehensive and effective and more suited to audit risk assessment and testing than fraud concepts. Interestingly, regulators and law enforcement have recognized the benefits of forensics and begun incorporating them into policies and procedures.
- Internal control is a relatively new (1949) and complex compilation of concepts, deficient in specific tools, techniques, methods, and methodologies.
- Legislative efforts and cumbersome guidance within the accounting profession have confused all parties regarding the scope and implications of internal control.

It makes little sense to identify a significant problem(s) without offering a solution(s). Therefore, the authors identify three steps essential to changing the status quo.

First, auditors must immediately implement legitimate forensic (beyond mere fraud) techniques throughout the entire process of auditing. This ranges from risk assessment through audit testing within the subject environment. Such techniques need not be complex, however. It is clear that the present complement of concepts used in auditing are simply insufficient and must be augmented by more appropriate forensic tools, techniques, methods, and methodologies.

Second, post-secondary education curricula must immediately implement education focused on legitimate forensic techniques. As mentioned elsewhere in this book, existing post-secondary and graduate curricula have a handful of programs alleging a forensic emphasis. Unfortunately, the vast majority these programs are merely accounting courses wrapped around one or two fraud (not forensic) courses.

Finally, financial information, users, and regulators should simply avoid being surprised until, and if, things change. It is clear that the present state of affairs is inadequate and will continue so until legitimate forensic tools, techniques, methods, and methodologies are implemented as integral to the audit process.

FINANCIAL STATEMENTS—WRITTEN CONFESSIONS

This is a training tool that the authors use to instruct parties seeking basic to intermediate level knowledge, for example, attorneys, during CPE sessions. According to textbooks, "Accounting is the language of business." This presumes a working knowledge of the mechanics of such a language. And unless you have extensive experience or hands-on training, developing a working knowledge is a challenge.

Most sessions on accounting and finance focus on the construction of the financial statements. However, unless you plan on a career in accounting, you do not need to construct the financials—you only need to know how to *read* the financials. This is particularly important in litigation matters, since the foundational assets and income stream must be translated into financial measures, typically consisting of financial statements. See Exhibit 4.2.

EXHIBIT 4.2 Financial Reporting Review Objectives

The Questions That You Must Answer	Explanation	The Tools You Will Receive During this Session
How do you read financial statements?	You must have some familiarity with financial statement composition in order to request the right data. You must then interpret what the financials claim to be telling you in order to validate them.	The 60-Second Method of financial statement analysis. A discovery checklist that you can modify as required.
How do you critique financial statements?	Even if you can interpret the financials, you must then convey your knowledge to the court, jury, or others lacking accounting and financial knowledge.	A completely preformatted example of what should be given to you. Visual techniques that convey the picture.
How are financial statements applied in litigation matters?	Financial statements can be applied in a myriad of litigation matters from personal injury to trademark infringement. You need to understand the "what, when, and how" of the application of financial data as pertinent to each matter.	Discussion regarding guidelines for application of financial statement data to applicable matters. A public *and* private question-and-answer session.

Therefore, this session will explore:

- How to read (interpret and analyze) financial statements.
- How to critique the financial statements.
- Use of financial statements in litigation-related matters.

How Do You Read Financial Statements?

There are a few key guidelines to keep in mind when financial information is necessary for your matter. The following items summarize the main guidelines.

1. Accounting and financial information are *not necessarily* the same information. The following definitions explain why:
   a. *Accounting* information is scorekeeping and includes financial statements (see further on) and is prepared by CPAs who are historians.
   b. *Financial* information is analytical and may include comparative and prospective financial statements.
2. The reason for the preparation of the accounting and financial information determines its results. For example:

a. By definition, income tax returns tend to *minimize* (legally, of course) taxable income, thus minimizing the income taxes paid. This is primarily a delaying tactic that results in account categories such as deferred taxes.
b. Other financial statements, for example, audited, reviewed, or compiled financial statements, *may* tend to *maximize* (legally, of course) income, especially if publicly held. These statements are intended to portray the results for third parties such as lenders or investors, or both, thus maximizing income.
c. Over long time periods, the two sources will not be materially different. But in the short term, they can be very different. The differences (primarily timing and recognition) can always be reconciled and thus explained. This presumes that the books are completely maintained.

3. You must have the Big Three financial statements in order to develop a complete picture of your matter. They are best remembered by the acronym BIC, indicating the *B*alance Sheet, the *I*ncome Statement, and the *C*ash Flow Statement, as follows:
   a. Balance Sheet—A snapshot of an organization's financial position at a specific point in time. Assets = Liabilities + Owner's Equity.
   b. Income Statement—Captures an organization's operating results over a period of time, shown by revenues and expenditures.
   c. Cash Flow Statement[11]—Reports the company's cash inflows and outflows by category for a specific period of time.
   d. Footnotes—Report any pertinent information explaining or clarifying items contained within the financial statements and making required disclosures.

Bear in mind that profit and cash flow are *not* synonymous. It is entirely possible to generate a great deal of profit but have very little cash. It is all a matter of timing.

Furthermore, GAAP[12] does *not* necessarily measure the economic benefit stream of the subject entity. GAAP-based financials may be significantly different from other financial guidelines required for litigation needs.

Finally, read the *footnotes* in detail.[13] The financial statements are incomplete without them, and they clarify and amplify the numbers.

How Do You Approach the Reading of Financial Statements? The approach to reading financial statements is illustrated by the following three-step method. It is the most effective means of reading, analyzing, and interpreting how the information applies to your client.

The steps are:

1. Gain a Clear Understanding of the Business by Interviewing Your Client. The most effective method to understanding a company's financial position is to learn about the company's history, operations, major changes, competition, people,

[11] Note that the cash flow statement is required for financial statements that purport to be prepared "in accordance with GAAP."

[12] Generally Accepted Accounting Principles.

[13] Note that footnotes are required for financial statements that purport to be prepared "in accordance with GAAP."

and so on. This is best obtained through the interview process and can be collected within the following five SCORE categories.

a. *Suppliers*—Who provides the products that your client sells?
b. *Customers*—Who are the buyers of your client's products or services?
c. *Owners*—Who are the lenders or equity participants?
d. *Regulators*—Who or what else has an impact on the business, including:
    i. Government (regulations and reporting).
    ii. Technology (innovation).
    iii. Economy.
    iv. Advisors.
    v. Competition, etc.
e. *Employees*—Who are the people essential to continuation of the business?

2. Form an Expectation in Your Mind of the Key Indicators of the Business
    a. *Trends in the Past*—Has the business's sales/revenues/receipts been growing or declining?
    b. *Trends in the Future*—What is the outlook for the business? Is it realistic, given your understanding of the industry?
    c. *Gross Profit*—As a percentage of sales, is it improving or declining for the past and for the future?
    d. *ROI* (return on investment, that is, net income or equity)—Is it improving or declining for the past and for the future?
    e. *Liquidity*—Is cash available to pay the bills?
    f. *Debt*—Has it been increasing or declining?
    g. *Owner's Compensation*—How does it compare to the industry? Is it growing or declining? Are the owners taking compensation through less traditional methods?

    Forming an expectation gives you a framework against which you can then compare the financial statements. For example, if your investigation leads you to conclude that the business is thriving, then the financial statements should support such a conclusion.
3. Use the 60-Second Method to Review the Client's Financial Statements. (Refer to following section on the 60-Second Method.)

What Is the Best Way to Present Financial Information? Financial information, by its nature, is composed of detailed quantitative measurements. The measurements provided by financial statements sometimes compare the two most recent complete fiscal periods. But financial statements are most meaningful when reformatted with the following two characteristics.

1. They should be prepared in a comparative (side-by-side) left-to-right format. This facilitates trend comparison, but it also accommodates other analysis such as common-sizing and ratio comparison. The following example illustrates the usefulness of such a format.

    Note that the side-by-side comparison (Exhibit 4.3) allows each line item to be scrutinized to spot favorable and unfavorable trends.
2. They should be translated to *simple graphics* that illustrate the trends of revenues, cost of revenues, and gross profit over time.

EXHIBIT 4.3 Income Statement for Sample Paint, Inc.

	Audited 12/31/2002	Audited 12/31/2003	Audited 12/31/2004
Paint	$2,000,000	$1,800,000	$1,700,000
Varnish	500,000	400,000	350,000
Lacquer	450,000	220,000	170,000
Less Returns (–)	(50,000)	(20,000)	(20,000)
Revenue	2,900,000	2,400,000	2,200,000
COGS—Paint	1,600,000	1,400,000	1,375,000
COGS—Varnish	300,000	200,000	190,000
COGS—Lacquer	362,000	200,000	135,000
Cost of Revenues	2,262,000	1,800,000	1,700,000
Total Gross Profit	638,000	600,000	500,000

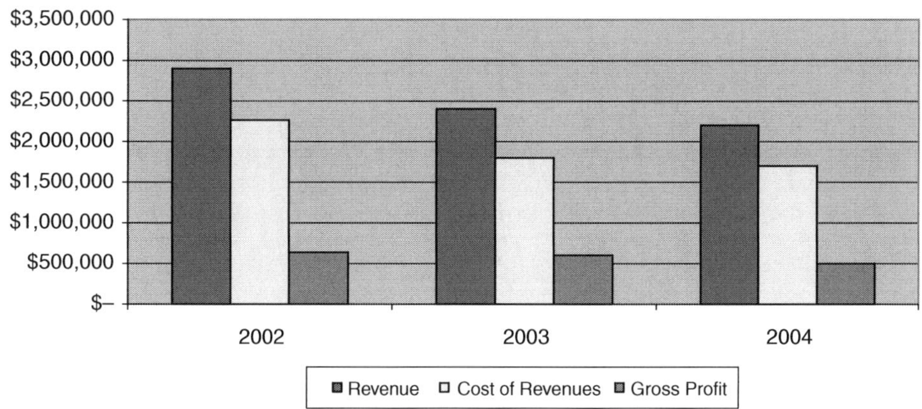

EXHIBIT 4.4 Income Statement Highlights

Note that the Exhibit 4.4 immediately conveys the same information quantitatively presented previously.

Notice the difference between the numbers and the picture—they both depict the same data, but the information instantly conveyed is quite different.

60-SECOND METHOD

The 60-Second Method is a system of ascertaining the financial status of a business or other entity in a few quick glances. It is a training tool that can be used to demonstrate how financial analysis works, or instruct decision makers and beginning to read and understand financial statement content. More comprehensive content is contained in the section titled "Financial Statements: Written Confessions" It will likely take longer than 60 seconds to learn the technique. However, as the name implies, it permits an evaluation of a company's financial strengths and weaknesses in a relatively short time. The method can also be employed when attempting to discuss financial matters with nonfinancial professionals such as attorneys and clients. It is very basic, yet informative. The authors have demonstrated the technique to hundreds, perhaps thousands, of people during the last 10 years or so.

WAR STORY

The 60-Second Method has been taught to literally hundreds of nonfinancial types, ranging from entry level to senior management people in the public, private, and government sectors of the economy. One participant remarked, "This is the code that unlocks the secrets to financial reporting. I now know how to approach almost any type of financial document without intimidation."

Foundation of Method

There are three essential financial statements when using the 60-Second Method:

1. *B*alance Sheet
2. *I*ncome Statement
3. Cash Flow Statement

Each statement is vital to the process and can be easily remembered with the acronym BIC (yes, like the pen) as illustrated by Exhibit 4.5.

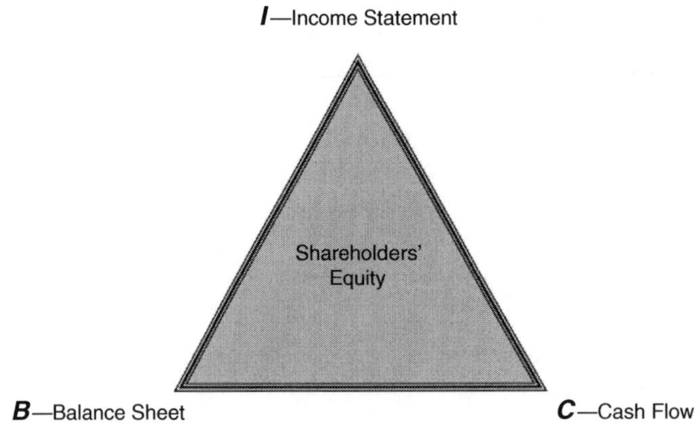

EXHIBIT 4.5 BIC

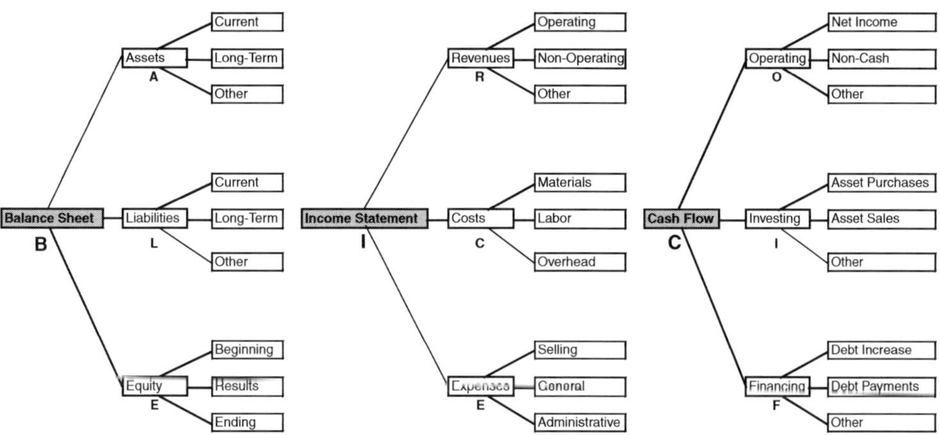

EXHIBIT 4.6 Tree Diagram of Three Main Components

Each of the three statements has three main components and each of those has three subcategories as displayed in the preceding tree diagram (Exhibit 4.6).

Application

The application of the 60-Second Method begins with understanding the three financial statements and the major components that make up each one. This structure supports the application of the method and assessing the results. The application of the method involves analyzing the changes in each financial statement's main component subcategories. Simply, did the amount increase or decrease (e.g., Year 2 compared to Year 1) and is that good or bad?

Balance Sheet The balance sheet reflects a company's assets, liabilities, and shareholder's equity. The amounts are reported as of a specific date. The date will often be as of the end of a month or year. It is called a balance sheet because the assets of a company will always equal or balance with the combination of the company's liabilities and shareholder's equity. See Exhibit 4.7.

EXHIBIT 4.7 Balance Sheet

Assets = Liabilities + Equity		
Generally, something that has value or future economic benefit. It includes those things that a company owns, such as machinery, inventory, and cash in the bank.	Generally, it is the amount that is owed to others. It includes amounts owed to the bank for outstanding loans, the government for taxes, or vendors for supplies.	Generally, it is the difference between the value of the company's assets if they were sold, and the outstanding amounts owed to others.

Assets Assets are reported on the balance sheet based on how quickly they can be converted to cash if sold. Although a real balance sheet typically has more subcategories, the three general groups are:

1. *Current*—Assets that the company expects to convert to cash within one year. Examples include cash, accounts receivable, and inventory.
2. *Long-term*—Assets that the company does not expect to convert to cash within one year. Examples include equipment, machinery, and leasehold improvements.
3. *Other*—Assets that would not typically fit in another category. Examples include goodwill and intangible assets.

Liabilities Liabilities are reported on the balance sheet based on when they are owed or to be paid. Although a real balance sheet would have more subcategories, the three general groups are:

1. *Current*—Assets that the company expects to pay within one year. Examples include accounts payable and accrued vacation.
2. *Long-term*—Assets that the company does not expect to pay within one year. Examples include equipment loans.
3. *Other*—Liabilities that would not typically fit in another category. Examples include contingent liabilities, a decidedly rare reporting category.

Equity Equity is the amount that was initially invested in the company and its accumulated yearly financial results, whether positive or negative. Although a real balance sheet typically has more subcategories, the three general groups are:

1. *Beginning*—The ending retained earnings (shareholder equity) amount from the prior period.
2. *Results*—The company's earnings or losses for the period.
3. *Ending*—The combination of beginning retained earnings (shareholder equity) and the current period results.

60-Second Method Application to the Balance Sheet

Once the major components and subcomponents are identified, changes to the account balances are assessed. A system of + (plus) and – (minus) is used to denote a favorable or adverse change, respectively. Exhibit 4.8 summarizes how to assess the changes in the balance sheet amounts.

EXHIBIT 4.8 Balance Sheet/Amount Changes

Balance Sheet		
Asset	Increase	+
Asset	Decrease	–
Liability	Increase	–
Liability	Decrease	+
Equity	Increase	+
Equity	Decrease	–

EXHIBIT 4.9 Asset Review Sequence

Assets	12/31/X1	12/31/X2	
2 Current assets	796,264	689,311	–
3 Long-term assets	1,128,467	1,147,612	+
4 Other assets	23,445	17,343	–
1 Total assets	1,948,176	1,854,266	–

Assets Assets are assessed in the following order:

1. Total assets.
2. Current assets.
3. Long-term assets.
4. Other assets.

Exhibit 4.9 illustrates the application of the 60-Second Method to the asset section of a balance sheet.

Assessing the results from period 12/31/X1 to 12/31/X2:

- Total assets decreased, denoting a –, or adverse change.
- Current assets decreased, denoting a –, or adverse change.
- Long-term assets increased, denoting a +, or favorable change.
- Other assets decreased, denoting a –, or adverse change.

Liabilities Liabilities are assessed in the following order:

1. Total liabilities.
2. Current liabilities.
3. Long-term liabilities.
4. Other liabilities.

Exhibit 4.10 illustrates the application of the 60-Second Method to the liabilities section of a balance sheet.

Assessing the results from period 12/31/X1 to 12/31/X2:

- Total liabilities increased, denoting a –, or adverse change.
- Current liabilities increased, denoting a –, or adverse change.

EXHIBIT 4.10 Liability Review Sequence

Liabilities	12/31/X1	12/31/X2	
2 Current liabilities	512,578	521,485	–
3 Long-term liabilities	1,008,467	1,016,112	–
4 Other liabilities	10,445	9,221	+
1 Total liabilities	1,531,490	1,546,818	–

EXHIBIT 4.11 Retained Earnings Review Sequence

2 Beginning retained earnings	389,122	416,686	+
3 Net income	27,564	(109,238)	–
1 Ending retained earnings	416,686	307,448	–

- Long-term liabilities increased, denoting a –, or adverse change.
- Other liabilities decreased, denoting a +, or favorable change.

Equity Equity is assessed in the following order:

1. Ending retained earnings.
2. Beginning retained earnings.
3. Results from business activity (net income or loss).

Exhibit 4.11 illustrates the application of the 60-Second Method to the shareholder equity section of a balance sheet.

Assessing the results from period 12/31/X1 to 12/31/X2:

- Ending retained earnings decreased, denoting a –, or adverse change.
- Beginning retained earnings increased, denoting a +, or favorable change.
- Results from business activity decreased, denoting a –, or adverse change.

Income Statement

The income statement reflects how much a company earned or lost over a specific period. The period will often be a year or month. It is called an income statement because it eventually reports the company's overall income as net profit or loss for the period. See Exhibit 4.12.

Revenue Revenue is reported first on the income statement and represents the total amount of money a company brings in from its operations. Although a genuine income statement will have more subcategories, the three general groups are:

1. *Operating*—All money received from normal business operations.
2. *Nonoperating*—All money received from nonbusiness operations (e.g., rental income).
3. *Other*—Money received that would not typically fit in another category (e.g., interest income).

EXHIBIT 4.12 Income Statement

Revenue minus Cost minus Expense		
The amount of money a company received in exchange for its goods or services.	The amount of money a company spent to produce the goods or services sold.	The amount of money a company spent to operate the company.

EXHIBIT 4.13 Income Statement/Amount Changes

Income Statement		
Revenue	Increase	+
Revenue	Decrease	–
Costs	Increase	–
Costs	Decrease	+
Expenses	Increase	–
Expenses	Decrease	+

Costs Cost of goods sold is generally reported next on the income statement and is deducted from total revenues. Costs include all amounts paid in order to produce the product or service sold. Generally, the three subcategories of costs[14] are:

1. *Materials*—Supplies, raw materials, and parts used.
2. *Labor*—Employee labor and labor costs directly incurred.
3. *Overhead*—The portion of company overhead that is allocated to production.

Expenses Expenses are all other amounts paid to support the general operation of the business. This would include items such as advertising, rent, insurance, and office expenses. The three main groups of expenses are:

1. *Selling*—Amounts incurred to sell the business product or service.
2. *General*—Amounts paid for the general business operation.
3. *Administrative*—Amounts incurred to direct and control the business operation.

60-Second Method Application to the Income Statement

Once the major components and subcomponents are identified, changes to the account totals are assessed. A system of + and – is used to denote a favorable or adverse change, respectively. Exhibit 4.13 summarizes how to assess the changes in the income statement amounts.

Revenue Revenue is assessed in the following order:

1. Operating income.
2. Nonoperating income.
3. Other income.

Exhibit 4.14 illustrates the application of the 60-Second Method to the revenue section of an income statement.

---

[14] In a service business, no inventory, per se, is reported. However, the cost to generate the revenue is equal to the labor and overhead expended.

EXHIBIT 4.14 Revenue Review Sequence

Revenue	12/31/X1	12/31/X2	
1 Operating income	1,055,791	992,521	–
2 Nonoperating income	34,564	65,464	+
3 Other income	654	522	–
Total Revenue	1,091,009	1,058,507	–

Assessing the results from year 12/31/X1 to 12/31/X2:

- Operating income decreased, denoting a –, or adverse change.
- Nonoperating income increased, denoting a +, or favorable change.
- Other income decreased, denoting a –, or adverse change.

Costs Costs of goods sold are assessed in the following order:

1. Materials.
2. Labor.
3. Overhead.

Exhibit 4.15 illustrates the application of the 60-Second Method to the costs of goods sold section of an income statement.

Assessing the results from year 12/31/X1 to 12/31/X2:

- Materials purchased increased, denoting a –, or adverse change.
- Labor costs increased, denoting a –, or adverse change.
- Overhead decreased, denoting a +, or favorable change.

Expenses Expenses are assessed in the following order:

1. Selling expenses.
2. General expenses.
3. Administrative expenses.

Exhibit 4.16 illustrates the application of the 60-Second Method to the expenses section of an income statement.

EXHIBIT 4.15 Costs of Goods Sold Review Sequence

Costs	12/31/X1	12/31/X2	
1 Materials	212,578	214,852	–
2 Labor	349,844	454,643	–
3 Overhead	182,488	179,741	+
Total costs of goods sold	744,910	849,236	

EXHIBIT 4.16 Operating Expenses Review Sequence

Expenses	12/31/X1	12/31/X2	
1 Selling expenses	115,495	97,242	+
2 General expenses	135,824	155,550	–
3 Administrative expenses	67,216	65,717	+
Total expenses	318,535	318,509	

Assessing the results from year 12/31/X1 to 12/31/X2:

- Selling expenses decreased, denoting a +, or favorable change.
- General expenses increased, denoting a –, or adverse change.
- Administrative expenses decreased, denoting a +, or favorable change.

Cash Flow Statement

The cash flow statement (Exhibit 4.17) reflects a company's inflows and outflows of cash over a specific period. The period will often be for a year or a month. The cash flow statement will reveal where the cash came from or went to, that is, cash generated from the sales of product or bank financing.

WAR STORY

An executive attending financial analysis training made the following observation to the instructor. "You previously commented that the double-entry system has been in operation at least since about 1494 when published by Luca Pacoli, an Italian monk. Therefore, the balance sheet and income statement have been in use for about 500-plus years. However, the accounting profession required the cash flow statement in 1987. Consequently, it took accountants *only* about 500 years to realize that cash might be important to business owners and investors."

EXHIBIT 4.17 Cash Flow Statement

Operating + Investing + Financing[15]		
The inflow (hopefully) or outflow of cash due to general business operations.	The inflow or outflow of cash due to investing activities. Outflow results from buying equipment or investments.	The inflow or outflow of cash due to outside borrowing and or equity activities.

[15] This represents the algebraic sum since they may be positive or negative amounts.

Operating Cash flow from operating activities is generally the profit or loss reported on the income statement adjusted for any noncash items that were included. Although some cash flow statements would have more subcategories, the three general groups are:

1. Profit (loss)—the amount reported on the income statement.
2. Depreciation—the amount included on the income statement.
3. Working capital—changes in working capital balances on the balance sheet, that is, accounts receivable and accounts payable.

Investing Cash flow from investing activities generally includes amounts for financial investing, that is, securities, but also includes investments in the company such as the purchase or sales of machinery or land. Generally, the three subcategories of investing are:

1. Operating Assets—assets used for operations.
2. Marketable Securities—investments with financial institutions, stocks or bonds.
3. Fixed Assets—property, buildings, and equipment.

Financing Cash flow from financing activities generally includes bank borrowing or loan repayment amounts. It also includes funds received from or paid to owners. The three main activities are:

1. Borrowing—amounts received from bank loans.
2. Repayment—amounts paid to repay outstanding bank loans.
3. Distributions—amounts paid to shareholders.

60-Second Method Application to the Cash Flow Statement

Once the major components and subcomponents are identified, changes to the cash flow statement totals are assessed. A system of "+" and "–" is used to denote a favorable or adverse change, respectively. Exhibit 4.18 summarizes how to assess the changes in the cash flow statement amounts.

The following schedule indicates how increases and decreases are represented by the pluses and minuses. This is a source of confusion to those unfamiliar with the cash flow statement. However, by recalling that this statement measures the flows of *cash* simplifies things. In other words, a decrease (–) in Investing cash reflects an outflow of cash, typically for the purchase of fixed assets. Therefore, cash flowing

EXHIBIT 4.18 Cash Flow Statement

Operating	Increase	+
Operating	Decrease	–
Investing	Increase	+
Investing	Decrease	–
Financing	Increase	+
Financing	Decrease	–

EXHIBIT 4.19 Operating Cash Flow Review Sequence

Operating	12/31/X1	12/31/X2	
1 Profit (loss)	27,564	(109,238)	–
2 Depreciation	65,212	75,968	+
3 Working capital	654	15,860	+
Total cash flow from operating activities	93,430	(17,410)	

out of an organization is not necessary bad, assuming it was used to purchase valid revenue-generating fixed assets.

In a like manner, cash flowing into an organization and resulting in an increase in Financing may or may not be bad. For example, cash flowing in from a loan could be positive, assuming it is prudent to borrow.

Operating Operating cash flow is assessed in the following order:

1. Net income
2. Noncash operating activities
3. Other operating activities

Exhibit 4.19 illustrates the application of the 60-Second Method to the operating section of a cash flow statement.

Assessing the results for the period 12/31/X1 to 12/31/X2:

- Profit (loss) from operating activities decreased, denoting a –, or adverse change.
- Depreciation increased, denoting a +, since it is a non-cash item.
- Working capital flow increased, denoting a +, presumably a favorable change, assuming prudent working capital management.

Investing Investing cash flow is assessed in the following order:

1. Asset purchases.
2. Asset sales.
3. Other investing.

Exhibit 4.20 illustrates the application of the 60-Second Method to the investing section of a cash flow statement. The plus or minus reflects the result assuming prudent overall asset and liability management.

Assessing the results from year 12/31/X1 to 12/31/X2:

- Operating assets cash flow decreased, denoting a +, or favorable change.
- Market securities cash flow increased, denoting a –, or adverse change.
- Fixed assets cash flow decreased, denoting a +, or favorable change.

EXHIBIT 4.20 Investing Cash Flow Review Sequence

Investing	12/31/X1	12/31/X2	
1 Operating assets	11,577	(6,703)	+
2 Marketable securities	(15,000)	51,254	–
3 Fixed assets	5,442	(12,442)	+
Total cash flow from investing activities	2,019	32,109	

Note: The preceding favorable or adverse conclusions depend upon the facts and circumstances. For example, a decrease in operating cash often occurs in early formation stages.

Financing Financing cash flow is assessed in the following order:

1. Debt increase.
2. Debt payments.
3. Other financing activities.

Exhibit 4.21 illustrates the application of the 60-Second Method to the financing section of a cash flow statement.

Assessing the results from year 12/31/X1 to 12/31/X2:

- Borrowed debt increased, denoting a +, or favorable change.
- Repayment of debt decreased, denoting a –, or adverse change.
- Distributions to shareholders decreased, denoting a +, or adverse change.

Note: The preceding favorable or adverse conclusions depend upon the facts and circumstances. For example, a decrease in cash resulting from debt repayment could be a favorable indicator.

The 60-Second Method quickly assesses financial statement components as favorable or adverse. In general, the assessment applies to almost any commercial, noncommercial, nonprofit, or government operation and accurately measures financial performance. However, it is important to note that occasionally an assessment results in a flawed conclusion of a company's financial position. For example, the

EXHIBIT 4.21 Financing Cash Flow Review Sequence

Financial	12/31/X1	12/31/X2	
1 Borrowing of debt	1,000	7,645	+
2 Repayment of debt	(75,314)	(62,545)	–
3 Distributors to shareholders	(15,000)	(10,000)	+
Total cash flow from financial activities	(89,314)	(64,900)	

60-Second Method for a start-up business would likely produce an adverse assessment of the company's investing cash flow. However, it is not unusual for a new company to purchase assets to begin business operations, thus creating an outflow of cash. When using this method, it is imperative that the forensic operator consider the results and then investigate specific variances as necessary.

How Do You Critique the Financial Statements?

After gaining an understanding of your client's business and the related financial statements (from the preceding section) you can now begin to consider how *well* the financial statements represent the business.

There are three categories of analysis used to guide forensic accounting activities. The methods are outlined for your reference and indicate the type of tests that we routinely employ. The examples are not necessarily all-inclusive, nor will every test apply in every situation. They illustrate the tools that you have at your disposal and that are typically applied by forensic accountants in order to support conclusions.

Indirect Methods These methods consist of comparing (and reconciling, where possible) key accounts on a year-to-year basis. For example, by comparing the year-to-year change in equity to the year-to-year difference between revenues (i.e., receipts) and expenses, the articulation of the financial statements can be tested. Any difference is investigated to determine whether it is merely an equity transaction, for example, capital infusion, or is determined to be unaccounted-for revenue or expense. This is often referred to as the Net Worth Method.[16]

The aberrant pattern detection technique (previously discussed) compares a time series pattern of observable data in order to identify observation points.

The *advantages* of the indirect methods are exploratory in nature. That is, areas meriting more intense investigation (see direct methods) can be identified to make the most time-effective use of resources. Likewise, areas determined to offer little promise are not needlessly pursued.

The *disadvantages* of the indirect methods may include lack of specificity to support conclusions. Such lack of evidence may require further investigation.

Direct Methods These methods consist of detailed scrutiny of transactions from the financial statements through the source document(s). The methods begin with a top-down approach so that the overall financial statements are progressively analyzed according to the following categories.

1. *Horizontal Analysis*—This test consists of comparing key account categories, such as officer compensation, travel and entertainment, etc., over a multiple-period time (e.g., year, quarter, month, day) to identify changes meriting further investigation. The test typically includes percentage changes, dollar changes, comparison changes, etc.

---

[16] The Net Worth Method gained notoriety with the case *Capone v. United States* (51 F.2d 609 (1931)).

2. *Vertical Analysis*—This test consists of comparing the relative (compared to revenues) size of accounts within financial statements over a multiple-period time. The test typically includes percentage changes, dollar changes, comparison changes, etc., and is further applied to trending, ratio, and common-sizing tests.
3. *Trending Analysis*—This test consists of comparing the rate of growth of items in comparison to the other financial items. The typical method consists of determining the compound growth rate (CGR) within and among the various account items. For example, if revenues exhibit a 10 percent CGR, and outside services exhibit a 30 percent CGR, further investigation is necessary.
4. *Common-Sizing*—This test consists of converting all financial statement items to a percentage of revenue or total assets. Income statement items are restated as a percentage of Revenue and balance sheet items are restated as a percentage of Total Assets. This method also accommodates a comparison to similar businesses that may be a much different size.
5. *Ratio Analysis*—This test consists of measuring the articulation of the financial statements among various categories, including liquidity, profitability, turnover, leverage, etc., to identify areas meriting further investigation. Also, this method provides the basis for comparison to similar businesses to identify variances. For example, if the current ratio of similar business approximates 2.6 and the subject entity exhibits 1.9, further investigation is necessary.
6. *Visual Testing*—This method consists of visually examining relationships within and among the financial statements and typically includes elements of all the preceding tests. An advantage of this test is the demonstration of findings to parties lacking technical knowledge of the preceding tests.
7. *Drill-Down*—This method consists of applying software tools in order to drill down from the highest to the lowest transaction levels, thus leading to source documents.
8. *Statistical Analysis*—These mathematical methods can be applied for sampling data, and they also can be applied to the ratio estimation techniques referred to later.
9. *Benford's Law*—This mathematical technique, developed by physicist Frank Benford in 1938, states that an analysis of supposedly randomly generated numbers compared to its statistical probability of distribution can indicate whether or not the preparer of the numbers was truthful.

The advantages of the direct methods include the ability to specifically resolve disputes by tracing to the lowest possible level. The obvious disadvantage is the labor intensity of such activities.

Comprehensive Methods These methods consist of the application of interrelated techniques that are based upon skill, experience, and even intuition. That is, no specific technique can be identified at the outset, but during the analysis, experience may lead to further investigation of the signature of a check. Also, tests that might be considered in either or both the indirect and direct methods may likewise be applied here, including the following:

1. *Full and False Inclusion*—This test is used to determine the appropriate universe of data under investigation. This ensures that no extraneous data is included and that no appropriate data is excluded.
2. *Background Investigation*—This test involves research (typically electronic) into a party's identity to identify other assets that may have been forgotten about.
3. *Event Analysis*—This test is used to identify activity changes coincident with key events. For example, by comparing trends before and after key changes in activity, aberrations may be detected, requiring further investigation.
4. *Attribute Testing*—This test is used to specifically identify characteristics that fall within or outside previously established norms. It can be applied either globally or statistically, using sampling techniques.
5. *Ratio Estimation*—This test is often used in connection with attribute testing and can estimate (on a statistically significant basis) the projected results based upon analytical sampling.
6. *"But For" Development*—This tool is used to forecast what a result would have been but for some particular event, such as misuse of corporate funds. The test is often applied in damages determination and pivots upon three major categories supported by eight detailed applications.
7. *Forensic Indices*—These techniques are quite sophisticated yet yield strong insight into the financial statements that make up operations. (Refer to the portion of this section titled "Forensic Indices," which is further on, for more information.)

The advantages of the comprehensive method include the ability to think outside the box and transcend the restrictions of traditional accounting and analytical methods.

The disadvantages typically relate to the difficulty of explaining the application of the various complex techniques.

How Do You Apply Financial Statements and Financial Data to Your Forensic Assignments?

Financial statement analysis is applicable to a myriad of litigation matters such as personal injury, breach of contract, patent infringement, etc. The key is to know what analysis must be performed and how it should be applied to the matter.

Types of Matters

1. *Business Interruption, Breach of Contract, Antitrust, etc.*—Financial statement analysis is necessary to compute lost profits applicable to a claim.
2. *Divorce*—Financial statement analysis or valuation analysis, or both, is typically required if a petitioner or respondent is a small-business owner.
3. *Fraud*—Detailed financial analysis is critical to any fraud matter (embezzlement, securities fraud, loan fraud, and so on). Investigations should be extremely thorough and assisted by a competent forensic operator, whether it be a civil or criminal matter.
4. *Intellectual Property Infringement or Theft*—Analysis of financial statements and detailed financial data is often necessary to determine damages as pertinent

to the matter (refer to damages types). Estimation of damages often involves a review of the plaintiff's *and* the defendant's financial data.

5. *Personal Injury or Wrongful Death*—Financial statement analysis would be applicable when the plaintiff is a small-business owner integrally involved with the day-to-day operations. Damages may be calculated as lost profits of a 100 percent or a fractional-interest owner.

Application of Financial Data to Damages

1. *Lost Profits*—Damages for most civil matters are calculated as lost profits.[17] Lost profit is normally considered synonymous with lost net income. However, in some cases, lost cash flow is a more accurate measure of damages.[18]
2. *Gross Profits (Contribution Margin)*—Damages are often estimated in intellectual property matters as lost gross profits as pertinent to the infringed-upon product or property.[19] These damages are usually estimated as lost revenues minus avoided costs. In essence, it is the profit generated by the sale of each unit.
3. *Other Damage Measures*—In some cases, the plaintiff may have incurred damages in addition to lost profits or lost gross profits. For example, the plaintiff may have expended additional funds on advertising to repair a damaged reputation. Additionally, in trade dress matters, permanent damage may have been done to the market because of the introduction of an inferior product, resulting in lower price points.

Financial statements and other financial data are often presented in the courtroom to support damage conclusions in myriad matters. It is critical that counsel and the expert have a thorough understanding of the damages methodology as applicable to their matter. Statute[20] and case law[21] often determine what methodologies are applicable.

Also, underlying financial data should always be tied out to financial statements or tax returns for the company. For example, if payroll documents are used for a damages element, then the total amount of the payroll should be tied in to the financial statements. This provides some level of assurance as to the accuracy of the underlying documents provided in litigation.

Ratio Analysis Commonly applied financial statement ratios are as follows:

Liquidity Ratios Liquidity ratios indicate the company's ability to meet its current obligations. In general, the higher the ratio, the greater the company's liquidity.

---

[17] Although the terms are not truly interchangeable, lost profits are often referred to as economic loss. Thus lost profits is a measure of the economic loss.

[18] Neil W. Freeman and James A. Spielmann, "Lost Profits" in *Litigation Services Handbook—The Role of the Accountant as Expert*, 2nd ed. (New York: John Wiley & Sons, 1995).

[19] Note that virtually all types of intellectual property matters (copyright, trademark, trade dress, patent, etc.) have very specific guidelines for what damages can be awarded and how they should be estimated.

[20] For example, The Lanham Act.

[21] Accepted damage theories often vary by jurisdiction.

Current Ratio

Formula = current assets/current liabilities

Quick Ratio

Formula = (cash + marketable securities + accounts receivable)/
current liabilities

Revenue/Accounts Receivable

Formula = sales/average accounts receivable balance

Cost of Goods Sold/Inventory

Formula = cost of goods sold/average inventory balance

Cost of Goods Sold/Payables

Formula = cost of goods sold/average accounts payable balance

Operating Cash Flow

Formula = cash flow from operations/current liabilities

Coverage Ratios Coverage ratios indicate the degree to which a company has covered its leverage requirements, that is, debt load of interest expense.

EBIT/Interest

Formula = earnings before interest and taxes/interest expense

(NI + NC)/Current LTD

Formula = (net income + noncash expenditures)/
current portion long-term debt

Coverage of Fixed Charges

Formula = (EBIT[22] + lease payments)/(interest + lease payments
+ current portion LTD)

Cash Interest Coverage

Formula = (operating cash flow + interest paid + taxes paid)/interest paid

[22] Earnings before interest and taxes.

Funds Flow Coverage

Formula = EBITDA[23]/(interest + tax-adjusted debt repayment + tax-adjusted preferred dividends)

Leverage Ratios Leverage ratios indicate the degree to which a company's capital structure is financed with debt. The higher the ratio, the riskier the company.

Total Debt to Total Assets

Formula = total debt/total assets

LT Debt to Total Capital

Formula = long-term debt/total capital

Debt/Net Worth

Formula = total liabilities/equity

Total Debt Ratio

Formula = operating cash flow/total debt

Operating Ratios Operating, or efficiency, ratios measure the efficiency at which a company is using its assets. Generally speaking, the higher the ratio, the more efficient its asset use.

EBT/Net Worth

Formula = pre-tax profit/net worth

EBT/Total Assets

Formula = pre-tax profit/total assets

Revenue/Fixed Assets

Formula = gross revenue/fixed assets

Revenue/Total Assets

Formula = gross revenue/total assets

[23] Earnings before interest, taxes, depreciation, and amortization.

Risk and Going Concern Ratios Risk ratios ascertain the uncertainty of the income flows to the company's various capital suppliers whereas going concern ratios measure the company's ability to meet future cash commitments.

Business Risk

Formula = standard deviation net income/average net income

Degree of Operating Leverage

Formula = percent change operating earnings/percent change gross revenues

Degree of Financial Leverage

Formula = percent change income to stockholders/percent change EBIT

Varying Measurement Baselines Forensic accountants often initiate investigations with an analysis of a company's financial statements, or at least documents that are referred to as financial statements by the owner(s). In practice, the degree of representation of the business, and thus the reliance by the forensic accountant, varies widely. Consequently, financial statements and related transactional documents requiring investigation span a continuum ranging from shoebox data to audited financial statements. Definable points along the continuum are:

- *Shoebox data*—Even midsized business owners sometimes rely on a primary or a few key measurements (as they perceive them) to manage the business. The authors have encountered a wide variety of individualized such practices.
  - For example, a rice farmer dutifully collected any and all business documents in a small cardboard box throughout the year. They could range from feed store cash register receipts to personal bank statements indicating deposits. The first week of each January he delivered the cardboard box and its contents (still unorganized) to his CPA. Interestingly, in the bottom of the box the rice farmer kept an old pair of dice and an old horseshoe "just for luck."
- *Checkbook management*—Many small business owners rely on a primary or a few key measurements (as they perceive them) to manage the business. The authors have encountered a wide variety of individualized such practices.
  - For example, one small specialty chemical manufacturer gauged the profitability of his business by his checkbook balance. When his business checking account carried a balance exceeding $1,000,000 he reasoned that his business was doing "okay." Otherwise, he would spur the salesmen into action. Another business owner "netted" the respective balances of accounts receivable against accounts payable every week. He was confident of success unless any week's "net" fell below his arbitrary "cushion" he periodically established.
- *OCBOA (Other Comprehensive Basis of Accounting)*—This category, under SAS No. 62 (Statement on Accounting Standards) Special Reports, can be any one of:
  - A statutory basis of accounting (e.g., a basis of accounting insurance companies use under the rules of a state insurance commission).

  - Income tax–basis financial statements.
  - Financial statements prepared using definitive criteria having substantial support in accounting literature that the preparer applies to all material items appearing in the statements (such as the price level basis of accounting).
- *Tax-basis accounting*— Even midsize business owners rely on annual income tax returns as their primary business management tool. Tax-basis accounting may or may not be based on GAAP but is typically cost-driven or fair market value–driven, depending upon the respective facts and circumstances. Furthermore, timing differences, for example, depreciation, revenue recognition, and inventory methods, can affect tax basis accounting.
- *Compilation*—This form of financial statement is prepared by a CPA, but contains virtually *no* reliance beyond the numbers provided by the client. It is slightly better than client-prepared financials, but not by much. It may contain footnotes or related disclosures.
- *Review*—This form of financial statement is prepared by a CPA, and contains considerably more scrutiny than a compilation, but still less than an audit. The reviewed financials prepared in accordance with GAAP contain footnotes explaining the financials.
- *Audit*—This is the highest level of assurance, since it reflects a CPA's attestation of client-prepared financial statements. It contains the highest level of scrutiny and disclosure, for example, footnotes that can be obtained from a CPA. Still, recall that it reflects only an attestation of client-prepared financials, and does *not* provide any assurance that fraud did not occur.

FORENSIC INDICES

The use of ratio analysis is commonplace throughout the world of finance and accounting. Its application spans many types of engagements, including, but not limited to, audit, review, business valuation, litigation consulting, and fraud investigation. As such, there are unlimited resources that discuss financial statement ratios, their purpose, and the appropriate formulas.

This section does not regurgitate the numerous ratios and their formulas that are commonly applied to financial and accounting engagements. Most ratios and their application have been discussed extensively in other resources, including textbooks, periodicals, websites, software, etc. Rather, the objective is to expose the reader to some lesser-used ratios and indices and explain their potential for application in financial forensic matters.

The Pitfall of Plug-and-Play Ratio Analysis

There are now a multitude of software packages that prepare boilerplate financial ratio analysis for the user. For example, valuation software will automatically prepare many of the common financial statement ratios once the user has input the historical financial statement data. While this may have increased the efficiency of forensic operators, it is not without its pitfalls.

Since a multitude of financial statement ratios can now be prepared with the click of a button, some forensic operators do not take the time necessary to fully analyze the ratio results, or worse yet, don't understand the specific ratios and how they relate to the subject company. Regardless of the engagement, it is critical to first gain a sufficient understanding of the company, the company's industry, and what the key financial drivers are. The forensic operator can then determine what ratios are appropriate to analyze the company or test their hypothesis.

With the advent of programs that automatically compute financial ratios, many forensic operators no longer take the time to review the ratio formulas and understand how they are computed. As such, forensic operators are not as proficient at reading and interpreting the ratio results. What is a positive result versus negative result for the ratio? Can ratios be too good? For example, a higher quick ratio is generally preferred. However, if the quick ratio is too high, could the company be inefficiently applying its assets? The subject company may be very liquid because it maintains a large balance of excess cash that could otherwise be reinvested in the company or distributed to stakeholders.

Finally, forensic operators need to review ratio results in tandem with each other and not as separate and distinct analyses. By selecting the proper ratios and reviewing the results in conjunction with each other, the forensic operator should be able to not only assess what is happening but why it is happening. For example, it is not sufficient to merely observe that net profit margins have declined. Through proper ratio analysis, the forensic operator should be able to develop a sound hypothesis or theory as to why net profit margins have declined.

Benchmarking

Benchmarking is defined as a standard or reference from which others can be measured or judged. In financial analysis, benchmarking is used to compare the subject company against itself and against its peers. The goal is to assess the financial health and viability of the subject company.

When conducting a financial investigation, the forensic operator can apply benchmarking for an entirely different purpose. For example, benchmarking can be used to assess the likelihood that financial statement fraud has occurred. This will be explored in detail later when discussing Beneish's model for detecting earnings manipulation.

Benchmarking can also be a valuable tool for embezzlement or other fraud investigations. A review of key financial ratios for the subject company may provide indicia of irregular variations in financial statement accounts meriting further investigation. The key is to establish a baseline for the company's financial ratio results. To do so, the forensic operator needs to obtain the company's financial statements for the periods outside of the investigation. Once the baseline has been established, the forensic operator can test the company's financial ratios against itself, comparing the period under investigation versus the period outside of the investigation.

For example, if the forensic operator is investigating a suspected fraud that occurred during 2008 through 2009, financial statements for the years preceding and following the suspected fraud should also be requested. These years are presumed to be the unaffected, or baseline, years. Once the pertinent financial ratios are calculated for the baseline years, the forensic operator can then prepare the same ratios for the years under investigation. The resulting financial ratios for the disparate time periods can then be compared and contrasted. Unusual variations that occurred in the suspect years should be investigated and may assist in refining the potential scope of the investigation.

When preparing ratio analysis and attempting to benchmark the subject company's results, it is critical that the forensic operator have a detailed understanding of the company's operating history and any significant events or factors, other than those under investigation, that may skew financial performance. Without this understanding, it is easy to misinterpret the analysis results, which may result in false positives and investigation inefficiencies.

Finally, the forensic operator needs to be cautious with benchmarking against industry peers. Two things must be understood for meaningful comparisons:

- What are the unique financial characteristics of the subject company that may not be common within the industry? For example, does the company hold a large piece of real property whereas industry peers typically do not have real estate holdings?
- What is the source of the industry data and how was it compiled? This may not always be evident or readily ascertainable, and for this reason, industry comparisons may not be as helpful.

When properly applied, benchmarking can be a valuable tool for assessing the health of a company as well as refining the scope of financial investigations.

The Other Financial Ratios

Standard financial ratios are grouped or categorized in many different ways, depending on the source. However, the standard financial ratios generally fall into one of the following four categories:

1. *Liquidity Ratios*—Liquidity ratios indicate a company's ability to meet its current obligations.
2. *Coverage Ratios*—Coverage ratios indicate the degree to which a company has covered its leverage requirements, that is, debt load of interest expense.
3. *Leverage Ratios*—Leverage ratios indicate the degree to which a company's capital structure is financed with debt.
4. *Operating Ratios*—Operating, or efficiency, ratios measure the efficiency at which a company is using its assets.

As mentioned earlier, the standard financial ratios are not covered here, as they are readily available through numerous other sources. The following sections focus on a few lesser-known ratios and their application for financial forensic matters.

Cash Flow Ratios Traditional financial statement ratios tend to focus on balance sheet and income statement accounts. However, one of the most important financial statements is the cash flow statement. The cash flow statement indicates the sources and uses of the company's cash. Furthermore, the cash flow statement is an articulation between the balance sheet and income statement. If the balance sheet and income statement are not in balance, then a proper cash flow statement cannot be prepared. As such the cash flow statement is an integral part of the financial statements.

Also, many financial forensic engagements focus on economic benefit streams other than net income. Net income is a product of generally accepted accounting principles. In litigation matters, net income may not always be a proper measure of economic damages because of noncash items and regulatory prescribed accruals. In business valuation engagements, many analysts tend to focus more on cash flow benefit streams, as they are a better measure of the cash available to the stakeholders. Therefore, cash flow measures tend to be more beneficial than the traditional measure of net income.

While cash flow ratios have been around for quite some time, they remain relatively unused in financial forensic matters, in spite of their ability to provide meaningful performance measures. For example, the operating cash flow ratio and total debt ratio are much more accurate measures of a company's liquidity and coverage. A company will likely be using cash flow from operations to repay its debt, not net income.

The following are a just few examples of cash flow ratios that may be applied to financial forensic engagements. There are a multitude of other cash flow ratios that the user can locate through textbooks, periodicals, and the Internet.

Operating Cash Flow Ratio–Liquidity

$$\frac{\text{Cash Flow from Operations}}{\text{Current Liabilities}}$$

Funds Flow Coverage Ratio–Liquidity

$$\frac{\text{EBITDA}}{(\text{Interest} + \text{Tax Adj. Debt Repayment} + \text{Tax Adj. Preferred Dividends})}$$

Cash Interest Coverage Ratio—Coverage

$$\frac{(\text{Cash Flow from Operations} + \text{Interest Paid} + \text{Taxes Paid})}{\text{Interest Paid}}$$

Cash Current Debt Coverage Ratio–Coverage

$$\frac{(\text{Cash Flow from Operations} - \text{Cash Dividends})}{\text{Current Debt}}$$

Total Debt (Cash Flow to Total Debt) Ratio—Coverage (the amount of time to repay debt)

$$\frac{\text{Cash Flow from Operations}}{\text{Total Debt}}$$

Total Free Cash Ratio—Going Concern

$$\begin{aligned}&(\text{Net Income} + \text{Accrued And Capitalized Interest Exp}\\&\quad + \text{Depreciation \& Amortization} + \text{Operating Lease \& Rental Exp}\\&\quad - \text{Declared Dividends} - \text{Capital Expenditures})/(\text{Accrued and}\\&\quad \text{Capitalized Interest Exp} + \text{Operating Leaes \&Rental Exp}\\&\quad + \text{Current Portion LTD} + \text{Current Portion of Capitalized Leases})\end{aligned}$$

Working Capital Ratios and Cash Gap

Working capital ratios measure the efficiency at which a company manages its working capital. Working capital ratios are an excellent tool for assessing a company's financial health and solvency. Furthermore, working capital ratios are an excellent tool for assessing the validity of a company's cash flow projections.

Similar to cash flow ratios, working capital ratios have been around for quite some time but are infrequently applied. The following methodology computes various working capital ratios. As with other financial ratios, different sources may present a slight variation on the ratio formulas. In general, except for days payable outstanding, a decrease in the working capital ratio signifies improvement.

Days Sales Outstanding

$$\frac{\text{Accounts Receivable}}{(\text{Gross Revenue}/365)}$$

Days Inventory Outstanding

$$\frac{\text{Inventory}}{\text{Gross Revenue}/365}$$

Days Payable Outstanding

$$\frac{\text{Accounts Payable}}{(\text{Gross Revenue}/365)}$$

Days Working Capital—Estimates how long it takes a company to convert its working capital into revenue. The faster a company converts its working capital, the better.

$$\frac{(\text{Accounts Receivable} + \text{Inventory} - \text{Accounts Payable})}{(\text{Gross Revenue}/365)}$$

The cash gap measures the amount of time from when a company pays cash for inventory to the time the company receives cash for the sale of said inventory. The company must have adequate cash reserves or access to financing to cover the cash gap.

$$\begin{aligned}\text{Cash Gap} = {} & \text{Days Accounts Receivable Turnover} \\ & + \text{Days Inventory Turnover} \\ & - \text{Days Accounts Payable Turnover}\end{aligned}$$

Companies experiencing strong or rapid growth in sales must closely monitor their cash gap, or they may quickly run out of cash. The cash strain experienced from a significant growth in sales is a primary reason why companies often cannot manage a long-term sustainable growth rate approaching 6 percent.

Financial Statement Manipulation Indices

Earnings management is practiced by thousands of companies every year. For example, most companies will take efforts to reduce their taxable income. The majority of companies manage their earnings through accepted or legal transactions.

Occasionally management will attempt to manage earnings through financial statement manipulation or misstatement. Management might be motivated by performance bonuses, debt covenants, or investor confidence. At this point, earnings management typically rises to the level of fraudulent conduct.

Professor Messod D. Beneish, of Indiana University, researched companies that had been required to restate their financial statements because of SEC enforcement actions. Professor Beneish's research is detailed in "The Detection of Earnings Manipulation."[24]

In Professor Beneish's research, he compared known manipulators to nonmanipulators. The objective was to determine if there were any identifiable indicators for companies that may be manipulating their earnings. Professor Beneish's paper delineates his M score (discussed later), which has some similarities to the Altman Z Score, but comprises nonbankrupt entities. The M score, composed of eight separate indices, indicates a probability as to whether the company has participated in financial statement manipulation or not.

The following indices were developed by Professor Beneish and used in the computation of the M score. A neutral value for all indices, except TATA, would be +1, as that would indicate no change from year to year.

Days Sales in Receivable Index (DSRI)

$$\left(\frac{\text{Accounts Receivable } cy}{\text{Sales } cy}\right) \Big/ \left(\frac{\text{Accounts Receivable } py}{\text{Sales } py}\right)$$

Disproportionate increases in receivables relative to sales may be suggestive of revenue inflation. Thus, a large increase in days sales in receivables may be associated with a higher likelihood that revenues and earnings are overstated.

Gross Margin Index (GMI)

$$\frac{\text{Gross Profit Percentage } py}{\text{Gross Profit Percentage } cy}$$

Gross margin deterioration is demonstrated by GMIs greater than 1. This is a negative signal about the subject's prospects. The assumption is that firms with poorer prospects are more likely to engage in earnings manipulation.

[24] www.bauer.uh.edu/~swhisenant/beneish%20earnings%20mgmt%20score.pdf.

Asset Quality Index (AQI)

$$\left(1-\left(\frac{\text{Current Assets } cy + \text{Net Fixed Assets } cy}{\text{Total Assets } cy}\right)\right) \Big/ \left(1-\left(\frac{\text{Current Assets } py + \text{Net Fixed Assets } py}{\text{Total Assets } py}\right)\right)$$

AQI measures the change in asset realization risk analysis. An AQI of greater than 1 indicates that the firm has potentially increased its involvement in cost deferral and therefore, earnings manipulation. An increase in asset realization risks leads to the propensity to make inappropriate capitalization.

Sales Growth Index (SGI)

$$\frac{\text{Sales } cy}{\text{Sales } py}$$

A disproportionate increase in sales unexplained by events such as a major acquisition can indicate manipulation.

Depreciation Index (DEPI)

$$\left(\frac{\text{Depreciation Expense } py}{\text{Depreciation Expense } py + \text{Net PPE } py}\right) \Big/ \left(\frac{\text{Depreciation Expense } cy}{\text{Depreciation Expense } cy + \text{Net PPE } cy}\right)$$

A DEPI of greater than 1 may be an indication that the company has revised upward the estimated useful lives of its larger assets. This could be an indicator of asset manipulation.

Sales, General, and Administrative Expenses Index (SGAI)

$$\left(\frac{\text{SG\&A Expenses } cy}{\text{Sales } cy}\right) \Big/ \left(\frac{\text{SG\&A Expenses } py}{\text{Sales } py}\right)$$

This index incorporates the same theory as the SGI index. Beniesh expects a positive relation between SGAI and the probability of manipulation.

Leverage Index (LVGI)

$$\left(\frac{\text{LTD } cy + \text{Current Liabilities } cy}{\text{Total Assets } cy}\right) \Big/ \left(\frac{\text{LTD } py + \text{Current Liabilities } py}{\text{Total Assets } py}\right)$$

An LVGI of greater than 1 indicates increased leverage. Higher leveraged companies are more prone to financial statement manipulation.

Total Accruals to Total Assets Index (TATA)

$$((\text{Working Capital } cy - \text{Working Capital } py) - (\text{Cash } cy - \text{Cash } py)) + (\text{Income Taxes Payable } cy - \text{Income Taxes Payable } py) + (\text{Current LTD } cy - \text{Current LTD } py) - (\text{Depreciation Expense } cy)/(\text{Total Assets } cy)$$

In its simplest form, if working capital (excluding cash) either increases or decreases dramatically, there could be a strong indication of financial statement manipulation. Accruals have always provided a common opportunity to commit and conceal a fraud. Total accruals are therefore defined as the change in working capital accounts other than cash and depreciation.

M Score The M score is computed through a weighting of the eight indices. While the M score is not foolproof, Professor Beneish found that companies with an M score higher than –2.22 had a higher probability to be financial statement manipulators.

The M score computation is reproduced as:

$$\text{M score} = -4.84 + \text{DSRI} \times .920 + \text{GMI} \times .528 + \text{AQI} \times .404 + \text{SGI} \times .892 + \text{DEPI} \times .115 + \text{SGAI} \times (.172) + \text{TATA} \times 4.679 + \text{LVGI} \times (.327)$$

Application of the Indices The M score was developed through the review and analysis of a specific population of companies, known manipulators that were required by the SEC to restate their financial statements. As such, the M score itself may not have application to many of the engagements a forensic operator will face. For example, most companies are much smaller than publicly traded companies and their financial statements are prepared on varying bases of accounting.

While the M score may have little application to most financial forensic matters, the underlying indices of the M score can provide valuable insight. For example, the asset quality index can still be used as an indicator of financial statement manipulation. Significant increases in nonoperating or other assets should be a red flag that warrants further investigation.

One of the unique aspects of Professor Beneish's indices is that they measure change year over year. Most financial statement ratios are stagnant and only measure performance for one year, thereby requiring two years of ratios for comparative purposes. Conversely, Beneish's indices attempt to quantify the change in key financial measures.

Finally, some of Professor Beneish's indices lend themselves to modification for applicability to the subject company under review. For example, total accruals to total assets can be easily modified to drill down and measure selected accrual elements.

The following is a formula to assess total accounts receivable to total assets (TARTA).

$$\text{TARTA} = \begin{pmatrix} ((\text{Accounts Receivable } cy - \text{Accounts Receivable } py) \\ -(\text{Depreciation Expense } cy))/(\text{Total Assets } cy) \end{pmatrix}$$

Similar formulas can be developed to assess changes in inventory (TITA), accounts payable (TAPTA), total current assets (TCATA), and total deferrals (TDTA).

Forensic indices are high-level tools that a properly trained forensic operator can use to assess the financial health of a company or to hone the road map for his investigation. However, as with many tools and techniques, forensic indices only provide indirect evidence and are not a substitute for the pick-and-shovel work.

FORENSIC FINANCIAL ANALYSIS

Financial analysis is an essential and never-ending responsibility for the forensic operator, since the analysis is foundational to forensic opinions. It is therefore essential to adopt and deploy an objective analytical process that considers all feasible data and techniques, and is easy for the various parties to understand. The chosen process must be thorough, avoid appearances of arbitrary selection, and lead other parties to the same conclusion.

Execution of such a process achieves two simultaneous objectives. First, it enables the forensic operator to meet his forensic assignment responsibilities. Second, it enables the forensic operator to defend against opposition attacks. Opposition parties will attack the forensic operator's selection and application of data and resultant analytical procedures. Consequently, diligence in identifying, collecting, validating, organizing, and examining the forensic assignment data blunts attacks.

This section and the companion sections indicated previously fill a vacuum in the financial forensics discipline. The vacuum exists due to the nature of the education and training common to most forensic operators. Their initial financial analysis education traces back to junior- or senior-level university accounting or finance classes, or both.[25] That is where they learned basic techniques such as horizontal and vertical analysis, trending, and possibly, simple ratio comparison, among other techniques.[26] Next, they learned analytical techniques used by their various employers. If the respective employers could offer nothing beyond initial university training, the forensic operator seldom progressed beyond this basic level. Finally, they learned analytical techniques through various CPE[27] offerings over the years. Unfortunately, many, if not most, CPE courses merely reinforce the basics already familiar to the forensic operator, thus providing little in the way of techniques that are more robust.

---

[25] Graduate-level education sometimes, but not always, goes beyond the basics of financial analysis.

[26] Curiously, even the universities and colleges offering forensic curricula offer very little in the way of new instruction. The substantial majority merely wrap a few accounting courses around a fraud course and refer to it as forensics.

[27] Continuing professional education.

Certain strengths and weaknesses inevitably result from such an educational process, with the weaknesses outweighing the strengths. The strengths include knowing how to calculate a few basic techniques, and possibly to interpret the implications of the results. The weaknesses include:

- Absence of a formalized methodology to consider and apply feasible techniques.
- Lack of awareness regarding the existence of forensic tools and techniques.
- Deficient knowledge regarding how or even whether to apply forensic techniques.
- Incomplete knowledge necessary to interpret and apply techniques.
- Inconsistency regarding the importance of one technique versus the other.
- Reliance upon a few techniques that become personal favorites.
- Absence of an objective means to evaluate and score the results.

These observations are common to practitioners throughout the United States. The authors often instruct forensic operators in forensic financial analysis techniques. The instruction session begins with basic financial analysis techniques to assess skill levels, and then proceeds to the forensic financial techniques contained in this section and the companion sections. The participants receive financial statement data and a reference handout containing basic analytical formulas, for example, current ratio, etc. Their assignment consists of three tasks: calculate all the analytical methods, interpret the results, and present their findings to the other participants.

Considering the heavy experience and skill levels of the participants, one can reasonably expect certain outcomes. Expectation of certain outcomes is reasonable because the vast majority of the participants have similar skill, knowledge, education, experience, and training in the analytical techniques. The expected outcomes include familiarity with most of the techniques, consistency in interpretation of the results, and consensus with respect to conclusions supported by the findings. Unfortunately, such outcomes are the exception.

The preceding expectations of commonality are no different from those expected from any profession, including physicians, attorneys, engineers, etc. That is, physicians (attorneys, engineers) of commensurate skill, knowledge, education, experience, and training, given the same set of facts, should arrive at similar conclusions. Forensic operators should be no different. Granted, opinions can differ, but differences should be a matter of degree rather than magnitude.[28]

This condition does not criticize forensic operators; rather, it merely describes the state of affairs regarding financial analysis. This section and the companion sections close the expectation gap by providing the knowledge to achieve three objectives. First, it outlines a framework of forensic financial techniques for forensic operators to use in actual assignments. Second, it clarifies the significance and importance of the various analytical measures using example data. That is, is the median more relevant than the truncated mean for the company under investigation? Third, and perhaps most important, it presents an objective scoring framework that forensic operators can use to support their opinions regarding financial data.

---

[28] "Can't Reasonable People Disagree?" *National Litigation Consultants Review* 3, no. 9 (February 2004).

All parties benefit when forensic operators apply these techniques. Forensic operators benefit because they achieve more with less effort, gain confidence in their assignment conclusions, produce more robust opinions less vulnerable to opposition attack, increase the capabilities of assigned staff, and differentiate themselves from competition.[29] Clients benefit from the empirical analysis used to arrive at conclusions, and less time and resources are invested in the project.

Forensic Financial Analysis

Fundamentally, forensic financial analysis is merely a form of data analysis. Consequently, one who understands data analysis can execute forensic financial analysis and vice versa. Granted, a party unfamiliar with financial statements lacks the insight that comes from financial knowledge. Nonetheless, the analytical processes parallel one another.

There are essential precedents commensurate with the analysis of and conclusions about data. Effective analysis requires five types of knowledge regarding the contents of a data set, including composition, boundaries, central tendencies, dispersion, and dynamics. Therefore, this section describes a schema that enables the forensic operator to discern the characteristics and the behavior of virtually any data set under investigation. The schema comprises five specific antecedents. That is, a forensic operator must know five key attributes regarding data before attempting to opine on the data. These attributes include the following:

1. The *composition* of the data, that is, the items that compose the data set.
2. The *boundaries* of the data to yield understanding of relative size.
3. The *central tendencies* of the data to identify data clustering.
4. The *dispersion* of the data to identify variation from central tendencies.
5. The *dynamics* of the data to identify the rate of change in the data.

In its most basic sense, forensic financial analysis (or forensic data analysis) seeks *aberrations* or *variability* in the data. Variability is important because, all other things being equal, the data created and resulting from business operations should behave in a predictable manner. In the most simplistic sense, variable expenses vary with revenue, while fixed expenses vary only over the long run. (See also the section of Chapter 3 titled "Aberrant Pattern Detection: What's the Difference?")

Therefore, the forensic operator compares data against two significant benchmarks to identify variability, itself and its peer group. This design mirrors the practice of medicine. For example, during one's annual physical examination, the physician considers two distinct sets of vital statistics benchmarks. First, he compares one's examination results against the patient's history of vital statistics, and second, against collective vital statistics from groups with similar sex, age, body composition, family history, and so on. This observation takes on more significance when considering that business peer data often lacks the similarity necessary to match the data set under investigation. Therefore, comparing data against itself (and its cohort from the same source) is often the best choice.

[29] In regulatory environments, *competition* is defined as competing agencies.

Consequently, the most effective deployment of forensic resources focuses on data exhibiting aberrations or variability. Manipulation may be the cause of the variability, as well as errors and explainable conditions. Nonetheless, the systematic investigation of target-rich, for example, varying data is far more efficient than arbitrary or random selection. This exploratory surgery approach further tunes the forensic operator to other indicators promising the greatest beneficial return on effort.

Forensic financial analysis comprises two major categories, data description and data analysis. The major categories mirror the process of analysis, whereby data requires description to determine which techniques are feasible. Analysis then produces observations for interpretation. The two major categories, in turn, are composed of five subcategories, executed in the following sequence: data composition, data boundaries, central tendencies, dispersion, and dynamics. Data composition presents an overall view of the data set, and may yield certain limited observations. Data boundaries presents a rough sizing of the data set as defined by its boundaries. Central tendencies indicates where the data set tends to cluster. Dispersion measures the breadth of the data set in comparison to its central tendencies. Finally, dynamics yields insight into the data set behavior in the form of rate, scale, and direction of movement.

The five subcategories are likewise composed of the individual measurements described in the remainder of this section. For example, data boundaries comprise minimum, maximum, and range measures of the data set. The 25-plus-or-minus individual measurements in the section are *not* all-inclusive. Literally hundreds, if not thousands, of potential measurements could apply. There is theoretically no limit to the number of individual measurements contained within the categories and subcategories. However, the practical limitations of a book compel a cutoff. If additional measurements merit inclusion or rejection for a particular data set, the schema framework described later in this section readily accommodates them.

The remainder of the section depicts the schema of the categories, subcategories, and individual measurements that constitute forensic financial analysis. The data set used in this section comes from an actual forensic assignment. The subject company in the actual forensic assignment manipulated financial statements to overstate reported net income, and concealed many of the journal entries in operating expense line items. The nature of the company under investigation suggested that operating expense line items exhibited relatively consistent behavior over time, journal entry distortion notwithstanding. Therefore, the forensic operator used forensic financial techniques to identify the line items exhibiting unusual variability. After the categories exhibiting the most variability surfaced, the respective accounts were investigated using drill-down techniques such as digital analysis, among others, to find concealing entries.

The actual forensic assignment comprised a very large data set, but using only a handful of the line items permits the reader to focus on the schema, techniques, and related observations. After completing the various measurements in the schema, the analysis aggregates to arrive at an overall conclusion using a technique known as multi-attribute utility analysis (MUA).[30] MUA is a widely accepted decision analysis

---

[30] Jacob W. Ulvila and Rex V. Brown, "Decision Analysis Comes of Age," *Harvard Business Review* 60, no. 5 (September–October 1982): 136–140.

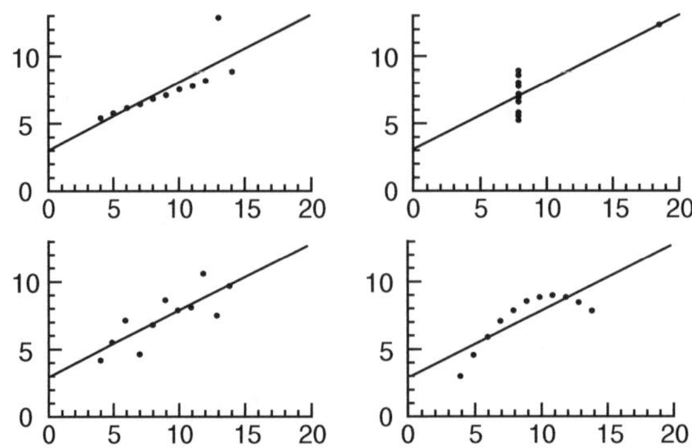

EXHIBIT 4.22 Anscombe's Quartet

technique formalized in the 1970s. It has wide use throughout virtually all disciplines, including biology, business, chemistry, physics, statistics, and many others.

The section contents provide a model that illustrates how a forensic operator should approach virtually all data analysis, regardless of the nature of the data. The example covers financial information, specifically, selected operating expenses for a subject company. However, the schema applies to virtually any type of required data analysis.

Generally, the schema structure accommodates a top down review with a bottom-up analysis. Each section disaggregates the respective category, for example, data boundaries, into the respective analytical measurements under the Measurement column in the tables. The table contains a description and example forensic application for each measurement. The respective data from the sample data set follows the table, with a visual, in turn, displaying the data. (See also the section in Chapter 6 titled Weapon (WPN).)

Visuals are essential to any form of data analysis. They not only indicate the shape and span of the data, but also often provide insight into clustering, dispersion, movement, and other indicators. Exhibit 4.22[31] displays a classic example of the necessity for visuals, described by Francis Anscombe and known as "Anscombe's quartet." Each of the data sets exhibits *identical* statistical properties: the mean and variance of both the X and Y coordinates are identical, the correlation between X and Y in each case is identical, and the linear regression line in each case is identical. Consequently, data description *requires* both a table containing the numbers, and a visual representing the numbers.

Schema The schema in Exhibit 4.23 conceptualizes the composition of the forensic financial analysis methodology. Analysis begins at the most detailed level, for example, individual measurements. After completing each individual measurement, they aggregate to the respective subcategory, which, in turn, aggregates to the respective

[31] F. J. Anscombe, "Graphs in Statistical Analysis," The American Statistician 27, no. 1 (1973): 17–21.

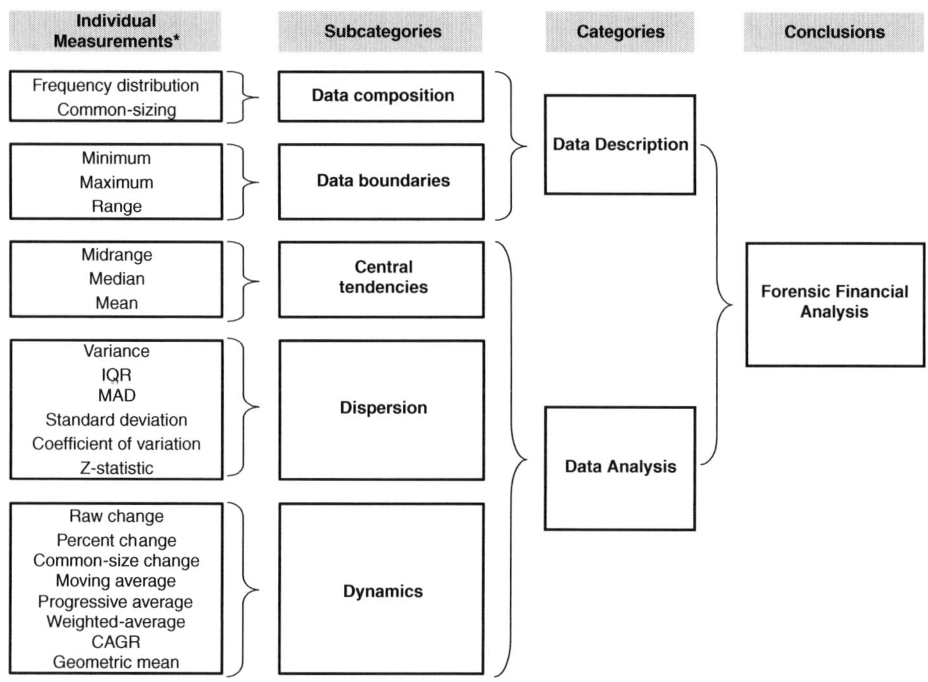

*There is no theoretical limit to the Measurements. They are determined by the assignment's dataset, and unique facts and circumstances.

EXHIBIT 4.23 Schema

category, which, in turn, aggregates and lends its findings to overall forensic financial analysis and related conclusions.

Data Description Data requires description before analysis. A simple example illustrates this point. Suppose a forensic operator's assignment required analysis of company X's cash disbursements over the last 42 months. The forensic operator received two different data sets, each of which contained cash disbursements data. The first data set contained 42 monthly journal entries reflecting summarized monthly cash disbursements for general ledger posting. The second data set contained 42 months of cash disbursement transactions reflecting the details of each check written, including date, payee, amount, account assignment, memorandum entry, and so forth. It comprised thousands of individual items and hundreds of pages. Despite both data sets agreeing in total, the applicable techniques for each would vary considerably.

The first data set's printout of the 42 items, and a bar graph displaying disbursements by month readily conveyed the contents, size, scale, trending, and other characteristics of the data set. The forensic operator learned a great deal about the data set by merely reviewing the printout and the bar graph. Most importantly, he instantly determined the types of analysis to complete so he could best complete his assignment. Data drives analysis.

The second data set's printout of the hundreds of pages displaying the detailed transactions, and a bar graph[32] displaying the disbursements, could not convey characteristics as readily as the first data set. Further description was necessary before the forensic operator could begin analysis. The necessary description included definition of the data set boundaries, range, central tendencies, dispersion, and dynamics so as to understand the contents. Most important, he realized that descriptive statistics were necessary to best describe the data. Data drives analysis.

The preceding example, although extreme, illustrates the importance of describing data, and thus gaining complete comprehension of its composition and boundaries, before analysis begins. As we already observed, the very act of description often produces observations that yield insight. Potential data set observations include indicators of cycles, variability, directional trending, and other characteristics. Furthermore, understanding the data within a data set makes possible the selection and application of various analytical techniques. For example, extremely large data sets require certain analysis, for example, central tendency, dispersion, etc., to best manage and interpret the data.

The data description category is composed of two subcategories, data composition and data boundaries, with data composition completed first. After data composition is completed the next subcategory, data boundaries is completed. Recall that the sample data set displayed further on comes from an actual forensic assignment. Note that generic category descriptors, for example, Category A, Category B, etc., prevent reader bias. For example, a forensic operator viewing two categories labeled *salaries* and *fuel* may impute (even subconsciously) behavior to the categories, that is, fixed and variable, respectively. (See also the section in Chapter 3 titled "Confirmation Bias: Clinical Thinking.")

Note to the reader: Practice using this technique. First, view the table and related visual on the following pages and use professional judgment, intuition, Kentucky windage, or any other means to identify the category that appears to exhibit the most variability. Make a note in the margin of this book so that the answer can compare to the conclusion at the end of the section.

The table in Exhibit 4.24 contains the measurement, description, and forensic application that makes up the subcategory, for example, composition, boundaries, etc., of the data set. For more explanation of the various measurement techniques, for example, geometric mean, there are an enormous variety of publications and references on the Internet. In fact, pursuing further explanation reinforces one's understanding of the technique. The forensic application listed for each measurement is by no means comprehensive. Rather, it provides a stimulus for other data sets under investigation.

Data Description and Data Composition The first step in forensic financial analysis typically requires identification of data composition, a subcategory supporting data description.

Frequency Distribution *Frequency Distribution—Data*—Data is most easily understood when logically presented. For example, a textual listing of category amounts

[32] Largely unreadable because of the volume of data.

EXHIBIT 4.24 Composition

Measurement	Description	Forensic Application
Frequency distribution[33]—data Frequency distribution—visual	The matrix or visual display of the values contained within a data set. In nearly all cases, the combination of the matrix and the visual maximize the forensic operator's description of the data.	These are typically the first two steps of forensic financial analysis. They describe the data set composition in its most basic form for the forensic operator, and may yield preliminary observation of patterns or trends or both.
Common-sizing	The measurement of each item compared to a common base. This provides a proportionate, or common, measure of comparison for all items.	This depicts comparative proportion among the items, and may yield preliminary observation of patterns or trends or both.

by year is less readily understood than presentation in a table format. Also, textual presentation inhibits observations that may be useful, which could include trending and other patterns.

Exhibit 4.25 displays the data for each category by year and contains annual totals.

- Category A exhibits 151,076 for 2007, which steadily increased to 475,680 for 2010, but declined substantially to 278,882 for 2011, and increased substantially to 362,338 for 2012.
- Category B exhibits 18,938 for 2007, increased substantially to 122,806 for 2009, but declined substantially to 1,576 for 2011, and increased substantially to 108,636 for 2012.
- Category C exhibits 87,830 for 2007 and was relatively stable until exhibiting 19,230 for 2011 and 16,160 for 2012.

EXHIBIT 4.25 Operating Expenses

	2007	2008	2009	2010	2011	2012
Category A	151,076	243,006	312,888	475,680	278,882	362,338
Category B	18,938	55,853	122,806	3,454	1,576	108,636
Category C	87,830	75,771	82,972	78,901	19,230	16,160
Category D	144,406	163,725	167,658	132,229	123,677	125,820
Category E	101,333	131,300	121,140	94,859	96,060	129,513
Category F	325,261	336,542	353,399	332,028	322,574	340,077
Total	828,844	1,006,197	1,160,863	1,117,151	841,999	1,082,544

[33] The presentation of the contents of a data set in a table or visual format or both.

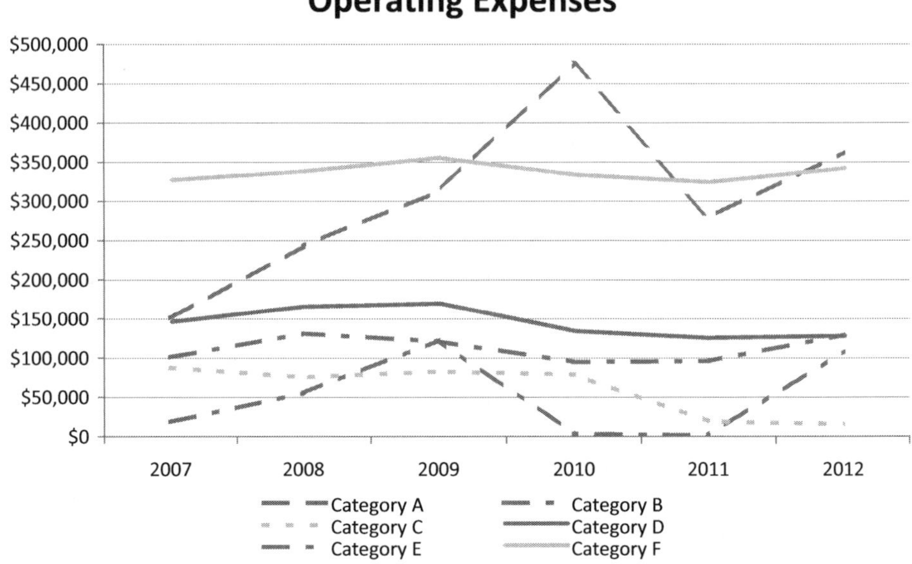

EXHIBIT 4.26 Operating Expenses Graph

- Category D exhibits 144,406 for 2007, and increased to 167,658 for 2009, decreased in 2010, and remained relatively stable until arriving at 125,820 in 2012.
- Category E exhibits 101,333 for 2007, increased to 131,300 for 2008, steadily decreased to 96,060 in 2011, and increased significantly to 129,513 for 2012.
- Category F exhibits 325,621 for 2007 and remained relatively stable until reporting 340,077 in 2012.

Frequency Distribution—Visual—Data should also be briefly presented in a visual format to maximize reader understanding. Furthermore, the visual format should supplement the table presentation. There is a wide array of visual formats that effectively display table contents. Also, there is no limitation, per se, on visual formats. It may be helpful to present multiple formats, such as a bar graph, stacked bar, pie chart, etc.

Exhibit 4.26 displays each data item within category by year and indicates the item's changes over the relevant time horizon.

- Category A and Category B appear to exhibit the greatest volatility, with the remaining categories appearing relatively stable.

Common-sizing Sizing *Common-sizing*—The measurement of each item compared to a common base. This provides a proportionate, or common, measure of comparison for all items. This depicts comparative proportion among the items, and may yield preliminary observation of patterns or trends or both. It also accommodates a comparison of items between two subjects of disparate size.

EXHIBIT 4.27 Common-Size

	2007	2008	2009	2010	2011	2012
Category A	0.64%	0.82%	0.78%	1.38%	0.95%	1.52%
Category B	0.08%	0.19%	0.31%	0.01%	0.01%	0.45%
Category C	0.37%	0.26%	0.21%	0.23%	0.07%	0.07%
Category D	0.61%	0.55%	0.42%	0.38%	0.42%	0.53%
Category E	0.43%	0.44%	0.30%	0.27%	0.33%	0.54%
Category F	1.37%	1.14%	0.88%	0.96%	1.10%	1.42%
Total	3.49%	3.40%	2.90%	3.23%	2.88%	4.53%

Exhibit 4.27 displays each data item in proportion to revenues (not shown) by year within a category.

- Category A exhibits .64 percent for 2007 and steadily increased to 1.38 percent for 2010, declined substantially to .95 percent for 2011, and increased substantially to 1.52 percent for 2012.
- Category B exhibits .08 percent for 2007, increased substantially to .31 percent for 2009, but declined substantially to .01 percent for 2011, and increased substantially to .45 percent for 2012.
- Category C exhibits .37 percent for 2007, decreased significantly to .26 percent for 2008, and was relatively stable until declining substantially, exhibiting .07 percent for 2011 and remaining steady for 2012.
- Category D exhibits .61 percent for 2007, and steadily declined to .38 percent for 2010, increased slightly to .42 percent in 2010, and increased again until arriving at .53 percent in 2012.
- Category E exhibits .43 percent for 2007, increasing slightly to .44 percent for 2008, substantially decreased to .30 percent in 2009, and remained relatively stable until increasing substantially to .54 percent in 2012.
- Category F exhibits 1.37 percent for 2007, declined slightly to 1.14 percent in 2008, declined again to .88 percent in 2009, increased to .96 percent in 2010 and remained relatively stable until substantially increasing to 1.42 percent in 2012.

Exhibit 4.28 displays each data item in proportion to revenues (not shown) by year within category and indicates the item's changes over the relevant time horizon.

- Category A exhibits the most dramatic proportionate increase from 2007 to 2012, while Category C exhibits the most dramatic decrease over the same time horizon.
- Category B exhibits a substantial proportionate increase from 2007 to 2012.
- Categories D, E, and F all exhibit significant change, but arrived at about the same position in 2012 as shown for 2007.

Scoring—Composition This section describes the composition of the data set. Therefore, the MUA format in Exhibit 4.29 scores comments and observations

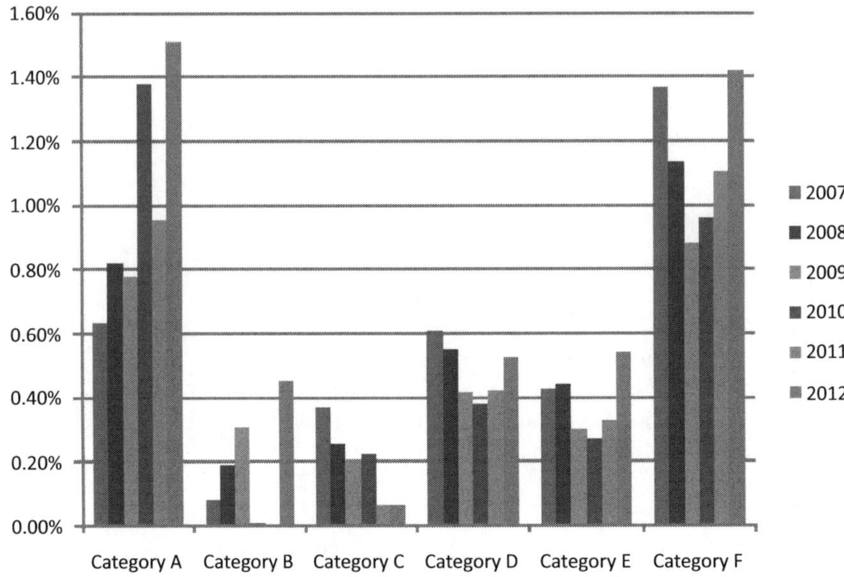

EXHIBIT 4.28 Common-Size Chart

resulting from the data set knowledge gained. No apparent pattern resulted from the annual totals. Categories A and B appear the most variable, and all categories display some variability. Categories A and B are each scored with a 1, indicating that they meet the condition stated in the comments and observation column. Since all categories display variability in a common sizing, no scoring is necessary.

Data Description and Data Boundaries The preceding section described the composition of the data set. The second step in forensic financial analysis is typically identifying data set boundaries. This section therefore describes the boundaries of the data set. The composition and boundaries of the data set make up the subcategories supporting data description.

Exhibit 4.30 contains the measurement, description, and forensic application composing the boundaries of the data set.

EXHIBIT 4.29 Comments and Observations

		Category						
	Measurement	A	B	C	D	E	F	**Comments & Observations**
Comp.	Frequency Distribution—Data							Annual totals present no apparent pattern
	Frequency Distribution—Visual	1	1					Categories A and B appear most variable
	Common-sizing							All categories display variability

EXHIBIT 4.30 Boundaries

Measurement	Description	Forensic Application
Minimum	The smallest value within a data set.	Sets lower data boundary and may apply in other techniques, for example, midrange (discussed next).
Maximum	The largest value within a data set.	Sets upper data boundary and may apply in other techniques, for example, midrange (discussed next).
Range	The difference between the highest and the lowest data value. Range sometimes calculates differently. For example, it could be described using "from and to" in lieu of the difference.	Indicates data spread and may help a forensic operator determine the scope of analysis likely to be necessary. Also, it is useful to compare other basic data sets.

Minimum, Maximum, and Range

Minimum—The minimum is the smallest value within a data set. The minimum sets the lower data boundary and may apply in other techniques, for example, midrange.

Maximum—The maximum is a largest value within a data set. The maximum sets the upper data boundary and may apply in other techniques, for example, midrange (discussed later).

Range—The range reflects the difference between the highest and the lowest data value. Range sometimes calculates differently. For example, it could be described using "from and to" in lieu of the difference, that is, Category A exhibits a range from 151,076 to 475,680, leaving the calculation to the reader. If negative numbers are involved, the algebraic sum is the proper means to calculate range. For example, if category A exhibited a minimum of –151,076 and a maximum of 475,680, the resultant range is 626,756 (475,680 minus –151,076). The range indicates data spread and may help a forensic operator determine the scope of analysis likely to be necessary. It is also useful to compare other basic data sets.

The range yields a poor measurement of variability since it considers only two extreme values, that is, the minimum and maximum, and ignores the remaining values.

Exhibit 4.31 displays the minimum, maximum, and range of values by category.

- Category A exhibits 151,076, 475,680, and 324,604 for the minimum, maximum, and range values, respectively.
- Category B exhibits 1,576, 122,806, and 121,230 for the minimum, maximum, and range values, respectively.
- Category C exhibits 16,160, 87,830, and 71,670 for the minimum, maximum, and range values, respectively.

EXHIBIT 4.31 Summary of Minimum, Maximum, and Range

	Min	Max	Range
Category A	151,076	475,680	324,604
Category B	1,576	122,806	121,230
Category C	16,160	87,830	71,670
Category D	123,677	167,658	43,981
Category E	94,859	131,300	36,441
Category F	322,574	353,399	30,825

- Category D exhibits 123,677, 167,658, and 43,981, for the minimum, maximum, and range values, respectively.
- Category E exhibits 94,859, 131,300, and 36,441, for the minimum, maximum, and range values, respectively.
- Category F exhibits 322,574, 353,399, and 30,825 for the minimum, maximum, and range values, respectively.
- The data set comprising all categories exhibits 1,576, 475,680, and 474,104 for the minimum, maximum, and range values, respectively.

Exhibit 4.32 displays the minimum, maximum, and range for each category.

- Categories A and F display the largest values of the data set.
- Categories B and C display the smallest values of the data set.
- Category A displays the greatest range of values of the data set.
- Category F displays the smallest range of values of the data set.

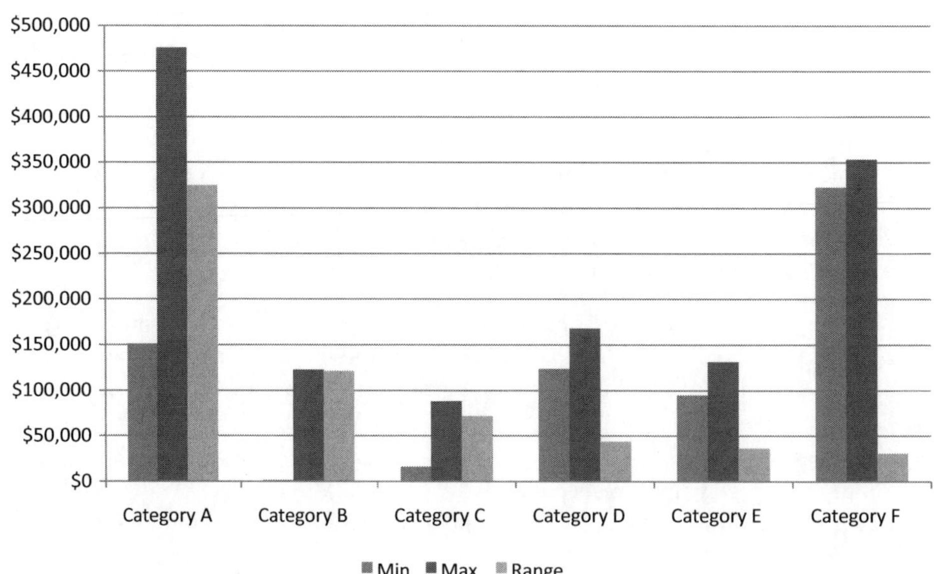

EXHIBIT 4.32 Data Description

EXHIBIT 4.33 Data Boundaries

	Measurement	Category A	B	C	D	E	F	Comments and Observations
Comp.	Frequency Distribution—Data							Annual totals present no apparent pattern
	Frequency Distribution—Visual	1	1					Categories A and B appear most variable
	Common-sizing							All categories display variability
Bnd-y.	Minimum						1	Largest minimum
	Maximum	1						Largest maximum
	Range	1						Largest range between minimum and maximum

Scoring—Boundaries This section described the boundaries of the data set. Therefore, the MUA format in Exhibit 4.33 scores comments and observations resulting from the data set knowledge gained. Category A contained the maximum value and the largest range, while Category F contained the largest minimum value.

Data Analysis and Central Tendencies The preceding section described the boundaries of the data set. The third step in forensic financial analysis is typically identifying data set central tendencies. Therefore, this section describes the central tendencies of the data set. The central tendencies of the data set comprise one of the three subcategories supporting data analysis. They are central tendencies, dispersion, and dynamics.

Exhibit 4.34 contains the measurement, description, and forensic application that make up the dispersion of the data set.

Mode, Midrange, Median, Mean (Arithmetic), and Mean (Truncated)

Mode—The mode, if any, is the data set value that occurs most frequently in a data set. If the data set does not contain a mode, it is identified to inform the reader that was considered, but is labeled as not present. In some cases, the mode saves time, since the analysis of one mode value is likely applicable to the other mode values. A typical example is recurring lease payments.

Midrange—The arithmetic mean of the minimum and maximum values. It is calculated by adding the minimum and maximum values and dividing by two. The midrange provides a measure of the expected value within a data set. The forensic operator can compare each actual value to the expected value to determine variability. For example, the actual invoice amount of customer K is compared to the expected (midrange) invoice amount of customer K. A discrepancy is one of the factors permitting the forensic operator to assess whether the invoice requires further investigation.

EXHIBIT 4.34 Central Tendency

Measurement	Description	Forensic Application
Mode	The data set value that occurs most frequently in a data set. The mode ignores all values except those considered modal. Its usage is nominal.	In some cases, the mode saves time since the analysis of one mode value is likely applicable to the other mode values. A typical example is recurring lease payments.
Midrange	The arithmetic mean of the minimum and maximum values. It is calculated by adding the minimum and maximum values and dividing by two.	Provides various measures of the expected or most likely value within a data set. The forensic operator can compare each actual value to the expected value to determine variability. For example, the actual invoice amount of customer K compared to the expected invoice amount of customer K permits the forensic operator to assess whether the actual invoice requires further investigation.
Median	The value reflecting the midpoint of the data set containing an odd number of values. The median of a data set containing an even number of values is the arithmetic mean of the two middle values. The median splits the data into two equal groups, one with values greater than or equal to the median and the other with values less than or equal to the median.	
Mean—arithmetic	The value resulting from the sum of all data set values divided by the number of data set values. The only measure of central tendency that gives equal representation to all values.	
Mean—truncated	The arithmetic mean, absent the highest and lowest values of the data set. The highest and lowest values can represent a proportion or absolute values within the data set. The proportion is typically based upon an objective measure.	
All means, dispersion	This compares all mean measurements for each category. The greater dispersion represented by the disparate means suggests skewed data. Despite being a dispersion measurement, it is included in the central tendencies section to reside with the respective findings.	Indicates variability away from the mean.

Median—The value reflecting the midpoint of the data set containing an odd number of values. The median of a data set containing an even number of values is the arithmetic mean of the two middle values. The median is not sensitive to any value in a data set, and is only sensitive to the number of values in the data set. It is useful when the arithmetic mean is known to be biased because of wide data set dispersion, but tends to have clustering. The median provides a measure of the expected value within a data set. The forensic operator can compare each actual value to the expected value to determine variability. For example, the actual invoice amount of customer K compared to the expected (median) invoice amount of customer K permits the forensic operator to assess whether the invoice requires further investigation.

Mean—arithmetic—The value resulting from the sum of all data set values divided by the number of data set values. The arithmetic mean is the only measure of central tendency that gives equal representation to all values. It provides a measure of the expected value within a data set. The forensic operator can compare each actual value to the expected value to determine variability. For example, the actual invoice amount of customer K, compared to the expected invoice amount of customer K, permits the forensic operator to assess whether the invoice requires further investigation.

Mean—truncated—The value resulting from the arithmetic mean, absent the highest and lowest values of the data set. The highest and lowest values can represent a proportion or absolute values within the data set. It is therefore important that the proportion or values to be ignored is based upon an objective measure. The proportion is typically based upon an objective measure. One measure is Chebyshev's Theorem. It applies to any data set and suggests that at least 75 percent of all the items fall within two standard deviations of the mean. The truncated mean provides a measure of the expected value within a data set. The forensic operator can compare each actual value to the expected value to determine variability. For example, the actual invoice amount of customer K compared to the expected invoice amount of customer K permits the forensic operator to assess whether the invoice requires further investigation.

All means, dispersion—The all means dispersion compares all mean measurements for each category to one another. The greater the dispersion, that is, variability represented by the disparate means, suggests skewed data. Despite being a dispersion measurement, it is included in the central tendencies category to reside with the respective findings.

Exhibit 4.35 exhibits the mode, midrange, median, mean (arithmetic), and mean (truncated) for the respective category.

EXHIBIT 4.35 Mode, Midrange, Median, and Means

	Mode	Midrange	Median	Mean Arithmetic	Mean Truncated
Category A	n/a	313,378	295,885	303,978	299,279
Category B	n/a	62,191	37,396	51,877	46,720
Category C	n/a	51,995	77,336	60,144	64,219
Category D	n/a	145,667	138,318	142,919	141,545
Category E	n/a	113,080	111,237	112,368	112,012
Category F	n/a	337,987	334,285	334,980	333,477

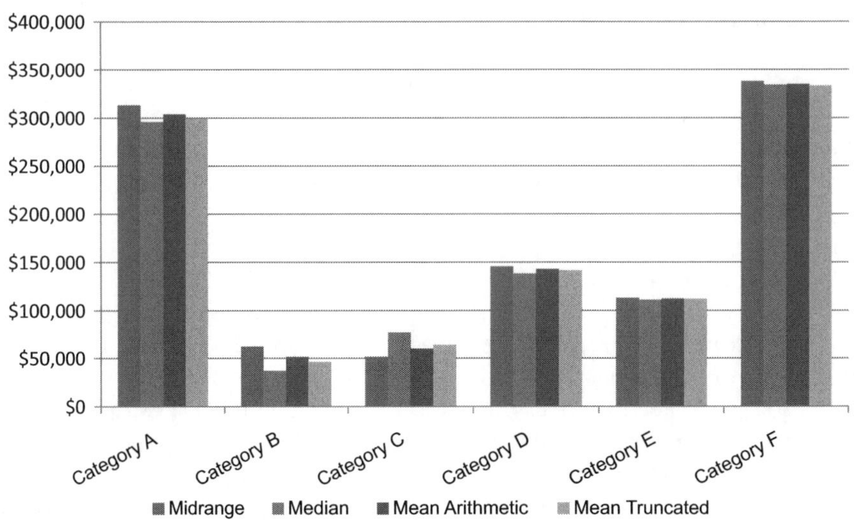

EXHIBIT 4.36 Mode, Midrange, Median, and Means

- Category A exhibits 313,378, 295,885, 303,978, and 299,279 for the midrange, median, arithmetic mean, and truncated mean, respectively.
- Category B exhibits 62,191, 37,396, 51,877, and 46,720 for the midrange, median, arithmetic mean, and truncated mean, respectively.
- Category C exhibits 51,995, 77,336, 60,144, and 64,219 for the midrange, median, arithmetic mean, and truncated mean, respectively.
- Category D exhibits 145,667, 138,318, 142,919, and 141,545 for the midrange, median, arithmetic mean, and truncated mean, respectively.
- Category E exhibits 113,080, 111,237, 112,368, and 112,012 for the midrange, median, arithmetic mean, and truncated mean, respectively.
- Category F exhibits 337,987, 334,285, 334,980, and 333,477 for the midrange, median, arithmetic mean, and truncated mean, respectively.
- The data set comprising all categories exhibits 283,103 and 286,757 for the all means dispersion arithmetic, and all means dispersion truncated values, respectively.

Exhibit 4.36 displays the midrange, median, mean (arithmetic), and mean (truncated) for each category.

- Categories A and D, and E and F exhibit very similar central tendencies.
- Categories B and C exhibit slightly different central tendencies.
- Categories A and F exhibit approximately the same central tendencies.

Scoring—Central Tendencies This section described the central tendencies of the data set. Therefore, the MUA format in Exhibit 4.37 scores comments and observations resulting from the data set knowledge gained. Categories A and F shared similar measurements as indicated by the format. The all means dispersion measurement is included with central tendencies (instead of dispersion) to reside with the respective findings.

EXHIBIT 4.37 Central Tendencies Comparison

	Measurement	Category A	B	C	D	E	F	Comments & Observations
Comp.	Frequency Distribution—Data							Annual totals present no apparent pattern
Comp.	Frequency Distribution—Visual	1	1					Categories A and B appear most variable
Comp.	Common-sizing							All categories display variability
Bndry.	Minimum						1	Largest minimum
Bndry.	Maximum	1						Largest maximum
Bndry.	Range	1						Largest range between minimum and maximum
Central Tendency	Mode							n/a
Central Tendency	Midrange	1					1	Categories A and F largest and similar value
Central Tendency	Median	1					1	Categories A and F similar value
Central Tendency	Mean—Arithmetic	1					1	Categories A and F similar value
Central Tendency	Mean—Truncated	1					1	Categories A and F similar value
Central Tendency	All Means Dispersion		1	1				Greatest disparity among central tendencies

Data Analysis and Dispersion The preceding section described the central tendencies of the data set. The fourth step in forensic financial analysis is typically measuring data set dispersion, or spread. Therefore, this section describes the dispersion of the data set.

Exhibit 4.38 contains the measurement, description, and forensic application that make up the dispersion of the data set.

Variance

Variance—The variance is arithmetic mean of the sum of the squared differences of the mean. (It is the square of the standard deviation; the standard deviation squared.) It is useful for comparing dispersion among different data sets. In addition, the squared nature of the variables is not intuitively understood.

Figure 4.39 displays the variance for category by year.

- Category A exhibits variances with a low of 8,910 for 2009 and a high of 171,702 for 2010.
- Category B exhibits variances with a low of 3,976 for 2008 and a high of 70,929 for 2009.

EXHIBIT 4.38 Dispersion

Measurement	Description	Forensic Application
Variance	The arithmetic mean of the sum of the squared differences of the mean. (The square of the standard deviation.)	Useful for comparing dispersion within and among different data sets.
Interquartile range (IQR)	Exhibits the dispersion between the third and first quartiles. It is sometimes referred to as the midspread, or the middle 50 percent.	Concentrates analysis on the middle 50 percent of the data values.
Mean average deviation (MAD)	The arithmetic mean of the absolute differences from the mean. Also, the median is sometimes used to derive the median average deviation.	Useful for comparing actual values that vary from the mean.
Standard deviation	A measurement reflecting the average distance of data from the mean of the data set. (The positive square root of the variance.)	Provides specific cutoffs for the forensic operator to categorize variability of data. For example, +/–1 standard deviation makes up 68.2 percent of the data.
Coefficient of variation	A measure representing the dispersion of data from the mean. It is calculated by dividing the standard deviation by the arithmetic mean. The smaller the measure, the closer the standard deviation approximates the mean. Thus, it measures the relative kurtosis of a data set. Kurtosis measures how peaked or flat the distribution of data relative is to a normal distribution. Data sets with a high kurtosis have a distinct peak near the mean, and vice versa.	This can be a useful measure of reliability. For example, recurring measures of the same data, airline on-time arrivals, should exhibit similar coefficients of variation. Significant differences suggest variability. Also, this is a useful measure when comparing data sets, since the lower the correlation of variation, the tighter the data toward the mean.
Z-statistic	Measures the distance of a value within a data set from the mean in terms of the number of standard deviations the value is from the mean.	Forensic operators use the Z-statistic to identify the extreme values, thus focusing attention on those values exhibiting greatest variability.

- Category C exhibits variances with a low of 15,627 for 2008 and a high of 43,984 for 2012.
- Category D exhibits variances with a low 1,487 for 2007 and a high of 24,739 for 2009.
- Category E exhibits a low of 8,773 for 2009 and the high of 18,933 for 2008.
- Category F exhibits a low of 1,562 for 2008 and a high of 18,419 for 2009.

EXHIBIT 4.39 Annual Deviation from Mean—Variance

	2007	2008	2009	2010	2011	2012
Category A	152,902	60,972	8,910	171,702	25,096	58,360
Category B	32,939	3,976	70,929	48,423	50,301	56,759
Category C	27,686	15,627	22,828	18,757	40,914	43,984
Category D	1,487	20,806	24,739	10,690	19,242	17,099
Category E	11,035	18,933	8,773	17,509	16,308	17,146
Category F	9,719	1,562	18,419	2,952	12,406	5,097

Exhibit 4.40 displays the variance for each category by year.

- Category A exhibits the largest overall absolute variances.
- Category B exhibits the second-largest overall absolute variances.
- Category C exhibits variances of relatively similar size for each year.
- Categories D, E, and F appear to exhibit variances of smaller proportion for the various years.

IQR, MAD, Standard Deviation, and Coefficient of Variation Exhibit 4.41 displays the IQR, MAD, standard deviation, and coefficient of variation by category.

IQR (interquartile range)—The IQR exhibits the dispersion between the third and first quartiles. It is sometimes referred to as the midspread, or the middle 50. The result of the IQR concentrates subsequent analysis on the middle 50 percent of the data. To calculate it, start with the median as a starting point, identify the data set above the median and the data set below the median. Then find the medians for each of those two sub–data sets. The median of the sub–data set below the median is Q1 and above the median

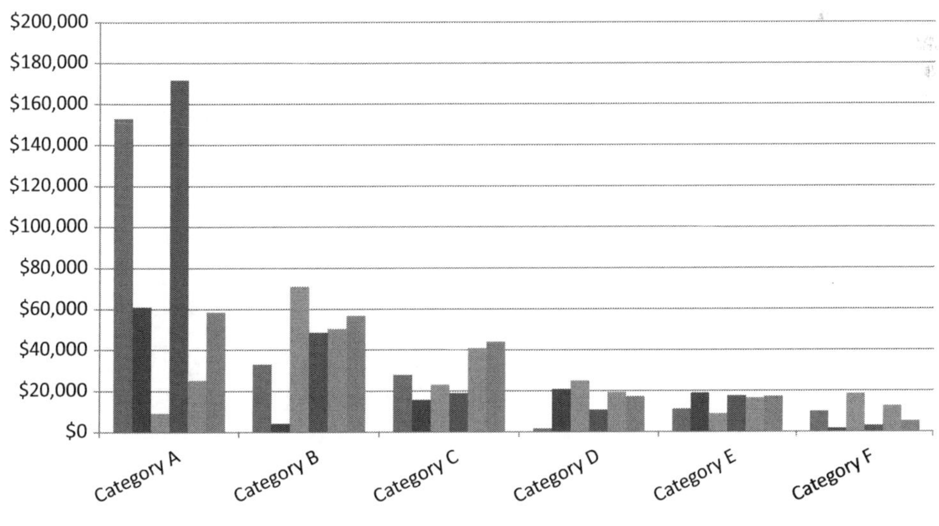

EXHIBIT 4.40 Dispersion and Deviation from Mean

EXHIBIT 4.41 IQR, MAD, Standard Deviation, and Coefficient

	IQR	MAD	Standard Deviation	Coefficient of Variation
Category A	98,001	79,657	110,176	0.36
Category B	88,115	43,888	53,345	1.03
Category C	48,589	28,299	33,143	0.55
Category D	31,474	15,677	19,100	0.13
Category E	30,042	14,950	16,874	0.15
Category F	12,240	8,359	11,178	0.03

is Q3. Finally, subtract Q1 from Q3 to derive the IQR. A data set must contain at least 50 items for the IQR to be meaningful. In such a condition, its measurement of dispersion is reasonably accurate.

MAD (mean absolute deviation)—The MAD is the arithmetic mean of the absolute differences from the mean. Also, the median is sometimes used to derive the median average deviation. It is useful for comparing actual values that vary from the mean.

Standard deviation—A measurement indicating the average distance of data from the mean of the data set. (It is the square root of the variance, explained earlier.) The standard deviation provides specific cutoffs for the forensic operator to categorize variability of data. For example, +/–1 standard deviation comprises 68.2 percent of the data, +/–2 standard deviations comprise 95.9 percent and +/–3 standard deviations comprise 99.7 percent of the data. Consequently, items following more than 3 (sometimes 2) standard deviations merit investigation.[34]

Coefficient of variation—A measure representing the dispersion of data from the mean. It is calculated by dividing the standard deviation by the arithmetic mean. A small coefficient of variation indicates that the standard deviation approximates the mean. Therefore, it can be used to compare the relative clustering of data among data sets. A kurtosis of zero indicates a data set with a standard or normal distribution. A kurtosis greater than zero indicates a peaked data set distribution: the greater the number, the sharper the peak. A kurtosis less than zero indicates a flat data set distribution: the greater the negative number, the flatter the data set distribution.

- Category A exhibits 98,001, 79,657, 110,176, and 0.36 for the IQR, MAD, standard deviation, and coefficient of variation, respectively.
- Category B exhibits 88,115, 43,888, 53,345, and 1.03 for the IQR, MAD, standard deviation, and coefficient of variation, respectively.
- Category C exhibits 48,589, 28,299, 33,143, and 0.55 for the IQR, MAD, standard deviation, and coefficient of variation, respectively.

[34] This is the Empirical Rule and only applies to Normal Distributions. For other than normal distributions, Chebyshev's Theorem applies, stating that 75 percent within +/−2 standard deviations, 89 percent within +/−3 standard deviations, and 94 percent of all data within +/−4 standard deviations.

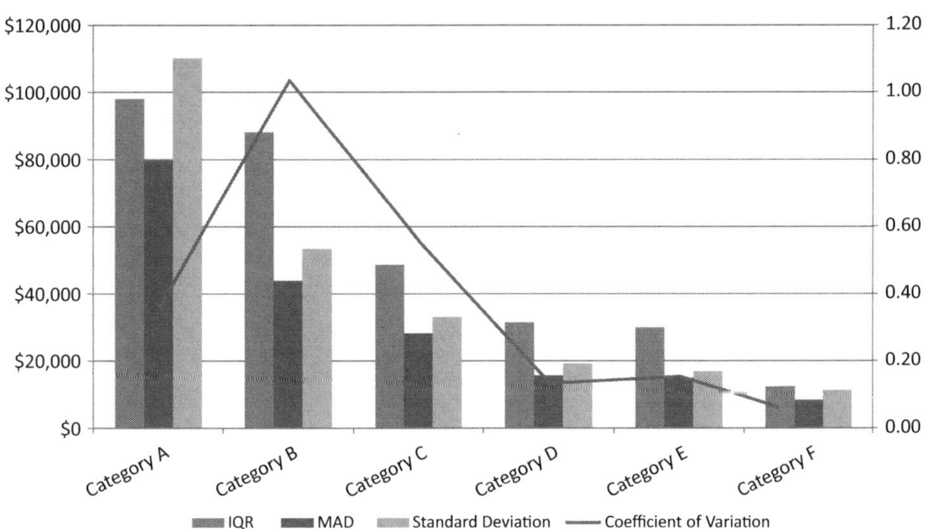

EXHIBIT 4.42 Dispersion

- Category D exhibits 31,474, 15,677, 19,100, and 0.13 for the IQR, MAD, standard deviation, and coefficient of variation, respectively.
- Category E exhibits 30,042, 14,950, 16,874, and 0.15 for the IQR, MAD, standard deviation, and coefficient of variation, respectively.
- Category F exhibits 12,240, 8,359, 11,178, and 0.03 for the IQR, MAD, standard deviation, and coefficient of variation, respectively.

Exhibit 4.42 displays the IQR, MAD, standard deviation, and coefficient of variation by category.

- Category B exhibits the largest coefficient of variation at 1.03, thus suggesting the largest relative disparity among the categories.
- Category F exhibits the smallest coefficient of variation at 0.03, thus suggesting the smallest relative disparity among the categories.

Z-Statistic

Z-statistic—The Z-statistic measures the distance of a value within a data set from the mean. Forensic operators use the Z-statistic to identify the extreme values, thus focusing attention on those values exhibiting greatest variability.

Exhibit 4.43 displays the Z-statistic for each category by year.

- Category A exhibits –1.39 for 2007 and 1.56 for 2010, thus displaying a range of 2.95.
- Category B exhibits –0.94 for 2011 and 1.33 for 2009, thus displaying a range of –0.29.

EXHIBIT 4.43 Z-Statistic

	2007	2008	2009	2010	2011	2012	Range
Category A	(1.39)	(0.55)	0.08	1.56	(0.23)	0.53	2.95
Category B	(0.62)	0.07	1.33	(0.91)	(0.94)	1.06	(0.29)
Category C	0.84	0.47	0.69	0.57	(1.23)	(1.33)	(0.27)
Category D	0.08	1.09	1.30	(0.56)	(1.01)	(0.90)	(0.64)
Category E	(0.65)	1.12	0.52	(1.04)	(0.97)	1.02	(0.38)
Category F	(0.87)	0.14	1.65	(0.26)	(1.11)	0.46	0.61

- Category C exhibits –1.33 for 2012 and 0.84 for 2007, thus displaying a range of –0.27.
- Category D exhibits –1.01 for 2011 and 1.30 for 2009, thus displaying a range of –0.64.
- Category E exhibits –1.04 for 2010 and 1.12 for 2008, thus displaying a range of –0.38.
- Category F exhibits –1.11 for 2011 and 1.65 for 2009, thus displaying a range of 0.61.

Exhibit 4.44 displays the Z-statistic for each category by year.

- Category F exhibits the largest Z-statistic of the data set that occurred in 2009.
- Categories A, B, and D exhibit the next largest Z-statistics that occurred in 2010 and 2009, respectively.
- Category A exhibits the largest negative Z-statistic of the data set that occurred in 2007.

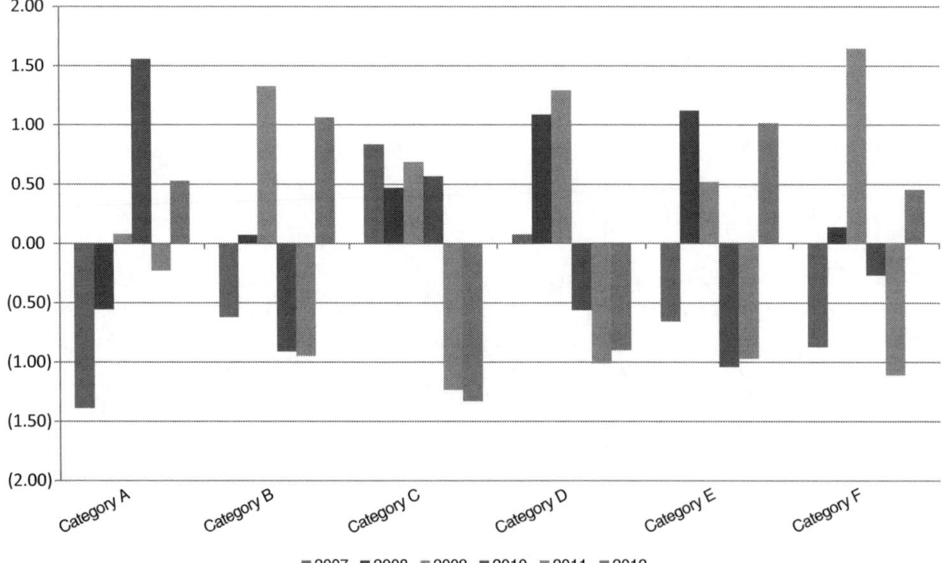

EXHIBIT 4.44 Dispersion Z-Score

- Category C exhibits the next largest Z-statistic that occurred in 2012, with categories C, D, and F exhibiting similarly large negative Z-statistics that occurred in 2011.

Scoring—Dispersion This section described the dispersion of the data set. Therefore, the MUA format in Exhibit 4.45 scores comments and observations resulting from the data set knowledge gained. Category A's variance, MAD, standard deviation, and Z score range scored the highest. Category B shared the IQR with Category A but had a very high coefficient of variation, with a low Z Score.

Data Analysis and Dynamics The preceding section described the dispersion of the data set. The fifth step in forensic financial analysis is typically measuring data set dynamics. Therefore, this section describes the dispersion of the data set. The dynamics of the data measures its rate of change, rate of direction, and so on, and generally reflects variability.

Exhibit 4.46 contains the measurement, description, and forensic application that make up the dynamics of the data set.

Year-to-Year Raw Change, Year-to-Year Percentage Change

Year-to-year raw change—This measurement computes the year-to-year increase or decrease in the value of a data set item.

Year-to-year percentage change—This measurement expresses the year-to-year increase or decrease in the value of a data set item as a proportion of the previous year.

Exhibit 4.47 displays the year-to-year raw change for each category by year.

- Category A exhibits a peak year-to-year increase of 162,792 for 2010 and a peak year-to-year decrease of –196,798 for 2011.
- Category B exhibits a peak year-to-year increase of 107,060 for 2012 and a peak year-to-year decrease of –119,352 for 2010.
- Category C exhibits a peek year-to-year increase of 7,201 for 2009, and peak year-to-year decrease of –59,671 for 2011.
- Category D exhibits a peek year-to-year increase of 19,320 for 2008 and a peak year-to-year decrease of negative –35,429 for 2010.
- Category E exhibits a peak year-to-year increase of 33,453 for 2012 and a peak year-to-year decrease of –26,281 for 2010.
- Category F exhibits a peak year-to-year increase of 17,503 for 2012, and a peak year-to-year decrease of –21,371 for 2010.

Exhibit 4.48 displays the raw change for each year by category.

- Category A exhibits the largest positive raw change in the data set that occurred in 2010.
- Category A exhibits the largest negative raw change in the data set that occurred in 2011.
- Category B exhibits the second-largest positive raw change in the data set that occurred in 2012.

EXHIBIT 4.45 Dispersion Comparison

	Measurement	Category A	B	C	D	E	F	Comments and Observations
Comp.	Frequency Distribution—Data							Annual totals present no apparent pattern
	Frequency Distribution—Visual	1	1					Categories A and B appear most variable
	Common-sizing							All categories display variability
Bndry.	Minimum						1	Largest minimum
	Maximum	1						Largest maximum
	Range	1						Largest range between minimum and maximum
Central Tendency	Mode							n/a
	Midrange	1					1	Categories A and F largest and similar value
	Median	1					1	Categories A and F similar value
	Mean—Arithmetic	1					1	Categories A and F similar value
	Mean—Truncated	1					1	Categories A and F similar value
	All Means Dispersion		1	1				Greatest disparity among central tendencies
Dispersion	Variance	1						Category A exhibits the largest absolute variances
	Interquartile Range	1	1					Category A largest, Category B similar in size
	Mean Absolute Deviation	1						Largest value
	Standard Deviation	1						Largest value
	Coefficient of Variation		3					Category B is 2X the next highest CV
	Z-Score—Highest						1	Largest score—2009
	Z-Score—Lowest		1					Lowest score—2008
	Z-Score—Largest Range	2						Category A is 5X the next highest score

- Category B exhibits the second-largest negative raw change in the data set that occurred in 2010.

  Exhibit 4.49 displays the year-to-year percentage change for year by category.

- Category A exhibits a peak year-to-year percentage increase of 60.85 percent for 2008 and a peak year-to-year percentage decrease of –41.37 percent for 2011.

EXHIBIT 4.46 Dynamics

Measurement	Composition	Forensic Application
Year-to-year raw change	Measures the year-to-year raw increase or decrease of each item.	Useful for establishing and comparing magnitudes of change.
Year-to-year percentage change	Measures the year-to-year percentage increase or decrease of each item.	Useful for establishing and comparing magnitudes of change.
Year-to-year common-size raw change	Measures the year-to-year increase or decrease of each common-size item.	
Year-to-year common-size percentage change	Measures the year-to-year raw percentage increase or decrease of each common-size item.	
Moving average (3 year)	The mean of a three-year sequence whereby the numerator adds the next year, and drops the first year, thus producing a moving, or rolling, average of three years throughout the sequence. The chosen years, that is, 2, 3, 4, and so on, should reflect a business cycle or other rationale.	Useful for measuring comparative central tendencies and rates of change.
Progressive average	The mean calculated by adding the amount in each successive year to the numerator, and adding one to the denominator for each successive year.	
Weighted-average (3-2-1)	The mean of a three-year horizon that weights the numerator to give more representation to the most current year, with successively less for presentations for prior years. The chosen weights should reflect a business cycle or other rationale.	
Compound annual growth rate (CAGR)	The smoothed annual rate that, when applied to the first year of the time horizon, arrives at the results of the last year.	Useful for measuring rates of change. For example, if a company's cost of goods sold CAGR of, say, 8.2 percent exceeded its revenue CAGR of, say, 6.0 percent, the trends can be extrapolated to converge on the critical year in the future.
Geometric mean	The mean calculated similarly to the arithmetic mean, except the numerator is the product of the values (that is, multiplied), taken to the nth root of the number of values.	Useful when measuring very skewed data, and when measuring rates of change.

EXHIBIT 4.47 Annual Amount Change

	2008	2009	2010	2011	2012
Category A	91,930	69,882	162,792	(196,798)	83,456
Category B	36,915	66,953	(119,352)	(1,878)	107,060
Category C	(12,059)	7,201	(4,071)	(59,671)	(3,070)
Category D	19,320	3,933	(35,429)	(8,553)	2,143
Category E	29,967	(10,160)	(26,281)	1,201	33,453
Category F	11,281	16,857	(21,371)	(9,454)	17,503
Total	177,354	154,666	(43,712)	(275,153)	240,545

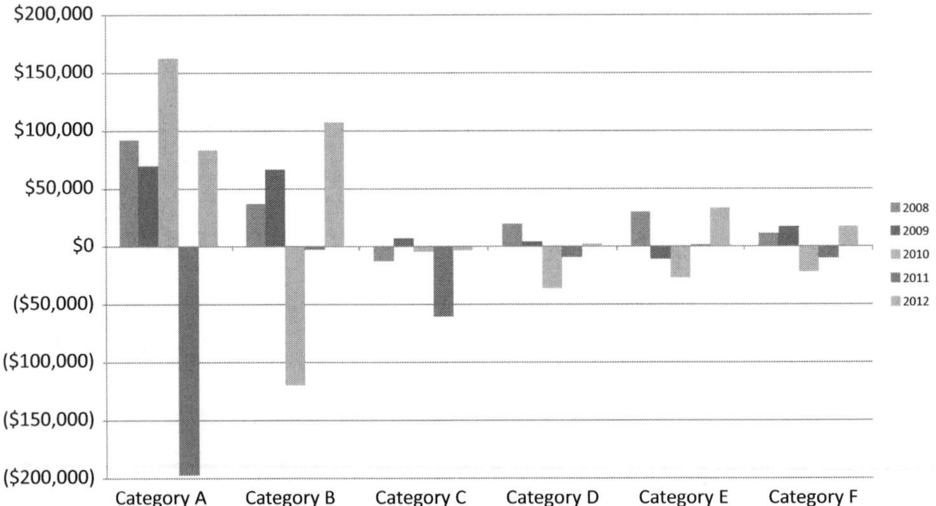

EXHIBIT 4.48 Dollar Changes over Prior Year

EXHIBIT 4.49 Annual Percentage Change

	2008	2009	2010	2011	2012
Category A	60.85%	28.76%	52.03%	(41.37%)	29.93%
Category B	194.93%	119.87%	(97.19%)	(54.37%)	6793.15%
Category C	(13.73%)	9.50%	(4.91%)	(75.63%)	(15.96%)
Category D	13.38%	2.40%	(21.13%)	(6.47%)	1.73%
Category E	29.57%	(7.74%)	(21.69%)	1.27%	34.83%
Category F	3.47%	5.01%	(6.05%)	(2.85%)	5.43%
Total	21.40%	15.37%	(3.77%)	(24.63%)	28.57%

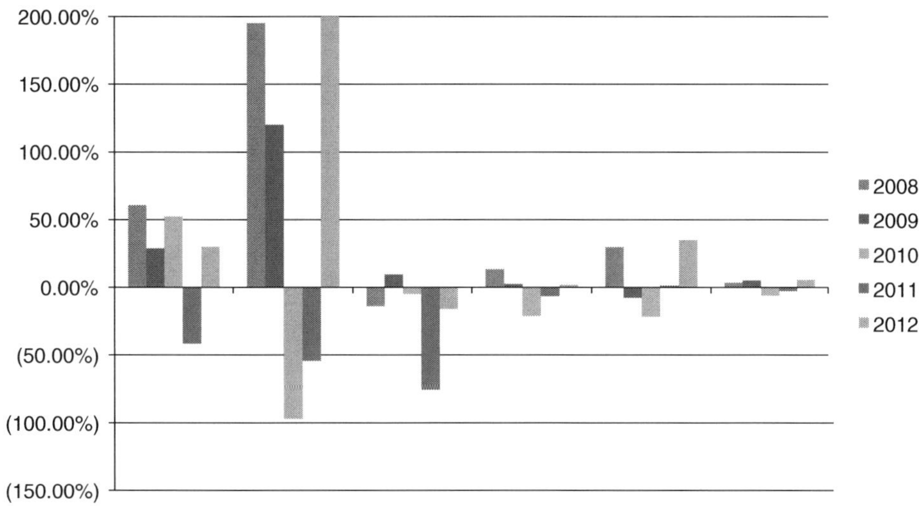

Note: The scale of the Y-axis has been modified to better illustrate the changes of all expense categories. The change for Category B for 2012 is greater than the Y-axis scale.

EXHIBIT 4.50 Percentage Changes over Prior Year

- Category B exhibits a peak year-to-year percentage increase of 6,793.15 percent for 2012 and a peak year-to-year percentage decrease of –97.19 percent for 2010.
- Category C exhibits a peak year-to-year percentage increase of 9.5 percent for 2009 and a peek year-to-year percentage decrease of –75.63 percent for 2011.
- Category D exhibits a peak year-to-year percentage increase of 13.38 percent for 2008 and a peak year-to-year percentage decrease of –21.13 percent for 2010.
- Category E exhibits a peak year-to-year increase of 34.83 percent for 2012 and a peek year-to-year percentage decrease of –21.69 percent for 2010.
- Category F exhibits a peak year-to-year increase of 5.43 percent for 2012 the peak year-to-year percentage decrease of –6.05 percent for 2010.

Exhibit 4.50 displays the percentage change for each category by year.

- Category B exhibits the largest positive percentage changes in the data set that occurred from 2007 to 2012.
- Category B exhibits the largest negative percentage changes in the data set that occurred from 2007 to 2012.

Year-to-Year Common-Size Raw Change, Year-to-Year Common-Size Percentage Change

Year-to-year common-size raw change—This measurement computes the year-to-year increase or decrease in the percentage of a data set item; for example, Years 1 and 2.

EXHIBIT 4.51 Common Size Change over Prior Year

	2007	2008	2009	2010	2011	2012
Category A	n/a	0.18%	(0.04%)	0.60%	(0.42%)	0.56%
Category B	n/a	0.11%	0.12%	(0.30%)	(0.00%)	0.45%
Category C	n/a	(0.11%)	(0.05%)	0.02%	(0.16%)	0.00%
Category D	n/a	(0.06%)	(0.13%)	(0.04%)	0.04%	0.10%
Category E	n/a	0.02%	(0.14%)	(0.03%)	0.05%	0.21%
Category F	n/a	(0.23%)	(0.25%)	0.08%	0.14%	0.32%
Total		(0.09%)	(0.50%)	0.33%	(0.35%)	1.65%

Year-to-year common-size percentage change—This measurement computes the year-to-year percentage change of a data set percentage; for example, Year 2 is expressed as an increase or decrease compared to Year 1.

Exhibit 4.51 displays the year-to-year common-size raw change for year by category.

- Category A exhibits a peak year-to-year common-size percentage increase of 0.60 percent for 2010 and a peak year-to-year common-size percentage decrease of –0.42 percent for 2011.
- Category B exhibits a peak year-to-year common-size percentage increase of 0.45 percent for 2012 and a peak year-to-year common-size percentage decrease of –0.30 percent for 2010.
- Category C exhibits a peak year-to-year common-size percentage increase of 0.02 percent for 2010 and a peak year-to-year common-size percentage decrease of –0.16 percent for 2011.
- Category D exhibits a peak year-to-year common-size percentage increase of 0.10 percent for 2012 and a peak year-to-year common-size percentage decrease of –0.13 percent for 2009.
- Category E exhibits a peak year-to-year common-size percentage increase of 0.21 percent for 2012 and a peak year-to-year percentage decrease of –0.14 percent for 2009.
- Category F exhibits a peak year-to-year common-size percentage increase of 0.32 percent for 2012 and a peak year-to-year percentage decrease of –0.25 percent for 2009.

Exhibit 4.52 displays the common-size raw change for each category by year.

- Category A exhibits the largest and second-largest peak year-to-year common-size percentage increases of the data set that occurred in 2010 and 2012.
- Category B exhibits the third-largest peak year-to-year common-size percentage increase of the data set that occurred in 2012.
- Category A exhibits the largest year-to-year common-size percentage decrease of the data set that occurred in 2011.

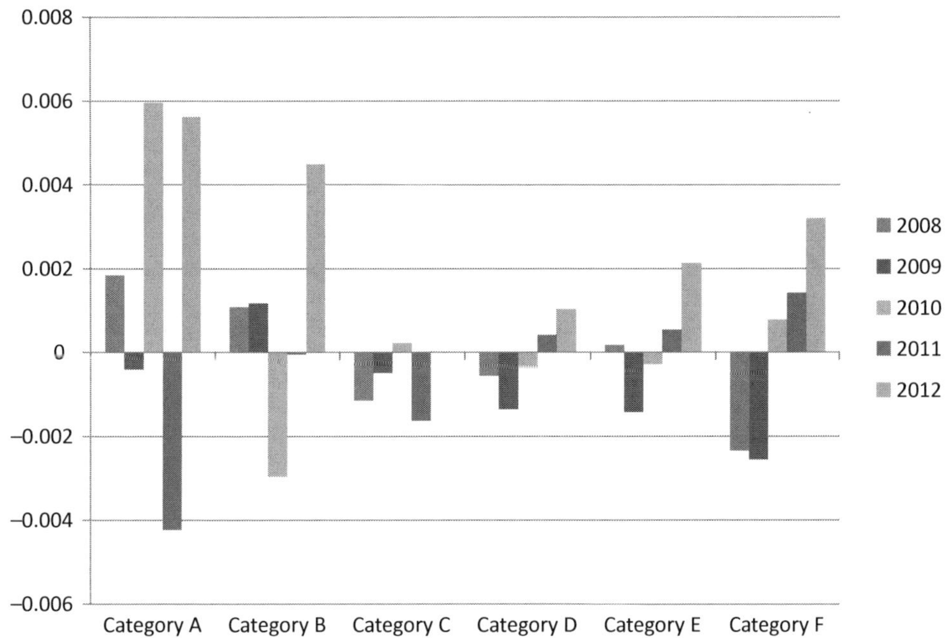

EXHIBIT 4.52 Change in Common-Size over Prior Year

- Category B exhibits the second-largest year-to-year common-size percentage decrease of the data set that occurred in 2010.

Exhibit 4.53 displays the year-to-year percentage change of a data set percentage. For example, Year 2 is expressed as an increase or decrease compared to Year 1.

- Category B exhibits substantial year-to-year percentage change for 2012, and large changes for 2008 and 2010.

EXHIBIT 4.53 Common-Size Percentage Change over Prior Year

		2008	2009	2010	2011	2012
Category A	n/a	28.95%	(4.83%)	76.21%	(30.70%)	58.90%
Category B	n/a	136.43%	62.51%	(96.74%)	(46.07%)	8330.24%
Category C	n/a	(30.84%)	(19.07%)	10.22%	(71.19%)	2.77%
Category D	n/a	(9.11%)	(24.31%)	(8.58%)	10.55%	24.42%
Category E	n/a	3.87%	(31.81%)	(9.24%)	19.70%	64.89%
Category F	n/a	(17.05%)	(22.39%)	8.90%	14.83%	28.93%
Total		(2.68%)	(14.73%)	11.54%	(10.91%)	57.24%

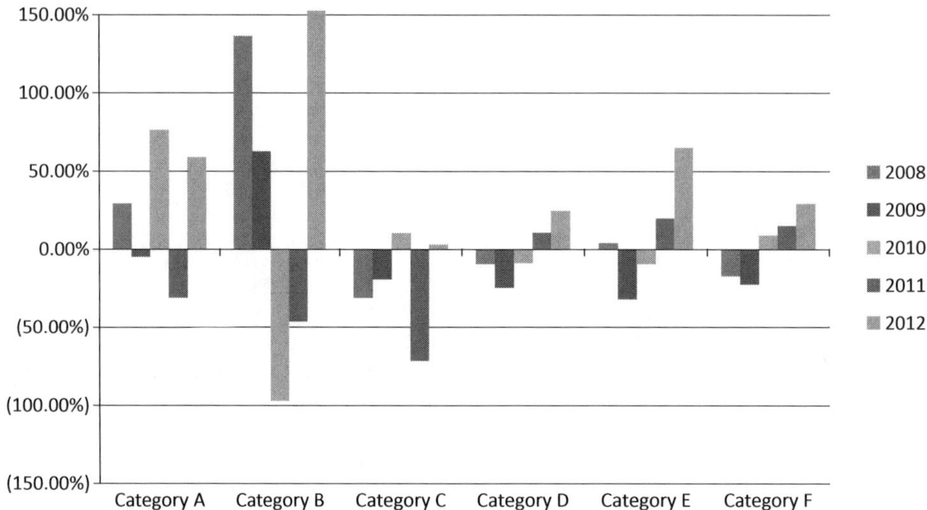

Note: The scale of the *Y*-axis has been modified to better illustrate the changes of all expense categories. The change for Category B for 2012 is greater than the *Y*-axis scale.

EXHIBIT 4.54 Common-Size Percentage Change over Prior Year

Exhibit 4.54 displays the year-to-year common-size percentage change for each data item in proportion to revenues (not shown) by year within category and indicates the item's changes over the relevant time horizon.

- Category B exhibits the largest and second-largest year-to-year common size percentage increases of the data set that occurred in 2008 and 2012.
- Category A exhibits the third-largest year-to-year common-size percentage increase of the data set that occurred in 2010.
- Category B exhibits the largest year-to-year common-size percentage decrease of the data set that occurred in 2010.
- Category C exhibits a second-largest year-to-year common-size percentage decrease of the data set that occurred in 2011.

Moving Average (Three-Year)

Moving average (three-year)—The mean of a three-year horizon that adds the next year and drops the first year, thus producing an average of three years. The chosen years should reflect a business cycle or other rationale. Useful for measuring comparative central tendencies and rates of change.

Exhibit 4.55. displays the three-year moving average for each category by year.

- Category A exhibits 235,657 for 2009 and steadily increases to 372,300 for 2012.
- Category B exhibits 65,866 for 2009 and steadily declines to 37,889 for 2012.

EXHIBIT 4.55 Moving Average (Three-Year)

Operating Expenses	2007	2008	2009	2010	2011	2012
Category A	n/a	n/a	235,657	343,858	355,817	372,300
Category B	n/a	n/a	65,866	60,704	42,612	37,889
Category C	n/a	n/a	82,191	79,215	60,368	38,097
Category D	n/a	n/a	158,596	154,538	141,188	127,242
Category E	n/a	n/a	117,924	115,766	104,020	106,811
Category F	n/a	n/a	338,401	340,656	336,000	331,560

- Category C exhibits 82,191 for 2009, gradually declines to 79,215 for 2010, and rapidly declines to 38,097 for 2012.
- Category D exhibits 158,596 for 2009 and steadily declines to 127,242 for 2012.
- Category E exhibits 117,924 for 2009, gradually declines to 104,020 for 2011, and slightly increases to 106,811 for 2012.
- Category F exhibits 338,401 for 2009, increases very slightly to 340,656 for 2010, and declines gradually to 331,560 for 2012.

Exhibit 4.56 displays the three-year moving average for each category by year.

- Category A exhibits a significant increase from 2009 to 2010, with small steady increases to 2012.
- Category B exhibits a relatively stable decline from 2009 to 2012.
- Category C exhibits similar levels for 2009 and 2010 and steadily declines to 2012.
- Category D exhibits a relatively stable decline from 2009 to 2012.
- Category E exhibits a relatively stable decline from 2009 to 2011, with a slight increase for 2012.
- Category F exhibits a gradual decline from 2010 to 2012.

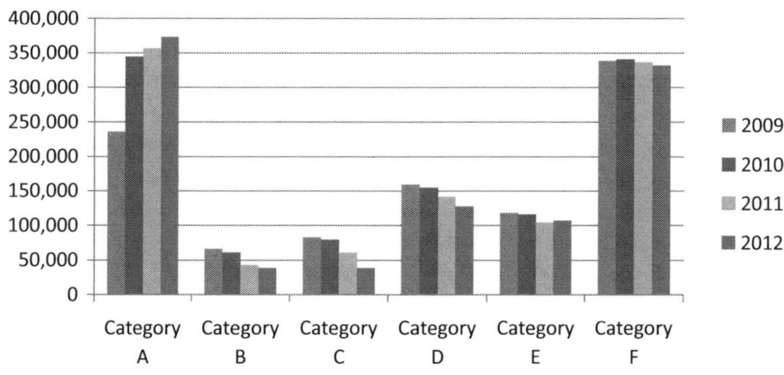

EXHIBIT 4.56 Moving Average (Three-Year)

EXHIBIT 4.57 Progressive Average

Operating Expenses	2007	2008	2009	2010	2011	2012
Category A	n/a	197,041	235,657	295,663	292,306	303,978
Category B	n/a	37,396	65,866	50,263	40,525	51,877
Category C	n/a	81,801	82,191	81,369	68,941	60,144
Category D	n/a	154,066	158,596	152,005	146,339	142,919
Category E	n/a	116,317	117,924	112,158	108,938	112,368
Category F	n/a	330,902	338,401	336,808	333,961	334,980

Progressive Average

Progressive average—The progressive average is the arithmetic mean calculated by adding the amount in each successive year to the numerator and adding one to the denominator for each successive year. It is useful for measuring comparative central tendencies and rates of change.

Exhibit 4.57 displays the progressive average for each category by year.

- Category A exhibits 197,041 for 2008 and rapidly increases to 295,663 for 2010, then declines slightly to 292,306 for 2011 and increases slightly to 303,978 for 2012.
- Category B exhibits 37,396 for 2008, increases significantly to 65,866 in 2009, declined steadily to 40,525 for 2011 and increases to 51,877 for 2012.
- Category C exhibits 81,801 for 2008, remains relatively stable through 2010, and then steadily declines to 60,144 for 2012.
- Category D exhibits 154,066 for 2008, decreases slightly to 152,005 in 2010, and subtly declines to 142,919 for 2012.
- Category E exhibits 116,317 for 2008, remains relatively stable through 2009, then declines gradually to 108,938 for 2011 and increases slightly to 112,368 for 2012.
- Category F exhibits 330,902 for 2008, increases slightly to 338,401 in 2009, decreases slightly to 333,961 for 2011, and increases slightly to 334,980 for 2012.

Exhibit 4.58 displays the progressive average for each category by year.

- Category A exhibits a steady increase from 2008 to 2010, a slight decrease to 2011, and a slight increase to 2012.
- Category B exhibits an increase from 2008 to 2009, decreases to 2011, and increases for 2012.
- Category C exhibits relative stability in 2008 to 2009 and then decreases rapidly to 2012.
- Category D exhibits a slight increase from 2008 to 2009 and then steadily decreases to 2012.
- Category E exhibits gradual decreases from 2008 through 2011, with a slight change for 2012.
- Category F exhibits a slight increase from 2008 to 2009, slightly decreases to 2011, and stabilizes for 2012.

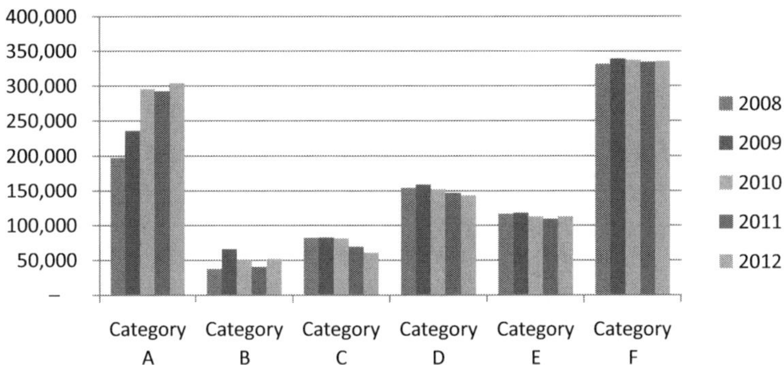

EXHIBIT 4.58 Progressive Average

Weighted Average (3-2-1)

> *Weighted-average (3-2-1)*—The weighted arithmetic mean of a three-year horizon that weights the numerator to give more representation to the most current year, with successively less for presentations for prior years. The chosen weights should reflect a business cycle or other rationale. Useful for measuring comparative central tendencies and rates of change.

Exhibit 4.59 displays the three-year weighted (3-2-1) average for each category by year.

- Category A exhibits 262,625 for 2009, a substantial increase for 2010, a slight decrease to 2011, followed by a slight increase to 2012.
- Category B exhibits 83,177 for 2009 with significant decreases to 22,407 for 2011 and a substantial increase to 55,419 for 2012.
- Category C exhibits 81,381 for 2009, a slight decrease to 79,736 for 2010, and rapid decreases to 27,640 for 2012.
- Category D exhibits 162,472 for 2009 and gradual decreases to 126,174 for 2012.
- Category E exhibits 121,226 for 2009, steady decreases to 99,840 for 2011, and increases to 112,586 for 2012.
- Category F exhibits 343,090 for 2009, slight decreases to 330,863 for 2011, and a slight increase to 332,901 for 2012.

EXHIBIT 4.59 Weighted Average (3-2-1)

Operating Expenses	2007	2008	2009	2010	2011	2012
Category A	n/a	n/a	262,625	382,637	350,149	353,410
Category B	n/a	n/a	83,177	51,971	22,407	55,419
Category C	n/a	n/a	81,381	79,736	49,744	27,640
Category D	n/a	n/a	162,472	149,288	133,858	126,174
Category E	n/a	n/a	121,226	109,693	99,840	112,586
Category F	n/a	n/a	343,090	339,904	330,863	332,901

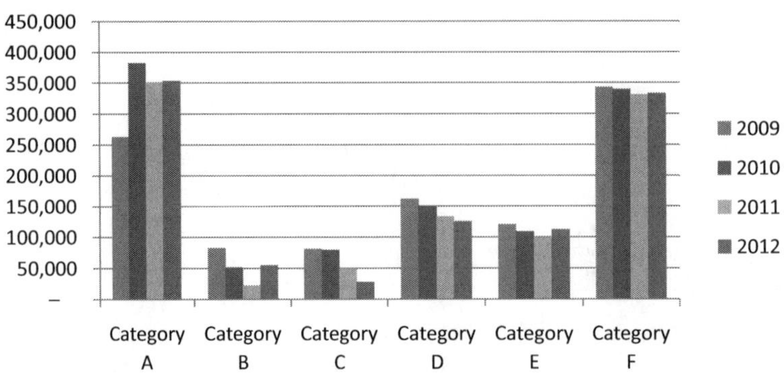

EXHIBIT 4.60 Weighted Average (3-2-1)

Exhibit 4.60 displays the three-year weighted (3-2-1) average for each category by year.

- Category A exhibits a significant increase from 2009 to 2010, and a decrease for 2011, where it remained relatively stable to 2012.
- Category B exhibits a steady decline from 2008 to 2011, with a significant increase to 2012.
- Category C exhibits slight decline from 2008 to 2009, with significant declines continuing to 2012.
- Category D exhibits a steady decline from 2008 to 2012.
- Category E exhibits a steady decline from 2008 to 2011, and an increase to 2012.
- Category F exhibits a slight decline from 2008 to 2011, where it remained relatively stable to 2012.

Compound Annual Growth Rate (CAGR)

Compound annual growth rate (CAGR)—The smoothed annual rate that, when applied to the first year of a time horizon, arrives at the results of the last year. It is calculated by calculating the percentage change resulting from dividing the ending amount by the beginning amount, applying the nth root to the percentage change, and subtracting 1. For example, a hypothetical 5-year series contains amounts of 5, 6, 7, 8, and 9. Dividing 9 (the ending amount) by 5 (the beginning amount) yields a growth rate of 180 percent over the five years. Then, calculating the 4th (for the 5-year period, there were only 4 years of growth) root of 180 percent results in 1.15829. Subtracting 1.00 from 1.15829 yields the series' compound annual growth rate of 15.829 percent. For proof, 5 compounded at 15.829 percent over 4 years yields 9.

Exhibit 4.61 displays the compound annual growth rate (CAGR) for each category by year.

- Category A exhibits a 2- and 3-year rate of 27 percent, an 18 percent 4-year rate, and 5- and 6-year rate declines of –2 percent and –4 percent, respectively.

EXHIBIT 4.61 Compound Annual Growth Rate (CAGR)

Operating Expenses	2007	2-Year	3-Year	4-Year	5-Year	6-Year
Category A	n/a	0.27	0.27	0.18	(0.02)	(0.04)
Category B	n/a	0.72	0.86	(0.50)	(0.58)	0.78
Category C	n/a	(0.07)	(0.02)	0.01	(0.25)	(0.23)
Category D	n/a	0.06	0.05	(0.05)	(0.06)	(0.01)
Category E	n/a	0.14	0.06	(0.08)	(0.05)	0.05
Category F	n/a	0.02	0.03	(0.00)	(0.02)	0.00

- Category B exhibits a 2-year rate of 72 percent 3-year rate of 86 percent, a 4-year rate decline of –50 percent a 5-year rate decline of –58 percent, and a 6-year rate increase of 78 percent.
- Category C exhibits 2- and 3-year rate declines of –7 percent and –2 percent, respectively; a 4-year rate increase of 1 percent, a 5-year rate decrease of –25 percent, and a 6-year rate decrease of –23 percent.
- Category D exhibits 2- and 3-year rate increases of 6 percent and 5 percent, respectively; a 4-year rate decline of –5 percent, a 5-year rate decline of –6 percent, and a 6-year rate decline of –1 percent.
- Category E exhibits 2- and 3-year rate increases of 14 percent and 6 percent, respectively; a 4-year rate decline of –8 percent, a 5-year rate decline of –5 percent, and a 6-year rate increase of 5 percent.
- Category F exhibits 2- and 3-year rate increases of 2 percent and 3 percent, respectively; a 4-year rate of zero percent, a 5-year rate decline of –2 percent, and a 6-year rate of zero percent.

Exhibit 4.62 displays the compound annual growth rate (CAGR) for each category by year.

- Category A exhibits relatively stable 2- and 3-year rate increases, and a rapid decline to a negative a 6-year rate.
- Category B exhibits significant 2- and 3-year rate increases, significant 4- and 5-year rate declines, and a significant 6-year rate increase.
- Category C exhibits 2- and 3-year rate declines, followed by a stable 4-year rate, with significant 5- and 6-year rate declines.
- Category D exhibits modest 2-and 3-year rate increases, followed by 4-, 5- and 6-year rate declines.
- Category E exhibits modest 2- and 3-year rate increases, followed by 4- and 5-year rate declines, with a small 6-year rate increase.
- Category F exhibits small 2- and 3-year rate increases, a 4-year stable rate, and a very small 5-year decline followed by no increase for year 6.

Geometric Mean

Geometric mean—The geometric mean is the mean calculated in a manner similar to the arithmetic mean. However, the numerator is the product of the

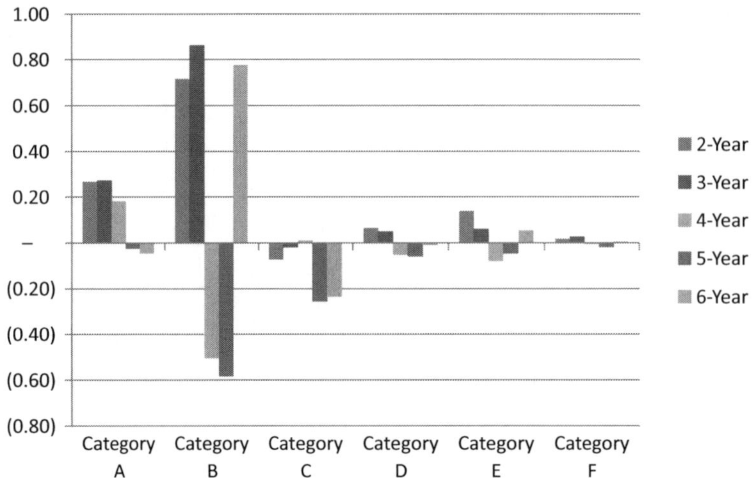

EXHIBIT 4.62 Compound Annual Growth Rate

values, while the denominator is the nth root of the number of values. For example, a hypothetical 5-year series contains amounts of 5, 6, 7, 8, and 9. Multiplying all the (absolute) numbers times one another, that is, 5 × 6 × 7 × 8 × 9, results in 15,120. Then, calculating the 5th root (to accommodate the five values), 15,120 results in 6.853. At least 50 items are necessary for the geometric mean results to be reliable.

The geometric mean applies only to nonnegative numbers, and is always equal to or less than the respective data set.

Exhibit 4.63 displays the geometric mean for each category by year.

- Category A exhibits a 2-year geometric mean of 191,605, steadily growing to the 6-year geometric mean of 286,423.
- Category B exhibits a 2-year geometric mean of 32,523, increasing to a 3-year geometric mean of 50,645, followed by a decline to the 5-year geometric mean of 14,788, with a six-year geometric mean of 20,618.
- Category C exhibits a 2-year geometric mean of 81,578, remains relatively stable until reaching a 5-year geometric mean of 60,901, and is followed by a 6-year geometric mean of 48,820.

EXHIBIT 4.63 Geometric Mean

Operating Expenses	2007	2-Year	3-Year	4-Year	5-Year	6-Year
Category A	n/a	191,605	225,632	271,881	273,267	286,423
Category B	n/a	32,523	50,645	25,881	14,788	20,618
Category C	n/a	81,578	82,040	81,244	60,901	48,820
Category D	n/a	153,762	158,261	151,308	145,328	141,878
Category E	n/a	115,347	117,247	111,198	107,990	111,311
Category F	n/a	330,853	338,204	336,649	333,786	334,826

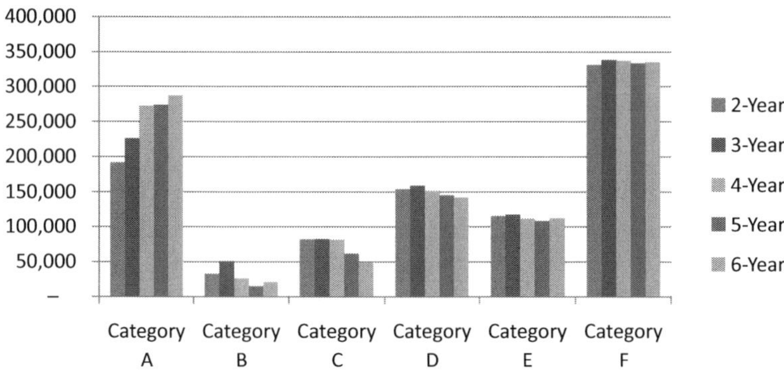

EXHIBIT 4.64 Geometric Mean

- Category D exhibits a 2-year geometric mean of 153,762, and a 3-year geometric mean at 158,261, followed by a steady decline to a 6-year geometric mean of 141,878.
- Category E exhibits a 2-year geometric mean of 115,347, followed by a slight increase for 3-year geometric mean of 117,247, declining gradually to a 5-year geometric mean of 107,990, with a 6-year geometric mean of 111,311.
- Category F exhibits a 2-year geometric mean of 330,853, followed by a 3-year geometric mean of 338,204 that slightly decreases to a 6-year geometric mean of 334,826.

Exhibit 4.64 displays the geometric mean for each category by year.

- Category A exhibits 2-year, 3-year, and 4-year increases in geometric mean, a stable 5-year geometric mean, and a slight increase for the 6-year geometric mean.
- Category B exhibits 2-year and 3-year increases in geometric mean, with a 4-year and 5-year decline, and a 6-year increase in geometric mean.
- Category C exhibits stable 2-year, 3-year, and 4-year geometric means, with 5-year and 6-year declines.
- Category D exhibits relatively stable 2-year and 3-year geometric means, and steadily declining 4-year, 5-year, and 6-year geometric means.
- Category E exhibits relatively stable 2-year and 3-year geometric means, with slight 4-year, and 5-year declines, and a slight 6-year increase in geometric mean.
- Category F exhibits a slight increase for the 2-year to the 3-year geometric mean, and relative stability for the 4-year, 5-year, and 6-year geometric means.

Scoring—Dynamics This section described the dynamics of the data set. Therefore, the MUA format in Exhibit 4.65 scores comments and observations resulting from the data set knowledge gained. Category B exhibits dramatic changes in year-to-year percentage changes or evolved values, compound annual growth rate (see CAGR), and the geometric mean.

EXHIBIT 4.65 Completed MUA Scoring

	Measurement	Category A	B	C	D	E	F	Comments and Observations
Comp.	Frequency Distribution—Data							Annual totals present no apparent pattern
	Frequency Distribution—Visual	1	1					Categories A and B appear most variable
	Common-sizing							All categories display variability
Bndry.	Minimum						1	Largest minimum
	Maximum	1						Largest maximum
	Range	1						Largest range between minimum and maximum
Central Tendency	Mode							n/a
	Midrange	1					1	Categories A and F largest and similar value
	Median	1					1	Categories A and F similar value
	Mean—Arithmetic	1					1	Categories A and F similar value
	Mean—Truncated	1					1	Categories A and F similar value
	All Means Dispersion		1	1				Greatest disparity among central tendencies
Dispersion	Variance	1						Category A exhibits the largest absolute variances
	Interquartile Range	1	1					Category A largest, Category B similar in size
	Mean Absolute Deviation	1						Largest value
	Standard Deviation	1						Largest value
	Coefficient of Variation		3					Category B is 2X the next highest CV
	Z-Score—Highest						1	Largest score—2009
	Z-Score—Lowest		1					Lowest score—2008
	Z-Score—Largest Range	2						Category A is 5X the next highest score

Dynamics	Year-to-year raw change	1						Category A largest, Category B similar
	Year-to-year % change of raw values		3					Category B dramatic changes 2008 & 2012
	Year-to-year common-size raw change	2	1					Category A exhibits largest; Category B second largest
	Year-to-year common-size % change	1						Category A largest, Category B similar
	Moving average (3-year)		1					Overall,Category B and C exhibits greatest change
	Progressive average	1						Category A largest change
	Weighted-average (3-year)		1					Category B largest variability
	Compound Annual Growth (CAGR)		3					Category B dramatic changes all years
	Geometric mean		2					Category B largest variability
	Total	18	18	1	0	0	6	

Scoring:
0 - Meets condition, but no consequence
1 - Meets condition
2 - Significant
3 - Critical

Scoring The completed scoring model scores each measurement within the respective attribute, for example, dispersion. The comments and observations section permits explanations of the rationale behind the category scoring. The model functions as is, or as changed, depending upon the facts and circumstances of each assignment. It will readily accommodate additions or deletions of measurements, for example, standard deviation; subcategories, for example, central tendency; and other descriptors, depending on the data set. For example, if a t-test merits inclusion, placing it within the dispersion category would merely increase the number of items. Furthermore, the comments and observations section permits expansion and could reference a separate section containing more description if necessary.

Another method of using the MUA technique is to significantly expand the respective subcategory, for example, dispersion, so that it contains, say, 20 measurements. Then, the respective conclusions would roll upward to an overall MUA scoring model.

The scoring scale, that is, 0 to 3, functions as is, or as changed, depending on the facts and circumstances of each assignment. The score in the example model indicates a tie between Category A and Category B. In effect, the model suggests those two categories represent the most promise for investigation based upon the importance of the measurements. But such a condition points out another feature of the MUA technique.

That is, although both categories display identical scores, the dynamics category indicates respective scores of 5 and 11 for Category A and Category B, respectively. Consequently, Category B exhibits the higher score, suggesting greater variability than Category A. Under these conditions, Category B would be the clear winner regarding investigation.

Alternatively, of course, additional refinement and scoring might materially change the conclusion for investigation. Furthermore, additional measurements could be added or deleted to finally select between categories. Regardless, the MUA model provides a facile means of sensitivity testing or modeling analysis that support the decision to investigate.

Note to the reader: Compare this quantified result to the selection of investigation made early in the chapter. Perhaps the conclusion is different; perhaps it is the same. Regardless, the contents of this chapter present a logical, structured, defensible, and easily explainable technique to support opinions.

CONCLUSION

This chapter (and the sections from other chapters that relate to it, as outlined earlier) achieved several objectives. First, it introduced the rationale of two categories and five subcategories necessary for analyzing data. Specifically, it laid out the seven attributes necessary for successful data analysis. The two categories comprised data description and data analysis. Then, five subcategories made up of composition, boundaries, central tendencies, dispersion, and dynamics were explained with respect to understanding and analysis to ensure that interpretation is accurate.

Next, it systematically disaggregated the individual, manageable components by identifying them as measurements. Each measurement supported the respective objective and included a potential forensic application regarding its use in an assignment.

Then the data set contents illustrated their characteristics with the data table and bar graph for each item.

Finally, an MUA model quantified, explained, and aggregated scoring for the respective measures. This chapter outlines the approach to virtually any data analysis, not merely financial. The forensic operator using this chapter gains knowledge regarding approach, components of data, foundational descriptive statistics, their application, summarization, and presentation, all of which are useful in virtually every forensic assignment.

Most importantly, note that this chapter and the respective model included apply to virtually any type of data analysis. For example, the forensic operator desiring to include more, and ratio analysis could use the same scoring methodology.

Regardless of the types of data analyzed, this chapter arms the forensic operator with essential tools, techniques, methods, and methodologies. Exhibit 4.65 contains all the scoring conclusions, indicating the quantified priorities.

CHAPTER 5

Data Collection and Analysis Phase: Part III

This chapter contains four valuable sections particularly beneficial to forensic operators investigating financial documents from the lowest level of detail to the highest level of summary. The sections include "Financial Status Audit Techniques (FSAT)," "Digital Analysis," "Valuation & Forensics—Why & How," and "Valuation's Orphan."

The section "FSAT" highlights the IRS's five indirect forensic methods that assess the veracity of reported income and expenses. Its techniques give forensic operators simple yet versatile tools.

The section "Digital Analysis" describes techniques applicable for forensic assignments, whether data-poor or data-rich. The data-poor methods include link and gap analysis; while the data-rich methods comprise analytical methods, including Benford's Law.

The section "Valuation & Forensics—Why & How" outlines why forensic operators conducting valuation-related assignments must deploy forensic techniques. A short list of the reasoning parallels technical guidance, comprising normalizations, guideline multiple application, and other tasks.

The section "Valuation's Orphan" covers the most under-addressed aspect of all valuation assignments in the profession: the economic benefit stream. It outlines a practical, technical, and defensible set of techniques forensic operators can immediately deploy to add an incremental dimension of rationale to all valuations.

This chapter permits forensic operators engaged in valuation assignments to take the next step toward sophistication in all aspects of financial forensics. The benefits apply across the spectrum of assignments, including litigation, fraud, transactions, estate and gift planning, solvency and insolvency analysis, and virtually all other related assignments.

FSAT—FINANCIAL STATUS AUDIT TECHNIQUES

The Internal Revenue Manual (IRM), Part 4 Examining Process, provides the SB/SE[1] examination field operations employees with the guidance to conduct an examination of small-business and self-employed income. The goal of an IRS examination is to determine whether the taxable income has been accurately reported on the tax return.

[1] Small business/self-employed.

These same methods outlined in the IRM can be employed by the forensic operator during his analysis of purported income. This may apply to many different types of assignments, including litigation, valuation, marital dissolution, fraud, or other civil or criminal disputes. There will likely be cases that have indications that the amount of reported income is inaccurate. Unlike IRS examinations, which look for understated income, the forensic operator can be considering whether income was either under- or overstated. Even though this section is mainly derived from the IRM as a guide for IRS examinations, the methods and calculations can be easily and effectively applied to forensic engagements.

The IRS examination process generally includes two methods: the specific item method and the indirect method. The specific item method involves the use of direct evidence, that is, a receipt, to determine the accuracy of the overall tax liability reported. The indirect method involves the use of circumstantial evidence to determine the accuracy of the overall tax liability reported. Based on the unique circumstances of the taxpayer, that is, incomplete books or records, this alternative examination method may be appropriate. In general, the method gathers all available documents, unique personal facts, and financial detail to draw a logical conclusion regarding the reported tax liability. Exhibit 5.1 is the section from the IRM that defines the indirect method.

Note to the reader: This section contains only a sampling of the extensive contents in the IRM. Some forensic operators have printed out the entire section for placement in a three-ring binder to support staff training.

EXHIBIT 5.1 IRM/Indirect Method

4.10.4.2.8 (08-09-2011)
Indirect Method

1. The indirect method involves the use of circumstantial evidence to determine the tax liability based on omitted income, overstated expenses, or both. Circumstantial evidence is evidence from which more than one logical conclusion can be reached. To support adjustments for additional taxable income, both the credibility of the evidence and the reasonableness of the conclusion must be evaluated before the determination of tax liability is made.
2. Analytical reviews and testing of the taxpayer's books and records, as required by the minimum income probes, may result in the identification of additional taxable income based on circumstantial evidence from which an inference can be made. The financial status analysis and bank account analysis are not prohibited by IRC 7602(e), *Limitation on the Use of Financial Status Audit Techniques*, simply because an adjustment to taxable income supported by indirect (circumstantial) evidence may be the result.

   Example:

   The minimum income probes for an individual business return include a bank account analysis. There is an identifiable potential source of additional taxable income. The records used for the analysis are the bank account statements, which are prepared by a third party, and are credible evidence. The characterization of excess funds as additional taxable income is reasonable because deposits of nontaxable funds are identified and eliminated. See *IRM 4.10.4.3.3.7*, *Bank Account Analysis (Individual Business Returns)*.
3. See IRM 4.10.7.3, *Evaluating Evidence*, for complete discussion.

EXHIBIT 5.2 IRM/Formal Indirect Method

4.10.4.2.9 (08-09-2011)
Formal Indirect Method

1. The formal indirect methods are audit techniques used to determine the tax liability based on the amount of unreported income.
   A. *IRM 4.10.4.6.3, Source and Application of Funds Method*
   B. *IRM 4.10.4.6.4, Bank Deposit and Cash Expenditures Method*
   C. *IRM 4.10.4.6.5, Markup Method*
   D. *IRM 4.10.4.6.6, Unit and Volume Method*
   E. *IRM 4.10.4.6.7, Net Worth Method*
2. The formal indirect methods are also known as financial status audit techniques. See *IRM 4.10.4.6.1* for additional discussion. They are distinguishable from other audit techniques by the following characteristics:
   A. Reliance on indirect evidence of income
   B. In-depth analysis of actual costs that requires the extensive collection of detailed information
   C. Subject to IRC 7602(e), which states, "the Secretary shall not use financial status or economic reality examination techniques to determine the existence of unreported income of any taxpayer unless the Secretary has a reasonable indication that there is a likelihood of such unreported income"
3. Formal indirect methods are appropriate when:
   A. The taxpayer's books and records are missing, incomplete, or irregularities are identified
   B. The financial status analysis indicates a material imbalance of cash flows after consideration of other adjustments identified during the examination

See *IRM 4.10.4.6.2* and *IRM 4.10.4.3.3.1.*

The IRS recognizes five formal indirect methods as audit techniques for use in the examination of taxable income. One particular method may be advantageous over another based on the particular circumstance of a taxpayer's business, books, and records. For example, the markup method would not be applicable to a business that has no inventory or cost of goods sold. Each of the formal indirect methods has particular factors to consider when applying the technique. Exhibit 5.2 is the section from the IRM that lists the formal indirect methods and their corresponding IRM section number.

Source and Application of Funds Method

The source and application of funds method is a frequently used technique. It is simple to apply and explain. Basically, it uses the taxpayer's cash flows to compare all known expenditures to all known receipts, both taxable and nontaxable. It also takes into consideration changes in assets and liabilities during the period. The method typically comes up with "Excess Applications over Sources (understatement of taxable income)" or "Excess Sources over Applications (overstatement of taxable income)." If income and expenses were accurately reported on the tax return, no excess would be computed; the application of funds would equal the sources of funds. Exhibit 5.3 is the IRM definition of the source and application of funds method.

Exhibits 5.4 and 5.5 are examples of the some of the sources and application of funds as well as an example displaying the format of the method.

EXHIBIT 5.3 IRM/Source and Application of Funds Method

4.10.4.6.3 (09-11-2007)

Source and Application of Funds Method

1. The Source and Application of Funds Method is an analysis of a taxpayer's cash flows and comparison of all known expenditures with all known receipts for the period. Net increases and decreases in assets and liabilities are taken into account along with nondeductible expenditures and nontaxable receipts. The excess of expenditures over the sum of reported and nontaxable income is the adjustment to income.
2. The Source and Application of Funds Method and the financial status analysis are both based on an evaluation of the taxpayer's cash flows. The only difference is the use of statistics to estimate unknown personal living expenses. Therefore, when the financial status analysis indicates a reasonable likelihood of unreported income and establishes a reasonable likelihood of unreported income, the Source and Application of Funds Method is an efficient method for determining the actual amount of the understatement of income.

EXHIBIT 5.4 IRM/Example of Source and Application of Funds Method

4.10.4.6.3.3 (08-09-2011)

Example of Source and Application of Funds Method

1. Sources of funds are the various ways the taxpayer acquires money during the year. Decreases in assets and increases in liabilities generate funds. Funds also come from taxable and nontaxable sources of income. Unreported sources of income, even though known, are not listed in this computation since the purpose is to determine the amount of any unreported income. Specific items of income are denoted separately. Examples of sources of funds include:
   A. Decrease in cash on hand, in bank account balances (including personal and business checking and savings accounts), and decreases in accounts receivable
   B. Increases in accounts payable
   C. Increases in loan principals and credit card balances
   D. Taxable and nontaxable income
   E. Deductions that do not require funds such as depreciation, carryovers and carrybacks, and adjusted basis of assets sold
2. Application of funds are ways the taxpayer used (or expended) money during the year. Examples of applications of funds include:
   A. Increases in cash on hand, increase in bank account balances (including personal and business checking and savings accounts), business equipment purchased, real estate purchased, and personal assets acquired
   B. Purchases, business expenses
   C. Decreases in loan principals and credit card balances
   D. Personal living expenses

   Determining the beginning amount of cash on hand and accumulated funds for the year is important. See *IRM 4.10.4.6.8.3* below for possible defenses the taxpayer might raise regarding the availability of nontaxable funds.
3. See *Exhibit 4.10.4-10* for an example.

EXHIBIT 5.5 IRM/Example of Computation for Cash- and Accrual-Based Taxpayer

Exhibit 4.10.4-10
Source and Application of Funds Method: Example of Computation for Cash- and Accrual-Based Taxpayer

Source and Application of Funds Method Example

Sources of Funds		Applications of Funds	
Wages		Withholdings (W-2)	
Interest Income		Investment Interest	
Dividends			
Tax Refunds			
Alimony Received			
Sch. C Receipts	$50,000	Sch C Expenses (net of depreciation	
		Sch C Purchases	
		Sch C Labor	$32,000
		Sch C Material and Supplies	
		Sch C other period costs	
Sch. D – Gross Sales		Sch. D Asset and Investment Purchases	
Sale of Business Property			
IRA/Pension Distributions		Contributions to IRA, annuities and pensions, Penalties for early withdrawal	
Rental Income		Rental Expenses (net of depreciation)	
Sch F Receipts		Sch F Expenses (net of depreciation)	
Unemployment Comp.			
Social Security Benefits			
Unreported Income (IRP)			
Cash Distributions:		Contribution of Capital	
– S-Corps		– S-Corps	
– Partnerships		– Partnerships	
– Fiduciaries			
Sale: Personal Residence		Sale of Residence Costs (Form 2119)	
Sale: Personal Property		Insurance Policies	
Advanced EITC			
Child Support Received			
Cash on Hand (beginning)		Cash on Hand (ending)	
Cash in Bank (beginning)	$300	Cash in Bank (ending)	$600
Credit Cards (End. Bal.)		Credit Cards (Beg. Bal.)	
Loans		Loan repayments	
Nontaxable Income – gifts, inheritances, etc.		Personal Capital Acquisitions	
Other sources of funds		Personal Living Expenses	$40,000

(continued)

EXHIBIT 5.5 IRM/Example of Computation for Cash- and Accrual-Based Taxpayer (*Continued*)

		Other "cash out" items		
Accrual Basis Taxpayer		Accrual Basis Taxpayer		
– Decrease in Accts/Rec.		– Increase in Accts/Rec.		
– Increase in Accts/Pay		– Decrease in Accts/Pay		
Total Sources of Funds:	$50,300	Total Expenditures:		$72,600
Computing understatement of taxable income				
Total Applications of Funds			$72,600	
Total Sources of Funds			$50,300	
Excess Applications over Sources (understatement of taxable income).			$22,300	

Bank Deposits and Cash Expenditures Method

The bank deposits and cash expenditures method is another frequently used technique. Although bank records are important to all methods, they are particularly critical to the bank deposits and cash expenditures method. The underlying theory of this method is that receipts are either deposited into the bank or spent (or kept on hand in the form of cash). It relies heavily on bank account transactions. Therefore, it does not lend itself to cash-intensive businesses, since significant amounts of cash may not be deposited and expenses may be paid directly from the cash till. The method calculates the "gross receipts as corrected" amount. If income and expenses were accurately reported on the tax return, the gross receipts as corrected would match the tax return's reported amount. Exhibit 5.6 is the IRM definition of the bank deposits and cash expenditures method.

Exhibits 5.7 to 5.10 illustrate the gross receipts formula and the explanation of formula for the bank deposits and cash expenditures method as well as displaying the format used in computing the gross receipts as corrected.

The Markup Method

The markup method reconstructs income based on the application of a reasonable business percentage, that is, gross profit, or ratio. The markup can be the taxpayer's actual amount, if known, or a generally accepted industry standard. This method can be particularly useful when applied to a business selling a single (or limited) product with a standard markup. Exhibit 5.11 is the IRM definition of the markup method.

Exhibit 5.12 is an example of the cost of sales to gross receipts ratio used to calculate sales.

Unit and Volume Method

The unit and volume method reconstructs income based on a definable unit of measurement that can be applied to determine gross receipts. For example, a taxi earns

EXHIBIT 5.6 IRM/Bank Deposits and Cash Expenditures Method

4.10.4.6.4 (05-27-2011)
Bank Deposits and Cash Expenditures Method

1. An important feature of any examination is the inspection or analysis of the taxpayer's bank records. This is particularly so in the examination of inadequate, nonexistent, or possibly falsified books and records. The depth of the bank account analysis (see *IRM 4.10.4.3.3.7*) will depend upon the facts and circumstances of the individual case. When the bank account *analysis* indicates a reasonable likelihood of unreported income, the examination of income may be expanded to include the use of the formal Bank *Deposits* and Cash Expenditures Method to determine the actual understatement of taxable income.
2. In summary, income is proven through a detailed, in-depth analysis of all bank deposits, canceled checks, currency transactions, and electronic debits, transfers, and credits to the bank accounts AND identification of the taxpayer's cash expenditures. The Bank Deposits and Cash Expenditures Method is distinguished from the Bank Account Analysis by:
   A. The depth and analysis of *all* the individual bank account transactions
   B. The accounting for cash expenditures
   C. Determination of actual personal living expenses
3. The Bank Deposits and Cash Expenditures Method computes income by showing what happened to a taxpayer's funds. It is based on the theory that if a taxpayer receives money, only two things happen with it: it is either deposited or it is spent.
4. This method is based on the assumptions that:
   A. Proof of deposits into bank accounts, after certain adjustments have been made for nontaxable receipts, constitutes evidence of taxable receipts.
   B. Outlays, as disclosed on the return, were actually made. These outlays could only have been paid for by credit card, check, or cash. If outlays were paid by cash, then the source of that cash must be from a taxable source unless otherwise accounted for. It is the burden of the taxpayer to demonstrate a nontaxable source for this cash.
5. The Bank Deposits and Cash Expenditures Method can be used in the examination of both business and nonbusiness returns.
6. The Bank Deposits and Cash Expenditures Method may supply leads to additional unreported income, not only from the amounts and frequency of deposits, but also by identifying the sources of such deposits. Determining how deposited funds are dispersed or accumulated (to whom and for what purpose) might also provide leads to other sources of income.
7. If the Bank Deposits and Cash Expenditures Method indicate an understatement of taxable income, it may be due to either underreporting of gross receipts or overstating expenses, or a combination of both.

income based on the miles driven and gross receipts can be reasonably extrapolated, based on the gasoline expense deducted on the tax return. Exhibit 5.13 is the IRM definition of the unit and volume method.

Exhibit 5.14 is an example of the unit and volume method computation.

The Net Worth Method

This method has been long recognized by the courts and upheld at the Supreme Court level. It is intuitively understood and relatively simple to prepare, depending

EXHIBIT 5.7 IRM/Gross Receipts Formula

4.10.4.6.4.6 (08-09-2011)
Gross Receipts Formula

1. The Bank Deposits and Cash Expenditures Method is used to determine gross receipts *from all sources*; i.e., it is not limited to consideration of business receipts and it is not necessary to audit or verify expenses deducted on the return. The basic formula for computing the understatement of taxable income is outlined here. An example is shown in *Exhibit 4.10.4-9, The Bank Deposits and Cash Expenditures Method.* Also, see the example of computation of gross receipts below:

1.	Total bank deposits
Less:	
2.	Nontaxable receipts deposited
3.	Net deposits resulting from taxable receipts
Add:	
4.	Business expenses paid by cash
5.	Capital items paid by cash (personal and business)
6.	Personal expenses paid by cash
7.	Cash accumulated during the year from receipts
Subtract:	
8.	Nontaxable cash used for lines 4–7.
For accrual-basis taxpayers:	
9.	For accounts receivable, subtract the beginning balance from the ending balance. A net increase represents additional taxable gross receipts and is added here. A net decrease represents payments included in prior year gross receipts and is subtracted here.
10.	For accounts payable, subtract the beginning balance from the ending balance. A net increase represents purchases on account during the year and is subtracted here. A net decrease represents payments on accounts and is added here.
11.	Gross Receipts as corrected

on the information available. The underlying theory is that increases to net worth, adjusted for nondeductible expenditures and nontaxable income, must result from taxable income. In general, net worth is calculated at the beginning and the end of the period. The difference between the two amounts is the increase (or decrease) in net worth. This amount is then compared to the amount of taxable income (or loss) reported as a source of the change in net worth. Exhibit 5.15 is IRM definition of the net worth method.

The formula for the net worth method is shown in Exhibit 5.16.

The section includes only examples of the actual IRM manual covering the formal indirect methods. The forensic operator must familiarize himself with the unique factors, requirements, and limitations of each technique before applying and relying on the results of any of these methods.

EXHIBIT 5.8 IRM/Explanation of Formula for Bank Deposits and Cash Expenditures Method—Page 1

4.10.4.6.4.6.1 (08-09-2011)
Explanation of Formula for Bank Deposits and Cash Expenditures Method

1. The following is an explanation of the specific items used in the above computation. The items are identified by the line number. See *Exhibit 4.10.4-9* for an example.
2. *Line 1*: Total bank deposits means total deposits in all of the taxpayer's bank accounts. this includes the taxpayer's business and personal accounts, the spouse's accounts, and dependent children's accounts. (Note: This could vary if the spouse files a separate return.) The deposits should be reconciled, if possible, so that only the receipts during the current year are included. This is accomplished by totaling deposits as shown on the bank statements, adding to this amount any current year's receipts (which were deposited in the subsequent year), and deducting any prior year's receipts, which were deposited in the current year. See *Exhibit 4.10.4-9* for an example.
   A. Analyze the deposits to identify those that appear unlikely to have resulted from the taxpayer's known business activity. Determining the source of the funds may result in the identification of additional sources of income.
   B. Look for amounts that are unusually large (or small) or in even amounts, received on a regular basis, or currency when deposits normally consist of checks. These irregular deposits may indicate that not all gross receipts are deposited.
3. *Line 2*: Eliminate nontaxable deposits representing duplicated and nontaxable items. See *Exhibit 4.10.4-9* for an example.
   A. Duplicated items include checks to cash where the proceeds are redeposited. An example is when the taxpayer writes a check payable to cash and obtains currency and/or coins from the bank in exchange for the check. This currency is then used to cash customers' checks, which are deposited into the taxpayer's bank account; in effect, redepositing the funds withdrawn. This deposit must be eliminated in determining deposits from taxable receipts.
   B. Transfers between accounts are another example of nontaxable receipts. Transfers can occur between different checking accounts, different savings accounts, and between savings accounts and checking accounts. Such transfers do not represent additional receipts since they are merely a shifting of funds from one account to another. Deposits from transfers must be eliminated in determining deposits from taxable receipts.
   C. Loan proceeds should be documented with loan applications and records of disbursement. The documents should be reviewed to confirm the amount and terms of the loan and determine if the information supplied by the taxpayer on the loan application is consistent with information on the return. Differences should be reconciled and may result in the identification of additional sources of income.
   D. Other common types of nontaxable receipts that are often deposited and must be eliminated in determining deposits from taxable receipts include gifts, inheritances, nontaxable Social Security benefits, nontaxable Veterans Administration benefits, tax refunds, etc.
4. *Line 3*: This line represents the total amount of net receipts *deposited* in bank accounts. At this point, the examiner has completed a detailed reconciliation of the bank deposits.
5. The next step in the Bank Deposits and Cash Expenditures Method is determining the amount of gross receipts *never deposited* in the bank accounts. The Bank Deposits and Cash Expenditures Method is incomplete and ineffective unless the cash expenditures are taken into account.

(*continued*)

EXHIBIT 5.8 IRM/Explanation of Formula for Bank Deposits and Cash Expenditures Method—Page 1 *(Continued)*

6. *Line 4*: Business expenses paid by cash are computed by determining the business expenses paid by check and subtracting this amount from the total business expenses reported on the tax return. Examiners should be satisfied that all checks have been presented. Should the taxpayer remove any portion of the nondeductible checks, the analysis would result in an understatement of unreported income. See *Exhibit 4.10.4-9* for an example.
   A. First determine total disbursements by adding the total deposits to the opening account balance, and then subtracting the ending balance. The resulting figure must then be adjusted for checks written during the year, which have not cleared the bank and checks written in the prior year, which cleared during the current year. This is merely a reconciliation of the checks so that only the current year's checks are taken into account.
   B. Then identify all the checks for personal expenses and purchases of assets (business and personal) that would not be deductible as a business expense on the tax return, and subtract from the total disbursements. The result will be the business expenses paid by check.

      Note:

      Generally, the number of nonbusiness checks written is less than the number of business checks. Nonbusiness checks include checks for personal living expenses, capital purchases (personal and business), checks to cash redeposited, check transfers between accounts, and payments on liabilities. Checks for these items would be included even if the taxpayer deducted them on the return.
   C. Analyze the business expenses claimed on the tax return to eliminate expenses which are not cash outlays; i.e., depreciation, depletion, bad debts, etc.

EXHIBIT 5.9 IRM/Explanation of Formula for Bank Deposits and Cash Expenditures Method—Page 2

   D. Subtract the business expenses paid by check from the expenses requiring cash outlays claimed on the tax return. The result is the amount of business expenses paid by cash rather than check.

      Note:

      This step is based on the assumption that outlays as disclosed on the return were actually made and could only have been paid for by either check or cash. The result could represent unsubstantiated business expenses. Effectively, the taxpayer is either underreporting gross receipts or overstating expenses. Either way, the adjustment amount is the same.
7. *Line 5*: Capital items paid by cash include cash purchases of capital assets, cash deposited in savings accounts, and cash used to make payments on liabilities or debt. For each item, determine how much the taxpayer paid during the year and subtract any payments made by check to arrive at the amount paid with cash.
   D. Review information in the file included with the case-building data.
   E. Personal assets may be identified by reviewing state registrations and licenses, property records, and building permits.
   F. Review the depreciation schedules to identify business assets for which the taxpayer is making payments; i.e., the taxpayer does not have clear title.

EXHIBIT 5.9 IRM/Explanation of Formula for Bank Deposits and Cash Expenditures Method—Page 2 (*Continued*)

8. *Line 6*: Personal expenses paid by cash include living expenses, income taxes, etc. Personal items paid for by cash can be determined in the same manner as the business expenses paid by cash. Add up all the actual personal living expense identified as part of the financial status analysis and by completing Form 4822 with the taxpayer's assistance, and then subtract the personal living expenses paid by check. The remainder will be the personal living expenses paid with cash. Personal living expenses purchased with credit cards must also be considered.
9. *Line 7*: Cash accumulated during the year is the cash (undeposited currency and coins) received by the taxpayer during the year which is on hand at the end of the year (it was neither expended nor deposited). There are two considerations:
   D. Increases in cash on hand at the end of the year that is associated with normal business practices and the need to complete cash transactions with customers.
   E. Increases in accumulations of funds that are not generally associated with normal business practices. Taxpayers may accumulate significant amounts of funds for personal use.
10. Examiners should establish the amount and verify the taxpayer's statements of cash on hand and cash accumulations early in the examination, before the likelihood of unreported income is established. This information is needed to complete the financial status analysis. Asking the taxpayer about cash on hand and cash accumulations does not violate IRC 7602(e), which requires the Service to establish a likelihood of unreported income before using a financial status audit technique (formal indirect method) to make the actual determination of tax liability. For additional information, see:
    D. *IRM 4.10.4.2.5* and *IRM 4.10.4.2.6*
    E. *IRM 4.10.4.3.3.2 (3)* and *IRM 4.10.4.3.3.2 (6)*
    F. *IRM 4.10.4.3.4.4 (4)*
    G. *Exhibit 4.10.4-1*
11. *Line 8*: Nontaxable cash used for (4) through (7) is nontaxable cash used to pay expenses, purchase capital assets, deposit into savings accounts, make payments on liabilities, and to accumulate. Nontaxable cash includes: loans not deposited, withdrawals from savings accounts not redeposited or transferred, gifts, inheritances, collection of loans receivable, nontaxable income, etc. It is important to get complete information about nontaxable income as efforts may be wasted if the taxpayer later provides information regarding the availability of nontaxable sources of funds to explain an understatement. See *IRM 4.10.4.6.8.3* for possible defenses the taxpayer might raise regarding nontaxable sources of funds.
12. *Line 9*: To account for changes in accounts receivable for accrual-basis taxpayers, subtract the beginning balance from the ending balance to determine the change. A net increase represents additional taxable gross receipts, a net decrease represents payments already included in prior year gross receipts. See *IRM 4.10.4.6.4.6.2* for a complete discussion of adjustments for accrual-basis taxpayers.
13. *Line 10*: To account for changes in accounts payable for accrual-basis taxpayers, subtract the beginning balance from the ending balance to determine the change. A net increase results from purchases on account during the year and is subtracted from gross receipts. A net decrease results from payments on account during the year in excess of purchases on account and is added to gross receipts. See *IRM 4.10.4.6.3.4* for a complete discussion of adjustments for accrual-basis taxpayers.
14. *Line 11*: Gross receipts as corrected should be compared to the gross receipts reported on the tax return to compute the adjustment to income.

EXHIBIT 5.10 IRM/Example of Computation of Gross Receipts

Exhibit 4.10.4-9
The Bank Deposits and Cash Expenditures Method: Example of Computation of Gross Receipts
Bank Deposits and Cash Expenditures Method Example

1.	Total reconciled bank deposits		$151,500
	Less:		
2.	Nontaxable receipts deposited		($35,000)
3.	Net deposits resulting from taxable receipts		$116,500
	Add:		
4.	Business expenses paid by cash	$50,700	
5.	Capital items paid by cash (personal and business)	$20,300	
6.	Personal living expenses paid by cash	$7,034	
7.	Cash accumulated during the year from receipts	$5,000	$83,034
	Subtotal		$199,534
8.	Less nontaxable cash used for lines 4-7		($15,000)
9.	Accts. Rec.: Add the difference between the ending and beginning balances		0
10.	Acct. Pay.: Subtract the difference between the ending and beginning balances		0
11.	Gross Receipts as corrected		$184,534

Line 1:			
	Deposits during the year		$150,000
	Add receipts deposited in the subsequent year		$13,000
	Substract prior year receipts deposited during year		($11,500)
	Reconciled bank deposits		$151,500
Line 2:			
	Loan proceeds		$12,000
	Checks to cash redeposited		$3,000
	Transfers between accounts		$6,000
	Nontaxable Veterans Administration pension		$14,000
	Total		$35,000

Line 4:		
Total business expenses per return	$200,000	
Non cash business expenses	$60,000	
Total business expenses requiring cash outlay per return	$140,000	

EXHIBIT 5.10 IRM/Example of Computation of Gross Receipts (*Continued*)

Computation of business checks for the year			
Account balance at beginning of year		$10,000	
Add deposits during the year		$150,000	
Subtotal		$160,000	
Less balance at the end of the year		($8,000)	
Subtotal		$152,000	
Add checks written this year but cleared in the subsequent year		$3,000	
Subtotal		$155,000	
Less checks written in prior year but cleared this year		($6,000)	
Total checks written this year		$149,000	
Less nonbusiness checks			
Checks to cash redeposited	$3,500		
Check transfers	$6,000		
Personal expenses paid by check	$34,500		
Capital expenditure paid by check	$15,700	$59,700	
Total business checks		$89,300	($89,300)
Total business expenses paid by cash			$50,700

EXHIBIT 5.11 IRM/Markup Method

4.10.4.6.5 (08-09-2011)
Markup Method

1. The Markup Method produces a reconstruction of income based on the use of percentages or ratios considered typical for the business under examination in order to make the actual determination of tax liability. It consists of an analysis of sales and/or cost of sales and the application of an appropriate percentage of markup to arrive at the taxpayer's gross receipts. By reference to similar businesses, percentage computations determine sales, cost of sales, gross profit, or even net profit. By using some known base and the typical applicable percentage, individual items of income or expenses may be determined. These percentages can be obtained from analysis of Bureau of Labor Statistics data or industry publications. If known, use of the taxpayer's actual markup is required.
2. The Markup Method is a formal indirect method that can overcome the weaknesses of the Bank Deposits and Cash Expenditures Method, Source and Application of Funds Method, and Net Worth Method, which do not effectively reconstruct income when cash is not deposited and the total cash outlays cannot be determined unless volunteered by the taxpayer. If personal enrichment occurs that cannot be identified, the effectiveness of these methods is diminished. For example, the possibility exists that significant personal acquisitions or expenditures are paid with cash and are not evident. The Markup Method is similar to how state sales tax agencies conduct audits. The cost of goods sold is verified and the resulting gross receipts are determined based on actual markup.
3. This method is most effective when applied to businesses whose inventory is regulated or purchases can be readily broken down in groups with the same percentage of markup.
4. An effective initial interview with the taxpayer is the key to determining the pertinent facts specific to the business being examined.

EXHIBIT 5.12 IRM/Cost of Sales to Gross Receipts Ratio

4.10.4.6.5.4 (08-09-2011)
Cost of Sales to Gross Receipts Ratio

1. Using the cost of sales to gross receipts ratio is a variation of the gross profit margin to sales ratio. It is also a comparison of costs to sales.

   Example:

   Example: A taxpayer sells two products, A and B, and reports $70,000 in gross receipts. The costs for product A are $20,000 and the costs for product B are $30,000. The costs are verified with the third-party supplier and adjusted for opening and closing inventory.

Sales per return:	$ 70,000
Cost of Sales (Product A)	$ 20,000
Cost of Sales (Product B)	$ 30,000

   The examiner determines that cost of sales is 75% of sales for product A and 50% of B by interviewing the taxpayer, analyzing the taxpayer's records, and reviewing industry standards.

   Step 1: Determine the COGS Percentage

	Product A	*Product B*
Cost of Sales %	75%	50%

   Step 2: Determine the correct Gross Receipts: (COS/COS % = Gross Receipts)

	Product A	*Product B*
$20,000/.75	$26,666	
$30,000/.50		$60,000

   Step 3: Determine the Adjustment to Gross Receipts

Sales of Product A:	$ 26,666
Sales of Product B:	+ $ 60,000
Sales as Recomputed:	$ 86,666
Sales per Tax Return:	− $ 70,000
Income Adjustment:	$16,666

EXHIBIT 5.13 IRM/Unit and Volume Method

4.10.4.6.6 (08-09-2011)
Unit and Volume Method

1. In many instances gross receipts may be determined or verified by applying the sales price to the volume of business done by the taxpayer. The number of units or volume of business done by the taxpayer might be determined from the taxpayer's books as the records under examination may be adequate as to cost of goods sold or expenses. In other cases, the determination of units or volume handled may come from third-party sources.
2. This method for determining the actual tax liability has been effectively applied in carry-out pizza businesses, coin operated laundromats, and mortuaries.

EXHIBIT 5.14 IRM/Example of Computation

4.10.4.6.6.4 (06-01-2004)
Example of Computation

1. This example is for a coin operated laundry, where the known unit is the amount of water needed for each unit of sale (load of laundry). Per the utility bills, the taxpayer consumed 3,000,000 gallons of water.

Gallons of water consumed:	3,000,000
Non washing machine consumption (spillage):	– 50,000
Net water available for paid loads (gallons):	2,950,000

   Gallons of water per load of wash, determined from manufacturer or credible oral testimony, is 27 gallons.
   The reconstructed number of loads of wash is 2,950,000/27 = 109,259.
   The price per washing machine load is $2.50. The gross receipts from washing machines is 109,259 loads × $2.50 / load = $273,148.
2. The price per dryer load is $1.50. Based on observations on different days of the week, the examiner determines that customers' use of dryers is 75% of their wash loads. The price per dryer load is $1.50. Therefore, the gross receipts for dryer use is .75(109,259) × $1.50 = $122,916.
3. Summarize the gross receipts for all the services and compare to the gross receipts reported on the tax return.

Gross Receipts from washers:	$ 273,148
Gross Receipts from dryers:	+ $122,916
Other Receipts (vending, arcade):	$ 25,000
Sales as Recomputed:	$ 421,064
Sales per Tax Return:	– $ 376,745
Income Adjustment:	$44,319

EXHIBIT 5.15 IRM/Net Worth Method

4.10.4.6.7 (06-01-2004)
Net Worth Method

1. The Net Worth Method for determining the actual tax liability is based upon the theory that increases in a taxpayer's net worth during a taxable year, adjusted for nondeductible expenditures and nontaxable income, must result from taxable income. This method requires a complete reconstruction of the taxpayer's financial history, since the government must account for all assets, liabilities, nondeductible expenditures, and nontaxable sources of funds during the relevant period.
2. The theory of the Net Worth Method is based upon the fact that for any given year, a taxpayer's income is applied or expended on items which are either deductible or nondeductible, including increases to the taxpayer's net worth through the purchase of assets and/or reduction of liabilities.
3. The taxpayer's net worth (total assets less total liabilities) is determined at the beginning and at the end of the taxable year. The difference between these two amounts will be the increase or decrease in net worth. The taxable portion of the income can be reconstructed by calculating the increase in net worth during the year, adding back the nondeductible items, and subtracting that portion of the income which is partially or wholly nontaxable.
4. The purpose of the Net Worth Method is to determine, through a change in net worth, whether the taxpayer is purchasing assets, reducing liabilities, or making expenditures with funds not reported as taxable income.

EXHIBIT 5.16 IRM/Formula for the Net Worth Method

4.10.4.6.7.3 (09-11-2007)
Formula for the Net Worth Method

1. The formula for computing income using the Net Worth Method is as follows:

Total Assets	$XXX
Less: Total Liabilities	(XXX)
Net Worth, end of year	$XXX
Less: Net Worth, beginning of year	(XXX)
Increase or decrease in net worth	$XXX
Add: Nondeductible expenditures	XXX
Sub-Total	XXX
Less: Nontaxable income	(XXX)
Adjusted gross income (this figure would be net or taxable income in the case of partnerships and corporations)	$XXX

2. A complete discussion of the computation for the Net Worth Method and associated audit techniques is included in IRM 9.5.9.5.4 through IRM 9.5.9.5.9.

APPLYING DIGITAL ANALYSIS TECHNIQUES IN FINANCIAL FORENSICS INVESTIGATIONS

Computer technology has been adopted as an integral part of business by both the private and public sectors. The growing proficiency of computer usage has consequently heightened an individual's ability to perform, hide, or otherwise aid unlawful or fraudulent activities. To meet these challenging demands, forensic operators must deploy more sophisticated and well-defined computerized forensic procedures.

Background

With the routine use of computers, the concept of digital analysis is an essential tool for the forensic operator. These techniques allow the forensic operator to efficiently accumulate and examine mass quantities of data, thereby enhancing the operator's findings and opinions. Digital analysis uses the speed, power, and storage capabilities of the computer to perform many different tests, such as data mining techniques for digital patterns.

Data mining is a computerized process of extracting digital patterns from large data sets with the goal of uncovering previously unknown hidden patterns, trends, and relationships that are too complex to discover manually. With the technical advances in computer processing, data mining has developed into a progressively more important tool for the forensic operator in converting large quantities of digital information into concise and targeted intelligence for further investigation. Other terms for data mining may include database reporting or data investigation, although all rely on the automated extraction of information from a database.

A database is defined as a collection of organized information that can be efficiently accessed, managed, and updated. The digital analysis techniques discussed in this chapter serve as a foundation for financial forensic investigations and the subsequent analytical procedures.

Removing the Roadblocks to Digital Analysis When computers first started to become part of the business landscape, they were expensive to buy and maintain. Some believed computers and the related software were too technical for the forensic operator, and their use should be left to computer experts. Extracting data from subject computers was often tedious and required certain computer expertise. Furthermore, there was a concern that by using computers, the forensic operator would be too far removed from the hands-on approach applied in the past.

Today, these issues and concerns are no longer true. Companies no longer run on mainframe computers and the cost to purchase computers has been drastically reduced. Furthermore, current software programs are more user-friendly and have reduced the complexity and risks of data extraction. Even with the use of computers, the forensic operator remains responsible for developing the investigative approach and analyzing the output.

Advantages of Digital Analysis Techniques Digital analysis techniques afford the forensic operator the ability to perform cost-effective financial forensic investigations. This is achieved through the following:

- The ability to test or analyze 100 percent of a data set, rather than merely sampling the data set.
- Massive amounts of data can be imported into working files, which allows for the processing of complex transactions and profiling of certain case-specific characteristics.
- Anomalies within databases can be quickly identified, thereby reducing the number of transactions that require review and analysis.
- Digital analysis can be easily customized to address the scope of the engagement.

Overall, digital analysis can streamline investigations that involve a large number of transactions, often turning a needle-in-the-haystack search into a refined and efficient investigation. Digital analysis is not designed to replace the pick-and-shovel aspect of an investigation. However, the proper application of digital analysis will permit the forensic operator to efficiently identify those specific transactions that require further investigation or follow up.

There are a growing number of software applications that can assist the forensic operator with digital analysis. A few such examples are CaseWare International Inc.'s IDEA, ACL Services Ltd.'s ACL Desktop Edition, and ActiveData, which can be added to Excel.

Application of Digital Analysis Techniques Some specific examples of digital analysis techniques that can be employed by the forensic operator include the following:

- Using Benford's Law to identify numeric pattern deviations and highlight unusual trends.

- Employing duplicate and rounded numbers testing to identify both simple and complex number patterns.
- Joining databases, for the purpose of performing link analysis, which matches certain common data characteristics.
- Performing gap analysis testing to identify missing invoices, checks, other numerical documents, and dates.
- Stratifying numeric values to identify unusual and outlying values.
- Developing visual illustrations to present the findings.

Digital Analysis Techniques

Some of the more widely used digital analysis techniques that can be employed in a financial forensic investigation include:

- Benford's Law
- Duplicate numbers test
- Rounded numbers test
- Link analysis
- Gap analysis
- Item listing
- Querying data
- Stratification

Of course, not every technique is applicable to each engagement, so proper planning is paramount. When selecting what techniques to apply, the forensic operator needs to consider what data is available, the medium or platform for said data, what the investigation objectives are, and what digital analysis techniques will assist in accomplishing those objectives.

Benford's Law One of the most popular digital analysis techniques is Benford's Law. It is based on a theory that there are expected frequencies of occurrence for the digits in a naturally generated data set of numbers. However, contrived numbers, which often represent illegal activity, will deviate from the benchmark frequencies of Benford's Law, revealing the irregularities.

History of Benford's Law Benford's Law, which was first identified in the 1880s by astronomer and mathematician Simon Newcomb, was developed by Frank Benford in the 1920s when he was a physicist for the General Electric Company. Benford noted that the first few pages of logarithm table books were more worn than the later pages. As an example, the logarithm tables beginning with the digits 1 and 2 were more worn than for the numbers 5 and 6. In those precalculator days, logarithm tables in books were used as a method to multiply two large numbers. Benford concluded that he and his fellow employees used pages with numbers of lower first digits more frequently and, therefore, more numbers with lower first digits existed. He confirmed this theory after extensive testing and analysis of 20,229 different observations on a wide variety of data ranging from population census figures to areas of rivers to baseball statistics. In 1938, Benford published an article on his

EXHIBIT 5.17 Benford's Law: Expected Digital Frequencies

	Position in Number			
Digit	**1st**	**2nd**	**3rd**	**4th**
0	N/A	.11968	.10178	.10018
1	.30103	.11389	.10138	.10014
2	.17609	.10882	.10097	.10010
3	.12494	.10433	.10057	.10006
4	.09691	.10031	.10018	.10002
5	.07918	.09668	.09979	.09998
6	.06695	.09337	.09940	.09994
7	.05799	.09035	.09902	.09990
8	.05115	.08757	.09864	.09986
9	.04576	.08500	.09827	.09982

work in the *Proceedings of the American Philosophical Society* journal, and scientists began to pay more attention to his findings.

Despite its origin many decades ago, Benford's Law was not recognized as a forensic accounting technique until the 1990s. Mark J. Nigrini, PhD, is responsible for pioneering new applications for this old mathematical phenomenon and promoting its use in the fields of audit, fraud investigation, and forensic accounting. Benford's Law provides a unique method of data analysis, allowing the forensic operator to identify fraud indicia, manipulative bias, processing inefficiency, errors, and other nonconforming abnormal patterns as they apply to a company's accounting records.

Benford's Law Explained Our number system uses the digits 0 through 9, and Benford was able to empirically demonstrate that in a large data set, the probabilities for the distribution of digit frequencies would follow the chart.[2] By way of application, the first digit of a number is the leftmost digit, so that the first significant digit of zero is ignored. For example, in the number sequence 582, the number 5 is the first digit, 8 is the second digit, and 2 is the third digit.

The forensic operator can employ this mathematical principle, using specialized software, to execute several compelling analytical tests. The chart indicates that under Benford's Law, the expected proportion of numbers with a first digit being 1 is 0.30103 rounded to 30.1 percent, while the expected proportion for numbers with the first digit being 2 is 0.17609 rounded to 17.6 percent, and so forth. As the numbers get higher in value, the percentage of their occurrence as the first digit becomes less frequent.

Benford also developed a distribution of frequencies for the second, third, and fourth digits. Exhibit 5.17 presents the expected digital frequencies for Benford's Law:

---

[2] M. J. Nigrini, "A Taxpayer Compliance Application of Benford's Law," *Journal of the American Taxation Association* 18 (1996): 72–91.

Criteria for the Use of Benford's Law The theory of Benford's Law is only applicable to data sets containing naturally occurring numbers, independent from human or categorical control. Based upon the experience of others in testing Benford's Law, the data set should meet certain criteria for the results to be meaningful. Not all data sets will conform to Benford's expected digit frequency. Therefore, the data set examined should:

- Describe the sizes of similar data; such examples include the lengths of rivers and populations of cities.
- Have no artificial limits, as well as no minimum or maximum amounts, such as the height of adults or a minimum bank charge (zero is an acceptable minimum).
- Not have numbers that are prearranged or assigned, such as Social Security numbers or zip codes.
- Contain more smaller numbers than larger numbers, such as there are more smaller cities than larger cities.
- Not be a subset of another set.
- Not represent aggregated totals, such as monthly invoices.
- Be large enough so that the expected proportions can manifest themselves.

Any numbers influenced by human thought would not be a good candidate for Benford's Law. Consideration should also be given to numbers that are set by psychological thresholds, such as the $19.99 sales item. These numbers may not be compliant with Benford's Law. There may be other numbers that may not follow a Benford distribution because they are company-specific.

Also, the forensic operator should be aware of repetitive payments such as monthly rent payments or the amount for monthly paychecks. The repetition of these numbers may produce false anomalies in the Benford's Law tests. The forensic operator may want to cleanse the data set of the known and accepted repetition and then perform the analysis again.

Applying Benford's Law Natural numbers, for this principle, are defined as naturally occurring and not manipulated, and these types of numbers, generated in the ordinary course of business, have a tendency to follow Benford's Law. The premise for Benford's application in fraud detection is that, over time, individuals invent numbers that tend to be repetitive in their selection, as people do not think like the natural-digit patterns of Benford's Law. This conclusion is based upon the theory that human actions are not random, and individuals will select the numbers they are accustomed to, or can easily create. Therefore, the numbers invented by fraudsters, for nonexistent goods or services, are unlikely to follow the sequence of Benford's Law. Alerted to this information, there are many practical applications for Benford's Law in a financial forensic investigation.

The forensic operator can apply Benford's Law to a company's various accounting records. The forensic operator might select disbursement journals, invoices, cleared checks, deposits, transfers, payment records, and so on. In applying these tests, the forensic operator compares the output data from selected accounting records to the anticipated digit frequency of Benford's Law to identify exceptions.

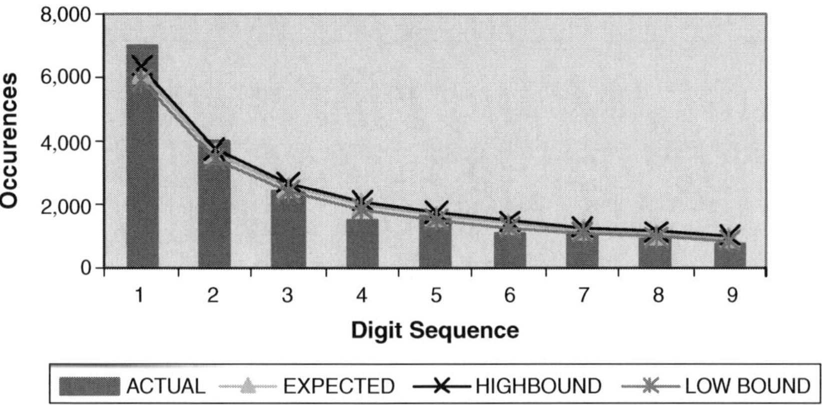

EXHIBIT 5.18 Chart-2, First-Digit Test

For example, if artificial or contrived values are present in a data set, the distribution of the digits data set will graphically contrast to the shape predicted by Benford's Law.

Benford's Law can be applied to the following digit combinations during the forensic operator's investigation:

- First digit
- Second digit
- First two digits
- First three digits
- Last two digits

The *First Digit* test is a test for reasonableness that compares the actual first digit frequency distribution of a target company's data set to Benford's Law. The geometric digit sequence expected from Benford's Law should match with the actual digit sequence of the company's transactions. At this test level, the data to be analyzed will be large and the test results would be used to identify suspected anomalies. This test will point the forensic operator in the right direction, as fraudsters will tend to overuse certain digit patterns when inventing numbers.

The graph in Exhibit 5.18 indicates (among other observations) that the numbers 1 and 2 both exceed the expected counts based upon Benford's Law, thus suggesting that anomalies exist within the company's financial data set.

Note that the numbers 4 and 6 fall below the predicted limit. This is not considered an anomaly warranting further investigation, as this is merely a byproduct of the other digits exceeding their expected counts. It is understood that if some digits exceed their respective proportion, then other digits must fall below their expected proportion.

The numbers across the bottom of this graph, and the other Benford graphs presented, represent the tested-digit sequence. The bars in the graph represent the actual number of occurrences for each digit sequence within the analyzed data set.

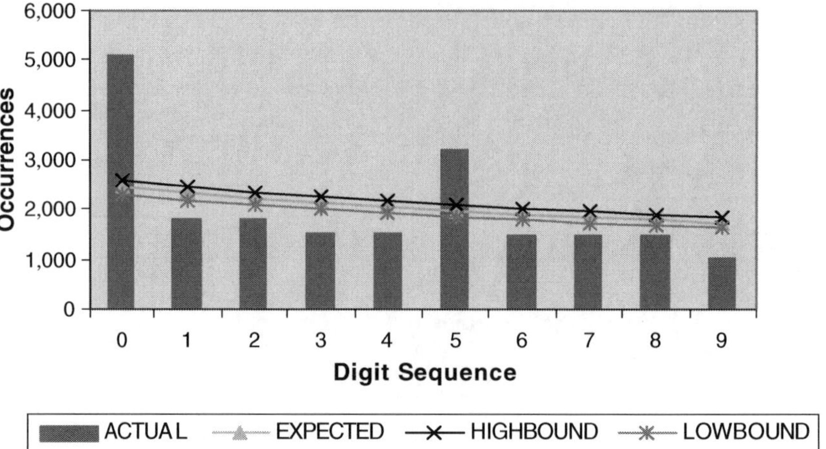

EXHIBIT 5.19 Chart-3, Second-Digit Test

The middle line indicates the expected number of occurrences for a particular digit sequence according to Benford's Law. For additional information, the low and high lines indicate the acceptable low and high range.

The *Second Digit* test is similar in analysis to the First Digit test and can assist the forensic operator in identifying possible irregularities in the data set under investigation.

The graph shown in Exhibit 5.19 indicates (among other observations) that the numbers 0 and 5 both exceed the expected counts based upon Benford's Law, thus suggesting that anomalies exist within the company's financial data set. For example, the data set may contain an inordinately large amount of payments containing 0 or 5 as the second digit, such as $10,000 or $150.

The *First Two Digits* test is a more refined procedure than the two preceding tests and uses the first two leading digits. For example, the first two digits of 7,380 are 7 and 3. There are 90 possible first-two-digit combinations ranging from the numbers 10 to 99. This test finds anomalies in the data that are not readily apparent from either the First Digit or Second Digit tests, when viewed on their own.

The graph in Exhibit 5.20 indicates (among other observations) that the numbers 10, 15, 20, 25 30, 50, and others exceed the predicted Benford's Law limit, thus suggesting that anomalies exist within the company's financial data set.

The *First Three Digits* test focuses on the 900 possible first-three-digit combinations ranging from 100 to 999. This is a highly focused test similar to the First Two Digits test and should produce a smaller sample size to be further analyzed.

Exhibit 5.21 indicates (among other observations) that the numbers 100, 150, 200, 250, 300, 500, and others exceed the predicted Benford's Law limit, thus suggesting that anomalies exist within the company's financial data set.

The *Last Two Digits* test is employed to find rounded numbers that may have been created. In the number sequence 7,500, the last two digits are 0 and 0, and indicate rounded numbers that may have been invented by the fraudster. This test is also useful in identifying unusual reoccurring patterns in the last-two-digit sequence that otherwise may not be readily apparent.

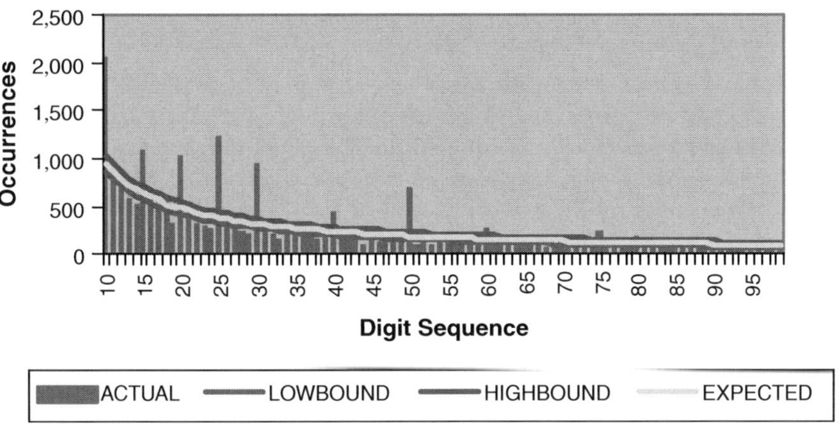

EXHIBIT 5.20 Chart-4, First-Two-Digits Test

Implementing Benford's Law To apply the tests previously outlined, the forensic operator must identify the company's specific databases that are suitable for Benford's Law analysis. The practical application of each test must be examined with regard to the database's overall volume of records, the specific assignment, and the pertinent characteristics that the forensic operator intends to examine.

The applicability of each Benford's Law test is highly dependent on the number of data points or observations available for analysis. For example, a data set with 1,000 observations is too small to produce meaningful results under the First Three Digits test. However, the same data set would be sufficient for the First Digit test and possibly the First Two Digits test. With experience, the forensic operator will gain a better understanding of the minimum data set size requirements to produce statistically significant results.

A preliminary investigation of the Benford's Law anomalies will often not immediately expose the source for the abnormality. Typically, this is due to the high

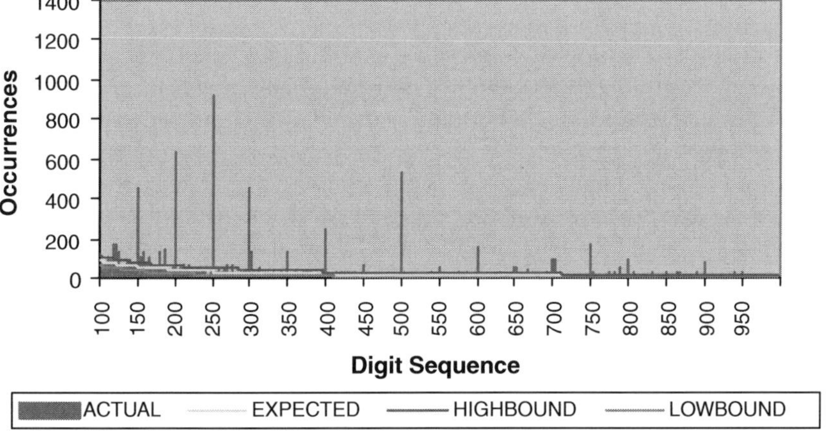

EXHIBIT 5.21 Chart-5, First-Three-Digits Test

number of anomalies produced from the First Digit test, thus necessitating further Benford Law digit testing. To illustrate, assume in the First Digit testing, the number 6 resulted in 3,521 disbursements to be reviewed. It may be difficult for the forensic operator to identify the source of the abnormality in 3,521 transactions. To narrow the scope of transactions requiring further investigation, the forensic operator can perform the First Two Digits and First Three Digits tests. For this example, assume these two tests resulted in an exception for the digit combination 64 with 1,541 disbursements to be reviewed and 647 with 337 disbursements to be reviewed. Therefore, after applying further Benford's Law tests, the forensic operator is now able to focus the analysis on a more manageable 337 disbursements than 3,521. Regardless of the results, the underlying investigation was performed on 100 percent of the data set, and the forensic operator's resources were allocated in a targeted and efficient manner.

Statistical Significance There is no specific method to measure how an actual data set compares to Benford's Law. Therefore, the forensic operator must determine the most appropriate goodness-of-fit for the actual data by applying one of the available methods. One such method is the Z-statistic, or Z Score, a mathematical formula that is used to compute the statistical significance of any deviations for a specific digit, or digit combination, when comparing the actual data set under investigation to the Benford's expected frequency.

By applying the Z-statistic, the forensic operator can establish if the anomalies are a genuine variation due to irregular activities, or a difference created by problems within the data itself or the method of data compilation. The Z-statistic calculates the error rate and assists the forensic operator in determining whether the error is worthy of any follow-up procedures. The formula for the Z-statistic is complex and beyond the scope of this book, but several digital analysis software programs can perform the computation.

When analyzing the results of a Z-statistic test, the forensic operator should identify occurrences where the Z-statistic exceeds a value of 1.96. A Z-statistic result in excess of 1.96 indicates that there is only a 5 percent probability that the difference between the expected and actual result is due to chance.

Case Study A company's senior management believes there may be some fraudulent activities within the organization. Although sales have continued to increase each year, profits within certain divisions have not been following a similar trend. Management has retained a forensic operator to perform a financial forensic investigation of its accounting records.

After examining the company's accounting systems, inspecting its available books and records, and interviewing key personnel, the forensic operator determined Benford's Law First Two Digits test should be applied to the company paid invoice amounts for period 20X1. The output of this test, Benford's Law results, is then interpreted by the forensic operator.

The graph in Exhibit 5.22 illustrates the application of Benford's Law applied to 100 percent of a company's paid invoices during the inspection period. The results represent a comparison of the actual numerical distribution of paid invoice amounts with the expected numerical distribution of invoice amounts when applying Benford's Law.

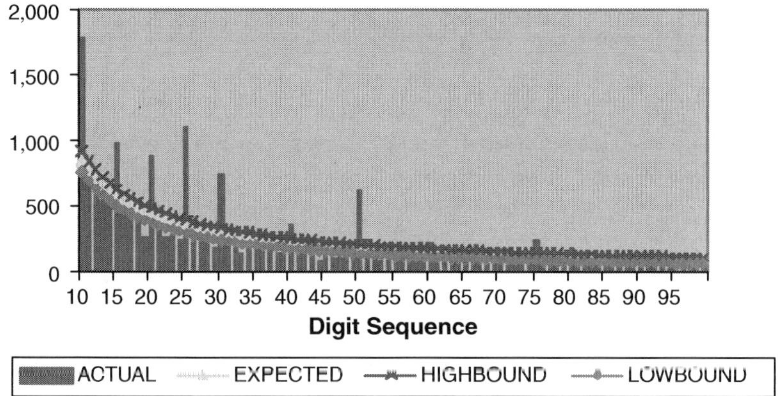

EXHIBIT 5.22 Chart-6, XYZ Company Inc. First-Two-Digits Test

The graph depicts the First Two Digits test results for the company and indicates that the numbers 10, 15, 20, 25, 30, 40, 50, 75, and others are above the distribution curve of Benford's Law expected frequencies. At this point, the forensic operator has identified the areas where the Benford's Law distribution does not agree with the actual distribution of the company's paid invoices. The number of transactions that comprise these eight different digit combinations likely makes it impractical and inefficient to obtain and analyze all the supporting documents.

The forensic operator then applied the Z-statistic to identify which of the combinations have an increased probability that the difference is due to chance and can therefore be eliminated from further investigation. The digit combinations of 40, 50, and 75 each resulted in a Z-statistic below 1.5 while the other combinations were above 2.0. Therefore, invoices should be obtained and investigated further for only the 10, 15, 20, 25, and 30 two-digit combinations.

The examination of the supporting documents will uncover whether the variation is an acceptable abnormality or a problem invoice(s). If the exceptions were an anomaly, no further investigation is required. If fraud is suspected, the investigation should continue to determine the individual, or individuals, connected with the suspicious invoices.

Duplicate Numbers Test The Duplicate Numbers test is used to identify abnormal recurrences of specific numbers, such as check numbers, invoice numbers, and dollar amounts. The objective is to draw attention to small groups of numbers that appear to be unusual because of their recurrence. The technique analyzes all the check (or other) numbers used by an individual or company during the period under investigation, and determines whether duplicate numbers exist. Once any duplication has been identified, meaningful inferences can be drawn through further investigation of the group or individual items.

When investigating duplicative dollar amounts, the forensic operator should review all significant numbers of duplicative transactions, as well as those duplicate transactions that are material in aggregate. The test can also be combined with the Rounded Numbers test to identify and investigate material recurrence of rounded numbers.

EXHIBIT 5.23 Chart-7, Duplicate Numbers Test Company Disbursements

Disbursement Amount	Total # of Records	Total Disbursement Amount	% of Total Records	% of Total Disbursements
10.00	469	4,690.00	2.21%	0.00%
15.00	144	2,160.00	0.68%	0.00%
18.50	129	2,386.50	0.61%	0.00%
20.00	201	4,020.00	0.95%	0.00%
25.00	651	16,275.00	3.07%	0.01%
100.00	204	20,400.00	0.96%	0.01%
150.00	41	6,150.00	0.19%	0.00%
200.00	91	18,200.00	0.43%	0.01%
250.00	38	9,500.00	0.18%	0.01%
300.00	208	62,400.00	0.98%	0.04%
301.50	111	33,466.50	0.52%	0.02%
400.00	34	13,600.00	0.16%	0.01%
450.00	22	9,900.00	0.10%	0.01%
500.00	91	45,500.00	0.43%	0.03%
550.00	16	8,800.00	0.08%	0.01%
600.00	34	20,400.00	0.16%	0.01%
650.00	10	6,500.00	0.05%	0.00%
700.00	23	16,100.00	0.11%	0.01%
750.00	38	28,500.00	0.18%	0.02%
800.00	26	20,800.00	0.12%	0.01%
900.00	14	12,600.00	0.07%	0.01%
950.00	10	9,500.00	0.05%	0.01%
1,000.00	117	117,000.00	0.55%	0.07%
1,100.00	26	28,600.00	0.12%	0.02%
1,200.00	18	21,600.00	0.08%	0.01%
1,300.00	14	18,200.00	0.07%	0.01%
1,400.00	13	18,200.00	0.06%	0.01%
1,500.00	71	106,500.00	0.33%	0.07%
2,000.00	174	348,000.00	0.82%	0.22%
2,500.00	82	205,000.00	0.39%	0.13%
2,700.00	17	45,900.00	0.08%	0.03%
3,000.00	130	390,000.00	0.61%	0.25%
3,400.00	16	54,400.00	0.08%	0.03%
3,500.00	30	105,000.00	0.14%	0.07%
4,000.00	48	192,000.00	0.23%	0.12%
4,500.00	17	76,500.00	0.08%	0.05%
5,000.00	253	1,265,000.00	1.19%	0.80%

Case Study The chart in Exhibit 5.23 summarizes Company ABC's transactions for the time under investigation, where 100 percent of the transactions were included for examination. The subject company was merely a vehicle used to facilitate a Ponzi scheme. Based on the company specific fact pattern, the duplicate numbers that required further analysis were identified. The amount $301.50 occurred 111 times. A review of the supporting documents for these 111 transactions revealed that they were ATM withdrawals of $300.00, plus $1.50 in transaction fees. There were also 30 suspicious checks written in the amount of $3,500 each, with an aggregate value of $105,000.

The results can also be examined by considering the percentage of total records, and the percentage of total disbursements, for each transaction category. In using the percentage of total records as a basis for investigation, the forensic operator may analyze the $25 amounts, which occurred 3.07 percent of the time. While this only aggregated to $16,275, the forensic operator may have been specifically alerted to this amount by interviews or other procedures during the investigation. In employing a percentage of total disbursements approach, the forensic operator may also investigate the $5,000 amounts, which occurred only 1.19 percent of the time, but aggregated $1,265,000, or the highest percentage of total disbursements, at 0.80 percent.

The forensic operator discovered many of the disbursements for $10, $15, $20, and $25 were bank charges. The majority of these bank charges were for insufficient funds, wire transfer fees, and cashier check fees. From this observation, several conclusions can be drawn. For example, the number of insufficient funds charges could indicate lack of proper cash management procedures, causing overdrafts. Also, the number of wire transfers and cashiers checks for the period examined pertained to investor inflows and returns.

Rounded Numbers Test The Rounded Numbers test operates on the same premise as the Duplicate Numbers test discussed earlier in this chapter. However, the objective is to identify abnormal recurrences of rounded numbers. Abnormal recurrences of rounded numbers are excellent indicators of estimation, since people tend to estimate when they create contrived numbers. For example, the test for rounded numbers may be beneficial to locate excessive rounded bank withdrawals, checks, or rounded vendor payments to the same vendor. For more on rounded numbers, see the Last Two Digits test in Benford's Law, discussed earlier in this chapter.

Case Study A financial forensic examination was conducted for all of the disbursements of the aforementioned Company ABC over the time period under investigation. As part of the assignment, the chart in Exhibit 5.24 was prepared for the Rounded

EXHIBIT 5.24 Rounded Numbers Test

Rounded Numbers Test Marital Estate Disbursements		
Rounded Disbursement Amounts	Number of Records	Aggregate Disbursements
10s	6,287	$108,667,550
25s	5,533	$106,764,875
100s	4,054	$104,427,800
1000s	2,369	$97,216,000

Numbers test and summarizes the forensic operator's initial findings. The results were used as a basis to identify and analyze the validity of transactions exhibiting rounded numbers.

The identified disbursements were individually investigated to determine the payees and the purpose. Upon analyzing supporting documents, it was determined that many of the rounded number transactions were cash withdrawals and bank transfers to suspects or beneficiaries of the Ponzi scheme.

Link Analysis Link Analysis identifies relationships among data and people that are not otherwise apparent. This technique is increasingly employed in fraud detection, counterterrorism, and other endeavors that use computer resources to analyze vast amounts of financial records. However, Link Analysis is also effective in its simplest form, as demonstrated in the chart shown in Exhibit 5.25.

The chart illustrates, by way of common color coding, how business records from the secretary of state were used to link parties and entities in a forensic accounting matter. It represents one of several actual court exhibits that were prepared to demonstrate the relationships of the various individuals and entities. The various colors indicate the links among the seemingly unrelated entities. Note how the same registered agent is linked with several of the entities.

Many forensic assignments involve vast amounts of information, including multiple databases. Using digital analysis software, two different databases can be joined to perform link analysis in order to discover patterns or commonalities in sets of business records. As presented in Exhibit 5.26, a company's master employee file and master vendor file are combined for Link Analysis testing. In this example, the two databases are joined, creating a new master database. Then a search for common characteristics, such as telephone numbers or addresses, can be employed.

Case Study A company suspects that an employee is using a fictitious vendor to misappropriate significant funds, and retains a forensic operator to perform a financial forensic investigation. The company had thousands of vendor disbursements totaling approximately $100 million annually, for each of the last three years, making manual testing impractical.

By employing Link Analysis, the forensic operator joined the master employee database and master vendor database. Using the new combined database, the forensic operator can search for certain commonalities within the two databases. In comparing addresses for 100 percent of the data, the forensic operator discovered that several vendors had the same or similar addresses as an employee who works in the accounts payable department. Further investigation of the records with address matches revealed multiple fictitious vendors that were being used to embezzle company funds.

Gap Analysis Gap analysis identifies missing items in a numerical sequence or a range of dates. Gap analysis is often used to review data that should be recorded in sequential order, such as checks, invoices, or credit memos. Gap analysis may also be performed on a range of dates to detect when a normally recurring journal entry does not occur.

Entity Name	Registry Date	Principal Place of Business	Registered Agent
Hobbies, Inc	8/11/78	2301 N Watermain Rd City ZIP	Old Attorney PC
Watermain Marketing Inc	8/11/78	Links to "Hobbies Inc"	Old Attorney PC
Regional Purchasing Inc	8/11/78	2301 N Watermain Rd City ZIP	Old Attorney PC
Hobbies, Inc	2/23/73	13367 Street Rd NE City ZIP	Old Attorney PC
Dog and Cat Hospital PC	7/31/81	976 SW Small Rd Hwy Example ZIP	**First Name Partner #2**
The Spouse Company	8/12/85	2 SW Heather Rd Small Town ZIP	First Name Spouse Jr.
Big-Ticket Services Inc	8/15/85	Links to "The Spouse Co"	First Name Spouse Jr.
Big-Ticket Services Ltd	8/12/85	Links to "The Spouse Co"	First Name Spouse Jr.
Spouse Partner Clinic Properties LLC	4/7/95	976 SW Small Rd Hwy Example ZIP	First Name Spouse Jr.
Spouse Partner Manage ment Co	4/7/95	976 SW Small Rd Hwy Example ZIP	First Name Spouse Jr.
Spouse Partner Manage ment Co	6/17/96	976 SW Small Rd Hwy Example ZIP	First Name Spouse Jr.
CSmall Townsed PC	4/7/95	433 Third St Small Town ZIP	First Name Spouse Jr.
Ark Manage ment Inc	4/7/95	Links to "Spouse Partner Management Co"	First Name Spouse Jr.
City Spouse Partner Clinic PC	5/1/96	976 SW Small Rd Hwy Example ZIP	C. First Name Spouse Jr.
Town Square Spouse Partner Clinic PC	11/22/96	111 SW Main #100 Town ZIP	C. First Name Spouse Jr.
Spouse Econometrics Inc	10/7/98	2 SW Heather Rd Small Town ZIP	First Name Spouse Jr.
Hobby Toy Ventures LLC	5/26/99	PO Box 459 City ZIP	New Attorney
Animal Allergy & Skin Clinic	8/12/99	4100 SW 109th City ZIP	**First Name Partner #2**
America's Dollhouse Co	8/20/99	2301 N Watermain Rd City ZIP	Old Attorney PC
Racings Farm	10/22/01	222 SW Alpine Road Town ZIP	First Name Spouse (auth. rep.)
Racings Farm LLC	10/22/01	222 SW Alpine Rd Town ZIP	First Name Spouse
Auto/Truck Specialties Inc	5/17/02	555 SW Advance Rd Town ZIP	Partner #3
Estates Shrunken LLC	3/7/03	2 SW Heather Rd Small Town ZIP	New Attorney
High-End Dollars Creation	4/10/03	222 SW Alpine Road Town ZIP	New Attorney
Tails & Paws	5/6/04	111 SW Main #100 Town ZIP	James New Partner
Regional Collect Cars LLC	12/12/05	n/a	Partner #3
Regional Tendon Cars LLC	12/12/05	Links to "Regional Collect Cars LLC"	Partner #3
Creative Transactions Inc	4/3/06	n/a	Regional Collect Cars LLC

EXHIBIT 5.25 Link Analysis, Examination of Relationships

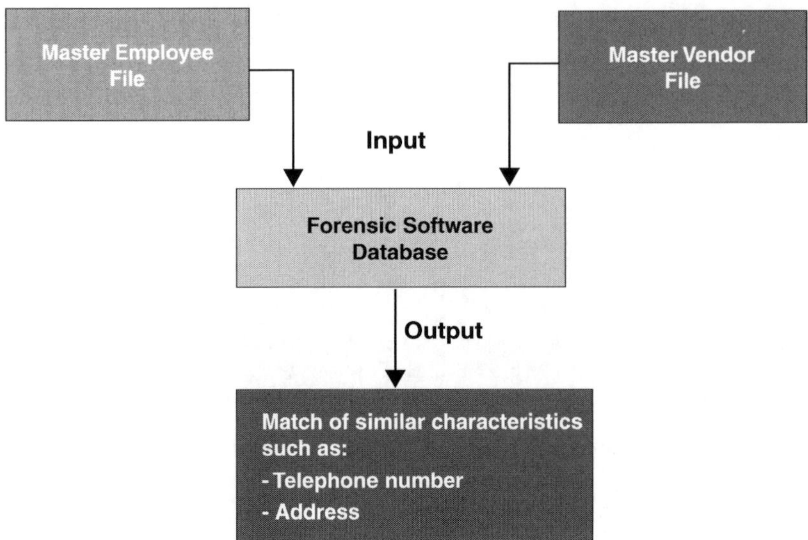

EXHIBIT 5.26 Link Analysis Joining Two Databases

Sequential numbering of checks, invoices, and other accounting records is critical for internal controls. In a good control environment, all document numbers should appear in the accounting records even if they are null or void. For example, every check number should be recorded in the accounting records even if the check has been voided. Furthermore, the company should retain all voided checks to ensure that they are not used for illicit activity.

The forensic operator should identify the characteristics to be examined, perform tests using digital analysis software, and develop a Gap analysis that can be used for further investigation. Many digital analysis software packages can perform Gap analysis at the click of a button once the appropriate database has been imported.

Case Study The analysis in the chart shown in Exhibit 5.27 reflects gaps in check numbers disbursed by a governmental agency. The initial analysis indicates all check numbers that have not been recorded within the accounting system. The forensic operator can then investigate these checks and determine whether they have been properly voided or have been used to suspect activity. The chart illustrates an efficient method to compile the investigation results, as information is obtained throughout the examination process.

Theoretically, the missing check numbers reflect voided checks. However, each item should be individually traced to determine that it was not misappropriated. All canceled, voided, and unused checks should be physically accounted for during an examination. In this case, the findings revealed that some of the unrecorded checks were actually written to a fictitious consulting company associated with the suspect's husband.

Check Number Gaps		Number	Missing	Have Void	Analysis of Located Checks		
Beginning	Ending	Missing	Check	Copy	Payee	Amount	Date Cleared
7233	7233	1	7233	y			
7314	7315	2	7314		Fictitious Consulting Co	$ 4,250.00	10/19/04
			7315	y			
7407	7408	2	7407	y			
			7408	y			
7543	7544	2	7543	y			
			7544	y			
7653	7654	2	7653		Fictitious Consulting Co	$ 4,970.00	11/7/04
			7654	y			
7777	7778	2	7777		Fictitious Consulting Co	$ 8,760.00	11/20/04
			7778	y			
7867	7868	2	7867		Fictitious Consulting Co	$ 8,070.00	11/27/04
			7868	y			
11321	11331	11	11321		Fictitious Consulting Co	$ 37,892.00	2/8/09
			11322		Fictitious Consulting Co	$ 36,756.20	3/24/09
			11323	n			
			11324	n			
			11325	n			
			11326	n			
			11327	n			
			11328		Fictitious Consulting Co	$ 34,694.00	3/29/09
			11329	n			
			11330	n			
			11331	n			
11341	11342	2	11341		Fictitious Consulting Co	$ 28,992.00	4/26/09
			11342	n			

EXHIBIT 5.27 Gap Analysis Missing Check Numbers

Note that Gap analysis may assist in detecting off-book transactions. In this particular case, none of the suspect checks were actually recorded within the governmental agency's accounting system.

Querying Data Querying data is a technique with which the forensic operator can identify and retrieve information based upon chosen criteria. The information may be extracted and isolated in a separate database for additional forensic testing. With the advances in computer technology and processing speeds, digital analysis software can typically query a massive number of records in a relatively short time.

Data can simply be queried by transaction date, amount, payee, or other recorded data. Or the forensic operator can develop formulas with conditional qualifiers to query the subject data. For example, formulas can be entered to extract all transactions that were entered on the weekends or all transactions that fell within a certain dollar threshold (to detect structuring of transactions).

Case Study The following example pertains to a company's accounts payable journal for the months of January and February 2009. The owner of the company suspects that an employee in the accounts payable department is stealing money.

EXHIBIT 5.28 Chart-15, Querying Data Entries Made on Weekends

INV NUM	INV DATE	INV AMT	CK NUM	CK DATE	MANUAL CK	BATCH	ENTER DATE
WNZ28C	1/2/2009	79571.88	701002	1/30/2009	N	33311	1/17/2009
871456BUZ	1/8/2009	37418.72	701009	2/3/2009	N	33103	1/24/2009
14598	1/8/2009	50.63	701010	2/3/2009	N	33097	1/24/2009
2828 BNA	1/5/2009	1185.46	701014	2/3/2009	N	33512	1/24/2009
9999-97-213	1/12/2009	59109.76	701049	2/13/2009	N	33507	1/24/2009
5745MCC	1/9/2009	17304.80	701062	2/4/2009	N	33295	1/25/2009
GR132 97	1/9/2009	26340.30	701013	2/3/2009	N	32965	2/1/2009
917328	1/12/2009	38309.89	701038	2/10/2009	N	33298	2/1/2009
659813	1/12/2009	9474.74	701040	2/10/2009	N	33298	2/1/2009
21G	1/13/2009	29033.80	701047	2/10/2009	N	33312	2/1/2009
216 A2Z	1/9/2009	24224.39	701025	2/10/2009	N	33513	2/1/2009
9359 NL	1/16/2009	83880.73	701069	2/17/2009	N	33420	2/7/2009
PPN98778	1/20/2009	32169.70	701076	2/17/2009	N	33420	2/7/2009
AZ279	1/12/2009	39900.83	701077	2/17/2009	N	33420	2/7/2009
PI7683	2/9/2009	21632.22	701046	2/10/2009	N	32882	2/8/2009
51498	2/9/2009	50067.31	701027	2/10/2009	N	32385	2/8/2009
L-1243/58	2/9/2009	56238.78	701132	3/6/2009	N	33119	2/8/2009
117-2293	1/30/2009	4735.39	701095	2/24/2009	N	32959	2/14/2009
FR-972 42	1/27/2009	3649.83	701094	2/24/2009	N	33223	2/14/2009
IN 6446 97	1/27/2009	24163.78	701096	2/24/2009	N	33238	2/14/2009
13597	2/13/2009	9264.18	701071	2/17/2009	N	32921	2/15/2009
CS-571-97	1/26/2009	2957.20	701093	2/24/2009	N	33420	2/15/2009
147870CTR	2/3/2009	1197.58	701113	3/3/2009	N	33302	2/21/2009
51522	2/6/2009	86780.44	701120	3/4/2009	N	32965	2/22/2009
97 2044.29J	2/5/2009	11375.26	701116	3/4/2009	N	33126	2/22/2009
25G	2/6/2009	21650.08	701118	3/4/2009	N	33126	2/22/2009

A forensic operator is hired by the owner to investigate the owner's suspicions. The employee had full access to the company's checkbook and could enter the premises at any time. Normal business hours were 8:00 A.M. to 5:00 P.M. Monday through Friday. The forensic operator therefore decided to query the disbursement data for those transactions that were entered or recorded on the weekends. The table in Exhibit 5.28 illustrates the results of the query performed, using digital analysis software to extract checks that were recorded on the weekends.

As an internal control function, many accounting software packages record the actual date the transaction was posted in addition to the date of the transaction. In this case, the forensic operator should be testing the transaction posting date, as that would imply that the transaction was entered during nonbusiness hours.

Stratification Stratification is defined as the "classification of a mass of data into categories and subcategories on the basis of one or more chosen criteria."[3] Many

[3] Definition from www.businessdictionary.com.

types of information can be stratified, including social, economic, and geological data. The increasing use of computers and digital analysis software advance the forensic operator's efforts to effectively use different forms of stratifications in a financial investigation. Stratification can be performed on data in various forms, such as numbers, characters, or dates.

Stratified Sampling Stratified sampling is used to extract a smaller representative group from data subsequent to stratification, therefore capturing key population characteristics within the sample. Stratified sampling is often used in auditing, fraud investigations, and other transactional testing. After stratification of the database, samples can then be selected on a truly random basis. Great care should be taken to verify that the selected samples are representative of the overall population.

The use of digital analysis software has greatly enhanced stratified sampling. Before the use of digital analysis software, a forensic operator frequently made a selection on a presumed random basis. The sampling basis was often not random, however, but rather systematic, whereas every nth transaction was selected for testing. Furthermore, sampling bias was also present in the selection made by the forensic operator, creating the uncertainty that the sample selection made was truly random.

The forensic operator can also use the digital analysis software to create a database profile. The profile will provide key database characteristics such as the number of records, range of values, mean, median, standard deviation, and other factors that can be considered in developing the stratification criteria.

VALUATION & FORENSICS—WHY & HOW

Despite all the attention focused on financial forensics in recent years, virtually *nothing* has been published regarding how to use the techniques in valuation.

Several reasons have prevented the techniques from being used in valuations, many of which are discussed later in this section. However, the primary impediment has been one of *misunderstanding*. That is, valuators unconsciously (or purposely) wrongly equate the term *forensics* with *fraud*. That posture supposedly somehow distances them from a perceived liability associated with financial statements used in valuation. That observation links back to the need to define financial forensics, and the need for a codified body of knowledge. This book addresses those issues.

Some valuators astonishingly claim that there is no requirement to conduct forensic analysis. Such comments demonstrate their lack of understanding of both the valuation discipline and the financial forensics profession. For example, consider the following:

- Do valuators analyze the subject's historical economic benefit stream?
- Do valuators derive the subject's future economic benefit stream?
- Do valuators analyze the subject's financial condition?
- Do valuators compare the subject against itself and its peer groups to determine financial strengths and weaknesses?
- Do valuators normalize income, cost, expense, asset, or liability items within the subject's financial statements?
- Do valuators assess and quantify the subject's required rate of return?

- Do valuators assess the capabilities of the executives and management of the subject company?
- Do valuators assess the impact of the economic outlook environment for the subject?
- Do valuators identify and calibrate against the subject guideline companies and transactions?
- Do valuators make secondary adjustments to the subject's interests reflecting adjustments for liquidity, control, and other factors?
- Do valuators opine on a point or range of value for the subject interest?

The answer, of course, to the preceding questions is a resounding yes. Valuators routinely conduct such exercises within the valuations that they perform. Furthermore, valuators are expected by their clients, the courts, and the public to use the necessary tools and techniques that refine the opinion resulting from the preceding tasks. The 250-plus-or-minus tools, techniques, methods, and methodologies within this book are ideally suited to achieving these tasks. And that is a benefit of the methodology described in this book—the multipurpose tools are exceptionally beneficial for a wide range of professional services having nothing to do with fraud.

The coverage sufficient to address how financial forensics applies to all the preceding tasks would require a separate book devoted strictly to the topic. Nonetheless, this distinct section contains guidance for valuators covering four primary topics.

First, summary discussion outlines the rationale for why it is essential that valuators immediately begin applying financial forensics tools, techniques, methods, and methodologies within their valuation assignments.

Second, a simplified how-to approach instructs valuators regarding the step-by-step process that will permit them to easily begin employing financial forensics methods.

Finally, a section on economic benefit stream refinement permits valuators use the step-by-step method to improve and update their present tasks.

Why?

In valuation, it is essential to grasp a keen understanding of the subject of economic benefit stream(s), regardless of its definition. Unfortunately, CPAs and appraisers lack familiarity with powerful analytical tools well known by others throughout the financial community. The tools have been widely used for decades, are heavily supported by the technical literature, and facilitate the dissection and estimation of requisite economic benefit streams. They're typically considered tools to detect earnings manipulation. All parties in valuation have a keen interest in discerning the veracity and volatility of the earning stream and its variants.

How?

Most CPAs and appraisers seeking to refine their valuation skills want to deploy forensic tools and techniques within their valuation assignment. Unfortunately, they lack familiarity with even basic forensic tools and are generally overwhelmed by the sheer array of tools available to them. Therefore, the following tools provide a means to begin using such tools to establish a base upon which to further enhance valuation responsibilities. The forensic operator should merely adopt one of the following in his next valuation assignment. Then the next assignment can include the next one, and so on until his repertoire has truly brought them up to speed with respect to the profession.

The alphabetized financial forensics techniques summary that follows are well known to the financial community (analysts, financial crimes investigators, investment bankers, investors, regulators, securities brokers, and others) *outside* of the CPA and appraisal professions. The specifics of why it is largely unknown to CPAs and appraisers are the topic for another article. Regardless, the three financial forensics techniques profiled next (that is, AQI, CRO, and TATA) are deeply rooted in technical literature and sophisticated accounting practitioners. They give CPAs and appraisers tools by which to evaluate earnings quality and thus accelerate and improve the valuation process.

AQI—Asset Quality Index The first forensic technique profiled in this section is AQI, that is, asset quality index.[4] It is described in *The Detection of Earnings Manipulation,* by Professor Messod D. Beneish, of Indiana University. Professor Beneish's paper delineates his M score (not reproduced here), which has a few similarities to the Altman Z Score but is more comprehensive and includes entities that are not bankrupt. The following items summarized Professor Beneish's writings regarding AQI. The TATA technique contained in this section is also described in Professor Beneish's paper.

AQI measures the index of noncurrent assets other than property, plant, and equipment (PPE), to total assets. It indicates the proportion of total assets that are proportionately less certain with respect to ultimate realization, that is, asset quality. Therefore, one can expect a positive relationship between AQI and the probability of earnings manipulation. That is, the greater the AQI (and diminished asset quality), the greater the probability of earnings manipulation. The technique is summarized later in this section.

$$\text{Asset Quality Index (AQI)} = \left(1 - \left(\frac{\text{Current Assets } cy + \text{Net Fixed Assets } cy}{\text{Total Assets } cy}\right)\right) \Big/ \left(1 - \left(\frac{\text{Current Assets } py + \text{Net Fixed Assets } py}{\text{Total Assets } py}\right)\right)$$

AQI measures the ratio of asset quality in year t, relative to asset quality in year *t*–1. If AQI is greater than 1.0, it indicates a potential increase in cost deferral or perhaps an increase in intangible assets, or both. Such a change could result from acquisitions or creative accounting treatment.

The AQI measurements are shown in Exhibit 5.29 (visual format) for two companies, that is, ABC and XYZ, respectively. They each represent actual companies encountered in the authors' financial forensics valuation work and are similarly sized

[4] A numerical scale used to compare variables with one another or with some reference number. http://wordnetweb.princeton.edu/perl/webwn?s=index.

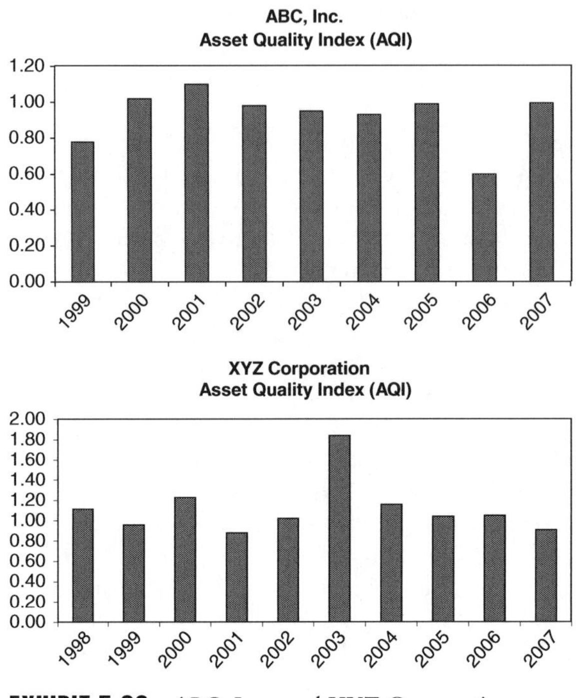

EXHIBIT 5.29 ABC, Inc., and XYZ Corporation Asset Quality Index

and similarly capitalized. One of the companies displays legitimate balance sheet indicators and one displays manipulated balance sheet indicators. Granted, there could be legitimate reasons for such divergence, for example, capital restructuring, but such explanations would account for variation. The reader is invited to identify the company displaying manipulated balance sheet indicators per the AQI measurement. (The answer is at the end of this section.)

CRO—Cash Realized from Operations The cash flow statement is arguably the single most important financial statement by which to assess earnings veracity and manipulation. It is also the most difficult statement driving this mistake, particularly over time, since it must tie to beginning and ending cash. Notably, since valuation driven by cash flow (or surrogates), it is often the most important statement for valuation conclusions. The reasons for the singular importance of the cash flow statement relate to the articulated nature of the balance sheet, the income statement, and the cash flow statement. That is, if a transaction is reported within the balance sheet or the income statement, it will be reflected in the cash flow statement. Likewise, nearly any accounting treatment would be reflected in the cash flow statement. Therefore, you can expect a strong correlation between reported net income, and resultant cash from operations.

Naturally, a lag may occur due to the accrual nature of net income (particularly among various industries), and cash may be affected by capital structure or other fundamental changes. Nonetheless, the correlation should be discernible, and variations explainable, thus lending strength (or requisite normalizations) to reported

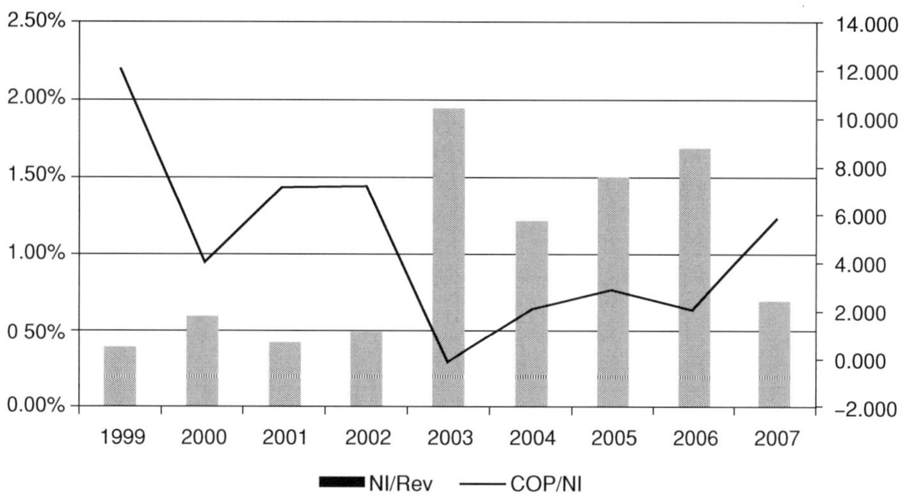

EXHIBIT 5.30 Cash Ops versus Net Income

net income. Specifically, the correlation between the reported operating cash and the reported net income should be very tight, everything else being equal. The technique is summarized as follows:

$$\text{Cash Realization Ratio (CRO)} = \frac{\text{Operating Cash Flow}}{\text{Net Income}}$$

CRO measures the ratio of operating cash in Year 1 relative to net income in Year 1. The measurements will vary greatly by industry and will usually be less than 1.0. However, the subject company's index should remain relatively consistent and ideally should increase over time. More precise measurements will be obtained using quarterly financials and can highlight end-of-year declines that suggest earnings management.

Operating cash and net income *should* demonstrate a strong correlation. That is "as earnings go (up *or* down), so goes operating cash." The reason is intuitive to those who understand financial statements. Specifically, accrual-based financials estimate future periods by accruing expected inflows and outflows. Divergence of *unexplainable* trends (e.g., income up, but operating cash down, and vice versa) suggests manipulation. Therefore, significant variations suggest manipulation. Granted, there could be legitimate reasons for such divergence, for example, capital restructuring, major change in business policies, and so on, but such explanations account for variation. When an explanation is lacking, manipulation may be present. Exhibit 5.30 is an example from the authors' financial forensics assignments and illustrates a divergence between operating cash and net income. The reader is invited to identify whether earnings manipulation occurred according to the CRO measurement. (The answer is at the end of this section.)

TATA—Total Accruals to Total Assets TATA is a technique that isolates a common source of financial statement manipulation: accruals. Accruals are short-term estimates (forecasts, if you will) made by management to reflect *expected* inflows and

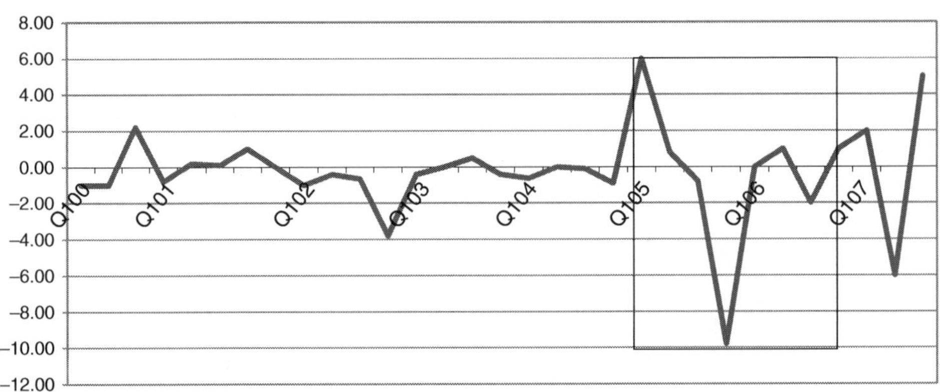

EXHIBIT 5.31 Accrual to Assets Ratio

outflows. Therefore, barring major structural changes such as new lines of business and so on, the relationship of yearly change in accruals to yearly change in assets should remain constant within a definable statistical variation.

TATA is composed of the change in working capital, less cash and depreciation or amortization. Year-to-year changes may indicate earnings manipulation resulting from management accrual decisions, particularly short-term decisions. Higher positive accruals (excluding cash) are correlated to earnings manipulation likelihood. TATA is ordinarily calculated for the respective periods as indicated.

$$\text{Total Accruals to Total Assets (TATA)} = \frac{\begin{array}{l}(\text{Working Capital}_t - \text{Working Capital}_{t-1}) - (\text{Cash}_t - \text{Cash}_{t-1}) \\ + (\text{Current LTD}_t - \text{Current LTD}_{t-1}) + (\text{Income Taxes Payable}_t \\ - \text{Income Taxes Payable}_{t-1}) - \text{Depreciation and Amortization}_t\end{array}}{\text{Total Assets}_t}$$

The example shown in Exhibit 5.31 is from the authors' actual forensic assignment, illustrating the power of measuring total accruals to total assets. Also note that the touted technique can be decomposed with other categories, such as TARTA (reflecting Total Accounts Receivable to Total Assets), and others. Such measurements provide similar insights. The reader is invited to identify whether earnings manipulation occurred according to the TATA measurement. (The answers are at the end of this section.)

What about Traditional Ratios?

The three financial forensics techniques presented earlier are virtually unknown to CPAs and appraisers. They are dramatically more effective, however, than using the mere traditional ratios such as liquidity, leverage, operating, profitability, and so on. The reason is that the traditional ratios were designed by lenders interested in liquidity, payback, and collateral considerations. They have their uses, but are inferior to the dozens of forensic indicators with regard to assessing earnings quality. Their use in lieu of forensic indicators results in inferior valuation conclusions. To wit, notice that the traditional ratios were used in all of the previous examples and none of them highlighted the inconsistencies shown earlier. Had reliance been placed on mere ratio analysis, the discrepancies in earnings would never have been determined, nor would the inordinate volatility surface, thus misstating the valuation conclusions.

Other Important Considerations

The power of these (and many dozens more) financial forensic tools is impressive. And they are nearly universally applicable to the scope of service typically rendered by forensic operators. Furthermore, additional observations compel their application as indicated.

Size-Independent The tools apply in virtually any entity, whether tiny or huge. Their principles transcend size, capital structure, industry, and other factors. The authors have used the techniques in an extraordinary array of industry and company types and are persuasive when demonstrating them to decision makers.

Risk Assessment If the CPA or appraiser identifies poor earnings quality (in contrast to the claims in the financial statements), he can account for the deficiency by adjusting the economic benefit stream or adjusting the discount or capitalization rate. Normalizations are a routine practice within valuation assignments, and normalizations to refine the earnings stream are no different.

Granularity More, rather than fewer, periods yield better results. This is true for virtually all financial analysis; that is, a five-year time horizon can be telling, but quarterly information over the same period provides 20 points instead of 5. And since manipulation is concealable (for a while) through annual journal entries, quarterly results make concealment more difficult.

Indices The measures previously described are *indices*, *not* ratios. Indices measure interrelated impacts while ratios are static and more applicable to lenders.

Statistics CPAs and appraisers can use simple statistics to further interpret the indices. For example, statistical volatility can be measured using Z-statistic, MAD (mean average deviation), t-statistic, and so forth, which are all powerful tools.

Vast Resources There are hundreds of financial forensics techniques available to the valuation profession. After forensic operators begin the process of deployment with one or two of the tools, the others will come far more quickly and become a natural part of the assignment.

Benefits The use of financial forensics tools, techniques, methods, and methodologies benefits two parties: the client and the forensic operator. The forensic operator benefits because less time is required in a typical engagement, and better results are achieved. The client benefits because the results are superior and the fees may be less. Consequently, everyone benefits.

Answers to the Three Questions

AQI—XYZ is the company displaying manipulated results in 2003, as measured by AQI.

CRO—Earnings manipulation started in 2003 and impacted through 2006 and 2007, as evidenced by the divergent trends of cash resulting from operations compared to reported net income.

TATA—Manipulation started in Q105 (because of the out-of-bounds index spike), and went the other way, the Q106, because manipulation did not result in cash.

The forensic operator reading this section should adopt one of the preceding techniques, for example, CRO and immediately implement it. That will propel the use of additional techniques, yielding benefits for all parties.

VALUATION'S ORPHAN

The valuation profession rests upon only three essential components: an economic benefit stream, a required rate of return, and secondary adjustments, all represented by the following formula:

$$V = \left[\frac{EBS}{R}\right] S_a$$

V	Value
EBS	Economic Benefit Stream
R	Required Rate of Return
S_a	Secondary Adjustments

The derivation of an economic benefit stream is a forward-looking concept, which can be derived through a wide variety of quantitative and qualitative forecasting techniques. The techniques can generally be categorized as historically driven, management driven, or independent variable driven in order to derive the outlook for the subject business.

The required rate of return and secondary adjustment components can be exceedingly complex, and thus require considerable deliberation. Nonetheless, one would be hard-pressed to find substantive guidance for constructing an economic benefit stream.[5] For example, assuming six years of financial statement history, valuation reports will often contain some weighted-average calculation intended to represent the near-term outlook of the stream. That is, a 3-2-1 (or other) weighting of the recent historical stream may be the only "science" applied. Worse, the report's supporting rationale may be nothing more than a statement that such method was used by the appraiser. Surprisingly, many valuation books and even a highly regarded and very recent valuation book recommend the same tired, stale approach.

[5] One notable exception is *Quantitative Business Valuation*, by Jay B. Abrams; see bibliography.

Economic benefit streams in damages calculations fare no better. While the literature and related technical guidance typically address issues regarding ex post[6] and ex ante[7] matters, very little practical substantive guidance for economic benefit stream construction can be found.

Therefore, this section delivers logical, practical, and defensible guidance for the forensic operator striving to develop a representative economic benefit stream in either valuation or damages matters. Furthermore, it provides a foundation upon which the forensic operator can continuously build and refine economic benefit streams.

A valuation premise is used for the section, but the same principles and techniques apply to economic damages calculations.

The economic benefit stream technique is outlined in the following seven steps, and is summarized as follows:

1. Array historical financial statements in both schedule and visual formats.
2. Array historical economic benefit stream(s) in both schedule and visual formats.
3. Identify historical benefit stream(s) comparison sources from three categories of independent variables as available:
   a. The subject entity's financial history, that is, itself.
   b. Management-prepared financial estimates (if any) such as business plans, budgets, forecasts, and projections.
   c. Independent variables such as GDP[8] or GDP-derived measures, GSP or GSP[9] measures, industry sector measures, and so forth.
4. Illustrate and quantify as available the relationships for each of the three categories listed in Step 3.
5. Estimate and visually array as available the history, planned, and correlated measures for each of the three categories listed in Step 3. Anything prepared by XYZ is considered a "dependent" variable, while GDP, GSP, and related sources are considered "independent" variables.
6. Compare and contrast the respective strengths and weaknesses of the quantitative and visual relationships.
7. Conclude upon a stream(s) that reflects the strongest quantitative and/or visual representations from the preceding steps. The selected stream may be best represented by a convergence of streams.

The preceding steps mirror the reasoning applied to the respective assignment, which in aggregate are persuasive in its simplicity, defensibility and logic. More important, for most audiences, the visualization of the history and alternative outlooks leads to the same logical and empirical conclusion reached by the forensic operator. Each step is explained as follows.

---

[6] Refers to past events when uncertainties have been eliminated; the opposite of ex ante.

[7] Refers to future, unknown events; the opposite of ex post.

[8] Gross Domestic Product—The total annual value of all goods and services produced by labor and capital within a country's borders.

[9] Gross State Product—The total annual value of all goods and services produced by labor and capital within a state's borders.

Step 1—Array Historical Financials

Array the historical financial statements in both schedule and visual formats. The financial statements should consist of at least the balance sheets, income statements, and cash flow statements; estimate them if unavailable. Construct detail sufficient for a reader to understand the forensic operator's analytical thought process.

The number of historical periods (years, quarters, months) is sometimes arbitrarily stated as three or five years without a valid supporting rationale as to why such a time horizon is preferred. Astonishingly, a recent valuation text stated that financial history beyond five years may be stale. Alternatively, the IRS's Revenue Ruling 59-60[10] is sometimes cited as the source of the five-year preference. However, a careful reading of 59-60's contents gives a very different viewpoint, as follows (emphasis added).

> *(c) Balance sheets should be obtained, preferably in the form of comparative annual statements for* two or more years *immediately preceding the date of appraisal, together with a balance sheet at the end of the month preceding that date, if corporate accounting will permit. . . . Comparison of the company's* balance sheets over several years *may reveal, among other facts, such developments as the acquisition of additional production facilities or subsidiary companies, improvement in financial position, and details as to recapitalizations and other changes in the capital structure of the corporation.*
>
> *(d) Detailed profit-and-loss statements should be obtained and considered for a* representative *period immediately prior to the required date of appraisal, preferably* five or more years. . . . *Prior earnings records usually are the most reliable guide as to the future expectancy, but resort to* arbitrary 5- or 10-year *averages without regard to current trends or future prospects will not produce a realistic valuation. (Emphasis added.)*

Therefore, the historical financial statements should cover a minimum number of years that represents the entity's business or operating cycle. Most entities, including the public sector, display distinct operating cycles. For example, federal government cycles often track closely with the respective administration in power. Certain state governments operate on a biennial cycle, thus suggesting an even number of historical financials. Also, certain industries operate with distinct cycles such as the pulp and paper industry, which operates in a 7- to 10-year cycle. Consequently, it is important to understand the subject entity's nature in order to capture and analyze sufficient periods.

Step 2—Array Historical Economic Benefit Stream(s)

The economic benefit stream composition can vary widely. Ideally, the economic benefit stream will be cash-based, but it can consist of a wide variety of streams,

[10] Rev. Rul. 59-60, 1959-1 CB 237—IRC Sec. 2031.

including revenue, cash flow, gross cash flow, net income, gross profit, EBT, EBIT, EBITDA, and so on. Also, the selected stream is sometimes predicated upon the information sources of guideline transactions. In this example, revenue is a significant value driver in the industry. Consequently, the previous income statement example provides the revenue contents and trends and served as the economic benefit stream. There is no need to duplicate the preceding income statement schedule and visual.

Step 3—Identify Historical Benefit Stream(s) Comparison Sources from Three Categories of Independent Variables

The various candidate economic benefit stream histories provide a perspective for the forensic operator, that is, how the subject has historically performed. Since "past results offer no guarantee of future performance," they must be compared to, and ultimately correlated to, an independent variable(s), say GDP, for estimation into the future. For example, if a subject entity's revenues are correlated with a market segment of GDP, then independent estimates of future GDP growth or decline provide a benchmark for the future.

In other words, if a subject entity's revenue historically correlated to GDP measures with a high indication, say .7439, then future GDP growth of say, 2.7 percent, can be regressed in order to derive an objective estimation of the subject's future revenues. In other words, apply a 2.7 percent growth rate to XYZ's revenue and multiply it by .7439 to derive the independent variable-driven estimate of XYZ's revenue.

Entity Financial History In this example, the most representative comparison results from observing the balance sheet, income statement, and cash flow statement, as contained in the previous description. Consequently, a forensic operator analyzes historical results visually (already displayed in this section's Exhibits) and quantitatively analyze them using techniques contained in other chapters in this book, e.g., Forensic Financial Analysis.

Balance Sheet XYZ's summarized historical balance sheets and illustrative visuals are presented in Exhibits 5.32 and 5.33. The period ended July 31, 2009, reflects TTM (trailing 12 months).

It is clear that XYZ's assets grew substantially through 2006 and have steadily declined to date. Likewise, liabilities grew slightly slower, resulting in a steadily increasing residual equity. It is clear that XYZ's relationship of assets to its liabilities has remained relatively stable. XYZ is able to maintain a stable relationship largely by the flooring financing necessary to maintain its large inventory of vehicles for sale.

Income Statement XYZ's summarized historical income statements and illustrative visuals are presented in Exhibits 5.34 and 5.35. The period ended July 31, 2009, reflects TTM (trailing 12 months).

Revenues grew substantially through 2006 and have since plummeted with net income following commensurately. Fortunately, XYZ's management is skilled at controlling expenses, thus declining revenues have not affected net income more severely.

EXHIBIT 5.32 Historical Summary Balance Sheets

ASSETS	2000	2001	2002	2003	2004	2005	2006	2007	2008	7/31/09
Cash	314,689	473,406	1,726,986	1,910,385	3,999,761	3,674,754	2,239,585	4,573,676	3,565,732	5,278,520
Accounts Receivable	3,566,999	2,867,792	2,648,404	3,378,354	3,093,784	2,986,615	6,384,009	4,633,780	3,792,366	2,764,790
Inventory	11,987,357	8,789,575	7,683,733	8,816,779	12,965,902	13,815,359	15,908,014	13,819,719	12,295,226	9,750,101
Other Current Assets	2,133,371	1,401,341	1,032,026	1,185,813	1,380,746	1,656,810	2,052,225	1,933,410	1,743,114	1,228,161
Total Current Assets	18,002,416	13,532,114	13,091,149	15,291,331	21,440,193	22,133,538	26,583,833	24,960,585	21,396,438	19,021,572
Fixed Assets	10,197,269	9,318,778	8,465,342	8,711,206	12,137,673	13,409,687	16,555,435	17,745,103	15,556,538	11,652,177
Net Intangible	0	0	0	0	0	0	0	0	0	0
Other Non-Current	4,570,941	4,210,002	3,736,708	3,763,990	4,594,697	4,602,581	3,486,910	3,423,429	3,209,551	2,203,224
Total Assets	32,770,626	27,060,894	25,293,199	27,766,527	38,172,563	40,145,806	46,626,178	46,129,117	40,162,527	32,876,973
LIABILITIES & EQUITY										
Accounts Payable	1,180,196	1,152,678	1,212,202	1,466,149	1,259,746	1,401,843	1,855,616	1,741,599	1,569,170	1,009,043
Short Term Notes Payable	831,267	829,426	664,177	696,649	635,407	483,896	480,249	384,439	320,623	0
Current Portion of LT Debt	2,859,595	2,701,533	2,247,704	2,123,096	2,890,563	3,133,736	3,767,647	4,173,810	3,415,498	2,894,542
Other Current Liabilities	13,944,049	9,535,087	9,525,802	10,872,284	15,670,669	16,514,936	18,449,649	16,583,585	13,848,032	11,241,215
Total Current Liabilities	18,815,107	14,218,724	13,649,885	15,158,178	20,456,385	21,534,411	24,553,161	22,883,433	19,153,323	15,144,800
Long-Term Debt	0	0	0	0	0	0	0	0	0	0
Other Non-Current Liabilities	7,678,854	6,687,417	5,976,942	6,508,876	10,773,955	11,320,489	12,143,316	12,029,235	9,661,036	7,555,540
Total Liabilities	26,493,961	20,906,141	19,626,827	21,667,054	31,230,340	32,854,900	36,696,477	34,912,668	28,814,359	22,700,340
Total Equity	6,276,665	6,154,753	5,666,372	6,099,473	6,942,223	7,290,906	9,929,701	11,216,449	11,348,168	10,176,633
Total Liabilities & Equity	32,770,626	27,060,894	25,293,199	27,766,527	38,172,563	40,145,806	46,626,178	46,129,117	40,162,527	32,876,973

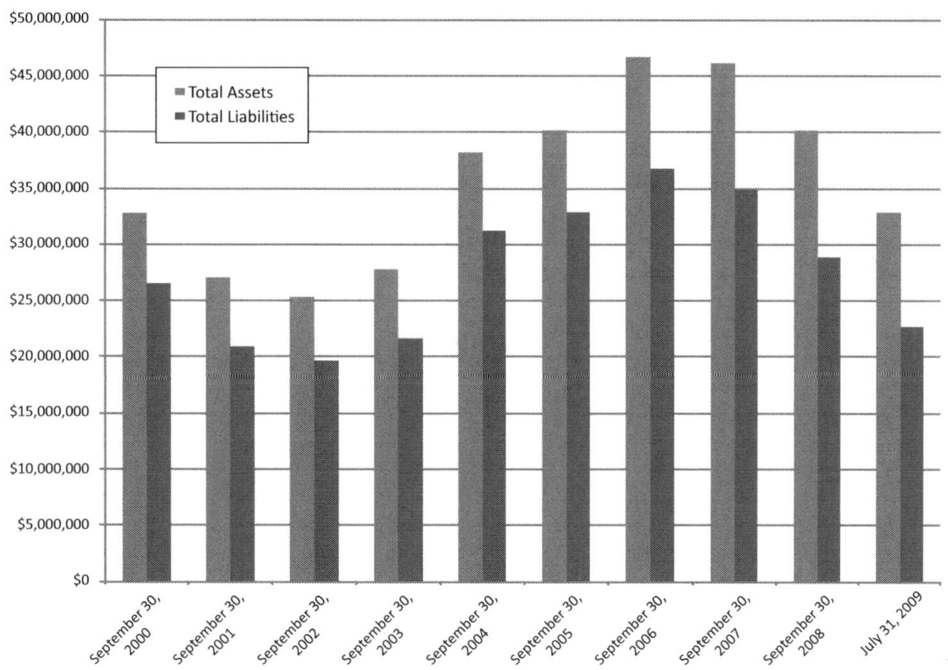

EXHIBIT 5.33 Chart of Historical Summary Balance Sheets

Cash Flow Statement XYZ's summarized historical cash flow statements and illustrative visuals are presented in Exhibits 5.36 and 5.37. The period ended July 31, 2009, reflects TTM (trailing 12 months).

XYZ's operating cash is reflected in the years of significant net income with negative flows resulting from recent economic declines. Also, note that the apparent investing cash inflows are affected by the independent accountants' recently adopted consolidated reporting for 2009.

Management-Prepared Financial Estimates Typically, smaller and midsized companies seldom have sufficient management-prepared financial estimates with which to compare against actual results. Consequently, this example reflects the most likely situation—there are no management-prepared financial estimates available. Nonetheless, an example from a different matter illustrates how such contents appear. Exhibit 5.38 illustrates eight years of history compared to five overlapping years of estimates, thus yielding a visual, demonstrating management's past record of estimation.

XYZ's steady historical growth is likely to continue based upon management's capabilities and expected continuity of the facts and circumstances. Consequently, their various forecasting of high, medium, and low outlooks can be considered reliable.

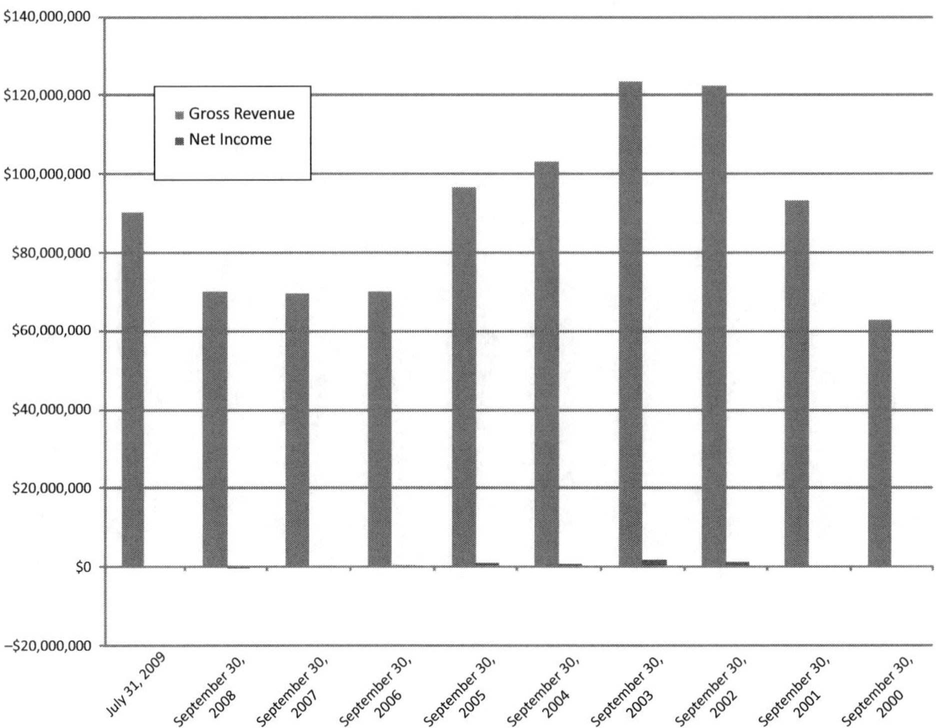

EXHIBIT 5.35 Chart of Historical Summary Income Statements

XYZ's steady historical gross margin is expected by management to increase slightly commensurate with expected revenue growth. Additional increases are expected if XYZ is successful in changing its primary supplier.

GDP and GDP-Derived Measures Since XYZ has experienced *fundamental*[11] economy-driven changes to its business model during the past two years, rigorous analysis is essential to avoid distortions to the resultant outlook. Therefore, XYZ's historical revenues stream is measured against U.S. GDP and the respective state's GSP, and the results are then applied to derive forward-looking estimates.

Step 4—Illustrate and Quantify Independent Variables

The logical progression indicates that independent variables must identified and then scheduled and displayed. This lays the foundation to demonstrate the correlation, or lack thereof.

Regression of XYZ's Revenues The XYZ Company's revenues and related financial performance are closely tied to economic conditions throughout the United States.

[11] Identified during company management interviews and ancillary industry research.

EXHIBIT 5.34 Historical Summary Income Statements

	2000	2001	2002	2003	2004	2005	2006	2007	2008	7/31/09
Revenue	90,292,699	69,989,079	69,687,496	70,026,654	96,595,009	103,112,607	123,415,189	122,477,164	93,202,364	62,808,395
Cost of Goods Sold	74,372,192	55,862,450	57,229,369	57,371,573	82,254,981	87,423,868	104,860,927	103,502,976	77,521,488	51,307,597
Gross Profit	15,920,507	14,126,629	12,458,127	12,655,081	14,340,028	15,688,739	18,554,262	18,974,188	15,680,876	11,500,798
Operating Expenses	14,495,407	13,538,473	11,898,609	11,514,518	12,656,787	14,062,721	14,895,456	16,000,470	14,231,169	11,636,431
Operating Profit	1,425,100	588,156	559,518	1,140,563	1,683,241	1,626,018	3,658,806	2,973,718	1,449,707	−135,633
Other Income/(Expense)	−943,151	−720,407	−358,560	−238,188	11,161	−495,605	−837,140	−1,044,986	−1,066,012	−39,218
Income Before Taxes	481,949	−132,251	200,958	902,375	1,694,402	1,130,413	2,821,666	1,928,732	383,695	−174,851
Income Taxes	252,877	−88,226	102,782	344,345	769,052	495,309	970,324	609,076	134,240	−326,760
Net Income	229,072	−44,025	98,176	558,030	925,350	635,104	1,851,342	1,319,656	249,455	151,909

EXHIBIT 5.36 Historical Summary Cash Flow Statements

Cash Provided by (used for) Operations	2001	2002	2003	2004	2005	2006	2007	2008	7/31/09
Net Income (Loss)	−44,025	98,176	558,030	925,350	635,104	1,851,342	1,319,656	249,455	151,909
Plus Depreciation & Amortization	2,125,192	265,989	263,645	259,734	256,824	260,365	263,286	283,052	316,794
Plus Non Cash Expenses	0	0	0	0	0	0	0	0	0
(Increase)/Decrease in Accounts Receivable	699,207	219,388	−729,950	284,570	107,169	−3,397,394	1,750,229	841,414	1,027,576
(Increase/Decrease in Inventory	3,197,782	1,105,342	−1,133,046	−4,149,123	−849,457	−2,092,655	2,088,295	1,524,493	2,545,125
(Increase/Decrease in Other Current Assets	732,030	369,315	−153,787	−194,933	−276,064	−395,415	118,815	190,296	514,953
(Increase/Decrease in Other Non-Current Assets	360,939	473,294	−27,282	−830,707	−7,884	1,115,671	63,481	213,878	1,006,327
Increase/(Decrease) in Accounts Payable	−27,518	59,524	253,947	−206,403	142,097	453,773	−114,017	−172,429	−560,127
Increase/(Decrease) in Other Current Liabilities	−4,408,962	−9,285	1,346,482	4,798,385	844,267	1,934,713	−1,866,064	−2,735,553	−2,606,317
Increase/(Decrease) in Other Non-Current Liabilities	−991,437	−710,475	531,934	4,265,079	546,534	822,827	−114,061	−2,368,199	−2,105,496
Total Cash Provided by (used for) **Operations**	1,643,198	1,871,768	909,973	5,150,952	1,398,590	553,227	3,509,600	−1,973,593	290,244

Cash Provided by (used for) Investing Activities									
(Increase)/Decrease in Net Fixed Assets	−1,246,691	587,447	−509,509	−3,685,201	−1,528,838	−3,406,113	−1,452,954	1,905,513	3,587,567
(Increase/Decrease in Net Intangible	0	0	0	0	0	0	0	0	0
Total Cash Provided by (used for) Investing	−1,246,691	587,447	−509,509	−3,685,201	−1,528,838	−3,406,113	−1,452,954	1,905,513	3,587,567
Cash Provided by (used for) Financing Activities									
Net Additions to/(reductions in) Notes Payable	−159,903	−619,078	−92,136	706,225	91,662	630,264	310,353	−822,128	−841,579
Net Investment in/(distribution of) Equity	−77,887	−586,557	−124,929	−82,600	−286,421	787,453	−32,908	−117,736	−1,323,444
Total Cash Provided by (used for) **Financing**	−237,790	−1,205,635	−217,065	623,625	−194,759	1,417,717	277,445	−939,864	−2,165,023
Total increase/(Decrease) in Cash	158,717	1,253,580	183,399	2,089,376	−325,007	−1,435,169	2,334,091	−1,007,944	1,712,798
Beginning Cash Balance	314,689	473,406	1,726,986	1,910,385	3,999,761	3,674,754	2,239,585	4,573,676	3,565,732
Ending Cash Balance	473,406	1,726,986	1,910,385	3,999,761	3,674,754	2,239,585	4,573,676	3,565,732	5,278,520

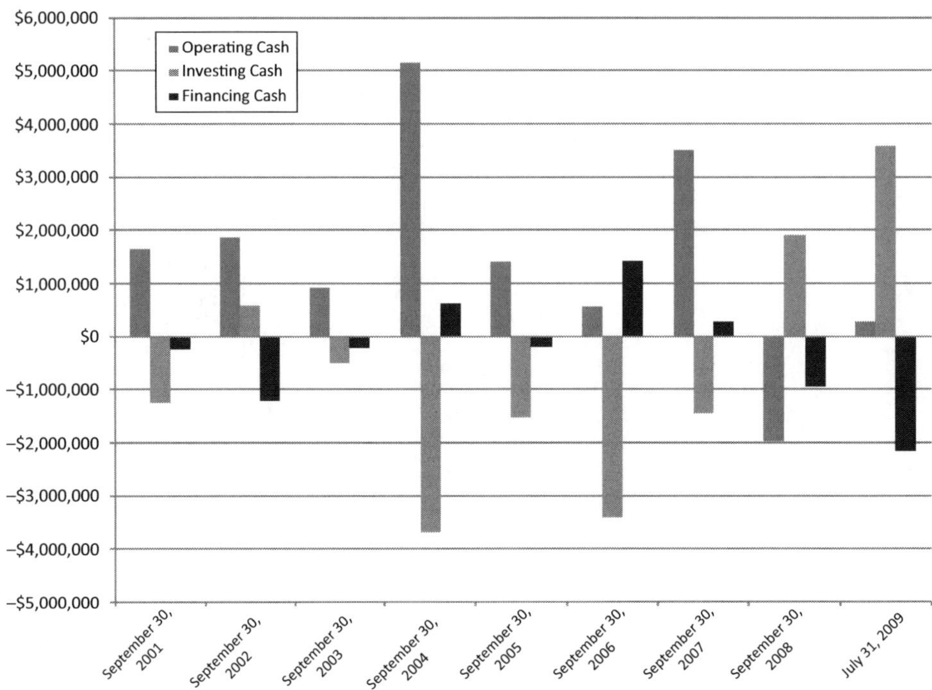

EXHIBIT 5.37 Chart of Historical Summary Cash Flow Statements

Therefore, a visual comparison and statistical regression analysis of XYZ's revenues for the past 10 years is compared against U.S. GDP and specific GDP segments, that is, personal consumption expenditures, gross domestic private investment, and all segments in aggregate.

It is clear from the following visuals and related analysis that a strong correlation exists between XYZ's revenues and U.S. GDP measures. Specifically, the

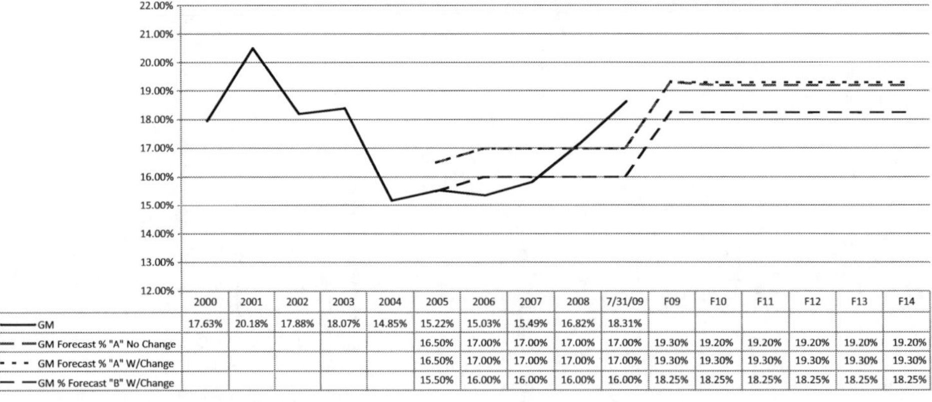

	2000	2001	2002	2003	2004	2005	2006	2007	2008	7/31/09	F09	F10	F11	F12	F13	F14
GM	17.63%	20.18%	17.88%	18.07%	14.85%	15.22%	15.03%	15.49%	16.82%	18.31%						
GM Forecast % "A" No Change						16.50%	17.00%	17.00%	17.00%	17.00%	19.30%	19.20%	19.20%	19.20%	19.20%	19.20%
GM Forecast % "A" W/Change						16.50%	17.00%	17.00%	17.00%	17.00%	19.30%	19.30%	19.30%	19.30%	19.30%	19.30%
GM % Forecast "B" W/Change						15.50%	16.00%	16.00%	16.00%	16.00%	18.25%	18.25%	18.25%	18.25%	18.25%	18.25%

EXHIBIT 5.38 XYZ Forecast to Actual Comparison

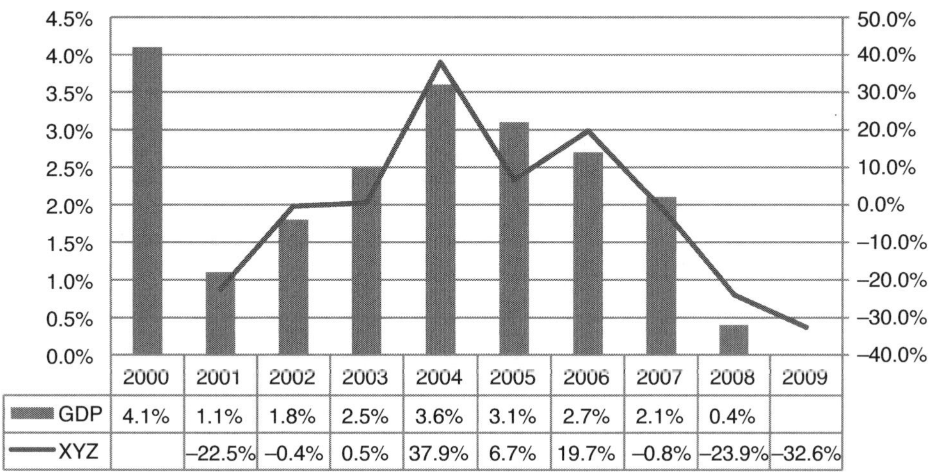

EXHIBIT 5.39 GDP Percentage Annual Change

year-to-year changes are quite evident in both the GDP comparison and the personal consumption expenditures comparison. For example, the following visuals contain annual percentage changes for both GDP and personal consumption measures, respectively, and XYZ's revenues.

Exhibit 5.39, GDP Percentage Annual Change, illustrates a strong visual match against the two variables.

Exhibit 5.40 personal consumption expenditures (PCE) shows some correlation, but lacks the tight fit of the GDP comparison.

Finally, Exhibit 5.41 private domestic investment (PDI) comparison, also shows a strong visual correlation, and contains the tightest statistical fit as measured by the remainder of this section of this section.

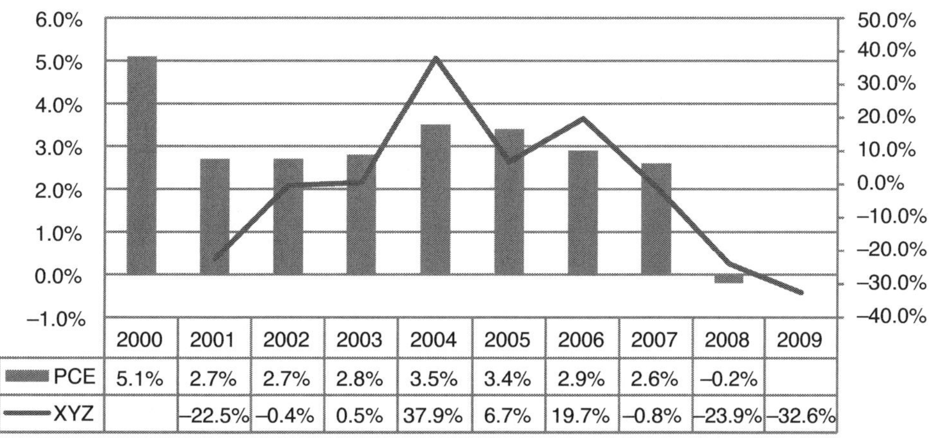

EXHIBIT 5.40 Personal Consumption Percentage Annual Change

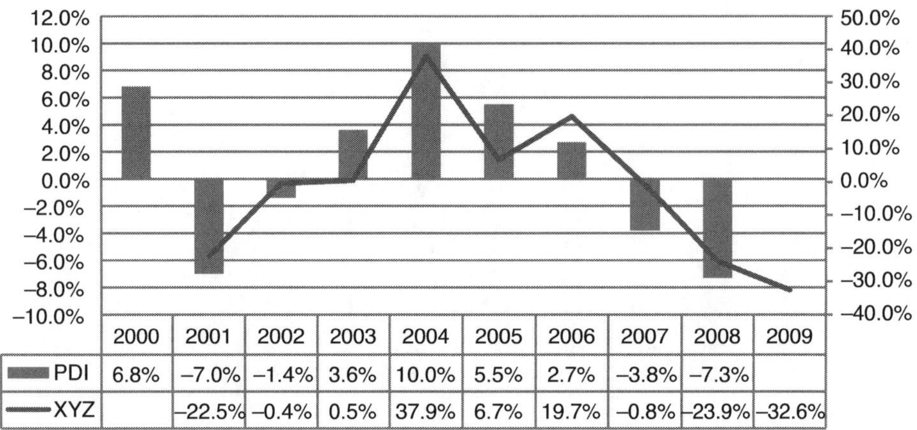

EXHIBIT 5.41 Private Domestic Investment Percentage Annual Change

Exhibit 5.42 displays a statistical regression[12] analysis based upon the data for XYZ revenues and the various GDP economic measurements as indicated.

Standard regression analysis techniques and derived relative comparative factors to establish test the robustness of the data fit. The table in Exhibit 5.43 summarizes the key measurements.

EXHIBIT 5.42 Regression Analysis

	Millions of Dollars			
Year	**GDP**	**PCE**	**PDI**	**XYZ Sales**
2000	9,951.5	6,830.4	1,772.2	90,292,699
2001	10,286.2	7,148.8	1,661.9	69,989,079
2002	10,642.3	7,439.2	1,647.0	69,687,496
2003	11,142.1	7,804.0	1,729.7	70,026,654
2004	11,867.8	8,285.1	1,968.6	96,595,009
2005	12,638.4	8,819.0	2,172.2	103,112,607
2006	13,398.9	9,322.7	2,327.2	123,415,189
2007	14,077.6	9,826.4	2,288.5	122,477,164
2008	14,441.4	10,129.9	2,136.1	93,202,364
7/31/2009	n/a	n/a	n/a	62,808,395

[12] The relation between selected values of x and observed values of y (from which the most probable value of y can be predicted for any value of x).
See http://wordnetweb.princeton.edu/perl/webwn?s=statistical%20regression. October 21, 2009.

EXHIBIT 5.43 Summary of Key Measurements

	Regressed Against Historical XYZ Revenue			
Regression Indicators	**GDP**	**PCE**	**PDI**	**Combined**
Multiple R	0.8083	0.7961	**0.9639**	**0.9821**
R Squared	0.6533	0.6338	**0.9292**	**0.9644**
Adjusted R Squared	0.5955	0.5728	0.9174	0.9378
Standard Error of the Y Estimate	14.237	14.630	6.435	5.584
t-Statistic	−1.12772	−1.03361	−3.42305	−0.29857
P-Value	0.30250	0.34117	0.01409	0.04051
95% Confidence Level Y Estimate	28.47	29.26	12.87	11.17

The findings from the preceding table are summarized below. Note: For more statistical support refer to the Internet sites referenced in the Laboratory Analysis Stage section of this book:

- *R*—The goodness of fit of an equation is measured by the degree of correlation between the dependent (XYZ revenue) and independent (GDP, PCE, PDI, combined) variables. An R value of +1 indicates a perfect direct relationship, while an R value of (minus) –1 indicates a perfect inverse relationship. The closer to +1 or –1, the better the relationship. Note that all the R values are statistically significant for the number of observations, with PDI and combined results of .9639 and .9821, respectively. They both exhibit the highest R measures.
- *R-Squared*—The R-Squared (or R^2) can range from near zero to +1 and measures the percentage of the variation in the dependent variable (that is, XYZ revenue) explained by the independent variable (that is, GDP, PCE, PDI, combined). R-Squared is the main measure of the goodness of fit. The R-Squared measures of 92.92 percent and 96.44 percent for PDI and combined, respectively, account for virtually all the variation of XYZ's Revenue.
- *The Standard Error of the Y Estimate*—The standard error calculates how far above or below an estimate may be yet still fall with an acceptable level of confidence, for example, 95 percent. The standard error for PDI and combined above is 6.435 and 5.584, respectively. Therefore, the approximate 95 percent confidence level is plus or minus two standard errors, equal to plus or minus 6.436 and 5.584, respectively, each of which approximate +/– 6 percent of the mean revenue.
- *T-statistic*—When calculating samples,[13] it is accepted practice to determine a 95 percent confidence level within a specific range of numbers, with the regression estimate at the midpoint. Therefore, the Student's t-distribution, or t-statistic, is used to calculate the range.

  Since part of the equations necessary to derive the t-statistic is unknown, an assumption is made for calculation. Typically a test of the probability, regardless

[13] XYZ financials are only available for monthly and annual comparisons. Therefore, quarterly amounts are not available for regression against quarterly GDP and related indicators.

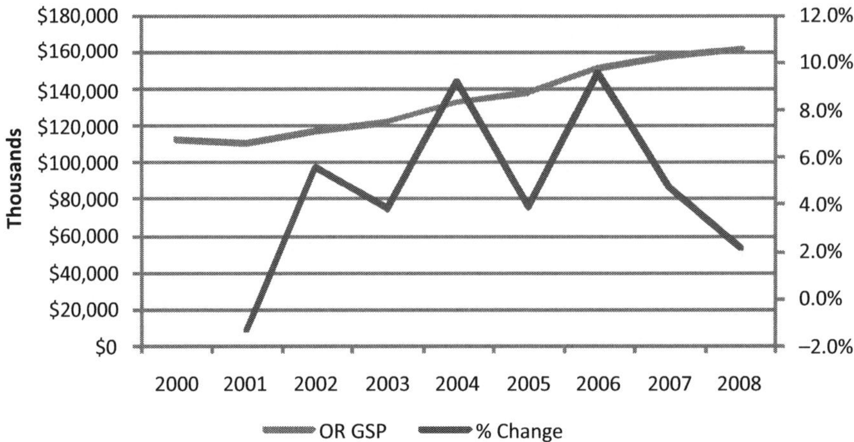

EXHIBIT 5.44 OR Annual GSP Dollar and Percentage Change

of the regression estimate, the true assumption of zero is made. This is known as the null hypothesis. Therefore, the magnitude of the t-statistic (the greater the better) indicates the ability to reject the null hypothesis for an individual variable in the regression equation. When the magnitude is sufficient to reject the null hypothesis, the regression estimate is statistically significant.

By referring to a t-statistic table and comparing to the degrees of freedom (*df*) we established the threshold necessary to reject the null hypothesis. Since our table indicates a threshold of 2.179 statistical significance is achieved for the PDI and combined *t*-statistics of (3.42305) and (2.98569), respectively.

- *P-value*—The easiest way to determine the level of statistical significance is through the *p*-value. One minus the *p*-value is the level of statistical significance; the smaller the *p*-value the better. The respective *p*-values per the preceding consist of .01409 and .04051, for PDI and combined statistics, respectively. Both the PDI and combined measures are therefore statistically significant, indicating that both are statistically significant at a level greater than 100 percent, *p*-value = 98 percent and 96 percent, respectively.

The same protocol applies to XYZ's home state, Oregon GSP[14] measures. Exhibit 5.44 contains Oregon GSP in dollars and annual percentage changes.

Exhibit 5.45 compares annual percentage change in Oregon GSP and XYZ's annual revenue. It appears to contain a visual match between the variables.

Exhibit 5.46 displays a statistical regression analysis based upon the data for XYZ revenues and the various GSP economic measurements as indicated.

Standard regression analysis techniques apply, and derived relative comparative factors produced so as to test the robustness of the data fit. The table in Exhibit 5.47 summarizes the key measurements.

[14] Gross state product.

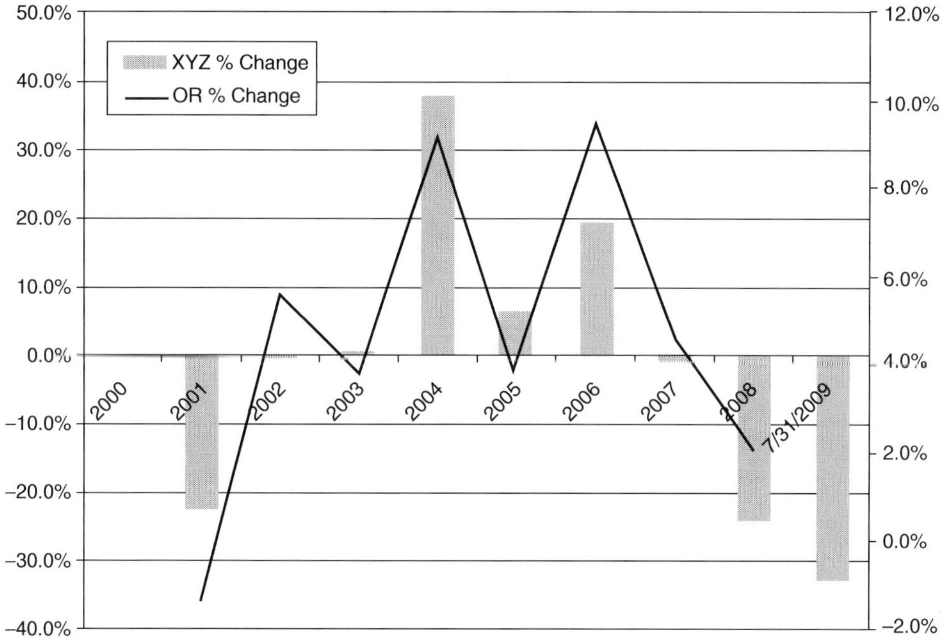

EXHIBIT 5.45 OR Annual GSP Percentage Change and XYZ percentage Change

Upon review of the preceding statistical regression measures, it is clear that Oregon GSP correlation, although strong, lacks the robustness of the U.S. GDP data, and also lacks the segmentation available to apply multiple regression techniques.

Consequently, U.S. GDP regression results are more reliable and a better fit that Oregon GSP regression results.

Estimation of XYZ's Revenues Having derived the regression statistics, estimates can be made of XYZ's future revenues, and ultimately its economic benefit streams, all driven by independently derived forecasts of GDP and related measures.

EXHIBIT 5.46 Regression Analysis

	Millions of Dollars	
Year	GSP	XYZ Sales
2000	112,438	90,292,699
2001	110,916	69,989,079
2002	117,131	69,687,496
2003	121,638	70,026,654
2004	132,835	96,595,009
2005	133,002	103,112,607
2006	151,205	123,415,189
2007	158,268	122,477,164
2008	161,573	93,202,364
7/31/2009	n/a	62,808,395

EXHIBIT 5.47 Regressed Against Historical XYZ Revenue

Regression Indicators	GSP
Multiple R	0.7719
R Squared	0.5959
Adjusted R Squared	0.5381
Standard Error of the Y Estimate	14.249
t-Statistic	−0.48700
P-Value	0.64114
95% Confidence Level Y Estimate	28.50

Since a strong correlation exists between XYZ's revenues and various GDP measures, a forward-looking estimate of GDP can be used to calculate XYZ's future revenues and long-term growth rates.

Therefore, although the world and US economies declined significantly at the valuation date, it appears that a recovery to previous levels is possible within two or three years. Since XYZ's customers are a function of the economy, their purchases occur after economic change and can be considered lagging[15] indicators. Consequently, XYZ's recovery will likely require a longer time horizon.

The factors listed in Exhibit 5.48 summarize near-term GDP measures and forward-looking estimates from the various sources that regularly publish forward-looking GDP outlooks. Note that the sources generally show consensus except for data (e.g., the 2010 federal budget, and so forth) from the Obama administration, which is an obvious outlier.

Therefore, XYZ's revenue outlook is nominal at best, and will not exceed the respective GDP measures for the near term. Note that during various conversations with XYZ management, they advised the following:

- We hope to reach the same sales level for fiscal 2010 that we reached in 2009.
- Although XYZ met its fiscal 2009 revenue budget, no 2010 budget was available.

Step 5—Estimate and Visually Array the Comparative Outlooks Using Quantitative and Qualitative Measures

XYZ's steady historical gross margin is expected by management to increase slightly, commensurate with expected revenue growth. Additional increases are expected if XYZ is successful in changing their primary supplier.

[15] An economic indicator that changes after the overall economy has changed. Examples include labor costs, business spending, the unemployment rate, the prime rate, outstanding bank loans, and inventory book value, October 21, 2009. www.investorwords.com/2713/lagging_indicator.html

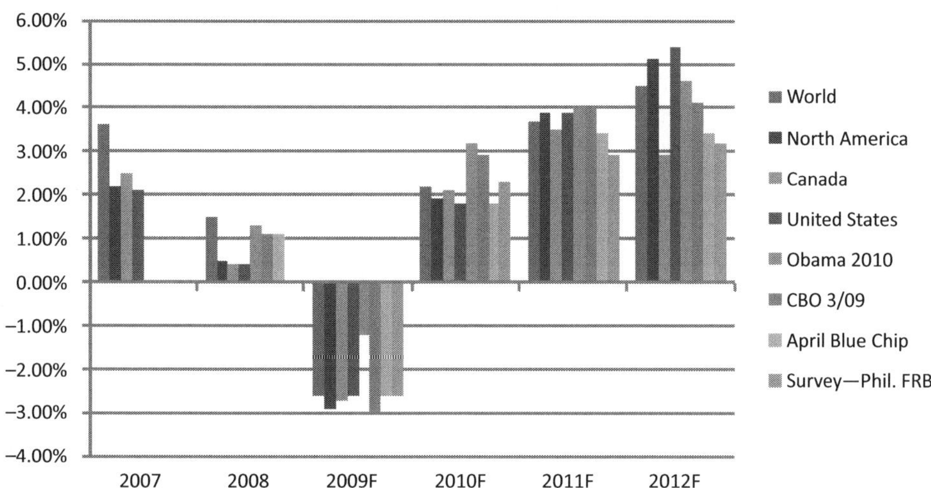

EXHIBIT 5.48 Year-to-Year Percentage GDP Change
Source: Moody's and as indicated.

Estimation of XYZ's Economic Benefit Stream The value of an entity requires an estimate of its future economic benefit stream. The most technically correct stream should reflect after-tax cash flow and account for other cash needs such as changes in working capital, capital expenditures, and other long-term needs. Therefore, the following section illustrates each of the cash flow components, as represented by XYZ's financials.

The following schedule contains a summary of each of the following items:

- *Net Income*—First, XYZ's net income is estimated based on the next fiscal period's likely revenues and net income. Since revenues for the next period will likely match the July 31, 2009, TTM period, the same revenue actually reported, that is, $62,808,395, is applied and rounded to $62,800,000. Then, the same net income that XYZ budgeted for fiscal 2009, that is, $109,245, is applied and rounded to $109,000. Although the net income applied related to an unmet revenue budget of $85,779,310, XYZ management has historically demonstrated a keen ability to achieve profits even in dire conditions.
- *Depreciation*—A five-year average of historical depreciation is applied.
- *Income Taxes*—Standard federal and state income tax rate schedules derive after-tax income, to which depreciation was added in order to derive gross after-tax cash flow before accounting for other cash flow impacts.
- *Working Capital*—XYZ's dealership status permits it to manage inventories and flooring in an inverse relationship as illustrated in Exhibit 5.49. Consequently, inventory and flooring tend to cancel one another out.

The other components of working capital are shown in Exhibit 5.50. The 2004 spike in ONCL (Other Noncurrent Liabilities) is predominantly driven by long-term

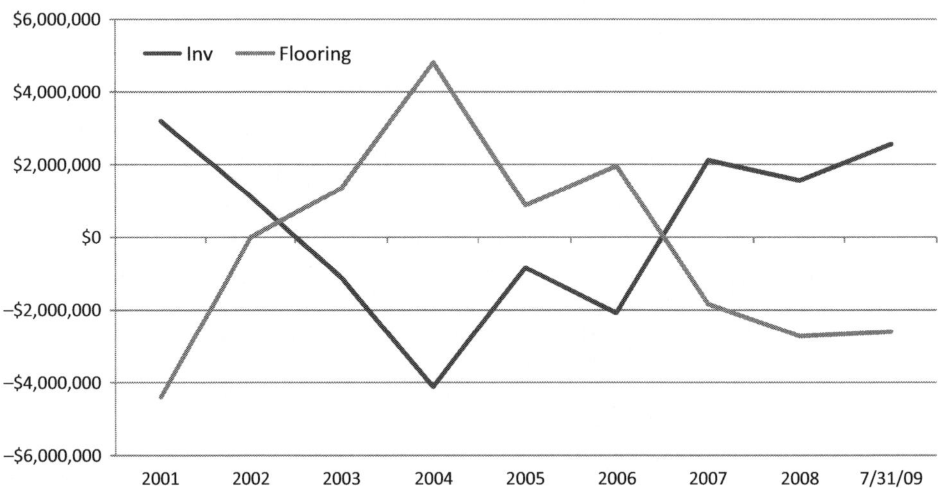

EXHIBIT 5.49 Change in Inventory and Flooring

debt, which XYZ has steadily paid down in recent years. Therefore, a portion is estimated to reflect the likely drawdown of working capital.

All the other components of working capital tend to remain relatively stable with the exception of A/R (accounts receivable). A/R is not expected to dramatically increase since sales will probably remain stable. Therefore, no other estimate was required. This conclusion is supported by the relatively large current assets ratio and XYZ's relatively large cash balance as of July 31, 2009.

- *Capital Expenditures*—XYZ has consistently replenished its revenue-generating assets over the years. Some years approached $4 million in acquisitions while

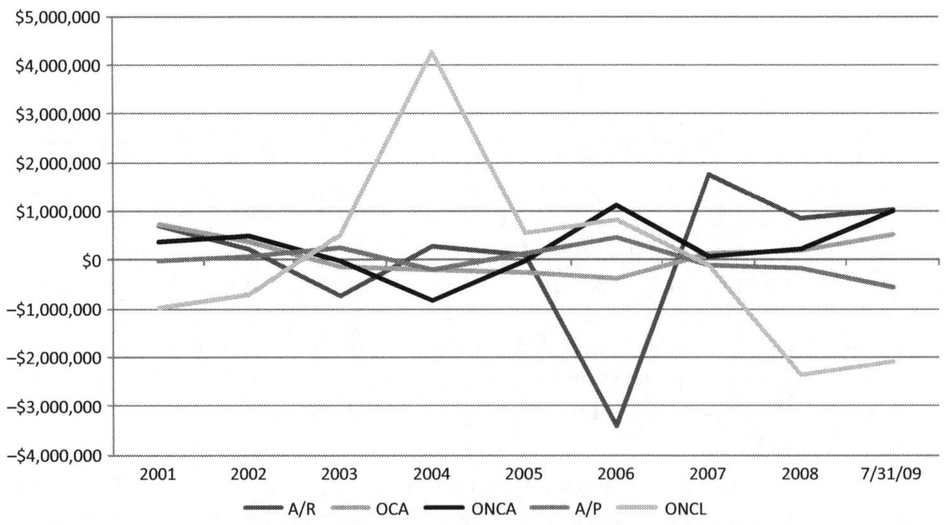

EXHIBIT 5.50 Change in Other Working Capital Components

EXHIBIT 5.51 Decomposition of Nonoperating Cash Flows

Transaction	July 31, 2009 Plus 1 Yr	W/C	Cap Ex	NP
Working Capital Changes, e.g. A/R	–	–		
Net Working Capital	–	–		
Capital Expenditures—	(5,800,000)		(5,800,000)	
Cap. Expend. Misc. ($10,000 per month)	(120,000)		(120,000)	
Total Capital Expenditures	(5,920,000)			
Depreciation on Capital Expenditures	1,184,000		1,184,000	
Net Capital Expenditures	**(4,736,000)**		(4,736,000)	
Notes Payable to	5,800,000			5,800,000
Expected NP Paydown	(3,100,000)			(3,100,000)
Net Notes Payable	**2,700,000**		–	
Net Change	**(2,036,000)**	–	(4,736,000)	2,700,000

the lowest year was about $1.5 million. Therefore, the amount is estimated that is deemed to be a minimum threshold reflecting the current conditions.

- *Long-Term Debt*—XYZ has consistently paid down its debt when cash and working capital were available. Therefore, an amount reflective of the condition is estimated.

The preceding items are scheduled as illustrated in Exhibits 5.51 based upon specific communications with executive management regarding the next fiscal period's expectations.

XYZ has consistently demonstrated dependable abilities to develop realistic annual revenue and profit budgets that closely estimate actual results. Therefore, the following schedules illustrate the respective sales and gross margin trends for both actual and forecasted results. (Note that forecasted sales for Model A—No Change and Model A—With Change are identical.)

Step 6—Compare and Contrast the Outlooks

Having constructed sufficient analysis for foundation, a visual display of the quantitative results leads to logical conclusions regarding which revenue stream(s) is the "best" one to use. In forward-looking financial matters, the term "best" is defined as the most likely scenario, which happens to be the scenario essential for the

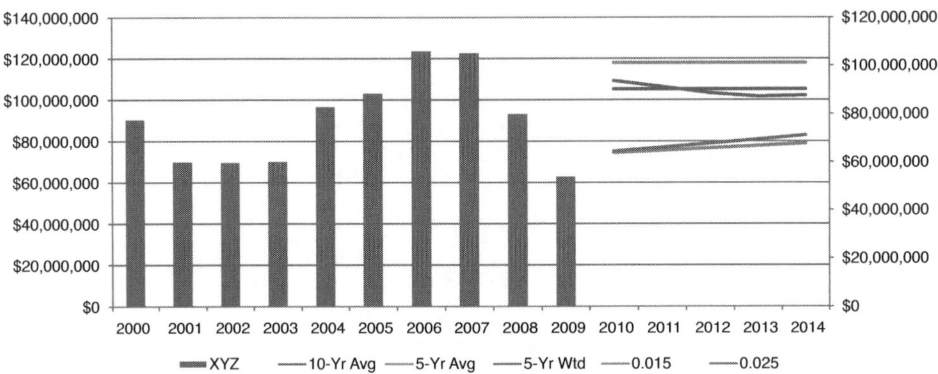

EXHIBIT 5.52 XYZ RevenuesVarious Forecasting Scenarios

assignment. Exhibit 5.52 illustrates XYZ's historical results and provides comparison of the various estimation scenarios used to proffer forward-looking estimates. Not all the methods are discussed since rationale for the approach is more important than mere number-crunching. Also, the mean and median for all the results (shown for comparison only) fall closely to one another and are supported by a relatively small standard deviation.

There are several benefits to Exhibit 5.52. First, it is comprised of quantitative support which can be used to demonstrate development as necessary. Second, it provides a historical perspective with respect to future estimates. Third, it demonstrates the convergence that typically results when using a variety of techniques to estimate the future. Finally, and perhaps most importantly, it permits a facile "eyeballing" of the feasibility of forward-looking alternatives.

The proper conclusion for a forensic operator falls with the lowest rate of estimate, falling within a 1.5–2.5 percent rate of growth.

Step 7—Conclusion Regarding the Selected Stream

The preceding contents demonstrated a methodical and empirical approach to analyzing XYZ's financial history and comparing it to various economic drivers. The strong correlations, as previously indicated, demonstrate a sound basis upon which to estimate future outcomes.

CONCLUSION

This chapter's contents achieve two key steps. It instructs the forensic operator in the derivation of an objective, technically correct, and defensible economic benefit stream. It also positions the forensic operator for the next and subsequent steps necessary to achieve a persuasive and defensible answer(s) for the subject parties. The next chapter describes those steps.

CHAPTER 6

Trial and Reports Phase

This chapter aggregates and conveys the forensic operator's entire assignment, with the degree of detail dependent upon many factors. They include: the court (whether bench or jury trial); the trial duration (a three-day trial has different dynamics from a three-week trial); the extent of discovery; the complexity of the data; the complexity of the matter; the opposition's likely approach; the forensic operator's trial experience; the client's or agency's comfort level; the chemistry among the various parties; and myriad other factors ranging from physical (e.g., weather, size of the courtroom), and psychological (e.g., small town, large city), etc.

This chapter explains simple yet effective tools to capture the nature and essence of a forensic assignment within the context of the output. Certain matters, for example, patent infringement in federal court, compel forensic operators to construct or explain a narrative supporting the data, analysis, observations, opinions, et al. Conversely, a short-duration dispute among two shareholders might merely require forensic operator testimony supported by a few schedules for demonstrative exhibits. Consequently, the forensic operator must have a facile grasp of the report and exhibit spectrum in order to communicate effectively and efficiently.

TRIAL PREPARATION STAGE

Purpose of Stage

This action defines the purpose of the trial[1] preparation stage. Also, it sets the stage for the reports, exhibits, and testimony that may be required.

The objective of this action is to insure that all prior data and analysis is appropriately included within a format admissible to the venue.

Some specific actions include:

- Prepare for the trial.
- Integrate parties and information.
- Ensure the completeness of all testimony and exhibits.

[1] Within the context of this chapter, "trial" could range from a semi-formal work session through more formal proceedings. They could include board meetings, mediation, arbitration, trial, et al.

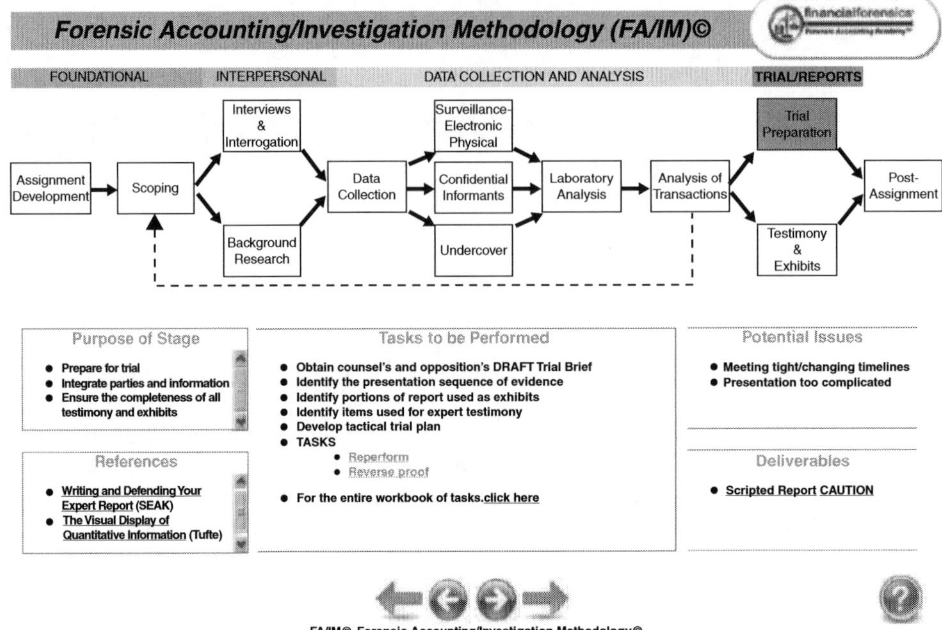

EXHIBIT 6.1 Trial Preparation

References

This action identifies and accesses all the data and guidance related to the report writing (including exhibits) and preparation for the trial.

The objective of this action is to maximize the communication to the involved parties.

Example of Reference Sources The following reference sources serve to jumpstart the forensic operator. The Key Internet Sites and Key Reference Materials are not all-inclusive, but provide starting points from which to build resources. Also, refer to the bibliography.

Key Internet sites

www.financialforensicsacademy.com

Key Reference materials

- *Envisioning Information*, by Edward R. Tufte
- *The Visual Display of Quantitative Information*, by Edward R. Tufte
- *Writing and Defending Your Expert Report*, by Steven Babitsky and James Mangraviti Jr.

Tasks to Be Performed

This action outlines likely tasks, but is not an all-inclusive checklist since each forensic assignment is unique. Use the tasks as a guideline and modify according to the unique facts and circumstances of the assignment.

The objective of this action is to ensure that the forensic operator *effectively communicate* the pertinent findings to the matter at hand.

Specific actions include:

- Obtain counsel's and opposition's draft trial brief.
- Identify the presentation sequence of evidence.
- Identify portions of the report to be used as exhibits.
- Identify items to be used for expert testimony.
- Develop tactical trial plan.
- Rehearse.
- Execute reverse proof.

Potential Issues

This action prompts the forensic operator to consider all possible roadblocks related to time, writing, and presentation that may arise during the trial preparation stage.

The objective of this action is to anticipate challenges to the forensic findings in order to blunt their impact.

Specific actions include:

- Meeting tight or changing timelines.
- Presentation may be too complicated.

Deliverables

The objective of this action is to identify and eventually finalize deliverables pertinent to the assignment. The forensic operator always develops deliverables designed with the end in mind so as to maximize efficiency.

Some specific deliverables include:

- Scripted Report—clear this with counsel first; this is likely discoverable. Exhibit 6.2 illustrates a sample testimony script. Note that it uses PowerPoint to

EXHIBIT 6.2 Testimony Scripting

What Is Forensic
Accounting/Accountant?

- **Forensic Accounting:**
  - *The art and science of applying financial techniques to matters of law.*
- **Forensic Accountant:**
  - Most CPAs, etc. *prepare historical* financial statements and income tax returns. Forensic accountants analyze them and *prepare future* estimates.

add "Notes" that counsel uses to query the forensic operator during direct testimony. *Caution:* This technique *must* be cleared before using to avoid violating any court or jurisdictional rules, procedures, or protocols.

Note to reader: Refer to Wiley Internet site for detailed examples of scripted reports. They can be found at www.wiley.com/go/financialforensics.

TESTIMONY AND EXHIBITS

Purpose of Stage

This action defines the purpose of the testimony and exhibits stage. Also, it sets the stage for the reports, exhibits, and testimony that may be required. See Exhibit 6.3.

The objective of this action is to insure that all prior data and analysis is appropriately included for delivery within a format admissible to the venue.

Some specific actions include:

- Prepare for the trial.
- Integrate parties and information.
- Ensure the completeness of all testimony and exhibits.
- Ensure admissibility.

References

This action identifies and portrays all the data, information and opinions supporting the trial testimony.

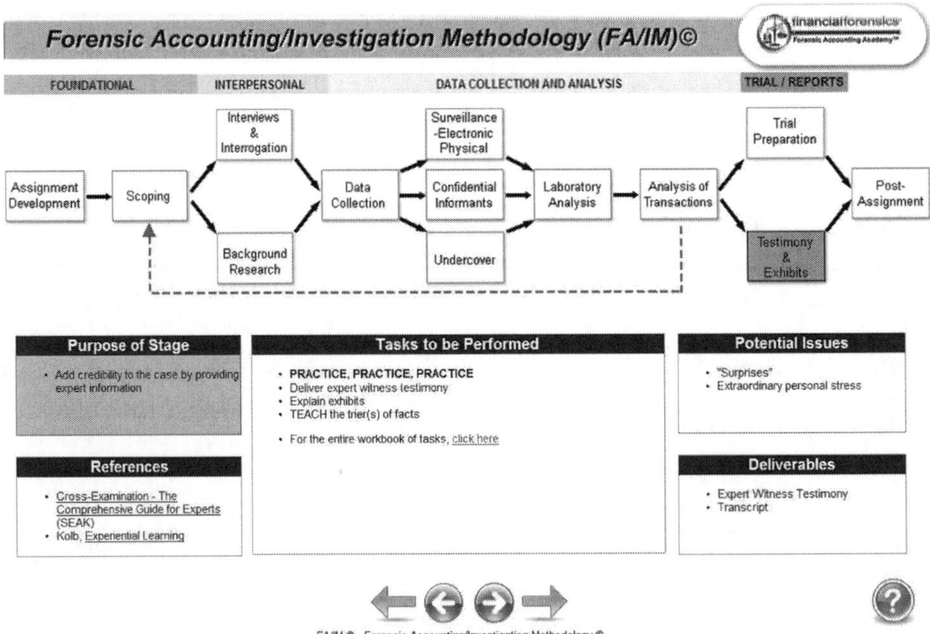

EXHIBIT 6.3 Testimony & Exhibits

The objective of this action is to maximize the communication to the judge, jury and related parties.

Example of Reference Sources

The following reference sources serve to jumpstart the forensic operator. The Key Internet Sites and Key Reference Materials are not all-inclusive, but provide starting points from which to build resources. Also, refer to the bibliography.

Key Internet sites www.financialforensicsacademy.com

Key Reference materials

- *Envisioning Information*, by Edward R. Tufte
- *The Visual Display of Quantitative Information*, by Edward R. Tufte
- *Writing and Defending Your Expert Report*, by Steven Babitsky and James Mangraviti, Jr.

Tasks to Be Performed

This action outlines likely tasks, but is not an all-inclusive checklist since each forensic assignment is unique. Use the tasks as a guideline and modify according to the unique facts and circumstances of the assignment.

The objective of this action is to ensure that the forensic operator *effectively communicates* the pertinent data, facts, evidence and opinions during the matter at bar.

Specific actions include:

- Obtain counsel's and opposition's exhibit list.
- Identify the presentation sequence of evidence.
- Identify portions of the report to be used as exhibits.
- Identify items to be used for expert testimony.
- Rehearse.
- Reverse proof.

Potential Issues This action prompts the forensic operator to consider all possible roadblocks related to time, writing, and presentation that may arise during the trial preparation stage.

The objective of this action is to anticipate challenges to the forensic findings in order to blunt their impact.

Specific actions include:

- Meeting tight or changing timelines.
- Presentation simplicity.

Deliverables The objective of this action is to identify and eventually finalize deliverables pertinent to the assignment. The forensic operator always develops deliverables designed with the end in mind so as to maximize efficiency.

WEAPON (WPN)

Forensic operators must have excellent report[2] writing skill. This requirement speaks to *persuasion* rather than grammar, lengthy prose, or hyper-technical content. Persuasion derives from the audience likely to read forensic reports, that is, parties to the matter, their attorneys, opposing experts, judges, court clerks, and juries. Since the report-reading audience is made up of adults, forensic operators must deploy adult-learning techniques within their forensic reports.

Many sources contain comprehensive details of adult learning theory, with Dr. David Kolb at the forefront.[3] Adult learning techniques are unavoidably comprehensive since adults exhibit vast and varied learning styles. However, three broad categories capture the styles: auditory, visual, and experiential, recognizing that most adults learn using a combination of styles. Fortunately, forensic operators capitalize on the categories by packaging forensic report contents to include all three styles for each major point in the report. The report packaging components are words, pictures, and numbers.

The acronym WPN (pronounced *weapon*) comprises the three categorized adult learning styles and guides forensic operators in report construction. Also, reports become easier to write and enhance audience comprehension.

WPN

The WPN technique ensures that forensic reports maximize the likelihood of audience comprehension. Therefore, each forensic report must contain the following for each major point in the report.

- *W* (Words)—Text that describes report content.
- *P* (Pictures)—Visuals (photographs, symbols, drawings, histograms,[4] diagrams, etc.) that reflect report content.
- *N* (Numbers)—Data that quantifies report content.

Naturally, the preceding description presupposes that the components amplify one another. For example, words describe a financial statement's fundamental trends, while pictures (in the form of a bar chart, line chart, etc.) illustrate the trends, and numbers are contained in the financial statement schedule.

The WPN technique often yields a valuable by-product, since the contents often serve as trial and testimony exhibits.

Actual WPN Example 1 The following WPN extract illustrates simple but effective use of photographs in reports.

---

[2] The definition of *report* (for this chapter) is any written communication the forensic operator prepares to convey forensic findings. Consequently, reports could range from one paragraph to hundreds of pages and still apply WPN throughout.

[3] David A. Kolb, *Experiential Learning* (Englewood Cliffs, NJ: Prentice Hall, 1984).

[4] Bar, line, scattergram, and other charts.

History of the Company
QRS Manufacturing was founded in YEAR in CITY, STATE by John C. QRS, as a sole proprietorship. Prior to founding the company, Mr. QRS had been trained as a Machinist and had learned the precision machining trade on the job as an employee of LARGE COMPANY. The Company relocated to CITY in YEAR and incorporated in STATE in YEAR.

[Insert photo of company here]

Services
The Company makes custom-machined component parts on a "job shop" or "discrete" basis. Customers are typically larger equipment and machine fabrication or production processors. The two primary costs of Company operations are Labor and steel. None of the Company's products or services are proprietary in nature, nor is their relationships to vendors or suppliers unique.

Since the year 2000, the Company has relied upon seven customers for approximately 86 percent of its sales. The Company has no long-term continuation or exclusivity contracts with its customers that would ensure a continued business relationship.

Actual WPN Example 2 The following WPN extract demonstrates a variation on WPN by using snippets of actual journal entry and general ledger components as part of the forensic report explanation.

February 28, 1995, USD$2,100,000 disbursement to EFG
The initial disbursement was recorded in the accounting ledgers as an investment in EFG FOREIGN ENTITY Telecommunications, Ltd., a wholly owned subsidiary of EFG.

```
01/1995* 28/02/95 P9502124  P   0000006   127        16,212,000.00 C
2,100,000.00 C USD  Rate    7.720000000
```

```
Account Code: 2013    Name: Investment    Type: BALANCE SHEET
 01/1995 28/02/95 9502020  P   0000011    11       2,100,000.00 D
16,212,000.00 D HKD  Rate   7.720000000
                     Re:
 01/1995 Period Total                 2,100,000.00 D
```

There was no valuation or financial analysis performed supporting why or how this investment would benefit QRP. Further, this disbursement was not discussed by, or approved by the QRP Board. In December 1995, EFG allegedly assigned their interest in one of their joint ventures (FOREIGN CITY) to QRP for USD$2,100,000, based on "costs incurred by the assignor." EFG's own internal documents indicate that costs incurred as of that date were significantly less than USD$2,100,000.

Actual WPN Example 3 The following WPN example illustrates key contents of an actual forensic report covering HOLDCO and XYZ (pseudonyms). The publicly held Hong Kong parent company diverted significant funds from its controlled, publicly held Canadian affiliate through several complex (alleged) transactions. The complexity and jurisdiction of the transactions required the forensic operators to write detailed reports to document the forensic findings. However, the complexity also compelled the forensic operators to use the WPN approach to enhance the court's understanding of the diversions. The visual contained in the example in Exhibit 6.4 (and others like it for other transactions) became exhibits during expert testimony.

Since the court required detailed descriptions of each (alleged) transaction the forensic report contained explanatory detail, shown here in italics. The underlying legal documents were extraordinarily complex, thus the narrative summarized and restated the contents of the legal documents. The visuals of the respective transactions further amplified the details.

Words Component of WPN

LLCO Transaction Detail

Background of the LLCO transaction

HOLDCO owned over 70 percent of LLCO, a publicly traded company engaged in the manufacturing of computer OEM equipment and storage devices. In Fall 2005, HOLDCO initiated a going-private transaction whereby it sought to acquire the remaining shares in order to achieve 100 percent ownership of LLCO's shares. In connection with the going-private transaction, HOLDCO granted its subsidiary, XYZ the right to acquire a 10 percent interest in LLCO.

Ownership Structure of XYZ's purchase

The Share Purchase Agreement contains complex and confusing language summarized by the following narrative.

1. The LLCO shares were indirectly acquired by XYZ through a newly formed two-tiered, non-control, non-liquid structure, that is, HCC and Ministerial.
2. XYZ's LLCO shares were actually held by Ministerial, which is 50 percent held (non-control, non-liquid) by HCC.
3. The other 50 percent non-control, non-liquid interest of Ministerial is held by Lackeys, and is controlled by HOLDCO.
4. Therefore, XYZ does *not* directly hold the 10 percent LLCO shares, but rather:
   a. controls an entity, that is, HCC; which
   b. holds a 50 percent interest in the entity, that is, Ministerial, that,
   c. holds 20 percent of LLCO shares.

What Did XYZ Spend for the Transaction?

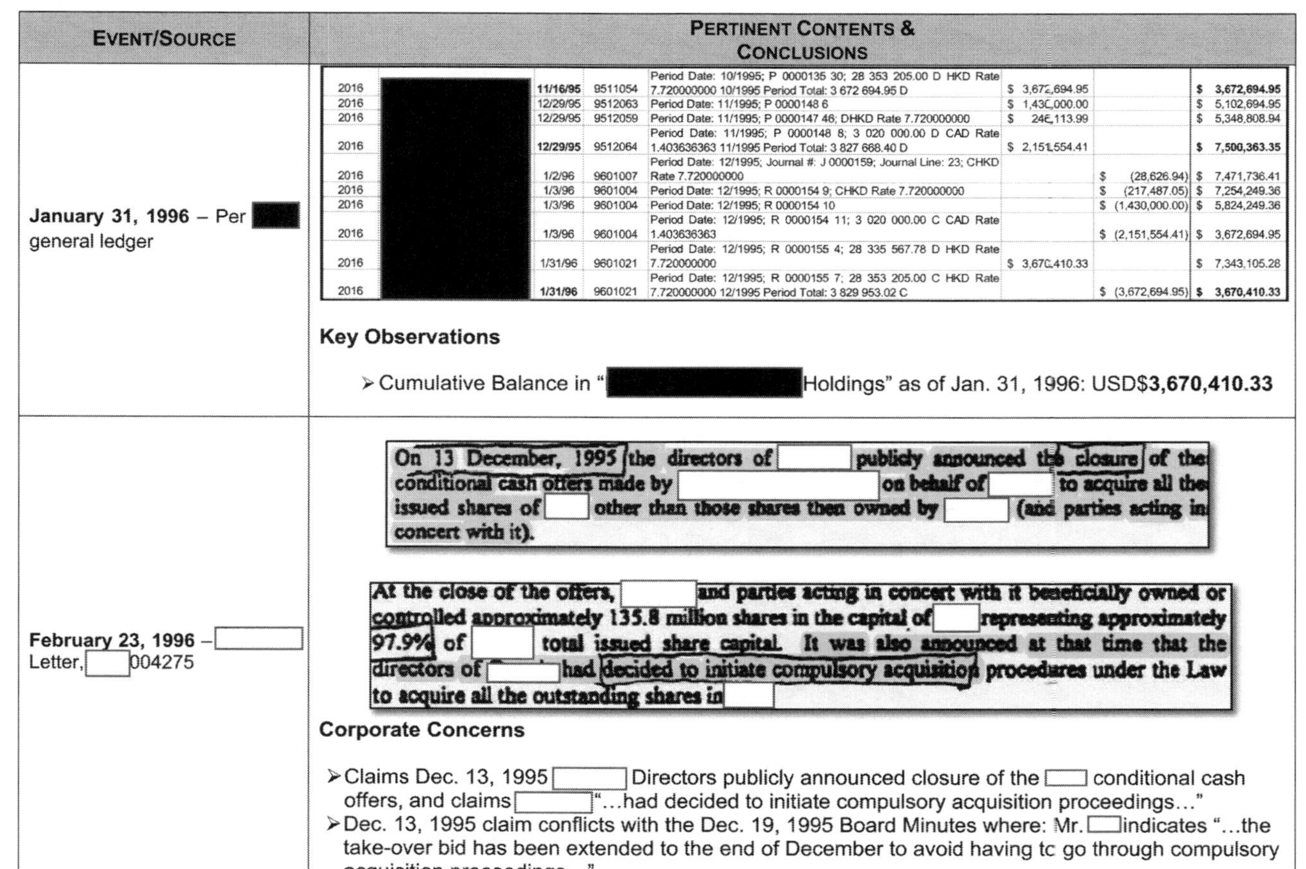

EVENT/SOURCE	PERTINENT CONTENTS & CONCLUSIONS
January 31, 1996 – Per [redacted] general ledger	(ledger extract and Key Observations below)
February 23, 1996 – [redacted] Letter, [redacted]004275	(letter extract and Corporate Concerns below)

January 31, 1996 – Per [redacted] general ledger

2016	[redacted]	**11/16/95**	9511054	Period Date: 10/1995; P 0000135 30; 28 353 205.00 D HKD Rate 7.720000000 10/1995 Period Total: 3 672 694.95 D	$ 3,672,694.95		**$ 3,672,694.95**
2016		12/29/95	9512063	Period Date: 11/1995; P 0000148 6	$ 1,430,000.00		$ 5,102,694.95
2016		12/29/95	9512059	Period Date: 11/1995; P 0000147 46; DHKD Rate 7.720000000	$ 246,113.99		$ 5,348,808.94
2016		**12/29/95**	9512064	Period Date: 11/1995; P 0000148 8; 3 020 000.00 D CAD Rate 1.403636363 11/1995 Period Total: 3 827 668.40 D	$ 2,151,554.41		**$ 7,500,363.35**
2016		1/2/96	9601007	Period Date: 12/1995; Journal #: J 0000159; Journal Line: 23; CHKD Rate 7.720000000		$ (28,626.94)	$ 7,471,736.41
2016		1/3/96	9601004	Period Date: 12/1995; R 0000154 9; CHKD Rate 7.720000000		$ (217,487.05)	$ 7,254,249.36
2016		1/3/96	9601004	Period Date: 12/1995; R 0000154 10		$ (1,430,000.00)	$ 5,824,249.36
2016		1/3/96	9601004	Period Date: 12/1995; R 0000154 11; 3 020 000.00 C CAD Rate 1.403636363		$ (2,151,554.41)	$ 3,672,694.95
2016		1/31/96	9601021	Period Date: 12/1995; R 0000155 4; 28 335 567.78 D HKD Rate 7.720000000	$ 3,670,410.33		$ 7,343,105.28
2016		**1/31/96**	9601021	Period Date: 12/1995; R 0000155 7; 28 353 205.00 C HKD Rate 7.720000000 12/1995 Period Total: 3 829 953.02 C		$ (3,672,694.95)	**$ 3,670,410.33**

Key Observations

➢ Cumulative Balance in "[redacted] Holdings" as of Jan. 31, 1996: USD$**3,670,410.33**

February 23, 1996 – [redacted] Letter, [redacted]004275

> On 13 December, 1995 the directors of [redacted] publicly announced the closure of the conditional cash offers made by [redacted] on behalf of [redacted] to acquire all the issued shares of [redacted] other than those shares then owned by [redacted] (and parties acting in concert with it).

> At the close of the offers, [redacted] and parties acting in concert with it beneficially owned or controlled approximately 135.8 million shares in the capital of [redacted] representing approximately 97.9% of [redacted] total issued share capital. It was also announced at that time that the directors of [redacted] had decided to initiate compulsory acquisition procedures under the Law to acquire all the outstanding shares in [redacted]

Corporate Concerns

➢ Claims Dec. 13, 1995 [redacted] Directors publicly announced closure of the [redacted] conditional cash offers, and claims [redacted] "...had decided to initiate compulsory acquisition proceedings..."

➢ Dec. 13, 1995 claim conflicts with the Dec. 19, 1995 Board Minutes where: Mr. [redacted] indicates "...the take-over bid has been extended to the end of December to avoid having tc go through compulsory acquisition proceedings..."

EXHIBIT 6.4 WPN Example

XYZ eventually spent HK$56,671,135.55 (USD$7,340,820.66), categorized as "Investments–LLCO Int'l holdings" on XYZ's balance sheet. The final amount resulted from a protracted series of bank transactions and accounting entries explained in the Transaction History, which follows.

What Did XYZ Receive for the USD$7,340,820.66 Expenditure?

Even though XYZ indirectly acquired the non-control, non-liquid LLCO share interest through a two-tiered, non-control, non-liquid, minority-held structure, XYZ was compelled to pay a *proportionate* percentage of HOLDCO's LLCO share purchase price. This resulted in XYZ paying a *disproportionate* 33 percent of HOLDCO's costs. Such amounts are excessive for reasons including:

- XYZ did not receive 10 percent of the LLCO shares, but rather a 50 percent non-control, non-liquid interest in a two-tiered structure that held 20 percent of the LLCO Shares.
- XYZ's payment of an allegedly proportionate share of HOLDCO's costs resulted in a disproportionate expenditure as indicated next.
  - HOLDCO needed to purchase only 29.9 percent of LLCO's outstanding shares to attain 100 percent LLCO ownership in the going-private transaction, since HOLDCO already held 70.1 percent of LLCO's shares.
  - XYZ paid HK$4.09 per share (HK$56,671,140 / 13,872,983 shares). Note that XYZ's share of the going-private warrant costs and acquisition costs, for example, legal, financial, advisory, printing, and so forth, aggregated to USD$512,150.
  - Based on the HK$4.09 per share that XYZ paid, HOLDCO paid HK$169,857,021 for the 41,529,834 shares.
  - Consequently, XYZ's purchase of an indirect 10 percent interest resulted in XYZ paying a *disproportionate* 33 percent of HOLDCO's expenditure, that is, HK$56,671,140/ HK$169,857,021.
- The amounts that XYZ paid contradict widely accepted valuation practice for several reasons.
  - The going-private transaction benefited HOLDCO, not XYZ.
  - XYZ paid a *premium* ranging from 5.6 percent to 40.7 percent for a non-control interest as illustrated in the LLCO share closing price schedule, which follows. A premium is ordinarily paid when some advantage is gained, for example, a control interest. A non-control interest such as that acquired by XYZ calls for a *discount* to reflect its lack of control.
  - Even a *direct* 10 percent shareholding is a non-control position in these circumstances. Indeed, the October 10, 2005,

board minutes described the [transaction] as [representing] a minority position. As such, it does not represent a proportionate value because of a lack of control characteristics.
  - Since LLCO was going private, the shares acquired by XYZ lack the liquidity ordinarily available to publicly traded shares, thus suggesting a further *discount* beyond non-control to account for LLCO shares' illiquidity.
  - The shares are distantly and indirectly held through a two-tiered entity structure, which XYZ does not control.
  - XYZ's LLCO interests were restricted even further when XYZ was compelled to submit them as collateral to BANK as part of a settlement agreement negotiated by Mr. CEO.
- In February 2007 (only nine months following the collateral requirement), XYZ was compelled to exchange its LLCO shares for non-control, non-liquid HIGH-END shares.
- XYZ received no dividends from LLCO during its ownership despite HOLDCO's agreement to pay dividends. XYZ recorded only accrued income for its proportionate shareholding, but never received the cash for the income.
- After XYZ's interest was exchanged for an interest in HIGH-END shares in February 2007, HOLDCO took LLCO public again in March 2010 and received large amounts of cash in which XYZ did not share.

Pictures and Numbers Component of WPN Even though the preceding narrative succinctly summarizes the (alleged) transaction, considerable thought is necessary to comprehend the entity structures, shareholdings, and fund flows.

Exhibit 6.5 combines both pictures and numbers into a summary that served as an exhibit during testimony at trial. The example extract of words, pictures and numbers from an actual forensic report illustrate the importance of using WPN.

Putting It All Together

Each reader will have his own respective preference for which of the words, pictures, and numbers were more persuasive. Actually, that proves the point—forensic operators must use all three components in forensic reports in order to reach anyone likely to read their report.

REPORTS AND EXHIBITS: TIPS AND TECHNIQUES

Report writing is one of the most significant challenges for the forensic operator who tends to practice in various disciplines. That condition exists because each assignment

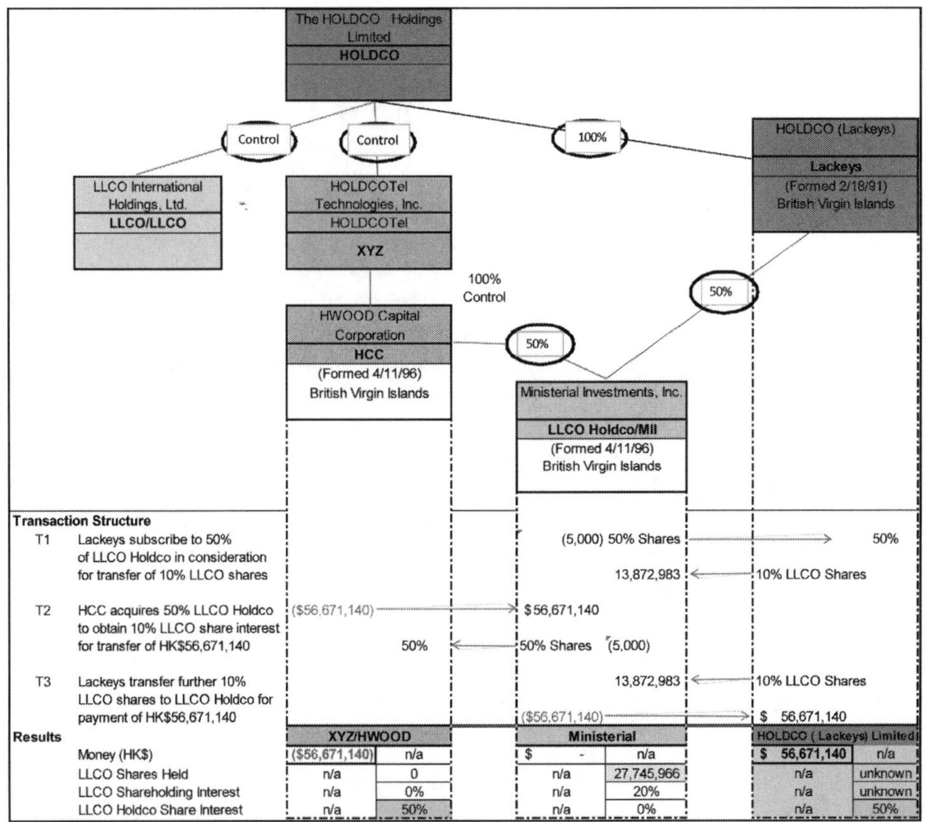

EXHIBIT 6.5 The HOLDCO Holdings Limited

is unique, the necessary tools and techniques vary, and each assignment's findings require disparate explanation. Therefore, several types of forensic assignments are included.

Actual BLINDED (all names and similar identifiers are changed) reports are available for the topics indicated here. The reports provide examples of forensic techniques used in the respective matters. They contain text and exhibits use in the original filing, with many exhibits produced as foam-core demonstratives for trial testimony support. For obvious reasons, supporting documentation for the respective book contents, for example, entity financial statements, industry outlook, detailed calculations, corroborating documents, etc. are not included.

The reports are offered as models for forensic operators seeking formats for the respective matters. Naturally, every matter—civil, criminal, or dispute—is unique. Consequently, the report contents, regardless of similarity to the forensic operator's matter, should not be merely lifted and modified for filing. Such an action poses a significant risk for the forensic operator.

Each report is highlighted by the following categories.

- *Matter*—This category alphabetically lists the type of forensic matter, for example, alter ego, damages, and so on. It contains a brief description of the nature and background of the matter.
- *Key Forensic Techniques*—This category references the key forensic techniques applied in the matter, such as timeline, regression, Cash-T, etc.
- *Key Report Contents*—This category refers to the key report contents applied in the matter. They include unique facts and circumstances, scorecard, MUA, etc.

Fortunately, certain report contents are common to nearly all forensic assignments. One example is the "Unique Facts and Circumstances" report section. The authors discovered this technique several years ago while constructing a Form 706[5] valuation report for an intestate decedent. The decedent's small chemical company was exceptionally dependent upon a single customer for the great majority of its business, that is, more than 98 percent of its revenues were from a public company whose CEO was the brother of the decedent. Since the company was extremely profitable and the decedent notoriously eccentric, the decedent's counsel encouraged us to make the valuation report as IRS-proof as possible. The Unique Facts and Circumstances section did the trick. It explained the customer dependence and supported the very large discount rate and secondary adjustments applied.

Exhibit 6.6 lists the various reports. Actual reports are available on this book's website at www.wiley.com/go/financialforensics. The following matrix summarizes the key report techniques, for example, "Deposition Matrix," and key report contents, for example," Unique Facts and Circumstances" to better plan the query through the Wiley site.

Forensic operators continually seek methods to make forensic assignments more efficient and effective. Report writing is no exception. Indeed, the authors often conduct training sessions exclusively devoted to writing forensic reports intended for civil, criminal, and dispute matters. One Internet application tailored to report writing is www.grammarly.com. It permits the upload, checking, and scoring of report content based on more than 150 common and advanced grammar rules. The rules include everything from subject-verb agreement to article use to modifier placement. It is very cost-effective and permits a seven-day free trial option. Forensic operators should investigate its features.

[5] Federal estate tax filing.

EXHIBIT 6.6 Reports

Matter	Key Forensic Techniques	Key Report Contents
Alter ego—Defendant engaged a forensic operator to assist counsel in the defense of an alter ego claim brought by the federal government. The matter involved a contract in a spotted owl forest. It was in process 17 years when the Court of Federal Claims bench trial was held.	Timeline—Interactive timeline used throughout testimony, displayed on the court's television screens. Photographs—records comprised 12,000 pounds, illustrated by photo research. Deposition Matrix—used against opposing expert. Research—Direct testimony began with 1921 to educate the court regarding the nature and extent of alter ego. Outcome: The judge delivered a bench ruling in favor of the defendant after the two-week trial.	Unique Facts and Circumstances Detailing extent of records analyzed Alter ego scorecard Multi-attribute analysis (MUA) Business definitions of terms, for example, *affiliate, intercompany, subsidiary,* and so on. Alter ego expertise—publications listed to emphasize experience. Alter ego expertise—speaking listed to emphasize experience.
Damages—Defendant engaged a forensic operator to rebut plaintiff's national BV firm expert's assertion of $30,000,000-plus damages from alleged harmful acts and punitive damages.	Timeline Market Scan Regression Causation Cash Flow Impact of Punitives	Assignment questions Unique Facts and Circumstances Cited judicial technical references. Cited state damages precedents. Cited state laws. Profiled specific damages and wholesale company expertise.
Damages—Lost Profits—Plaintiff engaged a forensic operator to assist in damages calculation. An excavation company had received a bank's verbal and faxed approval for an operating loan to proceed with a housing development, but reneged after work began.	Onsite—Forensic operator made several on-site visits to company and housing development, often when in proximity on other assignments. Interviews—Several interviews, some multiple Economic Drivers—Researched, compared, and applied pertinent county labor statistics to establish "but for" history and outlook. Economic and Industry Outlook—Applied matrix, linking specifics to results. Visual Extrapolation of "but for" revenues and gross profit. Outcome: Bank settled favorably with plaintiff on eve of trial.	"What Were We Asked to Do?" Unique Facts and Circumstances Cited judicial technical references. Cited state damages precedents. Cited state laws. Matter spanned 42 months due to court processes and setovers. New judge, thus counsel required two different approaches, valuation, and lost-profits computations. Two different write-ups, that is, 8 pages for jury submittal, and 42-plus pages for court filing, with same answers. Profiled specific damages and excavation company expertise. Reconciled lost profits and valuation approaches.

Forensic Accounting—Shareholder Oppression—An out-of-state sister to the local company CEO held a minority interest. As the company grew, she was frequently denied information beyond a K-1. Her suspicions compelled her to contact counsel, who engaged a forensic operator.	Limited Fee Budget Forensic Indices—Summarized in Matrix. Digital Analysis—Benford's Law Visuals. Photographs of Business Outcome: Counsel used the content to negotiate a favorable buyout.	Assignment Questions Unique Facts and Circumstances Matrix Indicator Summary: observations, impact and comments with scoring
Fraud—Individual—A dentist and his wife were trying a trial separation. He purchased her a separate home. His bookkeeper discovered wife had been stealing funds from the practice. Wife's neighbors reported wife leaving five- and six-year old children locked in a bedroom while she and her crack-selling boyfriend left for two and three days at a time. Even though county law enforcement believed prosecuting a wife would be difficult, a forensic operator was engaged to build fraud report. State's child protective services could use the felony to give husband custody of the children.	Detective and prosecuting attorney—Forensic operator worked closely with law enforcement to optimize trial output to expedite prosecution and husband's child custody case. Matrix—Events summarized by category and supplemented by detail. Outcome: Wife finally plead guilty after several missed court appearances; she was sentenced and began treatment for drug abuse; husband received custody of the children.	Constructed simple icon exhibit depicting how wife forged checks and used credit cards to steal funds. This permitted the detective and prosecuting attorney to comprehend theft. Constructed indictment matrix to established multiple counts based upon state statutes for felony alteration, fraud, forgery, ID theft. and money laundering. Thirty-three events yielded 144 counts.

(continued)

EXHIBIT 6.6 Reports (*Continued*)

Matter	Key Forensic Techniques	Key Report Contents
Fraud—Institutional—Small city discovered questionable transaction and asked the state's Department of Justice for assistance. State recommended a forensic operator because of the accounting complexity involved.	QDE-FAB—To identify document alteration. Digital analysis—Testing for gap detection; digital analysis of entire general ledger. Outcome: Analysis assisted City with insurance recovery and restitution. Suspect sentenced to 8 years.	Unique Facts and Circumstances Activity Summary Chronology of events
Fraudulent Transfer (including alter ego)—Defendant attempted transfer of partnership business assets pursuant to his pending loss of suit filed against him by partner. Counsel engaged forensic operator to assist in analysis of fraudulent transfer, and subsequently determined to also add alter ego analysis.	Scripting—Report contains scripting through Word Comments that guided counsel's questions of forensic operator during one of the trials. Deposition Transcripts—extracted key phrases, and populated within respective report card. Included state statutes in report appendix—judge expressed gratitude. Outcome: Judge concluded fraudulent transfer had occurred, and veil was pierced.	Assignment questions Unique Facts and Circumstances Fraudulent Transfer, scorecard—amplified using badges of fraud. Alter ego scorecard—amplified using indicia. Alter ego expertise—publications listed to emphasize experience. Alter ego expertise—speaking listed to emphasize experience.
Marital Dissolution—Forensic Accounting and Valuation—wife of divorcing couple claimed husband had significant unreported income in auto collision business. Husband engaged nominally qualified valuation person. Wife's counsel engaged forensic operator to conduct forensic accounting and a valuation of the business.	Forensic techniques Included: pattern analysis, Pareto's law, central tendency and variance, correlation coefficients, stratification, relative size factor, and so on. Cash T—Technique used to simultaneously identify marital estate's income while normalizing the business's economic benefit stream. IDEA—Used digital analysis, for example, Benford's law, stratification, questionable expenses identification, and so on.	Summary of assignment Unique Facts and Circumstances Explained how Forensic Accounting/Investigation Methodology (FA/IM) applied. Automotive industry expertise–emphasized assignment experience, including speaking.

	Outcome: Opposing expert opined on $138,000 FMV; forensic operator opined on $350,000 FMV before forensic analysis, and $875,000 FMV after forensic analysis. Parties *settled on $875,000* conclusion. Judge concluded fraudulent transfer had occurred, and veil was pierced.	
Observations Matrix—A company secured asset-based lending pursuant to an acquisition and intended expansion. Business collapsed within six months and counsel for the asset-based lender engaged a forensic operator to determine what happened.	Timeline—Highlighted key events tied to financing impact. Cash Flow—Identified acquisition flaw: EBITDA pricing for an income entity. Sensitivity Testing—Conducted pre- and post-acquisition sensitivity testing to illustrate working capital deficiencies. Background Investigation—Discovered third-party investment advisor was unqualified. Outcome: Counsel advised client to settle because of continuing liability.	Matrix used to rapidly assimilate and organize key findings by category.
Solvency/Insolvency—Counsel for a merged company engaged a forensic operator to identify the cause of a failed merger of two companies. They had spent 18 months planning with high-profile attorneys and accountants, but less than *90 days* after the merger, the new entity failed and closed its doors.	Solvency Tests—Applied balance sheet, cash flow and adequate capital sensitivity tests to isolate causation. Cash Flow—Demonstrated that cash flow projections were wildly overstated. Cash Flow Statement—Constructed cash flow statement driven by premerger estimates; parties had simply relied upon projected income statement. Pattern Analysis—Demonstrated that peak cash needs coincided with seasonality decline, thus "worst possible timing."	Unique Facts and Circumstances Defined standard for solvency testing. Visuals emphasizing three key failures, including erroneous sales, EBITDA, and total debt projections. Matrix highlighting findings by category.

(*continued*)

EXHIBIT 6.6 Reports (*Continued*)

Matter	Key Forensic Techniques	Key Report Contents
Valuation Matrix—Forensic operator prepared a valuation report containing several complex elements. Counsel requested that the forensic operator prepare a much simplified version to accommodate the arbitrator's limited understanding.	Matrix—Matrix, consisting of only 10 pages, highlighted succinct elements of valuation, simultaneously demonstrating opposition's errors. Photographs—Conveying company's operations in contrast to the opposition's characterizations. Visual regression—Demonstrated several visuals indicating strong correlation for various multiples. Comparative Matrix—Summarized valuation findings from more than 400,000 market sources, distilled to 28 distinct methods, demonstrating opposition's shortcomings. Numerous conclusions—Visually arrayed the 13 valuation conclusions to demonstrate convergence. Journalized Normalizations—Demonstrating balance sheet impact since arbitrator stated his position that the balance sheet was the most reliable measure of value. Outcome: Arbitrator compelled to modify his leanings closer to reality.	Unique Facts and Circumstances Cited state statutes coincident with the court's order. Photographs Explanatory visuals Emphasized specific industry experience. Comparative matrix Used methods matrix to narrate method selection and reconciliation of conclusions.
Valuation report card—Counsel engaged the forensic operator to critique a high-profile appraiser's valuation report.	Report Card—Pointed out appraiser's pivotal errors. Embedded Visuals—inserted visuals in matrix to illustrate opposition's major flaws. Visual Scoring—Objectively demonstrated appraiser's inherent bias. Outcome: Arbitrator compelled to modify his leanings closer to reality.	"What Were We Asked to Do?" Unique Facts and Circumstances Emphasized specific industry expertise. Referenced valuation report card publications. Report Card: Pinpointed pivotal opposition errors, including scoring, to measure dominant appraiser bias.

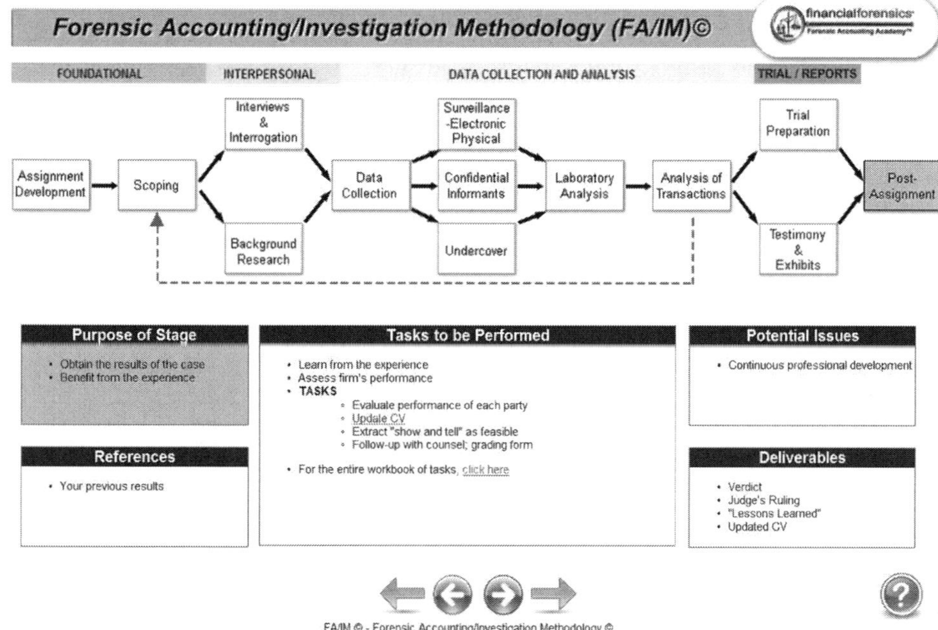

EXHIBIT 6.7 Post-Assignment

POST-ASSIGNMENT

Upon completion of the assignment, the forensic operator should take the following steps to review and evaluate the case. See Exhibit 6.7.

Purpose of Stage

This action plan defines the purpose of this stage. The specific action includes:

- Obtain the results of the case.
- Benefit from the experience.

References

This action identifies and accesses all documents pertaining to this trial and similar trials. Some sources could include your previous results.

Tasks to Be Performed

This action outlines the actions the forensic operator will most likely follow once the trial is complete. Use the tasks to create a list of steps necessary to complete the assignment. Some of the specific actions to be performed include:

- Learn from the experience.
- Assess the firm's performance.

- Evaluate performance of each party.
- Update CV.
- Extract show-and-tell components, if feasible.
- Follow up with counsel; grading form.

Potential Issues

This action provides the forensic operator with the potential issues that may be faced once the trial is complete. Some of these issues include continuous professional development.

Deliverables

This action prompts the forensic operator to generate deliverables at the completion of the trial. Some specific deliverables include:

- The verdict.
- The judge's ruling.
- Lessons learned.
- An updated CV.

CONCLUSION

This chapter's contents provided facile exhibit and report construction tools while emphasizing key report techniques and key report contents. Also, the 13 actual reports (BLINDED for confidentiality) contained on the Wiley website (www.wiley.com/go/financialforensics) give forensic operators outstanding reference material to maximize the pertinent phase of a forensic assignment.

PART

Two

Financial Forensics Special Topics

CHAPTER 7

Counterterrorism: Conventional Tools for Unconventional Warfare

Terrorists seek our annihilation. They conspire by any and all means to obliterate us. Their methods are insidious. They exploit our laws and freedoms, which, when compared to their home countries, offer nearly unfettered movement throughout our society to plot and execute their attacks. Consequently, they see our laws and freedoms as avenues by which to achieve their means.

The purpose of this issue of the *United States Attorneys' Bulletin* is to demonstrate how civil laws can be employed through forensic accounting tactics as new weapons in the counterterrorism arsenal. Paraphrasing the FBI's dictum, the United States should use any and all means to "[d]elay, disrupt or dismantle terrorist activities."

STOP THE MONEY—STOP THE TERRORISTS

Terrorists cannot function without money. Consequently, disrupting the flow of money disrupts terrorists' activities is a very effective law enforcement strategy. However, interrupting the money flow is more complex than it would seem.

There are several federal criminal statutes, such as the USA PATRIOT Act, Public Law No. 107-56, Statute 272 (2001), that are designed to disrupt the flow of terrorist money. The USA PATRIOT Act made major changes to the currency reporting laws and the money laundering laws. In addition, the Bank Secrecy Act, 31 U.S.C. §§ 5311-5330, requires many organizations to file suspicious activity reports (SARS) in the event evidence of suspicious transactions is uncovered. The Bank Secrecy Act also requires the filing of currency transaction reports (CTRs) to create a paper trail for large currency transactions.

In an effort to evade detection, terrorists can, and often do, operate on a shoestring. A prime example is the October 2000 bombing of the Navy ship USS

The terrorism content in this chapter was originally published in the United States Attorneys' Bulletin, U.S. Department of Justice, Executive Office of United States Attorneys (EOUSA), National Advocacy Center. They are referenced as: March 2005, Vol. 53 No. 2, Financial Forensics I- Counterterrorism: Conventional Tools for Unconventional Warfare, and May 2005 Vol. 53 No. 3, Financial Forensics II- Forensic Accounting: Counterterrorism Tactical Weaponry. Both issues were authored by Darrell D. Dorrell and Gregory A. Gadawski. The material is reprinted with permission by the National Advocacy Center.

Cole. The bombing killed 17 and wounded 39 US Navy personnel, and nearly sank a $924 million warship. By one estimate, the total cost to terrorists was less than $20,000. The Cole was procured in FY1991 at a cost of about $789 million. This is equal to about $924 million in FY2001 dollars.[1] Complicating matters, legitimate, quasi-legitimate, and fraudulent businesses and business fronts can obscure funds flow so that detection becomes extremely difficult. For example, international waste paper brokers routinely wire substantial sums worldwide in their industry. Conversely, retail storefronts such as restaurants deal in small, individual sums that are large in their aggregate. However, proving that the entities were operated as the instrumentalities of a target operator (terrorist suspect), or determining that the transactions were not executed at reasonably equivalent value, could demonstrate alter ego or fraudulent transfers, or both. This would result in a disruption of money flow or asset access, or both.

Complicating matters, legitimate, quasi-legitimate, and fraudulent business and business fronts can obscure funds flow so that detection becomes extremely difficult. For example, international waste paper brokers routinely wire substantial sums worldwide in their industry. Conversely, retail store fronts, such as restaurants, deal in small individual sums that are large in their aggregate. However, proving that the entities were operated as the instrumentalities of a target operator (terrorist suspect), or determining that the transactions were not executed at reasonably equivalent value, could demonstrate alter ego and/or fraudulent transfers. This would result in disruption of money flow and/or asset access.

Disrupting the money flow must comply with federal, state, and local laws; otherwise the terrorists win. However, not only criminal statutes can be employed. Civil laws and related forensic accounting tools can be employed, which adds to our prosecutorial arsenal.

CIVIL TOOLS USED BY FEDERAL LAW ENFORCEMENT

Federal law enforcement has employed civil tools since the early 1900s. In the 1930s, the US Treasury Department (Treasury) used a cutting-edge forensic accounting tool to defeat America's quasi-terrorist threat—organized crime.

The specific forensic accounting tool used by federal law enforcement was, and still is, known as the net worth method. It was used to help convict Alphonse (Al) Capone in *Capone v. United States,* 51 F.2d 609 (7th Cir. 1931). Using this technique, authorities compared his reported income with his evident income and proved that he had failed to accurately report his financial condition to the Internal Revenue Service (IRS).

Recent nationwide developments indicate that various federal agencies are pursuing civil tools such as alter ego. For example, the three-member Occupational Safety and Health Review Commission, which hears appeals from administrative law judges' decisions, will soon decide whether Occupational Safety and Health Administration (OSHA) regulators should be allowed to pierce the corporate veil and pursue the individuals running companies to hold them, or successor alter ego

[1] Congressional Research Service, Library of Congress, "Terrorist Attack on USS Cole: Background and Issues for Congress," Order Code RS20721, Updated January 30, 2001.

companies, responsible for fines and other enforcement actions.[2] Also, the IRS has routinely disregarded corporate entities in its pursuit of tax evaders in estate and gift matters. See *Strangi v. Commissioner,* 115 T.C. 478, 487 (2000); and *Hackl v. Commissioner,* 118 T.C. 1 (2002). A US District Court in *Baum Hydraulics Corp. v. United States,* 280 F. Supp 2d 910 (D. Neb. 2003), upheld an IRS lien against a corporate alter ego, citing 26 U.S.C. § 6321. Also, *United States v. Reading Co.,* 253 US 26 (1920), is an early example of how federal authorities pursued misuse of the corporate form (alter ego) in a restraint of interstate commerce case. As recently as July 2003, the use of alter ego has been discussed in connection with combating terrorist financing.[3]

Finally, certain statutes make corporate participants personally liable for actions they take or fail to take on behalf of the corporation. See Comprehensive Environmental Response Compensation and Liability Act of 1980 (CERCLA), 42 U.S.C. §§ 9601–9675 (1988). This Act imposes liabilities on certain owners or operators of polluting facilities, thus piercing the corporate veil.

THE CIVIL STATUTES AS COUNTERTERRORISM WEAPONS

The modern-day civil statutory weapons used in forensic accounting consist of the legal doctrine of alter ego, fraudulent transfer, and solvency analysis. These three techniques are discussed in detail next.

Alter Ego

The doctrine of alter ego is applied through various descriptors including:

- Corporate disregard
- Disregarding the corporate entity
- Disregarding its separate corporate existence
- Ignoring the (corporate) fiction
- Piercing the corporate veil

Alter ego in Latin means "second self."[4] In applying the legal doctrine of alter ego, one strives to persuade the court to remove an entity's corporate veil, or intended protection, to expose the owners to judgment. Such action provides access to owners who would otherwise be protected by the entity structure.

Alter ego is commonly employed in combination with a wide range of civil matters (antitrust, breach of fiduciary duty, fraudulent conveyance or transfer, lost

---

[2] Cindy Skrzycki, "Panel Weighs Letting OSHA Pierce the Corporate Veil," *The Washington Post,* March 23, 2004, E1. This article refers to three separate cases brought before the Panel. The cases involved Sharon and Walter Construction Corp., Altor Inc., and Avcon, Inc. The Sharon decision was issued 11/18/10 and the corporate veil was pierced. The Avcon and Altor decisions were issued on 4/5/11 and 4/26/11, respectively, and the corporate veil was not pierced. See the National Chamber Litigation Center website for further details. As of this writing, piercing the corporate veil continues to be pursued as a civil tool.

[3] Jeff Breinholt, "Terrorist Financing," *United States Attorneys' Bulletin* 51, no. 4 (July 2003).

[4] *Black's Law Dictionary* 6th ed. (St. Paul, MN: West Publishing, 1990), 77.

profits, misrepresentation, patent infringement, and others) that seek damages from parties otherwise protected by, or even disassociated with, an entity(ies). A critical component necessary for the court to invoke alter ego consists of control over an entity.

Alter ego is also commonly employed in criminal matters. Robert B. Thompson's 1991 alter ego study found that nearly 67 percent of criminal cases successfully pierced the corporate veil, which was intended to shield the acts of the shareholders. Thompson maintains that "piercing the corporate veil is the most litigated issue in corporate law."[5]

Fraudulent Transfer or Conveyance

The civil tool known as fraudulent transfer or fraudulent conveyance derives from common law and the Bankruptcy Code, 11 U.S.C. § 548. It is typically employed in connection with debtor and creditor relationships where an asset or liability has been transferred for less than reasonably equivalent value within one year of the filing of the bankruptcy petition, with the intent of defeating a creditor's rights.

The common law provisions typically originated from the Uniform Fraudulent Conveyances Act (UFCA) or Uniform Fraudulent Transfer Act (UFTA) and include measurements of badges of fraud that can be employed directly or indirectly. Thus, assets can be recovered and transfers voided when they constitute actual or constructive fraud.

Fraudulent transfer or conveyance is pursued in the same way among federal and state jurisdictions and can be used in combination with a wide array of other matters, including alter ego, solvency, merger, and acquisition.

Solvency

The concept of solvency (and insolvency) is generally familiar to most Americans. However, the definition of solvency is problematic in adjudication. Courts typically require an opinion regarding the solvency (or the lack thereof) of an entity or transaction at a particular time. In such cases, solvency is nearly universally defined as "a company's ability to meet the interest costs and repayment schedules associated with its long-term debt obligations."[6] Solvency analysis uses three tests. These are the balance sheet test, the cash flow test, and the adequate (reasonable) capital test. Each of them is set forth in detail in the Solvency section of this chapter.

Forensic Accounting Techniques

The selected forensic accounting techniques described earlier reflect only a fraction of the tools available to forensic accountants. Nevertheless, they illustrate the breadth and depth of tactics available to federal law enforcement. Selected forensic accounting techniques are defined further on, and a few highly pertinent techniques are highlighted.

---

[5] Robert B. Thompson, "Piercing the Corporate Veil: An Empirical Study," *Cornell Law Journal* 76, 1036 (July 1991).

[6] Robert N. Anthony, *Management Accounting: Text and Cases,* Richard D. Irwin, ed. (New York: McGraw-Hill, 1964), 301.

Benford's Law is the statistical technique for the objective analysis of numerical data sets. The result of a Benford's Law analysis can indicate when a significant portion of a numeric data set contains artificial or contrived numbers, which pinpoints potentially fraudulent transactions. The artificial or contrived numbers are evidenced by the vast numbers of nonrandom, duplicative, and rounded entries. Benford's Law states that digits and digit sequences in a legitimately prepared data set follow a predictable pattern, that is, a geometric sequence. Therefore, each digit and digit combination can be used as a statistical benchmark for the prepared data. The technique applies a data analysis method that identifies possible errors, potential fraud, or other irregularities. Benford's Law is such a potent forensic investigatory tool that it is separately addressed.

Expectations-based statement analysis consists of analyzing the language patterns used by a subject during interviews to assess his truthfulness. The FBI teaches its special agents that specificity can indicate veracity. That is, the statement, "I heard a shot and saw him standing over the body," is less specific than, "I saw him point the gun at the victim, I heard the shot, saw the recoil, and saw the victim clutch his chest and fall." All other things being equal, the second statement is more likely the truth.

A genogram is a diagram of the information gathered during background research, interviews, interrogation, and surveillance. It is often prepared in conjunction with other output such as event analysis. A genogram represents relationships among target subjects and reflects personal connections among other subjects. The genogram maps out relationships and traits that may otherwise be missed.

Proxemics, according to its founder, Edward T. Hall, is the study of humankind's "perception and use of space." It has parallels to kinetic and paralinguistic communications. Proxemics can be considered the forerunner of body language.[7]

A timeline analysis is a powerful tool for demonstrating causal elements of activity-based evidence and also assists in validating parties' claims.

Synergy of the Civil Statutory Weapons

The civil statutory weapons of alter ego, fraudulent transfer, and solvency exhibit unique characteristics that permit them to be used individually or in combination in a wide variety of matters. The forensic accounting techniques discussed earlier support them individually or in combination. Consequently, these weapons offer a synergistic approach that can be modified to the respective target scenario at hand.

The respective techniques can apply beyond the areas of law for which they were originally enacted. For example, solvency tests can be used in nonsolvency cases such as financial analysis in shareholder dissension suits. Fraudulent transfer can be used to analyze mergers and acquisitions.

WHY USE CIVIL LAWS IN ADDITION TO CRIMINAL LAWS?

Employment of civil statutory weapons against terrorists supplements, but does not supplant federal criminal statutes. Forensic accounting techniques are force

[7] Edward T. Hall, *The Silent Language* (New York: Anchor Books, 1990), 83.

multiplier tools. Specifically, low-level terrorist threats can be thwarted with civil tools. This allows scarce law enforcement resources to concentrate on the higher-level, higher-payback terrorist targets. Also, the civil evidence gathering process can be less labor- and-resource-intensive than criminal processes and readily available public information can be accessed and applied in civil processes. Furthermore, the stringent chain of custody evidence requirements do not apply in civil matters.

Civil Laws Supplement Criminal Law

Criminal prosecution can require years to achieve. Civil matters often progress more rapidly based upon evidentiary considerations and related attributes. Furthermore, civil objectives can sometimes be achieved through summary judgments and injunctions, thus accelerating the outcome significantly.

Levels of Proof for Criminal and Civil Laws

Another advantage to using civil laws is that the standard of proof for civil matters is less rigorous than the criminal standard, that is, beyond a reasonable doubt. Nevertheless, both criminal and civil levels of proof constitute a continuum of progressively more stringent requirements.

For criminal matters, such continuum is ordinarily presented as no significant proof, reasonable basis, probable cause, preponderance of evidence, prima facie case, proof beyond a reasonable doubt, and absolute proof of guilt.[8] Their respective measures are presented next.

- No significant proof implies complete doubt or suspicion or a lack of factual support.
- Reasonable basis is a belief that there is a significant possibility that the individual has committed or is about to commit a crime.
- Probable cause is belief that there is a substantial likelihood that the individual committed a crime.
- Preponderance of evidence is belief, based on all the evidence presented, that it is more likely than not that the individual committed a crime.
- Prima facie is belief, based on prosecution evidence only, that the individual is so clearly guilty as to eliminate any reasonable doubt.
- Beyond a reasonable doubt in evidence means fully satisfied, entirely convinced, or satisfied to a moral certainty. The phrase is the equivalent of the words clear, precise, and indubitable.
- Absolute proof of guilt is belief so certain that a defendant is so guilty as to eliminate even reasonable doubts.

For civil matters, the continuum is preponderance of the evidence and clear and convincing evidence.

Preponderance of the evidence is evidence that is of greater weight or more convincing than the evidence that is offered in opposition to it; that is, evidence that

[8] Hazel B. Kerper, *Introduction to the Criminal Justice System,* 2nd ed. (Toronto: Thomson Learning, 1979), 207.

as a whole shows that the fact sought to be proved is more probable than not... is that amount of evidence necessary for the plaintiff to win in a civil case. It is that degree of proof that is more probable than not.[9]

Preponderance is determined by more convincing evidence and its probable truth or accuracy, rather than the amount of evidence. Thus, a clearly knowledgeable witness could provide the preponderance of evidence over many other witnesses delivering weak testimony. Likewise, a signed agreement could carry more weight than testimony regarding the parties' intentions.

Clear and convincing proof results in reasonable certainty of the truth of the ultimate fact in controversy. It is proof that requires more than a preponderance of the evidence but less than proof beyond a reasonable doubt. Clear and convincing proof will be shown where the truth of the facts asserted is highly probable.[10]

Civil standards such as preponderance of the evidence and clear and convincing proof are less onerous than the criminal standard of beyond a reasonable doubt. With less rigorous evidence and proof standards, third parties can be even more effectively employed as consultants, contractors, and witnesses in civil matters.

DISCUSSION OF ALTER EGO

Alter ego, fraudulent transfer, and solvency are discussed in this article by profiling the respective technical and legal guidance. Each topic is supported by actual exhibits successfully employed in civil cases. Although the exhibits and related materials are matters of public record, they were altered so that the parties are unrecognizable.

The alter ego doctrine is addressed most extensively because:

- The doctrine holds the highest promise of directly linking and interrupting terror suspects.
- Alter ego is highly conceptual in nature and has the greatest overall potential for wide application in concert with other elements, both civil and criminal.
- The current technical literature covering alter ego is less comprehensive than either fraudulent transfer or solvency.
- Several comprehensive fraudulent transfer Internet sources already exist, including www.assetprotectiontheory.com, www.fraudulenttransfers.com, and www.irs.gov/irm/part5/.
- Solvency resources already exist, including www.insolvency.com.
- These materials add to the Assistant U.S. Attorneys' counterterrorism arsenal.

Alter ego statutes and precedents vary widely by jurisdiction. However, alter ego claims are ordinarily determined by evaluating the indicators, or indicia, of alter ego. That is, when the preponderance of evidence supports the indicia, then alter ego can

[9] *Black's Law Dictionary,* 6th ed. (St. Paul, MN: West Publishing, 1990), 1182.

[10] Hazel B. Kerper, *Introduction to the Criminal Justice System* 2nd ed. (Toronto: Thomson Learning, 1979), 251.

be granted by the court. Conversely, absence of sufficient indicia can persuade the court to leave the corporate structure intact.[11]

Determination of Alter Ego

In the traditional sense, alter ego is determined by evaluating a parent and subsidiary company's relationship to determine whether the parent (that is, through the controlling party) met the following three crucial conditions with respect to a complainant.

1. The parent exercised control and authority to the extent that the subsidiary was a mere instrumentality of the parent.
2. The parent committed a fraud or wrong with respect to the complainant.
3. The complainant suffered an injury as a result of the fraud or wrong (causation).

Note that all three conditions must be met for the court to invoke alter ego.

A parent company is defined as a "company owning more than 50 percent of the voting shares, or otherwise a controlling interest, of another company, called the subsidiary."[12] *Subsidiary* is defined as "[u]nder another's control. [The] [t]erm is often short for 'subsidiary corporation; that is, one that is run and owned by another company which is called the parent.''[13] A *holding company* is defined as "[a] company that usually confines its activities to owning stock in, and supervising management of, other companies."[14]

The classic alter ego matter is based on the traditional parent-child corporate structure in which a parent, or holding company, owns a controlling interest in a subsidiary entity. However, other relationships may exhibit alter ego characteristics, including sister corporations and brother-sister corporate structures. Finally, multiple parent-subsidiary-brother-sister corporate structures and tiered parent-subsidiary-brother-sister corporate structures may exhibit alter ego characteristics. *Sister corporation* is defined as "[t]wo corporations having common or substantially common ownership by same shareholders.[15] *Brother-sister corporation* is defined as "[m]ore than one corporation owned by the same shareholders."[16]

Improper Purpose

Use of the corporate entity for an improper purpose is at the heart of corporate veil cases. The types of situations in which such improper activities arise are classified under five headings, but the most pertinent activity is the violation of public policy, including evasion of statutes.

---

[11] Note that selected portions of this alter ego discussion have been adapted, with permission, from Darrell D. Dorrell and Christine A. Kosydar, "Alter Ego Diagnosis to Find Potentially Hidden Assets in Divorce Cases," *American Journal of Family Law* 18, no. 7 (2004).

[12] *Black's Law Dictionary*, 6th ed. (St. Paul, MN: West Publishing, 1990), 1114.

[13] Id. at 1428.

[14] Id. at 731.

[15] *Battelstein Inv. Co. v. United States*, 302 F. Supp. 320, 322 (S.D. Tex. 1969). Id. at 1387.

[16] Id. at 194.

The origin of the corporate veil doctrine arose as a result of violations or evasions of some statute or other strong public policy through the instrumentality of a subservient corporation.[17] *United States v. Reading Co.*, 253 US 26 (1920), is an early example of the misuse of the corporate form and demonstrates that the doctrine has long been wielded as a weapon by federal authorities.

The general rule cited by these authorities is usually cast in the words of Judge Sanborn in *United States v. Milwaukee Refrigerator Transit,* 142 F. 247, 255 (E.D. Wis. 1905).

If any general rule can be laid down in the present state of authority, it is that a corporation will be looked upon as a legal entity as a general rule and until sufficient reason to the contrary appears; but, when the notion of legal entity is used to defeat public convenience, justify wrong, protect fraud, or defend crime, the law will regard the corporation as an association of persons.

Beneficial Interest

Stock ownership, however, is not an absolute requirement for piercing the veil. A more precise requirement is that the dominant party must have some beneficial interest in the subservient corporation. In *Soderberg Advertising v. Kent-Moore Corp.,* 524 P.2d 1355 (Wash. Ct. App. 1974), the defendant had an option to acquire the subservient corporation but no actual stock ownership. Pursuant to contractual agreements, however, the optionee had effective control over the subservient corporation and a beneficial interest because of his right to purchase the company. In connection with other factors, it was found that the dominant party was, in fact, liable for certain actions taken through the instrumentality of the subservient corporation.

The doctrine can apply if the interest held is either control or minority interest in a subsidiary entity. Alter ego characteristics are also encountered between unrelated entities lacking any indication of formal corporate relationships. For example, a shareholder held separate controlling interests in corporation A and unrelated corporation B. Corporation A held a few subsidiaries, and unrelated corporation B held several multiple-tiered subsidiaries, some of which were inactive.

On paper, the two parent corporations appear separate and distinct and the only obvious relationship is the common controlling shareholder. Nonetheless, the group of companies exhibited many alter ego characteristics. Significant asset conveyances were conducted between and among the corporation's subsidiaries without fair market value consideration, and product marketing and labeling contained a confusing and inconsistent use of corporate names. The product names were portrayed to customers without identification of corporate ownership. Furthermore, legal and financial justification was obtained after the fact for certain event-specific transactions. Finally, receipts and disbursements were transacted through the subsidiary providing the most benefit to the parent.

[17] See Henry Ballantine, *Corporations* rev. ed. (Chicago: Callaghan, 1946), § 122; Harry G. Henn, *Law of Corporations,* 2nd ed., (Eagan, MN: West Publishing, 1970), § 252; Frederick J. Powell, *Parent and Subsidiary Corporations* (Chicago: Callaghan, 1931), § 1.

Exhibit 7.1 was constructed in a civil matter in which the plaintiff sought to pierce several of the defendant's corporate veils in order to recover payment pursuant to a triggered contingent lease liability. The Target Subject Group was a large, closely held multistate group of companies with a long history of acquiring smaller companies to enlarge its business. Target gained control of Acquired Subject & Sons, Inc. in its usual manner, noting that there was a contingent lease liability attached to the entity. The acquisition agreement attempted to indemnify the target from the contingent liability, but it did not provide sufficient protection.

The Target Subject Group acquired the smaller company for $21 million (cash, stock, and debt) in the year 2000 and duly recorded the transaction in various records (corporate purchase agreement, general ledger, audited financial statements, and income tax returns). In late 2001, however, the acquired company's $24 million contingent lease liability was triggered (post-acquisition). Consequently, the Target Subject Group attempted to rerecord the transaction at a near-zero value, advising the creditor that they could have the stock, now worth $700,000, instead of the original acquisition price.

The rerecording of the initial acquisition transaction was quite complex and involved competent attorneys and accountants who provided technical advice. The advisors recommended a framework that required the transfer of operating assets (without contingent liabilities) and the revaluation of a new class of stock. See Exhibit 7.1: Target Subject Group.

The plaintiff was faced with two significant challenges. First, if he began his challenge at the lowest level in the organization chart, Acquired Subject & Sons, Inc. (at the lower right-hand corner of Exhibit 7.1), he might be compelled to pierce the veils of several companies at successively higher levels. The second, and greater, challenge was almost insurmountable. The ownership was common among one shareholder, but separate and distinct between the two groups of companies as indicated by the dotted-line borders on the left-hand and right-hand sides of Exhibit 7.1. Therefore, the plaintiff sought to pierce the veil directly, through a one-shot–one-kill technique whereby the Acquired Subject & Sons, Inc. entity could be directly linked to the controlling shareholder. This is illustrated by the bold, double-arrowed line connecting Owner (shaded, in the upper left-hand corner of Exhibit 7.1) to Acquired Subject & Sons, Inc. (shaded, in the lower right-hand corner of Exhibit 7.1).

Exhibit 7.1 is the corporate organizational chart illustrating the entire group of entities comprising the defendant's companies. The chart indicates that 21 companies were contained within the overall target group, but some entities were not delineated for the sake of clarity (lower left-hand corner under the heading "Entities Unaccounted For"). The composition of Exhibit 7.1 is best reviewed from the left-right, top-down perspective as described next.

Beginning in the upper left-hand corner, the first item of information, containing the column headings of "Shares" and "%," identifies for each shareholder their respective ownership amounts and percentages for the left-hand dotted-line group of companies. Specifically, the Owner (name withheld) holds 1,178,628 shares, representing 65.5 percent of the group of companies contained within the left-hand dotted-line group of companies. Also, the same party holds 58,668 units, representing 3.3 percent of the outstanding units of the group of companies contained within the right-hand dotted-line group of companies.

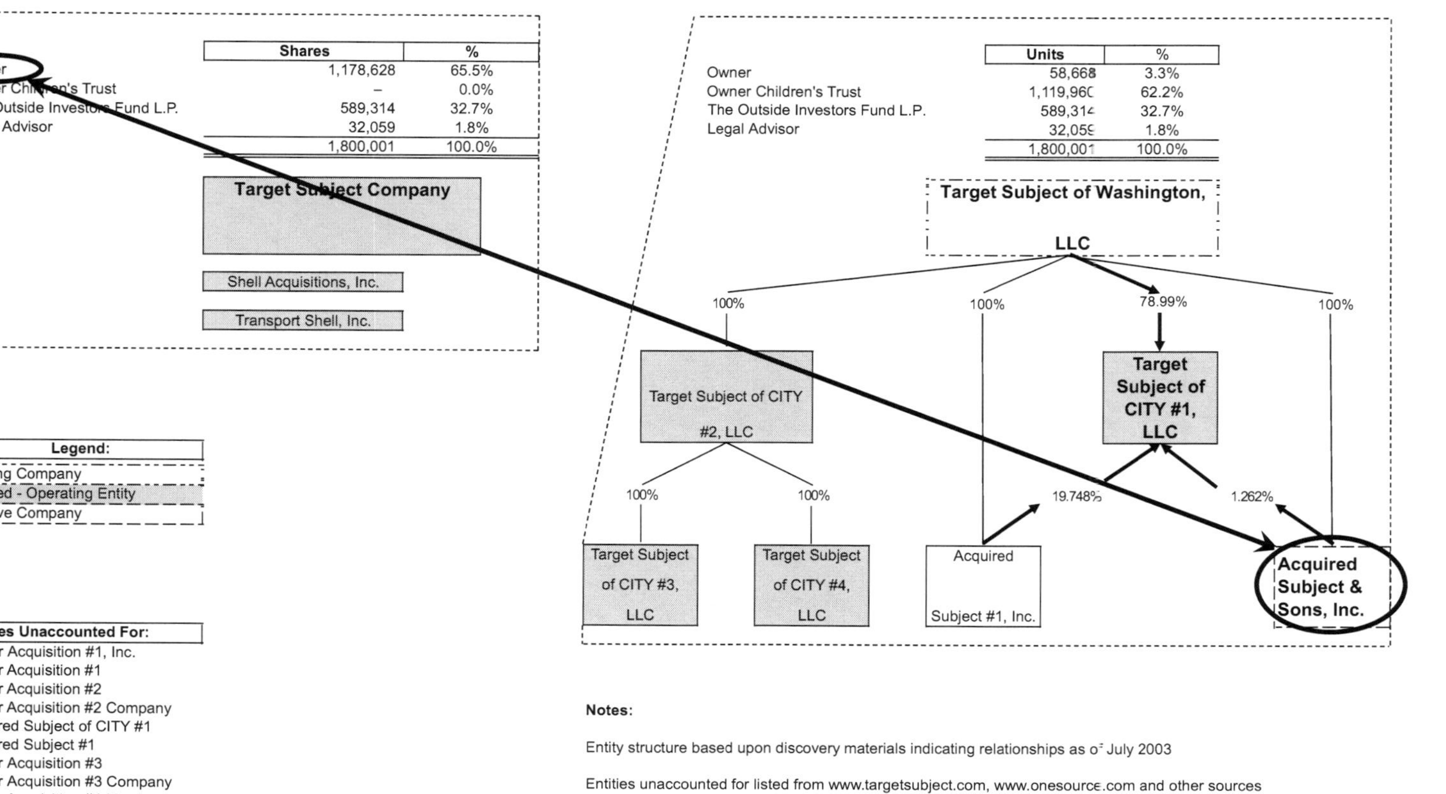

EXHIBIT 7.1 Target Subject Group

The left-hand dotted-line group of companies is composed of the Target Subject Company (bold font) and its wholly owned affiliates, Shell Acquisitions, Inc. and Transport Shell, Inc. Note that there are no ownership connections of any sort to the right-hand dotted-line group of companies.

The right-hand dotted-line group of companies is composed of the Target Subject of Washington, LLC (bold font) and its wholly owned, partially owned, and affiliate-owned affiliates. Note that Target Subject of Washington, LLC owns 100 percent of the Target Subject of CITY #2, LLC. That entity in turn owns 100 percent of Target Subject of CITY #3, LLC and also owns 100 percent of Target Subject of City 4, LLC. The names of the respective cities are withheld for confidentiality since the matter deals with territorial franchises.

Note also within the right-hand dotted-line group of companies that Target Subject of Washington, LLC (bold font) owns 78.99 percent of Target Subject of CITY 1, LLC (bold font). Target Subject of CITY #1, LLC is in turn partially owned (19.748 percent) by Acquired Subject #1, LLC and 1.262 percent of Acquired Subject & Sons, Inc., respectively. Note that there are no ownership connections of any sort to the left-hand dotted-line group of companies.

The litigation was triggered by post-acquisition transactions involving Acquired Subject & Sons, Inc. The legend at the middle-left portion of Exhibit 7.1 shows a dotted-line box for Acquired Subject & Sons, Inc. indicating that it was an "Inactive Company."

The challenge of persuading the court to invoke alter ego lay in the utter disconnectedness of the two groups of companies. That is, the groups of companies reflected by the left-hand and right-hand dotted-line rectangles had no legal connection. By design of the plaintiff, and upon advice of counsel, they were structured to appear separate and distinct.

The bold, double-arrowed line connecting the upper left-hand shaded Owner cell with the lower right-hand shaded Acquired Subject & Sons, Inc. cell demonstrates how alter ego was used to connect the seemingly disparate groups of companies. It was determined that if alter ego attributes could be shown, then the attempted separation of all the entities would be disregarded by the court, and the plaintiff would receive his desired award. The tactic was effective, since the defendant realized that connecting his actions to the right-hand group of companies through alter ego would expose his entire corporate empire to liability.

ALTER EGO LITERATURE

This section details primary alter ego sources from inception to date.

Frederick J. Powell

Frederick J. Powell's book *Parent and Subsidiary Corporations* (1931) is a landmark text that established guidelines for assessing the instrumentality rule and the 11 circumstances that may be indicative of alter ego. Mr. Powell's 1931 work must be read in its entirety to reap the full appreciation of his guidance. In particular, he is credited with establishing the instrumentality rule. Salient elements crystallize his viewpoint as indicated next.

Section 5: The Instrumentality Rule The Instrumentality Rule, in its shortest form, may now be stated:

> *So far as the question of control alone is concerned, the parent corporation will be responsible for the obligations of its subsidiary when its control has been exercised to such a degree that the subsidiary has become its mere instrumentality.*[18]

The instrumentality rule is recognized in all jurisdictions in this country and our problem therefore is to determine the circumstances which render the subsidiary an "instrumentality" within the meaning of the decisions. This is primarily a question of fact and of degree.

Section 6: The Circumstances Rendering the Subsidiary an Instrumentality It is manifestly impossible to catalogue the infinite variations of fact that can arise but there are certain common circumstances which are important and which, if present in the proper combination, are controlling. These are as follows:

1. The parent corporation owns all or most of the capital stock of the subsidiary.
2. The parent and subsidiary corporations have common directors or officers.
3. The parent corporation finances the subsidiary.
4. The parent corporation subscribes to all the capital stock of the subsidiary or otherwise causes its incorporation.
5. The subsidiary has grossly inadequate capital.
6. The parent corporation pays the salaries and other expenses or losses of the subsidiary.
7. The subsidiary has substantially no business except with the parent corporation or no assets except those conveyed to it by the parent corporation.
8. In the papers of the parent corporation or in the statements of its officers, the subsidiary is described as a department or division of the parent corporation, or its business or financial responsibility is referred to as the parent corporation's own.
9. The parent corporation uses the property of the subsidiary as its own.
10. The directors or executives of the subsidiary do not act independently in the interest of the subsidiary but take their orders from the parent corporation in the latter's interest.
11. The formal legal requirements of the subsidiary are not observed.[19]

Powell explained his rationale for each of the preceding circumstances as indicated next.

(a) The parent corporation owns all or most of the capital stock of the subsidiary.

It is familiar law in all jurisdictions in this country that ownership of stock alone will not render the parent corporation liable. This is but a statement of

[18] Id. at 8–9.

[19] Id.

the fundamental rule that stockholders are not liable for the corporate obligations. The result is the same whether the parent company owns all the stock, or all except directors' qualifying shares or a small amount in outside hands. The immunity, of course, extends to the normal exercise of a stockholder's rights, such as the election of directors, changes in the capital stock structure and the approval of the usual activities of the Board of Directors on behalf of the Corporation. This element of stock ownership is present in practically all the parent and subsidiary cases, and in the absence of unique circumstances (as where dominance is achieved through written contract or express agency), control by stock ownership is essential to the application of the Instrumentality Rule.

(b) The parent and subsidiary corporations have common directors or officers.

It is also clear that the parent corporation does not lose its immunity as a stockholder simply by furnishing from its own personnel the directors and principal officers of the subsidiary. In the case of principal subsidiaries, this is the usual practice. The officers of the two corporations are often the same in large part, and at least a majority of the subsidiary's directors are usually directors of the parent corporation. This common personnel, however, is an important factor in the application of the instrumentality rule, and in nearly all the cases in which the parent corporation has been held liable, we find this element or else dummy or subservient directors or executives of the subsidiary.

(c) The parent corporation finances the subsidiary.

The parent corporation is the natural source of the subsidiary's credit, and generally it is the most efficient source, for normally it has superior resources and can capitalize the increment in value due to the combination and co-ordination of several subsidiaries under a common supervisory management. Accordingly, the fact alone that the parent corporation finances the subsidiary will not subject the parent corporation to liability, although stock ownership and common personnel are also present. But this element of financing is important.

Thus far we find the law squaring with conventional business practice but we approach the danger line when we introduce additional elements showing a further exercise of control by the parent corporation. One or more of these additional elements is present in nearly all the cases in which judgment has been rendered against the parent corporation. As already indicated, a hard and fast rule cannot be laid down but, as a rough guide, it may be stated, generally, that proof of the following additional elements (sometimes one and often two) will be sufficient to hold the parent corporation. Some, of course, are more important than others.

(d) The parent corporation subscribes to all the capital stock of the subsidiary or otherwise causes its incorporation.

If the ownership of all the capital stock of a subsidiary and the normal exercise of the rights incident to that ownership do not destroy the immunity of the parent corporation, the acquisition of an existing corporation by purchase of its capital stock is of course equally harmless. And there is no reason why the parent corporation should not accomplish the same purpose—and with the same results—by itself causing the incorporation of the subsidiary in the first instance. Except in the case of railroads and public utilities, this is probably the commonest method by which a system of parent and subsidiary corporations is built up.

If, therefore, the degree of control exercised by the parent corporation is not sufficient to constitute the subsidiary a mere instrumentality, the further fact that the parent corporation caused the subsidiary to be organized will not force the case over the line. But in weighing all the circumstances in a given case, it is an evidential fact of value, particularly when it can be shown that the corporation was organized for a special purpose, such as the creation of a new or enlarged department.

Sometimes (particularly in the so-called one-man corporation cases), the courts point out that the purpose of organizing or maintaining the subsidiary was to secure the profits if it succeeded and to avoid the losses if it failed. This though must be applied with caution for of course this is a principal object of most incorporations and, by itself, is a lawful purpose. When a claim is based on the organization of the subsidiary as a step in an alleged scheme to defraud creditors [see § 13(a)], a finding of this special purpose is often vital.

(e) The subsidiary has grossly inadequate capital.

Manifestly, the fact that the subsidiary's capital is wholly disproportionate to the amount of the business that it actually conducts, is strong proof that it is a mere dummy or arm of the parent corporation. In the well-known Luckenbach Steamship case, two corporations were controlled by a common stockholder. One of them turned over steamers worth hundreds of thousands of dollars to the other which had a capital of only ten thousand dollars and which operated them under leases at a rental based on far below their real value. "Putting aside an inquiry into the motive for this arrangement" the Court found it would be "unconscionable to allow the owner" to escape liability by turning them over "to a $10,000 corporation, which is simply itself in another form."

This does not impugn the principle that the parent corporation may finance the subsidiary without subjecting itself to liability. That the parent corporation should be the principal or sole source of the subsidiary's credit from time to time, is one thing. But that it should launch the subsidiary in business without furnishing the appropriate funds or obligating itself to do so, is quite another. If the subsidiary is financially helpless and, through the fault of the parent corporation can call on the parent corporation for capital funds only when and if the parent corporation pleases to grant them, it is cogent evidence that the subsidiary is a mere tool in the hands of the parent.

It does not follow that a parent corporation may not organize a subsidiary, permit it to build up a business and then may not refuse in whole or in part to act as the subsidiary's banker. If there are no other circumstances on which to ground an application of the Instrumentality Rule, the mere fact that the parent has not furnished the subsidiary with adequate capital will not bring the Rule into play. In other words, this element of inadequate capital is merely persuasive but not controlling. The question of estoppel in these cases is discussed in § 13(e).

(f) The parent corporation pays the salaries and other expenses or losses of the subsidiary.

This reference is not to the case in which the parent corporation ultimately finances the expenses or losses of the subsidiary. The general right to finance is, as we have seen, clear. But where the subsidiary has no funds or means to meet its payroll or other current expenses, or its trade losses as they occur, and the parent corporation from its own treasury directly and regularly pays these bills as if the employees and business were its own, a strong case against the parent corporation is made out.

(g) The subsidiary has substantially no business except with the parent corporation, or no assets except those conveyed to it by the parent corporation.

These facts tend to show a position of subordination on the part of the subsidiary and lend color to the claim that it is not conducted as a separate corporation but just as if it were a mere department of the parent corporation. Here again a distinction must be made. A corporation which manufactures automobiles may have a wholly owned subsidiary that does nothing but supply it with batteries. If all the separate legal requirements of the subsidiary as a distinct corporation are observed, the parent corporation does not become subject to the obligations of the subsidiary, even though the latter, as a practical matter, is a department or division of the parent corporation. This "department" or "division" formula, enunciated in some of the cases as the test of the parent corporation's liability, should therefore not be regarded as an absolute equivalent of the Instrumentality Rule but rather as a concrete description or partial summary of certain circumstances properly entering into the application of the Rule.

(h) In the papers of the parent corporation or in the statements of its officers, the subsidiary is described as a department or division of the parent corporation, or its business or financial responsibility is referred to as the parent corporation's own.

Proof to this effect has a double function. It may create a so-called estoppel, and under the "department" or division" formula it is also probative of the fact of subordination. The former question is discussed later in § 13 (e); the latter, in the preceding subdivision.

(i) The parent corporation uses the property of the subsidiary as its own.

This reference is to cases in which the parent corporation helps itself to the cash and other property of the subsidiary as if it owned them directly. Direct appropriation by the parent corporation of the subsidiary's profits without any declaration of dividends by the latter's directorate, is an illustration. This is almost always fatal proof against the parent corporation.

(j) The directors or executives of the subsidiary do not act independently in the interest of the subsidiary, but take their orders from the parent corporation in the latter's interest.

The Instrumentality Rule cannot be circumvented by equipping the subsidiary with directors or officers who are ostensibly, but not actually, independent of the parent corporation. If, in fact, they took their orders from the parent corporation or someone who controlled it, and acted in the interest of the parent corporation rather than the subsidiary, the record names and formal setup will not avail. The result is the same where the same persons are directors of both corporations, but act in the interest of the parent corporation.

Direct proof of this affirmative subserviency of the subsidiary's officers is conclusive of the case against the parent corporation, insofar as the Instrumentality Rule is concerned. But such direct proof is not forthcoming. Usually this subserviency is an ultimate fact to be deduced from all the facts of the case and the other elements previously discussed indicate the circumstances which often are available for this purpose.

(k) The formal legal requirements of the subsidiary are not observed.

The observance of the technical formalities legally incident to the operation of the subsidiary as a separate corporation is very helpful in avoiding the Instrumentality Rule. Thus, proof that meetings of the subsidiary's stockholders and directors were held, that minutes were properly kept, that the subsidiary made its separate statutory reports, maintained its own books of account, had its own bank account and paid its own bills, is strong evidence against the parent corporation's liability. But the observance of these formalities is all of no avail when the proof as a whole shows that in the actual conduct of the business the parent corporation completely dominated the subsidiary and used it as a mere creature. Payment of rent by the subsidiary to the parent corporation, the use of separate letter or bill-heads, the existence of formal contracts between them, etc., are all futile when they are essentially nothing but sham or paper transactions.[20]

Finally, nearly all references to Powell overlook the following clarification found later in his book when he pulls together his commentary in application to an alter ego case:

Section 26: Complainant's Case

Except in cases of express agency of the subsidiary, or the actual commission of a tort by the parent corporation, either alone or jointly with the subsidiary, there are three essential elements in the complainant's cause of action against the parent corporation. He must prove first, that the parent corporation has exercised its control over the subsidiary, not in the manner normal and usual with stockholders, but to such a degree that it has reduced the subsidiary to a mere instrumentality; second, that this control has been exercised in such a way as to constitute fraud, wrong or injustice with respect to the complainant; and third, that (except in cases of so-called estoppel) a refusal to disregard the separate corporate entity of the subsidiary would result in unjust loss or injury to the complainant.

Taking up these three elements in order:

First Element: Defendant's Control The following constitute the exercise of normal and usual control over the subsidiary:

(a) Causing the subsidiary to be organized;

(b) Acquiring and holding all its capital stock;

(c) Exercising the usual voting rights of stockholders, including the election of directors, ratification of the acts of directors and officers, changes in capital stock structure, etc.;

[20] Id. at 10–19.

(d) Furnishing the subsidiary with the same directors and officers that the parent corporation has;
(e) Financing the subsidiary.

The following constitute the exercise of abnormal control and reduce the subsidiary to a mere instrumentality:

(a) Disregarding the formal legal requirements of the subsidiary as a separate corporation. Illustrations are: failing to hold meetings of its board of directors and stockholders or to keep separate bank accounts, books and other business papers, or to distribute dividends by way of declaration, etc. But observance of these formal requirements will not avail if the subsidiary is run as a mere puppet or creature of the parent corporation.
(b) Operating the subsidiary in the interests of the parent corporation and not in the interests of the subsidiary; in other words, using the subsidiary as a mere branch or division without regard to its separate interests and rights. The usual evidence of this is the fact that the subsidiary is managed on the direct orders of the parent corporation's officers in their capacity of the representatives of the parent corporation, or that the parent corporation directly handles the property of the subsidiary as if it were its own.

Persuasive evidence that the subsidiary is a mere instrumentality are the facts that it has no business except with the parent corporation or no assets except those conveyed to it by the parent corporation; that its capital is grossly disproportionate to the volume of its business; that the parent corporation pays its salaries or other expenses, or its losses; and that in the papers or statements of the parent company or its officers, the subsidiary is referred to as a mere department or division of the parent corporation, or its business of financial responsibility as the parent's own.[21]

Section 28: Working Chart of Proper Parent and Subsidiary Corporation Management To keep the parent corporation immune from liability for the obligations of its subsidiary, two pitfalls must be avoided: first, a violation of the formal corporate requirements of the subsidiary, and second, a disregard of its separate business interests.

The subsidiary, if a new corporation, must, of course, be incorporated and organized in accordance with statute. The representatives of the parent corporation may be its incorporators and subscribe to all its capital stock. After organization, periodic meetings of stockholders and directors should be held as required by statute and the by-laws. Minutes of these meetings should be permanently recorded in proper form.

A separate bank account, separate books of account and separate letter and bill-heads should be kept, and all other paperwork individual to the subsidiary's business, should be maintained separately.

The subsidiary should be furnished with a reasonable amount of capital. This may be done by the parent corporation and it is not essential that all the capital

[21] Id. at 103–104.

be supplied at the same time. Nor is it necessary that the parent corporation legally obligate itself to furnish any specific amount. But, on the other hand, the subsidiary should from time to time be furnished with an amount proportionate to its growing business and it should have a reasonable amount with which to begin business.

The subsidiary's receivables should, in the absence of good business reasons to the contrary, be collected and banked by it, not the parent corporation. Its expenses should be paid out of its own bank account unless they involve an apportionment of overhead expenses paid by the parent corporation in the first instance, but in that case the method of apportionment should be accurately and clearly agreed upon as a matter of record between the two corporations, and their respective books of account should precisely show the corresponding debits and credits. If care is constantly exercised, expenses chargeable only to the subsidiary and not involving any apportionment between it and the parent corporation or other subsidiaries can be paid in the first instance by the parent corporation and then charged to the subsidiary. In this practice, however, it is easy for things to drift into the position in which the parent corporation in the first instance is spending large sums for the account of the subsidiary and later seeing that the proper corporate action is taken by the subsidiary to reimburse or credit it. This is dangerous meddling with the immunity of the parent corporation as stockholder of the subsidiary, and carelessness or neglect may often result in just such a condition creeping into a large organization, although everyone concerned is acting in entire good faith. When circumstances will permit, it is preferable to have the parent corporation advance the necessary moneys to the subsidiary (on open account or otherwise) and then have the subsidiary expend them from its own treasury, and in accordance with antecedent corporate authority on its part. Such advances should be based on proper corporate authorization, and accompanied by proper corporate records, on behalf of both corporations. The authorization may be general or confined to specific instances from time to time.

The profits of the subsidiary should be distributed to the parent corporation by way of dividends with the usual declaration on board resolution, and not informally appropriated by the parent corporation. And in all ways, the parent corporation should never directly use assets of the subsidiary as if they were its own. The direct physical operation of the subsidiary must be through the subsidiary's own officers and through its own channels as a separate corporation, and not as a mere department of the parent corporation operated directly by the corporate organization of the parent corporation.

The second requirement that the business of the subsidiary must be run in its interest and not that of the parent corporation is not usually difficult to observe. It is safer to equip the subsidiary with the same personnel as that of the parent corporation than to use clerks or subordinates. Theoretically the latter's actions might be entirely for the benefit of the subsidiary and as judicious as those of an independent directorate—but a board of minor employees can hardly be independent, and this set-up breeds suspicion and is a badge of undue subserviency that will prove very damaging to the parent corporation in any suit against it by the subsidiary's creditors.

The subsidiary's directors, whoever they are, must, of course, run the business in its own interest. They must not be improvident with its resources even though their action may, for extraneous reasons, benefit the parent corporation. But the relationship between the two corporations, their normal identity in business interest and the fact that the parent corporation is in a position to benefit the subsidiary in so many ways, gives the subsidiary's directors ample discretion to adjust its affairs to those of the parent corporation for all legitimate purposes and within all reasonable limits. In the ordinary run of business, the interests of the parent and subsidiary are the same and no question should arise. If the time comes when the larger interests of the parent corporation conflict with the smaller interests of the subsidiary, the parent corporation should dissolve or merge the subsidiary and absorb its business or else dispose of the subsidiary and thus place it at arm's length.

The parent's executives should be most careful with respect to their written or oral representations regarding the relationship between the parent and the subsidiary. To say that the subsidiary is a subsidiary of the parent corporation or that the parent corporation owns all its capital stock or has financed it in the past, is unobjectionable. But to say that the parent corporation will finance the subsidiary in the future and that it will stand back of the subsidiary's obligations or that the situation is the same as if the customer or creditor were dealing with the parent corporation, is almost always fatal. And the common business practice of describing the subsidiary as a division or department of the parent corporation on letterheads, is dangerous, and in some jurisdictions would be sufficient to turn the scales against the parent corporation. Consolidated financial statements, if properly entitled, are in order.

The preceding requirements square with all legitimate business requirements. They are but an observance of good corporate practice and by insisting on those requirements, the law imposes no undue burden on business, but merely demands that there shall be no abuse of the privilege to do business in corporate form. If these limitations are not in accord with the exigencies of the case, the business is not adaptable to management through the medium of parent and subsidiary corporations.[22]

The Krendls' 1978 Study

The Krendls published a superb case summary titled *Piercing the Corporate Veil: Focusing the Inquiry,* cited earlier, which contains a list of factors that should be used when "attempting to keep the corporate veil intact." The factors are supported by the pertinent cases in their article and are summarized here.

- The shareholder is not a party to the contractual or other obligations of the corporation.
- The subsidiary is not undercapitalized.
- The subsidiary does not operate at a deficit while the parent is showing a profit.
- The creditors of the companies are not misled as to the company with which they are dealing.

[22] Id. at 108–111. See also *Beckeley v. Third Avenue Railway,* 155 N.E. 58 (N.Y. 1926); Henry Ballantine, "Parent and Subsidiary Corporations," *California Law Review* 14, no. 34 (1925); Maurice I. Wormser, *The Disregard of the Corporate Fiction and Allied Corporate Problems* (Greenfield, MA: T. Morey & Son, 1927); Cathy J. Krendl and James R. Krendl, "Piercing the Corporate Veil: Focusing the Inquiry," *Denver Law Journal* 55, no. 1 (1978); Robert B. Thompson, "Piercing the Corporate Veil: An Empirical Study," *Cornell Law Review* 76, no. 1036 (July 1991).

- Creditors are not misled as to the financial strength of the subsidiary.
- The employees of the parent and subsidiary are separate and the parent does not hire and fire employees of the subsidiary.
- The payroll of the subsidiary is paid by the subsidiary and the salary levels are set by the subsidiary.
- The labor relations of the two companies are handled separately and independently.
- The parent and subsidiary maintain separate offices and telephone numbers.
- Separate directors' meetings are conducted.
- The subsidiary maintains financial books and records that contain entries related to its own operations.
- The subsidiary has its own bank account.
- The earnings of the subsidiary are not reflected on the financial reports of the parent in determining the parent's income.
- The companies do not file joint income tax returns.
- The subsidiary negotiates its own loans or other financing.
- The subsidiary does not borrow money from the parent.
- Loans and other financial transactions between the parent and subsidiary are properly documented and conducted on an arm's-length basis.
- The parent does not guarantee the loans of the subsidiary or secure any loan with assets of the parent.
- The subsidiary's income represents a small percentage of the total income of the parent.
- The insurance of the two companies is maintained separately and each pays its own premiums.
- The purchasing activities of the two corporations are handled separately.
- The two companies avoid advertising as a joint activity or other public relations that indicate that they are the same organization.
- The parent and subsidiary avoid referring to each other as one family, organization, or as divisions of one another.
- The equipment and other goods of the parent and subsidiary are separate.
- The two companies do not exchange assets or liabilities.
- There are no contracts between the parent and subsidiary with respect to purchasing goods and services from each other.
- The subsidiary and parent do not deal exclusively with each other.
- The parent does not review the subsidiary's contracts, bids, or other financial activities in greater detail than would be normal for a shareholder who is merely interested in the profitability of the business.
- The parent does not supervise the manner in which the subsidiary's jobs are carried out.
- The parent does not have a substantial veto power over important business decisions of the subsidiary and does not itself make such crucial decisions.
- The parent and subsidiary are engaged in different lines of business.[23]

[23] Cathy J. Krendl and James R. Krendl, "Piercing the Corporate Veil: Focusing the Inquiry," *Denver Law Journal* 55, no. 1 (1978).

Thompson's 1991 Study

Robert B. Thompson's study, "Piercing the Corporate Veil: An Empirical Study," shows how alter ego was used by various courts to pierce the corporate veil. His study comprised 1,583 cases of alter ego, and found that certain factors tended to be associated with the courts' decisions to invoke alter ego and thus pierce the veil. The factors include:

- The subsidiary is an "instrumentality" of the parent.
- The subsidiary is the alter ego of the parent.
- The subsidiary is the "dummy" of the parent.
- The case involved misrepresentation of corporate separateness.[24]

Interestingly, Thompson found that when alter ego was not granted by the court, the plaintiff had most often failed to prove misrepresentation.[25]

ALTER EGO JURISDICTIONAL EXAMPLES

The following are some representative examples.

Federal Alter Ego

In general, a corporation is viewed as a legal entity separate and distinct from its shareholders, directors, officers, and affiliated corporations. Accordingly, as indicated in a 1998 U.S. Supreme Court ruling, a parent corporation will ordinarily not be held liable for the acts of its subsidiaries.[26]

Despite the disparity among jurisdictions, the standard for piercing the corporate veil is generally stated as having two aspects.

- The parent dominates a subsidiary's finances, operations, policies, and practices such that the subsidiary has no separate existence, but is merely a conduit of the parent.[27]
- The parent has abused the privilege of incorporation by using the subsidiary to perpetrate a fraud or injustice or otherwise circumvent the law.[28,29]

---

[24] Robert B. Thompson, "Piercing the Corporate Veil: An Empirical Study," *Cornell Law Review* 76, no. 1036 (July 1991).

[25] Roman L. Weil et al., *Litigation Services Handbook: The Role of the Financial Expert* 3rd ed. (New York: John Wiley & Sons, 2001), § 38.1.

[26] See *United States v. Bestfoods,* 524 U.S. 51, 60 (1998).

[27] See *Craig v. Lake Asbestos of Quebec,* 843 F.2d 145, 149 (3d Cir. 1988).

[28] See, for example, *Bestfoods,* 524 U.S. at 62; *Craig,* 843 F.2d at 149 (stating New Jersey law); In re *Hillsborough Holdings,* 176 B.R. 223, 231 (M.D. Fla. 1994).

[29] Richard M. Cieri, Lyle G. Ganske and Heather Lennox, "Breaking Up Is Hard to Do: Avoiding the Solvency-Related Pitfalls in Spinoff Transactions," *The Business Lawyer* 54 (February 1999): 533–552.

Certain federal alter ego matters use similar criteria. The United States Court of Federal Claims has adopted a three-part test in cases of corporate disregard wherein three questions must be considered.

1. Whether one corporation completely dominates the other so that it is merely an alter ego.
2. Whether such domination is used to commit fraud or injustice.
3. Whether such domination proximately causes the unjust loss.[30]

State Alter Ego

State courts have built upon the two characteristics of control and improper conduct (and injury) by constructing alter ego criteria ranging from 2 to 11 parts as indicated next.

Under California law and other state jurisdictions a two-part test may result in the disregard of a corporate entity.

1. Where there is such unity of interest and ownership that separate personalities of the two entities no longer exist.
2. Where an equitable result would follow if the corporations were treated as separate entities.[31]

   Plaintiffs in California are not required to demonstrate causation between improper conduct and harm to the plaintiff. An inequitable result is sufficient.

Oregon's strict requirements are more specific and perhaps more challenging to satisfy than the two-prong test used in California and other jurisdictions. Specifically, the Oregon Supreme Court has ruled that: "[t]he disregard of a legally established corporate entity is an extraordinary remedy which exists as a last resort, where there is no other adequate and available remedy to repair the plaintiff's injury."[32]

In Oregon's seminal alter ego case, *AmFac,* the court listed as four indicia of improper conduct.

1. Inadequate capitalization.
2. Milking.
3. Misrepresentation, commingling, and holding out.
4. Violation of statute.[33]

However, the court explained that these indicia were only examples and that other indicia might apply in other cases. The court did not list specific indicia or elements of alter ego. Oregon courts require the plaintiff to prove the following

[30] *Twin City Shipyard v. United States,* 21 Cl. Ct. 582 (Ct. Cl. 1990); *BLH v. United States,* 13 Cl. Ct. 265 (Ct. Cl. 1987).

[31] *Slottow v. American Casualty,* 10 F.3d 1355, 1360 (9th Cir. 1993).

[32] AmFac Foods. v. Int'l. Systems & Control Corp., 654 P.2d 1092, 1098 (Or. 1982).

[33] Id. at 1102.

three elements by a preponderance of the evidence in order for the court to invoke alter ego.

1. [T]he shareholder must have actually controlled or shared in the actual control of the corporation.
2. The shareholder must have engaged in improper conduct in the exercise of control over the corporation.
3. The shareholder's improper conduct must have caused plaintiff's inability to obtain adequate remedy from the corporation.[34]

The state of Washington generally holds that shareholders will not be personally liable for the acts of their corporations.[35] That is, a corporation as an entity is considered separate and distinct from its shareholders.[36]

Consequently, certain general principles are contained within Washington case law. For example, the condition that a corporation's assets are insufficient to cover its obligations does not, in and of itself, persuade the courts to disregard its separate corporate existence. Likewise, parent corporations owning all of a subsidiary's stock, loaning money to the subsidiary, or having the same president will not, by themselves, demonstrate the parent's domination over the subsidiary.

When Washington state courts invoke "piercing the corporate veil," they have applied the "doctrine of corporate disregard" based upon two elements. First, "the corporate form must be intentionally used to violate or evade a duty." Second, the "disregard must be necessary and required to prevent unjustified loss to the injured party."[37]

The first factor requires a showing of abuse of the corporate form, typically involving fraud, misrepresentation, or other action(s) by the corporation that harms the creditor and benefits the shareholder. The second factor requires that harm must actually occur (that is, causation) so that corporate disregard becomes necessary.

Although Washington courts have not proffered a comprehensive list of actions constituting intentional abuse of the corporate form, they have identified several types of actions that may meet the requirement, such as stripping corporate assets and undercapitalization.

Finally, Alaska has adopted an 11-part test to show whether a subsidiary is acting as the mere instrumentality of its parent. The tests virtually mirror Powell's 11 circumstances set forth in the Alter Ego section of this chapter.[38]

In summary, it is clear that although broad guidelines of alter ego evaluation are common, the state-by-state and jurisdictional specifics vary significantly.

---

[34] *Salem Tent & Awning Co. v. Schmidt,* 719 P.2d 899, 903 (Or. Ct. App. 1986).

[35] *R.C.W.,* 23B.016.220; *Barnett Brothers v. Lynn,* 118 Wash. 308, 203 P. 387 (1922).

[36] *Truckweld Equip. Co. v. Olson,* 26 Wn. App. 638, 618 P.2d 1017 (1980).

[37] *Meisel v. M&N Modern Hydraulic Press Co.,* 97 Wash. 2d 403, 410, 645 P.2d 689, 692 (1982) (quoting *Morgan v. Burks,* 93 Wash. 2d 580, 587 (1980)).

[38] See *Jackson v. General Electric Co.,* 514 P.2d 1170, 1173 (Ala. 1973).

THE CHALLENGES OF ALTER EGO INVESTIGATION

Despite the disparity discussed earlier, a more daunting challenge in alter ego matters lies in establishing the sufficiency of evidence in support of the indicia either for or against an alter ego conclusion. Despite broad guidelines of indicia within respective jurisdictions, there is generally no clear checklist of items comprising the indicia. Note, for example, the following reference.

> *There is no single approach, nor coherent set of principles that exists to govern the situations where alter ego should apply, but all the approaches bear similarities.... As a general rule, the courts have required that the party seeking to pierce the corporate veil satisfy a two-prong test: (a) such unity of interest and ownership exists that the corporation and the individual shareholders no longer have separate personalities; and (b) viewing the acts as those of the corporation alone will result in inequity.*[39]

Indicia of Alter Ego

Alter ego is decided based upon the extent of the evidence in support or rebuttal of the indicia. Such indicia of alter ego are sometimes composed of four categories summarized further on. Note that no priority is inferred by the sequence of their listing.

Financial dependence behaviors are behaviors that would cause another to infer that the parent corporation provides the majority of financial support or maintenance for the subsidiary(ies). The question to address is whether the subsidiary is financially dependent on its parent.

Confusion about corporate identity reflects behaviors that would cause difficulty in determining the nature and relationship of the parent corporation with the subsidiary(ies). The question to address is whether the subsidiary's identity is commingled with its parent.

Lack of separateness reflects behaviors by the subsidiary(ies) that would cause another to infer that it is not separate from the parent corporation. The question to address is whether the subsidiary functions in parallel with its parent.

Dominance and control reflect behaviors by the parent corporation that would cause another to infer that the subsidiary(ies) operate based on the best interests of the parent corporation. The question to address is whether the parent exercises inordinate authority over the subsidiary(ies).

Principles of Investigation for Alter Ego

Due to the complexities and lack of specific guidance in alter ego doctrine, it is essential that three principles be applied during the investigation. First, the party(ies) conducting the investigation must be deeply and broadly experienced in the financial, marketing, operational, and legal aspects of the subject entity's industry and business.

---

[39] Roman L. Weil et al., *Litigation Services Handbook: The Role of the Financial Expert* 3rd ed. (New York: John Wiley & Sons, 2001), § 38.1.

Second, each evidentiary item must be measured against two independent criteria: itself and its peer group, thus accommodating a continuum of evaluation. Finally, all of the evidence gleaned must be considered within the context of the facts and circumstances surrounding the alter ego claim.

Deep and broad experience is a must. The collection of evidence to be considered in alter ego investigations is a relatively straightforward process, but the assessment of such evidence is another facet entirely. For example, evidence of control is often cited as the portal through which improper conduct can be determined. Control can permit dominance, but control does not necessarily signify dominance. A person with nominal professional experience can readily determine that a party held control in a parent entity, which likewise held control in subsidiaries. Mere control, however, in and of itself, is not an indicator of alter ego. The control must be linked through improper conduct and causation (depending upon the jurisdiction) to opine on alter ego. For example, the presence of intercompany accounts (due to and due from) between the parent and subsidiary is sometimes considered as evidence of alter ego. However, a professional will recognize the extensive labor required to control and maintain intercompany accounts, which is more likely an indication of distinct separateness than alter ego.

Alter ego evidence is evaluated using techniques similar to those used in financial analysis. The evidence is compared against itself and its peer group. Measuring the pattern of evidence over a company's history will highlight anomalies that are often proximate to triggering events.

The same evidentiary item, when compared within two different matters, may lead to differing alter ego conclusions. For example, closely held businesses often pledge assets in cross-collateralization to acquire operating debt. Cross-collateralization is a formal lending agreement among borrowers to pool collateral, thus providing the lender recourse to all of the borrowers' collateral. Typically, closely held businesses have little choice in the matter, as the bankers insist on limiting their lending risk. On the other hand, cross-collateralization has been exercised in the form of a poison pill similar to publicly held companies attempting to avoid hostile takeovers. In such instances, cross-collateralization may be an indicator of alter ego. In other words, alter ego requires drill-down assessment, which is an investigative process that moves from top to bottom. It starts with summary information and moves downward through successively more detailed supporting data to focus on the pertinent component parts. Alter ego also requires a buildup conclusion, which is a process employed during a drill-down assessment, wherein the respective findings resulting from successively more detailed analysis are aggregated upwards in a manner demonstrating the preponderance of evidence in support of a conclusion.

Derivation of a self-evident alter ego conclusion is driven by the preponderance (or dearth) of evidence. Procedurally, it is achieved by assessing the unique elements that collectively compose the respective indicator. Therefore, the evaluation and assessment process drills down to successively deeper layers as necessary, subsequently aggregating upward to a conclusion.[40]

---

[40] See the alter ego report card from the article by Darrell D. Dorrell, "The Valuation Report Card," *American Journal of Family Law* 16 (2002), set forth at Exhibit 7.2.

Bear in mind the preceding comments regarding the continuum of alter ego investigation. With regard to evidence that "more is better," criticality is notwithstanding. This approach, however, is provided as a benchmark for investigation regardless of evidence detail. Note that the author has successfully employed the entire continuum of evidence, ranging from smoking gun to comprehensive scorecards of measurement.

Once the indicia are determined, criteria, elements, and sub-elements can then be applied to pertinent legal, financial, operational, and related evidentiary documents. During the screening of evidence, any and all items that could affect alter ego indicia are considered regardless of the likely result. This ensures that the universe of data is assembled and evaluated without bias (to the extent possible).

Once any and all material items potentially affecting alter ego indicia have been selected, each item of evidence is individually investigated, evaluated, and assessed within the context of the facts and circumstances previously determined.

Naturally, the evaluation and assessment criteria must be composed of objective and comprehensive components. Consequently, each indicator's foundational elements are constructed with regard to objective methods and techniques. For example, the elements of financial dependence are drawn (at least in part) from methods used to determine solvency analysis.

Then, based upon the preponderance of conclusions, aggregating upward from the sub-elements to the elements to the criteria to the indicia, and in concert with professional opinion, an overall conclusion can be formed for each indicator.

Each indicator may overlap other indicators and even a preponderance of conclusions one way or the other does not necessarily lead to an irrefutable conclusion. That is why it is necessary to develop a deep understanding of the nature and history of the business, and its financial, operational, marketing, management, and related elements.

Since the decomposition of indicia can lead to quite complex and detailed data, it is critical to organize the process into hierarchical categories. Furthermore, each category may require additional analysis and even cross-referencing to other categories and data.

Just as no checklist of criteria exists, no checklist of categories exists. However, Exhibit 7.2 illustrates a logical descending structure. The example demonstrates the decomposition of financial dependence. In practice, of course, the structure will vary, depending upon the facts and circumstances of each matter.

For purposes of this simplified example, the financial dependence indicator is composed of two basic criteria: legal criteria and financial criteria. The legal criteria

Indicator	Criteria	Elements	Sub-Elements
FINANCIAL DEPENDENCE	Legal Criteria	Legal Formation	Secy. State; Articles; Minutes; Resolutions; ByLaws; Stk. Reg.
		Legal Continuation	Filings; Minutes; Resolutions; Stk. Reg.
	Financial Criteria	Financial Formation	Initial Cap.; Initial Solv.; Open. Jes; Form. F/S; Sep. Equity
		Financial Continuation	Cont.Solv.; Cont. Prof.; Forward; Per. F/S
		Parent Relationship	Bus.Trans.; Funds Flow; Resources

EXHIBIT 7.2 Dorrell's Alter Ego Report Card

are further deconstructed into two elements: legal formation and legal continuation. Finally, legal formation and legal continuation are deconstructed into six and four sub-elements, respectively. The financial criteria are likewise deconstructed into their respective elements and sub-elements. See Exhibit 7.2.

Each indicator is deconstructed into three successively detailed levels, consisting of criteria, elements, and sub-elements. Note that criteria may be composed of one or multiple elements. Likewise, each element may be composed of multiple sub-elements. Sub-elements can continue indefinitely with the deconstruction process to provide as much detail as the facts and circumstances of the matter warrant.

Once all the factors have been scored, they can then, in the aggregate, lead to a conclusion (or rebuttal) of alter ego. For example, if 43 of 52 elements and sub-elements, or 83 percent, indicate alter ego conditions, then such conclusion will be relatively self-evident. Note that this assumes that each factor has similar weight with regard to the conclusion. (See the explanatory comments further on regarding relative weights.)

Self-Evident Conclusion

In theory, the determination of alter ego merely requires demonstrating how each indicator's underlying criteria drives a self-evident conclusion leading to one of four determinations.

1. Preponderance of criteria substantiating an alter ego conclusion could persuade the court to grant the claim of alter ego.
2. Preponderance of criteria rebutting an alter ego conclusion could persuade the court to honor the corporate structure.
3. Absence of criteria substantiating an alter ego conclusion could persuade the court to honor the corporate structure.
4. Absence of criteria rebutting an alter ego conclusion could persuade the court to grant the claim of alter ego.

Complexities Inherent in the Indicia

The criteria comprising the indicia are not well defined and often vary by jurisdiction. Furthermore, each matter contains unique facts and circumstances that frame the context and shape the analytical approach, which compounds the difficulty of evaluating the criteria.

Alter ego determination goes one step further. There are inherent complexities and interdependencies in alter ego determination that compound the assessment. The key complexities are set forth further on, but bear in mind that despite their discrete listing, they can, and often are, synergistic and interactive within and among one another.

Business relationships between otherwise unrelated entities may exhibit alter ego characteristics. Personally owned entities within family relationships may transact business with one another in a manner not complying with corporate governance requirements. Analysis of the entity's business history can yield revealing patterns of corporate behavior and can clarify decisions. For example, did an economic downturn or perhaps an acquisition, or even lenders, force the parent to cross-collateralize? Triggering events and their attendant corporate treatment (accounting recognition) can be compared against an entity's business history to determine if the event resulted in different treatment, potentially indicating alter ego.

The factual scenario set forth underlying Exhibit 7.1 is illustrative. A large multi-entity had an acquisition guided by financial and legal advisors who provided extensive due diligence with regard to the purchase price. Upon acquisition, the transaction was diligently measured and recorded in the parent's various audited financial statements, income tax returns, and related sources. The due diligence identified a contingent liability of the acquisition target in the form of a company-backed guarantee of a customer's long-term lease. The likelihood of triggering the contingency was deemed remote since it required insolvency on the part of the customer.

Approximately one year post-acquisition, the customer declared insolvency and defaulted on the long-term lease, thus triggering the acquisition's target guarantee. The resultant cost to the multi-entity of the guarantee exceeded the purchase price of the acquisition target. Seeking advice from the same pre-acquisition attorneys and accountants, the multi-entity company tried to rewrite history by soliciting new valuations and legal opinions that asserted the original acquisition had been vastly overvalued. Consequently, the multi-entity attempted to book complex accounting entries that obfuscated the actual transaction and appeared to reflect a zero balance for the acquisition purchase price. After forensic accounting analysis exposed the fraud, the case settled in favor of the plaintiff during trial and the disposition was sealed by a protective order.

Two key trial exhibits (Exhibits 7.3 and 7.4) illustrate the flow. Exhibit 7.3 gives a summary of the accounting transactions necessary to disguise the overall intent. Although such a schedule may be useful only to a duly qualified CPA, it presents a clear trail of the flow and journal entries that mirror the attorneys', outside CPAs', and advisors' guidance in order to avoid creditors' actions. Exhibit 7.4 is a pictorial representation of the accounting flows. Although less technical, it mirrors the trail of activities and also includes those items not necessarily reflected within the accounting records.

A detailed history of diligent corporate governance, board minutes and resolutions, timely corporate filings, and outside legal advice, among other things, can demonstrate a history of maintaining corporate distinction and separateness. Extensive business records spanning either the short or the long term can accommodate a comprehensive and detailed evidentiary analysis balanced against cost-effectiveness and practicality. Very limited business records preventing detailed analysis may rely upon extrapolated assumptions driven by available evidence. Note that routine business practices regarding discarding records may legitimately create gaps in the records trail.

The analysis of business records usually requires a balance between page-by-page and high-level document analysis to obtain the most cost-effective conclusion based upon optimal levels of evidence for the time periods investigated.

An entity's past practices can do much to demonstrate intent. A long history of acquiring, maintaining, or disposing of entities could indicate intent of separateness. Likewise, a long history of a single entity interrupted by the formation of a new entity proximate to an event could indicate an attempt at diversion. It bears repeating that interdependencies and complexities, despite their discrete listing, often are synergistic and interactive within and among one another.

Line	Column: A	B	C		D		E		F		G	H	I	J	K	L	M
1		Transaction Accounting and Subsequent Adjustments									Impact of Contributions			Consolidating Financials Combined Entities			
2		SUSPECT #2			10/10/2000		10/10/2000		Adjusted		Contribution		Post-	SUSPECT	SUSPECT		SUSPECT
3		Sons, Inc.	10/10/2000		Transaction		Purchase		10/10 SUSPECT #4		to	SUSPECT	Contribution	#7	Entities	Elimination	Entities
4		10/10/00	Transaction		Adjustments		Acctg. Adj.		Bal. Sht.		SUSPECT #5	#6	SUSPECT #4	9/30/2000	Combined 10/10/2000	Entries	Consolidated 10/10/2000
5																	
6	Current Assets	3,891,031							3,891,031	f	3,891,031			1,866,154	5,757,185		5,757,185
7	Inventory	11,530,225			(208,000)	d			11,322,225	f	11,322,225			6,124,784	17,447,009		17,447,009
8	Due from SUSPECT #1	2,283,676			(2,283,676)	d			–								–
9	Fixed Assets	911,364			(166,175)	d			745,189	f	745,189			1,171,102	1,916,291		1,916,291
10	Goodwill, Net	540,817			(199,800)	d			341,017	f	341,017				341,017		341,017
11	Distribution Rights, Net	299,852			5,514,416	d			5,814,268	f	5,814,268			17,670,631	23,484,899		23,484,899
12	Investment in SUSPECT #2 & Sons, Inc.	–	6,983,106	a			(5,172,620)	e	1,810,486	j		1,810,486			1,810,486	(1,810,486)	–
13	Investment—Retainage	–	600,000	a					600,000	j		600,000			600,000	(600,000)	–
14	Preferred Interest—SUSPECT #3										Plus		9,249,968		9,249,968	(9,249,968)	????????
15	Covenant not to Compete	–	1,000,000	b					1,000,000				1,000,000		1,000,000		1,000,000
16	All Other Assets	15,685							15,685	f	15,685			257,139	257,139		257,139
17	Total Assets	19,472,650	8,583,106		2,656,765		(5,172,620)		25,539,901		22,129,415	2,410,486	10,249,968	27,089,810	61,863,994	(11,660,454)	50,203,540
18											Minus						
19	Current Liabilities	12,679,223							12,679,223		12,679,223			5,072,675	17,751,898		17,751,898
20	Line of Credit	5,759,282	(5,759,282)	c					–		–						–
21	Current Portion, LTD	815,896	(815,896)	c					–		–	SUSPECT #4 Received					–
22																	–
23	Intercompany Debt - CDW		2,483,106	a					2,483,106		Minus		2,483,106	18,549,586	21,032,692		21,032,692
24	Intercompany Debt - CDO		6,839,482	c					6,839,482				6,839,482		6,839,482		6,839,482
25																	–
26	Long-Term Debt	1,616,049	(264,304)	c	(1,151,521)	d			200,224		200,224				200,224		200,224
27	Long-Term Debt—SUSPECT #2, CNTC		1,000,000	b			(72,620)	e	927,380				927,380		927,380		927,380
28	Long-Term Debt—Retainage		600,000	a			(600,000)	e	–								–
29	Subordinated Note—SUSPECT #2		4,500,000	a			(4,500,000)	e	–								–
30	Long Term Debt—Elands													4,000,000	4,000,000		4,000,000
31																	–
32	Treasury Stock													(12,000,000)	(12,000,000)		(12,000,000)
33	Common Stock—Old	672			(672)	d			–								–
34	APIC—Old	585,291			(585,291)	d			–		Equals						–
35	Common Stock—New				672	d			672	i		672			672	(672)	–
36	APIC—New				2,409,814	d			2,409,814	i	**9,249,968**	2,409,814			11,659,782	(11,659,782)	–
37	Retained Earnings	(1,983,763)			1,983,763	d			–					11,451,864	11,451,864		11,451,864
38	Total Liabilities & Equity	19,472,650	8,583,106		2,656,765		(5,172,620)		25,539,901		22,129,415	2,410,486	10,249,968	27,074,125	61,863,994	(11,660,454)	50,203,540

EXHIBIT 7.3 Summary Flow Sheet

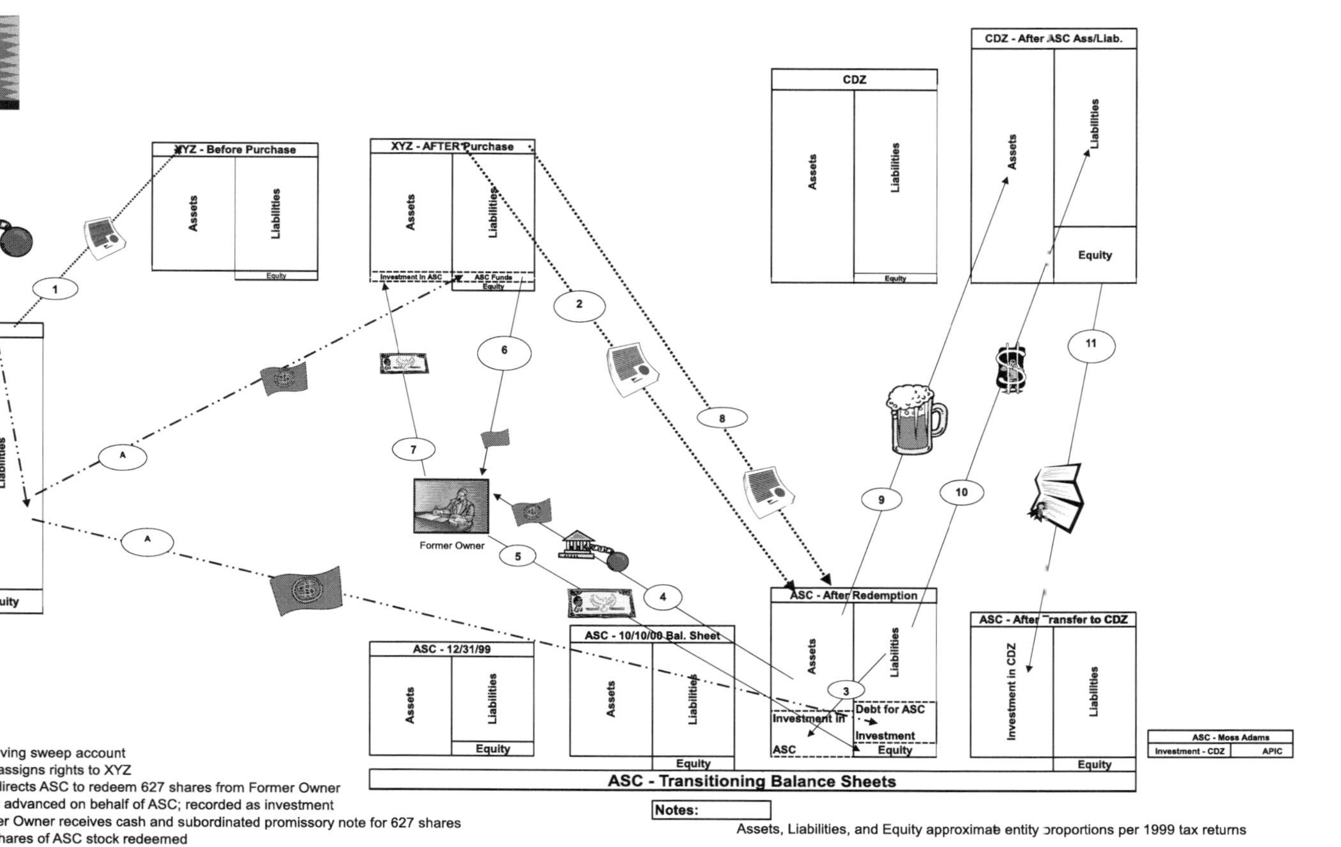

Legend:

A - Revolving sweep account
1 - CDX assigns rights to XYZ
2 - XYZ directs ASC to redeem 627 shares from Former Owner
3 - Debts advanced on behalf of ASC; recorded as investment
4 - Former Owner receives cash and subordinated promissory note for 627 shares
5 - 627 shares of ASC stock redeemed
6 - XYZ pays cash to Former Owner for 45 shares
7 - Former Owner tenders 45 shares of stock to XYZ
8 - XYZ directs ASC to redeem 627 shares from Former Owner
9 - ASC Inventory, Vehicles, etc. to CDZ
10 - ASC liabilities to CDZ
11 - CDZ tenders Preferred Series B Units ownership to ASC

EXHIBIT 7.4 Flow Diagram

The evidence evaluation method must be established before conducting the investigation to avoid confusion of indicia. Common forensic accounting techniques summarized next can accommodate such a need.

- The nomenclature encountered in alter ego, particularly for nonparent entities, is often pointed out as indicative of control. The mere labeling, however, of an entity as a subsidiary, affiliate, division, or branch, may or may not be indicative of alter ego.
- Certain indicators may tend to overwhelm other indicators despite the preponderance of evidence. Compelling evidence of financial dependence might carry more weight than the other indicators combined.
- Specific records might carry more weight than many of the other records within respective categories. Reliance upon outside legal or accounting advice could demonstrate an owner's intent to conduct due diligence within the various entities.
- The various factors may carry differing weight(s) regarding alter ego conclusions. A single bank account for the parent and subsidiaries may have little bearing if the various entities separately account for transactions. A truly commingled bank account, however, may carry a great deal of weight.
- Smoking gun evidence may carry more weight than more ordinary indicators. Smoking gun evidence can result in a favorable settlement during trial, immediately prior to expert testimony.
- The weighing of indicators depends greatly on the facts and circumstances of each matter.

A single piece of evidence can be so compelling that it might overshadow all other evidence in support or refutation of alter ego. Alternatively, the preponderance of evidence can be so compelling that it might overshadow even an extreme example in support or refutation of alter ego. In reality, most cases fall somewhere in between. See Exhibits 7.3 (spreadsheet) and 7.4 (pictorial of The Acquired Subject & Sons, Inc. transaction).

Exhibit 7.3 is the sort of schedule that causes an accountant's heart to race. It demonstrates (to an accountant) how, through the creative accounting process, an entity valued in excess of $9 million can be made to disappear on the financial statements, thus purportedly thwarting creditors. The disappearance is demonstrated by the two ovals at the right-hand side of the schedule. The $9,249,968 in entity assets is ultimately reported as zero on the consolidated financial statements. Consequently, an unsuspecting reader of the financial statements would overlook the disappearing entity assets.

Exhibit 7.4 is the same set of accounting transactions contained in Exhibit 7.3, but is constructed using a step-by-step pictorial technique. Exhibit 7.4's legend in the lower left-hand corner can be used to trace the transactions that we sequentially executed in the acquisition of the subject entity.

Following the legend, A refers to the various points at which the revolving sweep account (flexible line of credit) was used during the transaction. Step one refers to "CDX assigns rights to XYZ" and can be seen in the oval just below the ball and chain symbol on the left-hand side of the exhibit. Steps 2 through 11 can be followed in a similar manner, thus tracing the transaction through the various entities.

Exhibit 7.4 avoids the mind-numbing complexity of a convoluted accounting schedule and illustrates the business and accounting transactions in a story-line manner. This exhibit was actually used to demonstrate to the court how the defendant's claimed transaction was quite different from how they actually booked the entries within their financial records.

Contradictory Implications

Factors used to deconstruct alter ego indicia may have contradictory implications. Using the same law firm to advise both parent and subsidiary may indicate a lack of separateness, but could be a prudent business decision. Likewise, a subsidiary's operations residing in the parent's facilities could indicate lack of separateness, but paying market-based rent to the parent could negate the lack of separateness indication.

Factors used to deconstruct alter ego indicia may also have an overlapping application to the indicia. Using a common chart of accounts to record accounting transactions is a prudent business practice, but could conceivably serve as an indicator of a lack of separateness.

Some factors are subject to legitimate alternative interpretation. Consequently, a methodology by which to score the overall results becomes critical. (Refer to the preceding principles of alter ego investigation.) Furthermore, such methodology provides compelling evidence for an objective and critical analysis, persuasive to the court.

Varying Measurement Standards

The measurements standards used in assessing whether or not financial dependence is present will vary. A few examples follow.

- *Book Value*—This standard of measure rarely reflects anything beyond the nominal difference between assets (typically reported at cost) and liabilities (typically reported at fair market value).
- *Checkbook Management*—Even mid-size business owners sometimes rely on a primary, or a few key measurements (as they perceive them) to manage the business. A chemical manufacturer gauged the profitability of his business as either-or when his business checking account carried a balance exceeding $1,000,000. When the balance was over $1,000,000, he reasoned that his business was doing fine. Another business owner netted the respective balances of accounts receivable against accounts payable every week. He was confident of success unless any week's net fell below the arbitrary cushion he periodically established.
- *Fair Market Value*—"This standard of measure is ordinarily applied when restating cost-based assets, and sometimes liabilities, and is driven by the definition of fair market value as defined in Revenue Ruling 59-60 (1959-1 C.B. 237.)[41]
- *Generally Accepted Accounting Principles* (GAAP)—This standard of measure is composed of the conventions, rules, and procedures necessary to define accepted

[41] Readily accessible through the Internet.

accounting practices at a particular time, and includes both broad and specific guidelines. The source of such standards is the Financial Accounting Standards Board (FASB)."[42] GAAP statements are ordinarily available only when audited (or sometimes reviewed) financials are available.

Compilation-level financial statements may often offer very little assurance regarding their performance representation.

- *Guesstimates*—Often encountered in closely held businesses with regard to inventories, accounts receivable allowances, gross profit margins, warranties, and others when the business lacks competent internal financial resources to capture necessary information.

Some businesses seldom (if ever) conduct physical inventories, relying instead upon pricing guidelines that set gross profit margins that are applied to derive inventory levels.

- *Measurement gaps*—Even mid-size businesses ignore the importance of regular financial statements to track and control operating performance. Consequently, analysis often depends upon irregular annual measurements that preclude a finer calibration of trends and patterns.

Although annual financial analysis, common-sizing, trending, horizontal and vertical, ratio, growth rate, and similar techniques are helpful, frequent measurements are more specific. Note the annual resting requirements of lending institutions. The resting requirement lines of credit (LOC) demonstrate the business's solvency and limit the lending institution's risk.

- *Other Comprehensive Basis of Accounting* (OCBOA)—This category, under the Statement on Auditing Standards No. 62 Special Reports,[43] can be any one of the following: a statutory basis of accounting (e.g., a basis of accounting insurance companies use under the rules of a state insurance commission), income tax basis financial statements, or financial statements prepared using definitive criteria having substantial support in accounting literature that the preparer applies to all material items appearing in the statements (such as the price level basis of accounting).
- *Tax Basis Accounting*—Tax basis accounting may or may not be based upon GAAP, but is typically cost-driven or fair market value–driven, depending upon the respective facts and circumstances. Furthermore, timing differences, depreciation, revenue recognition, and inventory methods can affect tax basis accounting.

There is no definitive accounting literature that can be used to determine when or whether a subsidiary financially depends upon its parent. Consequently, financial

[42] *Black's Law Dictionary*, 6th ed. (St. Paul, MN: West Publishing, 1990), 685.

[43] Available at www.aicpa.org/research/standards/auditattest/pages/sas.aspx.

techniques such as solvency analysis, among others, are typically employed. Refer to the Solvency section of this chapter for guidance.

How Does One Determine Alter Ego?

Alter ego is ostensibly simple, but insidiously complex. The danger results from the inherent complexities and latent interdependencies of the indicia and their underlying evidentiary records. Which of the following evidence indicates a subsidiary's financial dependence on its parent? A subsidiary borrows start-up funds from the parent and:

- Pays it back right away and never again needs funds from the parent.
- Pays it back based upon prevailing market terms.
- Is capable of paying it back, but the parent never requests it, thus never accounts for it.
- Is capable of paying it back and the parent never requests it, but the subsidiary accounts for it and related interest through intercompany accounts.
- Is not capable of paying it back, and the parent never requests it.
- Is not capable of paying it back, but the subsidiary accounts for it and related interest through intercompany accounts.

The correct answer is, it depends upon the facts and circumstances surrounding the funds, the nature and history of the relationship between the parent and the subsidiary, industry practices, economic conditions, treatment over the life of the relationship, and a myriad of additional factors that may need consideration.

Fortunately, application of a few simple techniques and application of the preceding principles can simplify an otherwise complex exercise.

The complexities of alter ego determination are most easily analyzed by deconstructing each of the four indicators (financial dependence, confusion about identity, lack of separateness, and dominance and control) into progressively finer factors. The factors then are individually assessed, and when aggregated, can produce a scorecard for each indicator, clearly illustrating the extent to which the indicator lends support to an alter ego conclusion. Deconstructing the indicia into their factors, however, may not be sufficient. It may be necessary to further deconstruct the factors into elements, and perhaps even categories ad infinitum.

To best arrive at objective and supportable conclusions, the approach must be structured in accordance with professional technical guidelines, experience in alter ego investigation, and forensic accounting methodology. Forensic accounting is defined as "[t]he art and science of applying financial techniques to matters of law."[44]

Alter ego assessment is one of the most powerful, but complex, elements of corporate law. It requires a unique combination of financial, business, legal, operational, marketing, and related knowledge so as to serve the court's best interest.

---

[44] "How Do You Define Forensic Accounting?" *Financial Forensics Newsletter* (Financial Forensics, Lake Oswego, OR), September 1993 at 1, available contacting Financial Forensics.

FRAUDULENT TRANSFER

As previously stated, the concept of fraudulent transfer is typically employed in connection with debtor-creditor relationships in which an asset or liability has been transferred for less than reasonably equivalent value with the intent of defeating a creditor's rights. The principles derived from fraudulent transfer can also be applied to other types of law to illustrate intent and results.

The Bankruptcy Code grants a Chapter 11 debtor-in-possession (DIP) or bankruptcy trustee special powers to collect all of a debtor's assets in a bankruptcy matter. The powers include voiding prebankruptcy asset transfers that are fraudulent under applicable nonbankruptcy law, such as the Uniform Fraudulent Transfer Act (UFTA) or the Uniform Fraudulent Conveyance Act (UFCA). Under the UFTA or the UFCA, assets can be recovered and transfers voided when circumstances constitute actual or constructive fraud.

Actual fraud occurs when an asset is transferred with intent to hinder, delay, or defraud any creditor. Constructive fraud occurs when an asset is transferred for less than reasonably equivalent value or for other reasons, such as insolvency of the debtor or inadequate capitalization.

Constructive fraudulent transfer is determined by the following criteria.

- Did the subject receive reasonably equivalent value in connection with the transfer?
- Was the subject insolvent preceding the transfer?
- Did the subject become insolvent as a result of the transfer?

Actual fraudulent transfer is determined by various badges of fraud that indicate if the transfer was made with actual intent to hinder, delay, or defraud creditors, as evidenced by the following.

- Was the transfer to an insider?
- Was the transfer composed of substantially all of the subject's assets?
- Was a reasonably equivalent value received in the exchange?
- Was the subject insolvent at the time of transfer or did it become insolvent as a result of the transfer?
- Did the transfer occur proximate to substantial debt incurrence?
- Did the transferring entity retain possession, benefit, or use of the property(ies)?
- Did the transfer occur proximate to financial difficulties?
- Did the transfer occur proximate to a filed or threatened lawsuit?
- Is there any other evidence of actual intent to hinder, delay, or defraud the creditor(s)?

Another criterion is whether the transfer was for less than reasonably equivalent value. This element is ordinarily based upon fair market value consistent with the definition of fair market value in Revenue Ruling 59-60 (1959-1 C.B. 237), available by contacting Financial Forensics. Basically, fair market value is the amount at which property would change hands between a willing buyer and a willing seller when the former is not under any compulsion to buy and the latter is not under any compulsion to sell, both parties having reasonable knowledge of the relevant facts. Court decisions frequently state, in addition, that the hypothetical buyer and seller are assumed to be willing and able to trade, and are well informed about the property and the market for such property.[45]

The following eight factors are outlined in Revenue Ruling 59-60, § 4, under Factors to Consider.

- The nature of the business and the history of the enterprise from its inception.
- The economic outlook in general and the condition and outlook of the specific industry in particular.
- The book value of the stock and the financial condition of the business.
- The earning capacity of the company.
- The dividend-paying capacity.
- Whether or not the enterprise has goodwill or other intangible value.
- Sales of the stock and the size of the block of stock to be valued.
- The market prices of stock of corporations, engaged in the same or similar lines of business, having their stocks actively traded in a free and open market, either on an exchange or over-the-counter.

Some courts, however, apply value standards other than fair market value. Generally, tests regarding fair market value and other values require restatement of the transferring entity's balance sheet. Assets are restated to fair market value, and include all intangible assets such as copyrights, patents, trademarks, trade secrets (whether or not recorded by the transferring entity), but not goodwill. Liabilities are also restated to fair market value, and include recognition of contingent or unliquidated liabilities or both, whether or not recorded by the transferring entity.

Three other criteria must also be met.

1. Whether the entity was insolvent at the time of transfer or became insolvent as the result of the transfer.
2. Whether the transfer resulted in unreasonably small capital remaining in the transferring entity.
3. Whether the entity intended or expected to incur debts beyond its ability to pay.

Financial and empirical tests involving fraudulent transfers can be quite complex. However, a few simple examples illustrate the concepts.

Exhibit 7.5 illustrates how the transaction's equity had been legitimately recorded numerous times, all approximating $9 million. However, when a large contingent liability was triggered, unscrupulous attorneys and accountants rerecorded the transaction at $700,000, thus attempting to defeat the creditor. The rerecording was based on very complex legal and accounting maneuvers intended to obscure the deception. Nevertheless, the visualization in Exhibit 7.5 managed to simplify the defendant's complexity-by-design. That is, 10 times during the preceding year, the

[45] Title 26 C.F.R. 20.2031-2(2)(.02) available at ecfr.gpoaccess.gov and Revenue Ruling 83-120, available via the Internet. These two cites are parallel cites to Rev. Ruling 59-60.

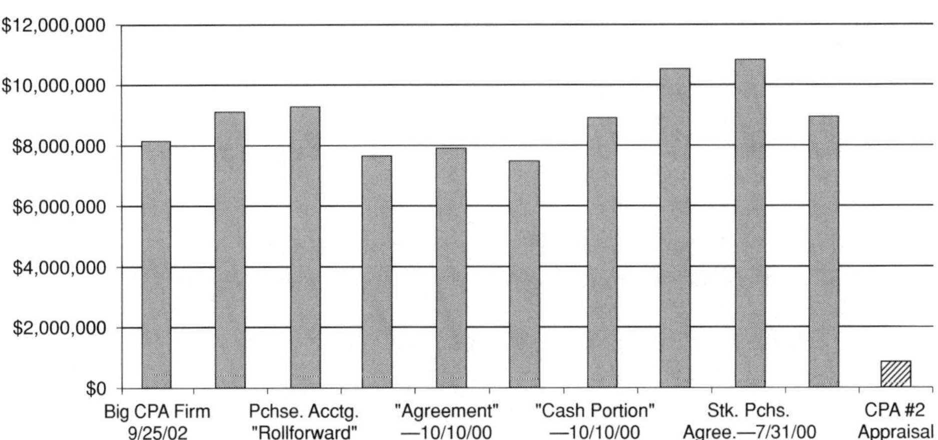

EXHIBIT 7.5 Comparative Purchase Price Indicators

defendant had documented that the transaction was worth $9 million. Immediately after a post-transaction liability surfaced, the company tried to rerecord the transaction at only $700,000 in order to deceive creditors into thinking that insufficient assets were available through the court.

The schedule in Exhibit 7.3 conveys meaning to perhaps only a CPA, but the trail is clear—assets were transferred and dispersed in an attempt to support a zero value for a subsidiary's stock. The schedule was used in the trial, and the flow exhibit (Exhibit 7.4) following it illustrates the visual representation of the accounting transactions, reflecting both the original transaction and the rerecording intended to defraud the creditor.

Such tools are commonly employed in fraudulent transfers, but their derivation requires skills well beyond mere accounting and finance. The practitioner must possess a broad array of eclectic legal, financial, and analytical skills to successfully make sense out of the disarray.

SOLVENCY

Solvency analysis can be applied to a wide array of litigation matters, including bankruptcy, alter ego, debt service capability, financing feasibility, pre- and post-merger due diligence, and other decisions geared to financial analysis.[46]

Solvency analysis is applied by testing the three following categories.

1. *Balance Sheet Test*—Used to determine whether, at the time of the transaction, a company's asset value (valued as a going concern) was greater than its liability value.

[46] Some of the solvency material discussed here was adapted from Darrell D. Dorrell and Gregory A. Gadawski, "Valuation in Solvency Analysis," *National Litigation Consultants' Review* 3 (July 2003): 1.

2. *Cash Flow Test*—Used to determine whether a business entity incurred debts that would be beyond the debtor's ability to pay as such debts matured.
3. *Adequate (Reasonable) Capital Test*—Used to determine if an entity was engaged in a business or a transaction for which it had an unreasonably low amount of capital.[47]

It is important to note that to be considered solvent, a company must pass all three tests. Furthermore, note that the occurrence of a bankruptcy following a leveraged transaction does not necessarily prove that the company was insolvent at the time of the transaction. Nor does the absence of a bankruptcy following a transaction guarantee that the company would have passed the solvency tests.

Solvency Analysis Terms

Financial analysts often perform a solvency analysis to determine whether, following some type of leveraged transaction, the company incurring the leverage is left in one of the following states.

- *Positive Equity*—Equity is measured by the excess or deficit of assets over liabilities.
- *The Ability to Repay Its Debts as They Come Due*—Debt-paying ability is measured by ratios including, but not necessarily limited to, debt to equity.
- *Debt to Equity*—The higher the ratio, the riskier the financial leverage.[48]
- *Times Interest Earned*—The lower the ratio, the riskier the financial leverage.
- *Adequate Capital to Operate Its Business*—Capital sufficiency is measured by ratios including tests that incorporate certain of the debt repayment ratios summarized earlier.[49]

Solvency ratios that measure liquidity include current ratio, quick ratio, and so on.[50]

Balance Sheet Test

As a first step in conducting the balance sheet test, the assets of the company are valued as a going concern as of the date of the transaction. Then the value of the company's liabilities is subtracted from the asset value. The balance sheet test is passed if the sum of the value of the company's assets is greater than the value of its liabilities. For example, if the going-concern (post-transaction) valuation of a

[47] Robert F. Reilly and Robert P. Schweihs, *The Handbook of Advanced Business Valuation*, ed. Richard D. Irwin (New York: McGraw-Hill, 2000), 340–342.
[48] Robert N. Anthony, *Management Accounting: Text and Cases*, ed. Richard D. Irwin (New York: McGraw-Hill, 1964), 301.
[49] Id. at 56–60.
[50] Michael R. Tyran, *The Vest Pocket Guide to Business Ratios* (Englewood Cliffs, NJ: Prentice-Hall, 1992) 77–86, 252–257.

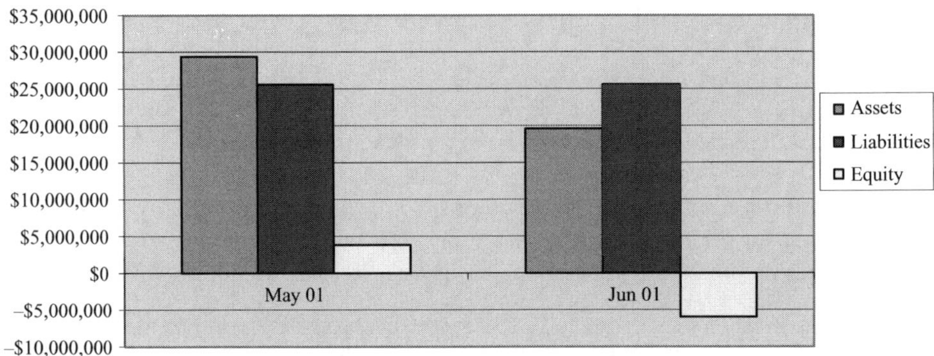

EXHIBIT 7.6 Pre- and Post-Merger Balance Sheet Test

company's assets arrived at $5.5 million fair market value, then the company's post-transaction liabilities of $4 million subtracted from the assets would result in an excess fair market value of $1.5 million. Such a condition would enable a company to pass the balance sheet test. Exhibit 7.6, "Pre- and Post-Merger Balance Sheet Test" illustrates a balance sheet indicating a positive equity before a transaction (May 1) and a negative equity following the transaction (June 1). This exhibit indicates how quickly solvency can change pursuant to a merger.

Cash Flow Test

As stated earlier, the cash flow test is used to determine whether a business entity incurred debts that would be beyond the debtor's ability to pay as such debts matured. Conclusions about the ability to pay debts are based on an analysis of a series of projections of future financial performance of the business that are created by varying some key operating characteristics of the business. These typically include, but are not necessarily limited to, revenue growth and profit per dollar of sales. The forensic accountant must judge which projection scenarios are reasonable in light of the company's past performance, current economic conditions, and future prospects. This is similar to what should be done in evaluating company projections for a discounted cash flow valuation.

In the cash flow test, future post-transaction debt payments of a company are computed and scheduled by a due date. Then a projection of the amount of liquidity available to the company to meet its debt requirements is estimated from each set of projections. To calculate a company's liquidity available for debt repayment, the valuation analyst could project each of the following for the company for several periods after the transaction: any excess cash on hand, free cash flows earned during each period, and the company's borrowing capability on each due date to repay its debts. A comparison would then be made between the amount of debt payments required during each period and the liquidity available to satisfy such requirements. A company will pass this test in any projected period if it can pay its debts as they come due through cash accumulated on its prior earnings, free cash flow earned in the period, or by having enough borrowing availability to pay its debts.

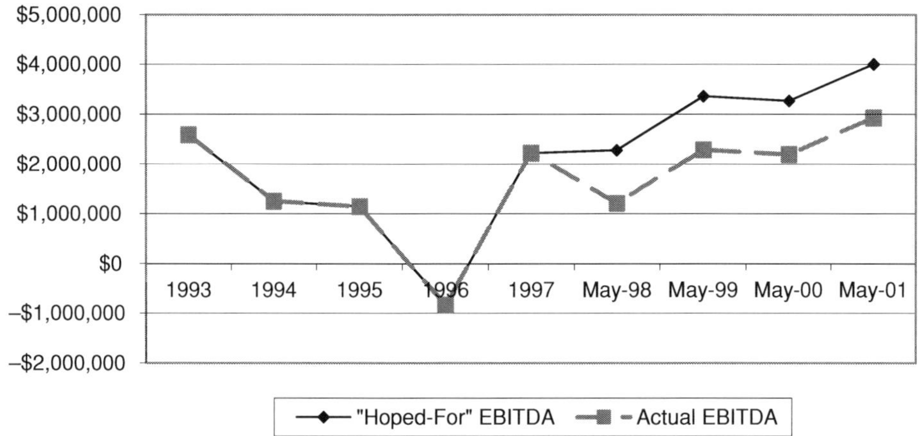

EXHIBIT 7.7 Hoped-for EBITDA Compared to Actual EBITDA

Exhibit 7.7 illustrates a failed cash flow test. The schedule demonstrates that cash flow can consist of various definitions. The example applies a form of cash flow commonly employed within the example company's industry. Specifically, the cash flow measure is an acronym consisting of the first letter of the components to which it applies: earnings before interest, taxes, depreciation, and amortization (EBITDA). A similar, but different form of cash flow, EBIT, is an acronym likewise consisting of the first letter of the components to which it applies: earnings before interest and taxes. In the example, the dark line indicates the hoped-for post-transaction cash flow, and the light line indicates the actual post-transaction cash flow. Consequently, the transaction failed the cash flow test.

Adequate Capital Test

The adequate capital test is used to determine if an entity was engaged in a business or a transaction for which it had unreasonably low amount of capital. The adequate capital test is related to the cash flow test in that a company that has adequate capital will be able to pay its debts as they come due and will have the capital to run its business under a wide range of financial circumstances and economic conditions. The adequate capital test is intended to determine whether a company is likely to survive, assuming reasonable business fluctuations in the future. Recognizing that all projections about the future are uncertain, one would like to be able to estimate the likelihood that the newly leveraged company has enough of a cushion in its post-transaction capital structure to withstand a typical amount of financial fluctuation.

One key measure of a company's reasonable capital is the availability of committed credit, given a variety of projected levels of performance. One would typically test the availability of committed credit under the lending covenants that were negotiated as part of the leveraged transaction. Exhibit 7.7 illustrates how the actual EBITDA resulted in a $1 million shortfall from hoped-for EBITDA. As a result, the company failed, since the shortfall exceeded the hoped-for cash flow resulting from the acquisition. See Exhibit 7.7 (Hoped-for EBITDA Compared to Actual EBITDA)

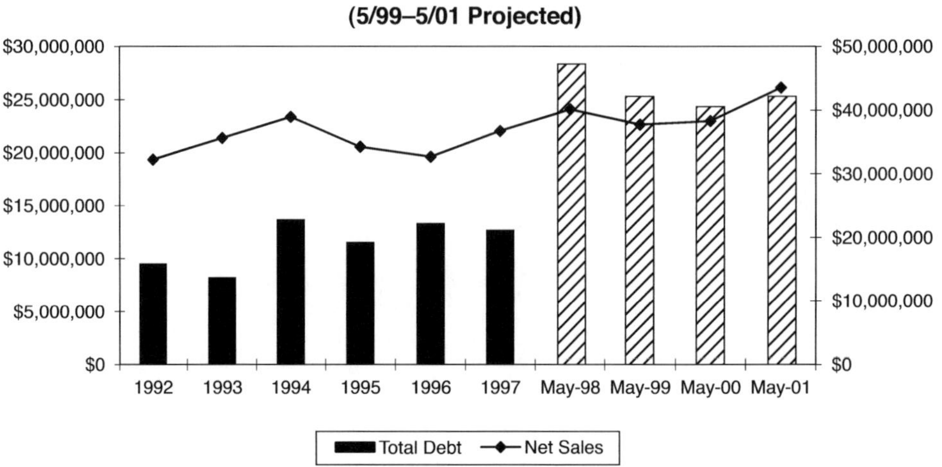

EXHIBIT 7.8 Pre- and Post-Merger Debt and Sales

and Exhibit 7.6 (Pre- and Post-Transaction Balance Sheet Test). Exhibit 7.6 clearly indicates the decline in equity resulting from a post-transaction asset decline and liability increase—a fatal combination.

Projected Cash Flow Sensitivity Analysis

When a cash flow sensitivity analysis is used to determine adequate capital, the projected future financial performance of the company is analyzed in a variety of scenarios and the sufficiency of its cash and credit to meet its needs is assessed. In addition to comparing the cash needs relative to its revolver limits, as is done in the cash flow test, one would analyze whether the company would pass each of the covenants on its term debt under a variety of presumed performance scenarios.

The results of this test will demonstrate under what circumstances the company would trigger a default under its lending covenants. The scenarios tested should include the following three factors.

1. Management's best estimate of the future.
2. No change from recent historical performance.
3. Some reasonable variations of revenue growth and profit margin assumptions.

Exhibit 7.8 indicates the pre- and post-transaction levels of debt in comparison to projected sales. The schedule is self-evident. The same level of sales was expected to service nearly twice the debt load, a classic example of hubris.

FORENSIC ACCOUNTING TECHNIQUES

Other techniques are often employed in support of civil tools. Perhaps the most recent and important statistical tool used in forensic accounting is Benford's Law, which is ordinarily supplemented by other, more traditional, financial tests.

Dr. Mark J. Nigrini's website contains a full-length forensic accounting report discussing the application of Benford's Law.[51]

Benford's Law

Benford's Law, set forth in this chapter under Civil Statutes as Forensic Techniques, is an analytical technique that grew out of observations made in the late 1800s by Simon Newcomb and was developed during the 1920s by Frank Benford, a physicist at General Electric's research laboratories. He noted that the first few pages of logarithm table books were more worn than the later pages. In those days, logarithm table books were used to accelerate the process of multiplying two large numbers by summing the log of each number and then referring to the table for the requisite integer.

Dr. Mark J. Nigrini of Saint Michael's College is responsible for promulgating Benford's Law as the modern-day DNA equivalent of forensic analysis. He built upon Frank Benford's work and used the topic of Benford's Law as the basis for his PhD dissertation. His website contains a wealth of information on the technique.

Benford's Law states that digits and digit sequences in a data set follow a predictable pattern. For example, in any set of numerical data, the number 1 will appear as the first digit approximately 30 percent of the time. Such a data set can consist of sales records, payroll records, journal entries, or virtually any other set of data that has been generated to record business and related transactions. A data set does not have to be large, but can consist of a very few records if the digit composition is sufficient to support the technique.

The technique applies a data analysis method that identifies possible errors, potential fraud, or other irregularities. For example, if artificial values are present in a data set, the distribution of the digits in the data set will likely exhibit a different shape, when viewed graphically, than the shape predicted by Benford's Law. Benford proved his theory by using 20 lists containing 20,229 numbers, and produced the statistical array that is still applied today.

The technique counts digit sequences of values in the sample data set and compares the totals to the predicted result according to Benford's Law. Nonzero digits are counted from left to right.

Despite its origin in the 1920s, Benford's Law was not recognized as an effective tool for forensic accounting analysis until the late 1990s. Data sets analyzed by Benford's Law require certain structural data conformity as summarized here.

- The data set must represent the sizes of similar phenomena.
- The data set must preclude built-in minimum or maximum values.
- The data set must not represent assigned numbers.

Results of Applying Benford's Law

The analytical tests contained within Benford's Law were applied to more than 25,000 financial transactions gathered during a forensic accounting matter. The transactions comprised a database from which the following exhibits resulted. Based

[51] It can be accessed by searching Dr. Nigrini's site for "Forensic Accountants' Report," at www.nigrini.com/images/ForensicAccountantReport.htm.

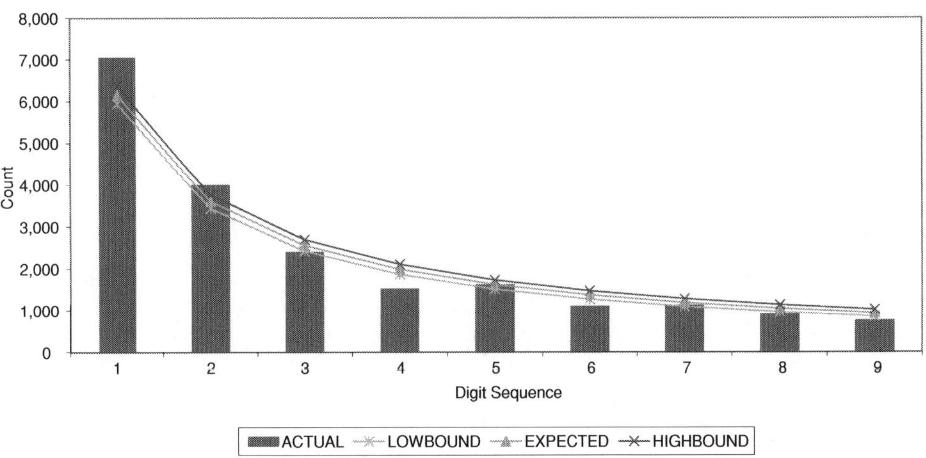

EXHIBIT 7.9 Benford's Law First Digit

upon the analysis of Benford's Law applied against 100 percent of the foundational transaction entries shown in Exhibits 7.9, 7.10, 7.11, and 7.12, it is clear that the transactions failed all four tests: first digit, second digit, first two digits, and first three digits. See Exhibits 7.9, 7.10, 7.11, and 7.12. The implications of the failures lead to the conclusion that a significant proportion of the example's foundational transaction data appears to be contrived and a significant proportion of the example's transactions containing rounded numbers appears to be excessive.

Major Digital Tests

Digital analysis is commonly defined as a set of procedures used to analyze the digit and number patterns of data sets, with the aim of finding anomalies and reporting on broad statistical trends. Digital analysis includes Benford's Law, duplicate numbers

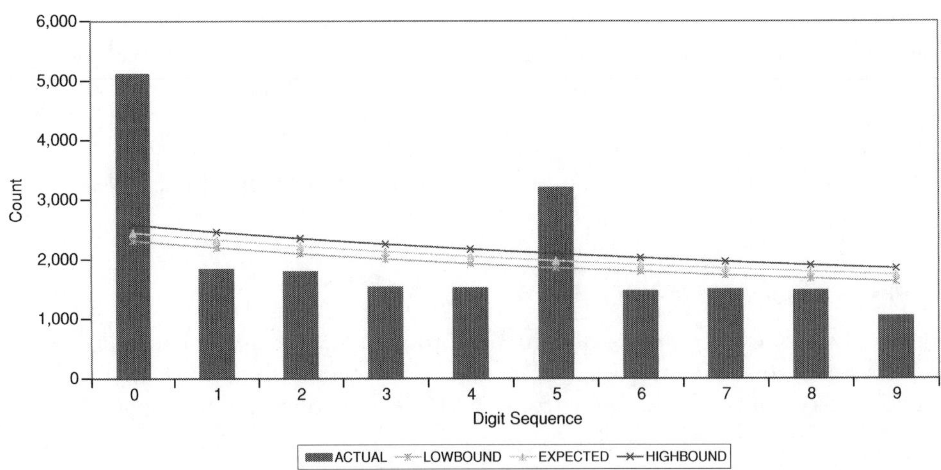

EXHIBIT 7.10 Benford's Law Second Digit

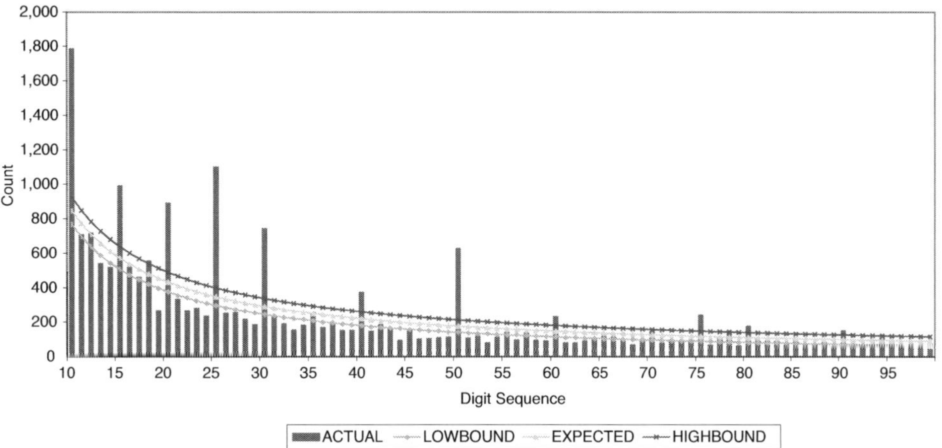

EXHIBIT 7.11 Benford's Law First Two Digits

testing, round numbers testing, and other statistical applications. These investigative tools are invaluable when properly applied to the case or matter at hand.

The digital analytical tests applied through Benford's Law are composed of the following.

- The first major digital test is a test of the first digit proportions, a test for reasonableness. The first digit of a number is the leftmost digit with the understanding that the first digit can never be a zero. For example, the first digit of 7,380 is 7.
- The second major digital test is a test of the second digit proportions, also a test for reasonableness. The second digit of a number is likewise determined by its placement within the number. The second digit of 7,380 is 3.

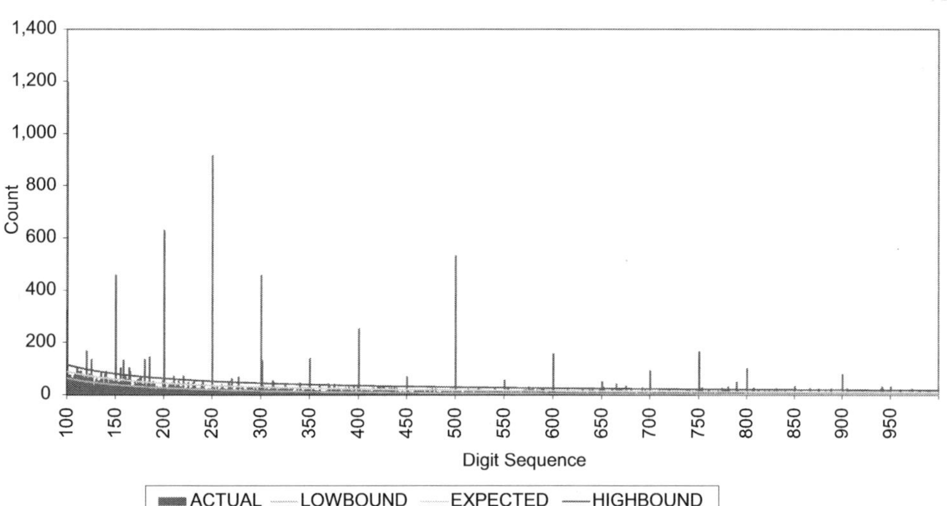

EXHIBIT 7.12 Benford's Law First Three Digits

- The third major digital test is more focused than the two preceding tests and uses the first two leading digits, again excluding zeros. For example, the first two digits of 7,380 are 73 and the first two digits of 0.07380 are also 73. There are 90 possible first-two-digit combinations—10 to 99 inclusive. This test finds anomalies in the data that are not readily apparent from either the first or second digits seen on their own.
- The fourth major digital test focuses on the 900 possible first three digit combinations—100 to 999 inclusive. This highly focused test indicates abnormal duplications.

The results of the first-digit test are indicated by Exhibit 7.9. The variations from the predicted norm suggest that anomalies exist throughout the example's financial data set.

Exhibit 7.9 indicates, among other observations, that the numbers 1 and 2 both exceed the expected counts by 14 percent and 11 percent, respectively. Additionally, the numbers 4 and 6 fall below the predicted limit, thus suggesting that anomalies such as contrivance, fraud, error, and so on exist within the example's financial data set. Such indicators point the investigator to areas where effort should be focused, thus avoiding hit-and-miss attempts.

The results of the second-digit test are indicated by Exhibit 7.10. Again, the variations from the predicted norm suggest that anomalies exist throughout the example's financial data set. Exhibit 7.10 indicates, among other observations, that the numbers 0 and 5 both exceed the expected counts by 110 percent and 61 percent, respectively, thus suggesting that anomalies exist within the example's financial data set. For example, an inordinately large number of payments contained 0 or 5 as a second digit such as $10,000 or $15,000.

The results of the first two digits test are shown in Exhibit 7.11. The testing criteria indicate several significant variations from the predicted norm, thus suggesting that anomalies exist throughout the example's financial data set. Exhibit 7.11 indicates, among other observations, that the numbers 10, 15, 20, 25, 40, and 50 all exceed the predicted limit. This suggests that anomalies exist within the example's financial data set.

The results of the first-three-digits test are indicated by Exhibit 7.12. Several variations from the predicted norm suggest that anomalies could occur throughout the example's financial data set. Exhibit 12 indicates, among other observations, that the numbers 100, 200, 150, 250, and 500 all exceed the predicted limit, thus suggesting that anomalies exist within the example's financial data set.

Numeric Tests

The numeric tests are composed of a numeric duplication test and a rounded numbers test. These tests can be conducted independently or in concert with a Benford's Law analysis. Once any significant duplication has been identified, meaningful inferences can be drawn through further investigation.

The numeric duplication test is used to identify abnormal recurrences of specific numbers. The objective is to draw attention to small groups of numbers that appear to be unusual. The rounded numbers test operates on the same premises as the numeric duplication test. The objective, however, is to identify abnormal recurrences of rounded numbers. Abnormal recurrences of rounded numbers are good indicia of estimation since people tend to estimate when they create contrived numbers.

Results of Applying Numeric Tests

The numeric tests were both applied against 100 percent of the example's foundational transaction entries. The numeric tests were also applied against 100 percent of the data that produced Exhibits 7.9, 7.10, 7.11, and 7.12. The implications of the results lead to the following observations. There appears to be significant duplication of numbers and significant use of rounded numbers. The results for both tests have been presented in a combined format explained next. Only the numeric duplications deemed significant have been set forth.

- Many of the debits for $10, $15, $20, $25, $30, $40, and $50 are bank charges. A large sum of these bank charges are insufficient funds fees (NSF), wire transfer fees, and cashier's check fees. From this, one can conclude that the subject lacked the capability to manage its cash flows, as illustrated by the amount of NSF fees, and that the subject transacted numerous wire transfers and cashier's checks.
- Upon further analysis, it was determined that many of the rounded transactions were cash withdrawals. In some cases, the withdrawals included the bank transaction fee. There are 111 transactions for $301.50. The components of most of these transactions are a $300 withdrawal with a $1.50 ATM fee. Note that $300 is the ATM withdrawal limit established by many financial institutions.
- Many of the larger rounded numbers are actually intercompany bank transfers. It is common for the individuals in charge to transfer large sums of money between the various corporate accounts.

Upon closer examination of these transactions, however, it is apparent that there was a lack of planning and accountability pertaining to these transfers. Furthermore, since there were never any check registers kept for any of the entities, the corporate finances were coordinated through the balances in the bank.

In some instances, the number of duplicate transactions for an amount may not be deemed significant. The aggregate value of these transactions, however, has made them noteworthy. For example, there are two transactions for $700,000 totaling $1,400,000. The aggregate value of these transactions is slightly less than 1 percent of all debit transactions for the company. There were four transactions for $1,000,000. Three of these transactions were payments in accordance with the sample acquisition. The remaining transaction was a wire transfer to a former defendant employee.

Counterterrorism Applications of Digital Analysis and Benford's Law

Digital analysis can streamline investigations that involve a large number of transactions, oftentimes turning a needle in the haystack search into a refined and efficient investigation. For example, in a (questionable) charitable organization conducting tens of thousands of transactions for both legal and illegal purposes, it may be extremely difficult to filter through all transactions and identify those for illegal purposes. However, tools such as Benford's Law may assist the investigator in refining the population of suspect transactions by identifying those transactions that are anomalies or irregularities. In essence, digital analysis may reduce the data population from tens of thousands of transactions to a more manageable number of transactions.

Also, digital analysis may provide indirect evidence of terrorist or criminal activity. An organization's everyday legal activities will result in benchmark transactions. As previously discussed, a truly random data set will normally conform to certain geometric patterns as in Benford's Law. However, contrived numbers, which often represent illegal activity, will deviate from the benchmark transactions revealing the irregularities. A classic example is the organization that has a disproportionate number of transactions in the $8,000 to $9,000 range since they may be structuring transactions (designed to fall below SAR and CTR levels). This fact would likely be revealed during a Benford's Law analysis as the amount of numbers beginning with the digits 8 or 9 would exceed their expected probability of occurrence.

In extreme instances, digital analysis can be used to illustrate that the entity is nothing more than a sham organization used for the furtherance of illicit purposes. A large percentage of contrived numbers for cash inflows and outflows should be easily detected through proper application of digital analysis. Two digital analysis benchmarks hold true for almost all entities reviewed. First, there should always be an exponentially larger proportion of small transactions than large transactions. Almost all entities will have more transactions under $100 than those over $100,000. Second, rarely do entities deal extensively in rounded numbers. Depending on the type of organization, cash inflows may be the exception to this rule. A charitable organization will often accept donations in multiples of $5, $10, $25, $100, and so on. However, the organization's expenditures should still abide by this rule.

ALTER EGO, FRAUDULENT CONVEYANCE, AND SOLVENCY MATTERS IN ACTION

The use of the civil weapons (alter ego, fraudulent conveyance, and solvency) in counterterrorism is understandably in the early stages. To wit, only since November 8, 2001, has the US Attorney General proclaimed that the federal prosecutor's core mission would be preventing terrorist attacks. Although only a handful of civil and criminal cases exist, there are sufficient references to illustrate the versatility of the civil weapons.

The references provided in this section are by no means the only avenues of application of alter ego, fraudulent conveyance, and solvency. Rather, the references reflect the gateway to further and expanded employment of civil tools that add to the prosecutor's arsenal.

Specifically, alter ego, fraudulent conveyance, and solvency are remarkably well suited to support the inchoate offenses of conspiracy and attempt contained in the key terrorist financing statute (18 U.S.C. § 2339B).

Under the Antiterrorism and Effective Death Penalty Act of 1996 (AEDPA), 8 U.S.C. §1189, the secretary of state, in consultation with the secretary of treasury and the attorney general, is empowered to designate an entity as a foreign terrorist organization (or FTO) after making certain findings as to the organization's involvement in terrorist activity. The designation by the secretary of state results in the blocking of any funds that the FTO has on deposit with financial institutions in the United States. Also, representatives and certain members of the FTO are barred from entry into the United States. Finally, all persons within or subject to the jurisdiction of the United States are forbidden from "knowingly providing material support or resources" to the FTO.[52]

In related actions, organizations or individuals found to be, in reality, a front for an FTO can be prosecuted under 18 U.S.C. §2339B. Section 2339B only requires proof that defendants knowingly provided material support or resources to a designated FTO. Also, the Secretary of State has found some organizations to be an alter ego or an alias of a previously designated FTO and subsequently designated that organization as an FTO.[53]

The National Council of Resistance of Iran (NCRI) and the People's Mojahedin of Iran (PMOI) petitioned for review of the secretary of state's designation of both organizations as foreign terrorist organizations under the AEDPA. By notice of October 8, 1999, the secretary of state redesignated the PMOI as an FTO, and also designated NCRI as an FTO. The State Department had determined two years earlier that NCRI was not an alias of PMOI. Nevertheless, the secretary found in 1999 that the NCRI was an alter ego or alias of the PMOI. Both petitioners argued that the secretary's designation deprived them of constitutionally protected rights without due process of law. Additionally, the NCRI argued that the secretary had no statutory authority to find that it was an alias or alter ego of the PMOI. The court agreed with the petitioners' due process argument, but rejected the NCRI's statutory claim. The court concluded that the secretary's designation of the NCRI as an alter ego or alias for the PMOI did not lack substantial support and that the designation was not arbitrary, capricious, or otherwise not in accordance with law.

The secretary did not expressly find that the NCRI engaged in terrorist activities under its own name. However, the secretary did find that the PMOI and the NCRI are one and the same. Therefore, if the NCRI is the PMOI, and if the PMOI is a foreign terrorist organization, then the NCRI is also a foreign terrorist organization. The court did conclude that the petitioners should be afforded the opportunity to file responses to the nonclassified evidence against them, to file evidence in support of their allegations that they are not terrorist organizations, and that they have an opportunity to be meaningfully heard by the secretary. The matter was remanded for further proceedings.[54]

While the court did not revoke the secretary of state's designation of the NCRI as a foreign terrorist organization, as it was an alter ego or alias of the PMOI, it is evident how the doctrine of alter ego could be applicable in defense of this type of matter. The doctrine of alter ego can also be applied to those organizations, charitable and noncharitable alike, found to be supporting designated FTOs. As the United States continues to aggressively pursue foreign terrorist organizations and those entities supporting them, the activities and underlying structure for these

---

[52] See 18 U.S.C. § 2339A.

[53] See *National Council of Resistance of Iran and National Council of Resistance of Iran, U.S. Representative Office v. Department of State and Madeleine K. Albright*, 251 F.3d 192 (D.C. Cir. 2001).

[54] Id. at 199–200, 209.

organizations will undoubtedly become more covert and convoluted. A comprehensive understanding of the jurisdictional law and various analytical techniques related to alter ego, fraudulent conveyance, and solvency analysis will allow those prosecuting such matters to maintain pace with the evolution of terrorist cunning. All of these tools can be applied in the following realms of terrorist financing prosecution.

- Identifying terrorists and supporters through financial analysis.
- Prosecution of financial crimes committed by terrorists and their supporters, including those involving terrorist financing.

Note also that a pre-9/11 case has pertinent application.[55]

WHAT TARGET-RICH SCENARIOS CAN BE EXPLOITED?

Numerous target-rich scenarios can be analyzed using the techniques described herein and civil statutes. The application of civil weapons in counterterrorism is said to parallel the war on illicit drugs. That is, drug dealers are compelled to employ the United States's financial systems (in a seemingly legitimate manner) so as to maximize the results of their efforts. Consequently, once drug dealing operations were understood, laws were passed to criminalize such activities, for example, money laundering.

In a like manner as terrorist activities became focused upon, funding sources migrated to so-called charities. Once charities are scrutinized, terrorists must migrate to the next avenue, that is, businesses, real and sham, that can facilitate their flow of funds. Therefore, it is a logical progression of law to apply civil statutes against terrorists' alleged civil activities in the business community.

The sample scenarios have been structured within the following framework:

- It makes no difference whether the funds under scrutiny are derived from legitimate or illegitimate sources.
- Terrorists are compelled to migrate to more seemingly legitimate business activities since their more recent avenues, that is, charities, are increasingly scrutinized.
- Tracking terrorist funds is more difficult than tracking the funds for which previous legislation, for example, the Bank Secrecy Act, was created, because terrorist funds are often very small amounts and fall under the radar screen of scrutiny provided by SARs and CTRs, and so on.
- Tracking smaller flows of money requires modern forensic accounting techniques that continue to grow in their sophistication.
- Since terrorist financing does not require a completed crime for prosecution, evidence in support of intent, gathered through forensic accounting, can support prosecution for domestic transactions even though the funds never reach their intended destination.
- With sufficient evidence such as that gained through forensic accounting, terrorist-connected assets can be seized through Executive Orders and the civil forfeiture provisions of US law, thus blocking, freezing, seizing, and forfeiting assets of terrorist supporters.

[55] See *People's Mojahedin v. Department of State*, 182 F.3d 17 (D.C. Cir. 1999).

The following examples of potential scenarios are by no means exhaustive, but illustrate the flexibility offered by the civil weapons. Each scenario is a composite constructed from various completed, in-process, and hypothetical civil and criminal matters, thus providing common circumstances in which the civil weapons can be applied.

The scenarios illustrate how alter ego, fraudulent conveyance, solvency, and related forensic accounting techniques, can be used individually or in combination to "[d]elay, disrupt or dismantle terrorist activities." As expected, not all the statutes or techniques apply in all cases.

The Restaurant That Never Opens

A small Portland, Oregon, restaurant offering ethnic foods was properly licensed and appeared to meet pertinent state and local operating ordinances. It contained a kitchen, counter, tables, chairs, utensils, and signage and was well lit at night. However, the doors were never unlocked or opened and customers were never observed inside. Furthermore, in addition to the lack of customers, no food, beverage, or supply deliveries ever occurred. Surveillance indicated that a subject periodically visited the site and was observed entering transactions on the restaurant's cash register system. He then made deposits (below CTR levels) at different local bank branches.

It was suspected that terrorist funds were somehow funneled through the sham business. Specifically, the store was believed to function as a collector that dutifully recorded, reported, and deposited receipts for sales that never occurred, and paid for merchandise that was never received. The party observed onsite was considered a low-level operative, but an offsite party who appeared to direct activities was the real target, that is, the terrorist suspect.

Alter ego indicia and statutes could be used to prove that the offsite party wielded instrumentality power over the restaurant through his direction of activities. Even though the offsite party held no ownership or business interest, for example, stock, debt, and so on, his actions could be proven to demonstrate his control over the business. Consequently, summary judgment or resultant court activities could pierce the veil of the restaurant to hold the offsite party accountable and thus make his personal assets accessible.

Fraudulent transfer tests and statutes would apply in this case since transactions were executed without receiving or giving reasonably equivalent value. Specifically, the restaurant received funds without exchanging value, that is, food and beverages, and the restaurant paid suppliers without receiving merchandise. Fraudulent transfer could also open the door against those so-called suppliers and so-called customers who were suspected of involvement.

Solvency analysis tests could be applied to prove the restaurant insolvent since the flow of funds resulted in a wash of cash inflows and outflows, normal expenses, for example, utilities, insurance, and so on, notwithstanding. Such insolvency determination could be used in support of alter ego and fraudulent conveyance techniques and statutes.

Forensic accounting techniques such as Benford's Law could be used to demonstrate that the deposited receipts (even if dutifully recorded, that is, through a cash register process) did not statistically compare with the restaurant's posted menu prices.

The result? By proving control through instrumentality (alter ego) the offsite target operator could be directly linked to the business, thus persuading the court to pierce the business veil. This would result in the cessation of business operations (through fraudulent transfer and solvency), thus making the target's personal assets subject to seizure.

Cases with potential application include: *National Council of Resistance of Iran and National Council of Resistance of Iran, U.S. Representative Office v. Department of State and Madeleine K. Albright*, 251 F.3d 192 (D.C. Cir. 2001); *Securities and Exchange Commission v. Health Maintenance Centers, Inc.*, C02-0153P, (W.D. Wash., Jan. 24, 2002); and *White Star Timber Co. v. United States*, 94-425C (United States Court of Federal Claims, Aug. 3, 2004).

Waste Paper Round-the-World

A Buffalo, New York, waste paper broker transacted large volumes of waste paper shipments throughout the world. Consistent with his industry's business practices, he seldom took title to the waste paper and often transferred large sums through international letters of credit (ILOC), depository transfer checks (DTCs), wire transfers, and so on, both domestically and internationally. Although his larger transactions were tracked through SARs and CTRs, the transactions appeared legitimate.

The target operator owned the waste paper brokerage as a holding company and passed the transactions through 10 wholly and partially owned multistate and nondomestic business entities. The entities were held in various states throughout the United States near waste paper processing facilities. It was suspected that terrorist funds were somehow channeled through some of the subsidiaries.

Alter ego could be used in concert with fraudulent transfer and solvency analysis to demonstrate that three of the subsidiaries were merely shell corporations, thus exposing the holding company to piercing and asset seizure. By using alter ego statutes and techniques, it could be demonstrated that the subsidiaries never functioned as legitimate stand-alone corporations. Consequently, their sham status could persuade the court to invoke the piercing of their corporate veils.

Fraudulent transfer would likely require proof for only the entry and exit points (where financial transactions initiated and terminated) within three of the selected subsidiaries, thus demonstrating that the remaining entities lacked corporate substance (solvency) in support of alter ego. Such analysis would determine that the transactions lacked reasonably equivalent value, thus supporting UFTA common law requirements. Specifically, when the owner's exchange of money for merchandise significantly exceeded market value, it could be proven that he did not receive reasonably equivalent value in the transaction.

Solvency analysis could further support alter ego and thus prove the lack of corporate substance in support of piercing the veil of the ultimate holding company. Balance sheet, cash flow, and adequate capitalization tests could be used to prove that the entities were not solvent.

A genogram could be used to illustrate the complex funds flow through the numerous wholly and partially owned subsidiaries. That would be necessary because some of the subsidiaries were held in wholly and partially owned shareholding blocks, and some subsidiaries held portions of other subsidiaries, thus complicating the corporate ownership trail.

The result? By proving corporate disregard for only a few of the subsidiaries, the holding company's corporate veil could be pierced, thus exposing the owner to judgment. All the subsidiaries would be required to cease operations, thus interrupting the flow of funds, and the owner's and holding company's funds could be accessed and seized.

Cases with potential application include: *National Council of Resistance of Iran and National Council of Resistance of Iran, U.S. Representative Office v. Department of State and Madeleine K. Albright*, 251 F.3d 192 (D.C. Cir. 2001); *U.S. v. Abdirahman Sheikh-ali Isse*, 342 F.3d 313 (4th Cir. 2003); *Securities and Exchange Commission v. Health Maintenance Centers, Inc.*, C02-0153P (W.D. Wash., Jan. 24, 2002); and *White Star Timber Co. v. United States*, 94-425C (United States Court of Federal Claims, Aug. 3, 2004).

Armored Car and Check Cashing Service

A Dothan, Alabama, armored car service transported coins, currency, and checks between banks and clearing houses. Armored car services throughout the United States similar to this business operate in a largely unregulated industry. The lack of regulation is presumed to exist because of the peripheral scrutiny placed on the respective banking institutions. However, consistent with industry practices, the company routinely cashed checks for otherwise undocumented parties, drawing upon its inventory of cash to process the transactions. Such transactions were typically overlooked by the banking institutions because they occurred between banking points.

It is suspected that the owner of a large Baltimore, Maryland, olive importing business exercised control over the Alabama armored car service. However, public records failed to show that the importer had any formal ties, for example, stock holdings or business debt, to the armored car service.

Alter ego indicia and statutes could be used to demonstrate that the Maryland olive importer wielded instrumentality control over the Alabama armored car service. This could be further supported by identifying selected check and cash transactions processed by the armored car service.

Fraudulent transfer techniques and statutes could be used to demonstrate that the proceeds transferred to undocumented parties in exchange for worthless checks supported the lack of reasonably equivalent value and met the common law requirements.

Solvency analysis would not likely apply in this matter, nor would it be necessary.

Forensic accounting techniques could include statistical tests such as attributes sampling. Attributes sampling is used to specifically identify occurrences that fall within and outside of previously established norms. Attributes sampling techniques can be applied either to the entire database or statistically, using sampling techniques, or both. The most common use of attributes sampling in forensic investigation is to test the rate of deviation from a prescribed or expected control perspective to support the forensic investigator's assessed level of assurance. A simple example is often applied in testing payroll records. That is, if 23 employees are paid weekly, then approximately 92 payroll checks are expected to be found (4 weeks times 23 employees) during a payroll month. If payroll checks exceed that amount, then phantom employees may be on the payroll.

Ratio estimation can further refine the investigation. Ratio estimation is sometimes referred to as extrapolation and is often used in connection with variables sampling. Ratio estimation can project statistically significant results based upon analytical sampling through probability-proportional-to-size sampling.

The legally separate operations could be shown to be operated as an instrumentality by the Maryland target operator. Thus the court would deem him in control and invoke piercing of the corporate veil to access his business and personal assets for seizure.

Cases with potential application include: *National Council of Resistance of Iran and National Council of Resistance of Iran, U.S. Representative Office v. Department of State and Madeleine K. Albright,* 251 F.3d 192 (D.C. Cir. 2001); *U.S. v. Abdirahman Sheikh-ali Isse,* 342 F.3d 313 (4th Cir. 2003); *Securities and Exchange Commission v. Health Maintenance Centers, Inc.,* C02-0153P (W.D. Wash., Jan. 24, 2002); and *White Star Timber Co. v. United States,* 94-425C (United States Court of Federal Claims, Aug. 3, 2004).

The $50 Cup of Coffee

The night manager of a local convenience store insisted on working the graveyard shift. About the middle of his shift, small groups of men appearing to be of Middle Eastern origin visited the store, appeared to transact business, exchanged pleasantries, and left, often three or more to a vehicle. Surveillance found that although significant currency (relative to the transactions) was exchanged, the men seldom left with significant amounts of merchandise. For example, one party was observed paying $50 for a cup of coffee. The night manager dutifully deposited his receipts (below CTR and SAR levels) at various bank branches—one used by the store and the others not related to the store.

It was suspected that the cash receipts were actually funds intended for terrorist purposes and that the night manager was a relatively highly placed operative. Although the store's actual owner appeared innocent, it would be helpful to prove that the late-night sales that occurred were not legitimate.

Even though the night manager held no ownership interest in the store, he could be proven to use the business as his instrumentality. That is, his graveyard shift responsibilities, consisting of stewardship of store assets, gave him functional control over business operations, including sales, merchandising, stocking, and ordering.

The target operator could be pursued with fraudulent transfer statutes and techniques since he executed transactions without receiving or giving reasonably equivalent value while using the store's facilities. Specifically, he received funds without exchanging value, that is, food, and other merchandise, from customers. This would also open the door against the customers who were suspected of involvement.

Solvency analysis would not need to be applied in this matter.

Forensic accounting techniques applied in this matter could include full-and-false inclusion testing and pattern analysis to identify the transactional inconsistencies and thus focus the respective analytical efforts. Full-and-false inclusion tests could be used to determine the appropriate universe of data under investigation. That would ensure that no extraneous data was included and that no appropriate data was excluded. Also, ratio estimation (sometimes known as ratio extrapolation) could estimate (on a statistically significant basis) the projected results based upon analytical sampling through probability-proportional-to-size sampling.

The court could deem the night manager to be in control of the store's night operations and thus access and seize his personal assets.

Cases with potential application include: *National Council of Resistance of Iran and National Council of Resistance of Iran, U.S. Representative Office v. Department of State and Madeleine K. Albright,* 251 F.3d 192 (D.C. Cir. 2001); *U.S. v. Abdurahman Muhammad Alamoudi,* C03-1009M (E.D. Va. Oct. 22, 2003); *Securities and Exchange Commission v. Health Maintenance Centers, Inc.,* C02-0153P (W.D. Wash., Jan. 24, 2002); and *White Star Timber Co. v. United States,* 94-425C (United States Court of Federal Claims, Aug. 3, 2004).

Conclusion

The most effective way for an AUSA to begin employing civil tools in a counterterrorism effort is to start with simple targets and begin applying the guidance on an experience basis. That is, consider all possible targets and organize them according to the ABC method. The As are the high-value targets, and the Cs are the low-value targets; the Bs fall in-between.

The array will resemble a bell curve, with a few As, a few Cs, and mostly Bs. Start targeting the Cs first and gain experience on low-value targets. Once all the Cs are exhausted, then begin with the As, and then the Bs. Such an approach will preserve precious resources while providing valuable experience.

As terrorists become more and more sophisticated in financing their activities, prosecutors must also become more resourceful. The forensic accounting weapons discussed in this article, when used effectively, will enable prosecutors to delay, disrupt, and dismantle terrorist activities.

FORENSIC ACCOUNTING: COUNTERTERRORISM WEAPONRY

This is the second of a two-part series that demonstrates how forensic accounting techniques fortify the identification, analysis, investigation, and prosecution of terrorist and terrorist-related organizations. Note that the forensic accounting techniques discussed apply to virtually all matters containing a money laundering and/or phantom business element such as white collar crime.

This knowledge grows in importance as terrorist money laundering migrates from charitable organizations into legitimate and illegitimate businesses to avoid the increasing scrutiny of AUSAs.

Terrorist Needs

Certain conditions are necessary for a terrorist to reside undetected in the United States until he is called upon to commit acts of terrorism. Such conditions accommodate *financial profiling* similar to behavioral profiling as applied to serial killers. The conditions and their detection through forensic accounting are described in this section.

Effective deployment of forensic accounting tools in the financial profiling of terrorists requires a comprehensive grasp of the money flows that terrorists rely upon. Fortunately, forensic accounting tools can be applied regardless of the source, disposition, or even the nature of the money flow. The tools are equally effective among all types of flows, including electronic transfers, checking accounts, credit cards, debit cards, traveler's checks, purchase and sale invoices, payroll records, letters of credit, cash, and other flows.

The following discussion profiles the nature of a terrorist's financial needs and outlines the likely sources and disposition of the money he acquires.

The Common Thread: Money

Even terrorists have basic needs that must be met in order to execute their plans. Their basic needs, in descending order, are composed of physiological needs, communications needs, and mobility needs. Significantly, the common thread of such basic needs is *money*. Each of their basic needs requires money to fulfill.

Terrorists cannot effectively attack our society unless they use our society's methods, which, by their nature, typically leave financial trails that can be traced by forensic accounting back to the terrorists. Therefore, the better we understand how and where terrorists acquire and expend their money, the more effective we will become in defeating their efforts.

Physiological Needs

Every human body must have air, water, and food to survive. The human body can live about three to five minutes without air, about eight days without water, and about 40 days without food before death occurs. In order to survive, the terrorist must breathe, drink, and eat so that his body will function when called upon. Air does not require a purchase, but purchases of water and food leave various trails of evidence.

After the basic physiological needs are met, the terrorist will also need shelter, clothing and (presumably) personal hygiene items to avoid attracting undue attention. Acquisition of such items generates a trail of evidence and activities through their provision or acquisition. Acquisition of such items continues to generate a trail of evidence and activities that can be traced by forensic accounting analysis.

Communication Needs

Communication needs are vital to a terrorist for three significant reasons. The most obvious reason is coordination among other terrorists in the execution of their schemes. Second, since several terrorists living together could attract attention, individual immersion is the most practical way to maintain a low profile. Therefore, periodic communication is necessary for planning. Finally, a less obvious need relates to a terrorist's persona. Specifically, he requires continual reinforcement by and with others sympathetic to his cause to ensure that his commitment is maintained and strengthened.

Installed landline phones require deposits, identification, and related trail indicators. Therefore, they are often avoided. Coin-operated phones leave little evidence, but are inconvenient, provide little privacy, and still leave a record of activities. Cellular phones can be purchased as throwaway units that preclude tracing except at the point of purchase and activation. Cellular phones have walkie-talkie and camera capabilities that are valuable to terrorists because of their mobility and multipurpose functionality.

Email communications, typically in code, are often used by terrorists since they are readily made at innumerable sources in most major cities, leave little trail (except for the purchase of online time) but also have limitations when not accessible at will. Mail communication is cost-effective but slow and leaves more of a trail than the terrorist desires, such as fingerprints, DNA, routing information, timing indications, and related data.

Mobility Needs

Mobility needs are vital to a terrorist for two significant reasons. First, mobility enables a terrorist to make himself a moving target, which, by definition is more difficult to track.

Second, a terrorist needs mobility so as to execute plans against targets of opportunity and in conjunction with other terrorists. Travel modes range from airline to public transportation.

Automobile ownership and related requirements such as a driver's license complicate a terrorist's mobility since their acquisition and operation compel documentation, providing evidence of activities. Therefore, a terrorist will minimize high-trail modes such as airline travel and maximize low-trail modes such as city bus routes.

Where Did The 9/11 Terrorists Get and Spend Their Money?

A summarized financial profile of the Pentagon/Twin Towers[56] financial investigation indicates that the 19 9/11 hijackers opened 24 bank accounts at 7 banks, and opened 12 international bank accounts. Their deposits and disbursements totaled $303,481 and $303,671, respectively, and are categorized in Exhibit 7.13 and Exhibit 7.14, respectively.

It is significant that the majority of their transactions for both money inflows and outflows were composed of *cash*. Note that Exhibit 7.13 indicates that 47 percent of the funds that the 9/11 terrorists received was in the form of cash.

Exhibit 7.14 illustrates that 42 percent of the terrorists' pre-9/11 expenditures occurred in the form of cash.

Other key points regarding the 19 hijackers' financial characteristics are significant. Specifically, none of the hijackers had a valid or issued Social Security number (SSN). They used foreign passports or visas from Saudi Arabia, the United Arab Emirates (UAE), Germany, Egypt, or Lebanon to open bank accounts. Most of the accounts were opened with cash and cash equivalents (such as travelers' checks) in

[56] ATF/FBI Joint Presentation, "Money Laundering and the Financing of Terrorism," American Institute of Certified Public Accountants' Annual Fraud and Litigation Conference, September 26–29, 2004.

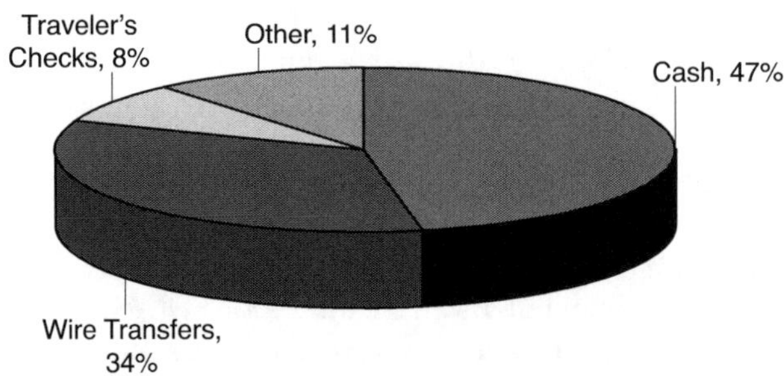

EXHIBIT 7.13 Pentagon/Twin Towers Terrorist Funds Received

the average amount of $3,000 to $5,000. Some hijackers opened joint accounts, and all the accounts were accessible with debit cards.

Interestingly, the 9/11 hijackers returned all unused money to the terrorist network immediately before executing their attacks. Marwan Al-Shehhi wired $5,400 from a Greyhound bus station in Boston, Waleed Al-Shehri wired $5,215 from Logan Airport in Boston, and Mohamed Atta wired $2,860 and $5,000 from two Laurel, Maryland, grocery stores. Al-Shehhi and Al-Shehri sent their funds through the Al-Ansari Exchange, and Atta sent his funds through the Wall Street Exchange, UAE.

In contrast, the alleged twentieth hijacker, Zacarias Moussaoui, obtained his funding directly from the al-Qaeda network, while Ahmed Ressam, the Millennium bomber, obtained his funds through criminal activity.

Sources of Terrorist Money

Generally, most terrorist money flows derive from two primary sources: operating entities, legal and illegal, and individuals. In theory, legal environments tend to have more comprehensive and accessible record-keeping systems than illegal operating entities. Forensic accounting tools, however, function regardless of the legality or extent of respective record-keeping systems.

Perhaps a more important distinction relates to whether the sources are sympathetic or unsympathetic to terrorist causes. A sympathetic source is a party who

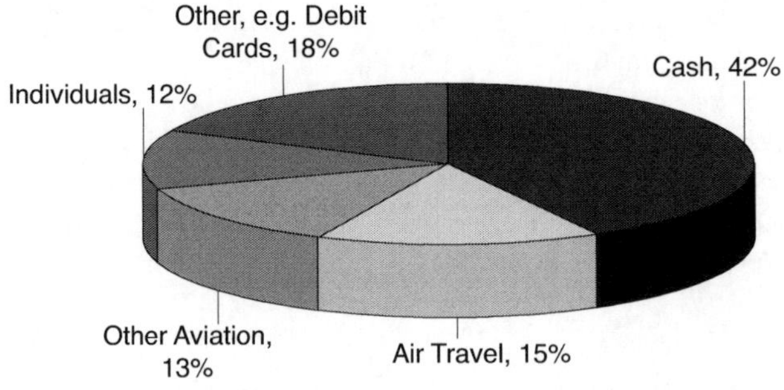

EXHIBIT 7.14 Pentagon/Twin Towers Terrorist Funds Disbursed

supports the terrorist's cause. An unsympathetic source could be an inner-city homeless shelter that unwittingly meets a terrorist's survival needs. Forensic accounting tools and techniques function well regardless of the predisposition of the source or the terminus of funds.

Critical Success Factors for Terrorists

Based upon the preceding terrorist financial profile, certain factors are critical to a terrorist's existence. These factors are highlighted here in a descending hierarchy of priority and serve as markers in support of forensic accounting analysis.

First, terrorists must minimize the evidence trail. Their day-to-day existence, spanning their physiological, communication, and mobility needs must be met in a low-profile manner that minimizes evidence generation. In short, they should deal in cash as much as possible.

Second, when evidence generation is unavoidable, they will use counterfeit identification before using legitimate, but easy to trace identification. For example, airline travel that requires identification may compel a terrorist to use legitimate foreign identification since counterfeit identification may raise red flags. Naturally, the counterfeit identification is time-sensitive since it is most effective when newly obtained, before authorities have had a chance to begin focusing on it.

Third, from the terrorist's point of view, criminal activities as a source of generating funds are undesirable and should be avoided. Criminal activities are avoided not because of their illegal nature, but because such actions may draw undue attention and potential disruption to the terrorist's actions.

Fourth, terrorists will seek donations (money, goods, services) from parties sympathetic to their cause to minimize the generation of evidence. Cash receipts from sympathetic donors leave almost no evidence trail. The receipt of goods and services (such as food and shelter) from sympathetic donors also leaves very little evidence trail. Still, a trail can be left from the donor source, which in turn leads to the terrorist.

Fifth, money and goods and services can flow through sympathetic parties that can consist of operating entities and individuals. Regardless of the source, such activities leave some evidence that can be traced, directly or indirectly or both.

Sixth, if sympathetic parties are not available, terrorists will extract resources through coercion, such as threatening family members residing in the source's foreign country. Even this source may leave a trail of activities when a comparison of resource consumption (food, communications, shelter) indicates that the (unwilling) donor has consumed more resources, such as food, than would otherwise be expected.

Seventh, a terrorist will strive to continually change his patterns to avoid generation of evidence and detection. Fortunately, human nature makes change an inherently difficult task and thus helps ensure that a trail of evidence is continually generated.

FINANCIAL STATEMENTS—THE SOURCES OF DATA

Virtually every business maintains some form of business activity record, whether for legitimate or illegitimate purposes. Therefore, even without a strong accounting system, internal controls or even honest management, transactional activity can be used to construct financial statements that represent even the most clandestine of operations. Consequently, if a source of terrorist funding flows from an operating entity, for example, a business, a charitable organization, an educational institution, a governmental organization, or a nongovernmental organization (NGO) forensic accounting tools and techniques can be used in the analysis.

Even the most basic financial statements can yield telling indicators when skilled analysis is applied to their composition. To provide a starting point for analysis, each of the basic financial statements found in a typical business is illustrated in this section, supported by examples and generally accepted accounting definitions, which are offered for reference.

Financial Statements

A financial statement is any report summarizing the financial condition or financial results of a person or organization on any date or for any period. Financial statements include the balance sheet and the income statement and sometimes the statement of changes in financial position,[57] currently identified as the cash flow statement. In most businesses, only a balance sheet and income statement will be available and the cash flow statement must be constructed by the forensic accountant.

Balance Sheet

The balance sheet, sometimes called the statement of financial position, lists the company's assets, liabilities, and stockholders' equity (including dollar amounts) as of a specific moment in time.[58]

Assets are probable future economic benefits obtained or controlled by a particular entity as a result of past transactions or events.[59] Assets are typically categorized into current, long-term, and other classifications, such as goodwill. Current assets include cash, accounts receivable, inventory, and prepaid items and are typically liquidated within one year or less. Long-term assets include land, buildings, fixtures, and equipment (and their related accumulated depreciation) and are expected to last longer than one year. Liabilities are probable future sacrifices of economic benefits arising from present obligations of a particular entity to transfer assets or provide services to other entities in the future as a result of past transactions or events.[60] Current liabilities include accounts payable, accrued expenses, lines of credit, and current portions of long-term debt and are typically liquidated within one year or less. Long-term liabilities include long-term debt and mortgages and are expected to last longer than one year. Other liabilities are seldom identified since they can consist of contingent liabilities such as pending lawsuits.

---

[57] *Black's Law Dictionary,* 6th ed. (St. Paul, MN: West Publishing, 1990), 631.

[58] Roger H. Hermanson and James Don Edwards, *Financial Accounting—A Business Perspective* 7th ed., (Boston: Irwin/McGraw-Hill, 1998), 20.

[59] Concept Statement No. 6, Elements of Financial Statements, Financial Accounting Standards Board, Norwalk, CT, 1985.

[60] Id.

EXHIBIT 7.15 Balance Sheet

	1999	2000	2001	2002	2003
ASSETS					
Cash	$45,161	$54,182	$98,179	$120,573	$101,355
Accounts Receivable	4,623	5,546	6,979	8,248	7,304
Inventory	13,513	16,212	20,400	24,108	21,350
Other Current Assets	15,290	18,345	23,084	27,281	24,161
Total Current Assets	78,587	94,285	148,642	180,210	154,170
Fixed Assets (net)	220,116	264,082	332,305	392,714	347,787
Net Intangible	9,957	11,946	15,032	17,764	15,732
Other Noncurrent	46,939	56,315	40,862	43,745	44,165
Nonoperating Assets	56,896	68,260	55,894	61,509	59,897
Total Assets	$355,599	$426,627	$536,841	$634,433	$561,854
LIABILITIES & EQUITY					
Accounts Payable	$35,560	$42,663	$53,684	$63,443	$56,185
Short Term Notes Payable	2,845	3,413	4,295	5,075	4,495
Current Portion of LT Debt	20,980	25,171	31,674	37,432	33,149
Other Current Liabilities	40,538	48,636	61,200	50,210	64,051
Total Current Liabilities	99,923	119,882	150,853	156,160	157,880
Long Term Debt	76,208	53,479	18,211	9,097	10,207
Other Non-Current Liabilities	—	—	—	—	—
Non-Operating Liabilities	13,868	16,638	20,936	24,743	21,912
Total Liabilities	190,000	190,000	190,000	190,000	190,000
Total Equity	165,599	236,627	346,841	444,433	371,854
Total Liabilities & and Equity	$355,599	$426,627	$536,841	$634,433	$561,854

Equity or net assets is the residual interest in the assets of an entity that remains after deducting its liabilities.[61] If liabilities exceed assets, a negative equity results and is technically insolvent, depending upon other measures.

A hypothetical balance sheet for a business with attributes conducive to terrorist money laundering is presented as Exhibit 7.15.

Exhibit 7.15 highlights the major components of the hypothetical balance sheet and thus establishes the starting point for financial analysis. A more apparent view of the data can be obtained by converting the data into a visual representation as illustrated in Exhibit 7.16. Exhibit 7.16 illustrates the total assets, total liabilities, and total equity contained in the balance sheet.

[61] Id.

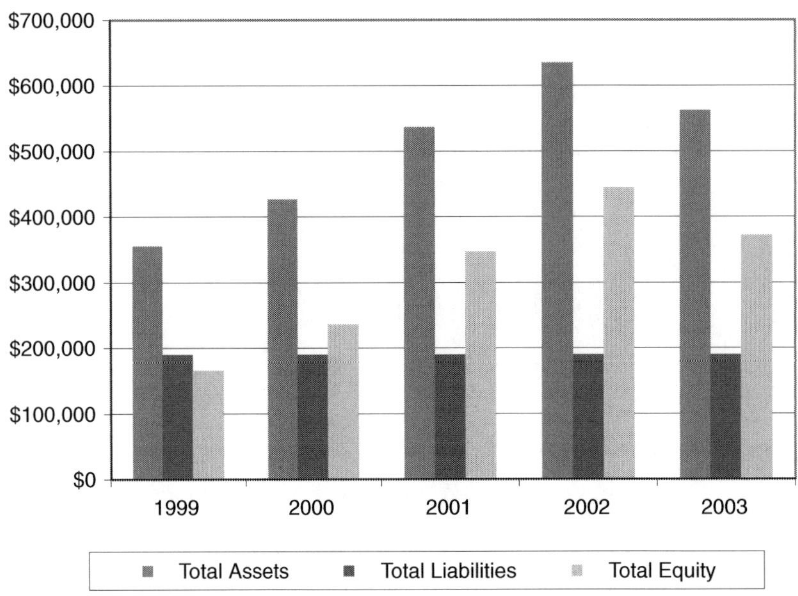

EXHIBIT 7.16 Balance Sheet Category Comparison

Also, a comparison technique known as *common-sizing* is provided in Exhibit 7.17 which in combination with the preceding exhibits enables a forensic analyst to formulate observations of the key items as indicated. Common-sizing consists of converting all financial statement items to a percentage of assets and revenues for the balance sheet and income statement, respectively. Results are then compared within and among one another over a multiperiod time horizon.

The common-sizing technique also accommodates a comparison to similar businesses that may be much larger or smaller than the subject under analysis. Bar graphs and line charts are useful to identify key variations warranting further investigation.

The data illustrated also supports other financial analysis methods such as vertical analysis and horizontal analysis. Vertical analysis consists of comparing each key account category item *within* its respective fiscal period. Horizontal analysis consists of comparing key account categories, such as officer compensation, travel and entertainment, and so on, over a multiperiod time horizon to identify changes meriting further inquiry. The technique typically includes percentage changes, dollar changes, comparison changes, and so on.

The sample balance sheet (Exhibit 7.15) and related visual and quantitative measures (Exhibits 7.16 and 7.17) indicate steadily growing assets driven primarily by growing cash balances, growing fixed asset balances, and steady nonoperating assets. The cash balances have resulted from stable revenues (Exhibits 7.18 and 7.19) and strong gross profit performance (Exhibit 7.20) while operating expenses have remained stable (Exhibits 7.18 and 7.20). Also, in comparison to the subject company's peer group (not shown for ease of illustration), the hypothetical balance sheet carries less accounts receivable than its competitors but employs substantially more fixed assets (Exhibits 7.15 and 7.17). Finally, the total current liabilities are

EXHIBIT 7.17 Balance Sheet Common-Sizing

	1999	2000	2001	2002	2003
ASSETS					
Cash	12.7%	12.7%	18.3%	19.0%	18.0%
Accounts Receivable	1.3%	1.3%	1.3%	1.3%	1.3%
Inventory	3.8%	3.8%	3.8%	3.8%	3.8%
Other Current Assets	4.3%	4.3%	4.3%	4.3%	4.3%
Total Current Assets	22.1%	22.1%	27.7%	28.4%	27.4%
Fixed Assets (net)	61.9%	61.9%	61.9%	61.9%	61.9%
Net Intangible	2.8%	2.8%	2.8%	2.8%	2.8%
Other Noncurrent	13.2%	13.2%	7.6%	6.9%	7.9%
Nonoperating Assets	16.0%	16.0%	10.4%	9.7%	10.7%
Total Assets	100.0%	100.0%	100.0%	100.0%	100.0%
LIABILITIES & EQUITY					
Accounts Payable	10.0%	10.0%	10.0%	10.0%	10.0%
Short-Term Notes Payable	0.8%	0.8%	0.8%	0.8%	0.8%
Current Portion of LT Debt	5.9%	5.9%	5.9%	5.9%	5.9%
Other Current Liabilities	11.4%	11.4%	11.4%	0.0%	11.4%
Total Current Liabilities	28.1%	28.1%	28.1%	24.6%	28.1%
Long-Term Debt	21.4%	12.5%	3.4%	1.4%	1.8%
Other Noncurrent Liabilities	0.0%	0.0%	0.0%	0.0%	0.0%
Non-Operating Liabilities	3.9%	3.9%	3.9%	3.9%	3.9%
Total Liabilities	53.4%	44.5%	35.4%	29.9%	33.8%
Total Equity	46.6%	55.5%	64.6%	70.1%	66.2%
Total Liabilities and Equity	100.0%	100.0%	100.0%	100.0%	100.0%

proportionately larger than its competitors and its long-term debt is proportionately smaller than its competitors, resulting in lower total liabilities than those of its competitors (Exhibits 7.15 and 7.17).

Generally, such indicators could point to money laundering, as cash balances and fixed assets are growing even though accounts receivable balances are small and stable. Consequently, further investigation is warranted.

Income Statement

The income statement, sometimes called an earnings statement or profit and loss (P&L) statement, reports the profitability of a business organization for a stated period of time. In accounting, profitability is measured for a period, such as a month

EXHIBIT 7.18 Income Statement

	1999	2000	2001	2002	2003
Revenue	$5,132,509	$5,090,135	$5,684,996	$5,696,025	$5,524,184
Cost of Goods Sold	1,703,993	1,837,539	1,659,199	1,669,128	2,039,819
Gross Profit	3,428,516	3,252,596	4,025,797	4,026,897	3,484,365
Operating Expenses	2,812,615	2,789,394	3,446,928	3,434,862	3,112,818
Officers' Compensation	—	—	—	—	—
Depreciation/Amortization	169,373	152,704	124,440	125,185	130,629
Interest Expense	—	—	—	—	—
Total Operating Expenses	2,981,988	2,942,098	3,571,368	3,560,047	3,243,446
Operating Profit	446,528	310,498	454,430	466,850	240,919
Other Income/(Expense)	(20,530)	(25,451)	(20,740)	(20,864)	(45,218)
Income Before Taxes	425,998	285,048	433,690	445,986	195,701
Income Taxes	170,399	114,019	173,476	178,394	78,281
Net Income	$255,599	$171,029	$260,214	$267,592	$117,421

or a year, by comparing the revenues generated with the expenses (and costs) incurred to produce the revenues.[62]

Revenues are inflows or other enhancements of assets of an entity or settlements of its liabilities (or a combination of both) from delivering or producing goods, rendering services, or other activities that constitute the entity's ongoing major or central operations.[63]

Costs are sacrifices of assets that result in the generation of revenues. Costs in manufacturing operations comprise materials, labor, and overhead. Overhead is typically applied in some manner related to the operations of the business, such as labor hours, labor dollars, machine time, and other techniques. Costs in retail operations are composed of purchased merchandise.

Expenses are period outflows or other consumption of assets or incurrence of liabilities (or a combination of both) from delivering goods, rendering services, or carrying out other activities that constitute the entity's ongoing major or central operations.[64] They are typically categorized within classifications of sales, general, and administrative expenses.

A hypothetical income statement for a business with attributes conducive to terrorist money laundering is presented in Exhibit 7.18.

Exhibit 7.18 highlights the major components of the hypothetical income statement and thus establishes the starting point for forensic analysis in concert with the balance sheet. A more obvious depiction is obtained by converting the data into a

[62] Hermanson, et al., 18.

[63] Ibid.

[64] Id.

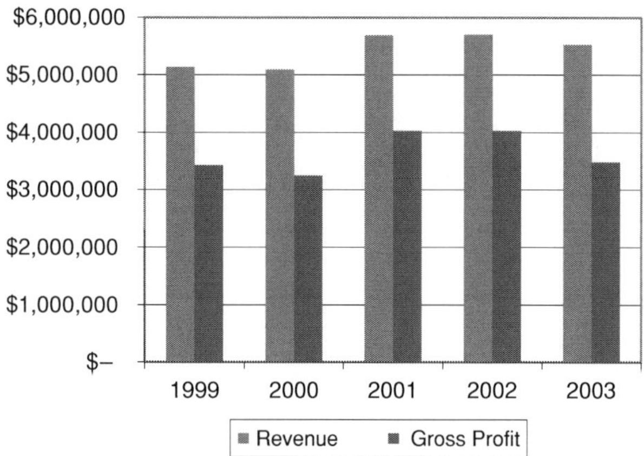

EXHIBIT 7.19 Income Statement Highlights

visual representation as illustrated in Exhibit 7.19, which shows the revenues and gross profit contained in the income statement.

Finally, the common-sizing technique is provided in Exhibit 7.20 which, in combination with the preceding Exhibits, enables an analyst to make the observations of the key items as indicated.

The sample income statement and related visual and quantitative measures shown here indicate generally that the hypothetical income statement's revenue base has remained relatively flat since 1999. The no-growth scenario results from the company's respective industry-related economic downturn following the mid to late 1990s. Despite the flat revenues, the gross profit margin has remained healthy relative to its competitors, even with the 2003 decline. Consequently, the gross profit margin peaked at 70.8 percent in 2001 and troughed at 63.1 percent in 2003. Since this hypothetical business operates in an industry notorious for aggressive price cutting, a relatively strong and stable gross profit margin during flat revenues is a flag meriting further investigation into money laundering.

Cash Flow Statement

The cash flow statement shows the cash inflows and cash outflows from operating, investing, and financing activities.[65]

Operating activities include all transactions and other events that are not defined as investing or financing activities. Operating activities generally involve producing and delivering goods and providing services. Cash flows from operating activities are generally the cash effects of transactions and other events that enter into the determination of net income.[66]

Investing activities include making and collecting loans and acquiring and disposing of debt or equity instruments and property, plant, and equipment and other

[65] Hermanson, et al., 20.

[66] FAS 95: Statement of Cash Flows, FASB (Financial Accounting Standards Board), Norwalk, CT, 1987.

EXHIBIT 7.20 Income Statement Common-Sizing

	1999	2000	2001	2002	2003
Revenue	100.0%	100.0%	100.0%	100.0%	100.0%
Cost of Goods Sold	33.2%	36.1%	29.2%	29.3%	36.9%
Gross Profit	66.8%	63.9%	70.8%	70.7%	63.1%
Operating Expenses	54.8%	54.8%	60.6%	60.3%	56.3%
Officers' Compensation	0.0%	0.0%	0.0%	0.0%	0.0%
Depreciation/Amortization	3.3%	3.0%	2.2%	2.2%	2.4%
Interest Expense	0.0%	0.0%	0.0%	0.0%	0.0%
Total Operating Expenses	58.1%	57.8%	62.8%	62.5%	58.7%
Operating Profit	8.7%	6.1%	8.0%	8.2%	4.4%
Other Income/(Expense)	−0.4%	−0.5%	−0.4%	−0.4%	−0.8%
Income Before Taxes	8.3%	5.6%	7.6%	7.8%	3.5%
Income Taxes	3.3%	2.2%	3.1%	3.1%	1.4%
Net Income	5.0%	3.4%	4.6%	4.7%	2.1%

productive assets, that is, assets held for or used in the production of goods or services by the enterprise (other than materials that are part of the enterprise's inventory).[67]

Financing activities include obtaining resources from owners and providing them with a return on, and a return of, their investment; borrowing money and repaying amounts borrowed or otherwise settling the obligation; and obtaining and paying for other resources obtained from creditors on long-term credit.[68]

Note that the cash flow statement is perhaps the single most powerful forensic accounting tool to deploy in money laundering investigations. Certain critical transactions will show up nowhere else unless a cash flow statement is prepared, such as cash distributions to and infusions from owners and outside parties. Unfortunately, the cash flow statement is very "young" relative to the balance sheet and income statement.

The balance sheet and income statements can be traced to Luca Pacioli, a 15th-century Franciscan Monk credited with formalizing the double-entry method of accounting in his 1494 treatise, *Summa de Arithmetica, Geometria, Proportioni et Proportionalita* (Everything About Arithmetic, Geometry and Proportion). It was written as a digest and guide to existing mathematical knowledge and bookkeeping was only one of five topics covered. The *Summa's* 36 short chapters on bookkeeping entitled *De Computis et Scripturis* (Of Reckonings and Writings) were added in "order that the subjects of the most gracious Duke of Urbino may have complete instructions in the conduct of business," and to "give the trader without delay, information as to his assets and liabilities."[69]

[67] Ibid.

[68] Ibid.

[69] All quotes from the translation by J.B. Geusbeek, *Ancient Double Entry Bookkeeping: Lucas Pacioli's Treatise* (Published by the Author in 1914).

The cash flow statement was only recently mandated by the FASB in 1987. Therefore, the 500 year-old familiarity of the balance sheet and income statement stand in stark contrast to the mere 24 year tenure of the cash flow statement. Simply put, even skilled accountants often lack a deep understanding of the cash flow statement's powerful capabilities and applications.

The cash flow statement is typically the most difficult statement to manipulate since it begins and ends with cash. A hypothetical cash flow statement for a business with attributes conducive to terrorist money laundering is presented in Exhibit 7.21.

Exhibit 7.21 highlights the key components of the hypothetical cash flow statement and thus enhances the starting point for operating analysis in concert with the balance sheet and income statement. Analysis is aided by converting the data into a visual representation as illustrated in Exhibit 7.22. Exhibit 7.22 illustrates the operating, investing, and financing flows contained in the cash flow statement.

Exhibit 7.23 focuses on the operating cash flows and highlights a key forensic observation: operating cash flow is declining despite continual increases in cash balances and fixed asset balances as contained in Exhibits 7.15, 7.16, and 7.17. This condition merits further investigation.

WHEN FINANCIAL STATEMENTS CONTAIN LAUNDERED MONEY

Money laundering is readily detectable since the related transactions disrupt the otherwise ordinary and predictable patters inherent in legitimate activities.

Cash Deposits Commingled with Routine Business Deposits

The most common goal of money laundering is to conduct cash transactions in such a way to conceal the true nature of the funds. Typically, there are three steps to this process. First, *placement* of cash in a financial institution reflects the entry point into our monetary system. Second, the *layering* of financial transactions in complex patterns to confuse the trail reflects continual and repeated transactions. Third, *integration* of the assets occurs back into the economy with the appearance of a legitimate business transaction.

Certain types of businesses have characteristics that accommodate money-laundering activities. The types of businesses can be broadly categorized into sale of products and sale of services. It makes little difference whether the business is selling high-profit or low-profit products. Likewise, the products can be genuine or counterfeit.

There are four important business characteristics that are conducive to money laundering for terrorist purposes. That is, businesses that sell consumer products, with a commodity-type demand, have low regulatory reporting requirements and deal in cash-based transactions are well suited to terrorists.

Note that such characteristics reflect the small-business nature of the United States' economy.

The types of business selling products conducive to money-laundering include clothing, cigarettes, perfumes, delicatessens, electronics, software, bakeries, restaurants, bars, bicycle repair, catering, and many others. Cash from sympathetic sources can be deposited along with the periodic deposits of an otherwise legitimate

EXHIBIT 7.21 Cash Flow Statement

Increase/(Decrease) in Cash	1999	2000	2001	2002	2003
Cash Provided by (Used for) Operations:					
Net Income/(Loss)	255,599	171,029	260,214	267,592	117,421
Depreciation	169,373	152,704	124,440	125,185	130,629
Amortization	—	—	—	—	—
(Increase)/Decrease in Accounts Receivable	(4,623)	(923)	(1,433)	(1,269)	944
(Increase)/Decrease in Inventory	(13,513)	(2,699)	(4,188)	(3,708)	2,758
(Increase)/Decrease in Other Noncurrent Assets	(15,291)	(3,054)	(4,739)	(4,196)	3,121
(Increase)/Decrease in Other Assets	(56,896)	(11,365)	12,366	(5,615)	1,613
Increase/(Decrease) in Current Liabilities	99,923	19,959	30,970	5,308	1,721
Increase/(Decrease) in Other Liabilities	13,868	2,770	4,298	3,806	(2,831)
Total Cash Provided by (Used for) Operations:	448,441	328,420	421,928	387,102	255,375
Cash Provided by (Used for) Investing Activities:					
Net (Additions to)/Disposal of Fixed Assets—Net	(389,489)	(196,671)	(192,662)	(185,594)	(85,702)
Net (Additions to)/Disposal of Intangible Assets—Net					
Total Cash Provided by (Used for) Investing Activities:	(389,489)	(196,671)	(192,662)	(185,594)	(85,702)
Cash Provided by (Used for) Financing Activities:					
Net Additions to/(Reductions in) Notes Payable	76,208	(22,729)	(35,268)	(9,114)	1,110
Net Investment in/(Distribution of) Common Stock	10,000	—	—	—	—
Net Investment in/(Distribution of) Retained Earnings	(100,000)	(100,000)	(150,000)	(170,000)	(190,000)
Total Cash Provided by (Used for) Financing Activities:	(13,792)	(122,729)	(185,268)	(179,114)	(188,890)
Total Increase/(Decrease) in Cash	45,161	9,021	43,997	22,394	(19,218)
Cash Balance at Beginning of Year	—	45,161	54,182	98,179	120,573
Cash Balance at End of Year	$45,161	$54,182	$98,179	$120,573	$101,355

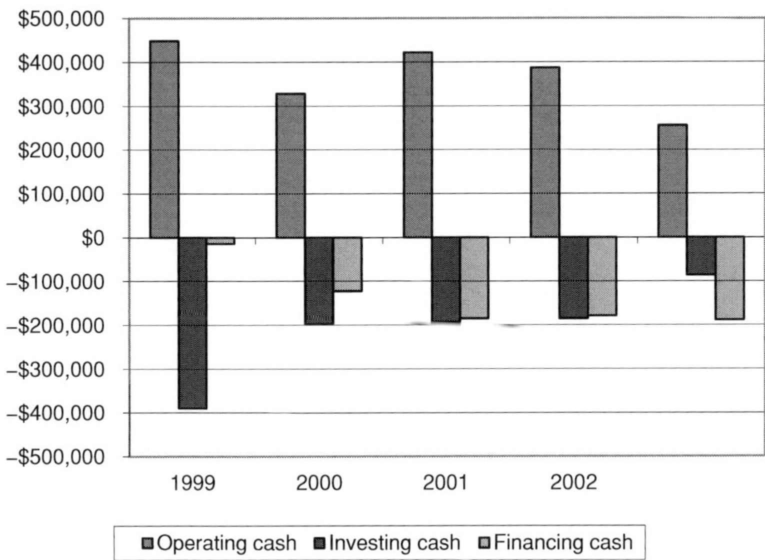

EXHIBIT 7.22 Comparison of Cash Flows

business. Fortunately, certain financial statement analysis can readily identify the result of terrorist deposits.

The primary methods of laundering money through a business are overstating revenues, overstating expenses, and balance sheet laundering. The overstatement of revenues and overstatement of expenses will typically occur concurrently so the culprit can avoid taxation on laundered funds. Balance sheet laundering can be as simplistic as merely adjusting balance sheet accounts to account for laundered funds (that is, increasing the cash account and increasing the equity account). However, balance sheet laundering schemes can easily be detected, as the change in equity will not agree with the net income or net loss reported on the income statement.

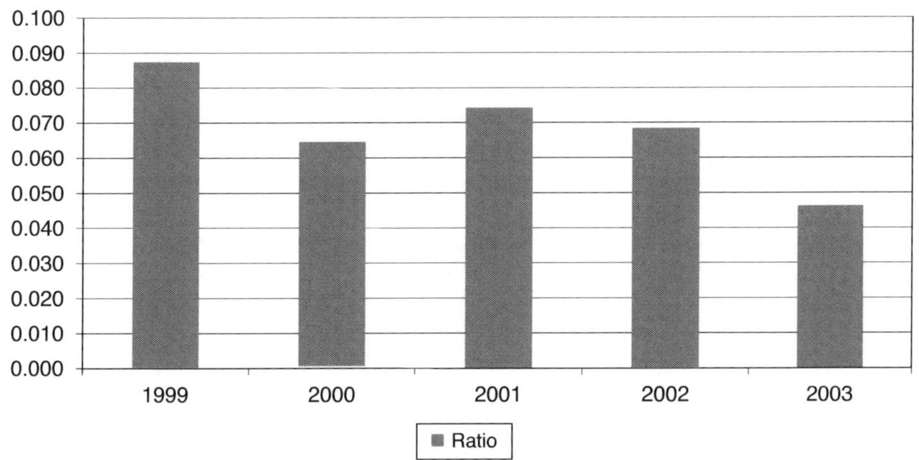

EXHIBIT 7.23 Comparison of Operating Cash Flow to Revenues

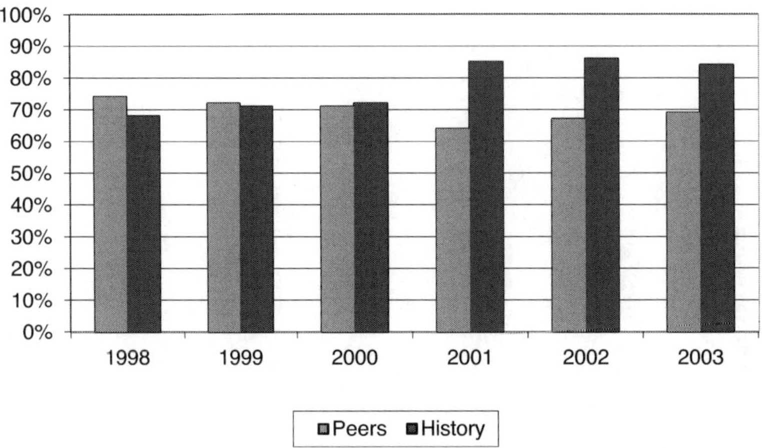

EXHIBIT 7.24 Gross Profit Margin Comparison

A primary forensic accounting test that highlights illicit deposits is known as the gross profit margin comparison test. The gross profit margin comparison test calculates the gross profit margin of the respective business and compares it to two key benchmarks: its peer group and itself over time. If anomalies are identified, then further investigation can be initiated. The following graphs illustrate the annual gross profit margin for a hypothetical Middle Eastern bakery.

The first graph, Exhibit 7.24 measures the bakery's gross profit margin expressed as a percentage ((sales – cost of goods sold = gross profit)/sales) against its peer group and itself (history) for the years 1998 through 2003. Exhibit 7.24 illustrates that the bakery's gross profit margin exceeds the industry's gross profit margin, and likewise increased in the early years. The peer group data can be obtained from various sources or can be constructed on an ad hoc basis to serve as a benchmark.

Exhibit 7.25 illustrates a more dramatic comparison resulting from applying the percentage change on a *year-to-year* basis. Exhibit 7.25 measures each individual

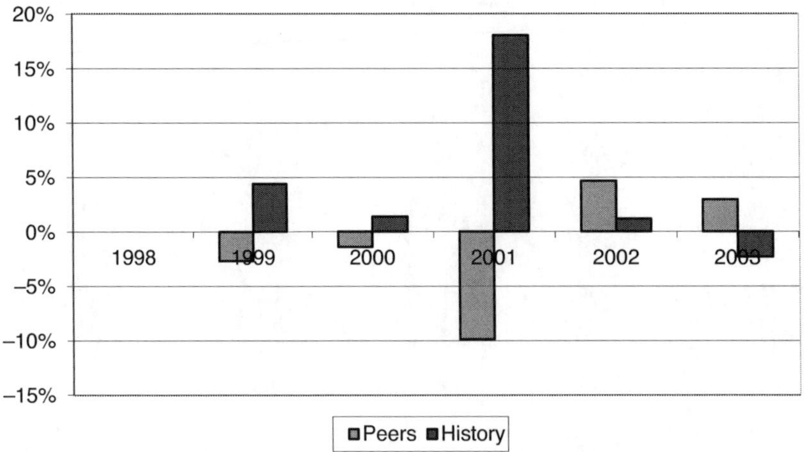

EXHIBIT 7.25 Percentage Change in Gross Profit Margin

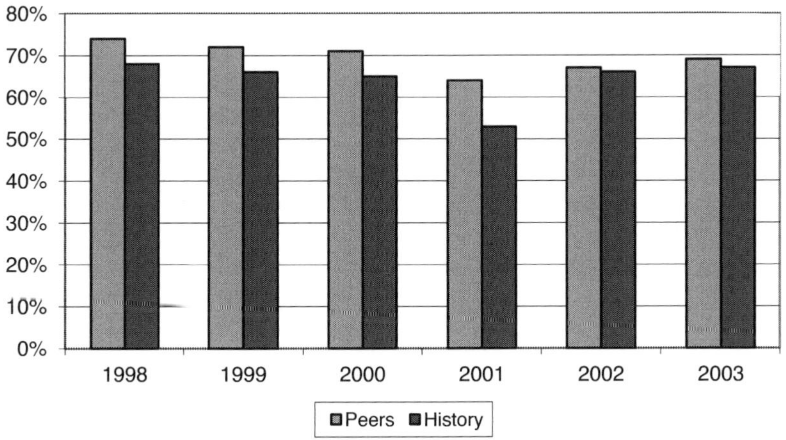

EXHIBIT 7.26 Gross Profit Margin Comparison

year's increase or decline in gross margin as a percentage change ((2003 gross profit margin – 2002 gross profit margin)/2002 gross profit margin). The percentage change in gross profit margin analysis shown in Exhibit 7.25 illustrates the significant change in gross profit margin coincident with and following the events of 9/11.

The percentage change in gross profit margin analysis contained in Exhibit 7.24 illustrates the significant change in gross profit margin coincident with and following the September 11, 2001, events.

The gross profit margin comparison test is based upon laundered monies flowing through a business to the *owners* of the business who then presumably direct the funds to their respective terrorist sources. The same test is used to determine when the *business* may have been used to direct the funds to terrorists, for example, when bogus payments are made to so-called vendors who are paid for merchandise such as flour never delivered to the bakery.

Exhibit 7.26 measures a *different* Middle Eastern bakery's gross profit margin expressed as a percentage ((sales – cost of goods sold = gross profit)/sales) against its peer group and itself (history) for the years 1998 through 2003. In this scenario, the bakery's gross profit margin *falls below* the industry's gross profit margin, and likewise decreased in the early years. Such a decrease in gross profit margin indicates that either revenues are not being reported or costs may be diverted to other purposes besides creating revenues. Either way, it is a tell tale flag requiring deeper inquiry.

Exhibit 7.27 dramatizes the comparison set out in Exhibit 7.26 by showing the percentage change on a year-to-year basis.

Note that Exhibits 25 and 27 illustrate the two different sides of the same coin. That is, Exhibit 25 illustrates a dramatic one-time (2001) increase in gross profit margin when compared to its own history and its peer group. A logical explanation is that more revenues flowed through the entity than could be explained by normal business fluctuation-a potential money laundering flag. Exhibit 27 illustrates a one-time dramatic increase (2002) with a corresponding decrease 2001 that could flag timing differences in revenues or costs or both. Both exhibits demonstrate cause for further investigation into money laundering.

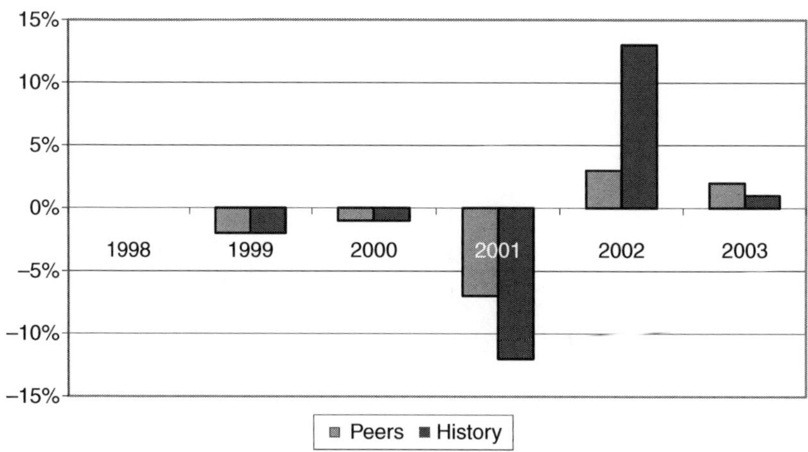

EXHIBIT 7.27 Percentage Change in Gross Profit Margin

As indicated by the preceding schedules, even simple tests such as the gross profit margin analysis comparison can identify and illustrate symptomatic indicators of money laundering for terrorist purposes.

WHEN NO RECORDS HAVE BEEN PREPARED BY THE TERRORIST

In virtually all cases, terrorists will lack any set of records that could be used against them. However, transaction-generated evidence such as food purchases provides a rich collection of data that can be aggregated by forensic accounting analysis. The data will then be analyzed and used to form both direct and indirect conclusions regarding its nature.

The types of forensic accounting analysis most likely applied in this scenario will consist of indirect methods such as the modified net worth method and direct methods such as the expenditures statement.

The Modified Net Worth Method

The modified net worth method derives from the net worth method long employed by the Internal Revenue Service (IRS). The most high-profile application of the net worth method was used by Treasury officials to help convict Alphonse "Al" Capone, *Capone v. United States* 51 F.2d 609 (1931). Its acceptance by the courts is well documented over the years.

To remove the complexities of income tax law, the net worth method was modified and popularized in 1974 as the *modified* net worth method, by Mr. Richard A. Nossen, a former IRS Special Agent.[70]

[70] Richard A. Nossen and Joan W. Norvell, *The Detection, Investigation and Prosecution of Financial Crimes*, 2nd ed. (Richmond, VA: Thoth Books, 1993).

EXHIBIT 7.28 Modified Net Worth Method

Net worth as of December 31, 2002	$$$,$$$		
Less: net worth as of December 31, 2001	$$,$$$		
Increase in net worth		$$,$$$	
Add: Living expenses		$$,$$$	
Total expenditures		$$$,$$$	
Less: Income from known sources		($,$$$)	
Expenditures in excess of known sources of funds			$$,$$$

The technique is effective at demonstrating a terrorist's apparent income by determining the increase in his wealth by deriving the year-to-year change in his overall net worth. Consequently, it can be shown that the terrorist has spent more than he had available to him from known, reported, or legitimate sources. For many years, the courts have accepted the method to infer (as admissible circumstantial evidence) that any excess of expenditures was made with funds from unknown or illegitimate sources or both.

Generally, the modified net worth method compares a year-end net worth estimate, say, December 31, 2002, with the December 31, 2001, year-end net worth estimate, identifying an increase. Then, living expenses are added to that amount and income from known sources is deducted from the subtotal. The residual identifies the expenditures in excess of known sources of funds.

The general format is depicted in Exhibit 7.28.

The modified net worth method is readily assembled from even widely disparate evidence and records. The method is ordinarily categorized by year, but it can also cover unusual time horizons such as from May 17, 1999, through February 20, 2002, to match pertinent statutory periods.

The following hypothetical schedule, Exhibit 7.29 illustrates how the modified net worth method is used to demonstrate that the terrorist had unreported funds. The respective lines are individually described following the schedule.

The preceding hypothetical schedule Exhibit 7.29 reflects the assets and records seized in a raid by Federal agents. Each line is described by the following explanations.

Line 1 reflects the currency seized during the raid. Note that the "Test." legend indicates that the subject terrorist testified that he had no currency as of the initial date, May 17, 1999.

Lines 2 to 6 reflect the amounts indicated through seized bank and related records. BR represents that the data is sourced through bank or other records; SR represents that the data was seized in the raid.

Line 7 reflects an estimate of the value of the large quantity of food stocks in the terrorist's custody at seizure. SRS represents that the data is based upon an estimated street value.

Lines 8 and 9 reflect the street value of the firearms, ammunition, and explosives seized during the raid.

EXHIBIT 7.29 Hypothetical Modified Net Worth Method

Line	ASSETS	Ref.	5/17/1999	2/20/2002
	Cash			
1	Currency	Test.	unknown	$71,000
2	Checking accounts	BR	1,732	8,434
3	Other accounts	BR	unknown	5,100
	Undeposited items			
4	Traveler's checks	SR	—	9,000
	Time deposits			
5	60-day CD	BR	unknown	5,000
6	120-day CD	BR	unknown	12,000
7	Food stocks	SR	unknown	2,932
8	Firearms, ammunition, explosives	SRS	unknown	16,700
9	Computers, cameras, software	SRS	—	16,256
10	Automobile	BR	—	3,600
	Total Assets		1,732	150,022
	LIABILITIES			
11	Automobile loan	BR	—	1,900
12	Net worth, beginning and end		1,732	148,122
13	Less: Beginning net worth			1,732
14	Increase in net worth			146,390
15	Add: Personal living expenses	CES		61,748
16	Total expenditures			208,138
17	Less: Funds carried into country	Test.		3,000
18	Funds earned through employment	BR		19,976
19	Wire transfers from family	BR		17,000
20	**Expenditures in excess of funds**			**$(168,162)**

Legend

Test. = Testimony
BR = Bank or other records
SR = Seized in raid
SRS = Seized, street value
CES = Consumer expenditure survey

Line 10 reflects the purchase price of the used automobile in the terrorist's custody.

Line 11 reflects the balance owing to a private individual as documented in a payment record.

Line 12 reflects the derivation of the net worth for both the beginning and ending periods by subtracting total assets from total liabilities.

Line 13 reflects the subtraction of the beginning net worth from the ending net worth.

Line 14 reflects the result of the items in Line 13, thus deriving the resultant increase in net worth over the respective time.

Line 15 reflects an estimate of the terrorist's estimated living expenses for the respective period as derived by adjusted third-party information sources such as the Consumer Expenditure Survey (CES) www.bls.gov/cex/. Since records were unavailable for living expenses (except in very scattered instances) and he refused to cooperate by describing his living patterns, the CES data was applied.

Line 16 reflects the result of adding Lines 14 and 15.

Line 17 reflects the amount that the terrorist declared when he entered the United States.

Line 18 reflects the total that the terrorist claimed as earned by his employment during the period.

Line 19 reflects the money wired to him by his family during his time in the United States.

Line 20 reflects the difference between the terrorist's expenditures and his claimed earnings, thus implying that he has significant unknown and unreported sources of income, (−$168,162).

The Source and Use of Cash Method

The preceding modified net worth method can be useful when a terrorist acquires relatively big-ticket items such as real estate, stocks and bonds, and tangible assets in general. Alternatively, a terrorist living a low profile, transient existence would require a different analytical technique such as the source and use of cash method.

The source and use of cash method lists each identified source and use of cash (or other funds) by category for the respective years under analysis. As in the modified net worth method, the years can be constructed for annual or other periods. The results of each method are exactly the same and sometimes the two techniques are used together to corroborate findings.

A hypothetical source and use of cash method is illustrated in Exhibit 7.30.

The preceding hypothetical schedule, Exhibit 7.30, reflects the sources and uses cash attributed to the terrorist based upon the various records collected and seized in a raid by federal agents. Each line is described by the following explanations.

Line 1 reflects the amount that the terrorist earned in employment during his time in the United States.

Line 2 reflects the total wire transfers from his family.

Line 3 reflects the amount of money declared by the terrorist when he entered the United States.

Line 4 reflects the currency in the terrorist's custody that was seized during the raid. Note that seizures are represented as *expenditures*. The corroborating theory is that the money was *available for expenditure* by the terrorist,

EXHIBIT 7.30 Hypothetical Source and Use of Cash Method

Line		1999	2000	2001	2002	Total
	Known sources of cash					
1	Earned in various jobs	$1,736	7,845	136	10,259	$19,976
2	Wire transfers from family	4,000	700	11,000	1,300	17,000
3	Carried into country	3,000	—	—	—	3,000
	Total known sources of cash	8,736	8,545	11,136	11,559	39,976
	Expenditures					
4	Seized currency				71,000	71,000
5	Increase in checking account				6,702	6,702
6	Seized in other accounts				5,100	5,100
7	Increase in traveler's checks	unknown			9,000	9,000
8	Increase in time deposits				17,000	17,000
9	Seized food stocks				2,932	2,932
10	Seized firearms, and so on				32,956	32,956
11	Net automobile purchase				1,700	1,700
12	Personal living expenses	9,952	14,871	16,589	20,336	61,748
13	Total expenditures	9,952	14,871	16,589	166,726	208,138
14	**Expenditures in excess of funds**	(1,216)	(6,326)	(5,453)	(155,167)	**$(168,162)**

and failing seizure would have eventually been expended since his outflows exceeded his inflows.

Line 5 reflects the increase in his checking account.

Line 6 reflects the other information contained in various accounts seized during the raid.

Line 7 reflects the increase in traveler's checks.

Line 8 reflects the increase in time deposits held in the terrorist's name.

Lines 9 and 10 reflect seizures during the raid.

Line 11 reflects the net automobile purchase as derived by the difference between the purchase at cost and the balance owed.

Line 12 reflects the terrorist's estimated living expenses for the respective period as derived by adjusted third-party information sources such as the Consumer Expenditure Survey (CES) www.bls.gov/cex/. Since records were unavailable for living expenses (except in very scattered instances) and he refused to cooperate by describing his living patterns, the CES data was applied.

Line 13 reflects the total expenditures for each respective year.

Line 14 reflects difference between the terrorist's expenditures and his claimed earnings, thus implying that he has significant unknown and unreported sources of income.

The Total column aggregates the years to validate that the totals compare (–$168,162).

Certain observations between Exhibits 7.29 and 7.30 are significant. First, note that the results of the analysis are *exactly the same* for both methods (–$168,162). Since the data used for each method derives from the same source, no difference should result if the methods are properly executed. Second, despite disparate time periods (one 32-month period for the modified net worth method, and 4-odd years for the source and use of cash method, the results of the analysis are *exactly the same* for both methods, (–$168,162). Finally, note the Unknown section, which indicates that yearly categorization was simply not possible for many items, and as demonstrated by the analysis, was not even required in aggregate.

SUMMARY OF FORENSIC ACCOUNTING OBSERVATIONS

Based upon the likely nature of terrorist activities, certain highlights regarding forensic accounting tools are summarized next.

Overall Approach

Generally, the approach to forensic accounting analysis should be initiated with indirect methods that accommodate an exploratory manner so that scarce resources can be most effectively deployed. That is, indirect methods can identify those areas offering promise in a manner comparable to exploratory surgery. After the promising areas are identified, direct methods can be deployed.

Operating Entities

Operating entities that provide financial statements, or for which financial statements have been prepared by the forensic analyst, exhibit certain key characteristics as follows.

A comparison of *operating cash flow* should be made to reported net income. Logically, operating cash flow should lag reported net income, due to the accrual nature of generally accepted accounting principles (GAAP). Manipulated financial statements will exhibit operating cash flow that trends differently from reported net income.

Put another way, financial statements that comply with GAAP are prepared on an accrual basis rather than a cash basis. Accrual-based financials report revenue and expenses as they are earned or incurred, whether or not they have been received or paid. Cash-basis financials report revenue and expenses only when cash is actually received or paid out, which by definition do not comply with GAAP. Accrual-based financial statements are the antithesis of cash-based financial statements.

Consequently, accrual-basis financials report net income before the commensurate cash is actually received. Logically, legitimate accrual-based financials will then show the statement of cash flow results lagging the income statement results. An obvious example is Enron, which reported enormous amounts of net income with relatively flat operating cash flow. Such anomaly is a clear flag for forensic accountants.

A *sustainable growth rate* should be calculated on the basis of reported net income and compared to actual growth. In manipulated financial statements, the actual growth rate will exceed the sustainable rate, since illegitimate funds are flowing through the operation. Estimation of the sustainable growth rate can be achieved by applying the sustainable growth model.[71] This model relies on two accounting concepts: return on equity and the plowback ratio. The equation follows:

$G_s = B_s \times \text{ROE}$

G_s = sustainable growth rate for a company,

B_s = plowback ratio, calculated as follows:

(Annual Earnings – Annual Dividends)/Annual Earnings; and

ROE = return on book equity, as follows:

Annual Earnings/Book Value of Equity

Use of *independent parallel indicators* can identify reporting anomalies. For example, in charitable organizations, the development department (or equivalent) typically maintains a donor log independent of management. Comparison of the log's entries to the reported donations can identify undesirable donors that require additional investigation.

More specifically, donor logs identify the parties responsible for individual sources of donation, for example, cash, checks, credit cards, services, and others. Therefore, the logs can be compared in aggregate and individually to the financial reporting system to identify discrepancies which can flag transactions meriting additional inquiry. Red flags might include the following:

Mixing of disparate types of deposits such as combining cash, third-party checks, wire transfers, traveler's checks and related items in a single deposit transaction.

Large withdrawals from a business account not ordinarily associated with cash transactions.

Individual Targets

Individual targets often exhibit behaviors that can identify terrorist actions as identified here.

Postal mailings can indicate shipments of cash outside the United States. Under current United States Postal Service (USPS) regulations, a first-class letter mail parcel can weigh up to four (4) pounds when mailed internationally, and up to sixty (60) pounds when mailed to Canada. A single, four-pound first-class letter parcel can accommodate about $180,000 in $100 bills while a 60-pound first-class letter parcel can handle about $2,700,000 in $100 bills.

Deposits are followed shortly by wire transfer of funds.

Beneficiaries of mailings and transfers reside in a problematic foreign jurisdiction.

Lifestyles inconsistent with stated employment streams such as irregular work habits without commensurate financial challenges.

[71] 2002 Yearbook, *Stocks, Bonds, Bills and Inflation,* valuation ed. (Chicago, IL: Ibbotson Associates, 2002, 62).

Involvement with multiple individuals from the same country, some of whom exhibit the preceding characteristics.

Inordinate or regular cell-phone conversations and no installed landline.

A FORENSIC ACCOUNTING METHODOLOGY TO SUPPORT COUNTERTERRORISM

Forensic accounting analysis in support of counter-terrorism efforts must be conducted in a methodical manner consistent with the high standards of federal law enforcement. Therefore, a proposed forensic accounting methodology is described that meets such requirements. The methodology is perhaps the only methodology in place in the United States today that combines the criminal investigation process with forensic accounting methods and techniques.

The criminal investigation process employed is the seven-step method popularized by Richard Nossen and still taught to key federal law enforcement agencies. The forensic accounting methods are those generally accepted techniques that support both civil and criminal expert witness analysis.[72]

Objectives of the Methodology

There are seven primary objectives intended for the methodology.

1. First, the methodology provides a starting point for the federal law enforcement profession to establish forensic accounting as its own discipline, that is, a codified body of knowledge.
2. Second, the methodology will serve as generalized or specific guidance to federal forensic accountants, thus ensuring that ancillary disciplines are appropriately considered.
3. Third, the methodology provides a framework through which forensic accounting techniques and methods can continually be refined.
4. Fourth, the methodology serves as a technical reference to those performing forensic accounting services on a part-time basis.
5. Fifth, the methodology ensures consistency of forensic accounting delivery, thus enhancing the likelihood of successful prosecutions.
6. Sixth, the methodology serves as a training tool for those entering the federal law enforcement profession.
7. Seventh, the methodology enhances expert witness and prosecution testimony credibility before Triers of fact.

This section describes the proposed forensic accounting methodology and thus enables practitioners to immediately apply its concepts. In recognition of the investigatory nature of forensic accounting, the methodology is built upon an integrated dual foundation of forensic accounting and criminal investigation.

---

[72] Richard A. Nossen and Joan W. Norvell, *The Detection, Investigation and Prosecution of Financial Crimes*, 2nd ed. (Richmond, VA: Thoth Books, 1993).

Many aspects of forensic accounting and related disciplines are referred to in the methodology. Most of the techniques will be familiar to practitioners, but where practitioners lack familiarity, the website version of the methodology links relevant technical aspects.

The methodology's embedded hyperlinks enable practitioners to readily access supporting documents, for example, a deposition matrix[73] to facilitate consistency and promote efficiency. Also, hyperlinks to explanatory text further support a forensic accountant's need to apply methods beyond one's immediate skill set.

Criminal Investigation

The traditional seven steps of criminal investigation is a process commonly taught and applied by federal, state, and local law enforcement authorities. Many variations of the seven-step method, that is, the four-step method, and so on, are used by law enforcement authorities. However, the seven-step method is preferable because of its comprehensive detail.

This customization capability enables forensic accounting practitioners to closely interface with respective law enforcement agencies, thus matching their approach when applying forensic accounting techniques.

The methodology is detailed next and consists of numerous components of criminal investigation processes, forensic accounting techniques, statistical methods, interviewing schema, sociopsychological constructs and adult learning theories. Consequently, the methodology offers a comprehensive and dynamic tool for analysis and evidentiary delivery.

The Methodology in Action—A Process Map

The methodology is constructed as a *process map* that visually guides the practitioner through the logical actions of a forensic accounting assignment. The methodology starts at the earliest stage of an assignment and progresses through the final stage, typically testimony delivery pursuant to prosecution.

The process map flows from left to right and top to bottom within the four phases and five stages, as shown in Exhibit 7.32. Therefore, a practitioner merely begins with the foundational (first) phase and progresses through the five stages where he then begins with the interpersonal (second) phase and again progresses through the five stages. Continuing in a like manner, the practitioner can address virtually every aspect of a forensic accounting assignment, whether complex or simple. Note the dotted-line flow indicating that the methodology is not merely static, but reflects the dynamic nature of forensic accounting that often requires looping back through tasks as new data surfaces, as shown in Exhibits 7.33 through 7.45.

Although the process map is visually self-explanatory, certain items require clarification. The language of forensic accounting can be applied to all types of investigative activities to clarify one's actions and findings, thus enhancing credibility during analysis, testimony, and prosecution. Forensic accounting techniques are readily

[73] Darrell D. Dorrell, "Deposition Matrix," *National Litigation Consultants' Review* 2, no. 9 (2002).

applicable to nonfinancial data. In fact, most readers of this chapter have probably applied forensic accounting techniques to nonfinancial data without realizing it. An example would be comparing salesmen's reported call logs with customer sales.

Other industry specific examples are commonly found. Note that physicians' appointment logs are often compared to billing and deposits to identify anomalies. Likewise, deliveries of sugar and flour (measured in pounds) can be compared to the output captured in a bakery's cash register receipts. Also, fund-raising donor logs of charities can be compared to reported receipts of goods and services. Finally, the IRS has been known to compare the towel laundry bills of a suspected brothel to its reported income.

Because of the size limitations of this chapter, not all the contents have been included, but the methodology is sufficiently populated to illustrate the intent and capabilities of the methodology.

Because of the two-dimensional nature of the written word, the process map appears sequential. However, the methodology is intended to be flexible, dynamic, integrated, and simultaneous and iterative, thus mirroring how information and conclusions develop. For example, interviews and interrogations might not be conducted until rather late in a forensic assignment.

Methodology and Linkage to Criminal Investigation

The methodology was constructed using a forensic accounting or investigation linkage to the seven-step criminal investigation methodology. The seven-step methodology is summarized in Exhibit 7.31, and the respective identifiers are provided that link to the detailed matrix.

A summary of the investigatory steps follows. Generic descriptions are provided since the focus of this chapter is forensic accounting, not criminology.

- Interviews and interrogation (I&I) reflects the personal aspect of data gathering, obtained through personal interviews and interrogation when under law enforcement authority. It is generally considered a source of primary data.
- Background research (BR) comprises two broad categories: primary data and secondary data. Primary data is acquired by the practitioner's efforts collecting data otherwise unavailable through secondary sources. Examples include performing an NCIC database query, or performing an Internet inquiry into a subject's asset holdings, and so on.

EXHIBIT 7.31 Matrix

Investigatory Steps	Identifier
1. Interviews and interrogation	I&I
2. Background research	BR
3. Electronic and physical surveillance	EP
4. Confidential informants	CI
5. Undercover	UC
6. Laboratory analysis	LA
7. Analysis of transactions	AT

- Electronic and physical surveillance (EP) is used to obtain evidentiary data through observation.
- Confidential informants (CI) provide information that is considered primary data and may include paid or voluntary informants.
- Undercover (UC) is used to obtain first-hand subject data.
- Laboratory analysis (LA) can range from statistical analysis, such as a duplicate-numbers test, to scientific analysis, such as ink composition to a wide range of investigatory procedures.
- Analysis of transaction (AT) compares and contrasts transactional and pattern-sensitive data measures to provide a record for forensic analysis. Full and false inclusion tests are used to determine the appropriate universe of data under investigation. This ensures that not extraneous data is included and that no appropriate data is excluded.

The Four Phases

The methodology is structured within a process map organized into four logically flowing phases covering 13 actions, with each action comprising five stages. (See Exhibit 7.32.) The 13 actions are executed throughout the process and contain many distinct techniques that closely track the seven-step criminal investigation methodology. The phases, actions, and stages mirror the activities ordinarily encountered in the forensic accounting investigation process and are indicated further on.

The foundational phase consists of assembling and preparing baseline data that will support and drive the investigation. The output must be continuously updated to provide a current record and status of the progress of investigation. For example, identification of all the bank accounts that may contain large wire transfers to offshore accounts would fall within this phase. They would have been identified within the full and false inclusion task to ensure that all relevant data is examined. The two actions in the foundational phase include assignment development and scoping, which is an allocation of responsibilities. (See Exhibits 7.34 and 7.35.)

The interpersonal communications phase consists of interviews and interrogation, surveillance, undercover, and the related activities necessary to extract pertinent information about the subject(s). Typical activities conducted by field officers would fall within this phase. A reasonably strong experience base is necessary to facilitate identifying the individual traits, habits, and characteristics that betray a subject's deceptions. The two actions in this phase include interviews and interrogations and background research. (See Exhibits 7.36 and 7.37.)

The data collection and analysis phase consists of applying the various indirect quantitative and qualitative data obtained during the earlier phases and developing output supporting observations, thus arriving at an appropriate conclusion(s). If such efforts prove inconclusive, the next segment of this phase—the direct analytical and conclusion phase—will provide additional evidence. Therefore, this phase consists of two subphases, that is, indirect (executed first as a diagnostic or exploratory tool, or both), and then direct, so that the labor-intensive efforts are most effectively applied. For example, by comparing the year-to-year change in equity to the year-to-year difference between revenues (that is, receipts) and expenses, the articulation of the financial statements can be tested. Any difference is investigated to determine whether it is merely an equity transaction, for example, capital infusion or is determined to

EXHIBIT 7.32 Forensic Accounting Methodology—The Framework

PHASES—4												
Foundational		Interpersonal Communications		Data Collection and Analysis (Direct and Indirect)						Trial		
ACTIONS—13												
Assignment Development	Scoping	Interviews and Interrogation	Background Research	Data Collection	Surveillance—Electronic and Physical	Confidential Informants	Undercover	Laboratory Analysis	Analysis of Transactions	Trial Preparation	Testimony and Exhibits	Post-Assignment
STAGES—5												
Purpose of Stage												
References												
Tasks to Be Performed												
Potential Issues												
Deliverables												

be an unaccounted-for revenue or expense. This technique is known as the net worth method, which is discussed earlier in this chapter.

Direct quantitative and qualitative analysis can follow the preceding indirect activities, or be executed either jointly with, or independent of them. The evidence provided by this phase is, by definition the most comprehensive, but is not necessary in every case. Also, since it is usually quite labor-intensive, it can require the highest resource usage. The six actions in this phase include data collection, surveillance—electronic and physical, confidential informants, undercover, laboratory analysis, and analysis of transactions. (See Exhibits 7.38 through 7.43.)

The trial phase consists of delivering the results of the forensic accounting analysis. The typical delivery target is comprised of a Trier of fact (a judge or a jury or both) that deliberates the evidence within the context of the law and other evidence. Also, this phase includes a post-assignment activity that is intended to capture benefits of the experiential process achieved from each assignment. The three actions in this phase include trial preparation, testimony and exhibits, and post-assignment activities. (See Exhibits 7.44 through 7.46.)

The Thirteen Actions

The assignment development action is the front end of a forensic assignment that shapes the context and defines the framework of the assignment.

The scoping action secures formal commitments and defines responsibilities among the parties with (and against) whom the forensic accountant is deployed.

The interviews and interrogation action consists of the face-to-face contact with key parties. These activities often comprise the most compelling, but nonquantitative evidence and can derive from actions ranging from conversations through depositions. This action can also be a reentry point in the process such as an admission-seeking interview conducted toward the end of an investigation.

The background research action permits independent verification against the oral claims made by the respective parties.

The data collection action is the entry point for several other stages, and likewise reflects the reentry when necessary.

The surveillance—electronic and physical action collects and categorizes data ranging from objective indicators such as the number of phone calls, through more subjective indicators such as behavioral symptoms.

The confidential informants action accesses parties willing to divulge data for their own reasons and which often opens doors to other evidence.

The undercover action is a form of ruse used to gain confidences so as to obtain data otherwise unavailable. It is sometimes irreplaceable, such as in drug cases.

The laboratory analysis action can range from statistical to chemical techniques that determine whether or not data converts to evidence.

The analysis of transactions action contains obvious efforts, such as tracing the evidence back to a source. It can also include less obvious efforts, however, such as establishing behavioral patterns demonstrating trends.

The trial preparation action is comprised of pre-deployment preparation, thus simulating the trial testimony and ensuring accuracy of content.

The testimony and exhibits action is the crucible within forensic accounting, and perhaps carries more weight than all the other stages combined. That is, even with superb foundational analysis, it may all be for naught if direct testimony is poorly delivered, or if withering cross-examination succeeds in diminishing the forensic accountant's opinions.

The post-assignment action recommends that each assignment should have a post-mortem lessons-learned review to capitalize on the experiences, whether favorable or disastrous.

The Five Stages

The methodology is organized into five foundational stages supporting the seven-step criminal investigation methodology described earlier. The stages mirror the activities ordinarily encountered in the investigation process and are indicated here:

- *Purpose*—This stage establishes the reasoning behind the necessity of the phase and its respective actions. Put another way, it shapes the context and defines the framework to ensure that the actions are properly focused.
- *References*—This stage lists key technical references for the pertinent phase and its respective actions. Naturally, the reference sources will vary. For example,

an excellent starting point for any forensic accounting matter is the *Litigation Services Handbook*[74] and its cumulative supplements. However, forensic accountants often need detail beyond the capabilities of the handbook. Therefore, references should be considered as matter-specific. In its electronic form, the methodology is hyperlinked to specific references and Internet URLs for further investigation.

- *Tasks to Be Performed*—This stage identifies key tasks that pertain to the context of the phase and its respective actions. Many tasks are linked to the narrative matrix following the process map so as to define and describe a generic set of activities. In its electronic form, the methodology is hyperlinked to the narrative matrix for easy reference to the pertinent activities.
- *Potential Issues*—This stage alerts the forensic accountant to the land mines of the respective matter. For example, during the interviews and interrogation action, the veracity of the respective party(s) can never be taken for granted.
- *Deliverables*—This stage suggests likely outputs that document the results throughout the methodology's process map. Such outputs can be merely documentary, but are likely to be eventually applied as exhibits in support of testimony. Several examples are included in the appendix of this chapter so as to provide forensic accountants with immediately applicable tools that have a proven track record. In its electronic form, the methodology is hyperlinked to the respective document's immediate application to the pertinent activities. The deliverables are incorporated into the testimony and exhibits action since they are typically applied during trial.

SUMMARY

The four phases, 13 actions, and five stages that underlie each of the 13 actions are illustrated in Exhibits 7.34 through 7.46 at the end of this chapter. Note that the methodology is constructed in an electronic, interactive format accommodating hyperlinked explanations that cannot be reproduced within the static pages of this chapter. The following is a summary explanation of each action.

After the Forensic Accounting Methodology Process Map is displayed, a table (Exhibit 7.47) outlining forensic techniques as they relate to the investigatory steps as listed in Exhibit 7.31. Next, a table of expectation attributes is presented (Exhibit 7.48) that can be used to characterize the financial environment of an entity by identifying the nature, form, extent, veracity, availability, and related elements of record keeping in order to set expectations about the entity(s)/party(s). Note that the table indicates a continuum of expectations, from the "best case" to the "worst case" scenario, with key indicators defining the reality of the circumstances.

As a supplement to this chapter, a summary of example reports as well as actual examples of applicable deliverables are on the book's website at www.wiley.com/go/financialforensics.

---

[74] Roman L. Weil et al., *Litigation Services Handbook: The Role of the Financial Expert* 3rd ed. (New York: John Wiley & Sons, 2001).

EXHIBIT 7.33 Summary of the 13 Actions

Exhibit	Phase	Action	Summary
33	Foundational	Assignment Development	This is the starting point for the methodology and clarifies the intent within the context of the assignment. Its formalized nature mirrors military mission planning, thus enhancing the likelihood of success within the resources available.
34	Foundational	Scoping	This is a reality check that balances expectations with constraints and reminds the participants of the ultimate output that may apply, thus establishing outcome-based efforts.
35	Interpersonal	Interviews and Interrogation	This encourages interviewers and interrogators to hone their skills, recognizing that even very experienced parties can always learn new methods and techniques. Likewise it enables less experienced parties to access the resources they need to enhance their effectiveness.
36	Interpersonal	Background Research	Background research is sometimes overlooked in the rush to proceed, but the formalization of this as a task ensures that readily available information is utilized as necessary.
37	Data Collection and Analysis	Data Collection	Output examples are used to inform all parties on the project of the expectations, thus ensuring focused efforts.
38	Data Collection and Analysis	Surveillance – Electronic and Physical	Surveillance activities are most productive when deployed consistent with the team's overall goals and objectives.
39	Data Collection and Analysis	Confidential Informants	Informants are most effectively deployed when they are directed to seek information in direct support of the team's efforts.
40	Data Collection and Analysis	Undercover	In a manner similar to surveillance, undercover activities are most productive when deployed consistent with the team's overall goals and objectives.

(*continued*)

EXHIBIT 7.33 *(Continued)*

Exhibit	Phase	Action	Summary
41	Data Collection and Analysis	Laboratory Analysis	Laboratory analysis can span the gamut of forensic analysis, including scientific, financial, psychological, biological, chemical and related topical subjects.
42	Data Collection and Analysis	Analysis of Transactions	This action pulls together all the preceding data collection and analysis, and brings it together within the context of the goals and objectives. Note also that it may be a logical point at which to "loop back" to another, earlier task to continue polishing and refining the evidence.
43	Trial/Reports	Trial Preparation	This action ensures that months or years of effort are effectively arrayed in order to maximize the prospects of obtaining a successful outcome.
44	Trial/Reports	Testimony and Exhibits	This is the last opportunity for the testifiers (experts and fact witnesses) to hone the delivery of their findings and opinions.
45	Post-Trial	Post-Assignment	This "lessons-learned" activity is perhaps the most overlooked of all prosecution efforts. However, it may also offer the greatest benefit to the team since virtually every prosecution has something which improves the overall capabilities of the team.

CONCLUSION

Forensic accounting, like most professional disciplines, is part art and part science. Therefore, it is most effective when applied in a methodical manner that considers all issues and alternatives, yet accommodates flexibility. This concept is what makes highly skilled professionals such as law enforcement, special operations military teams, and others so effective. They are so well trained that they know when to depart from the plan.

The extant methodology is the only known technique that simultaneously combines forensic accounting with criminal investigation. Therefore, it enhances law enforcement's technical skills in the pursuit of their prosecutions.

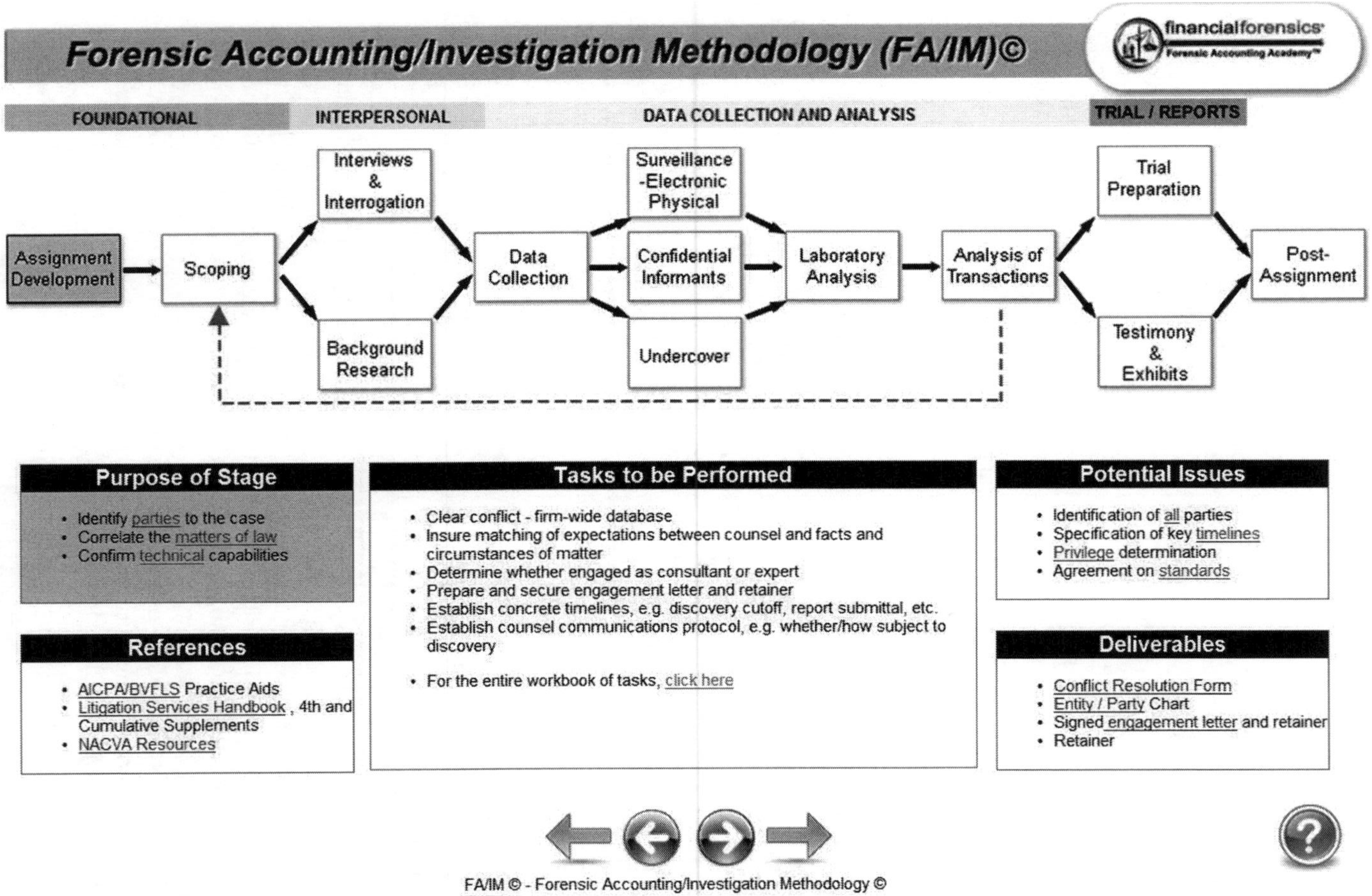

Forensic Accounting/Investigation Methodology (FA/IM)©

Purpose of Stage

- Identify parties to the case
- Correlate the matters of law
- Confirm technical capabilities

References

- AICPA/BVFLS Practice Aids
- Litigation Services Handbook , 4th and Cumulative Supplements
- NACVA Resources

Tasks to be Performed

- Clear conflict - firm-wide database
- Insure matching of expectations between counsel and facts and circumstances of matter
- Determine whether engaged as consultant or expert
- Prepare and secure engagement letter and retainer
- Establish concrete timelines, e.g. discovery cutoff, report submittal, etc.
- Establish counsel communications protocol, e.g. whether/how subject to discovery

- For the entire workbook of tasks, click here

Potential Issues

- Identification of all parties
- Specification of key timelines
- Privilege determination
- Agreement on standards

Deliverables

- Conflict Resolution Form
- Entity / Party Chart
- Signed engagement letter and retainer
- Retainer

FA/IM © - Forensic Accounting/Investigation Methodology ©

EXHIBIT 7.34 Assignment Development

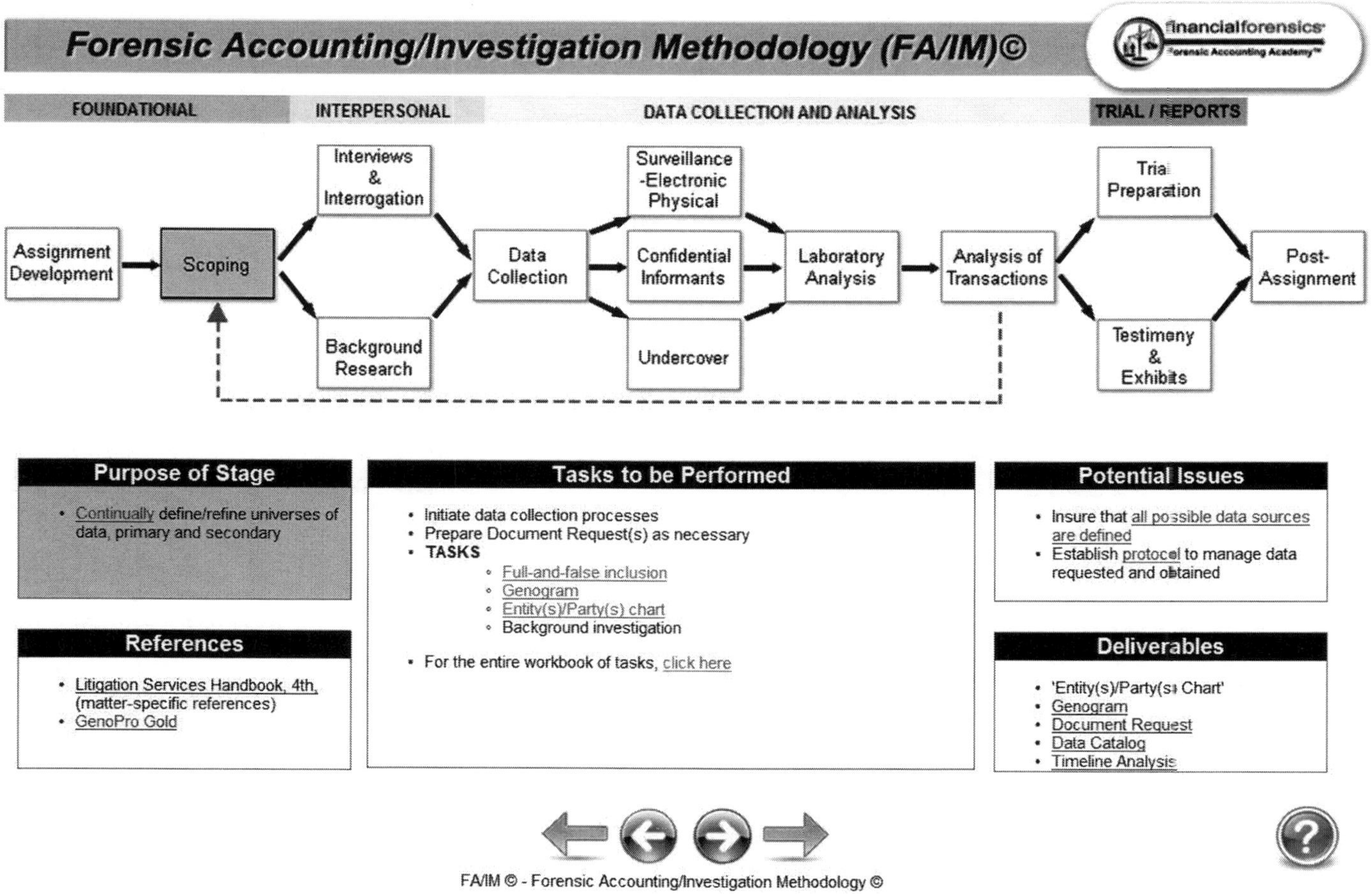

Forensic Accounting/Investigation Methodology (FA/IM)©

FOUNDATIONAL | INTERPERSONAL | DATA COLLECTION AND ANALYSIS | TRIAL / REPORTS

Assignment Development → Scoping → Interviews & Interrogation / Background Research → Data Collection → Surveillance -Electronic Physical / Confidential Informants / Undercover → Laboratory Analysis → Analysis of Transactions → Trial Preparation / Testimony & Exhibits → Post-Assignment

Purpose of Stage

- Continually define/refine universes of data, primary and secondary

References

- Litigation Services Handbook, 4th, (matter-specific references)
- GenoPro Gold

Tasks to be Performed

- Initiate data collection processes
- Prepare Document Request(s) as necessary
- **TASKS**
    - Full-and-false inclusion
    - Genogram
    - Entity(s)/Party(s) chart
    - Background investigation
- For the entire workbook of tasks, click here

Potential Issues

- Insure that all possible data sources are defined
- Establish protocol to manage data requested and obtained

Deliverables

- 'Entity(s)/Party(s) Chart'
- Genogram
- Document Request
- Data Catalog
- Timeline Analysis

FA/IM © - Forensic Accounting/Investigation Methodology ©

EXHIBIT 7.35 Scoping

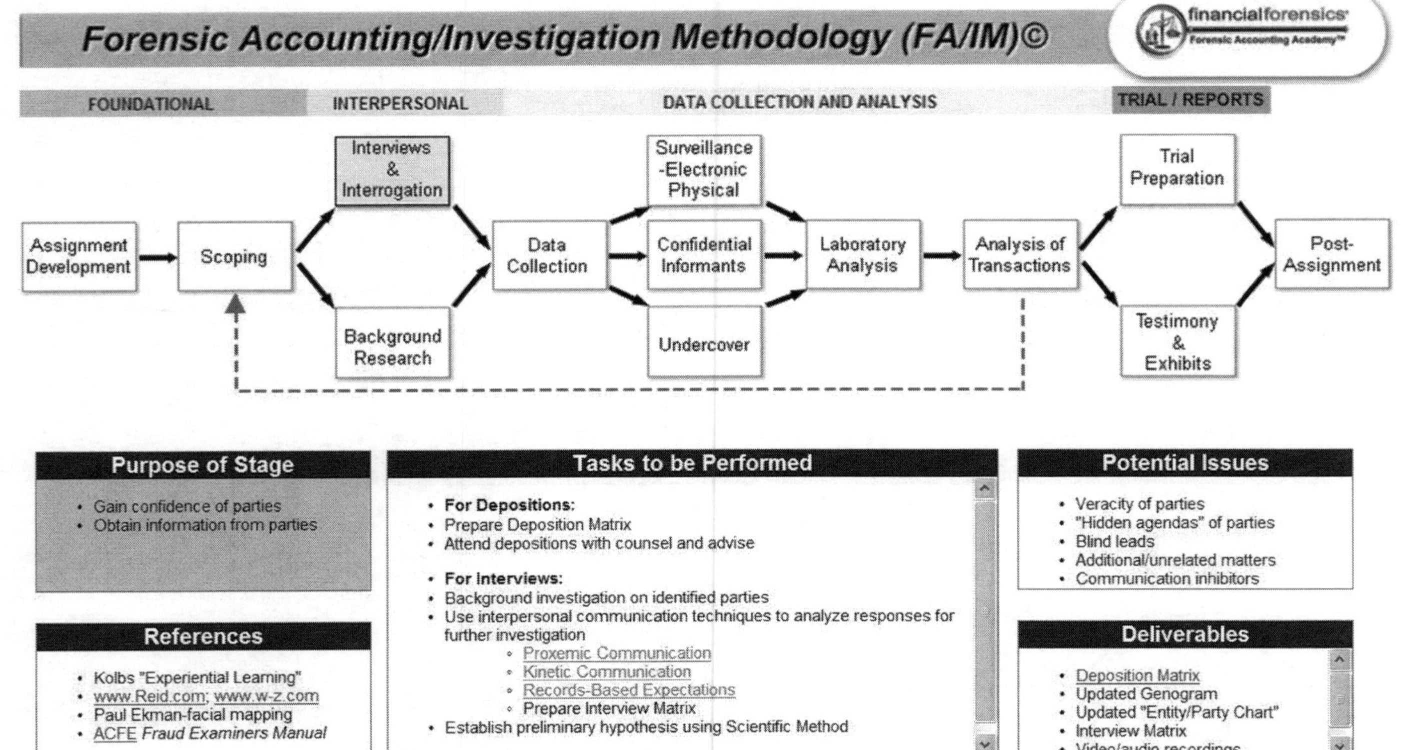

EXHIBIT 7.36 Interviews and Interrogation

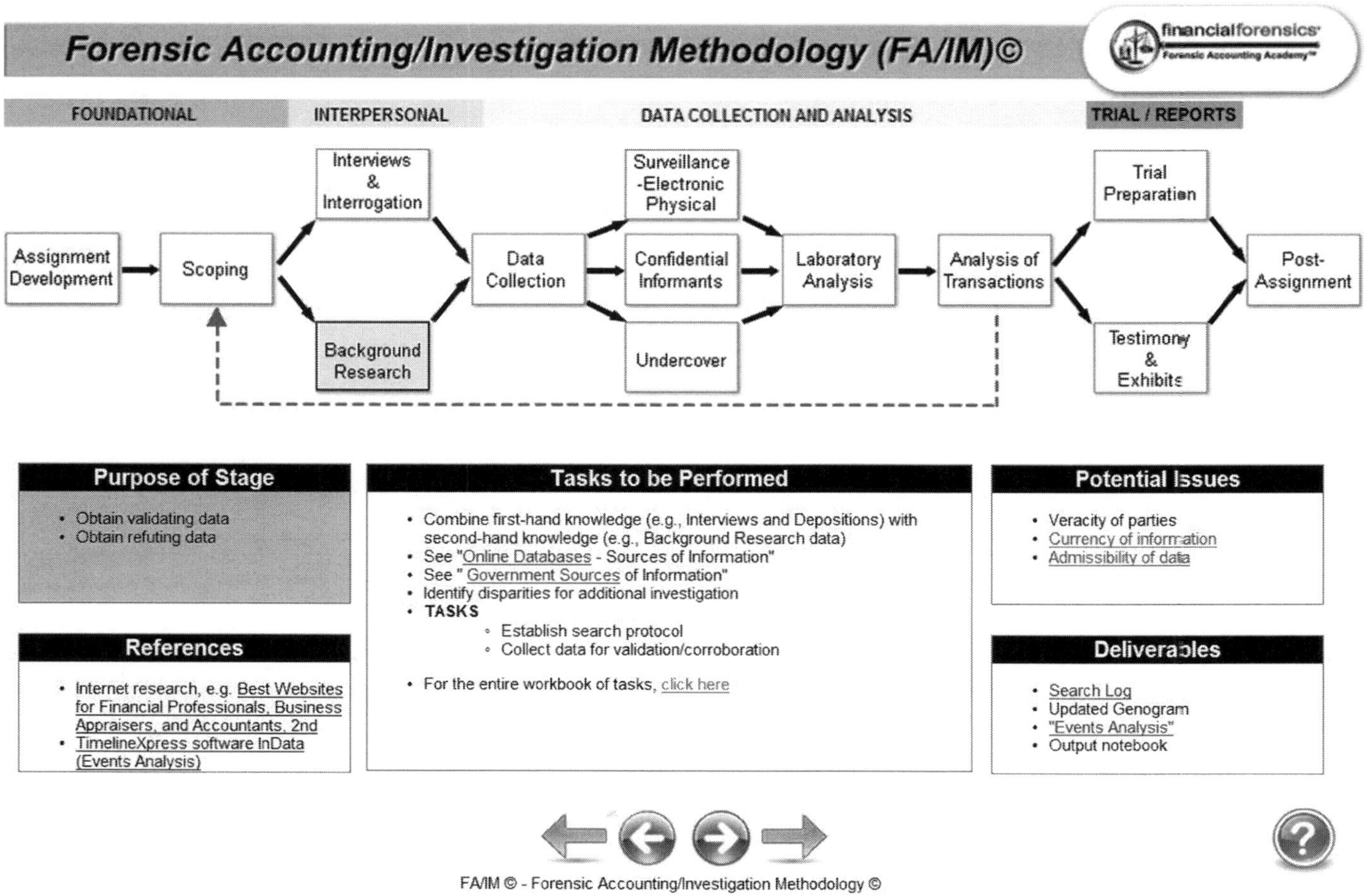

Forensic Accounting/Investigation Methodology (FA/IM)©

FOUNDATIONAL | INTERPERSONAL | DATA COLLECTION AND ANALYSIS | TRIAL / REPORTS

Assignment Development → Scoping → Interviews & Interrogation / Background Research → Data Collection → Surveillance -Electronic Physical / Confidential Informants / Undercover → Laboratory Analysis → Analysis of Transactions → Trial Preparation / Testimony & Exhibits → Post-Assignment

Purpose of Stage

- Obtain validating data
- Obtain refuting data

References

- Internet research, e.g. Best Websites for Financial Professionals, Business Appraisers, and Accountants, 2nd
- TimelineXpress software InData (Events Analysis)

Tasks to be Performed

- Combine first-hand knowledge (e.g., Interviews and Depositions) with second-hand knowledge (e.g., Background Research data)
- See "Online Databases - Sources of Information"
- See " Government Sources of Information"
- Identify disparities for additional investigation
- **TASKS**
    - Establish search protocol
    - Collect data for validation/corroboration
- For the entire workbook of tasks, click here

Potential Issues

- Veracity of parties
- Currency of information
- Admissibility of data

Deliverables

- Search Log
- Updated Genogram
- "Events Analysis"
- Output notebook

FA/IM © - Forensic Accounting/Investigation Methodology ©

EXHIBIT 7.37 Background Research

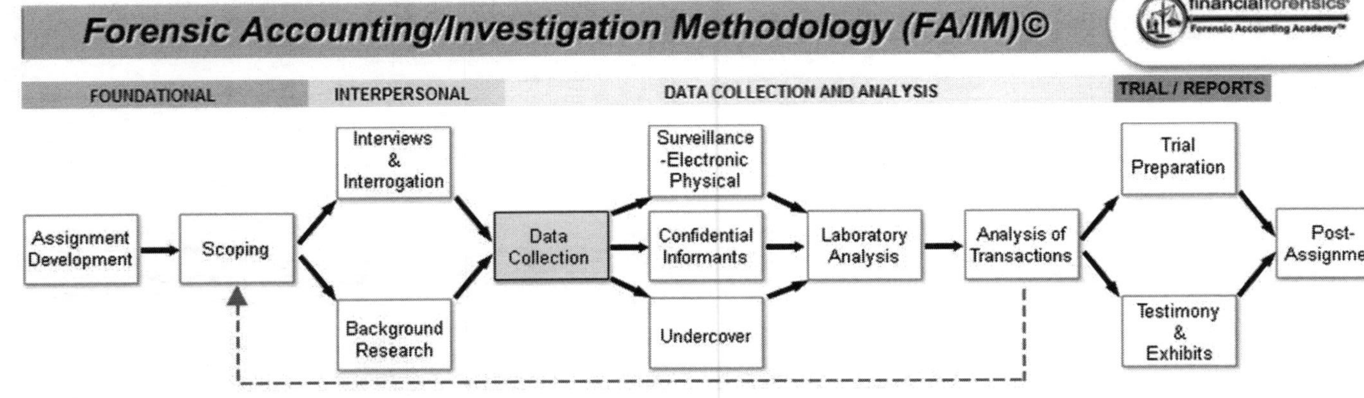

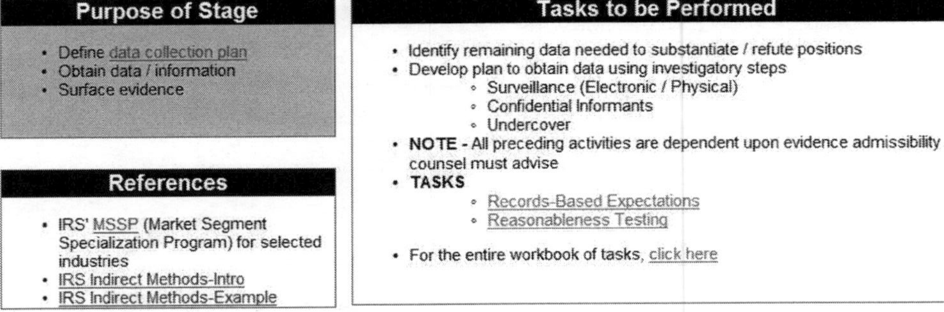

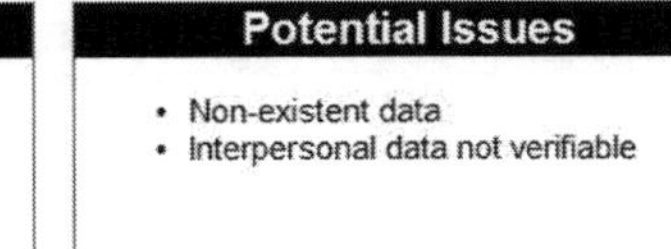

EXHIBIT 7.38 Data Collection

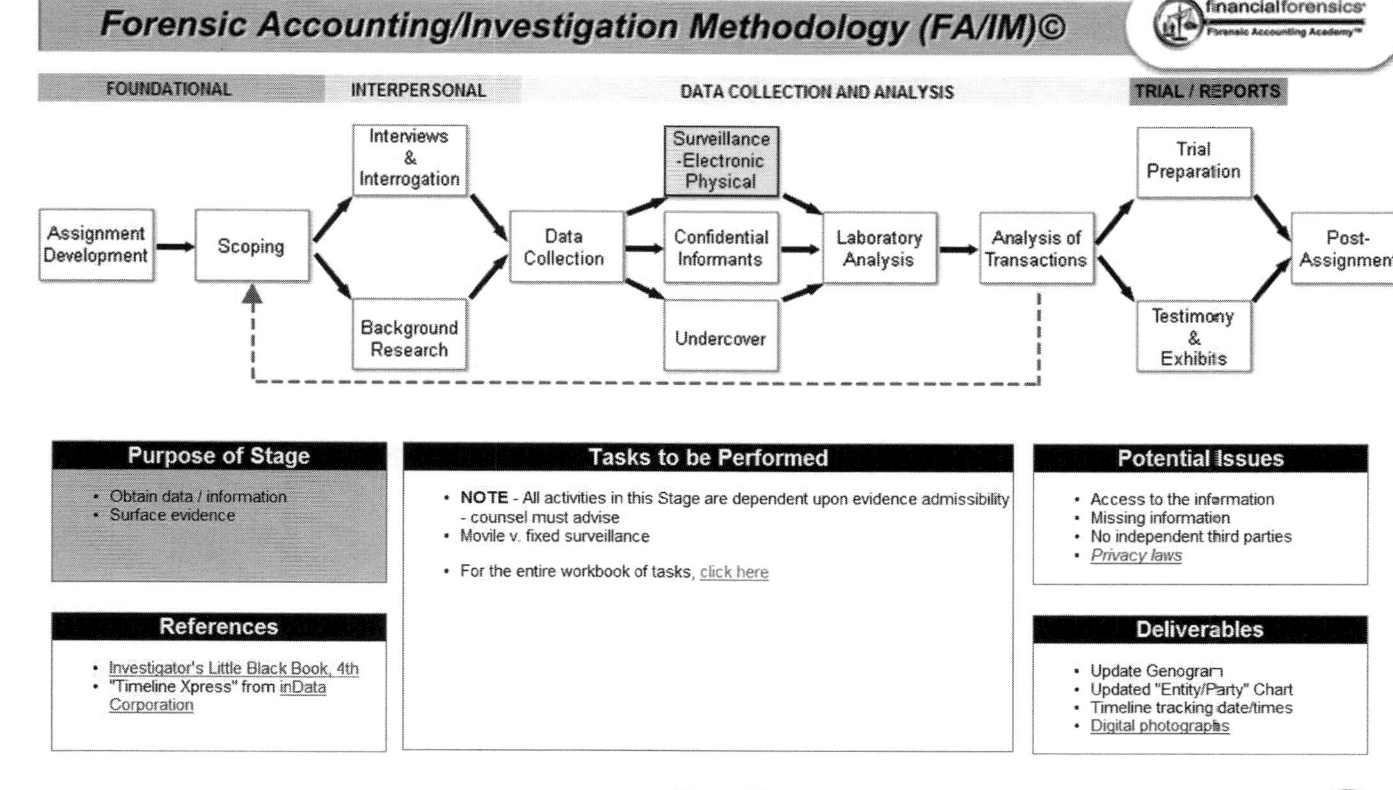

EXHIBIT 7.39 Surveillance – Electronic and Physical

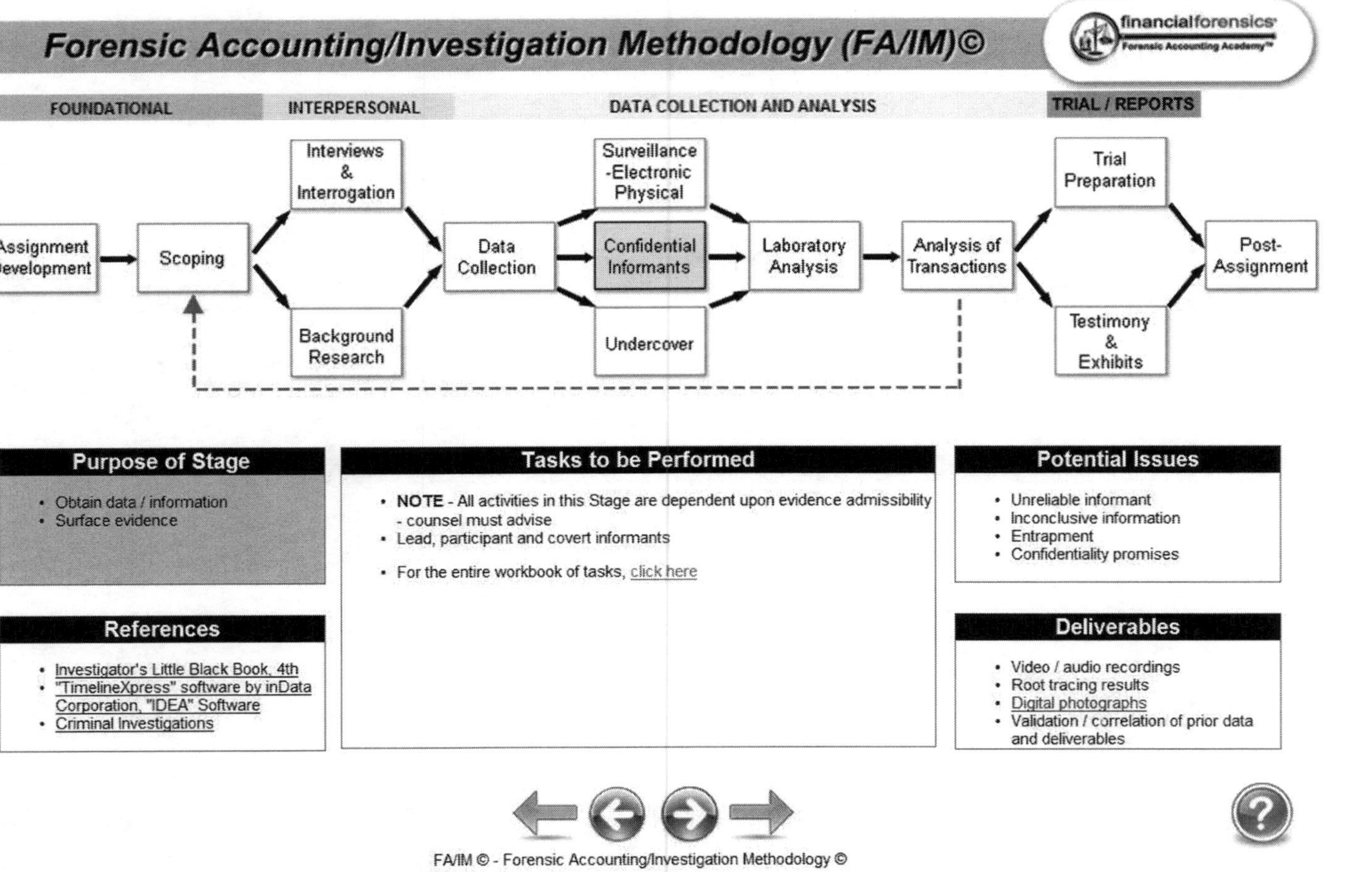

EXHIBIT 7.40 Confidential Informants

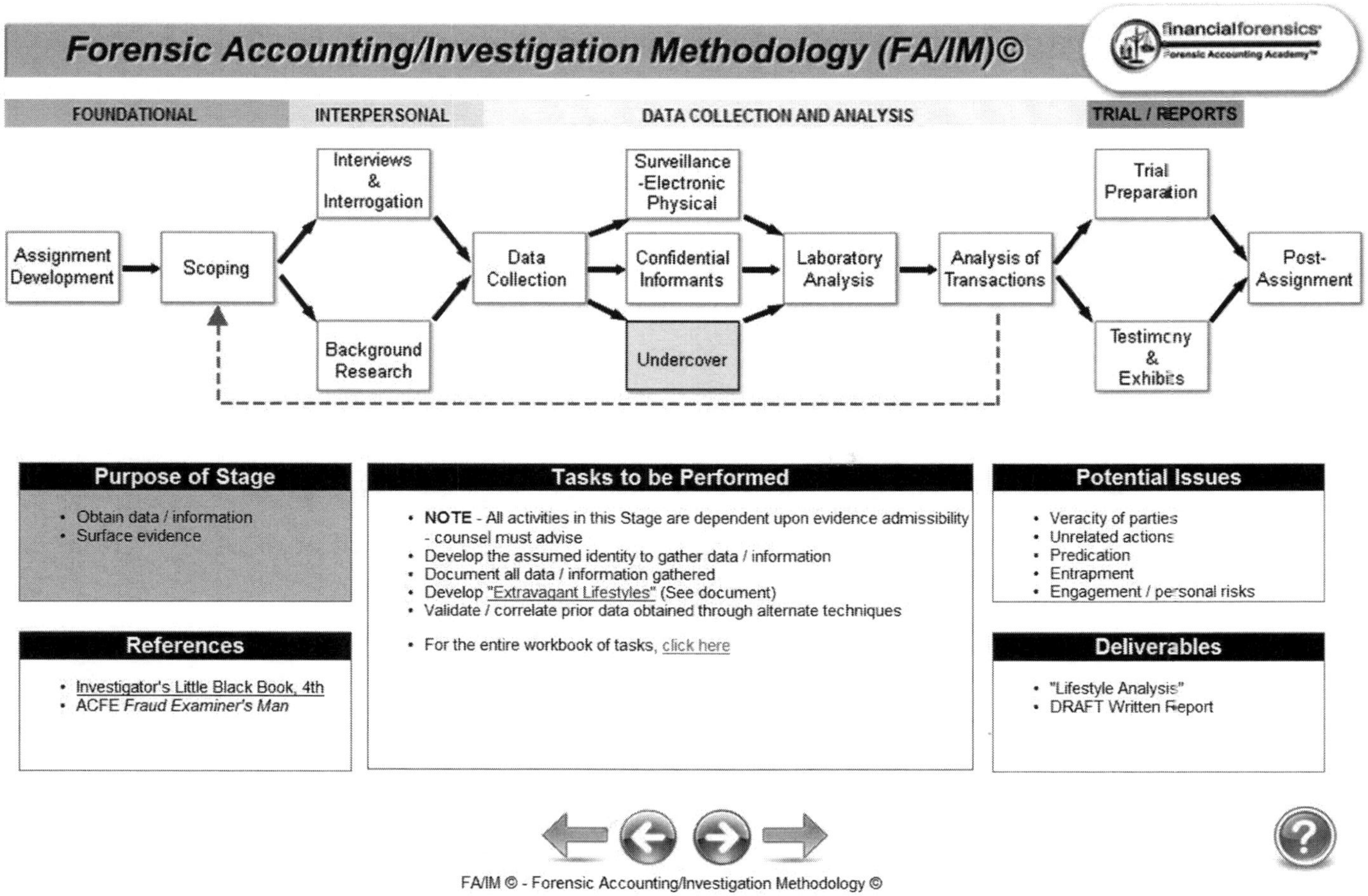

Forensic Accounting/Investigation Methodology (FA/IM)©

financialforensics
Forensic Accounting Academy™

FOUNDATIONAL | INTERPERSONAL | DATA COLLECTION AND ANALYSIS | TRIAL / REPORTS

Assignment Development → Scoping → Interviews & Interrogation / Background Research → Data Collection → Surveillance -Electronic Physical / Confidential Informants / Undercover → Laboratory Analysis → Analysis of Transactions → Trial Preparation / Testimony & Exhibits → Post-Assignment

Purpose of Stage

- Obtain data / information
- Surface evidence

References

- Investigator's Little Black Book, 4th
- ACFE *Fraud Examiner's Man*

Tasks to be Performed

- **NOTE** - All activities in this Stage are dependent upon evidence admissibility - counsel must advise
- Develop the assumed identity to gather data / information
- Document all data / information gathered
- Develop "Extravagant Lifestyles" (See document)
- Validate / correlate prior data obtained through alternate techniques

- For the entire workbook of tasks, click here

Potential Issues

- Veracity of parties
- Unrelated actions
- Predication
- Entrapment
- Engagement / personal risks

Deliverables

- "Lifestyle Analysis"
- DRAFT Written Report

FA/IM © - Forensic Accounting/Investigation Methodology ©

EXHIBIT 7.41 Undercover

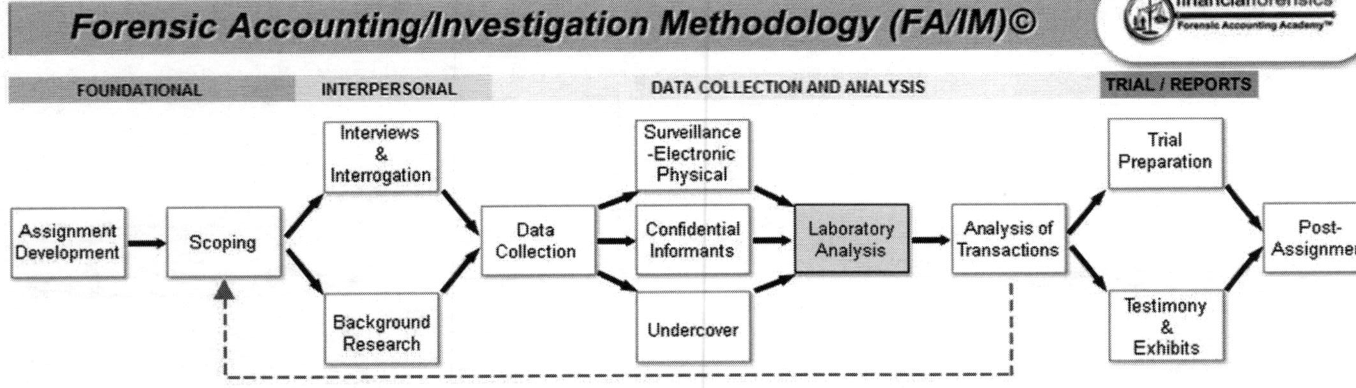

EXHIBIT 7.42 Laboratory Analysis

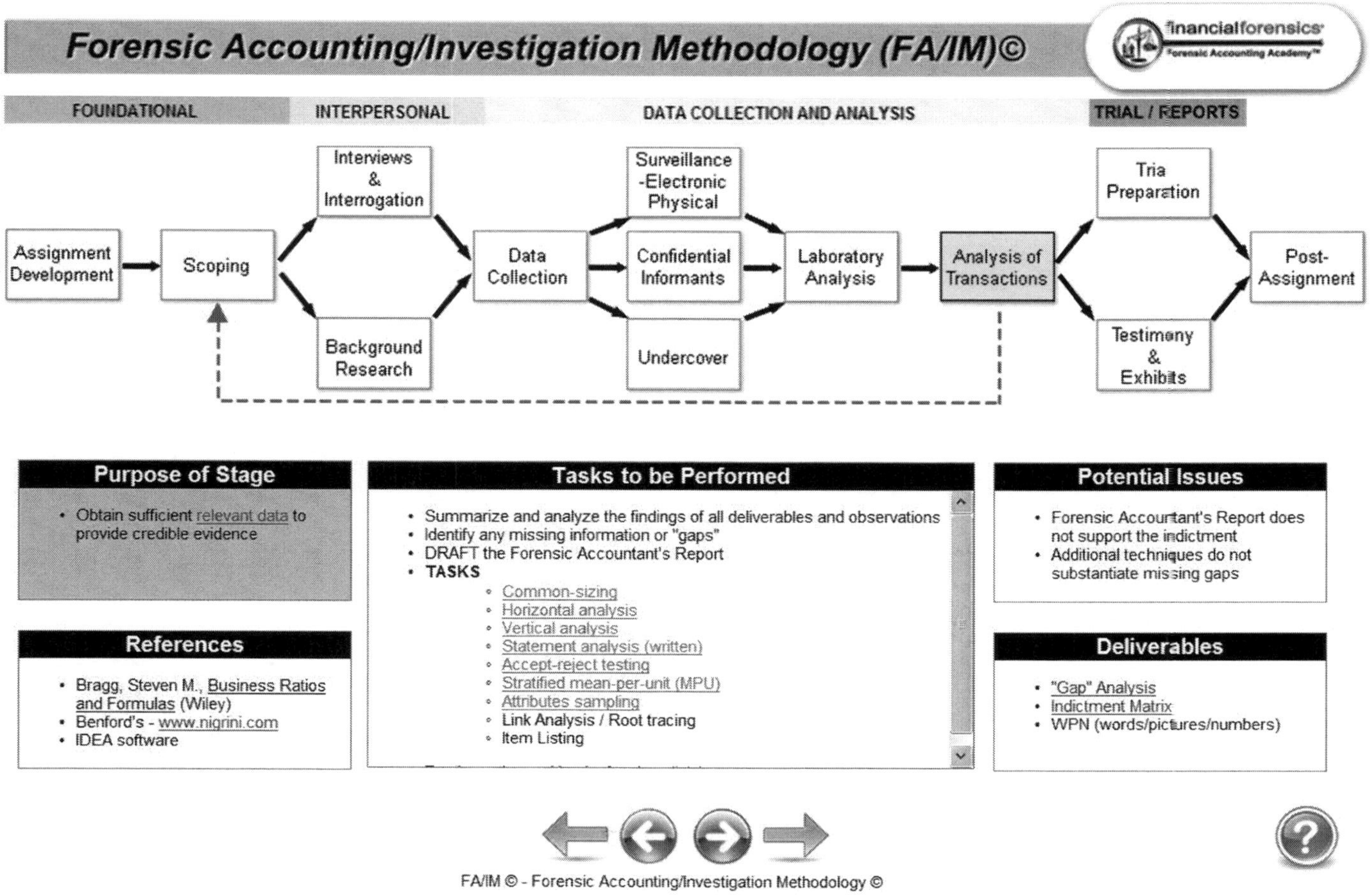

Forensic Accounting/Investigation Methodology (FA/IM)©

FOUNDATIONAL | INTERPERSONAL | DATA COLLECTION AND ANALYSIS | TRIAL / REPORTS

Assignment Development → Scoping → Interviews & Interrogation / Background Research → Data Collection → Surveillance -Electronic Physical / Confidential Informants / Undercover → Laboratory Analysis → Analysis of Transactions → Tria Preparation / Testimony & Exhibits → Post-Assignment

Purpose of Stage

- Obtain sufficient relevant data to provide credible evidence

References

- Bragg, Steven M., Business Ratios and Formulas (Wiley)
- Benford's - www.nigrini.com
- IDEA software

Tasks to be Performed

- Summarize and analyze the findings of all deliverables and observations
- Identify any missing information or "gaps"
- DRAFT the Forensic Accountant's Report
- **TASKS**
  - Common-sizing
  - Horizontal analysis
  - Vertical analysis
  - Statement analysis (written)
  - Accept-reject testing
  - Stratified mean-per-unit (MPU)
  - Attributes sampling
  - Link Analysis / Root tracing
  - Item Listing

Potential Issues

- Forensic Accountant's Report does not support the indictment
- Additional techniques do not substantiate missing gaps

Deliverables

- "Gap" Analysis
- Indictment Matrix
- WPN (words/pictures/numbers)

FA/IM © - Forensic Accounting/Investigation Methodology ©

EXHIBIT 7.43 Analysis of Transactions

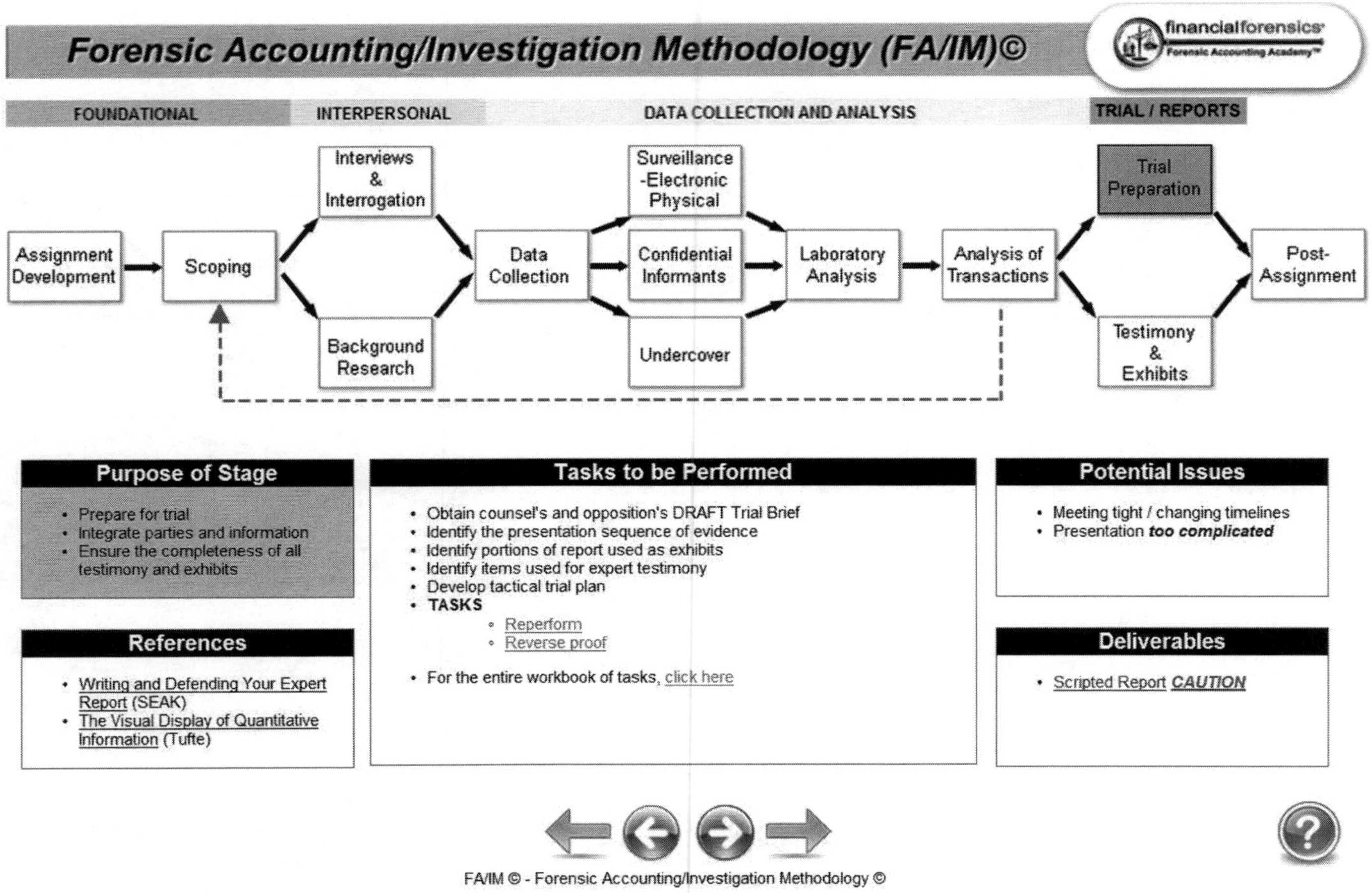

Forensic Accounting/Investigation Methodology (FA/IM)©

FOUNDATIONAL | INTERPERSONAL | DATA COLLECTION AND ANALYSIS | TRIAL / REPORTS

Assignment Development → Scoping → Interviews & Interrogation / Background Research → Data Collection → Surveillance -Electronic Physical / Confidential Informants / Undercover → Laboratory Analysis → Analysis of Transactions → Trial Preparation / Testimony & Exhibits → Post-Assignment

Purpose of Stage

- Prepare for trial
- Integrate parties and information
- Ensure the completeness of all testimony and exhibits

References

- Writing and Defending Your Expert Report (SEAK)
- The Visual Display of Quantitative Information (Tufte)

Tasks to be Performed

- Obtain counsel's and opposition's DRAFT Trial Brief
- Identify the presentation sequence of evidence
- Identify portions of report used as exhibits
- Identify items used for expert testimony
- Develop tactical trial plan
- **TASKS**
    - Reperform
    - Reverse proof
- For the entire workbook of tasks, click here

Potential Issues

- Meeting tight / changing timelines
- Presentation ***too complicated***

Deliverables

- Scripted Report ***CAUTION***

FA/IM © - Forensic Accounting/Investigation Methodology ©

EXHIBIT 7.44 Trial Preparation

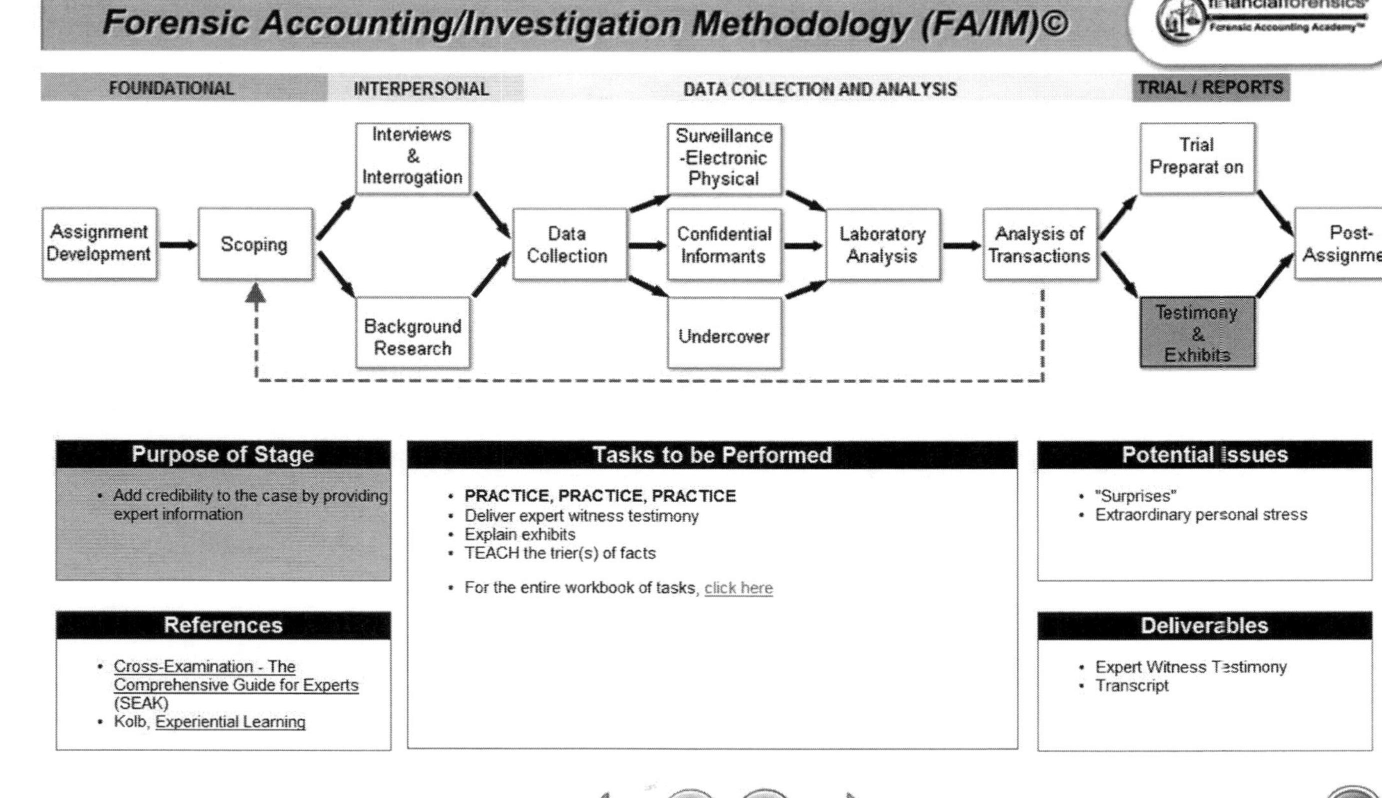

EXHIBIT 7.45 Testimony and Exhibits

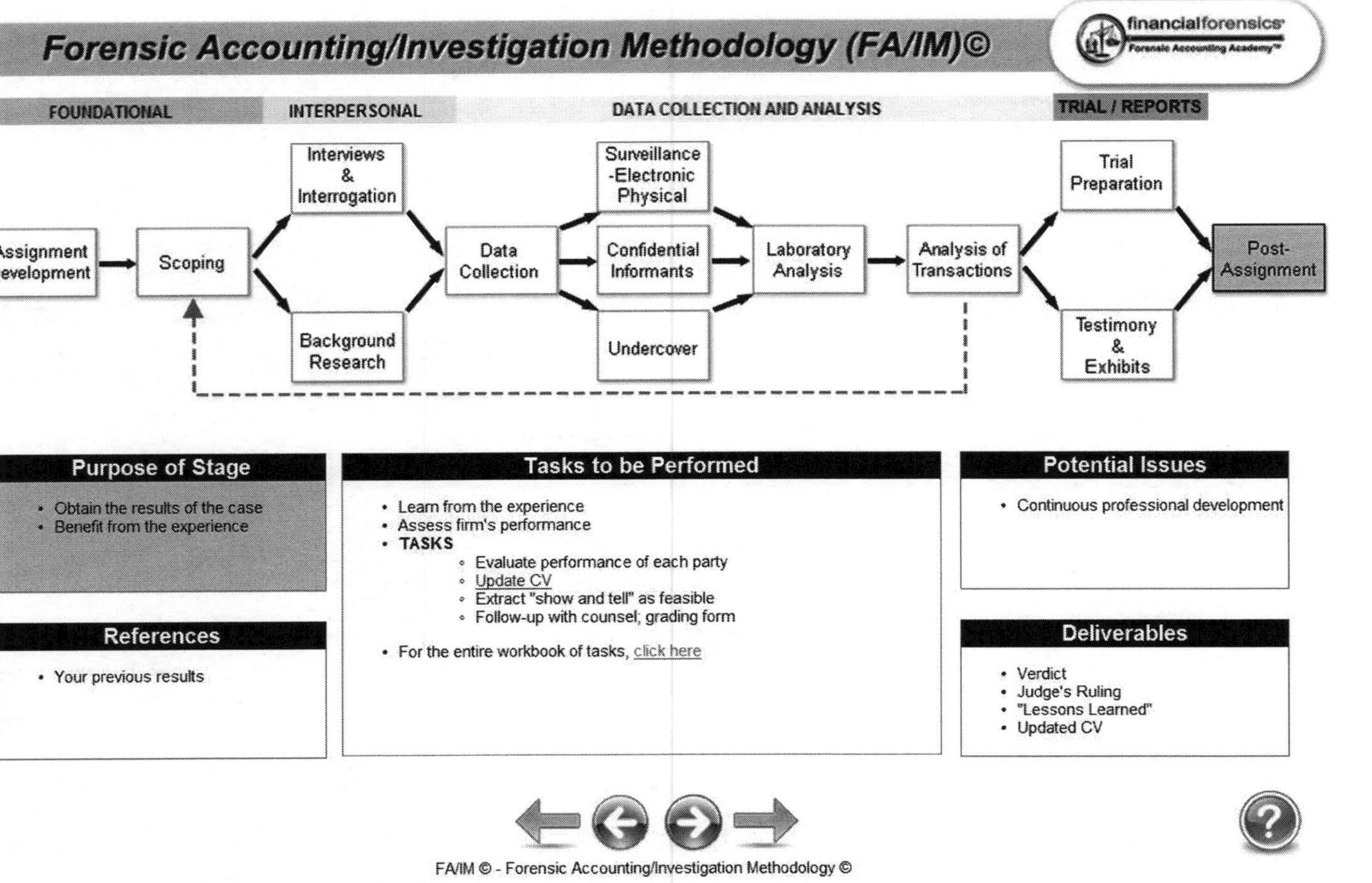

EXHIBIT 7.46 Post-Assignment

EXHIBIT 7.47 Forensic Accounting Techniques

Forensic Technique	Definition/Description (*Key Incremental* Findings in Blue)	Data Collection					Data Analysis	
		I&I	BR	EP	CI	UC	LA	AT
Foundational Phase: *This phase consists of assembling and preparing baseline output that will support and drive the investigation. The output will be continuously updated to provide a current record and status of the progress of investigation.*								
Full-and-false inclusion	*Full-and-false Inclusion* tests are used to determine the appropriate "universe" of data under investigation. This ensures that no extraneous data is included, and that no appropriate data is excluded. These types of tests are particularly useful for finding unreported assets. Also, this technique can/should be used throughout the various stages.	x	x	x	x	x	x	x
Genogram	A *Genogram* is a visual representation of the myriad of information gathered during Background Research, Interviews and Surveillance. It is often prepared in conjunction with *Events Analysis* output. It provides a common perspective for the forensic investigator to demonstrate patterns of behavior and identify other entities and parties meriting further investigation. Also, it can point to key indicators of the subject's behavior, leading to additional points of investigation.	x	x	x	x	x		
Entity(s)/Party(s) chart	*An Entity(s)/Party(s) Chart* is a visual representation depicting entity(s) or party(s) identification, and the associations among them. It is often prepared in conjunction with *Events Analysis* output. Entity(s)/Party(s) charts can be useful predictors of funds diversion. For example, identifying the formation date of an off-shore entity may be compared to funds decline, thus substantiating diversion. Also, identifying seemingly unrelated parties can indicate where further investigation is potentially warranted.	x	x	x	x	x		
Background investigation	*Background Investigation* first involves research (typically electronic, but also surveillance) into a party's identity to identify other assets that may have been "forgotten" about. The results are continuously updated to provide a comprehensive record of information about the target.	x	x	x	x	x		

(*continued*)

EXHIBIT 7.47 Forensic Accounting Techniques *(Continued)*

Forensic Technique	Definition/Description (*Key Incremental* Findings in Blue)	Data Collection					Data Analysis	
		I&I	BR	EP	CI	UC	LA	AT
Interpersonal Communications Phase: *This phase consists of Interviews, Interrogation, Surveillance, Undercover and the related activities necessary to extract pertinent information from/about the entity(s)/party(s).*								
Distance communication	*Distance Communication (or Proxemic Communication)* consists of comparing and contrasting the interpersonal distance involved in query responses. It has been suggested that (even subtle) movements away from an interviewer indicate avoidance, and thus merit additional investigation. Movements toward an interviewer can suggest a desire to be believed and/or a desire for assistance, such as a request for the interviewer to delve further into the matter. Note that cultural differences have a significant impact on interpersonal distance. For example, the "socially acceptable" distance in the US when 2 adults are communicating (while standing) is 18 to 24 inches. European norms are much closer.	×					×	×
Kinetic Communication	*Kinetic Communication* consists of observing bodily reactions to determine where additional investigation is warranted. It has been suggested that a person who averts his/her eyes to the left prior to responding may be lying. Alternatively, it has been suggested that averts his/her eyes to the right prior to responding may be recalling a memory. For example, it is well documented that when lying (and when passionate about a subject), blood flow increases to the subject's head and neck area, thus providing a "flush" that may warrant further investigation.	×					×	×
Paralinguistic Communication	*Paralinguistic Communication* consists of analyzing the volume, pitch and voice quality during verbal communication. Oral communication provides for a range of nonverbal accompaniment that can be used to convey certain emotions which may not be as easily discerned in written communication.	×					×	×
Expectations-based statement analysis	*Expectations-Based Statement Analysis* consists of analyzing the language used by subject during interviews to assess his/her truthfulness. For example, the reply "I don't remember" may require further investigation while the reply "I don't know" may indicate that no further inquiry is necessary.				×	×	×	

Data Collection and Analysis (Indirect) Phase: *This phase consists of applying the various indirect quantitative and qualitative data obtained during the earlier phases and developing output supporting observations, thus arriving at an appropriate conclusion(s). If such efforts prove inconclusive, the next phase – Direct Analytical and Conclusion Phase will provide additional evidence.*

Records-based expectations	*Records-Based Expectations* consists of identifying the nature, form, extent, veracity, availability and related elements of record keeping in order to set expectations about the entity(s)/party(s). For example, an entity handling a large sum of money from numerous investors would be expected, at a minimum to have in place very sound management and internal controls that provide solid foundation to the representative financial statements. Examples of the minimum types of records in such a case include the general ledger, receipts ledger, cost and expense ledgers, detailed shareholder records, comprehensive financial statements, current income tax returns, and related elements.	×	×	×			×	×
Common-sizing	*Common-Sizing* consists of converting all financial statement items to a percentage of revenue and assets, and then comparing the results within and among one another over a multi-period time horizon. This method also accommodates a comparison to similar businesses that may be a much different size. Bar graphs and line charts are useful to identify key variations warranting further investigation.		×				×	×
Horizontal analysis	*Horizontal Analysis* consists of comparing key account categories, such as officer compensation, travel and entertainment, etc. over a multi-period (e.g., year, quarter, month, day) time horizon to identify changes meriting further investigation. The technique typically includes percentage changes, dollar changes, comparison changes, etc. Also, bar graphs and line charts are useful to identify key variations warranting further investigation.		×				×	×
Reasonableness testing	In *Reasonableness Testing,* the forensic investigator formulates an expectation, (i.e. estimate) of an account balance based upon understanding and assumptions driving the account balance. For example, a reasonableness test of deposits could measure the actual deposits against the expected deposits could identify where further investigation is warranted.				×		×	×

(*continued*)

EXHIBIT 7.47 Forensic Accounting Techniques *(Continued)*

Forensic Technique	Definition/Description (*Key Incremental* Findings in Blue)	Data Collection					Data Analysis	
		I&I	BR	EP	CI	UC	LA	AT
Data Collection and Analysis (Direct) Phase: *This phase can follow the Indirect Phase, or be executed either jointly with, or independent of the Indirect Phase. The evidence provided by this Phase is, by definition the most comprehensive, but is not necessary in every case.*								
Benford's Law	*Benford's Law* is a financial "DNA-equivalent" technique developed during the 1920s by Frank Benford, a physicist at General Electric research laboratories. He noted that the first few pages of logarithm table books were more worn than the later pages. In those days, logarithm table books were used to accelerate the process of multiplying 2 large numbers by summing the log of each number and then referring to the table for the requisite integer. Benford's Law states that digits and digit sequences in a dataset follow a predictable pattern. The technique applies a data analysis method that identifies possible errors, potential fraud or other irregularities. For example, if artificial values are present in a dataset the distribution of the digits in the dataset will likely exhibit a different shape (when viewed graphically), than the shape predicted by Benford's Law.						×	×
Statement Analysis (Written)	In *Statement Analysis (Written)* investigators examine written documents in a manner similar to the Statement Analysis (Verbal) as described above. However, analyzing written documents focus on the words and the nature of the document, including the age, condition, and related physical document factors.						×	×
Accept-reject testing	*Accept-Reject Testing* is similar to sampling, but differs since sampling involves the projection of a misstatement amount and accept-reject testing does not. For example, "accepts" that the testing criteria have been met, or "rejects" that the testing criteria have not been met. If a "reject" occurs, additional testing may be carried out depending upon materiality and other considerations. Following are some examples of accept-reject applications when the projection of a misstatement amount is not practicable:						×	×

Stratified Mean per unit (MPU)	A *Stratified Mean-Per-Unit (MPU)* technique can improve the precision of the mean-per-unit technique without increasing the sample size. The technique uses stratification of the population and samples each stratum separately. By stratification, the forensic investigator segments the population into groups of items exhibiting similar value amounts. Once mean and standard error in each stratum are calculated, the results are combined for the individual strata to create an overall estimate. The first few strata reduce the necessary sample size, but diminishing returns and certain other factors result in from 3 to 10 strata as sufficient in many cases.	x	x
Attributes Sampling	*Attributes Sampling* is used to specifically identify occurrences that fall within and/or outside of previously established norms. It can be applied either globally and/or statistically using sampling techniques. Its most common use in forensic investigation is to test the rate of deviation from a prescribed (or expected) control perspective to support the forensic investigator's assessed level of assurance. In attributes sampling <u>each</u> occurrence of, or deviation from, a prescribed control perspective is given equal weight in the sample evaluation, regardless of the dollar amount of the transactions. In addition to tests of controls, attributes sampling may be used for substantive procedures, such as tests for under-recording inter-bank cash transfers or demand deposit accounts. However, if the audit objective is to obtain evidence directly about a monetary amount being examined, the forensic investigator generally designs a variables sampling application, described below. Substantive tests consist of tests of details of account balances and related transactions, and analytical procedures. They are intended to gather evidence regarding the validity/appropriateness of the treatment of transactions. Generally, such tests are performed in combination during investigation.	x	x

(*continued*)

EXHIBIT 7.47 Forensic Accounting Techniques *(Continued)*

Forensic Technique	Definition/Description (*Key Incremental* Findings in Blue)	Data Collection					Data Analysis	
		I&I	BR	EP	CI	UC	LA	AT
Ratio estimation; or extrapolation	*Ratio Estimation (sometimes Extrapolation)* is often used in connection with *Variables Sampling*, and can estimate (on a statistically significant basis) the projected results based upon analytical sampling via "Probability-Proportional-to-Size Sampling."						×	×
Reperform	The forensic investigator may *reperform*, sometimes on a test basis, procedures performed by employees, primarily to determine that a transaction was accurately recorded. Reperformance of computations, such as a bank reconciliation, also provides some assurance about the existence of the account balance, and solidifies a reference point for further investigation. If judgment drives the basis of a computation, such as in the valuation of accounts receivable, the forensic investigator reperforming the computation also should understand, evaluate and apply the reasoning process underlying the judgment.						×	×
Reverse proof	*Reverse Proof*. The examination of forensic investigation matters is approached from two perspectives: (1) that a fraud (or other deceit) has occurred, the proof must include attempts to prove it has not occurred; (2) that a fraud has not occurred, that proof must also attempt to prove it has occurred. The reason for reverse proof is that both sides of fraud must be examined. Under the law, proof of fraud must preclude any explanation other than guilt.						×	×

Trial Phase: *This Phase is perhaps the most critical and is highly experience dependent. Selected examples of actual (blinded and redacted) trial exhibits follow in order to provide the practitioner with illustrations of exhibits that have proven successful.*

	The following example Deliverables have all been successfully used in a wide variety of civil and criminal matters, and are offered to the reader as immediately applicable tools.

EXHIBIT 7.48 Expectations Attributes

	Expectations Attributes					
Case	Management	Planning	Financial Statements	Accounting System	Independent Attestation	Other
Best	Vision clearly defined Management structure and controls defined People linked to vision	Comprehensive business plan Comprehensive budgets	Monthly/Annual consolidated financials Compared to budget Accountability applied as appropriate	Strong financial and accounting resources Single comprehensive system Investor stewardship	Audits for pertinent years	Services/products well-defined Prototypes in place and working
Next-Best	Management structure defined Controls in place Key people in place	Comprehensive budgets	Monthly financials Annual consolidated financials	Strong financial and accounting resources Investor stewardship	Audits or Reviews for key years	Services/products well-defined
Most Likely	Key Controls in place	Budgets for selected elements	Annual consolidated	Single system	Reviews for key years	Some services or products in place
Undesirable	No internal linkage	"Back of the envelope"	Inconsistent	Multiple systems	Compilation	Ideas or concepts
Worst	Internal barriers	None	None	Patchwork	None	Pre-idea

CHAPTER 8

Civil versus Criminal Law Comparison

Financial Crimes

The public is generally more familiar with the criminal law process than the civil law process. Newspaper articles, news programs, movies, and endless television dramas portray the criminal offense, investigation, arrest, and subsequent prosecution. While the basic format of these television shows is usually accurate, they do not depict all the elements of the process because the case must be wrapped up within the allotted hour. The dramas often have an identifiable suspect and a smoking gun, so the viewer believes the crime is easily resolved. In reality, the process never concludes that quickly. It can be a long and arduous journey, especially for white-collar crime or related civil financial issues or both. They are never swiftly resolved because of the voluminous paper and hours of analysis involved. Civil financial lawsuits are frequently more complicated and more difficult than criminal lawsuits. The financial complexity is what often spurs the need for a forensic operator.

WAR STORY

A real estate holding company partner who also served as the partnership's CFO was believed to be taking more than his fair share of money. A forensic operator was engaged to assist in a clandestine investigation. Shortly after the forensic operator started, the company followed the forensic operator's advice and hired an attorney. Unfortunately, the attorney was a civil attorney with no criminal experience but apparently felt compelled to demonstrate his capabilities. Predictably, the attorney did what he knew and generally treated the case as a civil matter, frustrating the district attorney, the detective, and the forensic operator. The attorney was eventually replaced after much prodding from the forensic operator, but significant time and money had already been wasted.

This section compares and contrasts summaries of the civil and criminal processes that most forensic accounting matters follow. Also, the state and federal processes have different rules and procedures. The outline in Exhibit 8.1 describes

We gratefully acknowledge the technical assistance of Mr. Dennis Shen, Multnomah County, Oregon Deputy District Attorney in the criminal portion of this section.

EXHIBIT 8.1 Civil Law Process versus Criminal Law Process

Civil	Criminal
Alleged Event Occurs TRIGGERING EVENT—A party[1] suffers an apparent[2] legal wrong(s) at the hands of a perpetrator(s).[3] The wrong could have happened recently or in the past. It may be the same event as that which occurred in the criminal law process. STATUTE OF LIMITATIONS—The statute of limitations generally begins once the victim identifies the wrongdoing. The statute of limitations is the state or federal law that limits the amount of time within which to initiate legal action.	**Alleged Crime Occurs** TRIGGERING EVENT—A party suffers an apparent legal wrong(s) at the hands of a perpetrator(s). The wrong could have happened recently or in the past. It may be the same event that occurred in the civil law process. STATUTE OF LIMITATIONS—The statute of limitations generally begins at the commission of the wrongdoing. The statute of limitations is the state or federal law that limits the amount of time within which to initiate legal action. For example, if an employee embezzles funds for five years and the general statute of limitations is three years, then only crimes occurring within a three-year window apply. Statutes of limitation laws vary for the criminal process. For example, in many states murder and treason have no limitation, while sex crimes may be extended. The law often allows extensions beyond the time usually allowed, the basis of which are usually cited in the prosecutor's pleadings.
Victim Engages a Private Civil Attorney And a Forensic Operator OUTSIDE ASSISTANCE—If the party discovers sufficient evidence of a legal wrongdoing, she will engage a private civil attorney (at her own expense). The victim may also engage a forensic operator or delegate such authority to the attorney.	**File a Report with Law Enforcement** **Law Enforcement Report**—The party becomes a victim if the party's investigation uncovers sufficient evidence to support an alleged crime. The victim will file a report with law enforcement. The selection of law enforcement authority is critical and depends upon certain factors as summarized next.

The party retains a civil attorney.[4] The attorney will begin gathering facts and evidence and preparing various legal briefs, potentially including the complaint. The civil attorney may also assist the plaintiff in filing a report with law enforcement, and often seeks assistance from a forensic operator. In this case, the civil attorney becomes the plaintiff's advocate in the criminal prosecution process as well as the civil litigation.

FORENSIC OPERATOR—The attorney will likely recommend engaging a forensic operator to assist in the investigation. It is also likely that the forensic operator will testify at trial if events proceed to that end. Unlike plaintiff's counsel, forensic operators do not advocate for the plaintiff. Instead, they advocate for their opinion as supported by the evidence.

Jurisdiction—The crime must have occurred within the court's, prosecution's, and law enforcement agency's jurisdiction. This may be more complicated than it appears on the surface.[5]

For example, a victim may have to choose among city, county, state, or federal law enforcement authorities.

Resource allocation—Virtually all law enforcement authorities lack resources, particularly in white-collar crime.[6] Therefore, the victim must determine the magnitude of the crime, even if only from estimation. This helps the agency determine whether it can take on that matter at the respective point in time. A $500,000 crime will nearly always take precedence over a $50,000 crime, all else being equal. This is another reason to engage a forensic operator at the first opportunity.

Capabilities—City, county, and state law enforcement often lack accounting training and skills beyond basic levels. Therefore, the more sophisticated the crime, the less likely that city or county law enforcement can handle it. Federal law enforcement agencies, for example, the FBI, often possess training and skills beyond basic levels, but may seek outside expertise in complex matters. Both state and federal authorities may seek outside expertise because of a general lack of resources.

(continued)

---

[1]Person, company, agency department, etc.

[2]Recall the presumption of innocence.

[3]Perpetrate: to bring about or carry out (as a primer deception). www.Merriam-Webster.com.

[4]The attorney engaged must be qualified in white-collar crime matters; mere litigation or corporate experience is not sufficient.

[5]The authors worked a case where the perpetrator skimmed from a company in one state, but deposited the funds into her bank in a different state. Delicate coordination was required between the two district attorneys.

[6]Prosecution of violent crimes such as murder, rape, assault, etc. always takes priority over white-collar crimes.

EXHIBIT 8.1 Civil Law Process versus Criminal Law Process (*Continued*)

Civil	Criminal
Alleged Event Is Investigated The extent of the legal wrongdoing and the commensurate supporting evidence must be expeditiously determined as soon as practicable after the date of discovery. A forensic operator, if engaged, should employ at least one of the methodologies described in this book. Otherwise, his conclusions may be incorrect, and his work is open to challenge by opposition. The forensic operator can expect the outcome to result in some type of litigation. At this stage, it could be a civil lawsuit, criminal prosecution, or both. The forensic operator's process would be the same and would include but is not limited to: ■ Analyzing financial, corporate, and other records. ■ Interviewing witnesses. ■ Interrogating suspects. ■ Reporting findings. ■ Testifying as to facts and opinions.	**Alleged Crime Is Investigated** The extent of the legal wrongdoing and the commensurate supporting evidence must be determined as soon as practicable after the date of discovery. A forensic operator, if engaged, should employ at least one of the investigative methodologies described in this book. The forensic operator can expect the outcome to result in some type of litigation. At this stage, it could be a civil lawsuit, criminal prosecution, or both. The forensic operator's process would be the same and would include, but is not limited to: ■ Analyzing financial, corporate, and other records. ■ Interviewing witnesses. ■ Interrogating suspects. ■ Reporting findings. ■ Testifying as to facts and opinions.
Law Enforcement Does Not Investigate Each issue of wrongdoing is unique, and the victims and their legal counsel must determine whether to contact law enforcement based on the facts and circumstances. Not all disputes are potentially criminal or will warrant criminal prosecution. If the victim pursues only the civil law process, there is no involvement by law enforcement, and thus law enforcement does not conduct an investigation.	**Law Enforcement Investigates** If the forensic operator is not engaged to do a preliminary investigation, a highly trained financial crimes detective[7] will employ many of the same steps. Financial crimes detectives are usually law enforcement specialists first and accountants last. Therefore, they may lack the training and skill necessary to complete a complex financial crime investigation. This comment does not criticize financial crimes detectives. The reality is that government budgets are tight and the funds are unavailable to provide the education necessary to pursue complex financial crimes matters. Also, time is another drawback for overworked and understaffed agencies. Since financial crimes are time-consuming to investigate, most law enforcement authorities welcome the assistance of an experienced and trained forensic operator. Even if the forensic operator conducts an initial investigation, it may be incomplete and thus

require additional evidence. Law enforcement can serve subpoenas for the suspect's bank records and other information otherwise unavailable to the public or through the civil law process. Law enforcement also has access to confidential information and resources that can assist in the investigation and recovery of assets. The detective may also re-interview witnesses, re-interrogate the suspect, and review the analysis of the forensic operator.

Law Enforcement Submits Their Case to the Prosecutor for Review
When the detective has completed his case, he submits findings and suggests potential charges to the prosecuting attorney for review. The role of the prosecutor is to represent the State in seeking justice against a person charged with violating the law.

Prosecutor Accepts or Declines the Case or Requests Additional Investigation
For the most part, the prosecutor has the discretionary authority regarding whether or not to file charges. If there is insufficient evidence to proceed, the prosecutor is obligated to either decline the case or request further investigation to secure additional evidence to his satisfaction.

The Grand Jury Hears the Case Evidence and Testimony Regarding Felony Charges
If the prosecutor accepts the case, he submits the case to the grand jury for review. Some jurisdictions use an alternative process, such as a preliminary hearing. The purpose of such proceedings is to determine whether sufficient evidence exists to charge someone with a crime. The grand jury is a panel of seven people (depending upon the jurisdiction) selected from the jury pool and sworn in by the court. The grand jury hears the evidence in secret as presented by the prosecution and does not consider any evidence from the defendant. The preliminary hearing occurs with a judge, prosecutor, defendant, and defendant's counsel. Consequently, preliminary hearings typically last longer than a grand jury since defendant's counsel is permitted to ask questions. Prosecution will provide exculpatory evidence, if any.

(continued)

[7]This assumes that the respective agency has the commensurate talent on staff.

EXHIBIT 8.1 Civil Law Process versus Criminal Law Process (*Continued*)

Civil	Criminal
	The grand jury reviews only felony cases (and attendant and misdemeanors, if any), which comprises most embezzlement cases. Grand juries differ from trial juries; grand juries do not determine innocence or guilt. Rather, they decide whether the party will face charges for alleged crimes. Forensic operators may be subpoenaed to testify before a grand jury. Grand jury testimony is typically less formal than trial testimony. The witness may provide testimony with minimal direct questioning. Also, the grand jury may be permitted to ask questions directly of the witness.
The Victim Decides to Begin Litigation Based upon the facts and circumstances, and the evidence extant, the victim's attorney may declare that sufficient evidence exists to file a formal lawsuit against the wrongdoer. At this point, the victim becomes the plaintiff and the opposing party is the defendant.	**The Grand Jury Returns a Decision on the Indictment** After hearing the State's evidence, the grand jury votes on the proposed indictment. If the majority believes there is sufficient evidence to proceed, they return a *true bill* and the suspect becomes a defendant in a criminal proceeding. If they believe there is insufficient evidence to indict, they return a *not true bill* and no charges are filed.
Complaint Filed by Plaintiff(s)-Individual(s) and/or Organization(s) against the Defendant(s) The Complaint identifies the legal and factual bases that support the request for equitable relief or damages due to the legal wrong suffered by the plaintiff due to defendant's actions. Lawsuits can also seek injunctive relief, which means the plaintiff requests the court to order the defendant to cease certain actions. The lawsuit can comprise multiple plaintiffs against multiple defendants. Civil litigation is subject to the rules of civil procedure.	**Arrest Warrant Is Issued for the Defendant** The court issues an arrest warrant for the defendant based upon a grand jury indictment. Defendants have often previously retained a defense attorney in anticipation of pending legal issues. If the prosecutor and defense attorney have a working relationship, the prosecutor will work with the defense attorney to arrange for the defendant's voluntary appearance for the arraignment. In these cases, defendants in financial crimes are not arrested in the fashion portrayed on television. That is, they are not handcuffed and hauled off to jail in the back of a police cruiser. However, if the investigation has been undisclosed for some reason (e.g., concern that the defendant may flee), or the defendant has been willfully uncooperative, the normal arrest procedure would likely be followed. This includes handcuffs and a ride to the intake facility in the back of a police cruiser to be booked. Criminal prosecution is subject to the rules of criminal procedure.

Defendant(s) Files an Answer to the Complaint The defendant responds to each of the plaintiff's allegations of legal wrong by pleading the following: ■ Admitting the allegation ■ Denying the allegation ■ Pleading a lack of sufficient information to admit or deny the allegation The defendant may raise all the affirmative defenses, justifications, or excuses they may have. They may also file counterclaims against the plaintiff. For example, if a plaintiff filed a lawsuit against the bookkeeper for inappropriate use of funds, the bookkeeper could countersue for unpaid services rendered, wrongful termination, and other claims.	**Arraignment** The prosecutor informs the defendant of the charges against the party and the judge asks for a formal plea to the pending charges. The defendant typically pleads not guilty. Terms of release, such as bail, are determined. If the defendant cannot afford an attorney, he can request a public defender. If the defendant appears voluntarily per arraignment arrangements, he needs to be booked, or processed, into the justice system. The intake process includes photographs and fingerprints. If no bail was set at the arraignment, the court will release the defendant on his own recognizance.
Fact-Finding The pretrial discovery stage is a structured process of exchanging evidence and statements to preclude surprises at trial, and ensure that all parties are clear as to the reason(s) for the lawsuit. Each party tries to learn as much as they can about the opposing party and their position. There may be document requests by each party as well as interrogatories and depositions. Additional forensic analysis is applied to the production received from the opposing party. Findings may result in modifications and refinements to the original complaint. For example, the initial filing is captioned as the Complaint, so the first modification is captioned as the First Amended Complaint, and so on until all the complaints have been completed.	**Fact-Finding** The prosecution's criminal case is typically complete by this stage. The prosecution begins to provide the evidence against the defendant to the defense attorney. The evidence is often voluminous and is expensive to reproduce. The prosecution will make all the evidence available for the defendant's review but generally does not provide a complete copy of all documents. All pertinent documents identified by the defense are copied at their request. Discovery laws are reciprocal. However, Fifth Amendment[8] claims allow the defendant to restrict the information they would otherwise be required to provide to the prosecution.

(continued)

[8]The Fifth Amendment gives criminal defendants the right to decline to testify and requires that jurors be instructed that they cannot assume the defendant's guilt by their silence.

EXHIBIT 8.1 Civil Law Process versus Criminal Law Process (*Continued*)

Civil	Criminal
Plaintiff And Defendant Attorneys May Negotiate The fact-finding stage helps the parties realize whether they should settle or drop frivolous claims or defenses. During the pretrial phase, the attorneys may negotiate to reach a settlement offer or civil compromise. Whenever possible, a pretrial settlement agreement is beneficial to both parties. Trial can be extremely expensive and unpredictable for the plaintiff and defendant. Other alternative dispute resolutions are mediation and arbitration. Mediation helps the parties communicate and reach an agreement with the help of an independent mediator. The mediator can express an opinion as to the fairness of a settlement but cannot make a binding decision for the parties. Arbitration is similar to mediation. An arbitrator must remain neutral, however, does not participate in the settlement process, and may, depending on circumstances, impose a legally binding decision.	**Prosecutor and Defense Attorney May Negotiate a Plea Agreement** Generally, most financial crime cases settle with a plea agreement. After a thorough investigation and with sufficient corroborating evidence, the defendant's culpability is often undeniable. In such cases, the plea bargaining usually involves negotiating the charges and the sentence. As is often with financial crimes, the sentence is the driving force in the negotiations. For example, the court will reduce the number of felony theft counts to correlate with the agreed length of incarceration. With a plea agreement, the defendant, in some ways, has more control over the outcome than by going to the trial. A plea agreement will often result in a lesser sentence than would have been received if the defendant were found guilty at a trial. For many victims, a plea agreement is the optimal solution. The victim has the assurance of an acceptable outcome without the stress and delay of a trial. The criminal process can be long and arduous for the victim, as they have little or no control over the process. Unlike a plaintiff in a civil lawsuit who can push and prod a civil attorney because he pays the attorney's fee, the victim in a criminal case must be patient and work with the prosecutor and the criminal justice system timetable. On occasion, the defense attorney and prosecutor will discuss a civil compromise to the criminal charges. In general, the defendant must civilly admit his guilt and agree to restitution in exchange for removal of the criminal offense from his record. Prosecutors do not approve civil compromises very often. Even though such an argument saves the justice system time and money, it leaves no trace of the financial crime to protect future victims.

A Settlement or Civil Compromise Is Reached A settlement offer is an agreement to settle the dispute outside of court. The terms of the settlement can be whatever the parties agree to. A civil compromise is associated with criminal offenses and is reached with the defense attorney and prosecutor and then agreed to by the civil attorney on behalf of the client.	**Voluntarily Enter a Plea** A plea hearing is scheduled when the court is notified that the parties have reached a plea agreement and the defendant wishes to change his plea. The judge will ask the defendant a series of questions to ensure he is entering a guilty plea knowingly, voluntarily, and intelligently. Assuming the Court accepts the responses, the defendant pleads guilty or no contest to the charges against him as agreed to in the plea negotiation.
No Settlement or Compromise Is Reached If no settlement agreement is amenable, the lawsuit proceeds toward trial. Based on pretrial discovery, the defendant can make various motions such as a motion to dismiss or motion for summary judgment. If the Judge denies the motion, the case proceeds. Settlement discussions often continue up to the trial date and even after the trial has commenced.	**No Plea Agreement Reached** The criminal case proceeds to trial if the prosecution and defense do not reach a plea agreement. There are often various pretrial motions, such as a motion to dismiss or a motion for a directed verdict. If the motion is denied, the case proceeds. Plea negotiations often continue up to the trial date and even after the trial has commenced.
Trial Preparation The civil attorneys prepare for trial, witnesses are subpoenaed, and exhibits are prepared. All names of fact witnesses and pertinent documents relied upon must have been exchanged between each party. Most states require disclosure of expert witnesses and their reports prior to trial.	**Trial Preparation** The prosecutor prepares for trial, witnesses are subpoenaed, and exhibits are prepared. The defense receives notification of all the names of witnesses for the prosecution. All pertinent documents relied upon should have been previously provided as well as all evidence favorable to the defendant, known as exculpatory evidence. Discovery for the defense is more limited than a civil case because the defendant has certain constitutional rights, such as the right against self-incrimination.
Civil Trial Trials can be scheduled and then set over (rescheduled) multiple times because of scheduling conflicts or requests from the attorneys for more time to prepare for trial. Once the trial commences, each party's civil attorney represents the plaintiff and defendant, each bearing their own respective personal cost.	**Criminal Trial** Trials can be scheduled and then set over (rescheduled) multiple times because of scheduling conflicts or requests from the prosecution or defense for more time to prepare for trial. Once the trial commences, the prosecutor represents the state on the public's behalf and defense attorney represents the defendant. The jury trial proceeds unless the defendant waives his right to jury trial, whereupon a bench trial[9] proceeds.

(continued)

[9]Trial held before a Judge without a jury.

EXHIBIT 8.1 Civil Law Process versus Criminal Law Process (*Continued*)

Civil	Criminal
BENCH TRIAL—Most civil trials are bench trials, where the judge is both the Trier of fact and the Trier of law, unless a party requests a jury. A bench trial is similar to a jury trial with a few differences. A bench trial may be slightly less formal. The judge will often ask the witness clarifying questions during their testimony. Objections are less common as the judge is more familiar with the rules of evidence and acceptable testimony than would be a jury. JURY TRIAL—A jury trial is typically longer due to the jury selection process as well as the objections necessary to exclude certain testimony. Juries must weigh the evidence and testimony presented to determine the questions of fact, thus becoming the Trier of fact. Once they hear all the testimony and seal the evidence, the jury deliberates and applies the questions of fact to the complaint and the corresponding law. When deliberation is complete, they have reached a verdict.	JURY TRIAL—A jury is the finder of the facts in a trial. A jury trial is typically longer because of the jury selection process and the objections necessary to exclude certain testimony and evidence. Also, prosecutors or defense counsel may wish to elaborate on details with a jury. Juries weigh the evidence and testimony presented to determine the questions of fact, thus becoming the Trier of fact. Once they hear all the testimony and evidence, the jury deliberates and applies the questions of fact to the charges against the defendant, and the corresponding law violated is contained in the jury instructions. When deliberation is complete, they have reached a verdict with respect to the applicable law. BENCH TRIAL—There is no jury in a bench trial; the judge is the finder of the law and also applies the law. The defendant must waive his right to a jury trial. A bench trial progresses the same as a jury trial but with a few differences. A bench trial is less formal. The judge will often ask the witness clarifying questions during his testimony. Objections are less common, as the judge is more familiar with the rules of evidence and acceptable testimony than a jury would be.
Verdict The plaintiff has the burden of proving the facts and claims asserted in the complaint. The defendant must prove any counterclaims. The plaintiff's evidence, testimony, and exhibits must prove their claim by a preponderance of evidence. This means the plaintiff must convince the Trier of fact (judge or jury) that their case evidence makes it more likely than not that their claim is true, even by the smallest degree. If a jury trial, a majority (depending on the jurisdiction) of the jurors must agree on a verdict. The defendant's counterclaims must meet the same standard.	**Verdict** The state has the burden of proving the facts and charges alleged against the defendant. The prosecutor's evidence must prove the case beyond a reasonable doubt. This is the highest standard of proof used in court. Prosecutors and defense attorneys often argue over the definition of this term. However, reasonable doubt is amply described by the Supreme Court in *In re Winship*: "To this end, the reasonable-doubt standard is indispensable, for it 'impresses on the Trier of fact the necessity of reaching a subjective state of certitude of the facts in issue.'" The highest standard of proof reflects the overall effort to avoid mistakes "because of the possibility that he may lose his liberty upon conviction and because of the certainty that he would be stigmatized by the conviction."[10]

	If the Trier of fact believes beyond a reasonable doubt the defendant committed the criminal offense(s) for which they are charged, the verdict is guilty. If the Trier of fact has doubt of the defendant's guilt, the verdict will be "not guilty," never "innocent." If the jury cannot unanimously agree on a verdict, the jury is deadlocked resulting in a mistrial and a retrial may be necessary.
Reimburse Plaintiff for Losses Caused by Defendant's Behavior If the Trier of fact decides that the plaintiff has met the burden of proof, the defendant is held liable for damages, thus entitling the plaintiff to a judgment. The Trier of fact determines the financial damages amount, if any. The Trier may or may not include legal costs the prevailing party incurred to litigate the matter, depending upon the applicable laws. If the Trier of fact decides the plaintiff did not meet the burden of proof, the defendant is not liable for damages. The same process applies to any counterclaims. Either, or both, parties can be found at fault.	**Sentencing** States often have sentencing guidelines designed to alleviate sentencing disparities throughout the various state jurisdictions. The sentencing guidelines provide judges with the minimum and maximum punishment according to the crime for which the defendant is found guilty. Sentences imposed within a specific county tend to be equitable but can vary greatly between counties within the same state. For example, one county may routinely impose probation while another county sentences a defendant to prison for similar crimes.
Judgment The civil judgment is the final court order in a lawsuit. It documents the Trier's reasoning, and resolves the issues in the lawsuit by determining the rights and obligations of each party. The judgment clearly identifies the prevailing parties on each issue and the corresponding civil remedies (monetary damages, injunctive relief, or both). For financial cases, the judgment typically includes a finding that the defendant owes money to the plaintiff. Either party can appeal a final judgment.	**Restitution Order** Prior to sentencing, the prosecution investigates and presents to the court the nature and amount of economic damages the victim suffered. The court may include a victim restitution judgment against the defendant as part of the sentence. If so, the specific monetary judgment is entered for the victim. The state or local county may supervise restitution repayment for the victim. A restitution judgment is not a guarantee of payment. Many monetary judgments are never fully repaid because of the defendant's financial inability or unwillingness to reimburse the victim.

(*continued*)

[10] *In re Winship*, 397 U.S. 358, 363-64, 90 S.Ct. 1068, 1072-1073, 25 L.Ed. 2d 368 (1970).

EXHIBIT 8.1 Civil Law Process versus Criminal Law Process (*Continued*)

Civil	Criminal
Possible Appeal(s) Either party may appeal a judgment if they disagree with the decision. Appeals are usually based on arguments that there were errors in the trial procedure or that the law applied was unconstitutional or invalid. The appellate court can do one of the following: ■ Affirm the judgment (judgment is upheld). ■ Refuse to hear the appeal. ■ Reverse the judgment. ■ Remand the judgment (the case is sent back to the lower court to begin an entirely new trial or resolve an issue). Parties can continue appealing until the final appeal falls to the US Supreme Court. All decisions of the Supreme Court are final.	**Possible Appeal(s)** Only the defendant may appeal a guilty verdict. The prosecutor cannot appeal a not guilty verdict because double jeopardy forbids a defendant from being tried twice for the same crime. Appeals are usually based on arguments that there were substantial errors in the trial or sentencing, or that the law applied was unconstitutional or invalid. The appellate court can do one of the following: ■ Affirm the conviction (conviction is upheld). ■ Reverse the conviction (the case is sent back to the lower court to begin an entirely new trial or the case is dismissed and not retried). ■ Remand the case for resentencing. The defendant can continue appealing until the final appeal falls to the US Supreme Court. All decisions of the Supreme Court are final.
Enforcement of Judgment If final judgment included a monetary award, the losing party is legally obligated to pay the damages. If they fail to pay, it is necessary to bring additional court actions to enforce the judgment. A judgment does not guarantee the injured party will ever receive the monetary damages awarded.	**Enforcement of Conviction** If the defendant receives probation, the defendant is not imprisoned but instead is released to serve his sentence in the community under court-imposed conditions for a specified period. The conditions may include community service, jail, and mental health therapy, gambling treatment, and drug treatment. If the defendant is sentenced to state prison (over one year) or county jail (less than one year), he will complete his incarceration based on the sentencing provisions. Inmates are often paroled or released early due to good behavior, credit for time served, and early-release programs. In such cases, the defendant can serve the rest of his sentence under supervised release.
Purpose of Legal Outcome Civil law determines private rights and liabilities and is designed to settle legal disagreements between parties. Any judgment received is intended to right a legal wrong suffered by one of the parties.	**Purpose of Legal Outcome** Criminal law involves offenses against society and in violation of state law. The law strives to convict and punish the offender, deter future crime, remove criminals from society, rehabilitate offenders, and provide restitution to victims.

typical state processes, since state court has many actions filed. Another caveat is the legal process can vary from state to state and even different jurisdictions within the state. This section provides a general outline and guideline for comparison. Also, the outline should prompt forensic operators to become more familiar with the respective state or jurisdiction requirements.

COMPARISON

There are many similarities as well as differences between the civil and criminal law process. Each can stand on its own or be simultaneously executed. Regardless of how the parties pursue the processes, it is essential to maintain the integrity and justice of the criminal process. For example, evidence obtained in a criminal investigation cannot be shared with the civil process until the criminal process is complete and then typically only with a public disclosure request. Furthermore, never use the threat of criminal prosecution to coerce a favorable civil outcome.

Exhibit 8.1 outlines each process from inception to final adjudication. As each legal issue is unique, the timing and process that the event follows can be equally unique. Some events surface immediately while others arise many years later. The processing time will increase with the more time that has passed between the event occurrence and subsequent discovery. In addition, processing time increases with the duration of the event. It is time intensive to locate, obtain, and confirm older documents and evidence. The course the process takes can also cause variations in the total time elapsed from beginning to end. Numerous motions and rulings may occur along the way, and the outline that follows does not attempt to address all the different possibilities. Forensic operators involved in civil or criminal litigation must seek counsel's guidance to navigate this complicated process.

WHAT IF YOU SUSPECT EMBEZZLEMENT?—THE THREE BIG *DON'TS* AND SEVERAL *DO'S*

If you suspect that an employee is committing theft, your intuition is likely correct that something is amiss. However, what you sense may *not* be embezzlement[11]—it could be many things other than theft. Therefore, a prudent owner/employer/manager (the owner) will pause, take a deep breath, and read and apply the following advice before taking action. Then (assuming theft was indeed committed) you can demonstrate that you have taken a structured and measured approach that protects you and your company, agency, department, and so on (the company).

The comments in this section apply to all employees or related parties,[12] whether or not they handle money or are even involved with money. This could include a cashier, president or vice president, route driver, CFO, accounts receivable clerk, receptionist, bureaucrat, analyst, etc.—that is, virtually any person having a direct

[11] The term *fraud* is used throughout this chapter; terms such as *defalcation*, *embezzlement*, and *fraud* are often used synonymously despite distinct definitions.

[12] Prior employees, family members, suppliers, customers, lenders, etc.

or indirect relationship with the company's money or other assets. Theft other than money could include, for example, stealing inventory, "borrowing" office supplies, falsely reporting time worked, "padding" time sheets, exchanging favors for personal accommodations, etc.

Every significant employee matter (whether or not theft) requires thoughtful deliberation before taking action, since hasty actions will likely be detrimental to you and the company. Consequently, knowing what you should *not* do if you suspect fraud is often more important than what you should do.

That is where the Big Three *Don'ts* comes into play. They are the three most important actions that you should *not* take if you suspect fraud. They are listed in ascending priority further on under the *Don't* heading. The *Do* actions follow and will move you and your company back to where you need to be, and out of trouble. The *Do* actions are prioritized from most to least important. Read everything before doing anything. That framework enables you to understand the context of the advice.

Three Big *Don'ts*

The three most important actions that you should *not* take if you suspect fraud are described here.

WAR STORY

Physicians in a medical clinic discovered vendors were not being paid and hastily concluded their office manager was stealing. They immediately confronted her during an employee meeting and terminated her employment. Rumors and gossip spread around town. Later, the doctors called a forensic operator who determined the employee had not been stealing. Instead, the clinic had significant cash flow issues (mainly due to the doctors' excessive salaries). The office manager had failed to communicate the cash issues with the doctors while trying to keep the business afloat. The office manager sued for wrongful termination and her case was settled out of court.

Don't: Confront the Employee with Your Suspicions—Yet . . . The single most important *do not* item is: *Do not confront the employee with your suspicions until you have executed all the other issues as discussed here.* Even then, it may be necessary to use a different method of informing the employee regarding her status, imminent material harm notwithstanding.

False (or even valid) accusations can lead to defamation lawsuits or at the very least an extremely uncomfortable work environment. You will offend (or worse) an innocent person by questioning her integrity. Also, you may never be able to regain that person's trust or level of commitment. That downside is just one example of the collateral damage that can result from a fraud.

Even if the employee is ultimately found guilty,[13] your insinuation gives her time to alter records and conceal the theft, and perhaps even siphon off more assets. It takes only a moment for an experienced person to erase a computer's hard drive and shred documents. Virtually all business records can be reconstructed. However, reconstruction is a costly and time-consuming process that would aggravate an already stressful situation.

Don't: Terminate the Employee—Yet . . . The second most important *Don't* item is: *Do not terminate (or suspend) the employee until you have executed all the other issues contained in this section.*[14] The desire to take decisive action is understandable, but hasty actions may be detrimental to you and the company. Furthermore, there may be certain advantages to retaining the person's employment status for a short period as indicated by the section contents. That is because his employment status might compel them to take certain actions to your benefit. This condition does not apply to government employees since. Unlike the private sector, they cannot be compelled to participate in the investigation.

Don't: Share Your Suspicions with Other Employees—Yet . . . The third most important *Don't* item is: *Do not share your suspicions with other employees until you have executed all the other issues contained in this section.* Do not share your suspicions with other employees unless their assistance is crucial, and then they must maintain strict confidentiality. You place an arduous burden on anyone in whom you have confided. Shouldering such responsibilities is uncharted territory for nearly everyone (including you) and can aggravate an already stressful situation. You may view the confidence placed in an employee as a reflection of your trust. However, the employee may view the uninvited responsibility as taking sides with you at the expense of his relationship with other employees. Consequently, you should take this step only if necessary and *after* consulting with counsel and others.[15]

Do Actions

The *Do* actions that you should take are listed here.

---

[13] Guilt is used here in the generic sense. Only a court can determine whether or not someone is guilty of fraud.

[14] Granted, there can be occasions where it is absolutely necessary to immediately terminate the employee. For example, employees who serve in a position whose continued employment could put others at risk physically, financially, or otherwise may need to be terminated immediately. Such circumstances are rare, but if they do occur, document the entire process and advise counsel immediately.

[15] The authors have often encountered circumstances where other employees become distracted from their regular duties while they attempt to perform their own "rogue" investigations. Accountants are notorious for this transgression since they sometimes act as self-styled investigators. In every case encountered, such actions were detrimental, and not helpful, to the investigation.

Do: Begin Documenting All Pertinent Actions The instant that an employee fraud matter surfaces, you must begin a continuous documentation of all pertinent actions. Such documentation includes written narrative and pertinent hard copy with as much specificity as time permits. Its form can take many shapes, composed of handwritten notes, Microsoft Word files, emails to yourself, or almost any other method. This will, of course be time consuming but is another example of collateral damage resulting from employee fraud. The documentation should include reference to cost and expenses incurred because of the suspected fraud. Their documentation may permit them to be included as part of your insurance coverage or even within restitution.[16] Other business damages, such as the loss of customers, suppliers, other employees, etc., may also merit documentation.

Document your knowledge of the suspect's personal actions and your perception of the suspect's behavioral factors. Such information may include your knowledge of the suspect's hobbies, travels, interests, etc. and can be helpful in prosecution. These details may also help explain their motivation to execute fraud. Law enforcement sometimes refers to such motivators as the "Three B's" that drive fraud. When discussing motive for male suspects, the paraphrase is "Booze, Bucks, or Broads." When discussing motive for female suspects, the paraphrase is "Booze, Bucks, or Boys." Within the context of the reference, Booze implies alcohol, drugs, or other addictive substances; Bucks implies gambling, excessive spending, and credit problems; Broads and Boys imply pornography, prostitution, and extramarital affairs. Therefore, even seemingly innocent behavior indicators may assist in restitution.

PUTTING IT INTO PRACTICE

Behavior Patterns

Behavior patterns can help identify assets that may be recoverable, such as big-ticket purchases of automobiles, boats, collectibles, and other tangible assets. Likewise, patterns of behavior may save time by indicating when no assets are likely to be recovered. For example, a suspect known to spend significant time gambling is likely to have squandered any assets otherwise available for recovery.

Do: Meet with Your Business Attorney for Legal Advice An employee fraud situation is complex and fraught with risk for you and your company. The circumstances require broad and deep expertise in employment law, criminal law, insurance law, banking law, malpractice law, and various other legal potentialities. Fortunately, most attorneys will acknowledge when they need to seek additional expertise beyond themselves and their firm. For example, an attorney specializing in corporate matters

[16] Restitution—A legal action serving to cause restoration of the previous state. www.merriam-webster.com

may have little or no background in matters of fraud. Acknowledgment by an attorney that he needs additional expertise is a testament to his integrity. Furthermore, your attorney may contribute by participating throughout the duration of the investigation and prosecution, and can apply his cumulative knowledge of your company.

If you do not have an attorney, find one immediately. Contact your state bar and business associates[17] whom you trust. Do not proceed without sound legal advice. Employment law is complicated and you need to ensure you are following every federal, state, and local rule and regulation. Also, do not be surprised if, even with confirmed suspicion, a terminated employee sues you for wrongful termination, defamation, or other matters. Even if she does not prevail, it is expensive for you to defend.

WAR STORY

A nonprofit organization suspected the organization's founder of financial misappropriation and hired a CPA to audit the books. The CPA lacked the necessary skills to investigate the potential fraud. Based on the CPA's audit of the books, she concluded the founder misappropriated as much as $1 million. The organization sued and threatened prosecution. The accused founder hired a qualified forensic operator who determined, after a thorough investigation of the source documents, that there was no theft. In fact, the organization owed the founder money from unpaid loans. The lawsuit was settled out of court with the accused founder prevailing and the organization was left with a large legal bill, all due to an unqualified CPA's bumbling.

Do: Meet With Your Certified Public Accountant (CPA) Employee embezzlement must be scrupulously investigated to support any position you take. Remember that you are dealing with an employee who is keenly familiar with and skilled in your company's systems, procedures, and controls (or lack thereof) and has probably obscured the trail of evidence over a considerable duration of time. Therefore, you need someone with the expertise to assess the circumstances and possibly help build a case.

Exercise *caution* when meeting with your CPA. Your CPA may be well versed in their involvement with you through their work in income taxes, audit, review, and compilations, but not forensic analysis. Larger CPA firms may have departments that claim to specialize in financial forensics, although experience in these matters may vary widely. Furthermore, remember that the situation occurred under your CPA's watch, so they may not be free of conflict.[18]

Many CPAs are tempted to suggest that they are capable of assisting in a fraud even though they lack specific training. Their assertion could be true under certain limited conditions, for example, *knowing* that the suspect perpetrated the fraud

[17] Exercise discretion regarding comments you may make even to your closest business associates.

[18] In addition, they could potentially be a source of recovery.

within an isolated subsystem such as accounts receivable and nowhere else. In that case, the CPA might merely need to "tick, foot, and tie" any differences to document the loss. However, that unlikely scenario *presupposes* full knowledge regarding the means of perpetrating and concealing the fraud. Even such a supposedly simple scenario can become extremely complex very quickly and will require skills the CPA does not possess. Examples of the unexpected skills required include understanding the nature of criminal evidence, the chain of custody, gathering evidence in lieu of mere opinions, writing a report that is simple yet complete, navigating the civil/criminal law gauntlet, balancing the juggling act with disparate insurance coverage, conveying the circumstances to prosecution, standing up to a withering cross-examination, etc.

Not all CPAs are created equal, and most specialize in areas of accounting *outside* financial forensics, such as tax, auditing, consulting, or employee benefits. Some CPAs will have additional certification designations such as CFE (Certified Fraud Examiner), CFFA (Certified Forensic Financial Analyst), or CFF (Certified Financial Forensics). It is essential to note that designations do not automatically ensure expertise in the respective area of fraud or financial forensics. Furthermore, the training, testing, standards, and applicability of such designations vary widely and may or may not apply to fraud matters. Some certifications require the member to pass a test, demonstrate a minimum of qualifying experience, and maintain continuing education in the field; some designations do not.

Obtain and *follow up* with referrals for a specifically qualified forensic operator from your CPA if he or she lacks specific training and experience in fraud matters. Sources in addition to your CPA include your state's board of accountancy, local chapter (if any) of certified fraud examiners, and law enforcement representatives. Carefully review their experience in investigating employee fraud and employee embezzlement. Ask them specific questions, such as how many fraud matters have they investigated, how many times have they testified in court in fraud matters, what were the outcomes, was the testimony for the prosecution or defense, and other similar questions. The forensic operator you engage will need to review the evidence you have gathered and any other information that has led you to your conclusion to help advise you at the early stages of the investigation. He will work closely with you and your attorney to ensure that you optimize the effort for your company while minimizing the risk.

Computer Resources Even the tiniest of companies typically uses some form of computer software to track their finances. Consequently, you must immediately engage forensic computer expertise. Their expertise will permit you to establish and launch a defensible chain of custody for the data before making any changes or corrections to the accounting system. Computer investigation must begin with an image of the drive that alters none of the data contained. Conversely, merely copying the hard drive immediately destroys any chain of custody of the evidence, and thus potentially renders the data useless for criminal prosecution. If properly imaged, the computer drive can be an essential source of evidence for additional steps such as prosecution, insurance recovery, etc. Your CPA may be a logical person to help find such a resource, and potentially even manage that resource's activities.

Internal company computer operators often claim that they can conduct any data imaging for an investigation that may be necessary. Their good intentions may be for naught even if they are highly skilled in your company's technology. Fraud evidence requires a unique skill set and untrained technicians can destroy evidence otherwise useful to the court. It is invariably preferable to engage outside, third-party computer forensic expertise for several reasons. First, the internal computer people could be negligent in the tasks that permitted the fraud. Also, they might be directly or indirectly involved in the fraud. Finally, they probably lack familiarity with rules of evidence, chain of custody, and other requirements essential to successful prosecution.

Do: Decide What to Do with the Suspect Employee Decide how to handle the urgent matter of what to do with the employee by relying upon advice from your legal and forensics team. The level and availability of evidence often drive the actions relating to the suspect. For example, the best course of action may be to do nothing, closely monitor and document the employee's activities, suspend the employee with pay,[19] or immediately terminate the suspect's employment. There may be valid reasons to do any one of these options. Your advisory team is the best source to suggest the most advantageous alternative based on your unique circumstances.

You may be advised to merely monitor and document the employee's activities if you lack sufficient evidence to suspend or terminate the employee immediately. Your forensic operator and computer operator will both be an integral part of this option. They will design a plan based on your circumstances to protect you from further loss while they investigate behind the scenes. The investigation can take place after hours or under the guise of "efficiency audit," "business planning," or other labels. In any case, this option will probably require you to devote substantial time to oversee the employee and assist in the investigation.

The forensic operator will either assemble sufficient evidence to proceed or conclude there is inadequate substantiation to support the accusation. If this is the case, the forensic operator will likely have a plausible explanation for the cause of your fears.

Taking Action Assuming you have sufficient evidence, and the theft appears likely, suspension or termination may be necessary to protect you from further theft. At this point, your employee will become aware of your accusations. The initial confrontation of a suspected embezzler is the optimal, sometimes the only, time to obtain a confession from the employee. After coordinating with counsel, determine whether or to what extent you can use technology during the confrontation and potential confession. State laws vary widely regarding the permissibility of audio or video recording. At a minimum, however, obtain a signed confession and, if possible, obtain a hand-written signed confession.

An experienced and qualified forensic operator should possess the necessary interrogation skills to confront the employee and obtain a confession if appropriate. There should always be a second individual present to act as a witness to the proceedings. This protects the interrogator from false accusations and hinders the confessor from retracting an admission of guilt. Experience has shown that confrontations are most effective in an unfamiliar place, such as the forensic operator's

[19] Typically, "administrative leave."

office, or after hours so the employee can freely confess wrongdoings without the fear of judgment from the watchful eyes of her peers.

Do: Seize Company Property You must obtain company property from the suspended or terminated employee before he leaves, regardless of whether you obtain a confession. The receipt of all the company property items should have been documented upon the suspect's employment. They should be contained in the employee's file in accordance with your company personnel handbook (see comments further on). They typically include the following:

- Keys or entrance cards
- Credit cards
- Cell phones
- Desktop computers
- Computer laptops
- External disk drives
- Proprietary information, etc.

Document the receipt of such items and place the receipt in your file, which contains other pertinent documentation.

Accompany the employee to their desk or car to retrieve the items and then escort him out of the building. *Never* let the employee freely roam the business premises after he has been confronted with your suspicions. Critical evidence could disappear or be destroyed by the suspect. Furthermore, he could intentionally attempt to subvert or form alliances with other employees by lying about the circumstances. At the very least, the suspect can make things more difficult for you.

Do: Make Certain Immediate Changes The following changes should be made immediately after suspension or termination, to protect the business's assets from further loss.

Procedural Changes

- Change the locks if the employee had keys to the building.
- Change keyless entry codes.
- Remove the employee's access rights to the computer system.
- Change the employee's (and possibly other) computer passwords.
- Contact your ISP[20] to request a log of all the employee's activity.[21]
- Remove bank account access and signing authority, if applicable.
- Redirect all of the former employee's e-mail addresses to you or another designated person.

Consider keeping the employee's email address active for a period. Additional evidence can often be obtained from emails received after the suspension or termination.

[20] Internet service provider.

[21] Coordinate this action with counsel. In addition, ISP history retention procedures vary widely; thus speed is of the essence.

WAR STORY

The CFO of a successful company was terminated for embezzlement. All his company emails were redirected to the human resources officer to monitor and redirect as necessary. Two months after the CFO was terminated, an email was received from a paid escort service indicating that they missed his patronage. The information in the email led the forensic operator to identify large innocuous charges on his company credit card that were actually for adult entertainment.

Insurance Coverage Changes Immediately review your business insurance policy and have your attorney also review the policy. Do this before contacting your insurance agent. The terms can be confusing and require specific actions on your part. Since most policies have an employee theft clause but often require that you notify the insurance company within a short time after discovering the loss, time is of the essence in the contact. Your forensic operator and attorney should be able to help decipher the policy and file a claim if and when the time comes.

Do: Notify Remaining Personnel The employee grapevine is extraordinarily efficient (accuracy notwithstanding), particularly with important matters. As the saying goes, "... lacking information, employees will generate their own—real or imagined." After the employee is terminated or suspended, her absence will not go unnoticed. You must decide how to communicate the situation with the remaining personnel and other stakeholders. Various parties will make inquiries, including the media, people fishing for information (such as the employee, or their family members), creditors, customers, suppliers, and future employers, among others.

Legal counsel will assist in what information can be disclosed. If you can prosecute, revealing your stance sends a clear message to your staff that this type of conduct will not go unpunished. However, if you are unable to prosecute, carefully decide the level of detail you will disclose. The best method is to use a companywide memorandum drafted by your attorney simultaneous with appropriate all-hands meetings to announce details to the extent they can be disclosed. Such a document will also come in handy when dealing with inquiries from outside parties. The remaining employees should understand that crimes are not tolerated and such actions have consequences at your company.

Do: Replace the Employee You would not have been paying the employee unless you believe that you needed his skill set. Consequently, unless you intend to plan and execute a reorganization (usually not desirable under the circumstances), it is unlikely that you can continue without a similar skill set. Therefore, this is an excellent time to implement procedures you wish had been in place for the thieving employee. Such items should already be documented in your company's personnel handbook, but if not, this is an excellent time to include them.

When seeking replacements, indicate that you expect finalist candidates to provide you with credit reports from all three credit reporting agencies,[22] subject of course, to counsel's concurrence. Refer to the comments in the remainder of this section regarding free credit reports.

You must also carefully train the new employee and follow up on his performance on a regular basis. This will ensure you comply with the internal controls[23] that you need and that he is performing according to your expectations.

Do: Notification of Outside Parties Inevitably, a wide array of outside parties will contact you, directly or indirectly seeking information regarding the ex-employee. Your internal notification presented during the meeting with existing employees will serve as the basis for communication with outside parties. Designate a single person who is the sole point of contact for anyone seeking information regarding the terminated employee. That is, any contact from outside parties should be directed to that designated internal person. This will ensure that all communications are consistent, and it will help keep you out of trouble. If your company is large enough, the likely point of contact will be the human resources department. Otherwise, it should be someone relatively senior in the company who will maintain a log of all outside party contact.

WAR STORY

A bookkeeper embezzled a significant amount of money from a small glass-repair shop. During the investigation, the bookkeeper's previous employer was contacted. He disclosed he had also been a victim of theft but had agreed not to prosecute if she complied with a monthly repayment plan. Further investigation revealed that the bookkeeper was embezzling from the glass-repair shop to make the monthly payments to the previous employer.

Do: Contact Law Enforcement Many insurance policies require you to file a police report and cooperate with criminal prosecution in order to recover any losses under the policy. Filing a police report is an important decision and should be carefully considered. Your attorney and forensic operator should be a source of information regarding how your particular jurisdiction prosecutes white collar crime. Some jurisdictions have aggressive attitudes with considerable prison terms; others are lenient and sentence nothing harsher than probation. Some jurisdictions may be so inundated with crime that law enforcement and prosecutors will not consider indicting thefts under a certain dollar threshold. Therefore, it will be very beneficial if you have or can find personal contacts to the local district attorney. Personal conversation

[22] Equifax, Experion, TransUnion.
[23] Refer to the section titled "The Myth of Internal Controls."

with them can be very helpful regarding how or whether to proceed with prosecuting your matter.

Filing a complaint is often an ethical dilemma for the business owner. Frequently, the embezzler is a long-time employee and a (supposed) friend. They are typically married, have children, and are long-time and active members of the community. Those facts must be weighed against the stark reality that the long-trusted employee and "friend" embezzled and broke the law and your trust; actions have consequences.

Another point to consider is the impact the thief may have on other employers. This is particularly important for employees in accounting positions. Without prosecution, the next employer may unwittingly hire the embezzler; even the most thorough background check will not discover the past impropriety. Put yourself in that business owner's shoes. You will likely replace the terminated employee. Would you like to know if your new employee has a history of misappropriation? Finally, it is possible that future employers would be compelled to pursue you for failing to act.

In the end, whether or not to prosecute is a difficult and emotional decision for many employers. Carefully consider all the ramifications and try to make an objective decision. A word of caution—*do not* use law enforcement and the threat of prosecution to bolster any civil remedies you believe you may have. Once you choose to press charges and law enforcement begins to investigate, you must be willing to go the distance. Do not use the judicial system to coerce the embezzler into something you want. Our criminal justice system is overworked and understaffed; don't take undue advantage of their services.

Subsequent to the Investigation The initiation and (inevitable) conclusion of the civil and criminal process can be quite lengthy and only begins after the investigation is complete and your suspicions are confirmed. Many employers find this process frustrating and exhausting since the burden is incremental to the demands of their "day job," which continues unabated. Furthermore, there are potentially competing priorities between civil goals and criminal goals. Your main goal from the civil perspective is financial restitution, while law enforcement's main goal from the criminal perspective is conviction.

In restitution, the embezzler (theoretically) pays back what he stole. In other words, you measure success in terms of money. Unfortunately, the reality is that most embezzlers do not have any money to repay you; they spent it on the demon(s) that drove their fraud. Alternatively, they may have "given" it to friends, lovers, or family members. If the embezzler does not voluntarily agree to a restitution agreement, you will have to file a lawsuit to pursue financial recovery. Even if the employee has assets that are eligible for restitution, it often costs more (legal fees, time, etc.) to obtain the assets than they are worth. Consult with your attorney and carefully weigh the financial pros and cons of pursuing civil restitution judgments.

The prosecutor's main goal from the criminal perspective is conviction; restitution is incidental. Prosecutors measure success in terms of convictions. If you decide to criminally prosecute, you must be patient while the legal process gradually, but inexorably, advances. It is possible to pursue both civil and criminal remedies simultaneously. Simultaneous civil and criminal pursuit is a delicate legal balance for the attorneys involved, and the processes often have conflicting agendas. There are several steps in the criminal legal process. They may be called different things in different jurisdictions but are generally as described in the preceding part of this chapter titled "Civil versus Criminal Law Comparison."

The time frame from beginning to end varies. It can be as short as a few months or it can last a few years. It depends on many factors, including the egregiousness of the fraud, the current backlog of criminal cases in the court, the extent of evidence, and the overall cooperation of the suspect. Our judicial system may appear overly burdensome and taxing to the victim, but it essentially designed to protect innocent people from being wrongfully convicted. With that in mind, try to endure the process with tolerance and patience.

If the suspect pleads, or is judged, guilty at the conclusion of a trial, the sentence will likely include a restitution order. The individual will be required to repay a sum of money by court order. The guilty embezzler typically has no money to fulfill the judgment. Furthermore, if he is sentenced to prison, it may be a long time, if ever, before you begin to receive repayment. A restitution order and judgment is not a guarantee of payment. You may have to use the civil legal process to collect.

Do: Consider Counseling Owners, employers, managers, and other employees are victims of fraud in every sense of the word. They were victimized by the suspect's fraudulent acts of betrayal, which sometimes even places their continued employment and livelihood in jeopardy.

Reactions to such victimization vary widely, but the pain felt by people is no less real than physical pain. Few companies offer counseling resources for fraud-induced trauma even though some policies specifically provide coverage. Also, the authors are not aware of any study suggesting the extent of the emotional impact of fraud. Nonetheless, from years of experience, it is clear that the trauma has a very real impact on the company and its people. The decision makers should therefore carefully consider employing counseling expertise for anyone who may seek it.

Do: Reflect and Improve Finally, after the investigation (and often while you are waiting for the criminal process to conclude), you should consider possible improvements to your company. For example, if your business policy does not cover employee theft, consider purchasing insurance coverage, often known as *bonding*. Generally, there are three types of specialized bond coverage:

- Specifically named employees
- Specific positions
- Coverage for all business employees

Discuss which type of coverage is best for you with your insurance agent. Also, it is essential to review your internal controls[24] (such as they are), identify deficiencies, and correct weaknesses that permitted the embezzlement. Consult with a CPA who specializes in internal control assessments. You must make every effort to ensure

[24] Refer to the section titled "The Myth of Internal Controls."

that embezzlement does not happen again. If it does happen again, then the damage will be minimized, thanks to your post-fraud improvements.

How to Guard against Embezzlement

There are three basic steps that a company can take to reduce the risk of exposure to embezzlement.

Observe Employee Behavior Pay close attention to employee behavior—*all kinds* of behavior. For example, if a normally punctual employee begins to show up late, to leave early, becomes ill frequently, etc., such changes could be an indicator of personal stress manifesting itself. Alternatively, the disinterested employee becoming a model employee could be another indicator. There is no end to the examples that could be given. Any behavioral change could be indicative of fraud-induced stress. Granted, theft-induced stress may not be the cause of such behavioral changes, but they are a potential indicator, nonetheless. Theft could be one of those stressors affecting behavior.

Enlist Outside Resources Pay your outside CPA to reconcile your bank statement each month. The small amount of money that the CPA will (should) charge will be more than offset by the peace of mind that you receive and employee awareness of outside accountability.

Insist upon obtaining credit reports from all employees. Naturally, you should consult with your outside counsel regarding this issue. Very generally, however, it is acceptable to request credit reports from a candidate employee before completing the hiring process. The laws within the United States permit any person to obtain one's own credit report once a year from each of the three major credit reporting agencies. Refer to www.annualcreditreport.com.

Such a requirement makes a great deal of sense for any employees likely to be involved in a financial position. Existing employees, though, are a different matter. So contact your outside counsel regarding this issue and confirm its coverage in your company's personnel handbook.

Set the Tone The axiom that the tone starts at the top is true. If owners, employers, and managers treat employees, customers, creditors, tax authorities, and all others with honesty and integrity, that tone will be obvious. However, it does not occur by itself. You must also enforce such expectations.

CONCLUSION

A fraud is a devastating event within any company, but the advice in this chapter can minimize the damage and turn it to your advantage. The chapter emphasizes two key points. First, few entities and executives are familiar with the events that require forensic operator expertise. Consequently, their good intentions often make costly time, money, and people mistakes. Although many such mistakes can be repaired, they are sometimes devastating and irrecoverable.

Second, attorneys, accountants, and others in the service professions simply lack sufficient understanding to recognize the vast differences between civil and criminal processes. Granted, certain commonalities exist, but the differences are so consequential that untrained and unskilled attorneys, accountants, and others can provide the best service by referring and deferring to other, more capable sources. Also, otherwise inappropriate service providers can often play an ancillary role by providing background information, cumulative knowledge, and nonessential tasks.

Events requiring forensic operator expertise are similar to 500-year floods—they don't occur often, but when they do, they require expertise to address the problems.

APPENDIX

Forensic Inventory

Forensic Tools, Techniques, Methods, and Methodologies

This Forensic Inventory is the first assemblage of its kind known to exist. It comprises with the book's contents, more than 300 forensic tools, technique, methods, and methodologies, the majority of which are discussed in this book. It is integral to this book and will be updated with successive publications.

Forensic operators can use this inventory as a reference and/or a refresher.

Description	Explanation and Source	Source: Forensic Context
21-Foot Rule (reactionary gap)	A guideline for law enforcement developed by Lt. (ret.) Dennis Tueller, formerly of the Salt Lake City Police Department. Lt. Tueller is an internationally recognized Law Enforcement Instructor who first published his principle in the March 1983 issue of SWAT magazine. It suggests that an armed, i.e. knife, club male assailant can cover 21 feet in about 1.5 seconds. The time is that required for a skilled law enforcement officer to draw and fire his weapon to stop the assailant. www.theppsc.com. The Police Policies Safety Council.	Forensic operators often work in stressful and hostile circumstances. People under investigation often act impulsively. Thus, awareness of the reactionary gap permits forensic operators to maximize their safety.
60-Second Method	A simple method to evaluate the strengths and weaknesses of comparative financial statements.	Chapter 4 explains the 60-Second Method.

(*continued*)

Description	Explanation and Source	Source: Forensic Context
AAA	Anticipation, agility, and adaptation.	A mind-set established by a forensic operator throughout an assignment, particularly assignments in high-intensity circumstances. The forensic operator anticipates exigencies, is agile enough to respond to changes, and adapt to the circumstances in order to achieve the objective at hand.
Aberrant pattern detection	The concept of empirically measuring items outside the normal expected patterns.	For example, using statistical measures such as standard deviation and coefficient of variation to measure the variability of a data set.
Accept-Reject Testing	Similar to sampling, but differs since sampling involves the projection of a misstatement amount and accept-reject testing does not.	Accepts that the testing criteria have been met, or rejects that the testing criteria have not been met. If a reject occurs, additional testing may be carried our depending upon materiality and other considerations.
Adequate (Reasonable) Capital Test	See Solvency Analysis.	Used to determine if an entity was engaged in a business or a transaction for which it had unreasonably small capital.
Aguilar–Spinelli Test	A two-part test regarding the validity of a search warrant triggered by information from a confidential informant or anonymous source. Spinelli v. United States, 393 U.S. 410 (1969).	May apply in criminal matters when forensic operators use informant or anonymous sources.
Alter ego	In the traditional sense, alter ego is determined by evaluating a parent and subsidiary company's relationship to determine whether the parent (that is, through the controlling party) met the following three crucial conditions with respect to a complainant. 1. The parent exercised control and authority to the extent that the subsidiary was a mere instrumentality of the parent. 2. The parent committed a fraud or wrong with respect to the complainant.	Alter ego is said to be the most litigated matter in the United States, thus forensic operators should be familiar with the federal and state principles. Jurisdictions vary regarding the number of conditions, ranging from two to eleven.

Description	Explanation and Source	Source: Forensic Context
	3. The complainant suffered an injury as a result of the fraud or wrong (causation). Note that all three conditions must be met for the court to invoke alter ego.	
Altman Z-Score	An insolvency predictor created by Professor Edward Altman of NYU in the 1960s. It is comprised of five financial variables arriving at relative scores. Scores above 3 indicate sound results, while scores below 3 display varying degrees of risk	Forensic operators can use in a wide variety of forensic assignments, including bankruptcy, fraudulent transfer, insolvency, valuation, et al.
AQI	Asset Quality Index—see M-Score. Measures the ratio of non-current assets other than property, plant, and equipment to total assets in current year to prior year.	If AQI is greater than 1.0, it indicates potential increase in cost deferral and/or perhaps an increase in intangible assets resulting from acquisitions, or some other creative accounting treatment.
Arm's-length	A transaction where two or more parties act in their own best interests.	A principle that is used to determine whether a transaction was manipulated.
Articulated Cash Flow	The results of the cash flow statement rely on activity in both the income statement and the balance sheet. Darrell D. Dorrell, circa 2000; used as a training tool to explain the importance of the cash flow statement. See also, BIC.	Cash flows must reconcile to beginning and ending cash. Therefore, manipulations made to income or balance sheet items, must eventually be reversed for the cash flow statement to balance.
Attributes Sampling	Attribute sampling means that an item being sampled either will or won't possess certain qualities, or attributes. A certain number of records is selected to estimate how many times a certain feature will show up in a population. When using attribute sampling, the sampling unit is a single record or document.	Its most common use in forensic investigation is to test the rate of deviation from a prescribed (or expected) control perspective to support the forensic investigator's assessed level of assurance.

(continued)

Description	Explanation and Source	Source: Forensic Context
Audit	The purpose of a financial statement audit is to obtain reasonable assurance about whether an entity's financial statements are free of material misstatement. A financial statement audit includes examining, on a *test* basis, evidence supporting the amounts and disclosures in the financial statements. It also includes assessing the accounting principles used and significant estimates made by management, as well as evaluating the overall financial statement presentation. An audit is not a review of the entire population of an entity's financial transactions for a period. Performing tests on a specific set of data may also be referred to as an audit, but it is not providing the same level of assurance as a full financial audit and an audit report is not prepared and a CPA cannot provide an opinion on the results.	See also the section titled "The Myth of Internal Control."
Audit of the US Government, annual	The Secretary of the Treasury, in coordination with the Director of the Office of Management and Budget, is required to annually submit financial statements for the U.S. government to the President and the Congress. The USGAO (United States Government Accountability Office) is required to audit these statements. See www.fms.treas.gov/fr/index.html.	Forensic operators with accounting and auditing skills should read the GAO opinions for recent years. The contents are shocking and provide a benchmark for comparison against other audit opinions.
Authentication	In the law of evidence, the act or mode of giving authority or legal authenticity to a statute, record, or other written instrument, or a certified copy thereof, so as to render it legally admissible in evidence. *Black's Law Dictionary*, 6th ed. (St. Paul, MN: West Publishing, 1990), 132.	Certain sources are considered self-authenticating. For example, employment data from the Bureau of Labor Statistics, www.bls.gov is self-authenticating.
Background Investigation	Research into a party's identity to identify other assets that may have been forgotten about.	For example, a public records search may identify other business interests that have not been previously disclosed by the party.

Description	Explanation and Source	Source: Forensic Context
Badges of Fraud	The common law provisions typically originated from the Uniform Fraudulent Conveyances Act (UFCA) or Uniform Fraudulent Transfer Act (UFTA) and include measurements of badges of fraud that can be employed directly or indirectly. Thus, assets can be recovered and transfers voided when they constitute actual or constructive fraud.	Actual fraudulent transfer is determined by various badges of fraud, which indicate if the transfer was made with an actual intent to hinder, delay, or defraud creditors, as evidenced by the following limited examples. Was the transfer to an insider? Did the transfer comprise substantially all of the subject's assets?
	Actual fraud occurs when an asset is transferred with intent to hinder, delay, or defraud any creditor. Constructive fraud occurs when an asset is transferred for less than reasonably equivalent value or for other reasons, such as the insolvency of the debtor or inadequate capitalization.	If an alleged forensic operator uses badges of fraud as support for criminal fraud observations or conclusions, he likely understands *neither* fraudulent transfer nor fraud. Such entities are thus exposed to cross-examination for lack of competency.
Balance Sheet Test	See Solvency Analysis.	Used to determine whether, at the time of a transaction, a company's asset value (valued as a going concern) was greater than its liability value.
Ball and Brown	Study that used changes in a firm's stock price as a benchmark for measuring whether income and changes in income had information investors might find useful. *An Empirical Evaluation of Accounting Income Numbers,* by Ray Ball and Philip Brown, 1968.	Supports the hypothesis that accounting numbers do have information content.
Bank Deposits and Cash Expenditures	Internal Revenue Service Indirect Methods (IRM 4.10.4.6.4).	The bank deposits and cash expenditures method computes income by showing what happened to a taxpayer's funds. It is based on the theory that if a taxpayer receives money, only two things can happen: it is either deposited or it is spent. Income is proven through a detailed, in-depth analysis of all bank deposits, canceled checks, currency transactions, and electronic debits, transfers, and credits to the bank accounts *and* identification of the taxpayer's cash expenditures.

(*continued*)

Description	Explanation and Source	Source: Forensic Context
Be Prepared!	The Motto of the Boy Scouts of America, incorporated February 8, 1910. Excerpted from page 54, *Boy Scout Handbook,* 11th ed., Boy Scouts of America, 1998. Scouting's history goes back to the turn of the twentieth century to a British Army officer, Robert Stephenson Smyth Baden-Powell. While stationed in India, he discovered that his men did not know basic first aid or the elementary means of survival in the outdoors. Baden-Powell realized he needed to teach his men many frontier skills, so he wrote a small handbook called *Aids to Scouting,* which emphasized resourcefulness, adaptability, and the qualities of leadership that frontier conditions demanded. After returning from the Boer War, where he became famous by protecting the small town of Mafeking for 217 days, Baden-Powell was amazed to find that his little handbook had caught the interest of English boys. They were using it to play the game of scouting.	Superb guidance for forensic operators. Note the corollaries between the *Boy Scout Handbook, The Los Angeles Police Department Manual, The Marine Corp Manual,* and the Forensic Accounting/ Investigation Methodology, FA/IM.
Behavior Detection	Behavior Detection is a technique developed by the Israeli Security Agency (ISA) that allows trained professionals to detect people with harmful intentions such as carrying out a terrorist attack. ISA uses this technique every day at multiple high profile potential targets in Israel and throughout the world. Israel's Ben-Gurion International Airport and El Al Airlines are some of the places where this technique is in use. Behavior detection is the most effective method of preventing terrorist attacks versus responding to them. It puts the security or law enforcement agency on the proactive versus the reactive side. The effectiveness of behavior detection has been proven not only in Israel, but in the United States as well. www.rozinconsulting.com/services.html	Far more comprehensive people-assessment capabilities than mere interview or interrogation techniques. It has been described as "akin to NLP on steroids."

Description	Explanation and Source	Source: Forensic Context
Behavior Pattern Recognition	This site, offered by New Age Security Solutions (NASS) specializes in aviation and transportation security. They offer their proprietary Behavior Pattern Recognition (BPR) within their services. It is a behavior detection methodology built upon seven essential elements. NASS-USA: www.nass-usa.com.	Forensic operators must gain familiarity with the pertinent behavior detection tools and techniques in order to maximize the people component of investigation.
Benchmarking	Establishing a baseline for comparison purposes. For companies, the benchmark could be historical performance or performance of peers in the industry.	Benchmarking is critical for most financial forensic techniques. Without baseline data or benchmarks, it is difficult to assess whether observations are anomalies or deviations. Benchmarking is essential for behavior detection techniques.
Benford's Law	Benford's Law states that digits and digit sequences in a data set follow a predictable pattern. The technique applies a data analysis method that identifies possible errors, potential fraud, or other irregularities. www.nigrini.com	For example, if artificial values are present in a data set, the distribution of the digits in the data set will likely exhibit a different shape (when viewed graphically), than the shape predicted by Benford's Law.
BIC	Darrell D. Dorrell, circa 2000; used as a training tool for nonfinancial parties. The acronym refers to Balance sheet, Income statement and Cash flow statement.	This model visually depicts the interdependency of the basic financial statements and that they all affect equity. It is helpful in educating attorneys, clients, and triers of fact.
www.BlackBookOnLine.info	This is gateway site to hundreds of additional sources, many of which are free. www.blackbookonline.info	This is an excellent starting point for Internet research since the site contains numerous public record sources and other free information useful for background investigation. The authors consider this the "point of entry" for all Internet related investigations. Its contents facilitate subsequent information searches. See also Skiptracing.

(*continued*)

Description	Explanation and Source	Source: Forensic Context
Blogs	Web log is the root of the term's contraction. Blogs are usually created and maintained by a special interest user or group. The sites typically comprise regular entries of commentary from parties with specific interests.	Note: Receiverships and similar matters often attract bloggers and provide rich sources of easily obtained data. Blogs are located via various sources, but a quick Google search directs a search.
Business Judgment Rule	The reason for this rule is to acknowledge that the daily operation of a business can be innately risky and controversial. Therefore, the board of directors should be allowed to make decisions without fear of being prosecuted. The business judgment rule further assumes that it is unfair to expect those managing a company to make perfect decisions all the time. As long as the courts believe that the board of directors acted rationally in a particular situation, no further action will taken against them. www.investopedia.com/terms/b/businessjudgmentrule.asp Legal presumption that the management of a firm is acting in the firm's best interest and, therefore, its decisions are protected from judicial review. It protects the management from decisions that result in loss or turn out to be wrong. If the management is found, however, to be in violation of its fiduciary duties, the rule does not apply and its activities come under the scrutiny of the courts. www.businessdictionary.com/definition/business-judgment-rule.html	Often encountered in governance actions such as alter ego, fiduciary duty, fraudulent transfer, and others.
Business Ratios and Formulas	Analysis of relationships of elements of financial statements to help form a conclusion regarding an entity's financial condition. *Business Ratios and Formulas*, by Steven M. Bragg.	The major categories of ratio measurement include liquidity, coverage, leverage, operating, and working capital. For example, operating ratios measure the efficiency which which a company is using its assets.

Description	Explanation and Source	Source: Forensic Context
CAGR	Compound Annual Growth Rate The smoothed annual rate that, when applied to the first year of a time horizon, arrives at the results of the last year.	Used to compare rates of growth among financial measures. For example, a 9 percent CAGR for cost of sales over seven years is undesirable when compared to a 7 percent CAGR over the same period.
Cash Flow Test	See Solvency Analysis.	Used to determine whether a business entity incurred debts that would be beyond the debtor's ability to pay as such debts matured.
Cash-T, or Source and Application of Funds	Internal Revenue Service Indirect Methods Internal Revenue Manual (IRM 4.10.4.6.3).	An analysis of a subject's cash flows and comparison of all known expenditures with all known receipts for the period. Net increases and decreases in assets and liabilities are taken into account. The excess of expenditures over the sum of reported income is the adjustment to income. Statistics are used to estimate unknown personal living expenses.
Central Tendency	Measures of central tendency include mode, midrange, median, arithmetic mean, truncated mean, and all means—dispersion.	See Mean-Arithmetic.
Chain of Custody	The documented trail that authenticates evidence in civil or criminal matters. A method of keeping track of who has handled a piece of evidence, when, and for what purpose. Vital in ensuring that evidence is not damaged or altered in any way.	Gaps in the chain or mishandling of evidence can damage a case.
Changepoint Detection	The determination that a definite change has occurred, as opposed to normal fluctuations. *Solving Crime with Mathematics,* by Keith Devlin and Gary Lorden, 2007.	Looking for changes in the pattern of financial transactions that could signal criminal activity.
Chebyshev's Theorem	For other than normal distributions, Chebyshev's Theorem applies, stating that 75% within +/−2 standard deviations, 89% within +/−3 standard deviations, and 94% of all data within +/−4 standard deviations.	Forensic operators use Chebyshev's Theorem when dealing with non-normal distributions.

(*continued*)

Description	Explanation and Source	Source: Forensic Context
"Chewbacca Defense"	A "legal" strategy illustrated in episode 27 of the television program, *South Park*. The 38-second parody of defense counsel Johnny Cochran during the O. J. Simpson trial illustrates a fallacy causing jury confusion.	A humorous example that forensic operators can relate to with respect to opposition arguments from both alleged "experts" and counsel. Such circumstances occasionally arise and thus humor is a useful technique for stress relief.
Circadian Rhythms	The term *circadian* comes from the Latin *circa,* meaning *around,* and *diem,* or *dies,* meaning *day.* Circadian rhythms are physical, mental, and behavioral changes that follow a roughly 24-hour cycle, responding primarily to light and darkness in an organism's environment. www.nigms.nih.gov/Education/Factsheet_CircadianRhythms.htm	Sensitivity to circadian rhythms can help improve results when scheduling interviews with witnesses.
CICO	Simply stated, CICO (Concentric In-Concentric Out) The Concentric-In component starts conceptually with a very wide circle encompassing the subject company's and parties' business footprint and progressively becomes focused on the site. The Concentric-Out component starts conceptually with a very narrow circle encompassing the subject's eyes[1], and progressively expanding to include the forehead and temples, face[2], throat, shoulders, upper diaphragm and torso. Then, it starts conceptually again with a very narrow circle encompassing the subject's feet, and progressively expanding to include the legs, knees[3], thighs and lower midsection.	This is a behavior detection technique that permits a forensic operator to recognize that behavior detection comprises anything and everything that might represent a cause or effect of a subject's behavior.

[1] The progressive nature of the Concentric-Out technique mirrors individual behavior detection techniques.

[2] The human face is the only location on the body where the muscles are attached directly to the skin. Consequently, stress-induced physiologies typically manifest themselves through the face and related body parts.

[3] Knees can be very telling, suggestive of the subject's desire to leave by pointing toward the exit.

Description	Explanation and Source	Source: Forensic Context
Circularization, Accounts Receivable	Auditors use a statistical (or sometimes judgmental) sample to identify debtors to whom letters are sent requesting their agreement or disagreement, with an explanation regarding the respective amounts.	The concept or technique can be useful in certain forensic assignments.
Circularization, Cash	Auditors send a letter to each bank identified on the company's books requesting the company's cash balance as of the audit date. Also, the letter typically request that the banks confirmed debts incurred by the company, personal guarantees, funds transfer, check-signing authorities, and other matters affecting the cash reported on the company's books.	The concept or technique can be useful in certain forensic assignments.
Cleaning (data)	The removal of data extraneous to an investigation, thus permitting more focus on the remaining data. See also, outlier.	Cleaning must be done using only empirical considerations to avoid bias.
Coefficient of Variation	A measure representing the dispersion of data from the mean. It is calculated by dividing the standard deviation by the arithmetic mean. The smaller the measure, the closer that the standard deviation approximates the mean. Thus, it measures the relative kurtosis of a data set.	This can be a useful measure of reliability. For example, recurring measures of the same data, airline on-time arrivals, should exhibit similar coefficients of variation. Significant differences suggest variability. This is also a useful measure when comparing data sets, since the lower the correlation of variation, the "tighter" the data toward the mean.
Combat Breathing (tactical breathing, bell-shaped breathing, four-count breathing, diaphragmatic breathing)	A method of breathing that aids in calming the adrenaline dump often encountered by forensic operators in various high-stress situations, ranging from meeting deadlines, to on-stand testimony, to actual combat. The technique dates to the earliest martial arts. www.policeone.com	A simple description: sitting upright in a chair or on the floor, breathe in through your nose to a four-count until your lungs are fully expanded. Hold your lungs full to a four-count. Exhale through your mouth completely emptying your lungs to a four-count. Leave your lungs empty for a four-count (or less if uncomfortable). Repeat in groups of five sequences or until a calming effect is noted. Avoid hyperventilating.

(continued)

Description	Explanation and Source	Source: Forensic Context
CombatCPA©	A term used to compare and contrast the stresses of expert witness and combat. Darrell D. Dorrell, circa 2003; used as a training tool for aspiring expert witnesses. Also, a continuing series of CPE courses for forensic operators.	Forensic operators must recognize the stresses they encounter. Training and practice can mitigate their impact.
Common-Sizing	The measurement of each item compared to a common base. This provides a proportionate, or common, measure of comparison for all items.	This depicts comparative proportion among the items, and may yield a preliminary observation of patterns or trends or both.
Confirmation Bias	The tendency for people to recall and use information in a selective way that supports their preconceptions or hypotheses regardless of whether the information is true.	In performing analysis, the forensic operator must guard against confirmation bias.
Consumer Expenditure Survey	The Consumer Expenditure Survey program consists of two surveys, the Quarterly Interview Survey and the Diary Survey, that provide information on the buying habits of American consumers, including data on their expenditures, income, and consumer unit (families and single consumers) characteristics. The survey data are collected for the Bureau of Labor Statistics by the US Census Bureau. www.bls.gov/cex/home.htm	Provides estimates of personal living expenses when not available from records or information provided by the suspect.
Correlation of Cash Flow to Reported Net Income	Analysis of the ratios of net income to revenue and cash flow from operations to net income. See CRO.	These relationships are used to test the validity of financial statements.
CRO	Cash Realized from Operations Operating Cash/Net Income Darrell D. Dorrell, "Basic Forensic Techniques for Valuation," *National Litigation Consultants' Review* 9, no. 8 (March 2010).	Operating cash and net income *should* demonstrate a strong correlation. That is "as earnings go (up *or* down), so goes operating cash." The reason is intuitive to those who understand financial statements. Specifically, accrual-based financials estimate future periods by accruing expected inflows and outflows. Divergence of *unexplainable* trends (for example, income up, but operating cash down, and vice versa) suggests manipulation. Therefore, significant variations suggest manipulation.

Description	Explanation and Source	Source: Forensic Context
CTR	Currency Transaction Report. A requirement imposed by the Bank Secrecy Act (BSA) compelling reporting of currency transactions equal to or greater than $10,000. See SAR, structuring.	Used to detect money laundering.
Data	Organized information generally used as the basis for an adjudication or decision. Commonly, organized information, collected for specific purpose. *Black's Law Dictionary,* 6th ed. (St. Paul, MN: West Publishing, 1990), 395.	1640s, plural of *datum,* from Latin, *datum* "(thing) given," neuter pp. of *dare* "to give" (see date (1)). Meaning "transmittable and storable computer information," first recorded in 1946. *Data processing* is from 1954. www.etymonline.com/index.php?term=data
Data analysis	The process of identifying, collecting, validating, organizing, and examining data pursuant to forming findings, observations, and opinions reflected in the contents.	Note the implicit methodology of data analysis.
Data Mining	Efficient analysis of large amounts of financial data. IDEA Software. www.audimation.com	Data from spreadsheets, print files, and database files can all be imported into one software program and analyzed in one place. For example, check registers can be searched to identify potential fraudulent payees.
Dechow-Dichev Techniques	Defines accrual quality as the extent to which accruals map into cash flow realizations. Links accrual quality to earnings persistence. *The Quality of Accruals and Earnings: The Role of Accrual Estimation Errors,* by Patricia M. Dechow and Ilia D. Dichev, 2001.	Analysis of the residual of the change in working capital plus cash flows from operations compared to earnings can provide a sense of accrual quality and therefore the quality of earnings as well. Poor earnings or accrual quality can be indicative of earnings management or manipulation.
Defalcation	The act of a defaulter; act of embezzling; failure to meet an obligation; misappropriation of trust funds or money held in any fiduciary capacity; failure to properly account for such funds. Commonly spoken of officers of corporations or public officials. *Black's Law Dictionary,* 6th ed. (St. Paul, MN: West Publishing, 1990), 416.	Note the distinction referring to corporations or public officials.

(*continued*)

Description	Explanation and Source	Source: Forensic Context
Deposition Matrix/ Interview Matrix	Darrell D. Dorrell, "Deposition Matrix," *National Litigation Consultants' Review* 2, no. 9 (2002).	Used to guide an attorney in deposing witnesses. It includes the objective of the deposition or interview, pertinent background information, and a suggested series of questions and the purpose of the questions.
DI	Depreciation Index—see M-Score. DI measures the ratio of the rate of depreciation in prior year to the rate of depreciation in current year. The depreciation rate is composed of depreciation expense and net PPE.	A DI of greater than 1.0 suggests that the rate of depreciation has slowed, thus indicating changes to estimated useful lives or new methods.
Digital Analysis	Uses computer power to test for digit patterns.	Digit tests include gap analysis, duplicate numbers test, rounded numbers test, stratification percentage comparison, and Benford's Law.
Dispersion	Measures of dispersion include variance, IQR, MAD, standard deviation, coefficient of variation, and Z-statistic.	Measures the variability of a data set.
Document Map	A visual matrix of documents requested and received. Darrell D. Dorrell "Document Map," *National Litigation Consultants' Review* 9, no. 11 (2010).	Provides a visual representation of the cooperation levels of parties during discovery as well as a tool for investigators to index documents requested and received.
Drill-Down	An investigative process that moves from top to bottom. It starts with summary information and moves downward through successively more detailed supporting data to focus on the pertinent component parts.	Descriptive term when testifying and is a metaphor for forensic analysis.
DSRI	Days Sales in Receivables Index—see M-Score. DSRI is measured as receivables to sales in current year relative to receivables to sales in the prior year, "$t - 1$."	Should remain relatively stable, hence, approximately 1.0. This variable gauges whether receivables and revenues are in or out of balance in two consecutive years. Disproportionate increases in receivables relative to sales may suggest revenue inflation.

Description	Explanation and Source	Source: Forensic Context
Embezzlement	The fraudulent appropriation of property by one lawfully entrusted with its possession. *Black's Law Dictionary*, 6th ed. (St. Paul, MN: West Publishing, 1990), 522.	Typically refers to skimming and larceny.
Entity-Party Chart	Similar to a genogram. Its focus, however, tends to be more on business entities and the people affiliated with them. www.financialforensicsacademy.com	Entity(s)/Party(s) charts can be useful predictors of funds diversion. For example, identifying the formation date of an off-shore entity may be compared to funds decline, thus substantiating diversion. Also, identifying seemingly unrelated parties can indicate where further investigation is potentially warranted.
Evidence	Any species of proof, or probative matter, legally presented at the trial of an issue, by the parties and through the medium of witnesses, records, documents, exhibits, concrete objects, and so forth, for the purpose of inducing belief in the minds of the court or jury as to their contention. *Black's Law Dictionary*, 6th ed. (St. Paul, MN: West Publishing, 1990), 555.	Circa 1300, "Appearance from which inferences may be drawn," from O.Fr. *evidence*, from L.L. *evidentia* "proof," originally "distinction, clearness," from L. *evidentem* (see *evident*). Meaning "ground for belief" is from late fourteenth century, that of "obviousness" is 1660s. Legal senses are from circa 1500, when it began to oust *witness*. As a verb, from circa 1600. Related: *evidenced; evidencing*. www.etymonline.com/index.php?term=evidence
Ex-ante	Refers to future, unknown events; the opposite of ex-post. Latin: *ex*—from; *ante*—before.	Must be considered when present-valuing economic benefit streams.
Ex-post	Refers to past events when uncertainties have been eliminated; the opposite of ex-ante. Latin: *x*—from; *post*—after.	Must be considered when present-valuing economic benefit streams.
Expectations Attributes	See Records-Based Expectations.	
Experiential Learning	*Experiential Learning: Experience as the Source of Learning and Development*, by David A. Kolb.	Forensic operators are more effective in delivering opinions when adult learning techniques are applied.

(*continued*)

Description	Explanation and Source	Source: Forensic Context
FA/IM©	Forensic Accounting/Investigation Methodology© www.financialforensicacademy.com	A patent-in-process methodology to organize the process of the forensic accounting investigation.
FAB	Fabricated, Altered, Borrowed Darrell D. Dorrell, "Forensic Accounting—Beyond the Ordinary," *National Litigation Consultant's Review* 9, no. 6 (2010). See QDE.	Comparison of suspect documents to control documents to highlight areas of discrepancies to help determine whether a document was altered.
Facial Mapping	Facial expressions are universal and can be used to interpret communications. *Unmasking the Face: A Guide to Recognizing Emotions from Facial Expressions, by* Paul Ekman and Wallace V. Friesen.	Provides a reference for recognizing what the face is communicating versus what a person is saying.
FACS	Facial Action Coding System Developed by Paul Ekman to taxonomize every conceivable human facial expression. See reference under Facial Mapping^{+}.	Interpreting involuntary expressions to understand our real emotions, reactions, intentions; careful analysis can be used to gauge a subject's real reaction.
Factor Analysis	Applied as a data reduction or structure detection method. http://www.statsoft.com/textbook/principal-components-factor-analysis.	Used in forensic lexicology to quantify the number of occurrences of a particular word.
Fiduciary	The term is derived from the Roman law, and means (as a noun) a person holding the character of a trustee, or a character analogous to that of a trustee, in respect to the trust and confidence involved in it and the scrupulous good faith and candor which it requires. *Black's Law Dictionary,* 6th ed. (St. Paul, MN: West Publishing, 1990), 625.	Applicable in certain civil matters.
Financial forensics	"The art & science of investigating people & money." Circa 1993, **Financial Forensics** financialforensics® (see Forensic Accounting).	Registered in Oregon in 1993. Registered with the US Patent and Trademark Office in 2002, with logo.
Flagging and Tracing	Validation to source documents.	For example, whether a disbursement merits investigation and comparing the check register data to the cleared check.

Description	Explanation and Source	Source: Forensic Context
Flow Chart of Funds	Charting the path of funds through various financial institutions.	Creates a visual reference of inappropriate movement of funds alongside appropriate movements.
Forensic accounting	"The art & science of investigating people & money." Circa 1993, financialforensics® (see Financial Forensics).	The name, "**Financial Forensics**" was registered in Oregon in 1993, and registered with the U.S. Patent and Trademark Office in 2002, with logo. Also, it was re-registered in order to perfect the trademark.
"Forensic auditor"	A contradictory term, an oxymoron, akin to conducting a wellness check on a corpse (see Fraud Auditor).	Someone using such a term is exposed to cross-examination queries.
Forensic indices	Various techniques used to assess high-level financial statement veracity, often by focusing on accrual anomalies and interdependence anomalies. Creators of such techniques include Dechow-Dechev, Lev-Thiagarajan, Sloan, Beneish, and others.	Can apply to virtually any aspect of economic benefit streams.
Forensic Lexicology	The study of words and vocabulary and how they are used.	Can be used to analyze the responses to interviews, depositions, and other inquiries to consider what is meant by the types of words used in communications.
Forensic Linguistics	The analysis, measurement, and study of language in the context of judicial procedure, crime, or disputes in law. J. P. French and P. Harrison, (2006), "Investigative and Evidential Applications of Forensic Speech Science," In A. Heaton-Armstrong, E. Shepherd, G. H. Gudjonsson, and D. Wolchover (eds.), *Witness Testimony: Psychological, Investigative and Evidential Perspectives* (Oxford: Oxford University Press, 2006). See also Forensic Lexicology.	Forensic accountants and investigators can gain perspective on evidence by analyzing the speech patterns.

(*continued*)

Description	Explanation and Source	Source: Forensic Context
Forensic Operator, or Operator	Special operations—Operations conducted in hostile, denied, or politically sensitive environments to achieve military, diplomatic, informational, and/or economic objectives employing military capabilities for which there is no broad conventional force requirement. These operations often require covert, clandestine, or low-visibility capabilities. Special operations are applicable across the range of military operations. They can be conducted independently or in conjunction with operations of conventional forces or other government agencies and may include operations through, with, or by indigenous or surrogate forces. Special operations differ from conventional operations in the degree of physical and political risk, operational techniques, mode of employment, independence from friendly support, and dependence on detailed operational intelligence and indigenous assets. Also called *SO* (JP 3-05). *Department of Defense Dictionary of Military and Associated Terms,* Joint Publication 1-02, April 12, 2001 (as amended through September 30, 2010), Joint Chiefs of Staff (not classified). Special operations—Operations requiring unique modes of employment, tactical techniques, equipment, and training often conducted in hostile, denied, or politically sensitive environments and characterized by one or more of the following: time sensitive, clandestine, low visibility, conducted with and/or through indigenous forces, requiring regional expertise, and/or a high degree of risk. Also called *SO*. (Approved for incorporation into JP 1-02.) *Special Operations,* Joint Publication 3-05, April 18, 2011, Joint Chiefs of Staff (not classified).	United States Special Operations Command (USSOCOM) comprises special operations, special mission, and counterterrorist units. It comprises the US Navy Special Warfare Command, U.S. Army Special Operations Command, U.S. Air Force Special Operations Command, US Marine Corps Forces Special Operations Command, and others. The term *special operator* describes USSOCOM military personnel. Therefore, the term *forensic operator* describes financial forensics-capable personnel. Furthermore, *forensic operator* reflects the *necessity* for personnel to possess *unique and specific* skills, knowledge, experience, education, training, and integrity to function in the financial forensics discipline. Note the *extraordinary* similarity between special operator tasks and forensic operator tasks.

Description	Explanation and Source	Source: Forensic Context
"forensithist"	A whimsical term applied to forensic operators by Mr. Tom Hayes, deceased. Rest in peace.	Forensic operators need some humor in their lives.
"Fraud (audit) auditing"	A contradictory term, an oxymoron, akin to conducting a wellness check on a corpse (see Forensic Auditor).	Someone using such a term is exposed to cross-examination queries.
Fraud, Badges of	See Badges of Fraud.	
Fraud, civil	"*The difference between criminal and civil fraud is **prison**.*" Tennessee CPA, JD.	A simple means of differentiation for forensic operators.
Fraud, criminal	An intentional perversion of truth for the purpose of inducing another in reliance upon it to part with some valuable thing belonging to him or to surrender a legal right. *Black's Law Dictionary,* 6th ed. (St. Paul, MN: West Publishing, 1990), 660.	The distinction between civil and criminal fraud is described with one word: prison.
Fraudulent transfer, conveyance	The civil tool known as fraudulent transfer or fraudulent conveyance derives from common law and the Bankruptcy Code, 11 U.S.C. § 548. It is typically employed in connection with debtor and creditor relationships where an asset or liability has been transferred for less than reasonably equivalent value within one year of the filing of the bankruptcy petition, with the intent of defeating a creditor's rights. The common law provisions typically originated from the Uniform Fraudulent Conveyances Act (UFCA) or Uniform Fraudulent Transfer Act (UFTA) and include measurements of badges of fraud that can be employed directly or indirectly. Thus, assets can be recovered and transfers voided when they constitute actual or constructive fraud. Fraudulent transfer or conveyance is pursued in the same way among federal and state jurisdictions and can be used in combination with a wide array of other matters, including alter ego, solvency, merger, and acquisition.	Forensic operators often encounter fraudulent transfer matters in connection with bankruptcy, marital dissolution, receivership and related assignments.

(*continued*)

Description	Explanation and Source	Source: Forensic Context
Frequency Distribution—Data	The presentation of the contents of a data set in a table.	The data set's composition is described in its most basic form for the forensic operator, and may yield preliminary observation of patterns and trends.
Frequency Distribution—visual	The presentation of the contents of a data set in a visual format.	The data set's composition is described in its most basic form for the forensic operator, and may yield preliminary observation of patterns and trends.
FSAT	"Financial Status Audit Techniques," Internal Revenue Service Manual, Part 4, Chapter 10.	Methods used to reconstruct income when it appears that the data available is incomplete. See the Internal Revenue Service Indirect Methods in this table.
F-Score	A simple accounting-based analysis strategy using nine fundamental financial signals measuring three areas of a firm's financial condition: profitability, leverage/liquidity, and operating efficiency. The original purpose of this scoring system was to identify firms to retain or remove from a portfolio to maximize returns. *Value Investing: The Use of Historical Financial Statement Information to Separate Winners from Losers*, by Joseph D. Piotrosky, 2002.	This scoring system can be used to evaluate the relative financial strength of a firm.
Full-and-False Inclusion	Full-and-false inclusion testing commences with inception and continues throughout the duration of the assignment. It continually determines the appropriate universe of data under investigation. See Chain of Custody. Darrell D. Dorrell, circa 2002, and various publications.	Full-and-false inclusion testing ensures that all appropriate data is included, and extraneous data is excluded. It symbolizes the yellow crime-scene tape of a forensic assignment.
Gap Analysis	Identification of items not accounted for in a sequentially numbered or dated set of documents or transactions.	Gaps in sequences draw the investigator to items that may have been intentionally not recorded or provided. Items missing in a series, such as check numbers, should be traced to determine that they were not misappropriated.

Description	Explanation and Source	Source: Forensic Context
Genogram	Visual representation of the relationship of entities or people within the context of a case. www.genopro.com	It provides a common perspective for the forensic investigator to demonstrate patterns of behavior and identify other entities and parties meriting further investigation. Also, it can point to key indicators of the subject's behavior, leading to additional points of investigation.
GMI	Gross Margin Index—See M-Score. The ratio of gross margin in a prior year to the gross margin in the current year.	When GMI is greater than 1, it indicates that gross margins have deteriorated. When gross margins have deteriorated, it is more likely that a firm might engage in earnings manipulation.
Gross Margin Test	Gross margin of a business is calculated and compared to its peer group and itself over time. Peer data can be obtained from various sources, including RMA (Robert Morris & Associates) or can be constructed on an ad hoc basis to serve as a benchmark. See Darrell D. Dorrell, "Is the Moneyed Spouse Lying About the Money?" *American Journal of Family Law*, March 22, 2007.	It can highlight illicit deposits in cases in which the gross margin increases significantly from history or is significantly higher than the peer group. In the case of significant decreases, it can indicate skimmed or unreported receipts or both.
Horizontal Analysis	Direct method of financial statement analysis—Ratios or line items in a company's financial statement over a certain period of time such as percent increases or decreases in revenues or expenses.	Financial statements of businesses of all sizes can be compared.
Humintell	This is a resource site for forensic operators seeking training on interpreting facial expressions during interviews to determine veracity and other conditions. It offers free on-line training for up to one year. www.humintell.com.	Forensic operators can use these resources for free basic expression training, and purchase the periodic on-line training offered.

(*continued*)

Description	Explanation and Source	Source: Forensic Context
ICE/SCORE	See Chapter 3 for complete explanation.	ICE provides a model for considering the major categories of financial data to be analyzed. SCORE reminds you to consider the stakeholders and the types of information that might be available outside of the financial data.
Indicia, indicators	Latin plural of *indicium,* "information, disclosure, discovery."	Typically used in alter ego matters to assess the conditions extant.
Indictment Matrix	Visual representation listing details of evidence and linking them to potential charges	Provides clarity to the triers of fact.
Information	The result of data, that is, data becomes useful when it provides information. www.etymonline.com/index.php?term=information	Differentiates data from information.
Informants, confidential or open	Forensic operators sometimes assume that confidential (or open) informants can only be conducted by military or law enforcement agencies. However, any form of legal information gathering (after receiving approval from counsel, the director, and so on) is a type of informant access.	For example, a civilian forensic operator casually discussing incoming phone call volume to the CEO is a means of accessing an informant to gather evidence pertaining to damages.
Informed Judgment	Judgment deployed by a forensic operator relying upon empirical or similar objective means of reasoning to make a decision.	This is in contrast to professional judgment that typically lacks empirical methods or reasoning.
Internal Revenue Service Market Segment Specialization Program (selected industries)	Also known as MSSP and ATG (Audit Technical Guides).	These guides provide detailed information on how business operates within a particular industry, which may be useful in identifying areas of investigation, depending on the facts and circumstances of a case.
Interrogation	Questioning those suspected of having committed crimes as well as the questioning of 'hostile' and/or 'culpable' witnesses in order to obtain evidence of 'their' involvement in crimes. Nossen, Richard A. and Joan W. Norvelle. The Detection, Investigation, and Prosecution of Financial Crimes 2nd ed.	Interviewing and interrogation are closely related, but have distinct differences. Forensic operators must understand and discern the application depending upon the facts and circumstances.

Description	Explanation and Source	Source: Forensic Context
Interviewing	Questioning individuals in order to elicit information and to obtain documentary and physical evidence related to crimes committed by 'others.' Nossen, Richard A. and Joan W. Norvelle. The Detection, Investigation, and Prosecution of Financial Crimes 2nd ed.	Interviewing and interrogation are closely related, but have distinct differences. Forensic operators must understand and discern the application depending upon the facts and circumstances.
Invigilation	Close supervision of suspects during an examination period such that it is virtually impossible for a fraud to be committed.	Changes seen during the control periods highlight where fraud may be occurring.
IQR	Interquartile Range—Exhibits the dispersion between the third and first quartiles. It is sometimes referred to as the *mid-spread*, or the *middle fifty*.	Concentrates analysis on the middle 50 percent of the data.
Item Listing Method	Listing of items such as checks, deposits, and transfers and can include all or only certain amounts, such as only those exceeding a specified value.	Individual items are traced for leads to other items, including previously undisclosed bank accounts, payees, and so on.
Jones Method	In this study, the analysis of total discretionary accruals was used as a measure to detect earnings management. The model for discretionary accruals was adjusted to control for changes in nondiscretionary accruals caused by changing conditions. Discretionary accruals decreased during import relief investigations, as there was a clear incentive to decrease earnings in order to obtain import relief funds. Jennifer J. Jones, "Earnings Management During Import Relief Investigations," *Journal of Accounting Research* 29, no. 2 (1991).	This study provides further support in considering the levels of discretionary accruals when investigating potential earnings manipulation.
Khan Academy	A ***superb***, free Internet site containing more than 2,600 videos ranging from a few minutes to almost an hour. The topics cover "*. . . everything from arithmetic to physics, finance, and history . . .*" The topic is explained while the instructor writes out the equations, diagrams and related content on an electronic "chalkboard."	Forensic operators can learn or enhance their skills in a wide variety of pertinent subjects, including statistics, math, banking and money, computer science, et al.

(*continued*)

Description	Explanation and Source	Source: Forensic Context
Kinetic Communication	Observing bodily reactions to determine where additional investigation is warranted.	It has been suggested that a person who averts her eyes to the right prior to responding may be lying. Alternatively, it has been suggested that averting one's eyes to the left prior to responding may be recalling a memory. For example, it is well documented that when lying (and when passionate about a subject), blood flow increases to the subject's head and neck area, thus providing a flushed look that may warrant further investigation.
Knowledge Maps	Provide documentation of the information, knowledge, qualifications, and proficiencies held by individuals and groups within an organization.	Aids in identifying the source of information a forensic operator is looking for.
www.knowx.com	A data-rich pay site that provides progressively detailed and more expensive information. KnowX: www.knowx.com.	This is an extraordinarily rich site for forensic operators to conduct progressive levels of people related business, people and asset evidence. It is has a learning curve, but is well worth the time and money necessary to become proficient.
Kurtosis	Kurtosis measures how peaked or flat the distribution is of data relative to a normal distribution. Data sets with a high kurtosis have a distinct peak near the mean, and vice versa.	Forensic operators use kurtosis to measure and illustrate dispersion.
Lexicology	A branch of linguistics concerned with the signification and application of words. See www.merriam-webster.com	See Forensic Lexicology.
Lev-Thiagarajan Techniques	Identifies a set of 12 financial variables (also referred to as signals or fundamentals) claimed by analysts to be useful in security valuation. Their study supported the value relevance of these signals, particularly when evaluated in light of the macroeconomic conditions present during the period evaluated as well as the link between the identified signals and persistence (quality and growth) of reported earnings.	This is yet another tool to help the investigator determine the quality of earnings and as a result the potential of financial statement manipulation.

Description	Explanation and Source	Source: Forensic Context
	Fundamental Information Analysis, by Baruch Lev and S. Ramu Thiagarajan, 1993.	
LI	Leverage Index—See M-Score. Total debt to total assets in the current year to the corresponding ratio in a prior year.	An LVGI greater than 1 indicates an increase in leverage. It captures debt covenant incentives for earnings manipulation.
Lifestyle Analysis	Constructing the personal financial statements so that the subject's lifestyle in terms of income and expenditures can be compared to other individuals. Typically, sources used for comparison consist of governmental studies such as the *Consumer Expenditure Survey.*	Key variations indicated by the comparison warrant further investigation.
Likert Scale Protocol	A psychometric scale commonly used in questionnaires, and is the most widely used scale in survey research, such that the term is often used interchangeably with *rating scale* even though the two are not synonymous. When responding to a Likert questionnaire item, respondents specify their level of agreement or disagreement on a symmetric agree-disagree scale for a series of statements. Thus the scale captures the intensity of their feelings. The scale is named after its inventor, psychologist Rensis Likert. Rensis Likert, "A Technique for the Measurement of Attitudes," *Archives of Psychology* 140 (1932): 1–55. Alvin Burns and Ronald Burns, *Basic Marketing Research* 2nd ed. (Upper Saddle River, NJ: Pearson Education, 2008), 245.	This scaling method can be used to weight the levels of scoring in a report card.
Link Analysis/ Root Tracing	Establishes associations among people and data.	For example, a comparison of mailing addresses of company vendors and those of employees to determine if there are improper payments being made.
LSAT	Linguistic Style Analysis Technique. The technique evaluates veracity in verbal and written statements. Analysts parse content into structural components, for example, terms, phrases, and the like in order to compare (and develop) the facts.	For example, the comparison of the number of times the word *portion* versus the word *percentage* occurs in a subject's testimony versus the attorney brief in a case in which the transfer of an ownership interest is in dispute.

(*continued*)

Description	Explanation and Source	Source: Forensic Context
MAD	Mean Average Deviation. The arithmetic mean of the absolute differences from the mean. Also, the median is sometimes used to derive the median average deviation.	Useful for comparing actual values that vary from the mean.
Markup Method	Internal Revenue Service Indirect Methods (IRM 4.10.4.6.5).	The markup method is a formal indirect method that can overcome the weaknesses of the bank deposits and cash expenditures method, source and application of funds method, and net worth method, which do not effectively reconstruct income when cash is not deposited and the total cash outlays cannot be determined unless volunteered by the taxpayer. If personal enrichment occurs that cannot be identified, the effectiveness of these methods is diminished. For example, the possibility exists that significant personal acquisitions or expenditures are paid with cash and are not evident. The markup method is similar to how state sales tax agencies conduct audits. The cost of goods sold is verified and the resulting gross receipts are determined based on actual markup.
Maximum	The largest value within a data set.	Sets upper data boundary and may apply in other techniques, for example, midrange.
Mean—Arithmetic	The value resulting from the sum of all data set values divided by the number of data set values. The only measure of central tendency that gives equal representation to all values.	Provides a measure of the expected or most likely value within a data set. The forensic operator can compare each actual value to the expected value to determine variability. For example, the actual invoice amount of customer K compared to the expected invoice amount of customer K permits the forensic operator to assess whether the actual invoice requires further investigation.
Mean—Geometric	The mean calculated similarly to the arithmetic mean, except the numerator is the product of the values (that is, multiplied), taken to the nth root of the number of values.	Useful when measuring very skewed data, and when measuring rates of change.

Description	Explanation and Source	Source: Forensic Context
Mean—Truncated	The arithmetic mean, absent the highest and lowest values of the data set. The highest and lowest values can represent a proportion or absolute values within the data set. The proportion is typically based upon an objective measure.	See Mean-Arithmetic.
Means—Dispersion of All	This compares all mean measurements for each category. The greater dispersion represented by the disparate means suggests skewed data. Despite being a dispersion measurement, it is included in the central tendencies section to reside with the respective findings.	Indicates variability away from the mean.
Median	The value reflecting the midpoint of the data set containing an odd number of values. The median of a data set containing an even number of values is the arithmetic mean of the two middle values.	See Mean-Arithmetic.
Methodology	A body of methods, rules, and postulates employed by a discipline; a particular procedure or set of procedures. Simply put, a methodology is a formal or informal way of doing things. See www.merriam-webster.com/dictionary/methodology.	A party purporting to carry forensic capabilities can be discredited when lacking a methodology.
Midrange	The arithmetic mean of the minimum and maximum values. It is calculated by adding the minimum and maximum values and dividing by two.	See Mean-Arithmetic.
Minimum	The smallest value within a data set.	Sets lower data boundary and may apply in other techniques, for example, midrange.
MIMO (money-in/money-out)	An acronym describing a highly simplified conceptual methodology for forensic assignments.	Forensic operators can use the term to educate parties unfamiliar with forensic processes.
Miranda Rights	The formal warning law enforcement in the United States is required to be stated to criminal suspects in police custody before they are interrogated. *Miranda v. Arizona*, 384 U.S. 436 (1966)	Necessary for forensic operators in law enforcement.
Mode	The data set value that occurs most frequently in a data set. The mode ignores all values except those considered modal. Its usage is nominal.	In some cases, the mode saves time since the analysis of one mode value is likely applicable to the other mode values. A typical example is recurring lease payments.

(*continued*)

Description	Explanation and Source	Source: Forensic Context
Modified Net Worth Method	Removes the complexities of tax law from the Net Worth Method. *The Detection, Investigation and Prosecution of Financial Crimes* 2nd ed., by Richard A. Nossen and Joan W. Norvell, 1993.	The technique is effective at measuring a suspect's apparent income by determining the increase in wealth indicated by measuring the year-to-year change in the suspect's overall net worth. Consequently, it can be shown that the suspect spent more than he had available from known, reported, or legitimate sources. The excess then reflects underreported income sources.
Moving Average (3-year)	The mean of a three-year sequence in which the numerator adds the next year, and drops the first year, thus producing a moving, or rolling, average of three years.	Useful for measuring comparative central tendencies, and rates of change.
M-Score	Series of indices to measure potential of the existence of earnings management. "The Detection of Earnings Management," by Professor Messod D. Beneish, Harvard University. www.bauer.uh.edu/%7Eswhisenant/beneish%20earnings%20mgmt%20score.pdf	See AQI, DI, DSRI, GMI, LI, SGI, SGAI, and TATA.
Multi-Attribute Utility Analysis (MUA)	Multi-attribute utility analysis (MUA) is a widely accepted decision analysis technique formalized in the 1970s. It has wide use throughout virtually all disciplines, including, biology, business, chemistry, physics, statistics, and many others.	Jacob W. Ulvila, and Rex V., Brown, "Decision Analysis Comes of Age," *Harvard Business Review*, 60, no. 5 (1982): 136–140.
Net Worth Method	Internal Revenue Service Indirect Methods (IRM 4.10.4.6.7).	The taxpayer's net worth (total assets less total liabilities) is determined at the beginning and at the end of the taxable year. The difference between these two amounts will be the increase or decrease in net worth. The purpose of the net worth method is to determine, through a change in net worth, whether the taxpayer is purchasing assets, reducing liabilities, or making expenditures with funds not reported as taxable income.

Description	Explanation and Source	Source: Forensic Context
NGO	A nongovernmental organization (NGO) is any nonprofit, voluntary citizens' group organized on a local, national, or international level. Task-oriented and driven by people with a common interest, NGOs perform a variety of service and humanitarian functions, bring citizen concerns to governments, advocate and monitor policies, and encourage political participation through provision of information. Some are organized around specific issues, such as human rights, the environment, or health. They provide analysis and expertise, serve as early warning mechanisms, and help monitor and implement international agreements. Their relationship with offices and agencies of the United Nations system differs depending on their goals, their venue and the mandate of a particular institution. See www.ngo.org/ngoinfo/define.html.	The UN is an example, and illustrates the oversight and accountability risks associated with NGOs.
Night vision, improvement	In low-light conditions such as surveillance, a forensic operator can improve his vision by looking slightly to the left or right of the target.	The slight angle brings into play different color receptors than can enhance perception.
NLP: Neurolinguistic programming.	P. Tosey and J. Mathison, "Introducing Neuro-Linguistic Programming," Centre for Management Learning and Development, School of Management, University of Surrey, 2006. R. Dilts, J. Grinder, J. Delozier, and R. Bandler, *Neuro-Linguistic Programming: Volume I: The Study of the Structure of Subjective Experience* (Cupertino, CA: Meta Publications, 1980) 2; R. Bandler, *Richard Bandler's Guide to Trance-formation: How to Harness the Power of Hypnosis to Ignite Effortless and Lasting Change* (Deerfield Beach, FL: Health Communications, 2008).	A discipline applied in organizational change and other arenas, e.g. psychology to understand and modify behavior. Forensic operators can benefit by applying the techniques in concert with interviewing, interrogation and behavior detection.

(*continued*)

Description	Explanation and Source	Source: Forensic Context
Normalizations	Normalizations are adjustments to financial statements to eliminate the distortion of nonoperating, nonmarket and nonrecurring events.	*Not* limited to valuation; often necessary in many forensic matters. Akin to cleaning, except normalizations occur at a higher level.
NPO	Nonprofit organization—An entity organized for charitable, association, educational, or other purposes. It lacks the profit motive of the business entity, retains any economic benefits and any trustees, as related fiduciaries do not receive any personal financial benefit. Examples of NPOs include charities, such as the Red Cross, trade unions, and public arts organizations.	Reference only.
Numeric Duplication Test	Identification of items that have the same control numbers in a set of documents or transactions.	Duplicated control numbers may suggest manipulation or errors.
On-Book Data	Signifies the boundaries of data captured (whether or not self-reported) under any person's or entity's control.	Useful for forensic operators to clarify sources.
Off-Book Data	Signifies the boundaries of data under any person's or entity's control but *not* captured.	Useful for forensic operators to clarify sources.
OODA Loop	Observe, Orient, Decide, and Act. An entity (whether an individual or an organization) that can process this cycle quickly, observing and reacting to unfolding events more rapidly than an opponent, and can thereby get inside the opponent's decision cycle and gain the advantage. Developed by military strategist and USAF colonel John R. Boyd. *The Essence of Winning and Losing,* by John R. Boyd, 1995. *Certain to Win: The Strategy of John Boyd, Applied to Business,* by Chet Richards, 2004.	Forensic operators gather information (observe), develop strategies to pursue a case (orient), make decisions, and act on them. The cycle is repeated continuously. The aggressive and conscious application of the process gives one party an advantage over a competing party who is merely reacting to conditions as they occur, or has poor awareness of the situation. The FA/IM methodology follows an iterative process that applies the concept of the OODA Loop.

Description	Explanation and Source	Source: Forensic Context
Outlier	A data point(s) measurably distant from the remainder of data. Defined as: *An outlying observation, or outlier, is one that appears to deviate markedly from other members of the sample in which it occurs.* Grubbs, F. E.: 1969, Procedures for detecting outlying observations in samples. Technometrics 11, 1–21.	Forensic operators strive to rely on science more than art. Legitimate data outliers can be statistically measured. See also, cleaning data, Chebyshev's Theorem, standard deviation, among others.
PACER	Public Access to Court Electronic Records (PACER) is an electronic access service that provides case and docket information from federal appellate, district, and bankruptcy courts. Also, the PACER case locator functions through the Internet. "PACER is provided by the federal judiciary in keeping with its commitment to providing public access to court information through a centralized service." PACER: www.pacer.gov.	Forensic operators need to know all pertinent information on entities and parties, particularly in court-related matters. This source is the primary repository for such information.
Paralinguistic Communication	Analyzing the volume, pitch, and voice quality during verbal communication.	Oral communication provides for a range of nonverbal accompaniment that can be used to convey certain emotions that may not be as easily discerned in written communication.
Pattern	A natural or chance configuration such as the *pattern* of events; a reliable sample of traits, acts, tendencies, or other observable characteristics of a person, group, or institution such as *behavior patterns* or *spending patterns*.	Forensic operators seek to identify patterns in virtually every assignment.
Pretext	A purpose or motive alleged or an appearance assumed in order to cloak the real intention or state of affairs. www.merriam-webster.com	Forensic operators cannot use this technique unless appropriately authorized or explicitly permitted. See also subterfuge.

(continued)

Description	Explanation and Source	Source: Forensic Context
Privilege	A particular and peculiar benefit or advantage enjoyed by a person, company, or class, beyond the common advantages of other citizens. An exceptional or extraordinary power or exemption. A peculiar right, advantage, exemption, power, franchise, or immunity held by a person or class, not generally possessed by others.	Black, Henry C. Black's Law Dictionary 6th ed. St. Paul, MN: West Publishing, 1990.
Portfolio Theory	A collection of diversified financial investments intended to maximize earnings while minimizing risk to the investor or entity.	Occasionally used in corporate governance considerations.
Probability-Proportional-to-Size Sampling	Probability proportional to size sampling is also known as monetary unit sampling or dollar unit sampling. It is a method of sampling that takes the varying size of each item within the population into account when selecting the audit sample. When there are large items in the population (larger than the sampling interval), these are usually extracted first and will definitely be selected for testing. The remainder of the audit sample is then selected, using either cell selection or fixed interval.	This type of sampling focuses the sample selection on individually significant amounts. All amounts, however, have the opportunity to be selected.
Probative Evidence	Evidence that helps establish or contribute to proof.	Forensic operators are keenly focused on identifying probative evidence in both civil and criminal matters.
Process Map	Tool whereby a process such as a transactional process is depicted visually to facilitate understanding.	For example, a flow chart of how funds move through the various bank accounts of a company.
Professional Judgment	A catchall phrase used when an opposing expert cannot empirically substantiate his opinion. A forensic expert may reach the point at which *professional judgment* makes sense, but such occurrences should be very rare. A useful test of the opposition's positional strength consists of analyzing the number of times that *professional judgment* is used in testimony or reports or both; the relationship between opinion quality and the number is inverse. That is, the more times the phrase is used, the lower the opinion quality.	Competent forensic operators minimize the use of the term.

Description	Explanation and Source	Source: Forensic Context
Progressive Average	The mean calculated by adding the amount in each successive year to the numerator, and adding one to the denominator for each successive year.	Useful for measuring comparative central tendencies, and rates of change.
Proof of Cash	Validates reported receipts and disbursements to bank statement(s).	This is also known as a four-way bank reconciliation, and does not allow for entries to plug the balance.
Proxemics	Coined by researcher Edward Hall during the 1950s and 1960s and has to do with the study of our use of space and how various differences in that use can make us feel more relaxed or anxious. *The Hidden Dimension*, by Edward T. Hall, 1966. Edward T. Hall, "A System for the Notation of Proxemic Behavior," *American Anthropologist* 65 (1963): 1003–1026.	Distance Communication (or proxemic communication) consists of comparing and contrasting the interpersonal distance involved in query responses. It has been suggested that (even subtle) movements away from an interviewer indicate avoidance, and thus merit additional investigation. Movements toward an interviewer can suggest a desire to be believed or a desire for assistance (or both), such as a request for the interviewer to delve further into the matter. It is a component of the concept of communicating with body language.
P-Value	The probability, when the null hypothesis is true, of obtaining a sample result that is at least as unlikely as the observation, often referred as the observed level of significance. *NACVA Consultant's Training Institute* by Mark W. Shirley, CPA/ABV, CVA, CFFA, CFE, V & L Consultants, LLP, November 18, 2008.	Regression analysis.
QDE	Questioned Document Examination. A variety of scientific processes and methods are used to answer questions about a disputed document. See FAB. Jan Seaman Kelly and Brian S. Lindblom (eds.), *Scientific Examination of Questioned Documents* 2nd ed. (Boca Raton, FL: CRC Press, Forensic and Police Science Series), 2006.	Questions answered might include who wrote a document or whether a signature was forged or not.

(*continued*)

Description	Explanation and Source	Source: Forensic Context
R^2	The main measure of the goodness of fit in regression analysis. The R-Squared can range from near-zero to +1 and measures the percentage of the variation in the dependent variable explained by the independent variable.	Used by forensic operators in regression analysis.
Range	The difference between the highest and the lowest data value. Range sometimes calculates differently. For example, it could be described using "from-to" in lieu of the difference.	Indicates data spread and may help a forensic operator determine the scope of analysis likely to be necessary. It is also useful for comparing with other basic data sets.
Ratio Estimation; Extrapolation	Projecting the value of a misstatement based on a sample of transactions.	An example would be projecting the amount of disbursements to inappropriate payees based on the results of a properly selected sample.
Reasonableness Testing	Formulating an expectation (that is, an estimate) of an account balance based upon understanding and assumptions driving the account balance.	A reasonableness test of deposits could measure the actual deposits against expected deposits to identify where further investigation is warranted.
Reasonably equivalent value	A term used in fraudulent transfer possessing similarities and in some cases, equivalency to fair market value.	Used as the measurement standard in fraudulent transfers.
Records-Based Expectations	Identifying the nature, form, extent, veracity, availability, and related elements of record keeping in order to set expectations about the entity(s) or party(s).	For example, an entity handling a large sum of money from numerous investors would be expected, at a minimum, to have in place very sound management and internal controls that provide a solid foundation to the representative financial statements. Examples of the minimum types of records in such a case include the general ledger, receipts ledger, cost and expense ledgers, detailed shareholder records, comprehensive financial statements, current income tax returns, and related elements.

Description	Explanation and Source	Source: Forensic Context
Reid, John E.	This site offers highly regarded text and training resources. It is the source of The Reid Technique®, a well-known method of interviewing and interrogation taught to law enforcement. www.reid.com.	Forensic operators upgrade and refine their people investigation skills through the content on this site.
RSF (relative size factor)	The ratio of the largest data item compared to the second largest data item. Can also be applied in subsequent declining comparisons.	Used to measure data anomalies.
Reperform	Perform a test of data a second time to see if the results are consistent with how the original transaction was recorded or an amount was computed.	Reperformance of computations, such as a bank reconciliation, provides some assurance about the validity of an account balance and solidifies a reference point for further investigation.
Report Card	Method of summarizing the results of an investigation into categories and relating them to a score similar to what a student receives in school.	See Valuation Report Card, Damages Report Card.
Report Card (Damages)	See Report Card.	This form of report card tallies the damages within individual categories and overall in total.
Report Card (Valuation)	Methodology to quickly and objectively assess an opponent's valuation work product. Darrell D. Dorrell, "The Valuation Report Card," *American Journal of Family Law* 16, no. 2 (2002).	A matrix is used to identify and rate the tendency (viewpoint supported) of pivotal elements that are key to a business valuation. This concept has also been successfully adapted for use in evaluating alter ego elements.
Reverse Proof	The examination of forensic investigation matters is approached from *two* perspectives: (1) that a fraud (or other deceit) has occurred—the proof must include attempts to prove it has not occurred; (2) that a fraud has not occurred—that proof must also attempt to prove it has occurred.	The reason for reverse proof is that both sides of fraud must be examined. Under the law, proof of fraud must preclude any explanation other than guilt.

(continued)

Description	Explanation and Source	Source: Forensic Context
Rounded Numbers Test	This test filters transaction data for values that are rounded numbers.	Rounded numbers are not typically the norm in a set of transactions. Large or frequent round number transactions are a good indicator of estimation since people tend to estimate when they create contrived numbers.
Rule of Threes	Three minutes air, three hours shelter, three days water, three weeks food, three months companionship.	Guidelines for survival without: One can survive for three minutes without air, three hours without shelter, three days without water, three weeks without food, three months without companionship.
SAR	Suspicious Activity Report. A requirement imposed by the Bank Secrecy Act (BSA) compelling reporting of activities not otherwise flagged. See CTR.	Used to identify activities in addition to other reported conditions.
Scripting	Comments added to the expert witness report to guide the attorney in the flow of questioning to use with the expert witness during testimony to help highlight significant points in the report. Can be easily achieved by using the Track Changes feature in Microsoft Word, and the Notes feature in PowerPoint reports.	Caution: Do undertake this technique without prior consent from counsel; potentially subject to discovery. Comments might request the attorney to ask the expert why he is uniquely qualified to testify in the case.
Self-Reported Data	Data compiled or reported or both by any person or entity without the benefit of independent oversight or attestation. See Self-Reporting System.	See ICE/SCORE for further application.
Self-Reporting System	Signifies the boundaries of data captured under any person's or entity's control. See Self-Reported Data.	See ICE/SCORE for further application.
SGAI or SGAEI	Sales General and Administrative Expenses Index—See M-Score. Ratio of SGA in current year to the corresponding measure in prior year.	The variable is used following Lev and Thiagarajan's (1993) suggestion that analysts would interpret a disproportionate increase in sales as a negative signal about a firm's future prospects. A disproportionate increase may suggest manipulation. The index should remain relatively stable, at 1.0.

Description	Explanation and Source	Source: Forensic Context
SGI	Sales Growth Index—See M-Score. Ratio of sales in current year to sales in prior year.	Growth does not imply manipulation, but growth firms are viewed by professionals as more likely to commit financial statement fraud because their financial position and capital needs put pressure on managers to achieve earnings targets. Significant variations in this index could indicate manipulation.
SGR	Sustainable Growth Rate. Estimation can be achieved by applying the sustainable growth model. $G_s = B_s \text{ X ROE}$ G_s = sustainable growth rate for a company B_s = plow-back ratio calculated as follows: $$\frac{\text{Annual Earnings} - \text{Annual Dividends}}{\text{Annual Earnings}}$$ ROE = return on book equity as follows: $$\frac{\text{Annual Earnings}}{\text{Book Value of Equity}}$$ *Stocks, Bonds, Bills and Inflation,* Valuation Edition—2002 Yearbook, Ibbotson Associates, page 62.	Compares a claimed rate of business growth to its realistic growth rate.
Shaky Books Ratio	This ratio expresses an entity's nonrecurring expenses to revenues as a percentage, and compares it over a business cycle. Significant variations can signal earnings manipulation. Public companies do not consider nonrecurring expenses in their pro forma estimates. Harry Domash, MSNMoney, 2009.	A shorthand financial veracity test for forensic operators.
Skiptracing	A term that describes how bill collectors locate people who owe money, say on rent but have vacated the premises. The people are known as "skips" and the "tracing" describes the various means of locating the skips. www.skiptraceseminar.com.	Very useful for forensic operators seeking people information that is difficult to find and not otherwise available through routine queries. See also, www.blackbookonline.info

(*continued*)

Description	Explanation and Source	Source: Forensic Context
Sloan Method	Investigated whether stock prices reflect information about future earnings contained in the accrual and cash flow components of current earnings. The extent to which earnings persists in the future depends on the relative magnitude of the accrual and cash flow components of earnings. However, stock prices seem to indicate that investors fixate on earnings rather than reflecting the information available in the accrual and cash components of current earnings until they are reflected in future earnings. Richard G. Sloan, "Do Stock Prices Fully Reflect Information in Accruals and Cash Flows About Future Earnings?" *The Accounting Review* 71, no. 3 (1996).	This work emphasizes the importance of analyzing the cash versus accrual component of earnings and supports theories in detecting earnings manipulation by analyzing the magnitude of accruals.
Solvency Analysis	Method to determine "... a company's ability to meet the interest costs and repayment schedules associated with its long-term debt obligations." Robert N. Anthony, *Management Accounting Text and Cases,* (Homewood, IL: Richard D. Irwin, 1964), 301. Composed of the Balance Sheet Test, Cash Flow Test, and the Adequate (Reasonable) Capital Test. Robert F. Reilly and Robert P. Schweihs, *The Handbook of Advanced Business Valuation* (New York: McGraw-Hill Irwin, 2000), 340–342. Darrell D. Dorrell and Gregory A. Gadawski, "Valuation in Solvency Analysis," *National Litigation Consultant's Review,* July 2003.	Solvency analysis is used in alter ego cases to help assess whether a subsidiary is financially dependent upon its parent.
Source and Use of Cash Method	Lists each identified source and use of cash (or other funds) by category for the respective years under analysis.	Provides the same results as the modified net worth method and is used in cases in which a suspect is living a low-profile, low-record existence.
Splatter Vision	Looking at the big picture and not focusing on anything in particular and monitoring for deviation or change that then results in increased focus on the deviation.	This can aid in the efficiency of conducting forensic analysis. Used by the Secret Service for crowd observation.

Description	Explanation and Source	Source: Forensic Context
Spokeo	This site is a people search engine comprising vast amounts of information ranging from a large variety of public information sources. It reports the data in very informative formats, including earnings, occupation, marital status, age and other categories. It is very cost-effective. Spokeo: www.spokeo.com.	This site aggregates a great deal of people related information that aids in refining subsequent searches.
Stakeholder	Any party having an interest in an entity, including owner, employee customer, lender, regulator, supplier, government, and so on.	Useful in corporate governance matters.
Standard Deviation	A measurement reflecting the average distance of data from the mean of the data set. (The square root of the variance.)	Provides specific cutoffs for the forensic operator to categorize variability of data. For example, +/–1 standard deviation comprises 68.2 percent of the data.
Storyboard	A visual portrayal of events (often chronological) accompanied by explanatory text. The technique is often used in visual and other media production, including movies, commercials, television shows, theater plays, and so on.	Competent forensic operators deploy throughout all aspects of assignments, particularly when testimony is imminent.
Statement Analysis (Verbal)	Analyzing the language used by a subject during interviews to assess her truthfulness.	
Statement Analysis (written)	Examination of written documents in a manner similar to statement analysis (verbal). However analyzing written documents focuses on the words *and* the nature of the document, including the age, condition, and related physical document factors.	For example, a supporting document that is on a type of paper that would not have been used to create such a document suggests that it is not authentic.
Statistical Analysis	Mathematical analysis that describes and reasons from numerical observations or descriptive measures of a sample.	An analysis of the volatility of a set of financial results or transactions using statistical measures such as the coefficient of variation and the Z-score can identify the occurrence of outliers that may warrant further investigation.

(*continued*)

Description	Explanation and Source	Source: Forensic Context
Stratification Percentage Comparison	Categorizes check amounts into predefined strata, for example, high, medium, low, or perhaps "Above $10,000," "Between $5,000 and $9,999," and so forth. Darrell D. Dorrell, "Is the Moneyed Spouse Lying About the Money?" *American Journal of Family Law*, March 22, 2007.	Stratification can be used to focus efforts in an investigation.
Stratified Mean-Per-Unit (MPU)	A statistical method to estimate the value of a population using the means of samples from distinct categories within the population based on defined precision and confidence levels. Used in cases where no or only moderate monetary errors are expected. Vincent O'Reilly, Patrick McDonnell, Barry Winograd, James Gerson, and Henry Jaenicke, *Montgomery's Auditing* 12th ed., August 13, 1999.	For example, the total of a report could be estimated based on samples taken from each stratum or category of values and then adding the means of these samples together.
Structuring	Breaking large currency transactions into amounts below $10,000 to avoid triggering CTR reporting requirements. Treasury Department's Recordkeeping and Reporting regulation (affectionately called the BSA Reg) at 31 CFR 103.11(gg).	Used to detect money laundering.
Stylometry	Tests for author authenticity, plagiarism, multiple authors, and other factors. Patrick Juola, "Authorship Attribution, Foundations and Trends," in *Information Retrieval* 1, no. 3 (2006): 233–334.	Stylometry is often used to attribute authorship to anonymous or disputed documents.
Subterfuge	A deception by artifice or strategem in order to conceal, escape or evade. www.merriam-webster.com	Forensic operators cannot use this technique unless appropriately authorized or explicitly permitted. See also subterfuge. See also, pretext.

Description	Explanation and Source	Source: Forensic Context
Surveillance	Continual or intermittent covert observation of a party(s) who is a suspect or potential suspect in order to obtain evidence pursuant to an assignment.	The term, *surveillance* is most often associated with military or law enforcement activities. However, it is routinely used by civilian forensic operators. For example, observing the number of automobiles using a car wash over a one-week period in order to compare against reported revenues is a form of civilian surveillance. Note that in civilian and noncivilian matters, authority must always be obtained before attempting to gather evidence in such a manner.
TAPTA	Total Accounts Payable to Total Assets—A variation of TATA.	This ratio is a drill-down of TATA. Unusual changes in the pattern of the relationship may indicate that financial manipulations are being hidden in accounts payable. An increase in this ratio indicates increased pressure on the ability to meet current obligations, which provides an incentive for manipulation.
TARTA	Total Accounts Receivable to Total Assets—A variation of TATA.	This ratio is a drill-down of TATA. Unusual changes in the pattern of the relationship may indicate that financial manipulations are being hidden in accounts receivable. An increase in this ratio may indicate company growth if consistent with sales and gross margin growth. It may also be a signal, however, that receivables may not be realized in full and may have been manipulated.
TATA	Total Accruals to Total Assets—See M-Score. Total Accruals are calculated as the change in working capital accounts other than cash, less depreciation. Used to proxy for the extent to which cash underlies reported earnings.	A business usually has a relatively consistent or explainable pattern in its financial relationships. High levels of accruals (therefore, less cash) relative to assets can be an indicator of financial statement manipulation.

(continued)

Description	Explanation and Source	Source: Forensic Context
TCATA	Total Current Assets to Total Assets—A variation of TATA.	This ratio is a drill-down of TATA. Unusual changes in the pattern of the relationship may indicate that financial manipulations are being hidden in current assets. Alternatively, a decrease in this ratio signals a decrease in liquidity and may potentially indicate that the increase in noncurrent assets relative to current assets may have been manipulated.
TDTA	Total Deferrals to Total Assets—A variation of TATA.	This ratio is a drill-down of TATA. Unusual changes in the pattern of the relationship may indicate that financial manipulations are being hidden in deferrals.
Three Bs	Law enforcement sometimes refers to fraud motivators as the "Three B's." The motivators for male suspects are "Booze, Bucks, or Broads." The motivators for female suspects are "Booze, Bucks, or Boys."	Forensic operators can use the paraphrase as guidance when seeking input on suspect behavior patterns.
Three-Legged Stool	Cost, Precision, and Timing.	Phraseology used by forensic operators to deal with unreasonable clients, agencies, courts, and so on. For example, a client may demand certain things from a forensic operator, but cannot expect him to achieve all three, that is, cost minimization, precision results, and short-fuse timing. The retort is "Pick any two."
Time, Tools, and Talent	Phraseology suggesting that extraordinary achievements are possible with sufficient combinations of time, tools, and talent.	Forensic operators use the guidance to develop staff, i.e. insuring they have the requisite time, tools and talent necessary for the profession.
Timeline Analysis	Sequential visual representation of the timing of relevant events.	Assists with shaping of relevant facts and circumstances.
TITA	Total Inventory to Total Assets—A variation of TATA.	This ratio is a drill-down of TATA. Increases in this ratio (driven by increases in inventory) not commensurate with sales growth and gross margin growth may indicate manipulation of inventory accounts.

Description	Explanation and Source	Source: Forensic Context
Tobin's Q	$$\frac{\text{Equity Market Value} + \text{PS}^{*} + \text{Debt}^{**}}{\text{Total Assets}}$$ *PS = liquidated value of preferred stock **Debt = LTD + Current Liabilities – Current Assets Chung and Pruitt, "A Simple Approximation of Tobin's Q," *Financial Management* 23 (3), Autumn 1994.	Compares the market value of a firm to the replacement cost of its assets. Higher Tobin's Q = higher expectation of a firm's growth. Can be influenced by market hype and intangible assets.
Tools	Forensic operators should carry certain tools likely to be necessary in many circumstances.	Examples include: A cell phone containing a camera with both still shot and video and audio capabilities. A small magnifying glass; some models are credit card– sized and flexible and fit in a wallet. A small LED flashlight (www.surefire.com)
Trending Analysis	Direct method of financial statement analysis—Past trends of financial results are used to predict future results.	For example, in lost-profits cases, if a company historically did not make a profit before the event date, they will have to provide more compelling evidence to support that profits were actually lost due to the event.
Trust	A legal entity created by a grantor for the benefit of designated beneficiaries under the laws of the state and the valid trust instrument.[4]	Note the legal distinction.
Trustee	Person holding property in trust. Restatement, Second, Trusts, §3(3). The person appointed, or required by law, to execute, or trust.[5]	Note the legal distinction.

(continued)

[4] *Black's Law Dictionary*, 6th ed. (St. Paul, MN: West Publishing, 1990), 1508.
[5] Ibid., 1514.

Description	Explanation and Source	Source: Forensic Context
T-Statistic/ Distribution	A family of probability distributions often used to develop interval estimates of a population mean whenever the population standard deviation is unknown and the population has an approximately normal probability distribution or when the sample is small. Mark W. Shirley, CPA/ABV, CVA, CFFA, CFE, *NACVA Consultant's Training Institute,* V & L Consultants, LLP, November 18, 2008.	Regression analysis.
Tunnel vision	A stress-induced physiological condition where the field of vision is constricted.	Forensic operators must recognize the condition in order to counter it, i.e. during stressful circumstances such as trial testimony.
Unique Facts & Circum-stances	Report header phraseology that alerts the reader to the key drivers of the report analysis and conclusions.	Useful to guide readers toward the correct conclusion.
Unit and Volume Method	Internal Revenue Service Indirect Methods (IRM 4.10.4.6.7).	In many instances, gross receipts may be determined or verified by applying the sales price to the volume of business done by the taxpayer. The number of units or volume of business done by the taxpayer might be determined from the taxpayer's books, as the records under examination may be adequate as to the cost of goods sold or expenses. In other cases, the determination of units or volume handled may come from third-party sources.
Urine, color of	Normally, urine will be very pale yellow, similar to a manila folder. The darker the color, the greater one is dehydrated.	Forensic operators must stay hydrated, particularly in stressful environments such as interviewing, interrogation, behavior detection, surveillance, undercover, combat, trial testimony, and so forth.
Variables Sampling	When using classical variables sampling, auditors treat each individual item in the population as a sampling unit.	Based on the results of the sample, you can use estimating techniques to project the results to the population, such as mean per unit, ratio, and difference.

Description	Explanation and Source	Source: Forensic Context
Variance	The arithmetic mean of the sum of the squared differences of the mean. (The square of the standard deviation.)	Useful for comparing dispersion within and among different data sets.
Vertical Analysis	Direct method of financial statement analysis—Each entry for each of the three major categories of accounts (assets, liabilities, and equity) is represented as a percentage of the total category.	Balance sheets of businesses of all sizes can easily be compared. It also makes it easy to see relative annual changes within one business.
www.veromi.com	This is a gateway site that aggregates people specific information. Its contents are free at the first level and provide progressively more expensive information depending upon the length of time the user desires to access the site. Veromi: www.veromi.com.	The first level of information (free) is often sufficient for forensic operators and thus precludes the need to purchase additional access.
Weighted Average (3-2-1)	The mean of a three-year horizon that weights the numerator to give more representation of the most current year, with successively less for presentations for prior years. The chosen weights should reflect a business cycle or other rationale.	Useful for measuring comparative central tendencies, and rates of change.
Wicklander-Zulawski & Associates, Inc.	This site offers highly regarded text and training resources on interviewing and interrogation techniques. www.w-z.com.	Forensic operators upgrade and refine their people investigation skills through the content on this site.
White Yellow Orange Red	System to differentiate states of mind adapted from the U.S. Marine Corps. By John Dean "Jeff" Cooper. White—Unaware and unprepared Yellow—Relaxed alert Orange—Specific alert Red—Fight As the level of danger increases, your willingness to take certain actions increases. Jeff Cooper, *Principles of Personal Defense* (Boulder, CO: Paladin Press, 2006).	This concept can be applied to a subject's willingness to commit fraudulent or other criminal acts.

(*continued*)

Description	Explanation and Source	Source: Forensic Context
Wigmorean Chart	Graphical method for the analysis of legal evidence in trials. J. H. Wigmore, "The Problem of Proof," *Illinois Law Review* (1913), 77–103. Jean Goodwin, "Wigmore's Chart Method," *Informal Logic* 20, no. 3 (2000): 223–243.	A scheme for representing arguments in a tree diagram to help analyze the proof of facts at trial and assess the strength of an argument in meeting objections.
WPN (Weapon)	Words, Pictures, Numbers. Text that describes, visuals that reflect, and data that quantifies the contents of a document. Darrell D. Dorrell, "WPN, that is, "Weapon," *National Litigation Consultant's Review,* September 2004.	The most effective component in communicating a message to a reader depends on the reader. Some readers are textually oriented, some are visually oriented, and some are data oriented. Virtually all readers, however, are oriented toward a combination of these factors.
Year-to-Year Common-Size Percentage Change	Measures the year-to-year raw percentage increase or decrease of each common-size item.	Useful for establishing and comparing magnitudes of change.
Year-to-Year Common-Size Raw Change	Measures the year-to-year increase or decrease of each common-size item.	Useful for establishing and comparing magnitudes of change.
Year-to-Year Percentage Change	Measures the year-to-year percentage increase or decrease of each item.	Useful for establishing and comparing magnitudes of change.
Year-to-Year Raw change	Measures the year-to-year raw increase or decrease of each item.	Useful for establishing and comparing magnitudes of change.
Z-Statistic	Measures the distance of a value within a data set from the mean.	Forensic operators use the Z-statistic to identify the extreme values, thus focusing attention on those values exhibiting greatest variability.

Bibliography

This bibliography is noticeably shorter than typical bibliographies. The reason is simple. There is little coverage of the financial forensics discipline as discussed in the Introduction section of this book. Nonetheless, certain works as indicated here merit attention, at least in part. Also, note the dates on some of the works, because some were published near the turn of the last century. They contain timeless content.

Abrams, Jay B. *Quantitative Business Valuation.* New York: McGraw-Hill, 2001.

ACM IV Security Services. *Secrets of Surveillance: A Professional's Guide to Tailing Subjects by Vehicle, Foot, Airplane, and Public Transportation.* Boulder, CO: Paladin Press, 1993.

———. *Surveillance Countermeasures: A Serious Guide to Detecting, Evading, and Eluding Threats to Personal Privacy.* Boulder, CO: Paladin Press, 1994.

———. *Countering Hostile Surveillance: Detect, Evade, and Neutralize Physical Surveillance Threats.* Boulder, CO: Paladin Press, 2008.

Albrecht, W. Steven, and Chad Albrecht. *Fraud Examination and Prevention.* Mason, OH: South-Western, 2004.

Analyzing Financial Statements. New York: American Bankers Association, American Institute of Banking Section, 1939.

Babitsky, Steven, Esq., and James J. Mangraviti Jr., Esq. *Writing and Defending Your Expert Report: The Step-by-Step Guide with Models.* Falmouth, MA: SEAK Inc., 2002.

Ballantine, Henry Winthrop. *Ballantine on Corporations.* Chicago: Callaghan and Company, 1927.

Barson, Kalman A. et al., eds., *Income Reconstruction: A Guide to Discovering Unreported Income.* New York: American Institute of Certified Public Accountants, 1999.

Bellos, Alex. *Here's Looking at Euclid.* New York: Free Press, 2010.

Benson, Ragnar. *Ragnar's Guide to Interviews, Investigations, and Interrogations: How to Conduct Them, How to Survive Them.* Boulder, CO: Paladin Press, 2000.

Black, Henry C. *Black's Law Dictionary* 6th ed. St. Paul, MN: West Publishing, 1990.

Bragg, Steven M. *Business Ratios and Formulas: A Comprehensive Guide.* Hoboken, NJ: John Wiley & Sons, 2002.

Castenholz, William B. *Higher Accountancy: Auditing Procedure.* Chicago: LaSalle Extension University, 1918.

Constitution of the United States. September 17, 1787.

Dantzker, M.L. *Understanding Today's Police* 3rd. ed. Upper Saddle River, NJ: Prentice Hall, Inc., 2003.

Devlin, Keith and Lorden, Gary. *The Numbers Behind NUMB3RS: Solving Crime with Mathematics*, New York, New York: Penguin Group (USA), Inc., 2007.

Ekman, Paul and Friesen, Wallace V. *Unmasking the Face: A Guide to Recognizing Emotions from Facial Expressions.* Los Altos, CA: Malor Books, 2003.

Foundations of Freedom. Virginia Beach, VA: American Center for Law and Justice.

Fraud Examiner's Manual 3rd ed. vols. 1–3. Austin, TX: Association of Certified Fraud Examiners, 1998.

Frey, Bruce. *Statistics Hacks.* Sebastopol, CA: O'Reilly, 2006.

Fitzpatrick, Colleen. *Forensic Genealogy.* Fountain Valley, CA: Rice Book Press, 2005.

Golden, Thomas W., Steven L. Skalak, and Mona M. Clayton. *A Guide to Forensic Accounting Investigation.* Hoboken, NJ: John Wiley & Sons, 2006.

Gonick, Larry and Woollcott Smith. *The Cartoon Guide to Statistics.* New York: HarperCollins, 1993.

Graham, Benjamin and David Dodd. *The Classic 1934 Edition—Security Analysis.* New York: McGraw-Hill, 1934.

Gray, A. M. *War Fighting.* Washington, DC: United States Marine Corps, 1989.

Griffith, James B., et al. *Cyclopedia of Commerce, Accountancy, Business Administration.* Chicago: American School of Correspondence, American Technical Society, 1909.

Grudem, Wayne. *Politics According to the Bible: A Comprehensive Resource for Understanding Modern Political Issues in Light of Scripture.* Grand Rapids, MI: Zondervan, 2010.

Goldrick, Dr. Monica and Gerson, Dr. Randy. *Genograms in Family Assessment*, 3rd ed. W. W. Norton & Company, Inc., 2002.

Hetherington, Cynthia. *Business Background Investigations: Tools and Techniques for Solution-Driven Due Diligence.* Tempe, AZ: Facts on Demand Press, 2007.

Hill, Dan. *Emotionomics.* Edina, MN: Adams Business & Professional Publishing, 2007.

Holy Bible. 8th New International Version (NIV). Grand Rapids, MI: Zondervan, 1984.

Huber, Esq., Ezra and Donald A. Glenn. *Forensic Accounting for Divorce Engagements: A Practical Guide* 2nd ed. New York: American Institute of Certified Public Accountants, 2005.

Huff, Darrell. *How to Lie with Statistics.* New York: W. W. Norton & Company, 1954.

Interrogation Techniques and Tricks to Secure Evidence. Boulder, CO: Paladin Press, 1991.

Inbau, Fred E., Reid, John E., Buckley, Joseph P., and Jayne, Brian C. *Criminal Interrogations and Confessions, 5th.* Sudbury, MA: Jones and Bartlett Publishers, 2012.

Inbau, Fred E., Reid, John E., Buckley, Joseph P., and Jayne, Brian C. *Essentials of the Reid Technique: Criminal Interrogations and Confession, 5th.* Sudbury, MA: Jones and Bartlett Publishers, 2005.

Jablonsky, Stephen F. and Noah P. Barsky. *The Manager's Guide to Financial Statement Analysis.* New York: John Wiley & Sons, 1998.

Johnson, H. Thomas and Robert S. Kaplan. *Relevance Lost: The Rise and Fall of Management Accounting.* Boston: Harvard Business School Press, 1987.

Kennedy, D. James. *Reclaiming the Lost Legacy: The Founders and the First Amendment.* Fort Lauderdale, FL: Coral Ridge Ministries, 2001.

Kolb, David A. *Experiential Learning: Experience as the Source of Learning and Development.* Upper Saddle River, NJ: Prentice Hall, Inc., 1983.

Lang, Eva M. and Tudor, Jan Davis. *Best Websites for Financial Professionals, Business Appraisers, and Accountants*, 2nd ed. Hoboken, NJ: John Wiley & Sons, 2003.

Lee, Dr. Richard G., *American Patriot's Bible.* Nashville, TN: Thomas Nelson, 2009.

Licona, Michael R. *Paul Meets Muhammad: A Christian-Muslim Debate on the Resurrection.* Grand Rapids, MI: Baker Books, 2006.

Lindquist, Robert J., Tedd A. Avey, G. Jack Bologna, and Joseph T. Wells. *The Accountant's Handbook of Fraud and Commercial Crime* vols. 1–2. Toronto: The Canadian Institute of Chartered Accountants, 1999.

Lott, Jr., John R. *The Bias Against Guns: Why Almost Everything You've Heard About Gun Control Is Wrong.* Washington, DC: Regnery Publishing, 2003.

Lubet, Steven. *Expert Testimony: A Guide for Expert Witnesses and the Lawyers Who Examine Them.* Boulder, CO: National Institute for Trial Advocacy, 1999.

MacInaugh, Edmond A. *Disguise Techniques: Fool All of the People Some of the Time.* Boulder, CO: Paladin Press, 1984.

Maggio, Sharyn,Thomas Burrage Jr. *et al. A CPA's Guide to Family Law Services.* New York: American Institute of Certified Public Accountants, 2005.

Mason, R. Miles. *The Forensic Accounting Deskbook*. Washington, DC: ABA, 2011.

Mason, Robert D. *Statistical Techniques in Business and Economics* 4th ed. Homewood, IL: Richard D. Irwin, 1978.

Mlodinow, Leonard. *The Drunkard's Walk: How Randomness Rules Our Lives*. New York: Pantheon Books, 2008.

Nigrini, Mark J. PhD. *Digital Analysis Using Benford's Law: Tests & Statistics for Auditors* 2nd ed. Vancouver, BC, Canada: Global Audit Publications, 2000.

———. *Forensic Analytics: Methods and Techniques for Forensic Accounting Investigations*. Hoboken, NJ: John Wiley & Sons, 2011.

Nossen, Richard A. and Joan W. Norvelle. *The Detection, Investigation, and Prosecution of Financial Crimes* 2nd ed. Richmond, VA: Thoth Books, 1993.

Osborn, Albert S. *Questioned Documents*, 2nd ed. Albany, NY: Boyd Printing Company, 1929.

Paton, W. A. ed. *Accountant's Handbook*, 3rd ed. New York: Ronald Press, 1943.

Powell, Frederick J., *Parent and Subsidiary Corporations: Liability of a Parent Corporation for the Obligations of Its Subsidiary*. Chicago: Callaghan and Company, 1931. (Out of print—check a local law library.)

Rabon, Don and Chapman, Tanya. *Fraud-Related Interviewing*. Durham, NC: Carolina Academic Press, 2010.

Rabon, Don and Chapman, Tanya. *Interviewing and Interrogation*. Durham, NC: Carolina Academic Press, 2007.

Rabon, Don. *Investigative Discourse Analysis*. Durham, NC: Carolina Academic Press, 2007.

Rabon, Don. *Persuasive Interviewing*. Durham, NC: Carolina Academic Press, 2007.

Rabon, Don. *Interviewing and Interrogation*. Durham, NC: Carolina Academic Press, 1992.

Rand, Ayn. *Atlas Shrugged*. New York: Penguin Group, 1999.

Reference Manual on Scientific Evidence, Reference Guide on Economic Losses in Damages Awards, by Mark A. Allen, Robert E. Hall and Victoria A. Lazear, Federal Judicial Center, 2011.

Ritch, Van. *Rural Surveillance: A Cop's Guide to Gathering Evidence in Remote Areas*. Boulder, CO: Paladin Press, 2003.

Robinson, Maurice H. *Higher Accountancy: Organizing a Business*. Chicago: LaSalle Extension University, 1915.

Sample, John. *Methods of Disguise: Revised and Expanded*. Boulder, CO: Paladin Press, 1993.

Scott, Robert P. I. *The Investigator's Little Black Book: The Investigative Resource Used by Thousands of Private Investigators, Law Enforcement Agencies, Media Organizations* 3rd ed. Beverly Hills, CA: Crime Time Publishing, Co. Inc., 2002.

Scott, Robert P. I. *SkipTraceSeminar.com—The e-Book*. Beverly Hills, CA: Crime Time Publishing, Co., Inc. 2007.

Scoville, H. T. *Higher Accountancy: Principles of Accounting*. Chicago: LaSalle Extension University, 1916.

Senese, Louis C. *Anatomy of Interrogation Themes (The Reid Technique of Interviewing and Interrogation)*. Chicago: John E. Reid & Associates, Inc. 2008.

Silverstone, Howard and Michael Sheetz. *Forensic Accounting and Fraud Investigation for Non-Experts* 2nd ed. Hoboken, NJ: John Wiley & Sons, 2007.

Taylor, Frederick Winslow. *The Principles of Scientific Management*. New York: Harper and Brothers Publishers, 1911.

The United States Constitution Bill of Rights. December 15, 1791.

The Boy Scout Handbook. New Brunswick, NJ: National Council of the Boy Scouts of America, 1959.

The Unanimous Declaration of the Thirteen United States of America. July 4, 1776.

Thompson, George J. and Jerry B. Jenkins. *Verbal Judo: The Gentle Art of Persuasion*. Colorado Springs, CO: Quill, 1993.

Tudor, Jan Davis. *Super Searchers on Mergers & Acquisitions: The Online Secrets of Top Corporate Researchers and M&A Pros*. Medford, NJ: CyberAge Books, 2001.

Tudor, Jan Davis. *The Business Valuation Internet Research Guide*. Raleigh, NC: Lulu Press, 2008.

Tufte, Edward R. *Envisioning Information*. Cheshire, CT: Graphics Press, 1990.

Tufte, Edward R. *The Visual Display of Quantitative Information*. Cheshire, CT: Graphics Press, 1983.

Wall, Alexander and Raymond W. Duning. *Analyzing Financial Statements*. New York: American Institute of Banking Section, American Banker's Association, 1930.

Weil, Roman L., Peter B. Frank, Christian W. Hughes, and Michael J. Wagner, eds. *Litigation Services Handbook: The Role of the Financial Expert* 4th ed. Hoboken: John Wiley & Sons, 2007.

Weil, Roman L., Michael J. Wagner, and Peter B. Frank, eds. *Litigation Services Handbook: The Role of the Accountant as Expert* 2nd ed. New York: John Wiley & Sons, 1995.

Wells, Joseph T. *Corporate Fraud Handbook: Prevention and Detection* 2nd ed. Hoboken, NJ: John Wiley & Sons, 2007.

White, Gerald I., Ashwinpaul C. Sondhi, PhD, and Dov Fried, PhD, eds. *The Analysis and Use of Financial Statements*. New York: John Wiley & Sons, 1994.

Woods, Brett F. *The Art & Science of Money Laundering: Inside the Commerce of the International Narcotics Traffickers*. Boulder, CO: Paladin Press, 1998.

Wormser, I. Maurice. *Disregard of the Corporate Fiction and Allied Corporation Problems*. New York: Baker, Voorhis, and Company, 1927.

Zulawski, David E. and Wicklander, Douglas E. *Practical Aspects of Interview and Interrogation*. Boca Raton, FL: CRC Press, LLC, 2002.

About the Authors and Contributors

Darrell D. Dorrell, CPA, MBA, ASA, CVA, CMA, DABFA, ABV, CFF, is a founding partner of **financialforensics®**, a boutique financial forensics practice in Lake Oswego, Oregon. He practices in civil and criminal matters throughout the United States and has served as an expert witness or consultant in approximately 500 or so matters; additional assignments exceed 1,000. They include alter ego, antitrust, bankruptcy, breach of contract, breach of fiduciary duties, estate and gift taxes, family law, financial forensics, forensic accounting, fraud, fraudulent conveyance and transfer, intellectual property, lost profits, patent, solvency and insolvency, trademark, trade dress, and trade secrets, among others. He is a former Price Waterhouse partner.

Darrell is a nationally recognized speaker and author and has delivered more than 150 training sessions on forensic accounting–related topics since 2007. His presentations span 24 states (including 13 state CPA societies), Puerto Rico, and Canada, and include both continuing professional education (CPE) and continuing legal education (CLE) content. He has provided training to the Federal Bureau of Investigation (FBI), United States Department of Justice (USDOJ), Securities and Exchange Commission (SEC), American Bar Association, Bankruptcy Bar Association, Oregon Bar Association, Washington Bar Association, American Society of Appraisers (ASA), American Institute of Certified Public Accountants (AICPA), National Association of Certified Valuation Analysts (NACVA), Association of Certified Fraud Examiners (ACFE), Association of Insolvency and Restructuring Advisors (AIRA), Institute of Management Accountants, American Accounting Association (AAA), International Law Enforcement Auditors Association, SEAK (Skills, Education, Achievement, Knowledge), CPAA International, Inc., AGN, Inc., and Turnaround Management Association, among others. He has received several distinctive awards for his speaking and training.

Darrell has published more than 70 articles in the *American Journal of Family Law, Business Appraisal Practice, CPA Journal, Financial Valuation and Litigation Expert, Sarbanes-Oxley Compliance Journal, Litigation Counselor, National Litigation Consultants Review, Valuation Examiner,* RIA's *Valuation Strategies,* and the *United States Attorneys' Bulletin.* He has also been cited in *Bloomberg Wealth Manager, BusinessWeek, IR Magazine,* the Portland *Oregonian, Practical Accountant, Drunkard's Walk: How Randomness Rules Our Lives* (a *New York Times* best-seller), and authored the forensic accounting chapter in *Valuation for Dummies.* He has also been featured on National Public Radio (NPR) WYNC's RadioLab program, the Small Business Television network, and the "First Business News Network Television."

His financial forensics, forensic accounting, investigative, litigation, valuation, fraud, and related expertise are extensive. Most significantly, he developed the

Forensic Accounting/Investigation Methodology (FA/IM), and he co-authored with Greg Gadawski "Financial Forensics I—Counterterrorism: Conventional Tools for Unconventional Warfare," 53, no. 2, March 2005 issue and "Financial Forensics II—Forensic Accounting: Counterterrorism Tactical Weaponry" 53, no. 3, May 2005 issue for the United States Department of Justice. Both issues are contained in this book and are available on the website: www.usdoj.gov/usao/eousa/foia_reading_room/foiamanuals.html.

Gregory A. Gadawski, CPA/ABV, CVA, CFE, CIRA, is a partner of **financialforensics®**. He is a certified public accountant (CPA), accredited in business valuation (ABV), certified valuation analyst (CVA), certified fraud examiner (CFE), and certified insolvency and restructuring advisor (CIRA). He is a member of the Oregon Society of Certified Public Accountants (OSCPA), the American Institute of Certified Public Accountants (AICPA), the National Association of Certified Valuation Analysts, the Association of Certified Fraud Examiners, and the Association of Insolvency and Restructuring Advisors.

Mr. Gadawski has executed many complex fraud investigations on behalf of both victims and suspects. These investigations have ranged from small employee thefts to multimillion-dollar frauds. In addition to conducting the investigations, Mr. Gadawski has assisted the victims with the identification of assets and recovery of losses from fraud. He has also served as forensic accountant to the receiver in multiple receiverships. These receiverships are typically the result of various types of securities fraud or Ponzi scheme or both. As forensic accountant to the receiver, Mr. Gadawski has provided transaction analysis, asset tracing, identification and investigation of targets for third-party litigation, solvency analysis, testimony in civil and criminal matters, and other services for the benefit of the receivership estate.

Mr. Gadawski has served as an expert witness or consultant in a variety of complex litigation matters, including breach of contract, business valuation, alter ego, lost profits, marital dissolution, personal injury, wrongful death, intellectual property infringement, fraudulent conveyance, solvency, and others. His expertise encompasses a wide scope of industries, including professional service organizations, brokerages, financial services, construction, retail, timber, utilities, municipalities, not-for-profits, manufacturing, and others. He has authored and co-authored several forensic accounting and litigation consulting related articles. He has presented continuing education courses (both CPE and CLE) on forensic accounting, financial statement analysis, fraud investigation, and litigation-related topics. Mr. Gadawski also serves as an instructor for the Forensic Accounting Academy as sponsored by National Association of Certified Valuation Analysts (NACVA) and the Consultants' Training Institute. NACVA acknowledged him as Instructor of the Year for 2010. He co-authored, with Darrell D. Dorrell, "Financial Forensics I—Counterterrorism: Conventional Tools for Unconventional Warfare" 53, no. 2, March 2005 issue and "Financial Forensics II—Forensic Accounting: Counterterrorism Tactical Weaponry" 53, no. 3, May 2005 issue for the United States Department of Justice. Both issues are contained in this book and are available on the website: www.usdoj.gov/usao/eousa/foia_reading_room/foiamanuals.html.

CONTRIBUTING AUTHORS

The following experts devoted extraordinary time, effort, patience, and wisdom to the construction, review, and editing of this book. Their efforts were in addition to their thriving professional practice and busy personal lives. The book simply could not have been completed without their collective knowledge, expertise, experience, and integrity. The authors are deeply grateful to have them as friends and colleagues. The authors are also privileged to have the contributing authors' vast capabilities represented in this book.

Heather D. Barnette, BS, is the chief financial officer for **financialforensics®** in Lake Oswego, Oregon. She is responsible for the preservation and development of the firm's people and financial assets, human resources policies, and IT and communications infrastructure and security. She specializes in background and asset searches in forensic assignments and often augments the firms "second set of eyes" review policy by adding a cold third review, particularly in prefinal reports and reports requiring permanent binding. She demonstrates unwavering personal commitment to the firm by working many late nights and weekends, often on short notice. This book would not have been possible without her contributions.

Heidi Bowen, CPA, CFE, is an associate with **financialforensics®**. She was formerly a criminal financial investigator with the Oregon Department of Justice and has served in the Oregon Department of Revenue. She has 20 years of professional experience in fraud investigation, business and personal taxation, and litigation support services. Ms. Bowen's litigation and fraud investigation–related experience includes a variety of complex matters in a wide scope of industries, including construction, retail, not-for-profit, municipalities, securities, and several others. Furthermore, she is a graduate of the Forensic Accounting Academy. She has served as an expert witness in various cases, including embezzlement, arson, elder abuse, and murder. Heidi has specialized expertise in subject interrogation, digital analysis using IDEA software, and has uncommon abilities in report review and editing. She holds a BS in business from Portland State University. Heidi demonstrates her forensic operator nature by applying new forensic tools, techniques, methods, and methodologies to each assignment. She demonstrates her personal commitment to the firm by her willingness to work late nights or weekends, often on short notice. This book would not have been possible without her contributions.

Cynthia A. Dorrell, LPN, is the marketing director for **financialforensics®** in Lake Oswego, Oregon, and is responsible for the firm's security and safety, maintaining logistics infrastructure uptime readiness levels and document and archival control. She serves in forensic assignments requiring specialized skill deployment in troubled companies and crisis situations such as hotels, automotive equipment, and investment advisors. She also maintains the firm's intellectual property (IP) assets such as compliance with United States Patent and Trademark Office (USPTO) requirements. Furthermore, she often augments the firm's "second set of eyes" review policy by adding a cold third review, particularly in prefinal reports and reports requiring permanent binding. She demonstrates unwavering personal commitment to the firm by working many late nights and weekends, often on short notice. This book would not have been possible without her contributions.

Kevin J. Gadawski, CPA, CVA, is the principal of NL Strategies, Inc. in Dana Point, California. He specializes in business consulting focused on litigation support for both valuation and forensic accounting matters such as alter ego, receivership, bankruptcy, fraud investigation, and shareholder actions. Mr. Gadawski also conducts financial and operational strategy sessions for distressed private and public companies focused on developing and executing initiatives to enable sustainable and profitable growth. Mr. Gadawski has successfully led companies through turnaround situations and has guided numerous companies through successful merger and acquisition (M&A) transactions. Mr. Gadawski has previously served as the president and owner of a successful medical device manufacturer, where he introduced and obtained regulatory clearance to market the first-of-its-kind device aimed at detecting prescription drug abuse, ultimately growing the product into the leading brand at major retailers. He has also served as the chief financial officer for several public entities in various industries, including software, medical device, and financial services and has led the internal audit department for a Fortune 500 company, where he developed a comprehensive program of fraud detection and prevention. This book would not have been possible without his contributions.

Janet F. Hunt, CPA, is an associate with **financialforensics**® in Lake Oswego, Oregon. She has several years' experience in public accounting, including auditing, taxation, and consulting services to companies in a wide variety of industries. She has also worked in a privately held business and local governmental agencies. Her expertise includes analysis of financial systems and transactions in small-to-medium-size privately held businesses. She has provided support in several forensic accounting matters, covering issues including lost profits, misappropriation of assets, and alter ego, and is a graduate of the Forensic Accounting Academy. She holds a BA in business from Oregon State University. Janet demonstrates her forensic operator nature by her exceptional diligence, eagerness, and perseverance to learn and apply new forensic tools, techniques, methods, and methodologies. She demonstrates her personal commitment to the firm by her willingness to work late nights or weekends, often on short notice. This book would not have been possible without her contributions.

Brien K. Jones is the director of education and conferences for the Consultants' Training Institute (CTI) and its affiliate organizations, the National Association of Certified Valuators and Analysts (NACVA), the International Association of Consultants, Valuators and Analysts (IACVA), the Institute of Business Appraisers (IBA), the Financial Forensics Academy (FFA), the Financial Forensics Institute (FFI), the American Institute for Expert Witness Education (AIEWE), and the Middle Market Investment Banking Association (MMIBA), all based in Salt Lake City, Utah. He has been directing business valuation and financial forensic certification and training programs for both live and online delivery for these organizations for nearly 15 years. He is well known throughout the business valuation and financial forensic industry as a seasoned association executive with extensive professional experience in continuing professional education management, online and distance learning, business development, building and maintaining strategic alliances, member recruitment and retention, marketing, graphic design, public relations, and managing association governance. He was honored as one of the first 40 Under 40 Rising Stars by *Utah Business* magazine (2003), has received a Diploma from the International Olympic Committee for his volunteerism as an international placard bearer for the Salt Lake City Winter Olympic Games (2002), and is recognized as an ambassador by the Salt Lake Convention and Visitors Bureau (1999). He serves on the industry advisory council for Associated Luxury Hotels International and is an advisor to the NACVA executive advisory board. Mr. Jones received his bachelor of behavioral science degree in public communication from Hardin-Simmons University.

Odalys Z. Lara, CPA, CVA, CFF, CFFA, CFD, is a principal of Perzel & Lara Forensic CPAs, PA, in Clearwater, Florida, and co-chairs the firm's litigation support department. Her extensive experience in providing a broad spectrum of professional services, including forensic accounting, auditing, tax, pension and estate planning, provides the technical foundation required to excel as a certified business valuation analyst (CVA), certified forensic financial analyst (CFFA) and certified fraud deterrence analyst (CFD). Over 20 years as a certified public accountant, with a wide variety of experience in many different industries, with differing accounting practices and methods, as well as significant tax issues, has provided the technical background needed in a professional providing business valuations, forensic and fraud prevention services, expert witness, and litigation support services. Odalys's ability to communicate clearly as well as withstand cross-examination and other courtroom dynamics strengthen a case by adding an unparalleled level of credibility and expertise. Clients depend upon her business valuation recommendations in the areas of divorce, mergers and acquisitions, buy-sell agreements, partner and stockholder agreements, damage losses, and succession and estate planning. Her experience includes valuation services for medical and professional practices, service businesses, construction, manufacturing, and so forth. Her varied background in working in many industries as well as her thirst for up-to-date technical information keeps her on the forefront of business valuation issues.

Miles Mason Sr., JD, CPA, is the founder of the Miles Mason Family Law Group, PLC, located in Memphis, Tennessee. He practices family law exclusively. An active member of the ABA Family Law Section, Mr. Mason serves as its liaison to the American Institute of Certified Public Accountants (AICPA), has served on its CLE committee, has attended its Trial Advocacy Institute, has presented at conferences, and has written for the *Family Advocate*. He is past chair of the Tennessee Bar Association's Family Law Section, served as editor of the section's newsletter, and served on the editorial board of the Tennessee Bar Journal. Mr. Mason has also presented at numerous national and regional conferences, including the AICPA's National Business Valuation Conference and National Forensic Accounting Conference, as well as at conferences and seminars held by NACVA and IBA, the Tennessee Society of CPAs, and the Mississippi Society of CPAs. He has authored articles for publications by the ABA Family Law Section, the Tennessee Bar Association, and the Georgia Bar Association Family Law Section. Mr. Mason is married and has three children.

To learn more about Mr. Mason and his practice, see www.MemphisDivorce.com. He demonstrates his unwavering personal commitment to the financial forensics discipline in many ways, including Internet marketing, exceptional technical guidance, and instruction in the Forensic Accounting Academy. This book would not have been possible without his contributions.

Patricia A. Perzel, CPA, CVA, CFFA, CFF, is the founder of Perzel & Lara Forensic CPAs, PA, in Clearwater, Florida, and has more than 30 years of experience testifying in both criminal and civil matters in state and federal courts, serving as an expert witness or consultant in the following types of cases: forensic accounting investigation, business valuations, hidden asset tracing, divorce litigation, money laundering, fraud deterrence, breach of contract, intellectual property infringement, patent, trademark, cyber piracy, estate and gift taxes, mergers and acquisitions, damage claims, business interruption claims, economic loss analysis, securities fraud, Ponzi schemes, personal injury, complex fraud schemes, shareholder and partner disputes, insurance damage claims, and embezzlement. Pat is frequently designated as a joint expert or a court-appointed expert in various litigation matters. Pat teaches and was also a contributing author for the development of the following publications and educational courses for the National Association of Certified Valuation Analysts (NACVA): The Fundamentals, Techniques and Theory of Business Valuations training course, Forensic Accounting Academy, Fraud Prevention and Detection training course, and Business Interruption and Damage Claims training course.

Andrew P. Ross, CPA, CVA, CFE, PFS, is a partner at Gettry, Marcus, Stern & Lehrer, CPA, PC, in Long Island, New York City, and Westchester, New York. Mr. Ross has more than 25 years of experience providing audit, tax, and litigation services to his clients, many of whom are in the service, manufacturing, and wholesale industries. He is also a member of the firm's Business Valuation and Litigation Support Group and Quality Control committee. Mr. Ross has constructed and contributed technical forensic indices materials and has instructed in the Forensic Accounting Academy curriculum. A graduate of Syracuse University, Mr. Ross is active in the New York State Society of Certified Public Accountants, Nassau Chapter, and in 2004, was elected chairman of the accounting and auditing committee, a position he held for six years. As committee chair, he lectured to members of the society in the areas of accounting and auditing updates. He is also a member of the American Institute of Certified Public Accountants.

Mark W. Shirley, CPA, ABV, CFF, CVA, CFFA, CFE is the managing partner of V & L Consultants, LLC, in Baton Rouge, Louisiana. His professional discipline and experience is in business valuation, forensic and investigative accounting, and financial analysis and modeling. Technical and academic materials have been published by Wiley Law Publications, Aspen Legal Press, and Business Valuation Resources (BVR), including: *Cost of Capital,* third and fourth editions, the *4th edition Workbook,* and *BVR's Guide to Personal v. Enterprise Goodwill.* Technical articles have been published in the *Valuation Examiner, BewertungsPraktiker* Nr., *The Practical Accountant, CPA Litigation Services Counselor, Gatekeeper Quarterly,* and the *Journal of Forensic Accounting.* Mr. Shirley has developed several training and continuing education courses for professional organization accrediting advanced accounting and finance disciplines. Also, advanced training courses have been developed in applied statistics and financial modeling. Mr. Shirley is an adjunct faculty member at the National Judicial College, University of Nevada at Reno, and on the advisory panel for *Mdex Online;* the *Daubert Tracker,* an online *Daubert* research database. Since 1996, Mr. Shirley has presented lectures in more than 50 U.S. cities, Puerto Rico, and Canada, including AICPA, the New York Society of CPAs, Louisiana Certified Public Accountants (LCPA), NACVA, the American Academy of Matrimonial Lawyers, the National Judicial College, the LSU Law Center, the FBI Academy, and numerous civic and professional organizations. Expert witness testimony has been provided before the U.S. Tax Court, federal district courts, U.S. Bankruptcy Court, Louisiana district courts, Tunica-Biloxi Indian Tribal Court, and local specialty courts.

Gabe Shurek, CFE, is a senior manager in the business valuation and litigation support group at Gettry, Marcus, Stern & Lehrer, CPA, PC, in Long Island, New York City, and Westchester, New York. Mr. Shurek has played active roles in health care–related fraud investigations, including medical practices suspected of being fraudulently incorporated. He has extensive knowledge of the uses and applications of data mining software (IDEA). He has 10 years of experience in forensic accounting and fraud detection, and has been engaged by attorneys to perform services and various complex litigation matters, including shareholder dispute, breach of contract, and damage calculations. He has managed engagements and various types of federal and state commercial matters and applied forensic techniques in the bankruptcy cases in which he represented bankruptcy trustees, debtors, and creditors' committees, and assignments such as solvency analysis and investigation for fraudulent conveyance. Mr. Shurek is a contributing author and co-presenter for the Forensic Accounting Academy concerning data mining techniques and other fraud detection methods. Mr. Shurek received his bachelor of business administration and accounting degree from Dowling College.

Mark S. Warshavsky, CPA, ABV, CFF, MBA, CVA, CBA, CFE, DABFA, CFFA, is partner in charge of the Business Valuation and Litigation Support Group at Gettry, Marcus, Stern & Lehrer, CPA, PC, a multi-office accounting and advisory firm in Long Island, New York City, and Westchester, New York. He's also a member of the firm's executive committee. He has been a consultant to individuals, businesses, law firms, financial institutions, and insurance companies, providing services in varied areas of litigation support, forensic accounting, and business valuation. He has served as an expert witness and consultant, as well as a court-appointed expert and arbitrator, and has been retained in both federal and state cases. Some of his engagements have covered lost profits and commercial damage modeling, shareholder dispute resolutions, contract disputes, marital dissolution, wrongful termination, fraud investigations, business bankruptcy, and gift and estate tax filings. Mr. Warshavsky also represents high net worth individuals and was a featured guest on WNYW-TV Fox 5's *Good Day New York,* discussing "Uncovering Hidden Assets During a Divorce." Mr. Warshavsky dedicates his expertise to his profession and community through participation in various organizations. He is a past president of the New York State Society of CPAs, Nassau County Chapter, which has more than 5,000 members. He is a member of Adelphi University's School of Business Administration

Advisory Board and is a past member of the board of directors of the American Heart Association, Long Island region, and the Professional Experience in Placement Advisory Board for Long Island University, C.W. Post College.

Mr. Warshavsky is a national instructor for the National Association of Certified Valuation Analysts and has lectured to its Consultants' Training Institute and various state CPA societies. Mr. Warshavsky has been presented with the Instructor of Exceptional Distinction award by NACVA for the past several years. His lecture audiences have included CPAs, business valuators, forensic accountants, and attorneys. He is a founding member of the five-day Forensic Accounting Academy, where he provides course materials and instruction. Mr. Warshavsky is on the editorial advisory board of several national publications, peer-reviewing transcripts in the fields of business valuation, forensic accounting, litigation support services, and expert testimony. He has also been a contributing author for courses in the areas of business valuation and forensic accounting for NACVA's accreditation curriculums. He serves on NACVA's exam-grading committee, critiquing business valuation reports of candidates for the Certified Valuation Analyst (CVA) designation. He is the immediate past chairman of the New York State Society of CPAs statewide Business Valuation Committee. He demonstrates his unwavering personal commitment to the financial forensics discipline in many ways, including Internet marketing, exceptional technical guidance, and instruction in the Forensic Accounting Academy. This book would not have been possible without his contributions.

Paul E. Zikmund, CFE, CFFA, serves as senior director for forensic audits at Tyco International, which has corporate offices in Schaffhausen, Switzerland, and Princeton, New Jersey. He is responsible for managing a global team providing fraud investigation, detection, and deterrence services to help reduce and manage the company's fraud risk. He has nearly 20 years of experience in this field and has effectively managed global fraud and forensic teams at various Fortune 500 companies. Paul, who is a certified fraud examiner and certified forensic financial analyst, designs and implements programs and controls to detect fraud. He manages investigations conducted in response to allegations of fraud, misconduct, or abuse occurring within Tyco. Paul also leads Tyco's fraud risk assessments and fraud awareness training. His years of public and private sector experience includes the investigation of complex financial frauds, conducting forensic audit engagements and fraud risk assessments, and providing litigation support for a variety of industries. Paul is a former Pennsylvania state trooper.

Index

Aberrant pattern detection
about, 131, 132, 472
and confirmation bias, 128
in counterterrorism, 390
data and patterns, 133, 134
in Laboratory Analysis stage, 120, 122
time-based patterns, 134, 138–146, 197, 214
use of, 132, 133
in valuation and litigation, 123
variation in patterns, 134, 147–149
visual, 134–137
Accept-reject testing, 440, 472
Accounting information versus financial information, 182, 183
Accurint, 75
ACL Desktop Edition, 271
ACL Services Ltd., 271
Actions of criminal investigation methodology, 419, 420
ActiveData, 271
Activity-based evidence, 341
Adequate (reasonable) capital test, 331, 340, 375, 377, 378, 388
Admissibility of evidence, 76, 81, 112–114, 116, 118, 315, 318, 409
Aguilar-Spinelli Test, 116, 472
All means dispersion, 227, 228, 497
Alter ego doctrine
about, 339, 340, 343, 344, 472, 473
beneficial interest, 345–348
civil cases, 338–340
corporate parent and subsidiary, 344–356
criminal cases, 340
determination of, 371
elements of, 344
federal cases, 358, 359
improper purpose, 344, 345
indicia of, 343, 344, 361, 364–369
investigations, 361–371
Krendls' study (1978), 356, 357
piercing the corporate veil, 338–340, 344–346, 356–361, 388–390
reports, 328
resources and references, 348–358
as source of terrorist funding, 338, 339, 387–390
state cases, 359, 360
tax liability cases, 339
Thompson's study (1991), 358
use of in counterterrorism, 384–386
use of with other civil actions, 341
Alter Ego Report Card, 363
Altman Z Score, 209, 289, 473. *See also* Z-statistic (Z Score)
American Institute of Accountants, 178
American Institute of Certified Public Accountants (AICPA), 28–30, 32, 176, 178, 179
Analysis of Transactions stage. *See* Transaction analysis
Anscombe, Francis, 216
Anscombe's quartet, 216
Antiterrorism and Effective Death Penalty Act of 1996 (AEDPA), 384, 385
Appeals, civil and criminal, 456
Arithmetic mean, 225–228, 496
Asset Quality Index (AQI), 210, 211, 289, 290, 294, 473
Attributes sampling, 389, 441, 473
Audits
about, 474
financial statements, 204
internal control, 175–181
interviews, 63, 64. *See also* Interviews
IRS audit technique guides. *See* Financial Status Audit Techniques (FSAT)
Myth, internal control, 175
use of ICE/SCORE, 106. *See also* ICE/SCORE
Authentication, 54, 474
Aversion cues, 66

Background investigation, 60, 75, 119, 199, 331, 437, 474, 477
Background research stage
about, 77, 420, 422
chart, 427
criminal investigations, 417–420
deliverables, 76, 77, 427
FA/IM diagram, 427
genograms, 341. *See also* Genograms
for interviews, interrogation, and behavior detection, 60, 63
potential issues, 76, 427
purpose of, 73, 74, 427

Background research stage (*Continued*)
  resources and references, 74–76, 427
  tasks to be performed, 76, 427
Badges of fraud, 330, 340, 372, 475
Balance sheet
  about, 396, 397
  BIC (Balance Sheet, Income Statement, Cash Flow Statement) methodology, 1, 173, 183, 186, 187, 477
  in economic benefit stream calculation, 296–299
  example, 397
  financial statement analysis, 183, 186–190, 397–399
  historical background, 402
  money laundering, 405. *See also* Money laundering
  test, 340, 374–376, 475, 508
Bank deposits and cash expenditures method, 257, 260–267, 475
Bank Secrecy Act, 337, 386
Bankruptcy, 340, 372. *See also* Solvency analysis
Behavior detection
  about, 55, 62, 77, 476
  background research for, 60, 63, 73–77
  deliverables, 61
  facial mapping and micro-expressions, 66, 67
  during Interview and Interrogation stage, 55, 56, 64
  tasks to be performed, 60
  verbal and nonverbal cues, 63–66
Behavior Pattern Recognition (BPR), 59, 477
Behavior patterns, 48, 59, 460, 477, 501, 512
Benchmarks/benchmarking
  about, 477
  transaction analysis, 205, 206
  variability in data, 214
Beneish, Messod D., 205, 209–211, 289
Benford, Frank, 272, 379. *See also* Benford's Law
Benford's Law
  about, 273, 341, 379, 440, 477
  application of, 274–277
  case study, 278, 279
  criteria for use of, 274
  First Digit test, 275–278, 381, 382
  First Three Digits test, 276–278, 381, 382
  First Two Digits test, 276–279, 381, 382
  historical background, 272, 273, 379
  implementation of, 277, 278
  Last Two Digits test, 276, 281
  Second Digit test, 276, 380–382
  statistical significance, 278
  use of in counterterrorism, 300, 379, 384
Bias. *See* Confirmation bias
BIC (Balance Sheet, Income Statement, Cash Flow Statement) methodology, 1, 173, 183, 186, 187, 477
BlackBookOnline, 75, 477
Blogs, 58, 478
Body language, 341, 503
Bonds, 468
Book value, 369
Bowen, Murray, 48
Bowen Theory, 48
Boy Scouts, 476
Breach of contract cases, 106, 199
Burden of proof, 342, 343, 454
Business Background Investigations (Hetherington), 75
Business Risk ratio, 203
"But for" development, 199

Capone, Alphonse (Al), 9, 338, 408
CaseWare International Inc., 271
Cash, mailing, 414
Cash current debt coverage ratio – coverage, 207
Cash flow
  profit compared, 183
  ratios, 206, 207
  statement. *See* Cash flow statement
  test, 340, 375–377, 508
Cash flow statement
  about, 401, 402
  BIC (Balance Sheet, Income Statement, Cash Flow Statement) methodology, 1, 173, 183, 186, 187, 477
  in economic benefit stream calculation, 296, 297, 302–304
  example, 404
  financial statement analysis, 183, 186, 187, 193–197, 403, 405
Cash Gap, 208
Cash Interest Coverage, 201, 207
Cash Realized from Operations (CRO), 144, 289–291, 294, 482
Cash-T technique, 327, 330, 479
Central tendencies, 148, 214, 215, 218, 225–229, 236, 237, 242, 244, 245, 250, 252, 479
Certified Financial Forensics (CFF), 462
Certified Forensic Financial Analyst (CFFA), 462
Certified Fraud Examiner (CFE), 462
Certified Public Accountants (CPAs), 461, 462
Chain of custody
  about, 479
  assignment development stage, 23
  and civil actions, 342
  computer evidence, 462, 463
  form, example, 23, 24
  Scoping stage, 38
Charitable organizations, 383–386, 391, 396, 414, 417, 500
Chebyshev's Theorem, 227, 479
Checkbook management, 203, 369
Chewbacca Defense, 480

Chi-square test
aberrant pattern detection, 147, 148
in stylometry, 165, 168–172
CICO (Concentric In-Concentric Out), 62, 480
Circadian Rhythms, 60, 62, 480
Civil actions, use of in counterterrorism. *See also* Counterterrorism
about, 337–343, 384–386
alter ego doctrine. *See* Alter ego doctrine
civil law, use of, 338–343
criminal versus civil actions, 341–343, 445, 456, 457
evidence of terrorist activities, 337, 341–343, 384–386, 392, 393, 395, 409
forensic accounting techniques, 340–342, 378–384, 390–423
fraudulent transfers. *See* Fraudulent transfers
solvency analysis. *See* Solvency analysis
Civil versus criminal actions, 341–343, 445–457
Classes of People Reliant Upon Financial Information
Originators of financial information, 10, 11, 125
Users, 10, 11, 125
Regulators, 10, 11, 125
Coefficient of Variation, 217, 230–233, 235, 236, 481
CombatCPA, 8, 482
Combat, xii, xv, 4, 339
breathing, combat, 481
Committee of Sponsoring Organizations of the Treadway Commission (COSO), 176, 179
Common-sizing, 184, 198, 217, 219–222, 237, 239–242, 370, 398, 399, 401, 402, 439, 482
Compound Annual Growth Rate (CAGR), 81, 217, 237, 246–249, 479
Comprehensive methods for financial statement analysis, 198, 199
Concentric In-Concentric Out (CICO), 62, 480
Confidential informants. *See* Informants, confidential
Confirmation bias
about, 122–124, 482
defined, 122
overcoming, methods for, 128–131
and roles of forensic operators, 124–128
Conflicts, 23, 25–27
Congress of Accountants (1904), 4, 8
Consumer Expenditure Survey (CES), 411, 412, 482, 495
Contradiction cues, 66
Control cues, 66
Corporations. *See also* Alter ego doctrine
parent and subsidiary, 344–356
piercing the corporate veil, 338–340, 344–346, 356–361, 388–390
Cost of goods sold, 191, 201, 257, 266, 268, 496, 514
Counterterrorism. *See also* Civil actions, use of in counterterrorism
and charitable organizations, 383–386, 391, 396, 414, 417, 500
criminal laws, 337
criminal versus civil actions, 341–343
digital analysis, use of, 383, 384. *See also* Digital analysis
evidence of terrorist activities, 337, 341–343, 384–386, 392, 393, 395, 409
financial profiling, 391–395
financial statement analysis, 395–408, 413, 414
forensic accounting techniques, 340–342, 378–385, 390–423
indirect methods, use of, 408–411, 413
money laundering, 337, 386, 391, 397, 399–403, 405–408, 483
9/11 terrorists, 393, 394
terrorist acts, 337, 338
terrorist funding sources, 386–395
Coverage of Fixed Charges, 201
Coverage ratios, 201, 202, 206
Credit reports, 466
Criminal investigation. *See also* Counterterrorism
embezzlement, 466–468. *See also* Embezzlement
and forensic accounting, 415–423
phases of, 418, 419
process map, 416, 417
seven-step method, 416–418
Criminal versus civil actions, 341–343, 445–457
CRO. *See* Cash Realized from Operations (CRO)
Currency Transaction Reports (CTRs), 337, 384, 386, 388, 483
Current ratio, 201, 375

Damages
"but for" test, 199
civil cases, 455, 456
economic benefit stream calculations, 207, 295. *See also* Economic benefit stream, calculation of
ICE/SCORE, use of, 96, 97, 103, 106
measures of, 200
reports, 328
Damages Report Card, 505
Data analysis phase. *See also* Forensic financial analysis
about, 423, 483
analysis of transactions. *See* Transaction analysis
Benford's Law. *See* Benford's Law
criminal investigations, 418, 419
of forensic accounting methodology, 14–16, 418, 419, 439–442

Data analysis phase (*Continued*)
laboratory analysis. *See* Laboratory analysis
self-reported data, 93–106, 506. *See also* ICE/SCORE
Data catalogs, 38, 48–52
Data collection
about, 420, 422
chart, 428
confidential informants. *See* Informants, confidential
criminal investigations, 418, 419
deliverables, 82–93, 428
FA/IM diagram, 428
forensic techniques, 439, 440. *See also* specific techniques
Interview and Interrogation Stage, 56
phase of forensic accounting methodology, 14, 15, 418, 419, 439
potential issues, 81, 82, 428
prerequisite phases, 79
purpose of, 79, 428
resources and references, 80, 81, 428
Scoping stage, 38
Surveillance. *See* Surveillance
tasks to be performed, 81, 428
transaction analysis. *See* Transaction analysis
undercover. *See* Undercover data collection
Data description, 252
Data dynamics, 252
Data investigation, 270. *See also* Digital analysis
Data management, 38, 39
Data mining, 270, 483. *See also* Digital analysis
Data set boundaries, 214, 217–225, 252
Database reporting, 270. *See also* Digital analysis
Dating sites, gathering information from, 57, 58
Days Sales in Receivable Index (DSRI), 20, 484
Days Sales Outstanding, 208
Days Working Capital, 208
Debt/Net Worth, 202
Decision analysis. *See* Multi-attribute Utility Analysis (MUA)
Degree of financial leverage, 203
Degree of operating leverage, 203
Depositions
about, 67
matrix, 61, 67–73, 416, 484
preparation for, 67
Depreciation Index (DEPI), 210, 484
The Detection of Earnings Manipulation (Beneish), 209, 289
Development stage of assignment
about, 54, 422
chart, 424
deliverables, identifying, 25–36, 424
FA/IM diagram, 424
potential issues, identifying, 25, 424
purpose of, 21, 22, 424
resources and references, 21, 22, 424
tasks to be performed, outlining, 23, 424
Digital analysis
about, 255, 270, 271, 380, 381, 484
advantages of, 271
Benford's Law. *See* Benford's Law
counterterrorism cases, 383, 384
duplicate numbers test, 272, 279–281, 380–383, 500
and forensic financial analysis, 215, 270
gap analysis, 255, 272, 282, 284, 285, 490
item listing, 272
link analysis, 272, 282–284, 495
querying data, 272, 285, 286
rounded numbers test, 272, 279, 281, 282, 381–383, 506
stratification, 272, 286, 287
stratified sampling, 287
techniques, 272
use of, 271, 272, 383, 384
Direct methods of financial statement analysis, 197, 198
Discovery, 38, 49, 67, 315, 451
Dispersion, 214, 227–236, 252, 484. *See also* Coefficient of Variation; Interquartile Range (IQR); Mean Average Deviation (MAD); Standard deviation; Z-statistic (Z Score)
Distance communication. *See* Proxemics
Divorce cases, 15, 74, 105, 199, 256, 330, 331, 489
Document maps, 38, 49, 52–54, 484
Document requests, 38
Donor logs, 414, 417
Double-entry method of accounting, 402
Drill-down method, 96, 157, 198, 211, 362, 484
Duplicate numbers test, 272, 279–281, 380–383, 500

Earnings before interest, taxes, depreciation, and amortization (EBITDA), 202, 207, 296, 331, 377
Earnings before interest and taxes (EBIT), 201, 203, 296, 377
Earnings before taxes (EBT), 202
Earnings manipulation, 205, 209–212
Earnings quality, 289–293
Economic benefit stream
calculation of. *See* Economic benefit stream, calculation of
composition of, 296, 297
and GAAP, 183
net income compared, 207
and reconciliation of internal and external data, 97
use of ICE/SCORE technique, 106
in valuation, 287, 288, 293. *See also* Economic benefit stream, calculation of

Economic benefit stream, calculation of
about, 294, 295
array historical economic benefit stream(s) (step 2), 295–297
array historical financial statements (step 1), 295, 296
compare and contrast outlooks (step 6), 295, 313, 314
conclusion regarding selected stream (step 7), 295, 314
estimate and visually array comparative outlooks (step 5), 295, 310–313
identify historical benefit stream(s) comparison sources (step 3), 295, 297–304
illustrate and quantify independent variables (step 4), 295, 301, 302, 304–311
Ekman, Paul, 66
Embezzlement
about, 485
financial statement analysis, 205, 206
response to suspected embezzlement, 457–469
risk reduction and protection against, 464, 469
Employees
employment law issues, 460, 461
termination of, 459, 463
Engagement letter, example, 27–33
Entity-party charts, 34–36, 38, 61, 437, 485
Event analysis, 119, 199, 341
Evidence
about, 485
activity-based, 341
admissibility, 76, 81, 112–114, 116, 118, 315, 318, 409
alter ego cases, 361–371
assessment of, consultative role of forensic operator, 127
authentication, 54, 474
burden of proof, 342, 343, 454
chain of custody. *See* Chain of custody
circumstantial evidence, 256, 409
confidential informants, 114, 420. *See also* Informants, confidential
criminal cases, 384, 453, 454, 457
data collection, 79. *See also* Data collection
depositions, 67. *See also* Depositions
direct evidence, 256
discovery requests, 49
fraudulent transfers, 372
patterns, 132, 133. *See also* Aberrant pattern detection
scoping, 40
surveillance, 111. *See also* Surveillance
suspicious transactions, 337
terrorist activities, 337, 341–343, 384–386, 392, 393, 395, 409
testimony and exhibits. *See* Testimony and exhibits
trial preparation, 317, 319, 420
types of, 49
undercover operations, 117, 420. *See also* Undercover data collection
Evidence-based analysis, 93. *See also* ICE/SCORE
Excel. *See* Microsoft Excel
Expectation attributes, 443, 485
Expectations-based statement analysis, 341, 438

FAB (Fabricated, Altered, Borrowed), 106, 330, 486
Facebook, 58
Facial Action Coding System (FACS), 67, 486
Facial mapping, 14, 54, 66, 67, 486
Fair market value, 369, 372, 373
FBI (Federal Bureau of Investigation), xi, xii, 11, 36, 125, 126, 337, 341, 393, 447
Fiduciaries and fiduciary duties, 339, 486
Financial forensics
defined, 6, 7, 63, 486
diagram, 6, 7
financial analysis. *See* Forensic financial analysis
Financial information
accounting information compared, 182, 183
presentation of in financial statements, 184, 185
reliance on, 10, 11, 125
Financial statements
about, 396
and accounting methods, 203, 204
analysis of in counterterrorism, 395–408, 413, 414
analysis of in litigation, 182, 199, 200
audited, 204
balance sheet. *See* Balance sheet
benchmarking, 205, 206
cash flow statement. *See* Cash flow statement
checkbook management, 203
compiled, 204
comprehensive methods of analysis, 198, 199
critiquing, 182, 197–199
direct methods of analysis, 197, 198
economic benefit stream calculation. *See* Economic benefit stream, calculation of
footnotes, 183
forensic indices, 204–212
Generally Accepted Accounting Principles (GAAP), 183
income statement. *See* Income statement
indirect methods of analysis, 197
manipulation indices, 209–212
measurement baselines, 203, 204
money laundering, detection of, 403, 405–408. *See also* Money laundering
normalization, 97, 287, 290, 293
OCBOA (Other Comprehensive Basis of Accounting), 203
ratio analysis, 200–205

Financial statements (*Continued*)
reading, 181–197
reviewed, 204
shoebox data, 203
tax-basis accounting, 204
60-Second Method for reading, 185–197
Financial Status Audit Techniques (FSAT)
about, 255, 256, 490
bank deposit and cash expenditures method, 257, 260–267, 475
indirect methods, 256, 257
markup method, 257, 260, 267, 268, 496
net worth method, 257, 261, 262, 269, 270, 338, 408, 419, 498
source and application of funds method, 257–260, 479
specific item method, 256
unit and volume method, 257, 260, 261, 268, 269, 514
Financing activities, 402
Flesch-Kincaid Grade Level scale, 152–155
Flesch Reading Ease Scale, 152–155
Foreign terrorist organization (FTO), 384, 385
Forensic accounting
defined, 6, 63, 487
reports, 329
techniques, summary of, 437–442
techniques used in counterterrorism, 340–342, 378–384, 390–423
Forensic Accounting/Investigation Methodology (FA/IM)
about, 1, 11, 14, 486
phases of. *See* Phases of forensic accounting methodology
purpose of, 4
reviews of, 1
U. S. Department of Justice publication of, 6
use of methodology, 14
Forensic data analysis, 214. *See also* Forensic financial analysis
Forensic Document Request
during data collection stage, 82
example, 84–93
ICE/SCORE methodology, use of, 83. *See also* ICE/SCORE
importance of, 84
preparing, 83, 84
Forensic financial analysis
about, 212–216, 252, 253
central tendencies, 148, 214, 215, 218, 225–229, 236, 237, 242, 244, 245, 250, 252, 479
data analysis component, 214, 215
data composition, 214, 218–222
data description component, 215–218
data set boundaries, 214, 222–225, 252
data set dispersion (spread), 214, 229–236, 252, 484
data set dynamics, 214, 235–251
digital analysis. *See* Digital analysis
Financial Status Audit Techniques. *See* Financial Status Audit Techniques (FSAT)
large data sets, 215, 218, 270, 273
methodology schema, 214–217
multi-attribute utility analysis (MUA), 215, 216, 221, 222, 225, 228, 229, 235, 236, 249–253, 327, 328
scoring model, completed, 252
scoring of central tendencies, 228, 229
scoring of data composition, 221, 222
scoring of data set boundaries, 225
scoring of data set dynamics, 249–251
scoring of dispersion, 235, 236
training and education, 212, 213
valuation assignments, use in. *See* Valuation and forensics
variability in data, 214, 215, 218
visuals, use of, 216, 220
Z-statistic, 233–235. *See also* Z-statistic (Z Score)
Forensic indices, 204–212, 293, 487
Forensic lexicology
about, 150, 487
Flesch-Kincaid Grade Level scale, 152–155
Flesch Reading Ease Scale, 152–155
intuition, 152
in Laboratory Analysis stage, 120, 122
Linguistic Style Analysis Technique (LSAT), 155–157, 495
Microsoft Word, use of, 152–155, 157
myWordCount, 157–163
Signature software, 163–172
stylometry, 163–172, 510
word analysis, 150, 151
Forensic linguistics, 487
Forensic operator(s)
about, 488
combined roles of, 128
commonalities, xii
consultative, 124, 127, 128
derivation of term, 5
enforcement role, 124, 126, 127
environmental hazards, 8
independent, 124–126
reliance on methodologies, xiii
requirements, 4
training, xi
use of this book, 5, 6, 10, 11, 14–17
Foundational phase
assignment development. *See* Development stage of assignment
criminal investigations, 418, 419

of forensic accounting methodology, 14, 418, 419, 422, 437
forensic techniques, 437. *See also* specific techniques
scoping. *See* Scoping stage of assignment
summary of, 422
Four-way bank reconciliation, 107. *See also* Proof-of-cash technique
Fraud. *See also* Embezzlement; Fraudulent transfers
actual, 372, 475
benchmarking, use of in financial statement analysis, 205, 206
civil, 489
constructive, 372, 475
counseling for victims, 468
criminal, 489
detection of and internal control, 175
reports, 329, 330
response to, 458–469
"Three B's" (booze, bucks, broads/boys) motivators, 460
truthfulness, assessment of, 64, 65
Fraudulent conveyance. *See* Fraudulent transfers
Fraudulent transfers
about, 340, 341, 372, 489
determining, 372, 373
examples, 373, 374
reports, 330
as source of terrorist funding, 338, 387–390
use of in counterterrorism, 384–386
Frequency distribution, 217–220, 275, 490
FSAT (Financial Status Audit Techniques). *See* Financial Status Audit Techniques (FSAT)
Full-and-false inclusion testing, 23, 38, 199, 390, 418, 437, 490
Funds Flow Coverage, 202, 207

Gap analysis, 255, 272, 282, 284, 285, 490
Generally Accepted Accounting Principles (GAAP), 183, 369, 370
Genograms, 38, 44–48, 61, 77, 114, 119, 341, 388, 437, 491
Genograms in Family Assessment (Goldrick and Gerson), 48
GenoPro, 46–48
Geometric mean, 217, 218, 237, 247–249, 496
Gerson, Randy, 48
Goldrick, Monica, 48
Goodness-of-fit, 278, 306, 307
Gross Margin Index (GMI), 209, 491
Gross profit margin comparison test, 406–408, 491
Gross profits (contribution margin), 184, 200, 370, 401

Hall, Edward T., 66, 341
Hay, David, 177
Hetherington, Cynthia, 75, 77
Historical background
Benford's Law, 272, 273, 379
events between 1910 and 1930, 8–10
internal control, 177–180
Horizontal analysis, 197, 212, 370, 398, 439, 491
Humintell.com, 59, 491

ICE/SCORE
about, 1, 93, 94, 492
components of methodology, 94, 95
and financial data analysis, 173
flow chart, 95
SCORE component, importance of, 104–106
Step 1, ICE–Reconcile, 95–98
Step 2, ICE–Validate, 98–100
Step 3, correlate using SCORE, 100–106
as submethodology of FA/IM, 15, 93
use of, 93, 106
IDEA, 271
Income statement
about, 399, 400
BIC (Balance Sheet, Income Statement, Cash Flow Statement) methodology, 1, 173, 183, 186, 187, 477
in economic benefit stream calculation, 296, 297, 300, 301
example, 400
financial statement analysis, 183, 186, 187, 190–193, 400, 401
historical background, 402
InData Corporation, 40
Independent parallel indicators, 414
Indirect methods
financial statement analysis, 197
IRS examinations, 256–270
use of in counterterrorism, 408–411, 413
Informants, confidential
about, 420, 422, 492
chart, 430
criminal investigations, 417, 418
deliverables, 117, 430
FA/IM diagram, 430
potential issues, 116, 430
purpose of stage, 114, 115, 430
resources and references, 115, 116, 430
tasks to be performed, 116, 430
Instrumentality rule, 348–353
Insurance coverage, 465, 468
Intellectual property infringement/theft, 182, 199, 200, 315, 340
Internal control
confusion concerning, 175–177
economic factors, 180

Internal control (*Continued*)
historical background, 177–180
professional factors, 181
recommendations for, 181
societal factors, 180
and transaction analysis, 175–181
Internal Control: How It Evolved in Four English-Speaking Countries (Hay), 177
Internal Revenue Service (IRS)
Audit Technique Guides (ATGs), 80, 81, 492
Financial Status Audit Techniques (FSAT). *See* Financial Status Audit Techniques (FSAT)
Internal Revenue Manual (IRM), 255, 256
Market Segment Specialization Program (MSSP), 80, 492
Revenue Ruling 59-60, 296, 372, 373
Interpersonal phase
about, 55, 56, 77
background research, 60, 63, 73–77, 422
behavior detection, 60–67
criminal investigations, 418, 419
of forensic accounting methodology, 14, 418, 419, 438
interviews and interrogation, 56, 59–61, 422
Interquartile range (IQR), 217, 230–233, 235, 236, 493
Interrogation
about, 55, 77, 420, 422, 492
background research for, 60, 63, 73–77
chart, 426
criminal investigations, 417
deliverables, 61, 426
employees, 463, 464
FA/IM diagram, 426
interviews and behavior detection, relationship to, 64
potential issues, 60, 61, 426
purpose of, 56, 426
resources and references, 59, 426
tasks to be performed, 60, 426
use of, 63
Interview Matrix, 60, 61, 484
Interviews
about, 55, 77, 420, 422, 493
background research for, 60, 63, 73–77
chart, 426
criminal investigations, 417
deliverables, 61, 426
FA/IM diagram, 426
importance of, 63
interrogation and behavior detection, relationship to, 64
potential issues, 60, 61, 426
purpose of, 56, 426
resources and references, 59, 426
tasks to be performed, 60, 426
verbal and nonverbal cues, 63–66
Interview Matrix, 60, 61, 484
Intuition, 152, 198, 457
Inventory, forensic, 471–516
Investing activities, 401, 402
IQR. *See* Interquartile Range (IQR)
Israeli Security Agency (ISA), 62, 476
Item listing method, 272, 493

Juola, Patrick, 163

Khanacademy.com, 121, 174, 493
Kinetic communication, 60, 61, 66, 341, 438, 494
KnowX.com, 75, 494
Krendl, Cathy J., 356, 357
Krendl, James R., 356, 357
Kurtosis, 230, 232, 494

Laboratory analysis
about, 420, 423
chart, 432
criminal investigations, 417, 418
deliverables, 122, 432
FA/IM diagram, 432
potential issues, 121, 122, 432
purpose of, 119, 120, 432
resources and references, 120, 121, 432
tasks to be performed, 121, 432
Law enforcement
filing reports with, 446, 466, 467
investigations, civil and criminal matters compared, 448–450
Legal and regulatory compliance
assignment development stage, 23
personal information, collecting, 57, 58
Leverage Index (LVGI), 210, 211, 495
Leverage ratios, 202, 206, 292
LexisNexis, 75
Lifestyle analysis, 117, 119, 495
Likert Scale Protocol, 495
Linguistic Style Analysis Technique (LSAT), 155–157, 495
Link analysis, 272, 282–284, 495
LinkedIn, 58
Liquidity ratios, 200, 206, 292, 375
Litigation Services Handbook (Weil), 421
Living expenses
bank deposits and cash expenditures method, 261, 264–266
modified net worth method, 409–411
source and application of funds method, 258, 259, 411–413, 479
Long-term debt to total capital, 202
Lost profits, 96, 97, 103, 106, 199, 200, 328, 513
LSAT (Linguistic Style Analysis Technique), 155–157, 495
Lying, 64–66, 74. *See also* Truthfulness, assessment of

M score, 209, 211, 289, 498
Marital dissolution. *See* Divorce cases
Markup method, 257, 260, 267, 268, 496
Mean
all means dispersion, 227, 228, 497
arithmetic, 225–228, 496
geometric, 217, 218, 237, 247–249, 496
truncated, 226–228, 497
Mean absolute deviation (MAD), 232, 236, 250
Mean average deviation (MAD), 148, 217, 230–233, 235, 236, 250, 293, 496
Median, 226–228, 497
Median average deviation, 230, 232, 496
Mergers and acquisitions, 340, 341, 374–376, 489
Methodologies
about, 1–5
counterterrorism forensic accounting, 415–422
defined, 1, 497
examples of, 2
Forensic Accounting/Investigation Methodology (FA/IM). *See* Forensic Accounting/Investigation Methodology (FA/IM)
FSAT (Financial Status Audit Technique), 1, 16, 255, 490
need for, 79
60-Second Method, 1, 16, 173, 182, 184–204, 471
Micro-expression, 63, 66, 67
Microsoft Excel
digital analysis software, 271
document maps, construction of, 52–54
entity-party charts, 34–36
forensic timeline, construction of, 40
genograms, construction of, 46
Microsoft PowerPoint, 34
document maps, construction of, 52–54
forensic timeline, construction of, 40
genograms, construction of, 46
Microsoft Word
document maps, construction of, 52–54
entity-party charts, 34
forensic timeline, construction of, 40
genograms, construction of, 46
Midrange, 225, 227, 228, 497
Millican, Peter, 163
Mode, 225, 227, 497
Modified net worth method, 408–411, 498
Money laundering, 337, 386, 391, 397, 399–403, 405–408, 483
Moving average, 217, 237, 242, 243, 498
MUA. *See* Multi-attribute Utility Analysis (MUA)
Multi-attribute Utility Analysis (MUA), 215, 216, 221, 222, 225, 228, 229, 235, 236, 249–253, 327, 328, 498
Myth, internal control, 175
MyWordCount, 157–163
MyWriterTools, 157

Nass-usa.com, 59, 477
National Council of Resistance of Iran (NCRI), 385
Negation cues, 66
Net worth method, 257, 261, 262, 269, 270, 338, 408, 419, 498
New Age Security Solutions, 59, 477
Newcomb, Simon, 272
(NI + NC)/Current LTD, 201
Nigrini, Mark J., 273, 379
Normalization, 97, 287, 290, 293, 500
Nossen, Richard A., 408, 415

Occupational Safety and Health Administration (OSHA), 338, 339
Off-book transactions, 285, 500
The Online Secrets of Top Corporate Researchers and M&A Pros (Tudor), 75
Operating cash flow, 201, 207, 401, 413
Operating ratios, 202, 206, 207, 292
Originators of financial information, 10, 11, 125
Other Comprehensive Basis of Accounting (OCBOA), 203, 204, 370
Outliers, 155, 501
Owners compensation, 184

P-value, 308, 503
PACER (Public Access to Court Electronic Records), 76, 501
Pacioli, Luca, 402
Paralinguistic communication, 63, 66, 341, 438, 501
Parent and Subsidiary Corporations (Powell), 348
Patterns
aberrant patterns. *See* Aberrant pattern detection
about, 501
Behavior Pattern Recognition (BPR), 59, 477
behavior patterns, 48, 460, 501, 512
evidence, 132, 133
People & money principle, 63, 133. *See also* Interpersonal phase
People's Mojahedin of Iran (PMOI), 385
Percentage change, 197, 198, 203, 217, 235–242, 246, 249, 304–306, 308, 309, 398, 406–408
Performance cues, 66
Personal injury/wrongful death cases, 182, 199, 200
Personal liability, 339
Phases of forensic accounting methodology
about, 14
data analysis, 14–16, 418, 419, 439–442. *See also* Data analysis phase

Phases of forensic accounting methodology (*Continued*)
  data collection, 14, 15, 418, 419, 439. *See also* Data collection
  foundational, 14, 418, 419, 422, 437. *See also* Foundational phase
  interpersonal communications, 14, 418, 419, 438. *See also* Interpersonal phase
  trial, 16, 419, 442, 443. *See also* Post-assignment review and evaluation; Testimony and exhibits; Trial preparation
Physiological considerations, 60, 62
Piercing the corporate veil, 338–340, 344–346, 356–361, 388–390. *See also* Alter ego doctrine
"Piercing the Corporate Veil: An Empirical Study" (Thompson), 358
Piercing the Corporate Veil: Focusing the Inquiry (Krendl and Krendl), 356, 357
Plaxo, 58
Post-assignment review and evaluation
  about, 420, 423
  chart, 436
  criminal investigations, 419
  deliverables, 333, 334, 436
  FA/IM diagram, 436
  potential issues, 333, 436
  purpose of, 327, 436
  resources and references, 327, 436
  tasks to be performed, 333, 436
Powell, Frederick J., 348, 360
PowerPoint. *See* Microsoft PowerPoint
Preliminary hypothesis, 61
Privilege, 25, 29, 30, 502
Probability-proportional-to-size sampling, 391, 502
Process maps, 11, 416–418, 421, 502
Professional judgment, 128, 129, 131, 502. *See also* Confirmation bias
Profit, 183
Profitability ratios, 292
Progressive average, 217, 237, 244, 245, 503
Proof-of-cash technique, 107–111, 503
Proxemics, 60, 63, 66, 341, 438, 503
Public Access to Court Electronic Records (PACER), 76, 501

QDE (Questioned Document Examination), 106, 330, 503
Querying data, 272, 285, 286
Quick ratio, 201, 375

R-Squared (R^2), 307, 504
R value, 307, 310
Range, data set boundaries, 223–225, 504
Ratio analysis, 200–208, 292, 293, 478
Ratio estimation (ratio extrapolation), 390, 391, 442, 504
Raw change, 217, 235–237, 239–241
Reader Lookup Table, 10, 12, 13
Reasonableness testing, 81, 439, 504
Reasonably equivalent value, 338, 340, 372, 387–390, 475, 489, 504
Records-based expectations, 439, 504
Regression analysis, 301, 306–310
Regulators of financial information, 10, 11
Reid, John E., 59, 505
Reid Technique, 59, 505
Relative size factor, 214, 330, 505
Reperform, 442, 505
Report cards, 330, 332, 363, 505
Reports
  contents of by subject matter, 327–332
  examples available on website, 326, 327, 334
  scripting, 317, 318, 506
  WPN *(weapon)* technique, 320–325
  writing, 320–327
Required rate of return (R), 287, 294
Return on investment (ROI), 184
Revenue/Accounts Receivable, 201
Revenue/Fixed Assets, 202
Revenue Ruling 59-60, 296, 372, 373
Revenue/Total Assets, 202
Reverse proof, 317, 319, 442, 505
Risk and going concern ratios, 203
Risk assessment, 293
Rounded numbers test, 272, 279, 281, 282, 381–383, 506

Sales, General, and Administrative Expenses Index (SGAI), 210, 506
Sales Growth Index (SGI), 210, 507
SAR. *See* Suspicious Activity Report (SAR)
Sarbanes-Oxley Act (SOX), 179
Scoping stage of assignment
  about, 54, 420, 422
  chart, 425
  deliverables, 39–54, 425
  FA/IM diagram, 425
  potential issues, identifying, 38, 39, 425
  purpose of, 36, 37, 425
  resources and references, 37, 38, 425
  task list, developing, 38
  tasks to be performed, 425
SCORE (Suppliers, Customers, Owners, Regulators, and Employees), 101, 102, 184. *See also* ICE/SCORE
Secondary adjustments (S_a), 288, 294, 327
Self-actualization method (for countering confirmation bias), 128–131
Self-reported data, 93–106, 506
Seven-step methodology of criminal investigation, 417, 418

Shaffer, Bob, 155
Shareholder disputes, 48, 83, 329, 341
Shoebox data, 203
60-Second Method, 1, 16, 173, 182, 184–204, 471
Skepticism, 64, 97
Skip Trace, 75
Skiptraceseminar.com, 75, 507
Social media as source of information, 57, 58
Software
 accounting, 286
 Benford's Law, 273
 data mining, 483
 data query, 285, 286
 digital analysis, 271, 278, 282, 284–287
 drill-down technique, 198
 Forensic Accounting/Investigation Methodology (FA/IM), 1, 11
 forensic lexicology, 150, 152–155, 157–172
 gap analysis, 284
 genograms, 46–48
 link analysis, 282, 284
 ratio analysis, 24, 204, 205
 stratification and stratified sampling, 287
 stylometry, 163–172
 timelines, 40–43
 valuation, 204
 Z-statistic test, 278
Solvency analysis
 ability to repay debts, 375
 about, 340, 374, 375, 508
 adequate (reasonable) capital test, 375, 377, 378
 adequate capital to operate business, 375
 balance sheet test, 374–376
 cash flow test, 375–377
 positive equity, 375
 projected cash flow sensitivity analysis, 378
 reports, 331
 resting requirement line of credit, 370
 solvency ratios, 375
 times interest earned, 375
 use of, 374
 use of in counterterrorism, 384–388
 use of with other civil actions, 341
Solvency ratios, 375
Source and application of funds method, 257–260, 411–413, 479, 508
Special operator, 5, 488
Specific item method, 256
Splatter vision, 508
Spokeo, 75, 509
Stages of forensic accounting methodology, 14, 416, 418–421
 Analysis of Transactions, 173
 Assignment Development, 21
 Background Research, 73
 Confidential Informants, 114
 Data Collection, 79
 Laboratory Analysis, 119
 Interviews and Interrogation, 56
 Post-Assignment, 327
 Scoping, 36
 Surveillance, 111
 Testimony and Exhibits, 318
 Trial Preparation, 315
 Undercover, 117
Standard deviation, 203, 217, 227, 229–233, 235, 236, 252, 287, 314, 509
Standard error of Y estimate, 307, 310
Statement analysis, 440, 509
Statutes of limitations, 446
Storyboards, 39, 40, 509
Stratification, 272, 286, 287, 510
Stratified mean-per-unit (MPU), 441, 510
Stratified sampling, 287
StumbleUpon, 58
Stylometry, 163–172, 510
Summa de Arithmetica, Geometria, Proportioni et Proportionalita (Pacioli), 402
Surveillance
 about, 420, 422, 511
 chart, 429
 criminal investigations, 417, 418
 deliverables, 114, 429
 FA/IM diagram, 429
 potential issues, 113, 114, 429
 purpose of, 111, 112, 429
 resources and references, 112, 113, 429
 tasks to be performed, 113, 429
Suspicious Activity Report (SAR), 337, 384, 386, 388, 508
Sustainable Growth Rate (SGR), 209, 413, 414, 507

T-statistic, 81, 293, 307, 308, 514
Tax-basis accounting, 204, 370
Tax returns, 54, 95–97, 183, 204. *See also* Financial Status Audit Techniques (FSAT)
Technical capabilities, 23
Terrorism. *See* Counterterrorism
Testimony and exhibits
 about, 420, 423
 chart, 435
 deliverables, 319, 435
 FA/IM diagram, 435
 potential issues, 319, 435
 purpose of, 318, 435
 resources and references, 318, 319, 435
 tasks to be performed, 319, 435
 testimony scripting, 317, 318, 506
 and WPN technique, 320, 325
Thompson, Robert B., 340, 358
"Three B's," 460, 512

Timeline analysis, 341, 512
Timelines/schedules
  Assignment Development stage, 25
  forensic timelines, 38–44
TimelineXpress, 40–43
Total Accounts Payable to Total Assets (TAPTA), 212, 511
Total Accounts Receivable to Total Assets (TARTA), 212, 511
Total Accruals to Total Assets Index (TATA), 144, 145, 209, 211, 289, 291, 292, 294, 511
Total Current Assets to Total Assets (TCATA), 212, 512
Total Debt Ratio, 202
Total Debt (cash flow to total debt) Ratio – coverage, 207
Total Debt to Assets, 202
Total Deferrals to Total Assets (TDTA), 212, 512
Total Free Cash ratio – going concern, 207
Total Inventory to Total Assets (TITA), 212, 512
Transaction analysis
  about, 420, 423
  benchmarking, 205, 206
  chart, 433
  comprehensive methods, 198, 199
  criminal investigations, 417, 418
  damages, measures of, 200
  deliverables, 175, 433
  direct methods, 197, 198
  FA/IM diagram, 433
  financial statements, 181–204
  forensic indices, 204–212
  indirect methods, 197
  and internal control, 175–181
  potential issues, 175, 433
  purpose of stage, 173, 433
  ratio analysis, 200–208
  resources and references, 173, 174, 433
  60-Second Method, 185–197
  tasks to be performed, 175, 433
  and types of forensic assignments, 199, 200
Tree diagram, financial statements, 187
Trending analysis, 198, 212, 513
Trial phase of forensic accounting methodology, 16, 419, 442, 443. *See also* Post-assignment review and evaluation; Testimony and exhibits; Trial preparation
Trial preparation
  about, 420, 423, 453
  chart, 434
  criminal cases, 419, 453
  deliverables, 317, 318, 434
  FA/IM diagram, 434
  potential issues, 317, 434
  purpose of, 315, 316, 434
  resources and references, 316, 434
  tasks to be performed, 317, 434
  testimony and exhibits. *See* Testimony and exhibits
Trials, civil versus criminal, 453, 454
Truncated mean, 226–228, 497
Truthfulness, assessment of, 64–66, 73, 74, 77
Tudor, Jan Davis, 75, 77
Twitter, 58

Undercover data collection
  about, 420, 422
  chart, 431
  criminal investigations, 417, 418
  deliverables, 119, 431
  FA/IM diagram, 431
  potential issues, 119, 431
  purpose of, 117, 118, 431
  resources and references, 118, 431
  tasks to be performed, 118, 119, 431
Uniform Fraudulent Conveyances Act (UFCA), 340, 372
Uniform Fraudulent Transfer Act (UFTA), 340, 372
Unique Facts and Circumstances, 23, 25, 38, 60, 76, 79, 81, 82, 113, 114, 116, 118, 175, 217, 317, 319, 327, 328–330, 332, 364, 514
Unit and volume method, 257, 260, 261, 268, 269, 514
USA PATRIOT Act, 337

Valuation and forensics
  applicability of forensic techniques in valuation, 287, 288
  benefits of forensic techniques in valuation, 293
  economic benefit stream. *See* Economic benefit stream; Economic benefit stream, calculation of
  implementation of forensic techniques, 288, 289
  misconceptions, 287
  ratio analysis, use of, 292, 293
  reports, 332
  techniques used, 289–292, 294. *See also* Asset Quality Index (AQI); Cash Realized from Operations (CRO); Total Accruals to Total Assets index (TATA)
Variability in data, 214. *See also* Aberrant pattern detection; Forensic financial analysis
Variables sampling, 390, 441, 442, 514
Variance, 132, 165, 172, 197, 198, 216, 217, 229–232, 235, 236, 515
Veracity. *See* Truthfulness, assessment of
Verbal and nonverbal cues, 63–66
Veromi, 75, 515
Vertical analysis, 198, 212, 370, 398, 515

Weapon. *See* WPN (words, pictures, numbers) technique *(weapon)*
Websites
Benford's Law, 379
data collection and analysis resources, 80, 81, 113, 115, 116, 118, 121, 174
Financial Forensics Academy™, 5
Financial Forensics Body of Knowledge, 1, 5, 10, 327, 334, 421
Forensic Accounting/Investigation Methodology (FA/IM), 1, 5, 6
foundational phase resources, 22, 37, 38
interpersonal phase resources, 57–59, 75, 76
online dating sites, 57–59
personal information, sites for obtaining, 57, 58
social media, 57, 58
trial and reports phase resources, 316, 319
Weighted-average, 217, 245, 246, 294, 515
WestLaw, 76
White collar crime, 391, 445, 466
Wicklander-Zulawski & Associates, 59, 515
Word. *See* Microsoft Word
Working capital ratios, 208
WPN (words, pictures, numbers) technique *(weapon)*
about, 320, 516
examples, 320–326
pictures and numbers component, 325, 326

Year-to-year change, 235–241, 516

Z-statistic (Z Score), 209, 217, 230, 233–235, 278, 279, 293, 473, 516

Printed and bound by CPI Group (UK) Ltd, Croydon, CR0 4YY

24/04/2025

14661404-0001